THE TRIPLE KNOWLEDGE

THE
TRIPLE
KNOWLEDGE

An Exposition of the
Heidelberg Catechism

by
HERMAN HOEKSEMA

COMPLETE IN THREE VOLUMES
VOL. 1

REFORMED FREE PUBLISHING ASSOCIATION
Grand Rapids, Michigan

(Distributed by Kregel Publications)

Library of Congress Catalog Card No. 71-129740
ISBN 0-916206-06-8 (This Volume)
ISBN 0-916206-05-X (Complete Set, 3 Volumes)

THE TRIPLE KNOWLEDGE, An Exposition of the Heidelberg Catechism. Volume One was originally published by the William B. Eerdmans Publishing Co. in three volumes. Volume One: In the Midst of Death, 1943; Volume Two: God's Way Out, 1944; Volume Three: The Death of the Son of God, 1946.

Complete set of 3 volumes
First edition 1972
Second edition 1976

Printed in the United States of America

EDITOR'S PREFACE

This is the first volume of a planned three-volume reprint of the late Reverend Herman Hoeksema's *The Triple Knowledge, An Exposition of the Heidelberg Catechism*. The original edition of this series was published by the Wm. B. Eerdmans Publishing Company in ten volumes over a span of years from 1943 to 1956. It remains the only extensive work in the English language on the Heidelberg Catechism. However, several volumes of the original edition are now out of print; and in order to make this valuable commentary available in its entirety to the Reformed community this reprint is being prepared.

This first volume contains three sections, originally published under the three titles, *In The Midst Of Death*, *God's Way Out*, and *The Death Of The Son Of God*. No editorial changes have been made, nor have these volumes been abridged. We have attempted to eliminate as much as possible any printing errors which appeared in the original edition.

May the Lord bless this publication and use it for the preservation of this part of our Reformed heritage and the revival of interest in the Reformed faith.

— Homer C. Hoeksema

PREFACE

If in God's inscrutable purpose there are left to me a sufficient number of days to work and to labor, I intend to complete the work the beginning of which I offer to the public in the present volume. There is room, it seems to me, for an explanation of the Heidelberg Catechism in the English language. This part of our Reformed heritage still occupies a large place in the hearts and minds of those that love the Reformed truth, and to them this exposition should be welcome. And for those who "lost their first love" even for this best known part of the *Three Forms of Unity*, it may under God's indispensable blessing serve the purpose of reviving their interest in it, and in Reformed truth in general.

Even as proper preaching on the Heidelberg Catechism should never offer mere exegesis of its contents, so an exposition of this book of instruction should be more than a mere commentary. While intending to be an explanation of the Catechism, therefore, the present work also purposes to be a development of the different doctrines presented therein, and that, too, in the direction in which the Instructor points us. How extensive the completed work will be (if with God's blessing I may be granted the opportunity to complete it), I will not attempt to predict, but as it appears now it should fill several volumes of approximately the same size as the present one.

For more than twenty-seven years I have faithfully preached once a Sunday (except on special occasions) on the Heidelberg Catechism, and it is my experience that when this is faithfully done, so that with every new series the preacher enters upon his task with new zeal and a firm resolution to make study of the material presented by the Heidelberger, neither he nor his congregation ever grow weary of this form of doctrinal preaching, but rather grow in their appreciation of it, and, of course, increase in their capacity to receive it. May this also be the experience of those that will take the trouble to read this exposition!

H. HOEKSEMA

vii

CONTENTS

CONTENTS

x

CONTENTS

SECTION I

IN THE MIDST OF DEATH

Introductory

The Heidelberg Catechism As A Symbol

Our Heidelberg Catechism is part of our Reformed heritage. It belongs to the Reformed Symbols or Confessions. The other parts, that with the Heidelberger constitute the Three Forms Of Unity, are the Netherland or Belgic Confession, and the Canons of Dordrecht. Our age is not characterized by a clear knowledge of and love of distinct doctrine. Creeds do not meet with much favor in the church of today. Some churches still have creeds but without being acquainted with their contents; others have so abbreviated their confessions that they contain no distinctive doctrine at all; many have adopted the deceiving slogan: "no creed but Christ." Our churches still value their Reformed heritage as contained in the Forms of Unity. An attempt is made to acquaint our people with their contents. Often our young people are instructed in the doctrine as expressed by the Netherland Confession and the Canons. And it is still the established custom in our churches to preach once a Sunday from the Heidelberg Catechism in such a way that no Lord's Day is omitted. Before we enter upon the exposition of our Heidelberg Catechism, as we shall try to do in the following chapters, it may not be superfluous to say a few words about creeds or symbols in general, and about our Heidelberg Catechism as a symbol in particular.

A symbol may be defined as a declaration by a church or group of churches of what such a church

3

or group of churches believes to be the truth of the Word of God or the true doctrine concerning salvation. Symbols are also called confessions or creeds. By the name symbol is expressed that the church or group of churches that framed a particular statement of doctrine consider this their ensign. Just as a nation has its flag which serves as a symbol of its nationality in distinction from other nations, so a church has its authoritative declaration of doctrine as a symbol or ensign, representing the catholic faith of the church over against the world, or the particular faith of a certain church in distinction from other churches. The word *creed* is derived from the Latin word *credere* meaning "to believe." By this term, therefore, is expressed that a church or group of churches regards its statement of the truth as an object of faith. A symbol is not a mere compendium of doctrine or system of dogmatics, but it is the setting forth of those truths, which a whole church or denomination of churches embraces as the object of its belief. It is living truth. And by the term *confession* the idea is set forth that a group of believers or churches openly profess their faith in unison with one another and with their Lord Jesus Christ. There are many different kinds and forms of creeds. Some are very brief and comprehensive, setting forth the mere essentials of the catholic Christian faith, as the "Apostles' Creed" and the Nicene Creed. Others are more elaborate and specific, and offer a more or less detailed exposition of the truth as professed by a certain church, as the Westminster Confession. To the latter belong also the Netherland Confession and the Heidelberg Catechism. Still other confessions limit themselves to the exposition and defense of certain particular points of doctrine. To these belong the Canons of Dordrecht, setting forth the faith of the Reformed Churches concerning the "Five Points of Calvinism."

True creeds or symbols are not the result of abstract theological contemplation. They are rather to be conceived as spiritual children of the faith of the church. The believers individually, and also the Church of Christ collectively, are set in the midst of the world to be witnesses of the truth of God. The Church may not be silent, especially not as it stands in antithetical relation to the world of darkness. Its calling is to bear testimony in opposition to the lie. It partly meets this obligation through its confessions or symbols. But it also lives by faith in Christ. And faith has in it the urge to speak. The believing Church loves the truth as it is in Christ Jesus, and as it is contained in the Holy Scriptures. It loves to contemplate that truth, strives more and more fully to understand it and to appropriate it by faith, and has the desire to witness of that truth before all the world. Thus creeds are born from the faith of the Church in contact with the Holy Scriptures. Schaff says: "Faith, like all strong conviction, has a desire to utter itself before others—'Out of the abundance of the heart the mouth speaketh'; 'I believe, therefore I confess' (*Credo, ergo confiteor*)." Although, therefore, theology certainly may and does aid the Church in formulating its creeds, they are never the product of abstract theological thinking but the spontaneous expression of the faith of the church. They are born, not made. A live church will certainly have its creed, just as a living believer must needs bear testimony of the truth.

And thus we already touched upon the question of the value of symbols or creeds. They are valuable because they serve as a means whereby the whole church may express her faith over against all the

world, or by which a group of churches may declare
what they believe to be the truth of the Word of God
in distinction from other churches. As has been stated,
it is the calling of the Church in the midst of the world
to let her light shine and bear witness of the truth,
to maintain that truth in opposition to every form
of the lie. She does this through her confessions as
her medium. In the second place, they serve as a bond
of union and a basis upon which a certain group of
churches may unite. Just as a flag is not merely an
ensign representing the distinctive nationality of a
certain people in the midst of other nations, but also
serves as a symbol around which a particular nation
rallies; so a particular group of churches rallies around
a certain confession as the symbol of its unity. In
the third place, confessions or creeds are means to preserve the truth as it is delivered to us from the past in
the line of generations. It is true that the whole truth
is contained in the Holy Scriptures. But the Scriptures are the revelation of God in Christ as it was
given in the process of a history of many centuries and
culminated in Christ. They offer no ready made
system of doctrine. It is the need, and also the calling
of the Church to elicit from these Scriptures the truth
in doctrinal form. This is difficult labor, which often
finds an incentive in the opposition of false teachers.
However, this work need not and may not be started
anew by the Church of every age. God establishes His
covenant and Church in the line of continued generations, in order that one generation may enter into the
fruit of the labor of another. Thus the truth is preserved from age to age under the guidance of the
Holy Spirit. And creeds serve as means to transmit
the truth and preserve it from one generation to the
next. In close connection with the immediately pre-

ceding, finally, must be mentioned that symbols or confessions are excellent means of instructing the youth of the Church. If a creed is to remain the expression of the faith of a church or group of churches, it stands to reason that the individual members of such a church or churches must be acquainted with its contents. The Church must instruct its members, particularly its children and youth, in its doctrine. For this purpose its creeds may be found to be excellent aids, if not textbooks. For many reasons, therefore, it is expedient that the Church preserve and maintain her symbols.

Confessions have no authority other than derivative, that is, their authority can never replace or be put on a par with that of the Holy Scriptures. The Word of God is and must remain the sole authority in the life of the individual believer and of the Church of Jesus Christ. This does not mean, of course, that they have no authority whatsoever. For, they are a reflection of the truth of the Word of God in the believing consciousness of the Church, and authoritatively expressed by the Church, unto which our Lord Jesus Christ has given the power of the keys and the promise of the guidance of the Holy Spirit into all the truth. And those that submit themselves to the government of the Church that is based upon a certain creed are certainly under the authority of that creed and bound by it. But it does mean that a creed can never be the final court of appeal. Confessions and traditions must always be based on the Scriptures. And with the Scriptures they must constantly be compared, and in their light their truth must be judged. The contents of the Scriptures can never be subject to the criticism of the believer or of the Church, but the doctrinal declarations of the confessions must

really constantly be subject to such criticism. Scripture cannot be altered or developed, confessions may
and should. The Bible is infallible, the creed of the
Church is not. Hence, the confessions must constantly be gauged by the Scriptures. A church that fails
to do this lapses into confessionalism and dead intellectualism.

This does not mean that the individual believer has
the right or power to alter the confession of the church
of which he is a member, nor does he have the right to
propagate views that are in conflict with the creed of
his church. One that takes his confession seriously will
not even easily reach the conclusion that the doctrine
as set forth in the symbols of his church is erroneous.
He will remember that the symbols are the product
of long and earnest labor and struggle on the part of
the Church, and that she was guided, too, by the
Holy Spirit. But if, after serious consideration and
prayerful study, a believer cannot escape the conviction that with respect to a certain doctrine the creed
of his church is in conflict with the Bible, he will reveal his objections to the church, and try to persuade
her to rectify the error. He will do this in the proper
way, which in the Reformed Churches is the way of
consistory, classis and synod. If he fails to convince
the church, and if the doctrinal point of difference
is sufficiently serious and fundamental, the way is always open to him to join himself to a purer manifestation of the body of Christ on earth. However, this
may be, the confession can never have other authority
than such as it derives from the Scripture, and appeal
from the creed to the Bible must always remain possible.

If this is borne in mind, one will find little difficulty in answering the various objections that have been and still are often raised against creeds as such. Some of the main objections are the following: 1. The church needs no creed; the Bible is sufficient for the faith and instruction of the believers. 2. Creeds impede the development of the truth and stand in the way of unprejudiced exegesis of Holy Writ. 3. Confessions force and bind the conscience of the believer, subjecting him to doctrines of men rather than to the Word of God only. 4. They are the cause of much false religious zeal, engender strifes and contentions, breathe the spirit of sectarianism and cause hopeless division in the Church of Christ. 5. The result is often doctrinal indifferentism and skepticism. This explains why the age of Confessionalism in the church of the seventeenth century was followed by that of Rationalism and apostasy in the eighteenth. Our general reply to these objections may be that improper emphasis on the importance of symbols may be the occasion of the abuses mentioned, but all these objections fall away as long as the Church remembers that the confessions can never take the place of, nor be placed on a par with Holy Writ, and that their contents must always be gauged by the teaching of the Bible. The truth of the sufficiency of Holy Scripture cannot be used as an argument to defend denial or ignoring of the labor of the Church in the past as it is expressed in the confessions. If symbols, moreover, are kept in their proper place, that is, in subjection to Scripture, they will surely not impede the development of the truth, or obstruct free exegesis, for then the principle will be maintained that in no case may the doctrine of the Church dominate the interpretation of the Bible. Again, as long as the Church maintains the truth that the authority of creeds is only derivative, individual believers will always find the way open to appeal to Scripture if they have objections against the confessions, and their conscience is not bound. Nor can it be said that the symbols of the Church are the cause of division and contention; on the contrary, it is heresy and false doctrine that must be blamed for these evils. And the movement to establish church-union by obliterating distinctive creeds can only impoverish the Church doctrinally, and induce doctrinal indifferentism, thus making the Church a prey to the false philosophy of the world.

The many symbols that have been framed and adopted by the different churches in the course of their history may be divided into four classes (see Schaff: *Creeds of Christendom*, I, 9-11). The first class contains the ecumenical symbols of the early church, chiefly relating to the doctrines of the Holy Trinity and of the natures and Person of Christ. The second division embraces the symbols of the Greek Church, differing from the Western Church on the wellknown question of "filioque" or the double procession of the Holy Spirit, and on the doctrine of the papacy. In the third category belong the symbols of the Roman Church from the Council of Trent, which was convoked to counteract the movement of the Reformation and closed in 1563, to the Council of the Vatican, which finally established the doctrine of the infallibility of the Pope, in 1870. And, finally, there is the fourth class in which are comprised all the different creeds of the Evangelical Protestant Churches, mostly dating from the period of the Reformation. The two main divisions of these are those that are of Lutheran and those that are of the Calvinistic persuasion, chiefly differing with respect to the doctrines of God's decrees and of the nature and efficacy of the Sacraments.

To the last named belong the Three Forms of Unity of the Reformed Churches, comprising the Heidelberg Catechism, the Netherland or Belgic Confession, and the Canons of Dordrecht. A comparison of these three parts of our Reformed heritage will show that each is quite distinct from the other. The Netherland Confession contains thirty-seven articles, setting forth in the main the chief doctrines of the Reformed Churches and following the objective dogmatic order. The Heidelberg Catechism is much more practical in character, and follows the subjective-experiential order of the doctrines of sin, redemption, gratitude. And the Canons of Dordrecht, having their occasion in the Arminian controversy of the last part of the sixteenth and the beginning of the seventeenth century, are designed to defend the doctrine of divine predestination, together with the related doctrines of particular atonement, total depravity, irresistible grace, and perseverance of the saints.

As to the Heidelberg Catechism, its name is derived from the fact that it is cast into the form of questions and answers, originally designed for the instruction of the youth, and from the fact that it was composed in the city of Heidelberg, situated in the Palatinate, of which at that time Frederick III was elector. It was originally the Lutheran Reformation that about the year 1546 gained foothold in the Palatinate. In the year 1556, however, Frederick III succeeded Otto Heinrich, and was elector until 1576. And under his reign a complete reformation was accomplished. As he himself had become thoroughly Reformed in his convictions, he desired to introduce the Calvinistic faith into his dominions, where hitherto the Augsburg Confession had been the sole norm of faith. He, therefore, commissioned Zacharias Ursinus, who at that time

occupied a theological chair at Heidelberg, and Caspar
Olevianus, who had formerly been incumbent of the
chair then occupied by Ursinus but was then minister
of the church of Heidelberg, to compose a book of instruction developing the Reformed line of doctrine.
Both men had enjoyed the personal acquaintance of
Calvin and the reformers of Switzerland, and were
well fitted for the task. Schaff writes: "The peculiar
gifts of both, the didactic clearness and precision of
the one, and the pathetic warmth and unction of the
other, were blended in beautiful harmony, and produced a joint work which is far superior to the separate
productions of either." *Creeds of Christendom*, I, 535.
The Catechism was completed and accepted by the
Synod of Heidelberg in 1563. Frederick III had added
a short preface, in which he informed the clergy and
schoolteachers of his domain that the book was composed at his injunction in order that it might be used
for the instruction of the youth in churches and
schools. From the outset, therefore, the Heidelberg
served the double purpose of catechetical textbook and
symbol of the Church. It soon found its way into the
Netherlands, where it was highly esteemed, adopted
by several particular synods, and finally ratified and
officially included in the Forms of Unity of the Reformed Churches by the Synod of Dordrecht in 1618-
19.

As we all know, the Heidelberg Catechism is divided
into three parts, the first treating of the doctrine of sin
and misery, the second of the doctrine of redemption
and deliverance from sin, following the general line
of the so-called Apostles' Creed, while the third part,
under the general heading of gratitude treats of the
subjects of the law and prayer. This division reveals
the practical, spiritual character and viewpoint of the

Heidelberger: it considers the contents of Christian doctrine from the experiential standpoint of the believing Christian. For the same reason this little textbook of instruction in the truth is direct and personal in form throughout. It addresses the conscious believer. It is further divided into fifty-two Lord's Days, a division that was not found in the original editions, but was soon introduced with a view to its being used as a basis for instruction on the Sabbath. In the first edition there appeared only one hundred and twenty-eight questions and answers. The eightieth question which refers to the popish mass as an accursed idolatry was inserted in the second and third editions, according to Schaff "by the express command of the elector, perhaps by his own hand, as a Protestant counterblast to the Romish anathemas of the council of Trent, which closed its sessions Dec. 4, 1563." (*Creeds of Christendom*, I, p. 536). Hence, the Catechism now contains one hundred and twenty-nine questions and answers, in which is set forth in brief the whole content of the Christian faith from a Reformed viewpoint. Introducing its instruction with a question concerning the only comfort in life and death, and by stating that knowledge of sin and misery, of deliverance, and of gratitude are the indispensable elements of this all-embracing comfort, it speaks of the law as the source of the knowledge of sin and misery, of the greatness of this sin and misery, of man's original state, his wilful disobedience and total depravity, of the wrath of God and the punishment of sin, and of the impossibility of man's ever saving himself or being saved by another creature. This in the first part. The second part follows in the main the exposition of the "Apostles' Creed" and treats of the character of saving faith, of the Trinity, creation and providence, the names and natures, the offices and states of the Mediator, His death and descension into hell, His resurrection, ascension and exaltation at the right hand of God, and His return to judge the quick and the dead. It continues to treat of the Holy Spirit and His work, of the holy catholic church and the communion of saints, of the final resurrection and eternal life. Lord's Day 23 stops to consider the fruit of believing all this and speaks of justification by faith only. It further discusses the means of grace, the Word and the Sacraments, and closes this second part with a few questions and answers concerning the keys of the kingdom of heaven. The third part is introduced by a few questions concerning the true conversion of man, which is followed by a discussion of the law of God as a guide for the Christian's walk, and by a treatment of each commandment separately. This discussion is concluded with the well-known question: "Canst thou keep all these things perfectly" and the beautiful reply that even the very holiest in this life has only a small beginning of the new obedience, but so that he has a sincere desire to live according to all the commandments of God. It closes with a discussion of the subject of prayer in general, and of the contents of the Lord's Prayer in particular.

Thus the Heidelberg Catechism is a veritable treasure of that triple knowledge of which it speaks in its second question and answer, and which is indispensable for the possession of the true comfort in life and death. It is the most widely known and generally used of all Reformed symbols. It is rich in content, beautifully simple in form, highly spiritual in tone and character. And although, perhaps, were it composed in our own time, some of its chapters, notably those on the sacraments, would be considerably abridged, while others would be enlarged, both from the viewpoint of its being a symbol of the Reformed Churches and of its being intended as a catechism, the Heidelberg Catechism is one of the most beautiful and masterful compositions of all times.   And our Reformed fathers gave evidence of their sound practical judgment when they ordained that one of the sermons on each Sabbath should be based on one of the Lord's Days of this precious little book.

LORD'S DAY I

Question 1. What is thy only comfort in life and death?

Answer. That I, with body and soul, both in life and death, am not my own, but belong unto my faithful Saviour Jesus Christ; who, with His precious blood, hath fully satisfied for all my sins, and delivered me from all the power of the devil; and so preserves me that without the will of my heavenly Father not a hair can fall from my head; yea, that all things must be subservient to my salvation; and therefore, by his Holy Spirit, he also assures me of eternal life, and makes me sincerely willing and ready henceforth to live unto him.

Question 2. How many things are necessary for thee to know, that thou, enjoying this comfort, mayest live and die happily?

Answer. Three; the first, how great my sins and miseries are; the second, how I may be delivered from all my sins and miseries; the third, how I shall express my gratitude to God for such deliverance.

I

The Viewpoint Of The Heidelberger

The text of the first Lord's Day that is quoted above is the one that occurs in our Psalter, and that is most commonly used. The English version that is offered by Schaff, and which, according to him, is much better than the one we quote, was prepared by a committee of the Synod of the German Reformed Church of the United States. Its text of the first Lord's Day differs in some minor details from ours. Instead of "delivered me from all the power of the devil" it has "redeemed me" etc. The German text has: "und mich aus aller Gewalt des Teufels erlöset hat." It is true that "redeemed" is a more literal translation of "erlöset" than "delivered"; yet the latter most probably expresses the thought more correctly than the former. Instead of "all things must be subservient to my salvation," it offers "all things must work together for my salvation." But the former adheres more closely to the German text: "mir alles zu meiner Seligkeit dienen muss." Like the German text it begins a new sentence with "Wherefore, by his Holy Spirit, he also assures me of eternal life," etc.; and more correctly than our text it renders "von Herzen willig" by "heartily willing." More important, perhaps, is the difference in the rendering of the second question. Our text has: "that thou, enjoying this comfort, mayest live and die happily?" The version Schaff presents translates: "that thou in this comfort mayest live and die happily?" The latter is certainly the correct rendering of the German: "das du in diesem Troste seliglich leben und

sterben mögest?" But it is also more objective as to
meaning and certainly stronger than "enjoying this
comfort." "In this comfort" presents the comfort not
merely as a matter of feeling and joy, but as the basis
of our living and dying happily, as the sphere and cause
of it. Our whole life, our thinking and willing and desiring, our speech and our action, is characterized and
spiritually determined by this all comprehensive comfort. And this is expressed much more correctly and
forcefully by "in this comfort" than by "enjoying this
comfort." Finally, Schaff's text renders the first part
of the second answer: "First, the greatness of my sin
and misery," where our text, however, is a more correct translation of the German: "Erstlich, wie gross
meine Sunde und Elend seien."

So much about the text.

As to the contents of this first Lord's Day, it will
be evident at once that it is designed to serve an introductory purpose. The teacher or preacher who would
enter into a detailed interpretation of the various
elements of the truth that appear in this first chapter
of the Heidelberger would make a serious mistake.
He would find that there would be very little left for
him to explain in connection with the rest of our
instructor. And so does the preacher err, who, in
expounding this first Lord's Day, offers a *general* explanation of all the different parts of the truth that
are here mentioned. He would merely scan the surface
of many points of doctrine, would lack the time to explain any one of them sufficiently, surely would fail to
present the truth as living reality, and would bring his
congregation from the very start in a state of mind
in which it will be difficult for him to make them believe that preaching on the Heidelberg Catechism is
either important or interesting. In this Lord's Day

the Catechism speaks of an only comfort, of life and of death, of body and soul, of not being our own but belonging to our faithful Saviour Jesus Christ, of satisfaction through the precious blood of Christ, of deliverance from all the power of the devil, of our preservation by our heavenly Father, so that not a hair can fall from our head contrary to His will, and so that all things must serve the purpose of our salvation, of the personal assurance of being heirs of eternal life and of sanctification, so that we are heartily willing and prepared to live unto God, of the Holy Spirit, of the knowledge of sin and misery, of salvation, and of the gratitude we owe to God for such deliverance. How could a preacher mould all these different elements into the contents of his sermon without sacrificing the unity of his discourse, and without becoming guilty of offering to his audience mere generalities, unless he would commit the foolishness which was, in fact, committed by some, of preaching more than two score times on the first question of our instructor alone? Neither a detailed interpretation of this Lord's Day, nor a general survey of the various doctrines mentioned therein, therefore, is required or expedient, when one expounds this chapter of the Heidelberg Catechism to his congregation. Rather must he understand that this Lord's Day is introductory, and that as such it presents the viewpoint from which the entire system of doctrine is considered, the standpoint from which the instructor would have his audience look at the truth of the Word of God.

This viewpoint is immediately and concisely expressed in the very first question: "What is thy only comfort in life and death?" There can be no doubt about the fact, that the Heidelberg Catechism considers and explains the truth from the viewpoint of the consciousness and subjective experience of the believing Christian in this world. In this respect it differs radically from the Westminster Catechisms, both the larger and the shorter. The Westminster Larger Catechism begins as follows: "What is the chief and highest end of man? Man's chief and highest end is, to glorify God and fully to enjoy him forever. How doth it appear that there is a God? The very light of nature, the works of God declare plainly that there is a God: but his Word and Spirit do sufficiently and effectually reveal him unto men for their salvation. What is the Word of God? The Holy Scriptures of the Old and New Testament are the Word of God, the only Rule of Faith and obedience." And then it continues to treat the doctrine of God, His virtues, the Trinity, the decrees, creation, man, the fall, etc. Now, look at the first Lord's Day of the Heidelberg Catechism. You at once discern the difference. The Westminster starts out from the question of the objective end and calling of man: to glorify God and to enjoy Him forever; the Heidelberger speaks of the subjective appropriation and experience of this truth by the individual Christian: my comfort is that I belong to my faithful Saviour Jesus Christ. The viewpoint of the Westminster Catechism is doctrinally objective; that of the Heidelberg Catechism is experientially subjective. The standpoint of the former is general and impersonal: it addresses no one, it speaks of *man;* that of the Catechism is specific and personal: it speaks to the man of God.

Let us not misunderstand this viewpoint of our Heidelberger.

When we insist that our catechism proceeds from the standpoint of the subjective experience of the individual believer in this world, we do not imply at all that it is anthropocentric. This has often been alleged. It is pointed out that this is the characteristic difference between the Catechism of Heidelberg and some other symbols, such as the Netherland Confession, and the Westminster Catechisms. The Heidelberg Catechism is anthropocentric, i. e., it makes man the center and end of all things, his redemption and deliverance, his happiness and eternal life are the things that count. But symbols such as the Westminster Catechisms are theocentric, i.e., they place God in the center of things and present Him as the end and purpose of all existence. But this judgment is not quite correct. And it surely is not our intention to characterize the Heidelberg Catechism in this way, when we claim that its viewpoint is subjectively experiential. It is, we judge, surely not impossible to present a theocentric truth from the viewpoint of its being appropriated by the faith, and experienced in the consciousness of the Christian. And this is what, in our opinion, the Heidelberg Catechism attempts to do. It is not anthropocentric to appeal to the law of God as the criterion and source of the knowledge of man's misery, or to begin a discussion of the contents of the Christian's faith with an exposition of the first article of the Apostles' Creed, or to teach that man was created rightly to know God his Creator, to heartily love Him, and to live with Him in eternal happiness to glorify and praise Him. It is not anthropocentric to describe the quickening of the new man as a "sincere joy of heart in God, through Christ, and with love and delight to live according to the will of God in all good works," nor to limit good works to those "which proceed from a true faith, are performed according to the law of God and to His glory." Lord's Day 33. And it certainly is not anthropocentric but positively

theocentric to present true prayer as the highest expression of thankfulness, or to close the discussion of
the subject of prayer with the words: "all this we
pray for, that thereby not we, but thy holy name may
be glorified forever." Q. 128. But we do claim that
the Heidelberg Catechism considers the truth which,
of course, is always theocentric, from the viewpoint of
its being appropriated and experienced by the believing
Christian in this world, and, more particularly, from
the point of view that it is his comfort, his sole comfort in life and death.

This already removes, in part, the danger of another
possible misunderstanding. By saying that the Heidelberg Catechism is subjective and experiential in viewpoint, we do not imply that it makes man the criterion
and source of the truth. The latter is done in two
ways. Man's intellect, his reason, may be presented
as the final court of appeal to determine what is truth.
To do so is *Rationalism*. It is not rationalism to present the truth as reasonable, as adapted to the understanding of man. The truth is not illogical or un-
reasonable, or contrary to the mind of the Christian.
But it is rationalism to elevate reason to the position
of supreme judge, in order to let man's mind decide
what shall be considered truth. The Christian lives
by revelation, not by the conclusions of reason. But
man may also be presented as the measure and source
of the truth in the way of *Mysticism*. In that case the
objective revelation and Word of God is replaced by
"feeling," by certain states of consciousness, by the
"inner light," by the direct whisperings of the Spirit
of God to our spirit. There is really no essential or
principal difference between Rationalism and Mysticism. Both deny the objective Word or revelation of
God as the sole rule for faith and life. Both make

man the measure and source of the truth. This, however, is not the method of the Heidelberg Catechism. It does not pretend to derive the knowledge of the truth from the mind or feeling of the individual believer, nor from the consciousness of the Church, but it always appeals to the Word of God. The objective law of God is the source of the knowledge of our misery. The question: "Whence knowest thou this?" (i.e. that Jesus Christ is the Mediator) is answered by pointing to "the holy gospel, which God Himself first revealed in Paradise; and afterwards published by the patriarchs and prophets, and represented by the sacrifices and other ceremonies of the law; and lastly, has fulfilled it by His only begotten Son." Q. 19. The Decalogue is recommended as a guide for the Christian's life, and the prayer which the Lord Himself taught us is taken as the perfect model for all our prayers. Throughout, therefore, it is the Word of God that is recognized as the sole source and criterion of the truth. The Heidelberger instructor is neither a Rationalist nor a Mystic.

Yet, we repeat, the viewpoint is that of the subjective experience or, if you prefer, that of the spiritual knowledge of the objective truth of the Word of God as possessed by the believing Christian in this world. There is an evident difference between the questions: "What is the chief end of man?" and "What is thy only comfort?" There is an obvious difference between the threefold division of the Heidelberger: sin and misery, redemption, gratitude, on the one hand, and the well-known six loci of dogmatics. The Catechism treats the truth, not merely as a science, but as the spiritual knowledge that is eternal life. John 17:3. It discusses the system of doctrine from the viewpoint of his faith to whose heart the objective Word of God has been applied by the Holy Spirit, the Spirit of Christ, Who dwells in the Church, and Who leads into all the truth. It is not a theology, it is knowledge of God. The one that speaks here is regenerated and called. The Word, the truth of which he discusses, has been applied to his heart. He has ears to hear, eyes to see. And as he stands in the midst of the present world, full of misery and darkness, and as he himself, outside of Christ, lies in the midst of death, the clear understanding of that Word, or rather, that Word itself as it reveals to Him God in Christ, redemption and deliverance from the power of sin and death, and as he by faith lays hold upon that Word, is his comfort, his sole and all-sufficient comfort in life and death. In that thoroughly sound sense of the word the Heidelberger is experiential and subjective in its approach of the truth.

In close connection with this viewpoint of the Heidelberg Catechism stands the fact that the Catechism is very personal, and that it addresses throughout the child of the Church as "the man of God" that must be thoroughly furnished unto all good works. It speaks in the singular throughout: "What is *thy* only comfort?" "How many things are necessary for *thee* to know, that *thou* in this comfort mayest live and die happily?" "Whence knowest *thou* thy misery?" "What believest *thou*," etc, etc. And the one addressed is the baptized child of the Church, considered as a *living member*. In this respect the Heidelberg Catechism proceeds from the same standpoint as the Baptism Form. The child of the covenant is sanctified in Christ, and is baptized as member of His Church. God has forgiven us and our children all our sins, and received us through His Holy Spirit as members of His only begotten Son, and adopted us to be His children, and sealed and confirmed the same unto us by holy baptism. That is the standpoint of the Baptism Form. It is no different with the Heidelberg Catechism. The children of the covenant that must be instructed are living children of God. This does not mean that the Catechism teaches presupposed regeneration. It does not speak on the basis of a supposition: it speaks with certainty. Neither does it mean that the instructor lives in the illusion that all the members of the church on earth are spiritual members of Christ's body. When it speaks of the keys of the kingdom of heaven it reveals quite clearly that it knows that there is a carnal seed of the covenant. But it does mean that this carnal seed is not addressed, it is left out of view. It is the spiritual seed that must be instructed in the Word of God. This spiritual seed, "the man of God," must be made perfect, thoroughly furnished unto every good work. It is the only seed that can be instructed and that can be made perfect in the truth. And, therefore, it is to this spiritual seed that the Catechism addresses itself throughout. It has nothing for "the others."

In this respect the Catechism stands far above the level of the Church of our own day, even above the level of those that call themselves Reformed. They administer the sacrament of baptism to the children of the covenant; and they ask of the parents the confession that their children, though conceived and born in sin, are sanctified in Christ and members of the Church; they lead their people in the thanksgiving, that God has forgiven us and our children all our sins. and adopted us to be His children; but when it comes to actual application of this sound and strong doctrine, they rather deny it all, and, instead of instructing and confirming the true seed of the covenant in the truth of the Word of God, they come with "offers of grace"

and altar calls and what not! If many spoke their
mind, they would have to confess that they do consider
it a rather dangerous practice to confront the children
of the Church with the pertinent question: "What is
thine only comfort in life and death?" And they would
rather substitute another: "Hast thou the only comfort
in life and death?" And still more dangerous they
would consider the business of placing upon the lips
of the congregation, believers and their children, the
answer: "That I, with body and soul, am not my own,
but belong to my faithful Saviour Jesus Christ." Yet,
in the age of the Reformation this was a common practice. The Heidelberg Catechism in this respect is no
exception. It agrees with other Catechisms. Luther's
Small Catechism has a different approach from that
of our Heidelberger: it commences with a discussion
of the Ten Commandments. But when it discusses the
articles of our faith, it becomes very personal and
direct. Following the article concerning Jesus Christ
our Lord in the Apostles' Creed comes the question in
this Catechism: "What does this mean?" And the
following answer is placed upon the lips of the pupil:
"I believe that Jesus Christ, true God, begotten of the
Father from eternity, and also true man, born of the
virgin Mary, is *my* Lord; who has redeemed *me*, a lost
and condemned man, secured and delivered *me* from
all sins, from death and from the power of the devil,
not with gold or silver, but with his holy, precious
blood, and with his innocent sufferings and death; in
order that *I* might be his own, live under him in his
kingdom, and serve him in everlasting righteousness,
innocence and blessedness, even as he is risen from the
dead. This is most certainly true."

This Small Catechism of Luther was written in
1529.

The Anglican Catechism, written in 1662, has a peculiar approach, but it proceeds from the same principle: the one instructed is the living child of the covenant. Let us quote a little of it:

"Question. What is your name?

"Answer. N. or M.

"Question. Who gave you this name?

"Answer. My Godfathers and Godmothers in my Baptism; wherein I was made a member of Christ, the child of God, and an inheritor of the kingdom of heaven.

"Question. What did your Godfathers and Godmothers then for you?

"Answer. They did promise and vow three things in my name. First, that I should renounce the devil and all his works, the pomps and vanity of the wicked world, and all the sinful lusts of the flesh. Secondly, that I should believe all the articles of the Christian Faith. And thirdly, that I should keep God's holy will and commandments, and walk in the same all the days of my life.

"Question. Dost thou not think that thou art bound to believe and to do as they have promised for thee?

"Answer. Yes, verily; and by God's help so I will. And I heartily thank our heavenly Father that he hath called me to this state of salvation through Jesus Christ our Saviour. And I pray unto God to give me grace, that I may continue in the same unto the end of my life."

We do not quote all this to express agreement with everything that is here taught, or with the practice of the Anglican Church in the seventeenth century. But it shows how in the period of the Reformation, and shortly after, the Church instructed its spiritual seed in the truth of the Word of God.

This, then, is the viewpoint of the Heidelberg Catechism. There can be no question about this fact. They that are called to preach from this book of instruction will do well to bear this in mind. Approaching the truth from the standpoint of the conscious experience of the believing Christian in this world, and addressing the living member of the Church, it aims to bring the "man of God" to a conscious knowledge of the living truth, of the only comfort in life and death!

The Idea Of An Only Comfort

The first question of the Heidelberg Catechism speaks of an "only comfort in life and death." There are three elements in this question that at once draw our attention and that require explanation. The first is the fact that the Catechism here speaks of "comfort," and the question arises: what is the implication of this concept? What is true comfort? The second element is expressed in the adjective "only." By this qualification the Christian comfort is characterized as an exclusive and quite sufficient comfort. One who has this comfort needs no other. And the third element is expressed in the words "in life and death," by which phrase the comfort of which the Heidelberg speaks is described as an all-embracing comfort. It covers all. It meets all possible exigencies. And, at the same time, it presupposes that "life" requires comfort as well as "death." We must briefly explain these three closely related conceptions.

The first question, therefore, is: what is the idea of comfort, particularly of Christian comfort?

Zacharias Ursinus, one of the authors of the Heidelberg Catechism, gave an explanation of our Catechism in the form of lectures to his students. These were collated and edited by David Parëus; and they were translated and published, in 1657, in the Holland language under the title "Schatboek der Verklaringen over den Heidelbergschen Catechismus." (Treasurebook of Explanations of the Heidelberg Catechism.) The translation is by Festus Hommius. It was edited

and published again in 1739, enriched by a rather
lengthy preface of approximately one hundred and
sixty pages. And more recently it was translated from
the edition by Parëus into the Holland language by
C. Van Proosdij. Whenever I speak of or quote from
the "Schatboek," as the work is generally known, the
reference is to the last named translation. In this
"Schatboek," then, Ursinus offers the following definition of comfort: "Troost is een zeker besluit van het
verstand, waardoor we tegenover iets ongelukkigs, dat
we hebben, eenig goed stellen, en door dit goede te be-
schouwen de smart verzachten en het ongeluk geduldig
dragen," p. 21. We may translate this definition as
follows: "Comfort is a certain determination of the
mind, whereby we posit some good thing over against
a certain evil which we experience, by the contemplation of which we alleviate the grief and patiently bear
the evil." And Dr. A. Kuyper agrees with the chief
notion of this definition. Also according to him comfort is "een overlegging in ons verstand," a consideration in our mind or intellect. E Voto, I, p. 3.

An important truth is expressed here, upon which
we should insist, provided we do not give it all the
emphasis. I refer now to the statement, that comfort
is a determination, or conclusion, or consideration of
the mind.

Of course, if we should say no more than this, the
definition would not be correct. It would be untrue
because of its one-sidedness. And if we, then, in the
subsequent exposition of the truth, should follow the
lead of this definition, the result would be intellectualism, dead orthodoxy. Man is more than mere intellect,
mind or reason. He is also a volitional being. He has
a will, emotions, desires, imagination, feelings. He
is a being with "heart and mind and soul and strength."

And comfort concerns the whole man. It is not merely a consideration of the mind, a decision of the intellect, a conclusion of reason. Faith is more than knowledge, it is also confidence. Religion is more than doctrine, it is life and joy. And comfort is more than a mere decision of the mind, it is also a determination of the will, affecting all the desires and emotions. And Christian comfort is a matter of the heart, whence are the issues of life.

Yet, it should be maintained that comfort is also a consideration and conclusion of the mind; in the specific case under discussion, that of the Christian comfort, it is also a determination of the believing mind. This must be emphasized over against all forms of emotionalism and false mysticism, in opposition to all who deny or belittle the value and necessity of Christian knowledge and Christian doctrine and, therefore, also of Christian instruction. There are those, especially since the last part of the eighteenth century, that would separate the emotional life of man from his intellect, that would make of "emotion" a separate power or faculty of the soul, and give it a more or less independent place. And it is amazing how much is relegated to the domain of the emotions or "feeling." It is through "feeling" that we distinguish ourselves from the outside world, that we become individuals, personal beings. "Feeling expresses the fact that all is not purely objective and universal, but that it also exists in individual and subjective form" (John Dewey). The same author distinguished between Sensuous, Formal, and Qualitative Feelings, and to the latter category is relegated the "feeling" of sympathy and antipathy, of pride and humility, of good and evil, of guilt and remorse, of dependency and obligation, of peace and rebellion, of love and hate, of faith and hope!

Religion and morality become matters of feeling. One can readily understand that this is the deathblow to Christian doctrine. Feelings certainly are no "decisions of the mind," the intellect has nothing directly to do with them, you can hardly construe a dogmatics of your feeling or on the basis of your emotions. All that pertains to religion and morality becomes subjective and vague. And the Word of God cannot serve as the source or criterion of this religion of the feelings. It would, in that case, have no sense to ask the question: "what is thy only comfort in life and death?" For an intelligent account of the "feelings" is quite impossible. And in opposition to this it is significant to maintain the truth that comfort is a consideration of the intellect, that without this intellectual consideration and conclusion no Christian comfort is possible. Faith is more than knowledge, but it is, nevertheless, also knowledge; and without the knowledge of faith the confidence of faith is impossible. You cannot make a Christian by instruction, but the Christian can be indoctrinated, and by growing in the knowledge of Jesus Christ may increase in the conscious possession of the true comfort in life and death.

Of course, it should be added that, in the case of Christian comfort, this "consideration of the intellect," this "conclusion of the mind," is not a mere rational process or the result of a syllogism. The "only comfort in life and death" is concerned with a good, which "eye hath not seen and ear hath not heard, and has never arisen in the heart of man." It is, therefore, a good that can be posited over against the evil of life and death only by the mind of faith. And this faith lays hold upon that which the Spirit of God reveals to us, not by inner light, as the mystics would have it, but by the Word of God as we possess it in the

Scriptures. It is the believing mind that lays hold upon the promise of God, is certain of that promise, contemplates that promise, so that the believing heart embraces the thing promised and esteems it so great and gracious, that the sufferings of this present time are not worthy to be compared with it. Thus Abraham by faith, when he was called to sacrifice the child of the promise, posited the good that God was able to raise him from the dead. And Moses esteemed the reproach of the people of God, the reproach of Christ, greater riches than all the treasures of Egypt, for he had respect unto the recompence of the reward. Both actually did some accounting, some figuring. In the case of Abraham this is even literally expressed in the original of Hebrews 11:19. Both performed an act of the mind, both reached a conclusion concerning a good which they placed over against an evil. But it was a consideration of faith, that laid hold on the promise of God, yea, on Himself, who calleth the things that are not as if they were, and who raiseth the dead. Rom. 4:17. And thus this "consideration of the mind" which is implied in Christian comfort, is based on the Word of God, and is an activity of faith in the promise.

What, however, is true comfort? It is, indeed, the positing of a good over against an existing evil. But must not more be said? Is comfort perfect when we are aware of both, an existing evil and, over against it, an existing good? Evidently not, for the fact remains that the evil also exists. It is true, that in that case the contemplation of the good may alleviate the suffering, relatively lighten the burden we bear, but it cannot possibly reconcile us to the evil we experience. As long, therefore, as our experience is dualistic, and we are conscious of a good and of an evil in juxtaposition, our comfort cannot be perfect. We can conceive of a far happier state, that in which the good alone exists. Nor can comfort be said to be perfect, when the good of which we are aware and which we posit over against the evil we suffer, is greater, even much greater than the existing evil. For the evil still remains, and the possibility is still there of conceiving of a happier lot for ourselves, that in which the evil has no place. Perhaps we are inclined to say, that comfort is complete and perfect, when, over against the prevailing evil, we know of a good that is not only far greater than the evil, but by which the evil will ultimately be removed. We know of a good that overcomes the evil! We are contemplating a good that is victorious over the evil! Yet, although in that case our comfort is far greater because of the prospect of final deliverance from the evil, the dualism still remains. And the question must needs arise: why should there have been an evil at all? Still we can conceive of a more blessed situation: that in which we enjoyed the good from the beginning, the joy of which was never for a moment marred by the suffering of the evil. We must go a step further in order to arrive at the conception of full and perfect comfort. It is the consciousness and contemplation of a good so great and precious that the evil we suffer cannot be compared with it, *and unto the attainment of which the evil we bear for the time being is strictly subservient and necessary!* Only when we may contemplate the evil as a means to the end of the great good do we have full and perfect comfort. Only in that case do we have an answer, the final answer, to the question: why should the evil exist at all, even for a time? Only in that light can we see that the evil is only relatively an evil, while absolutely it is a good. I may have to walk a steep and rugged road, to travel which means toil and suffering; but if it is the only way that leads me to my destination, the almost impassable road is, nevertheless, a good, and I become reconciled to my suffering. A surgical operation may cause much pain and suffering, and I may dread to submit myself to it; but if I have the assurance that it is the only and sure way to recovery, I consider it a good. Perfect comfort, therefore, is the knowledge and contemplation of a great good over against an evil which is subservient to the good and necessary to the attainment of the latter.

Such, indeed, is the comfort of the Christian, the only comfort in life and in death!

Ursinus may not have conceived of the Christian comfort in this light, as his definition would give us reason to surmise, but surely, it is the underlying notion of the first question and answer of the Heidelberg Catechism. How otherwise could it have spoken of an *only* comfort, and that *in life and in death?*

Let us consider the deep seriousness of the realities of life and of death, of life-and-death as moving on the same plane and belonging to the same category, as they are viewed and evaluated in this amazing question of the catechism. It draws the lines sharply. It speaks of an *only* comfort. Consider the implication of this qualification. It is not a "great" comfort, or a "chief" comfort with which our instructor is concerned. That would make it relative. It would leave us many comforts among which there is one that is easily the greatest. But if that should be our view of life-and-death we cannot possibly agree with the first question of the Heidelberger. The comfort of which it speaks is exclusive. It brooks no competition, no comparison. It will have sole sway, or it will have nothing to do with you. It is like a physician that offers you just one particular treatment of your disease, on condition that you refrain from taking any other medicine. It takes all your other comforts away from you! It wants to be all or nothing!

But even so we probably did not make quite clear the seriousness of the situation as presented by this bold question. To do this we must also consider that this comfort of which we now speak presents itself as all-embracing and fully sufficient in all cases: It is not an only, an exclusive comfort in a given case, let us say in the most serious case: death. Perhaps we could more readily agree with the Heidelberger if it had not spoken of life-and-death but simply of death in connection with the only comfort. Indeed, that would make the question quite intelligible. Even the "flesh" can understand the question quite well in this slightly altered form: what is thy only comfort in death? Death! Death in distinction from life, even from our present life! Yes, indeed, that is the great evil, for which there is no remedy, over against which the mind cannot posit any good derived from this life that is sufficient to serve as comfort, even in the slightest degree. Life is rather good to us. True, there are also many evils, but these are more than counter-balanced by the goods. There is much that is un-pleasant, much toil and labor, much pain and suffering, much sorrow and grief, but there are also many com-forts that alleviate the suffering. For there is a good deal of "common grace" in this world that causes us to enjoy life. And so, the mind "considers." We do some accounting. We divide our experiences into two classes. We put the things of this present life on two piles. And evaluating the one class, we complain of our lot and way, and conclude that there is a good deal of evil and suffering; but we turn to the other pile for our comfort, and say: "we have much to be thankful for." And so we do, indeed, speak of comfort-in-life, meaning that there is a silver lining to every dark cloud, that there is a good deal of sweet mixed with the bitter, that there are many things that make life worth living. But to speak of an *only* comfort in life sounds rather unintelligible, absurd, too absolutistic. If it were not for death, the death that makes an end to this life, we could get along quite well without any other comfort than those we find in this life itself! In fact, is not this exactly the unique terror of death that it cuts off this present life? Indeed, we admit: over against death we can think of nothing that can comfort us. All our other comforts we can find in life itself, in this world; but for a comfort in death life offers nothing. To obtain this comfort we go to church on Sunday. When we die we call in the minister to pray for us (and, if it seems at all reasonable, to pray that we may recover and stay in this life), or the priest to administer extreme unction. And so all is well. My comfort in life is that it rains and that the sun shines, that I have enough to eat and to drink, that I have a good job, that there is a doctor when I am sick and that I may look forward to recovery, that I have some money in the bank on which to fall back, that I have a pleasant home, a lovely wife, dear children, that there is peace and prosperity in the country or that they will surely return when war rages and depression makes life less pleasant; and if, besides, I may also have comfort in death, an only comfort, I am well off, and have nothing to complain.

Indeed, that would seem a reasonable philosophy, the philosophy of common grace *and* special grace, of *many* comforts in life and an *only* comfort in death!

Any normal intelligence can grasp such a world-and-life-and-death view. And who could possibly be offended by it?

But consider, now, the conception of life-and-death that is implied in this first question of the catechism: what is thy *only* comfort *in life and death?* What does it mean? Clearly, it can express only one thing: *that life and death are both evils when considered apart from this comfort after which our instructor inquires!* It speaks of life-and-death in one breath. It puts them in the same class. You need the same comfort in both, over against both: life and death! It means that life is also death, "nothing but a continual death" as the prayer before baptism in our Form has it, when evaluated by itself, without the light of this only comfort. This life, such as it is, as I live it in this mortal and corruptible body, as it is hemmed in on all sides by death, as it inevitably, inexorably ends in death, is an evil, offers no comfort. Life, the life in which I am born through "the will of the flesh," on whose pathway I move, and move inevitably and from my very first breath in the direction of death and in the domain of death, the limit of which is threescore years and ten or fourscore years at the utmost, is an evil unless you can bring into account the only comfort in life and in death. Life and all it implies, life in which I eat and drink, labor and toil, marry a wife and bring forth children; life and all its activity in labor and industry, business and commerce, science and art; life in all its relationships of natural love and friendship, of parent and child, of brother and sister, of man to man, group to group, nation to nation; life with its sorrows, but also with its joys, with its moaning but also with its singing, with its sickness and pains but also with its health,—life such as it is in this world, is, in this first question of our catechism, mentioned in one breath with death. It is, together with death, in inseparable connection with death, the evil over against which the believing mind posits a good that overcomes the evil of life and of death, nay more: that presses it into its service!

Such, then, is the idea of this only comfort. It is a decision of the believing mind, that clings to and takes into account the promise of God. It is the knowledge and personal assurance of a great good, without which life-and-death are an evil from which there is no escape; of a good that cannot be found within the scope of life-and-death, that comes from without, that transcends it, that is both exclusive and all-embracing, and unto the attainment of which the present evil of life and of death are necessary and subservient as a means to an end.

III

The Contents Of The Christian Comfort

The question now is: what is that great good, the knowledge and consideration of which is sufficient to be a true and sole comfort in life and in death? The Heidelberg Catechism answers: "That I with body and soul, both in life and death, am not my own, but belong unto my faithful Saviour Jesus Christ." Here, too, one might easily be tempted to elaborate so as to anticipate practically the entire contents of the Catechism. He might set out to explain the meaning of "my faithful Saviour," and to set forth in detail what it implies to belong to Him, how one becomes His property, that God has given the elect to Him from eternity, that Christ purchased us to be His own by His precious blood, and that we are united by faith with that faithful Saviour. But, evidently, this is not the purpose of this first Lord's Day. It intends to be introductory, and as such it must be treated. And, therefore, the central idea must be clearly grasped, it must receive all the emphasis in our exposition, and all the details that are mentioned in this first answer must be used only in as far as it is necessary to set forth that central thought in all its significance. And that one idea is this: the fact that I belong to Christ is an all sufficient comfort to me in life and in death, a comfort beside which no other comfort is either necessary or conceivable! To belong to Christ means that all is well. He that is conscious of this relationship to Christ considers all things, in life and in death, in the light of it, and evaluating things in that light, is quite sure that the evil of this present time, including death, must be subservient to the attainment of a great good that could not otherwise be realized!

Clearly and fully you realize the evil of "life and of death." You do not close your eyes to reality. You know that "life and death" are both "death." And there is no way out, as far as you can see. You realize your sin. You know that there is a load of guilt, increasing day by day, that makes you damnable in the sight of God, worthy of eternal desolation. You know that you are hopelessly in the power of death and corruption, so that sin has dominion over you, and that you can never liberate yourselves from that slavery of sin. You know, too, that God is righteous and just, and that He is angry with the wicked every day. He will never excuse you or acquit you when you appear before Him in judgment. You realize that He judges you every day, every moment of your life, and that His sentence is always: "Cursed is every one that abideth not in all things written in the law, to do them!" And you say: "My sole comfort over against this crushing evil is that I belong to Christ!" And presently you lie on your deathbed. You feel how impotent you are in your struggle against that last enemy. But what is more, you clearly understand that even death is of God. You do not merely die somehow, according to some "law of nature," perhaps. No, death is the hand of God! God speaks in and through death. And He speaks the language of wrath: "By Thy wrath we pine and die." And in that last moment of struggle and anguish, when the chill hand of death chokes you, and the cold sweat of suffocation is upon your brow, the "murderer from the beginning," the devil, that "accuser of the brethren," reminds you of all your sins and transgressions, and brings them

into causal connection with the fact of your death.
He impresses upon your mind that death is, indeed, the
hand of God, and that it is the punishment for sin.
He brings you before the tribunal of God, and shows
you that you will never be able to stand before Him.
Sorrows of death are compassing you and pains of
hell get hold upon you. And you do not try to mini-
mize the seriousness of the evil. You do not appeal to
extenuating circumstances. You make no attempt to
diminish the greatness of your sin. You agree with
the tempter, that you are, indeed, damnable. But you
do not despair. Facing the full reality of the evil that
engulfs you, you say triumphantly: "But this is my
only and all sufficient comfort, that I belong to Christ!"

Yes, an only comfort in "life and in death" it is that
we belong to our faithful Saviour Jesus Christ!

It is your answer, too, in all circumstances of your
present life. For life, too, "is nothing but a continual
death." All things seem to go against you, and it
seems that your punishment awaits you every morning.
There is "depression" in the land, and in vain do you
walk the streets of the city to find employment that
you may provide for your family. Whatever savings
you were able to lay up for such times are soon consumed. You lose your home. You are forced to live
on "relief," or on charity. What is your only comfort?
That soon the evil days may be over and prosperity
will return to the land? No, but that you belong to
Christ! Sickness attacks your frame and day after
day, week after week, month after month, you travel
a way of suffering. What is your only comfort? That
there are physicians and means to alleviate your suffering; or that you may look forward to recovery?
No, but your only consolation is that you belong to
Christ! Death enters your home and takes away a

dear child, tearing it from your very heart. And again, your only, mark you well, emphatically your only comfort is that you are not your own, but belong to your faithful Saviour Jesus Christ! War rages in the world, and the very foundations of the earth are shaken. Perhaps you are called to take up arms, or your sons are sent to the battle. What is your comfort in the midst of all this confusion and suffering of this present time? That the war may soon cease and peace be restored, and your sons return from the battle in safety? No, but your only comfort in all this is that you belong to Christ! Your relationship to Christ is always sufficient!

But why is this true? How is this possible? What, then, is there in this relationship to Christ that causes it to be the source of such an all-comprehensive comfort? Who is this Christ, to Whom to belong means that all is well?

He is the Christ! That, in brief, explains fully why it is a comfort, why it is the only possible comfort, why it is an all-embracing comfort, to belong to Him. He is the Christ of God! He is the image of the invisible God, the firstborn of every creature. By Him were all things created, that are in heaven and that are in the earth, visible and invisible, whether they be thrones, or dominions, or principalities, or powers: all things were created by him, and for him. And he is before all things, and by him all things consist. And he is the head of the body, the Church, and as such he is the beginning, the firstborn from the dead, that in all things he might have the preeminence. For it pleased the Father that in him should all the fulness dwell; and having made peace through the blood of his cross, by him to reconcile all things unto himself, whether they be things in earth,

or things in heaven! Col. 1:15-20. O, but don't you
see, why it is an all-comprehensive comfort to belong
to Him? He is Christ, the Lord! He is the Lord
of heaven and of earth! God's Lord is He, the Christ,
ordained by Him from before the foundation of the
world. He is the firstborn of every creature, and the
first begotten of the dead! All things were created
with a view to Him, to His revelation, to His final
glory and victory! He is the Alpha, and also the
Omega! Nothing exists that does exist, nothing moves
that does move, nothing develops that does develop,
nothing happens that does happen, whether light or
darkness, whether sin or grace, whether the devil or
antichrist, whether life or death, whether sickness or
health, whether prosperity or adversity, whether joy
or sorrow, whether war or peace, whether angels or
principalities or powers,—nothing in heaven or in
earth or in hell exists or acts but for Him! The very
world is upheld by Him, governed by Him. All the
lines of history converge in Him. He is the center of
all things, the reason for all things, the pivot on which
all things turn, in order that in and through Him all
things might be to the praise of Him that created them!
No, "things are not what they seem." They may
seem a hopeless chaos, vanity of vanities, encircled by
death, from which there is no way out. But in Christ,
God's Christ, the Lord of life and of death, the Lord
of all, they have their reason and their unity. And
in Him all things, yes, absolutely all things must and
do actually tend to the final and eternal state of glory,
in which all things shall be united in Him and God
will be all in all. For such was the good pleasure
which God has purposed in Himself, that in the dispensation of the fulness of times he might gather
together in one all things in Christ, both which are

in heaven, and which are on earth. Eph. 1:10.

Christ, the Lord!

The firstborn of every creature; *and* the first-begotten of the dead!

O, but do you not see that to belong to that mighty Lord, Who was revealed as Christ, the Lord, in the fulness of time; Who came into the world as Christ, the Lord; Who spoke as Christ, the Lord; Who suffered and died as Christ, the Lord; Who was raised from the dead on the third day as Christ, the Lord; Who ascended into the highest heavens, and is seated at the right hand of the Most High, as Christ, the Lord; Who has all, yes, absolutely all power in heaven and on earth as Christ, the Lord; and Who will come again in due time to judge the quick and the dead, as Christ, the Lord;—that to belong to Him, I say, is absolutely your only comfort in life and in death?

If you do not belong to Him, you are, in a sense, your own, with body and soul, in life and in death. In a sense, for still you are God's, and strictly you have nothing you can call your own. To Him you owe your very breath and existence. And still He demands of you that you shall love Him with all your heart and soul and strength, that you glorify Him and be thankful. But you are your own in that you stand alone, at your own responsibility, left to help yourself. You are outside of that whole, of that communion, in which Christ is the Lord. And still there is "life and death." Still there is the load of guilt which you can never pay. Still there is the dominion of the devil and of corruption from which you can never liberate yourself. Still there is death encompassing you on every side. And in the midst of it all you are your own! Your lord is the devil, your god is your belly, your way is corruption, your end is destruction.

And you have no answer to anything, no solution of
the problem of existence, no way out of death, no comfort in either life or in death!

But I am not my own!

I belong to Christ, the Lord! And that means that
He is *my* Lord in every sense of the word. It means
that He owns me, and that I am His property, with
body and soul, in life and in death, for time and
eternity. It implies that He is responsible for me, for
my body and for my soul, for my all in life and in
death, responsible, that is, for me as part of that
whole of which He is the appointed Lord, and which
He must keep and preserve and lead into the eternal
glory of His kingdom. It signifies that He is ordained
to rule over me, and that He actually does have dominion over me, over my body and over my soul, my
mind and my will, over all that I am and have, in life
and in death, in time and in eternity! Christ, the
Lord, is my Lord! It means that all things are mine;
whether Paul, or Apollos, or Cephas, or the world,
or life, or death (yes, indeed, even death!), or things
present, or things to come,—all things are mine. For
I am Christ's; and Christ is God's! I Cor. 3:22, 23.
It implies, too, that I am more than conqueror, through
him that loved us, for neither death nor life, nor
angels, nor principalities, nor powers, nor things present, nor things to come, nor height, nor depth, nor
any other creature, shall be able to separate me from
the love of God, which is in Christ Jesus my Lord.
Rom. 8:37-39. How could they? Are they not all
Christ's? Do they not all belong to that scheme of
things that is created unto Him, and that is all arranged to cooperate in the final revelation of Him, as
my Lord, in glory?

Yes, indeed, a sure comfort it is that I belong to

Him. For the fact of my relationship to Him as my Lord is not my work, nor of my choosing. It is of grace, of sovereign grace, and absolutely of grace only. It is a relationship that is rooted in eternity, in the unchangeable good pleasure of the almighty God Himself. For He is the God and Father of our Lord Jesus Christ. He ordained Him Lord of all. It was His good pleasure that He should be the firstborn of every creature, and the firstborn of the dead, and that in Him all the fulness should dwell. It is He, too, that predestinated His own to be conformed to the image of His Son, that He should be the firstborn among many brethren. He gave me to Him. He is my Lord from before the foundation of the world. He it was, Who sent His Son into the likeness of sinful flesh, and Who caused Him to die for me, an ungodly in myself, in due time. And my Lord purchased me at the price of His own precious blood. He it is, that established the unity between Him and me, by ingrafting me into Him by a living faith through His Spirit. And so I am assured that I belong to Him, and that nothing can separate me from His love. Christ, the Lord of life and of death, is my Lord forever; to Him I belong with body and soul. And that is my all sufficient and only comfort in life and in death!

The Heidelberg Catechism enumerates the implications of this relationship somewhat in detail. He, Christ the Lord, is my faithful Saviour, who with his precious blood hath fully satisfied for all my sins, so that He is my only comfort over against the present evil of my guilt and damnableness before God: I am justified! He delivered me from all the power of the devil, so that he is no longer my lord, I am no longer his slave, and sin hath no more dominion over me. He preserves me according to the will of my heavenly

Father, even so that no hair can fall from my head without His will, for He is my Lord and with body and soul I belong to Him! Nay more, He so governs me and all things,—for He is Lord of all—that they must be subservient unto my salvation! All things! Life and death, sin and grace, heaven and earth, the world and the devil, suffering and sorrow, angels and principalities and powers,—all things must work together for my good, because I belong to Christ, my Lord! And so, this Lord of life and death, Who is the firstborn of every creature and firstborn of the dead, assures me of eternal life! Even in this life which is nothing but a continual death, He assures me of life eternal in everlasting glory and perfection through His Holy Spirit! What a comfort! In the midst of guilt and condemnation I am justified, and know that there is no condemnation for them that are in Christ Jesus! In the midst of my present sin and corruption I know that I am delivered from all the dominion of sin and all the power of the devil! And while I still lie in the midst of death, I am assured of eternal life!

And gladly I acknowledge His lordship! Indeed, not as a response on my part to what He did for me, but as the fruit of His own work for me and within me. For He it is, too, Who as my Lord makes me His subject, and constantly makes me sincerely willing to live unto Him!

It follows that only in the way of this willingness to serve Him with a thankful heart, I can be conscious of His Lordship and of my belonging to Him, and that, therefore, outside of this way the only comfort in life and in death cannot be my conscious possession.

It is this conscious possession of the only comfort in life and death, to which the Heidelberg Catechism refers in the second question and answer of this Lord's Day: "How many things are necessary for thee to know, that thou, enjoying this comfort, (or: in this comfort) mayest live and die happily? Three; the first, how great my sins and miseries are; the second, how I may be delivered from all my sins and miseries; the third, how I shall express my gratitude for such deliverance." It is, indeed, possible for one to possess this comfort in principle, without "enjoying it" consciously, or rather, without having this comfort as the deep, motivating principle of his whole life in the world. How often are we, in our actual life, far below the standard that is set up in the first question and answer of the Catechism! Yes, we are Christians, and we belong to Christ. We confess it, if we are asked, more or less hesitantly. And we believe that we have a comfort in death, that is: we hope to have a comfort when we die. But what becomes of "living and dying in this comfort"? Where is the manifestation of this "happy life-and-death" in our everyday walk and conversation? Where is it, when we move about in the world, in our shop or office or on the street; where is it in our home life? Is the Lordship of Jesus Christ really the dominating factor in our life? You know better. If it were, that which is really the only comfort in life and death, that we belong to Him, would also actually occupy the only place in our consciousness; while now the reverse is often true: we have many comforts, and the only comfort is allowed to sink into oblivion, below the threshold of our believing consciousness. If it were, we would surely seek the kingdom of God and His righteousness first, always first, believing that all things are ours; while now we are often foolish and seek the things that are below. If it were, we would surely be more than conquerors, while now we often suffer defeat, and are afraid that the world will frown upon us! What, then, is necessary for thee to know?

Yes, comfort is also knowledge. Hence, we may be instructed in this comfort, instructed by the Word of God, and through instruction we may grow in the conscious and full possession of this comfort in life and death. Three things we must know, the Catechism teaches us, know with the spiritual knowledge of faith: our sins and miseries, and the measure of them; the way of our deliverance; and the expression of our gratitude according to the Word and will of God. Do not misunderstand the intention of the Catechism here. It does not mean that we must first learn to know all about our sins and miseries in order, then, to come to the knowledge of our salvation; and, when the latter is finished, enter into the knowledge of the expression of our gratitude. The three things we must know do not successively replace one another; they are simultaneous. The Christian possesses this knowledge in its threefold fulness. Always he must know his sins and miseries; always he must know how he is delivered; and always he must know how he may express his thankfulness to God for such deliverance. They are three indispensable elements of the one knowledge. They are "the triple knowledge." And until the day of his death he must increase in this threefold knowledge. There is no end to it in this life. He never graduates. And the more he grows in true spiritual knowledge along the triple line of sin, deliverance, gratitude, the more he will approximate the high standard set up in the first question and answer of this Lord's Day and be able to say triumphantly: "This is my only comfort in life and death, that I belong to Christ my Lord!"

LORD'S DAY II

Q. 3. Whence knowest thou thy misery? Out of the law of God.

Q. 4. What doth the law require of us? Christ teaches us that briefly, Matt. 23:37-40, "Thou shalt love the Lord thy God with all thy heart, with all thy soul, with all thy mind, and with all thy strength. This is the first and great commandment; and the second is like unto it, Thou shalt love thy neighbor as thyself. On these two commandments hang all the law and the prophets.

Q. 5. Canst thou keep all these things perfectly? In no wise; for I am prone by nature to hate God and my neighbor.

I

The Law As Norm

Proceeding now from the standpoint that true comfort, also true Christian comfort, is not a mere matter of the emotions, nor of inexplicable mystic experience, but is also a consideration of the mind, of which one is able to give an intelligent account and in which one may be instructed, the Catechism asks the question: "Whence knowest thou thy misery?" Three things, we recall, one must know in order to live and die happily in this true comfort. And the first of these was: "how great my sins and miseries are." Upon a discussion of this part of the Christian comfort our instructor now enters.

We must clearly understand the meaning and purpose of the question. The question does not mean the same as: "how knowest thou that thou art miserable?" This would have no sense. That man is miserable is simply a matter of universal experience. The misery of "life and death" is too real to be in need of verification. Every individual man can testify for himself that he is aware of a good deal of evil, of suffering and sorrow, of "misfortune" and adversity in life; and he knows that he is encompassed by death on all sides, so that there is no way out. Man may attempt to drown the consciousness of his misery by drunken revelry, like a man that enjoys his last feast in a death-cell; or he may try to find the golden mean of moderation in sinful pleasure and indulgence in order to elicit from life the greatest possible amount of enjoyment; or he may proudly steel himself to endure suffering without complaint or show of emotion, like the Stoic,—the fact remains that the consciousness of misery is universal. To ask a man in this world how he knows that he is miserable would be quite superfluous. That there is something wrong, something very seriously defective with the world, yea, even that man is sinful, morally corrupt to an extent, everybody knows from his individual experience, and the report of it reaches him every day through his newspaper and over the radio. Or what note is more dominant in the tumult of the world that reaches your home through the air or by the printed sheet, than that of human corruption and human sorrow and death? But it is not the purpose of the Heidelberger to inquire as to whether and how we are aware that we are miserable. But it would instruct us with regard to the true nature and seriousness of our misery, and to realize this purpose it inquires after the source of our knowledge: "whence knowest thou thy misery?"

It must be admitted that the Catechism here applies the correct method to arrive at true knowledge of our misery. It applies a standard, a criterion, whereby to determine the real nature and cause, as well as the greatness and extent of our misery. It proceeds from the assumption that misery is something abnormal and that in order to discover just what is the character of the abnormality a *norm* must be applied. Abnormal is that which departs from the standard, the norm. A man may, in a general way, realize that his condition is abnormal, that there is something wrong with him, but only when he applies the proper criterion and gauges his condition with it can he know the character and seriousness of the abnormality. It is this truth that is implied in the question that introduces the discussion of our misery in this second Lord's Day

of the Heidelberg Catechism. The question means:
what norm do you apply to find out what is the nature
of your trouble?

And the question is very important. For it stands
to reason that the kind of remedy you seek depends
upon the knowledge you have of your misery, and the
latter again is certainly determined by the norm you
apply. And, in the case under consideration: the
misery of man in "life and death," there are only two
possibilities in this respect: either you find the norm
to be applied in man himself, or you apply a norm from
without. Whence knowest thou thy misery? What
norm did you and do you apply to determine its nature?
In the world man is always measured by himself.
Various standards are put up and applied, and accordingly, different remedies are tried to deliver humanity
from its misery of "life and death." Sometimes the
standard of the philosophy of evolution is applied,
according to which man constantly ascended the steep
and difficult slope of progress from a very low state.
And when this criterion is applied as the "norm,"
the result is rather satisfactory and flattering to man.
After all, the misery of life and death is quite normal.
Already the progress man has made is really amazing.
And there is a well founded hope that in course of time
he will advance to perfection! Or, perhaps, a certain
standard of living is applied and we speak of "the
abundant life" (rather profanely!) as the normal state
for which to strive. In that case, it is conditions,
environment that are to blame for the misery of life,
at least, not to speak now of death. Or the standard
is found in man's conscience, or in intellectual attainment, and we set ourselves to "build character" or to
improve education to overcome the misery of man and
to eliminate evil from the world.

Whence knowest thou thy misery? the instructor asks of the Christian. What is your criterion? What determines for you what is normal? And the answer is placed upon the lips of the pupil: "Out of the law of God." The law is "normal." Whatever is in agreement with the law is "normal." And whatever departs or is in conflict with the law of God is "abnormal," and therefore, miserable!

What, then, is that law of God?

In general, law is the will of God concerning the nature, position and relationship, operation and movement and life of any creature. We must not think of law as a code, as a rather arbitrary set of precepts, which one may obey or disregard without any necessary evil result. Thus it is with laws of man. You may violate them with impunity as long as there is no representative of the law to arrest you. But the law of God is the living will of God, of the immanent God, Who is present in all creation, and Who always maintains and executes His will, and deals with the creature accordingly. You cannot escape it. It besets you from every side. It is a power that blesses you as long as you are and act in harmony with it, but that crushes and curses you, the moment you transgress. Nor is the law of God an arbitrary expression of the will of God concerning the creature, something that bears no relation to the creature's nature. On the contrary, God's law for each creature is in harmony with the nature of that creature, the one is adapted to the other. And to be and operate in agreement with the law is "normal" for every creature. Disagreement with the law of God is abnormal and results in instant misery.

Thus there is a law for the fish that it shall be and move in the water; the nature of the fish is formed so as to be in harmony with this sphere of its law. To transgress this sphere of the law of God means death. There is a law for the bird in the air, for the tree in the soil, for the course of the sun and moon and stars in the firmament, for the temperature of your blood, the count of your pulse, the digestion of your food, the breathing of your lungs. And always that law of God is "normal," and the transgression of that law means misery, destruction, death. For the law of God is the living and mighty will of God, within the sphere of which He created, and within whose bounds it pleases Him to bless the creature.

And so there is a law of God for man as a volitional and intellectual being, as a rational, moral creature, as a personal nature, a free agent, who thinks and wills and speaks and acts as he is motivated from within, from the heart, by the determination and choice of his mind and will. For thus man was created. He was formed from the dust of the ground, and God breathed into his nostrils the breath of life, and thus man became a living soul. Indeed, he is a living soul, and as such he is related to the animals. But in distinction from the animals God *formed* him as to his physical organism, and by His Spirit breathed into him, so that he became a personal being, standing in a definite relation to God and to all creation. The issues of his life are from his heart. He is capable of moral self-determination. And it is of the law of God for this personal, rational and moral nature of man, the law that is in harmony with this free agent and that is "normal" for him, that the Catechism speaks in this second Lord's Day, and which it designates as the source of the knowledge of our misery. Remember that also this law is not a mere code of precepts. Its essence is not the two stone tables which Moses brought with him from the mount. It is not the "ten words" of the Decalogue. These are merely the expression, the revelation of the contents of the law of God. No, also this law is rather to be conceived as the living will of God, which is quite in harmony with the being and nature of man, God's will concerning man's will and life in relation to Himself and to all things; the law which God always maintains and according to which He always blesses man if he moves within the sphere of that law, and curses him when he transgresses.

What is that law of God?

The Catechism answers this question by quoting the Lord Jesus Himself: "Thou shalt love the Lord thy God with all thy heart, with all thy soul, and with all thy mind, and with all thy strength. This is the first and great commandment; and the second is like unto it, Thou shalt love thy neighbor as thyself. On these two commandments hang all the law and the prophets." The quotation is from Matt. 22:37-40. The context of the passage in Matthew is interesting. We read: "But when the Pharisees had heard that he had put the Sadducees to silence, they were gathered together. Then one of them, which was a lawyer, asked him a question, tempting him, and saying, Master, which is the great commandment in the law?" The Sadducees, the rationalistic sect among the Jews, who did not believe that there is a resurrection of the dead, had first tempted the Lord and tried to entrap Him by their sophistry. They had concocted a subtle story about a woman that had been the wife successively of seven brothers; and they were wondering how the Lord could possibly solve the problem as to whose wife this woman was supposed to be in the resurrection. The only possible solution would seem to be that of polyandry. And the Lord had put them to shame by pointing out their fundamental error which concerned their conception of the resurrection itself. "For in the resurrection they neither marry, nor are given in marriage, but are as the angels of God." vs. 30. And at the same time the Lord had attacked them in the very purpose for asking the question and concocting the story: to refute the whole idea that there is a resurrection: "But as touching the resurrection of the dead, have ye not read that which was spoken unto you by God, saying, I am the God of Abraham, and the God of Isaac, and the God of Jacob? God is not the God of the dead, but of the living." The Sadducees had been put to silence.

Well, the Pharisees had a double interest in this incident, although their interest did not concern the truth at all. On the one hand, they could only rejoice that their enemies, the Sadducees, had been overcome in argument, and had been put to shame in public. But on the other hand, they must surely regret the fact that it was Jesus of Nazareth that had scored this victory over the Sadducees, for Him they hated. They have a conference about the matter. And they decide that now they ought to make an attempt to ensnare the Lord in His own arguments. And they delegate one of them, a theologian of first rank, to make the attempt. Hence, he approaches the Lord with the question: "which is the great commandment of the law?"

The learned theologians of that time had developed "the law" into minutest detail. When they spoke of the law, they referred to a body of hundreds of precepts. But they made a distinction between more or less important commandments. They were even divided among themselves on the question which of the precepts were to be regarded as essential and important, and which might be relegated to the category of non-essential commandments. And when they come to Jesus with the question concerning the "great commandment," they see a possibility to entrap Him, to compel Him to select one of all the commandments as of sole importance, and thereby to characterize the rest of the law as of minor significance. And in the eyes of the public he would be branded as a liberal, a modern! But in His answer the Lord again proves that the question is based upon a very fundamental error. They do not understand the law. They have no proper conception of the essence and true nature of the law. They think it is a code of many precepts, and that they can distinguish mechanically between "the great" commandment, as one of many, and less important precepts. In this they err. If you want to discover the "great commandment," you cannot apply the method of selection from a code; you must rather search for the root of the whole law, for the essence of every precept, for that which touches not the external forms of life but the inner motives of the heart. If you do this, then there is, indeed, a "great commandment," but then it is one that governs all other commandments of God, and from which all are derived. It is the commandment of the love of God!

Love the Lord thy God! Yes, indeed, that is the one great commandment, beside which and apart from which there is none other! For the love of God is emphatically the love of GOD! To love Him means perfection. For God is good. He is the implication of all infinite perfections. He is righteous and holy and true, merciful and just, gracious and faithful. He Himself is love, the bond of perfectness. And you must love *Him!* You must not make or conceive a God of your own imagination, that is like yourself, in

order to love that idol. No, you must love the living
God, Who is GOD indeed. You must learn humbly
from Him Who He is and what He is, and love Him
for His own sake, just because He is God and because
He is good. And you must *love* Him. Your whole
life must be motivated by an intense desire to be in
harmony with Him, your mind with His mind, your
will with His will, your desires with His desires, your
word with His Word, your deed with His deeds; to be
pleasing to Him, so that He looks upon you in divine
favor and you taste His goodness; to seek and to find
Him, and to live in perfect fellowship of friendship
with Him.

Yes, that is the great commandment. From this
all possible precepts must be derived. It is their root.
It expresses the living will of God that besets man on
every side, from which there is no escape, according
to which the living God deals with man. And it concerns the whole man. It is not satisfied with any
outward performance or show of goodness in the
spoken word or the visible act: it lays hold on the
heart of man. It does not merely prescribe what man
shall *do* or even what he shall think or what he shall
contemplate, purpose or desire: it expresses what he
shall *be*, that is, what he shall be from a spiritual,
ethical viewpoint. For love is a matter of the heart,
and the heart concerns the spiritual, ethical status of
man's whole nature. His own heart he does not control: the heart controls him. From the heart are the
issues of life. As the heart is, so are man's inner
desires, thoughts, purposes, motives, aspirations, words
and deeds: as the heart is, so is man! And, therefore,
this great commandment involves the whole man: all
his heart and mind and soul and strength. "Love God"
means that you love Him for His own sake with your

whole being, with all your thinking and willing, with all your strength, every moment of your existence, in every relationship of your life, with all that you possess. Love of God is all-inclusive. It is either that or nothing, or rather: it is either love God or hate Him! Here you cannot divide or compromise. You cannot serve two masters. The great commandment is inexorable in its absoluteness. It brooks no competition. God is a jealous God!

And, mark you well, it is *the great* commandment. The Lord, in His reply to the tempting lawyer, does not evade the issue. The question was not concerning the greatest commandment, as if there were, indeed, a comparison possible, as if starting from the greatest there is a descending scale of precepts down to the very least of them all. No, the Pharisee had inquired definitely after the one great commandment. And the Lord takes him up. He is not speaking of the greatest commandment. Nor does He reply that there are really two great commandments, a great and a greater, the latter requiring the love of God, the former the love of the neighbor. On the contrary, there is only one first and great (not greatest or greater) commandment, and that is: "thou shalt love the Lord thy God." And if you remark that the Lord, nevertheless, speaks of two commandments, we must call your attention to the fact, that Christ also declares that the second is "like unto the first." And this cannot mean that there are after all two separate commandments of equal value and force, or that you could just as well say that the first commandment is like unto the second. It can only mean, that the second is rooted in the first, or, if you please, that the second, requiring love of the neighbor, is also principally love of God! You must love the neighbor with the same love wherewith you

love God! You must love the neighbor *as yourself*,
because also yourself you may not love otherwise than
with the love of God and for God's sake! You cannot
love yourself unless you love God. You cannot love
the neighbor as yourself unless the love of God is the
motive power of your life! Yes, indeed, the love of
God is the one great commandment!

Take it away and everything falls into ruins! For
"on these two commandments hang all the law and
the prophets"! And "the law and the prophets" denote
the entire Scriptures of the Old Testament. So that
we may safely say: the whole Bible depends on these
two commandments. For the law is norm. If you distort the norm, you distort everything. If the plumb-
line is not normal, your whole house in every line of
it is abnormal, and the whole city in which you live
stands awry. The love of God is norm. Take it away
or distort it, and everything tumbles down: the law
and the prophets, the sacrifices and the shadows, repentance and redemption, sin and grace, Christ and
the cross and the resurrection, yea, God Himself!

O, indeed, the law of God is norm, and if you want
to know the real nature, and the extent of our misery,
the very love of God must give us the amazing audacity
to apply that norm to ourselves!

II

Prone To Hate

Normal for man, who is made a rational, moral creature, is that he love God with all his heart and mind and soul and strength. Such is the living will of God for him. It is the great commandment. All other commandments are implied in this. Even the love of the neighbor is "like unto it." For you may love the neighbor only for God's sake, even as you may love yourself only as existing and living unto Him. Hence, love of the neighbor is impossible if you do not love God. The love of God is and remains the one great commandment. And this means that the law of God is not merely concerned with our outward deeds, or even with our inmost thoughts and desires, but that it points its finger at our very nature, for love is a matter of the heart, whence are the issues of life, and, therefore, concerns the very condition of our nature from a spiritual-ethical viewpoint. If we love God, it indicates that our nature is sound: that we are normal. If we hate God, it is because our nature is corrupt: we are abnormal. And if the latter is the conclusion that must be reached when we apply the norm of the law of God to ourselves, this abnormal condition of our nature and of our whole life is, at the same time, the explanation of our misery. For within the scope and sphere of the law God deals with us in His favor and blesses us with His friendship; but outside of that sphere we meet with His wrath on every side, and He curses us. And that wrath and curse of God is unspeakable misery.

And now the Heidelberg Catechism, in the fifth question and answer, applies this norm of the law of God, makes the comparison between it and man "by nature" and so comes to a diagnosis of the real misery of man "in life and death." The application is made personally. The fifth question, like all the preceding, is addressed to the individual Christian. It is he that is asked by the instructor to compare himself with the law of God and to express the result of this comparison: "Canst *thou* keep all these things perfectly?" And it is he that replies: "In no wise; for I am prone by nature to hate God and my neighbor." The natural man, as long as he lives in the sphere of the lie in this world, will never admit this naked truth. This does not mean that he cannot see the truth of it. Intellectually he can very well understand what it implies that the law of God demands that we shall love Him and love the neighbor for His sake. And intellectually he is also able to make the comparison between himself and that perfect law of God, and to discover that instead of love there is hatred in his heart. Ursinus writes in his "Schatboek" (I translate): "The conscience causes all men to make such a syllogism. For conscience is nothing else than a practical syllogism in the spirit of every man; of which syllogism the prescription of the law of God is the major premise, while the minor premise is the thought of our departure from that law. The conclusion is the acknowledgement that the law is good in its condemnation of us on account of sin," p. 33. That the natural man is capable of making this comparison, is due to the fact that there remains in him "since the fall, the glimmerings of natural light, whereby he retains some knowledge of God, of natural things and of the difference between good and evil and discovers some regard for virtue,"

etc. Canons of Dordrecht, III, IV, 4. He does not even
have to be acquainted with the law of the ten commandments in order to make this comparison and draw
this conclusion. For even the "Gentiles, which have
not the law do by nature the things of the law" (the
Revised Version offers the correct translation here).
This does not mean, of course, that they do "the things
contained in the law," that they keep the law of God,
but that they do themselves what the external written
code of the law did in Israel: distinguish between good
and evil with application to themselves. Hence, they
"are a law unto themselves," and they "show the work
of the law written in their hearts." Again, this does
not imply that the law of God, the law of love, is
written in their hearts, but the "work of the law,"
that standard, that criterion, that norm according to
which they must needs judge themselves and their
whole life, is always present with them, in their very
hearts. And so it happens that "their conscience" is
also "bearing witness, and their thoughts the meanwhile accusing or else excusing one another." Rom.
2:14, 15.

We may go a step further, therefore, in the light
of Scripture, and assert positively, not only that the
natural man is *capable* of making a comparison between himself and the law of God, and to draw a
fundamentally correct conclusion of self-condemnation,
but also that in his deepest heart he also actually makes
the syllogism of which Ursinus speaks in the lines
quoted above. He cannot possibly escape the necessity of doing this. For God always judges him. He
judges every man. He writes his sentence of condemnation, through the "work of the law" and by His
convicting Spirit in the heart of every man. And in
the day of the revelation of the righteous judgment

of God, "when God shall judge the secrets of men by
Jesus Christ" (Rom. 2:16), the books of the consciences will be opened, and all men will be compelled
to confess that God is righteous when He judges.

In fact, all men plainly reveal, in spite of themselves, that they constantly make this comparison.
For although they refuse to admit that they are enemies of God and of one another when it concerns themselves, they constantly pass this very judgment upon
one another. It is of this very corrupt but also very
revealing business among men that the apostle writes
in Rom. 2:1-3: "Therefore thou art inexcusable, O man,
whosoever thou art that judgest: for wherein thou
judgest another, thou condemnest thyself; for thou
that judgest doest the same things. But we are sure
that the judgment of God is according to truth against
them which commit such things. And thinkest thou
this, O man, that judgest them which do such things,
and doest the same, that thou shalt escape the judgment of God?" Life is full of this. It was thus
among the Jews. They taught others, but failed to
teach themselves; they preached against stealing, but
stole themselves; they condemned adultery and committed it; they abhorred idols and committed sacrilege;
they boasted in the law but dishonoured God by breaking the law. Rom. 2:17ff. And the same sordid
business is going on in the world today, both among
individuals and nations. At gossip parties men and
women will indignantly condemn the gossip and back-
biting of someone at the very moment that they are
engaged in the same sinful activity. Business men
berate the underhanded dealings and shady trans-
actions of others which they themselves practise.
Nations are horrified when another nation applies
the same ruthless methods of warfare followed by

themselves. We cry out in indignation, when Germany violates our "neutrality" and sinks our ships that are intended to carry aid to Great Britain. And so on. We condemn in others what we practice ourselves. And by so doing we clearly reveal that we are able to make the syllogism of which Ursinus speaks, and agree with the righteous judgment of God.

Yet, the natural man would never give the answer which the Heidelberg Catechism puts in the mouth of its pupil in reply to the fifth question: "I am prone by nature to hate God and my neighbor." He is even offended at this truth. He far prefers his own philosophy. Man may fail occasionally. He may blunder. There may even be some that habitually sin. But inherently he is good. And he loves to extol his own virtues, and sing the praises of his good deeds in public. Only, it must be understood that this lie concerning himself, this closing of his eyes to the righteous judgment of God, is not due to any lack of natural light. The lie is an ethical one, not an intellectual mistake in judgment. Just as the "fool saith in his heart" that there is no God, so he persuades himself of his own goodness. Man lives in the sphere of the lie, both with regard to God and with respect to himself.

Hence, the answer of the Catechism to the fifth question is the reply of faith, given in the light of revelation that is caused to shine in the heart of the believer by the Spirit of truth. It is, therefore, the answer of him in whose heart the love of God is already shed abroad, and who in principle loves God and His precepts. For the same reason, there is more in this answer than a cold syllogism, more than a mere logical conclusion. The believer who answers here is discovering and characterizing his misery. And he now finds that his misery is his corruption, his guilt

and sin, his hatred of God and of the neighbor. It is
this sinful condition that troubles him. With a spiritual
judgment of the mind and heart he passes sentence
upon himself, declares himself corrupt and guilty.
He stands, therefore, on God's side in passing sentence
on himself. And he does so as being of the party of
the living God. He condemns himself and repents in
dust and ashes.

Let us look a little more closely at the question and
its answer. The Catechism asks: "Canst thou keep
all these things perfectly?" Perhaps you say, that
the phrase "all these things" is hardly proper here.
Had not the Catechism summed up the law in just one
thing: the love of God? But let us remember that
this love of God is the principle of all the commandments of God, and that we must love the Lord our God
with all our heart and mind and soul and with all
our strength, i.e. all the time and in our whole life
and all its relationships. It is with a view to this, that
the catechism now puts the fifth question in this form.
"Canst thou keep all these things?" that is, canst thou
live thy whole life, with body and soul, with mind and
will and all thy powers, all the time and everywhere,
in home and church, in school and office, in the shop
and on the street, from the principle of the love of
God; and from that same principle canst thou always
love thy neighbor? "All these things," therefore, it
must remain. And notice that the adverb "perfectly"
is added. Canst thou keep all these things *perfectly?*
That is: canst thou keep them without flaw or blunder,
without ever being motivated to the slightest degree
by anything else than the love of God? Dost thou wake
up with that love of God in thy heart and mind in the
morning, and dost thou go to sleep with it in the evening? Does it motivate thee in thy eating and drinking,

in every thought of thy mind, in every desire of thy
heart, in every word thou speakest, in every deed thou
performest? Yes, it must be that or nothing. For
this adverb "perfectly" is not added in order to suggest that it is possible that you keep all these things
imperfectly; but on the contrary, to emphasize the
fact, that you must either keep them perfectly or cannot keep them at all. For it is a question of *love,* and
that of the love of *God.* And love is a matter of the
heart. Hence, here you cannot compromise; you must
choose. It is "either—or," not "both—and." It is
"Yes" or "No," never "Yes" and "No." And, what is
more, here there is no possibility of neutrality. You
cannot evade the issue. If your answer is "No," you
say "No" to the living God, to the Lord of all, and that
means that you hate Him, and hate Him perfectly, with
all your heart and mind and soul and strength. Thus
the question must be put. What is your answer?

The answer of the Christian, who stands on God's
side and in His light when he passes judgment upon
himself, is absolute and uncompromising: "In no wise;
for I am prone by nature to hate God and my neighbor." Every word here has its weight. "In no wise":
this is the direct reply to the question as to my *ability*
to keep all things perfectly, i.e. to love God. Mark you
well, it is a question of *ability,* of *capability,* not merely
of *activity.* It is an answer to the question *Canst*
thou? not to the totally different question *Dost* thou?
The answer, therefore, means: *I cannot!* The Catechism, therefore, here teaches *total incapability* to love
God. And that emphatically: "in no wise"! Keep all
these things perfectly? Impossible! I could not even
begin to keep them. And this impossibility is due to
incapability. I have not the power to love God. And
this incapability is not a physical defect, it is ethical,

moral, spiritual. I cannot, I will not, I cannot will.
I have not the light in my mind; I have not the inclination in my will; I have not the desire in my heart to
love God and to keep all these things! Yes, such is
the implication of the verdict the Christian passes
upon himself. "Canst thou?" . . . ."In no wise"!

And notice that the rest of this verdict which the
believer passes on himself as he compares himself with
the law, is a reason or ground for the opinion or conclusion expressed in the words "in no wise." Often
the words: "for I am prone by nature to hate God and
my neighbor" are understood as if they stood in ad-
versative relation to the first part of the answer. If
that were correct the sense would be: "No, I am
not capable of keeping all these things, but, on the
contrary, I am prone by nature to hate God and my
neighbor." But that is not the meaning. The last
sentence is put in the form of a reason: "*For* I am
prone," etc. It answers the question why I am incapable of keeping the law of God. It is because I am
prone by nature to hate. The reason for my incapability must be found in the condition of my nature.
The words "by nature" refer to the condition of my
mind and will and heart as they are apart from grace,
as they are by virtue of my birth and my being part
of the human race, the human nature as such. Later,
indeed, the Heidelberger repeats virtually the same
question: "But can those who are converted to God
perfectly keep these commandments?" And then the
answer is principally different from the one we are
now discussing: "No; but even the holiest of men,
while in this life, have only a small beginning of this
obedience; yet so, that with a sincere resolution they
begin to live, not only according to some, but all the
commandments of God." Q. 114. But this small

beginning, and this sincere resolution, are "by grace," not "by nature." By nature, i.e. as far as my condition is concerned apart from grace, "I am prone to hate God and my neighbor." And because of that condition of my nature I cannot possibly love God or will to love Him.

Now, this is important. To hate is the very opposite of to love. To love God is to have my delight in Him, to hate Him is to abhor Him, to dislike Him with all my heart. To love God is to seek Him, His revelation, His Word, His precepts and His fellowship; to hate Him is to depart from Him, to flee far from Him, to gainsay and oppose His Word and to trample under foot His commandments. To love God is to stand in relation of intimate friendship and fellowship to Him; to hate Him is to be an alien, a stranger to Him and His house. To love God is to reverence Him, to glorify Him and be thankful; to hate Him is to curse Him and to destroy His name, if possible, from the earth. And even as "by nature" I am prone to hate God instead of loving Him, so I am also prone to hate my neighbor. My neighbor is the one that lives next to me in this world, with whom I share my name, my position, my honor, my possessions, my business; the one that rubs elbows with me, that crosses my path. It is of him that I must think in this connection. It is true, that in a very wide sense all men are my neighbors. But if I would feel the force of this answer of the Heidelberger, I must not think in general of "all men," nor of the poor Chinese whom I never see, and whom to love seems rather easy; but I must bring before my mind the man with whom I come into contact daily, and because of whose existence I am limited in my place in the world. Well, my nature is such, that I am prone to hate God; and, therefore, also to hate my neighbor.

As my neighbor who crosses my path and who limits my place, I dislike him, and like to destroy him. If that neighbor is my employer, I simply try to get my wages out of him; if he is my employee, I try to keep those wages down as far as possible; if he is in the same business I am in, I try to force him out of business; if he is my competitor for a certain job or office, I do all in my power to disqualify him and spoil his reputation. If he is in authority over me, I rebel against him; and if he is subject to me, I lord it over him. These and many other things are daily manifestations of this hatred of my neighbor.

And do not misinterpret the words of the Heidelberger. When we read in this fifth answer that *we are prone* to hate God and our neighbor, the purpose of these italicized words is not to weaken the sense They have often been explained as if they were a mitigation of the severity of this judgment. The meaning of the words in that case is supposed to be that we are, indeed, somewhat inclined to hate God and to hate the neighbor, but this does not necessarily imply that we always actually hate them. It is true, that if we just follow the inclination of our nature, we reveal ourselves as enemies of God and of one another. But we can restrain this inclination, and then we appear rather loving and lovable. But this is a corruption of the sense of the Heidelberger, certainly no interpretation of it. The word "prone" denotes here a state of departure from a certain standard, a decline, a state of non-conformity to a certain criterion. In this case, it denotes that our nature has fallen away, declined from its upright position, is perverse, contrary to the standard of the law of God. This proneness, therefore, is such a corruption of my nature that it is impossible for me to keep the things of God's law of love, and that I do indeed hate God and my neighbor!

When the believer gives this answer and expresses this verdict upon himself, he is taught by the Spirit, Who instructs him in the Word of God. For that this is, indeed, the teaching of Scripture concerning "man by nature," no one can deny. In proof of this the "Schatboek" refers to several passages of Holy Writ, such as Rom. 3:10, 20, 23; I John 1:8, 10; Rom. 8:7; Eph. 2:3; Tit. 3:3, etc. No, indeed, there is none righteous, no not one. There is none that seeketh after God, they are all become unprofitable; their throat is an open sepulchre; with their tongues they have used deceit; their mouth is full of cursing and bitterness, their feet are swift to shed blood; destruction and misery are in their ways. That is the testimony of Scripture throughout. And that testimony is amply corroborated by actual experience as well as by the history of the world. But in the fifth answer of the catechism it is the confession of the Christian, whose only comfort over against this evil of "life and death" is that he belongs to his faithful Saviour Jesus Christ!

LORD'S DAY III

Qu. 6. Did God then create man so wicked and perverse?

A. By no means; but God created man good and after his own image, in true righteousness and holiness, that he might rightly know God his Creator, heartily love him and live with him in eternal happiness to glorify and praise him.

Qu. 7. Whence then proceeds this depravity of human nature?

A. From the fall and disobedience of our first parents, Adam and Eve, in Paradise; hence our nature is become so corrupt, that we are all conceived and born in sin.

Qu. 8. Are we then so corrupt that we are wholly incapable of doing any good and inclined to all evil?

A. Indeed we are; except we are regenerated by the Spirit of God.

I

Good And After His Image

The text as it is found in our psalter of this third Lord's Day gives a good translation of the original German. The English version made in the name and by the direction of the German Reformed Church, to which we referred before, differs from ours in a few minor details. The most important of these is, perhaps, the insertion of "that is" in the answer to the sixth question between "his own image" and "in true righteousness and holiness." This is in accord with the original German text: "Nein: sondern Gott hat den Menschen gut and nach seinen Ebenbild erschaffen, das ist, in wahrhaftiger Gerechtigkeit und Heiligkeit." And the insertion is not without significance as it serves to express clearly and definitely that, according to the Heidelberg Catechism, the image of God consisted in the original integrity of man's nature. We may also note that the German text of question eight is very emphatic on total depravity: "Sind wir aber dermassen verderbt, *das wir ganz and gar untüchtig* sind zu einigem Guten und geneigt zu allem Bösen?" This the English version authorized by the Synod of the German Reformed Church of the United States mentioned above renders rather weakly: "But are we so depraved that we are wholly unapt to any good, and prone to all evil?"

As to the contents of this third Lord's Day, it first traces the origin of the depravity of our human nature; and, secondly, it describes the extent or degree of that depravity. The contents, therefore, are very

important. Many fundamental questions are implied
in this Lord's Day, which ought to be discussed rather
thoroughly and answered as clearly and definitely as
possible. A line drawn in the wrong direction at this
point is bound to have a disastrous effect upon the
entire system of doctrine. And it is, therefore, expedient for the preacher that expounds the truth implied in this chapter of the Catechism, to take his
time and proceed carefully. Rather than to scan the
surface of the doctrine, he can better devote two or
three sermons to a discussion of its contents.

Our instructor introduces the subject matter here
by a bold question: "Did God then create man so
wicked and perverse?" I say bold, because it broaches
the problem of sin and evil with relation to God, the
problem of the theodicy. Or rather, the question introduces one aspect of this problem. How can there be
evil in the world in view of the truth that God is God,
and that He is good? God is surely sovereign. To
attribute independent existence to the forces of sin
and evil is to deny that sovereignty of God. He is the
Almighty, and He certainly could have created a world,
in which sin had no place and could not find entrance.
And not only is He the almighty Creator of all things,
"who of nothing made heaven and earth," who calls
the things that are not as if they were, but He is
also the sole and supreme Governor, without Whose
will nothing ever happens, and Who, therefore, could
surely have prevented evil to make inroads into His
creation. But this is not all. God is not only the
absolute Sovereign, Who hath done whatsoever hath
pleased Him, but He is also just and wise and good.
He is a light and there is no darkness in Him. Evil
cannot dwell with Him. He is too pure of eyes than
to behold evil. How, then, can the presence of evil be

explained? Such is the general problem of the theodicy, i.e. of the justification of God in connection with
the fact of sin and evil in the world.
And various answers have been given to this question. Some have tried to solve the problem by postu-
lating a separate source of sin and evil, next to God,
the Creator and Ruler of the Universe. The material
from which this world is formed is inherently evil;
hence, when God created the world it was inevitable
that evil should express and reveal itself. However,
God is combating the forces of iniquity and death, and
will surely overcome them in the end. Or, sin has its
ultimate origin and explanation in the sovereign, free
will of the moral creatures, angels and men. When
God created a moral being, it was inevitable that He
should leave the destiny of the world to a large extent
in his hands. Whether he should remain in his state
of integrity in which he was created or choose against
God, righteousness and truth and thus introduce evil
into God's handiwork, was entirely contingent upon the
sovereign choice of his will. God had nothing to do
with it, neither did He control it. And thus the ultimate source of all the evil, sin and suffering and death,
is the devil. This dualistic solution of the problem is
really no solution at all. Rather does it remove the
difficulty and destroy the problem by denying the
sovereignty of the Most High in relation to the forces
of darkness. Others, realizing that the existence of
evil cannot very well be entirely separated from the
will and sovereignty of God, have tried to go a step
further, rather carefully feeling their way, and explain that evil is in the world by God's permissive will.
They dare not say that God willed the entrance of evil
into His creation, for it seems to them that this would
be tantamount to making God the author of sin, which

they justly abhor. On the other hand, they try to maintain God's sovereignty as far as possible, realizing that independent existence cannot be ascribed to the powers of darkness and death. And they flatter themselves that they have found an answer which is satisfactory in the view expressed by the term "God's permissive will." However, it should be apparent at once, that this conception fails to maintain the sovereignty of God, while it does not succeed to avoid what is, from their viewpoint, the error of making God the author of sin. For, on the one hand, the term "permission" presupposes that there is a power outside of the one who permits, that can operate independently from the latter. With application to the subject under discussion, it means that there was some power of evil that had energy to work apart from God and outside of Him. The operation of this power God might have prevented, but He chose not to do so; instead He permitted that power to do its evil work. In so far, then, the view expressed by the term "permissive will" is dualistic, denies the sovereignty of God. On the other hand, it does not succeed in explaining how God can be said to have no responsibility for the presence of evil in the world. If a child is on the verge of drowning, and I have but to put out my hand and grab it in order to save it, but I choose not to do this, but permit it to drown, am I not virtually as responsible for the child's death, as if I had actually thrown it into the water? If I know that down the track along which a train is speeding there is a washout and a bridge was destroyed, and I have the opportunity to flash a danger signal to the engineer, but I choose not to do so, but permit the train to rush to its certain doom, am I not responsible for the crash and its results? And if God could have prevented the entrance of evil into the world through the restraining of the pride of the devil and the preservation of Adam in first paradise (as, no doubt, it must be granted that He could have done), but He willed to permit it, does this "permissive will" theory explain how God is not the author of sin anymore than the view that God willed it? It ought to be evident to all that it does not.

Now, strictly speaking, the Catechism does not introduce this problem in all its implications; it refers to only one aspect of it: is God the *Creator* of evil? It is, therefore, not necessary to go into the problem here. But we wish to make a few remarks about it, nevertheless. First of all, it ought to be emphasized that we cannot and may not and need not call God before the bar of our human judgment in order to determine whether He can be justified in His work or not. We cannot, for He is God, the Holy One of Israel, the incomparable One: to whom or what shall we liken God, or what standard of judgment could we possibly apply to Him? He is absolute goodness in Himself. We may not, for He alone is Judge of heaven and earth, and to call Him before the tribunal of our human judgment would be the height of presumption: "who art thou, O man, that answerest against God?" And we need not, for God justifies Himself. He justifies Himself in the cross of Jesus Christ, in the consciences of His people through faith, and in the consciences of all men; and He will justify Himself, i.e. He will clearly reveal that He is the absolute Sovereign and at the same time absolutely righteous and just, in the day of the revelation of the righteous judgment of God. Hence, *we* do not have to solve the problem. The only question that remains for us to answer is: what does God reveal of Himself with respect to His relation of sin and evil in the world? And then, two

truths seem to be very clear in the Scriptures: that
God is strictly sovereign also in relation to sin and
suffering; and that He rules in righteousness and
judges in equity, that He is a light and there is no
darkness in Him at all. This is not the place to quote
texts in proof of these two statements; but they can
easily be furnished. God hates sin, yet it is here, not
by His permission, but according to the will of His
sovereign counsel and by His own providence. And it
must serve His purpose. Sin and evil always have
been and always will be strictly subject to Him. Also
with regard to it, He hath done whatsoever He hath
pleased. So that we understand the Scriptures to
teach us this: Without ever becoming the author of
sin and evil, and without ever taking pleasure in iniquity, yea, so, that He always hates sin and judges
it to condemnation, God has nevertheless willed that
sin should enter into the world to serve His own holy
purpose.

And this is in full agreement with the teaching of
our Catechism in as far as it broaches this question:
"Did God then create man so wicked and perverse?
By no means; but God created man good and after His
own image, in true righteousness and holiness, that he
might rightly know God his Creator, heartily love Him
and live with Him in eternal happiness to glorify and
praise Him." Bold though the question may be, it follows here naturally enough. The last answer in the
preceding Lord's Day stated that we are "so wicked
and perverse" that we are wholly contrary to the law
of God, so that, while it demands that we love God
above all and our neighbour as ourselves, we hate Him
and one another. And the Catechism had stated that
this hatred of God and of our neighbour is not a matter
of a sinful *deed* only, nor does it arise from a sinful

habit we have formed, but that it arises from the perversity and wickedness of our *nature.* We are *by
nature* prone to hate God and the neighbour! But
we did not make our own nature! How, then, is it so
corrupt? What was more natural than to put the question in this form: "Did God create man so wicked and
perverse?"

And the answer is an emphatic denial: "by no
means." And this is followed by a statement concerning man's original state as he came from the hand of
his Creator: "God created man good and after his own
image." He created man *good.* In this connection
this means: without corruption and sin; and, positively, so that man could reach the purpose of his existence
in relation to God and to all things. And this goodness
of man in the state of his original integrity consisted
in this, that he was made after the image of God.
The question is: what does this mean? What is implied in the image of God?

The general meaning of the phrase "image of God"
is clear enough. It signifies that man was so created
that there was a creaturely likeness of God in him,
that there was a reflection of the perfections of God
in man. Thus we must understand the statement of
Scripture in Gen. 1:26: "And God said, Let us make
man in our image, after our likeness." About the
interpretation that would read this text as if it intended to make a distinction between "image" and
"likeness" in such a way that "image" refers to the
body while "likeness" refers to the soul of man, we
need not say much. This distinction is rather arbitrary. It is much more natural to understand that
"likeness" is meant as a further definition of "image,"
so that the text means: "let us make man in our image
in such a way that the image is also a likeness." All

images are not likenesses. There are images that only
represent the objects for which they stand. Thus, for
instance, the images of the cherubim in the holy of
holies were representative images, but not necessarily
meant to be likenesses of spiritual beings. But man is
so made in the image of God, that the image is also a
likeness, so that his very nature reflects some of God's
own perfections. There is a creaturely likeness of God
in man.

Of more importance, however, is the question: just
what belongs to this image of God in man? And this
question is not always answered in the same way.
Augustine, too, made a distinction between "image"
and "likeness," and explained that the former consisted especially in the knowledge of the truth, while
the latter implied the love of virtue. Later, during the
time of Scholasticism, the image was explained as referring to mere natural attributes of the soul, such as
reason and knowledge, intellect and will; while likeness
was a spiritual, ethical concept, including righteousness and holiness and true spiritual knowledge of God.
This led later to the Roman Catholic distinction be-
.tween man as he is *naturally* good, and man with the
additional gift of the likeness of God, according to
which he is able to seek the higher, spiritual things of
God. Man, therefore, can lose the image of God and
still be *naturally* good, although he is no longer able
to perform spiritual works. Others identified image
and likeness, and taught that the image of God included both natural endowments, such as man's rational and moral nature, his conscience and will, his freedom and "immortality," and man's original righteousness and holiness, his conformity to the will of God.
Some even went to the extreme, especially among the
Greek theologians, of letting the image of God consist

exclusively in the natural gifts of his rational and moral nature. Remonstrants and Socinians identified the image of God in man with the dominion God gave him over all the earthly creation. The Reformers, it seems, were inclined to limit the image of God to man's original integrity, his true knowledge of God, righteousness and holiness. Especially Lutheran theologians are very explicit on this point. They deny that the "rational soul" of man as such is part of the image of God. And they argue that man's reason and will as such cannot be lost, while plainly, according to the Bible, man lost the image of God, whence it follows that the former cannot belong to that image that was lost. It is sometimes suggested that Calvin included more in the image of God than what belonged to Adam's original rectitude, because he speaks of the image as being nearly wiped out after the fall: "prope deleta." But this is, to say the least, very doubtful. For, in his Institutes, Book I, chap. XV, par. 4 he writes as follows: "However, it appears that no complete definition is as yet given of that image, unless it be set forth more clearly in which faculties man excells by which he must be considered a mirror of the glory of God. Now this can be known better from no other source than from the restoration of the corrupt nature. (Id vero non aliunde melius quam ex reparatione corruptae naturae cognosci potest.)" And later in the same paragraph Calvin refers to the contents of this restored image by quoting from Col. 3:10 and Eph. 4:24, and he explains: "Whence it appears what Paul comprehends chiefly under the image of God. In the first place he mentions knowledge (Priore loco agnitionem ponit), and further true righteousness and holiness (altero autem sinceram iustitiam et sanctitatem); whence we gather that in the beginning the image of God was conspicuous by the light of the mind, the rectitude of the heart, and the soundness of all the parts (unde colligimus initio in luce mentis, in cordis rectitudine, partiumque omnium sanitate conspicuam fuisse Dei imaginem.)" And as concerns the "prope deleta" (well-nigh wiped out), the phrase occurs in the following sentence: "since then the image of God consists in the original excellency of the human nature (integra naturae humanae praestantia), which shone forth in Adam before the fall, afterwards however is so corrupted and nearly wiped out, (vitiata et prope deleta), that in the ruins there is nothing left than what is confused, mutilated and infected by filth (ut nihil ex ruina nisi confusum, mutilum, labeque infectum supersit)" etc. Calvin may have taught that the image of God was not entirely wiped out through the fall, but he certainly tells us here in the strongest language that what is left is nothing but miserable ruins and corruption. And that also man's body and his rational soul as such belong to this image cannot be found in the Institutes.

Later Reformed theologians, however, made a distinction, that has found a way into the Reformed Churches through preaching and instruction, and is rather generally accepted as belonging to Reformed doctrine. I am referring, of course, to the distinction between the image of God in a wider and in a narrower sense. To the former then belong man's rationality and morality and immortality; to the latter his true knowledge of God, righteousness and holiness; the former implies all that distinguishes man from the lower animals, the latter is his original state of righteousness. The latter was lost through the fall; the former, however, was retained. Man still possesses the image of God in a wider sense, though he no more possesses his original integrity.

How is to be judged of this distinction?

It cannot be claimed that the distinction: "image of God in a wider and in a narrower sense," is confessionally Reformed. Our Three Forms of Unity rather leave the impression that they favor the idea of limiting the image of God to man's original integrity, true knowledge of God, righteousness and holiness. This is true of our Catechism in the Lord's Day we are now discussing. In answer to the question: "Did God create man so wicked and perverse?" it states: "No; but God created man good, and after His own image, that is, in righteousness and true holiness." It certainly leaves out of view the image of God in a wider sense altogether, and confines the scope of that image to "righteousness and true holiness." This does not mean that the authors of the Heidelberg Catechism were not acquainted with the distinction, or even themselves did not favor it. From Ursinus' *Schatboek* it is quite evident that they did. He answers the question: "In how far is it (the image of God) lost; and what is left of it in man?" as follows:

"This image of God, after which God created man in the beginning, and that, before the fall, shone in man as a light; this very beautiful image of God man has lost through sin after the fall, and he is changed after the ugly image of the devil. A few remnants and sparks, however, of this image were left after the fall, which are even now present in unregenerated men. 1. The essence of the soul is still incorporeal, rational, immortal and still has its faculties; also the freedom of the will, so that man freely wills what he wills. 2. Great knowledge of God, of nature, of the difference between good and evil; this knowledge is the principle of all science. 3. A few vestiges and seeds of moral virtues, and a certain possibility of external order. 4. The enjoyment of much temporal good. 5. A certain dominion over the creatures; for also this has not entirely been lost, many creatures are still subject to the power of man and he can rule over them and use them to his advantage. These remnants of the image of God in man, even though through sin they have become terribly dark and unstable, are, nevertheless, in one way or another left in the nature of man; and that too: 1. In order that they might serve as witness of God's mercy toward us who are unworthy; 2. in order that God might use them for the restoration of His image in us; 3. in order that the reprobate might have not a single excuse." pp. 39, 40.

Nevertheless, all this additional material, much of which is derived from Scholastic philosophy, and through it from Plato and Aristotle, rather than from Scripture, is not incorporated in the Catechism. And this shows that the authors of the Catechism considered the image of God as consisting chiefly in the original integrity of man. Also the Belgic Confession limits the image of God in the same fashion in Art. 14: "We believe that God created man out of the dust of the earth, and made and formed him after His own image and likeness, good, righteous, and holy, capable in all things to will agreeably to the will of God." And the Canons of Dordrecht, III, IV, 1, have this to say about the subject: "Man was originally formed after the image of God. His understanding was adorned with a true and saving knowledge of his Creator, and of spiritual things; his heart and will were upright, all his affections pure, and the whole man was holy." The distinction between the image of God in a narrower and in a wider sense, therefore, even though it is embodied in many works on dogmatics, and commonly taught through the media of question books in catechetical classes, as well as from the pulpit, has never received official standing in the Reformed Churches.

Nor is the distinction an innocent one and without danger to true doctrine. It is dangerous, because it prepares room for the further philosophy that there are remnants of the image of God left in fallen man, and that, therefore, the natural man cannot be wholly depraved. The argument is, that man lost the image of God in a narrower sense, but he retained that image in a wider sense. By the latter, then, is usually meant, that man still has an immortal, rational soul, in distinction from the animals. Now, except for this heresy about man's "immortal soul," very little harm results as long as nothing more is said, and as long as it is strictly remembered that nothing of man's original righteousness is contained in this image of God in a wider sense. But the trouble is that words have meaning, and that the real meaning of words will assert itself regardless of false distinctions we may try to maintain. After all, the term "image of God" conveys a meaning that cannot very well be applied to a man that is changed into the image of the devil. It carries a favorable connotation. It denoted goodness, moral, ethical, spiritual integrity. To state that man after the fall is an image bearer of the devil, and at the same time to maintain that he still bears the image of God or a remnant of it, does not harmonize with each other, contains a flat contradiction. And so it happens, that the distinction of image of God in a narrower and wider sense, gradually but irresistibly is used to teach that there is still a remnant of man's original righteousness and integrity in fallen man, and that he is not totally depraved. It is a distinction that lends itself very easily to support the view of those who insist that there is a certain common grace by virtue of which natural man is not so depraved as without that grace he would have been. And if this is not a denial of the doctrine of total depravity, words certainly have lost their plain meaning.

It may not be superfluous to insert a paragraph here about the so-called "immortality of the soul." Above I spoke of "the heresy" that man's soul is immortal. And a heresy it certainly is, for the which there is no item of proof in the Word of God; which, on the contrary is condemned by Scripture throughout. It is one of those doctrines that have been inherited by the Church from Platonic philosophy, that have simply been received without criticism and without being judged in the light of Scripture, and that have been accepted by the Church ever since. It has become a very "gangbare meening," a generally current opinion that man has an immortal soul. So general and so deeply rooted is this philosophical tenet, that I have often experienced that the statement "the heresy about man's immortal soul" will act like a boomerang, so that many consider the statement itself a heresy! People have been taught to speak of man's immortal soul so persistently; they pray so often that the "immortal soul" may be saved; and they admonish one another so earnestly that they have "an immortal soul" to lose, that it is considered almost sacrilegious to maintain that man's soul is not immortal, and what is more, very really dead, unless he is regenerated by the Spirit of God. The trouble is that immortality is often identified with unending existence. When philosophy speaks about immortality, it does not take eternal death and hell into consideration. According

to its view, man is either immortal, that is, the soul
continues to live after this life, or physical death ends
all.   But this is not the view of Scripture.   Surely,
there is a continued existence after temporal death,
but this is not the same as immortality.   The latter
term in Scripture signifies the state in which man is
exempt from death, the state of incorruptibility, of
eternal life.   And this state can be attained only in
Christ.   No man is by nature immortal, either as to
body or soul.   No man outside of Christ has an immortal soul.   Even though it is certainly true, that the
soul of every man will continue to exist, and that the
body of every man will be raised from the dust, neither
this continued existence nor this resurrection means
that he is or will be immortal.   For the wicked shall
suffer eternal death both in body and soul; and it is
only the righteous that shall be raised incorruptible.
And, therefore, we should not follow the language of
philosophy, and we should refuse to adopt its terminology.   The truth is that man is mortal.   He has a
body that can die and so he has a perishable soul.
God can destroy both soul and body in hell.   And immortality is the word that can be applied only to the
state of the glorified saints in Christ.

II

The Image And Its Bearer

If a distinction must be made in the image of God, after which man was created, we prefer to make the distinction between the image in a formal and in a material sense. By the former is meant the fact that man's nature is adapted to bear the image of God. Not every nature of the creature is capable of bearing the image of God, showing forth a reflection of God's own ethical perfections, of knowledge, righteousness and holiness. It is evident that it requires a rational, moral nature to bear that image of God. And by the image of God in a material sense is meant that spiritual, ethical soundness of the human nature, according to which he actually shows forth the virtues of knowledge of God, righteousness and holiness. If you will, we may distinguish between man as the image-*bearer*, i.e. as being capable of bearing the image of God, and man as actually bearing God's image.

In Gen. 2:7 we read: "And the Lord God formed man of the dust of the ground, and breathed into his nostrils the breath of life; and man became a living soul." We learn here that man was created by one, special, very distinct, twofold act of God, which emphasizes from the beginning the two aspects of man's being. Thus, no doubt, we must understand this passage. Often this creative act of God, whereby He gave being to man, is understood as consisting of two separate acts: first God formed a sort of clay image;

and when it was finished, He made the image alive by breathing into it. According to this conception, man is really two beings. He is a body with a soul in it. And the soul is really the life of the body. When he dies, his soul leaves the body, and this departure of the soul is the cause of the death of the body. But it is evident that this is not the correct conception of man, and surely not of the text in Gen. 2:7. Do not misunderstand this. God certainly created man by a twofold act: by forming him as to the physical side of his nature out of the dust of the ground, and by bringing into existence the spiritual side of his nature by breathing into him the breath of life. Nor do we agree with those who proceed on the assumption that Scripture uses the word "soul" always in the same sense, and who insist that we cannot properly make the distinction between man's body and his soul. Scripture certainly teaches that man's body can die, while his "soul" or "spirit" continues to lead a conscious existence, either in life or in death. Does not the preacher emphasize that, when the body returns to the dust, the spirit returns to God who gave it? Does not the Lord speak of those that kill the body, but cannot destroy the soul? Does not Christ Himself commend His spirit into the hands of the Father, when He is about to die? And does not the apocalyptic seer of the book of Revelation behold "the souls of them that were beheaded for the witness of Jesus and for the Word of God. . . . and they lived and reigned with Christ a thousand years"? Rev. 20:4. But even so man is not two beings but one, with a physical and spiritual side, a living physical organism, formed out of the dust of the ground, and this living organism most intimately united with a rational spirit: one physical and psychical, intellectual and volitional rational and moral being, adapted to be lord of the earth and servant of the living God.

Notice, that in Gen. 2:7 the statement: "and man became a living soul" is predicated of the *whole man.* Man did not *receive* a living soul, but he *became* a living soul. He is not a body with a living soul in it, but he *is* a living soul. And he *became* a living soul, not merely by the inbreathing of God into his nostrils, but by the whole of God's creative act: His forming man out of the dust and His breathing into him the breath of life. Thus, i. e. by this twofold act of God, man became a living soul. *Man* is the subject about which is spoken throughout the text: *man* is formed, into *man's* nostrils is breathed the breath of life, *man* became a living soul. "Living soul" in Gen. 2:7, there-fore, does not at all refer to man's spiritual being in distinction from his body. This will be all the more evident if we consider that the same term "living soul" is used also in reference to the animals. In our English translation of Gen. 1 this is not apparent, but the Holland rendering is more faithful to the original, when it speaks of the animals as "levende zielen." Gen. 1:20 should have been translated: "Let the waters swarm with swarms of living souls." And Gen. 1:24 should read: "And God said, Let the earth bring forth living souls after their kind." In both cases identically the same words are used as in Gen. 2:7 with respect to man. Fish and fowl, cattle and beasts of the field and creeping things are living souls. And thus man also was made a living soul. The term as such, therefore, as it is used in Gen. 1 and 2, denotes nothing more than a creature with locomotion, a creature that is free to move about by an act that has its impetus from within the creature. Plants are not living souls. They are fixed in the earth. They do not freely determine their own movement on the earth. But animals and man are living souls.

However, there is a sharp distinction between the animal as a living soul and man. This is indicated by the way in which man is created in distinction from the creation of the animals. Like the animals he is, indeed, taken out of the ground. He is of the earth earthy. He is not the Lord of heaven. I Cor. 15:47, 48. To the earth he is closely related. The chemical composition of his physical organism is earthy. He is created to live on the earth. As he was created he could not possibly live in heaven. Flesh and blood cannot inherit the kingdom of God! Dependent on the earth he is for his very subsistence and life. From the earth his life must constantly be replenished. And if he cannot eat of the tree of life, he must needs return to the dust sooner or later. Gen. 3:22. And he has a psychical body, a body that is wholly adapted to serve as instrument of a "soul," to live an earthly life. He has earthly sensations and earthly perceptions. He has an earthly ear to catch earthly sounds; he has an earthly eye to catch earthly sights; an earthly sense of taste and touch and smell that brings him into contact with earthly things only. There are things which his eye cannot see, and his ear cannot hear, and that cannot even arise in his heart without special revelation. Even his thinking and willing, his ideals and aspirations, his ties of friendship and love,—all assume earthly forms. The first man is of the earth earthy!

But let us note the distinction between man as a living soul and the animals. This distinction is indicated by a twofold difference between the creation of man and that of the animals. First of all, the animals

were simply called forth from the ground (the fish
and fowls from the waters) ; man is *formed* as to his
physical side by the very fingers of the great Artificer.
Man did not simply find his origin in the ground.
There is no continuous line of evolution from the
animals to man. The line is broken. God formed
man out of the dust of the ground. The "missing link"
is missing indeed! Closely man is related to the
animals. Both are living souls. We may even say
that there is a kind of image of man in the animals.
This is very evident in the life of the higher animals.
Within their limited sphere they reflect an image of
the life of man. Also the animal remembers, dreams,
rejoices and evinces deep sorrow, loves and hates,
shows fear, courage, faithfulness, and even shows a
sense of guilt in relation to man. But withal there is
a sharp boundary fixed by the very act by which man
was created. The animals are called forth by God's
Word out of the ground, man is formed by God's
creative hand. The very act that forms Adam out
of the earth elevates him above it! Being closely
related to the earth because he is formed of its substance, he is capable of living and moving on the earth,
can enter into communion with its creatures, share
his life with them, use their resources as means to
labor with them and to support and enrich his own life
from them; yet, by being formed by God's own fingers,
he is elevated above the earth: his relation to the dust
of the earth is one of freedom. For he was made to
be lord of the earthly creation, and even his physical
organism is adapted to this lordship. His upright
position, his noble form bespeak royalty; his finely
formed hand was shaped for the sceptre; his face is
the face of a king. And by his being *formed* out of
the dust of the ground even his physical organism

was worthy of a being that was adapted to be the image-bearer of God!

But there is another distinction between the way in which God created the animals and that in which He gave being to man: the breathing into man's nostrils of the breath of life. This act of God is absent in the creation of the animals altogether. It is an act of the Spirit of God. While God took and formed man out of the dust of the ground, He so belabored him by His Spirit that he became a living soul which is also a personal spirit. Of the animals nothing more is said than that they were called forth out of the ground and out of the waters. They are purely material living souls. Their soul is in their blood. Not so with man. He is made a psychical body, a body that is so finely and delicately constructed as to be adapted to be the instrument of a personal soul; and he is made a personal spirit by the very inbreathing of God into his nostrils of the breath of life. By this second aspect of God's creative act man's whole nature became adapted to be the bearer of God's image. This is not the same as saying that he is God's image. But it means that he is a personal being, with a rational, moral nature, capable of standing in a conscious, personal relation to God, capable of knowledge of God, of righteousness, and holiness. And this *capability* of being endowed with God's image, we would prefer to call God's image in a *formal* sense. No matter what becomes of man, whether he actually shows forth the beauty and glory of the image of God, or whether he turns into the very opposite and reveals the image of the devil, always you can distinguish him as a creature *that ought to show forth God's image,* always he remains the living soul that was formed by God's fingers out of the dust of the ground, and into whose

nostrils God breathed the breath of life originally;
always he remains a personal, rational and moral
being, who *ought to* live in covenant fellowship with
the living God!

However, man was originally created so that he
actually possessed the image of God. He was not only
formally adapted to bear the image of God, but he was
also materially endowed with the spiritual-ethical virtues of that image. These virtues are usually distinguished as true knowledge of God, righteousness,
and holiness. The Catechism in its answer to question
6 directly mentions only "true righteousness and holiness"; yet, the element of true knowledge of God is
clearly implied in what follows: "that he might rightly
know God his creator." Fact is, that true righteousness and holiness cannot be divorced from true knowledge of God. Without the latter the former are impossible, and without true righteousness and holiness
true knowledge of God cannot exist. All three are
often expressed in the one term: "man's original righteousness." It is that original goodness of man's
nature, according to which it was wholly motivated
by the love of God, and with all its faculties and powers
moved in the direction of God, so that the operation of
his heart and soul and mind and will and all his
strength were in accord with the will of God. And
this one virtue of complete integrity is distinguished
as true knowledge, righteousness, and holiness.

That this is, indeed, the contents of the image of
God is evident from Scripture. For it presents man's
redemption and deliverance from sin as the restoration
of the image of God in him, and the image of God
as restored in the redeemed sinner is said to consist of
this true knowledge of God, righteousness, and holi-

ness. Thus the apostle instructs us in Eph. 4:23, 24, that believers have so learned Christ, and are so instructed by the truth as it is in Jesus (vss. 20, 21) that they are renewed in the spirit of their mind, and that they put on "the new man, which after God is created in righteousness and true holiness." And the admonitions to the believers of Colosse in Col. 3:5ff. are based on the fundamental truth that they "have put off the old man with his deeds; and have put on the new man, which is renewed in knowledge after the image of him that created him." Col. 3:9, 10. And this is confirmed by all the rest of Scripture in so far as it has reference to the renewal of man through the grace of the Lord Jesus Christ. They are called to present their bodies a living sacrifice, holy, acceptable to God, and not to be conformed to this world, but to be transformed by the renewing of their mind, that they may prove what is that good and acceptable and perfect will of God, Rom. 12: 1, 2. They must cleanse themselves from all filthiness of the flesh and spirit, and perfect holiness in the fear of God, II Cor. 7:1. For they were sometimes darkness, but now they are light in the Lord, and as children of light they must walk, Eph. 5:8. The Father bestowed the great love upon them that they should be called children of God. And now they are children of God, and it is not yet revealed what they shall be; but when it shall be manifest, they shall be like God, for they shall see Him as He is. I John 3:1, 2. Everywhere the Bible teaches that redemption and deliverance from sin restores the likeness of God in us, and that this likeness consists in a reflection of God's ethical perfections, particularly those of knowledge, righteousness, and holiness. For this is life eternal that they know the only true God, and Jesus Christ whom He has sent. John 17:3.

By these three spiritual virtues, that originally
adorned the nature of man, the rectitude of his whole
being in relation to God and all things is denoted.
By holiness is meant, not any acquired purity, but that
original rectitude of his nature, according to which he
was consecrated to God in love with all his mind and
heart and soul and strength. His whole soul yearned
after the living God, and had its delight in His favor
and fellowship. His righteousness was not an imputed
righteousness, nor was it acquired, but it was that
virtue of his whole nature according to which he was
wholly in harmony with the will of God and that according to the judgment of God, so that he was fully
capable of doing the will of God, and to do that will
was his delight. And his knowledge of God was not a
mere intellectual or natural knowledge of the Most
High, so that he knew who and what God is; nor was
it a ready made system of theology or dogmatics with
which Adam was endowed from the beginning; but it
was that original rectitude of his mind by virtue of
which he immediately and spontaneously knew God,
both through the revelation of all the works of God
round about him, and through the direct Word of God
that was addressed to him in paradise. And through
this positive knowledge of God he had a living contact with the Most High, the fellowship of friendship,
that was his life. And thus Adam was "good." He
was so made that he was quite capable of serving the
Lord his Creator, to be His representative in all the
world, His prophet to know and to glorify Him, His
priest to consecrate himself and all things unto Him,
and His servant-king to rule in righteousness over the
works of God's hand, and thus to live in "eternal happiness to glorify and praise Him."

And even on this point the truth differs radically from the Pelagian errors, that teach "That the spiritual gifts, or the good qualities and virtues such as: goodness, holiness, righteousness, could not belong to the will of man when he was first created, and that these, therefore, could not have been separated therefrom in the fall"; and "that in spiritual death the spiritual gifts are not separated from the will of man, since the will itself has never been corrupted, but only hindered through the darkness of the understanding and the irregularity of the affections; and that, these hindrances having been removed the will can bring into operation its native powers, that is, that the will of itself is able to will and to choose, or not to will and not to choose, all manner of good which may be presented to it." Canons III, IV, Rejection of Errors, 2, 3. The fundamental error of Pelagianism in all its forms is always that it denies any other righteousness and holiness than that which is the result of the choice and act of the will of man. Hence, righteousness and holiness cannot be virtues with which the nature of man was originally endowed. Man could be either righteous or unrighteous, holy or unholy, according as he chose to be. Only the *deed* of righteousness makes a man righteous. And according to the same fundamental principle, man could never become corrupt in nature. It may have become more difficult for him to choose for righteousness and holiness because of the fall; but essentially he is the same as before the fall: a being that can be either righteous or unrighteous by the choice of his own will. And grace may "give him a lift" in his efforts to be righteous after the fall, it never is a radical change of his nature. Over against this Pelagian corruption, which is as superficial as it is pernicious, stands the plain truth of the Word of

God and of our Confessions, that God created man good and after His own image in true knowledge, righteousness and holiness.

What became of this image of God in man must be discussed in another connection. But even here we may be reminded of two facts: 1. that man did not possess this image of God as a treasure that could not be forfeited and lost; it was amissible; and 2. that it is not enough to say, that man merely lost this image of God, but that through the fall it was changed into reverse. As to the first, man was created lapsible. He was, indeed, the son of God by creation, but he was not the Son of God in the flesh. He could fall. He was free, but he had not attained to the highest freedom. His freedom consisted in this that he was capable of doing the will of God, for this alone is freedom; but he could, nevertheless, by an act of his own will subject himself to the slavery of sin. The highest freedom is the state in which it will be forever impossible for man to choose contrary to the will of God. But this is attainable only in the Lord Jesus Christ, the Son of God united with our nature. Adam could lose the image of God. And as to the second, merely to state that through the fall man lost that image is not expressing the whole truth. Surely, he did lose it, and lose it completely. There is nothing left of man's original integrity, of his knowledge of God, righteousness, and holiness. But it is equally true, that through the fall his rational-moral nature became wholly corrupt. The spiritual-ethical operation of his heart and mind and will and strength was put into reverse, so that his knowledge became darkness and love of the lie, his righteousness became rebellion and iniquity, his holiness became aversion to God and impurity in all his affections. The being that was designed to be the image of God changed into the image of the devil! And only through the grace of Christ, our only comfort in life and death, is this image restored and raised to a heavenly level and glory that can be lost nevermore!

III

The Covenant With Adam

To the relation in which Adam stood to God the
Catechism refers in the words: "that he might rightly
know God his Creator, heartily love Him, and live with
him in eternal happiness to glorify and praise him."
That this relation is a covenant relation is not expressly stated, nor is it implied in the words that the relation
between God and man in paradise was that of the so-
called "covenant of works." Nor does Ursinus, in
his "Schatboek" speak of this relation as a covenant-
relation, still less does he mention a "covenant of
works." And also the rest of our Confessions are
silent on this matter. They all teach, to be sure, that
the sin of Adam is the source of the corruption of the
whole human race, and that by the fall and disobedience of our first parents our nature is become so corrupt that we are all conceived and born in sin. But
this refers to the relation between Adam and the
human race, not to that between God and Adam. And
of a "covenant of works" our confessional standards
know nothing. A brief statement concerning this
covenant is found in "The Irish Articles Of Religion,"
1615, as follows: "Man being at the beginning created
according to the image of God (which consisted especially in the wisdom of his mind and the true holiness
of his free will), had the covenant of the law ingrafted
in his heart, whereby God did promise unto him everlasting life upon condition that he performed entire
and perfect obedience unto His Commandments, according to that measure of strength wherewith he was

endued in his creation, and threatened death unto him if he did not perform the same." (Schaff: *Creeds of Christendom*, Vol. III, p. 530.) And also the Westminster Confession expresses itself on this subject in ch. VII, 2 in the following words: "The first covenant made with man was a covenant of works, wherein life was promised to Adam, and in him to his posterity, upon conditions of perfect obedience." Here, therefore, we meet with the term "covenant of works."

But although this idea of a "covenant of works" was not incorporated into our Reformed Standards, it has become a rather common term, and the doctrine represented by it was developed in works on dogmatics and taught in sermons and catechetical classes, until it was quite generally accepted in Reformed circles as a part of the Reformed heritage. It is rather common to speak of the relation of Adam to God as being that of a covenant of works. A rather elaborate discussion of this covenant is found in Dr. Charles Hodge's *Systematic Theology,* II, pp. 117-122. He writes: "God having created man in his own image in knowledge, righteousness, and holiness, entered into a covenant of life with him, upon condition of perfect obedience, forbidding him to eat of the tree of knowledge of good and evil upon the pain of death". p. 117. He admits that this statement does not rest upon any express declaration of the Scriptures. But he argues as follows: "It is, however, a concise and correct mode of asserting a plain Scriptural fact, namely, that God made to Adam a promise suspended upon a condition, and attached to disobedience a certain penalty. (Let us note here, however, that also this "plain Scriptural fact" that God made a promise of eternal life to Adam, again "does not rest upon any express declarations of the Scriptures.") This is what in Scriptural language is meant by a covenant, and this is all that is meant by the term as here used.   Although the word covenant is not used in Genesis, and does not elsewhere, in any clear passage, occur in reference to the transaction there recorded (however, Gen. 2 does not speak of any *transaction* at all), yet inasmuch as the plan of salvation is constantly represented as the New Covenant, new, not merely in antithesis to that made at Sinai, but new in reference to all legal covenants whatever (it would be quite difficult to find Scriptural proof for this statement), it is plain that the Bible does represent the arrangement made with Adam as a truly federal transaction.   The Scriptures know nothing of any other than two methods of attaining eternal life: the one that which demands perfect obedience, the other that which demands faith.   If the latter is called a covenant, the former is declared to be of the same nature." p. 117.

The elements of this "covenant of works," according to Dr. Hodge, are the usual "condition, promise, and penalty." Thus he writes: "The reward promised to Adam on condition of his obedience was life. (1) This is involved in the threatening: 'In the day that thou eatest thereof, thou shalt surely die.' It is plain that this involved that he should not die, if he did not eat. (This may be true, but this is quite different from saying that Adam would attain to "eternal life," if he did not eat.) (2) This is confirmed by innumerable passages and by the general drift of Scripture, in which it is so plainly and so variously taught, that life was, by the ordinance of God, connected with obedience. 'This do and thou shalt live.' 'The man that doeth them shall live by them.' This is the uniform mode in which the Bible speaks of that law or covenant under which man by the constitution of his nature and by the ordinance of God, was placed. (But again, that man shall live by obedience is quite different from the statement that he should attain to "eternal life.") (3) As the Scriptures everywhere present God as a judge or moral ruler, it follows of necessity from that representation, that his rational creatures will be dealt with according to the principles of justice. If there be no transgression there will be no punishment. And those who continue holy thereby continue in the favor and fellowship of him whose favor is life, and whose lovingkindness is better than life. (This is true, but still fails to prove that Adam would have attained to a higher state of life and glory, had he not sinned, or that God made such a promise to him.) (4) And finally, holiness, or as the Apostle expresses it, to be spiritually minded, is life. There can be therefore no doubt, that had Adam continued in his holiness, he would have enjoyed that life which flows from the favour of God." (Nor can there be any doubt that in the state of his original rectitude he did enjoy that life; but the question is: would he have attained to that higher glory which is "eternal life"?), p. 118.

This life, which was promised to Adam, according to Dr. Hodge, was "the happy, holy, and immortal existence of soul and body." Nor would *perpetual* obedience have been necessary as a *condition* of the covenant. For he writes: "The question whether perpetual, as well as perfect obedience was the condition of the covenant made with Adam, is probably to be answered in the negative. It seems to be reasonable in itself and plainly implied in the Scriptures that all rational creatures have a definite period of probation. If faithful during that period they are confirmed in their integrity, and no longer exposed to the danger of apostasy. Thus we read of the angels who kept not

their first estate, and those who did. Those who remained faithful have continued in holiness and in the
favor of God. It is therefore to be inferred that had
Adam continued obedient during the period allotted
to his probation, neither he nor any of his posterity
would have been ever exposed to the danger of sinning." pp. 119-120.

Hence, according to the presentation of Dr. Hodge,
there would have come a moment in Adam's life, had
he not sinned, when the period of probation was finished, and when the promise would have been fulfilled to
him, so that he would have entered into immortality
and eternal life. He would have been changed. What
he understands by this promised change may be
gathered from his commentary on I Cor. 15:45, where
Paul compares Adam as a "living soul" with Christ as
"the quickening spirit." Writes Dr. Hodge: "From
what the apostle, however, here says of the contrast
between Adam and Christ; of the earthly and perishable nature of the former as opposed to the immortal,
spiritual nature of the latter, it is plain that Adam
as originally created was not, as to his body, in that
state which would fit him for his immortal existence.
After his period of probation was passed, it is to be
inferred, that a change in him would have taken place,
analogous to that which is to take place in those believers who shall be alive when Christ comes. They
shall not die but be changed. Of this change in the
constitution of his body, the tree of life was probably
constituted the sacrament."

Here, then, we have a rather clear and comprehensive exposition of what is commonly meant by the so-
called "covenant of works." We may summarize the
various elements as follows. 1. The covenant of works
was an arrangement or agreement between God and

Adam entered into by God and established by Him after man's creation. It was not given with creation, but an additional arrangement. 2. It was a means to an end. Adam had life, but did not possess the highest, i.e. eternal life. He was free, but his state was not that of highest freedom. He was lapsible. And the covenant of works was arranged as a means for Adam to attain to that higher state of freedom and eternal life. 3. The specific elements of this covenant were a promise (eternal life) ; a penalty (death) ; and a condition (perfect obedience). 4. In this covenant Adam was placed on probation. There would come a time, when the period of probation was ended, and when the promise would be fulfilled. 5. At the end of the period of probation Adam would have been translated into a state of glory, analogous to the change of believers that shall live at the time of Christ's second advent. 6. The fruit of this obedience of Adam would have been reaped by all Adam's posterity.

Many and serious objections may be raised against this rather generally accepted doctrine of the "covenant of works." That the relation between God and Adam in the state of righteousness was a covenant relation, we readily admit. But that this covenant should be an established agreement between Adam and his Creator, consisting of a condition, a promise, and a penalty, and that it was essentially a means whereby Adam might work himself up to the higher state of eternal life and heavenly glory that is now attained by the believers through Christ, we deny. First of all, there is the chief objection that this doctrine finds no support in Scripture. We do read of the "probationary command" prohibiting man to eat of the tree of knowledge of good and evil, and of the penalty of death threatened in case of disobedience.

But nowhere do we find any proof in the Scriptures for the contention that God gave to Adam the promise of eternal life if he should obey that particular command of God. It is true, of course, that Adam would not have suffered the death penalty if he had obeyed. But this is quite different from saying that he would have attained to glory and immortality. This cannot be deduced or inferred from the penalty of death that threatened. Adam might have lived everlastingly in his earthly state; he might have continued to eat of the tree of life and live forever; but everlasting earthly life is not the same as what the Scriptures mean by "eternal life," and that Adam would have attained to this higher level of heavenly glory, that there would have come a time in his life when he would have been "translated," the Scriptures nowhere suggest. Besides, this giving of the probationary command and this threat of the penalty of death are no covenant or agreement, constitute no transaction between God and Adam. The latter simply receives a command and is threatened with just punishment if he disobeys. Such a command might conceivably be connected with the covenant relation, but that it *is* the covenant Scripture does not even suggest. A command is no covenant. Nor is the command imposed on man in the form of a *condition* unto eternal life. It is true, of course, that elsewhere in Scripture it is emphasized that obedience and life are inseparably connected: "the man that doeth them shall live in them." But even this does not mean that man by the keeping of the law could ever attain to the higher level of heavenly life and glory. In vain does one look in the Word of God for support of this theory of a "covenant of works."

But there are other objections. First of all, it is quite impossible that man should merit a special re-

ward with God. Obedience to God is an obligation.
It certainly has its reward, for God is just, and He
rewards the good with good. But obedience has its
reward in itself. To obey the Lord our God is life
and joy. For "the statutes of the Lord are right,
rejoicing the heart: the commandment of the Lord
is pure, enlightening the eyes. The fear of the Lord
is clean, enduring forever: the judgments of the Lord
are true and righteous altogether. More to be desired
are they than gold, yea, than much fine gold: sweeter
also than honey and the honeycomb. Moreover by
them is thy servant warned: and in keeping of them
there is great reward." Ps. 19:8-11. Sin is misery
and death; life and joy there are in obedience. To
keep the commandments of the Lord is a privilege.
But the covenant of works teaches that Adam could
merit something more, something special by obeying
the commandment of the Lord. And this is quite impossible. What the Lord says to His disciples is applicable to man in relation to God always: "So likewise ye, when ye shall have done all those things
which are commanded you, say, We are unprofitable
servants: we have done that which was our duty to
do." Adam was God's with all his being and life in
the world. To consecrate himself with all things in
love to the living God was simply his obligation. He
could do nothing for God. He could work no over-
time with God. He could never earn anything extra.
The privilege of serving God was all his. Suppose
that Adam had served the Lord in perfect obedience
a thousand years, could he possibly have felt that it
was about time that his God should reward him with
something special? Suppose the Lord had inquired of
him at that time: "Adam, thou hast served me faithfully all these years; how much do I owe thee?" What

would Adam have answered? He would have said this: "Thou owe me, O Lord my God? All these thousand years Thou hast filled me with Thy goodness; pure delight it was to me that I might live before Thee and serve Thee in love; I owe all to Thee, but Thou canst not possibly owe me anything at all!" Suppose this conversation had continued, and the Lord would have inquired of Adam: "But wouldest thou not rather be taken out of thy earthly paradise and be translated into another glory?" What would the earthy first man have answered? Conceivably this: "No, Lord, I do not like to be unclothed. I am perfectly satisfied here in the earthly paradise. And I am serenely happy here by the tree of life. I cannot long for anything else than that I may stay here forever, and live with Thee in the friendship of Thy covenant." And suppose further that the Lord would have asked: "But hast thou not merited another thousand years in this earthly paradise by thy faithful obedience?" What would have been the inevitable answer? This: "Thou Lord art my benefactor every day anew. Surely, I could never earn my next breath. If Thou shouldest drop me back into nothingness, Thou wouldest do no injustice." No, indeed, as long as Adam obeyed, God could not in justice inflict upon him the suffering of death; but this does not mean that He owed to His creature another moment of existence at any time of his life. Never can man merit anything with God. Nor is there any indication in Scripture that God voluntarily placed man in a position in which he could merit eternal life.

Besides, how must we conceive of this promise of eternal life to Adam? Suppose that Adam would have obeyed the commandment of God. Then, according to the covenant of works doctrine, he would have been glorified and raised to a heavenly plane of immortal life. The question arises: when would this have happened? The usual answer is that the matter would have been decided within a comparatively short time, perhaps soon after Adam and Eve had resisted the temptation of the devil. At any rate, it is usually supposed that this moment of Adam's reward would have come before there would be any descendants, because Adam stood in paradise as the representative of the whole human race. But what then? Adam and Eve would have been translated to a kind of immortal, heavenly glory. Would they have brought forth the human race in that state of glory? This seems quite impossible, for the propagation of the human race and the replenishing of the earth appears inseparably connected with the present earthy state of man in his physical body. In heaven they do not marry or bring forth children. And what of the earth and all the earthly creation? Would it also have been glorified, or would Adam simply have been taken out of it? Someone might object to this way of argumentation that we speak of things that did not actually happen and that, therefore, were not in the counsel of God. True, but I claim that God's promises are sure, and that He does not promise anything that is not even possible of fulfillment within the economy of His counsel and the whole of His works. It is, of course, quite conceivable that Adam would have obeyed, and that in the way of obedience he would have continued and perpetuated his earthly life and happiness. It is also conceivable that in this earthly state of perfection he would have represented the whole human race and brought forth children. But the theory that Adam had the promise of God that he would inherit eternal life, had he obeyed the probationary command, does not fit in with the rest of Scripture, nor with any possible dogmatic conception.

This conception, moreover, presents the covenant relation as something incidental and additional to man's life in relation to God. It is a means to an end, not an end in itself. It is not given with man's creation and, therefore, it is not a fundamental and essential relationship, but it is an agreement established sometime after man was called into being. The question, how long after Adam was created God made this agreement with him, is quite irrelevant. Whether it was a week, or a day, or even an hour after he was created that the probationary command was given him, the fact remains that this covenant was imposed upon the relation Adam already sustained to God by reason of his creation. And the question arises: what, then, was Adam's relation to God apart from this "covenant of works"? However, the Word of God does not present the covenant relation as an accidental relationship, but as fundamental and essential. It is not a means to an end, but an end in itself. In its highest perfection, that is, in Christ, it is life eternal itself. For this is life eternal that they know the only true God and Jesus Christ whom He has sent. John 17:3.

Finally, from the viewpoint of God's sovereignty and wisdom, this theory of a "covenant of works" appears quite unworthy of God. It presents the work of God as a failure to a great extent. Even though God may be and will be victorious in the end and the devil will suffer defeat, the latter, nevertheless, succeeded in inflicting heavy damage upon the works of the Creator, if this theory were true. Consider that, according to the covenant of works conception, Adam stood in a position in which he could attain to eternal life and glory, and merit that same glory and life for all his posterity, by obeying God's command. The glory he could inherit for himself and all his descendants was the same or similar to that believers now receive in Christ. But now it is attained only through the deep way of suffering and sin and death; now it is merited only through the death and perfect obedience of the Son of God in the flesh; and now it is attained only by some, the elect, while the majority of the race perishes. But will this not everlastingly appear as a failure on the part of God? Or rather, can this possibly be true in view of the wisdom and absolute sovereignty of the Most High? If eternal life and glory could have been attained in the first man Adam, would God have chosen the long and deep way through the death of His Son? He would not. And the fact is, that it was quite impossible for Adam to attain to the heavenly level of immortal life. Immortality and heavenly glory are in Christ Jesus alone, and outside of the Son of God come into the flesh they were never attainable.

However, even though the first three chapters of the book of Genesis do not mention the term "covenant," there can be no doubt that the relation between God and Adam was such a covenant relation. This truth does not have to be based upon a single text such as Hos. 6:7, although this passage certainly may be quoted with reference to this truth. The Lord in that passage accuses His apostatizing people that they have transgressed the covenant "like Adam." Some prefer here the translation "like man" instead of "like Adam." Although the former is most probably correct, it does not make a great deal of difference with respect to the question we are now discussing. If "like man" or "like men" is considered correct, the

text speaks in a broad sense of the relation between
God and man as fundamentally a covenant relationship; if the rendering "like Adam" be preferred, it
refers directly to the covenant relation between Adam
and God. But all of Scripture proceeds from the truth
that man always stands in covenant relation to God.
All God's dealings with Adam in paradise presuppose
this relation, for God talked with Adam and revealed
Himself to him, and Adam knew God in the wind of
day. Besides, salvation is always presented as the
establishment and realization of God's covenant. By
the flood God destroys the first world and saves His
Church in Noah and his seed, and with these He
establishes His covenant embracing all creation. With
Abraham and his seed He makes His covenant as an
everlasting covenant, and gives them the sign of cir-
cumcision as a seal of the righteousness which is by
faith. Gen. 17:7ff. And this covenant could not be
disannulled by the law which came four hundred and
thirty years later, so that the covenant of Sinai is
essentially the same covenant as that with Abraham
and his seed, even though for a time the law is super-
imposed upon that relationship. Gal. 3:17. And in
the new dispensation God establishes a new covenant
with His people, a higher realization of the same
covenant as the old, based on the blood of Jesus, and
consisting in this, that He will remember their iniquities no more, and that He will write His law upon
their hearts and minds, that all may know Him. Jer.
31:21ff.; Heb. 8:8ff.; 10:16.

Moreover, the Scriptures often refer to this covenant relation without expressly mentioning it. Thus
we read that Enoch walked with God, Gen. 5:22. And
the same is said of Noah. Gen. 6:9. Abraham is
called the friend of God. Isa. 41:8; Jas. 2:23. The

tabernacle and temple foreshadow the truth that God dwells with His people under one roof, in the same house, as a Friend with His friends. And this covenant relationship is centrally realized in the incarnation of the Son of God, for "the Word was made flesh and dwelt among us." John 1:14. And through the death and resurrection and exaltation of the Lord Jesus Christ and the outpouring of His Spirit upon the Church, the latter is become "the temple of the living God; as God hath said, I will dwell in them and walk in them; and I will be their God and they shall be my people." II Cor. 6:16. And the highest realization of the glory God prepared for them that love Him is expressed in the words of Rev. 21: "Behold, the tabernacle of God is with men, and he will dwell with them, and they shall be his people, and God Himself shall be with them and be their God." Indeed, all Scripture presents the covenant relation as fundamental and essential, and if the work of redemption and that of creation are related to each other, there can be no doubt that Adam stood in covenant relation to God in his state of integrity.

For the same reason, however, this covenant relation is not to be conceived as something incidental, as a means to an end, as a relation that was established by way of an agreement, but as a fundamental relationship in which Adam stood to God by virtue of his creation. It is not essentially an agreement, but a relation of living fellowship and friendship. It was given and established by Adam's creation after the image of God. For fellowship, the intimate relation of friendship requires likeness as its basis. Like knows and can have fellowship with like. For this reason the ultimate covenant-life is to be found in God Himself, and is based on the Trinity. Being essentially

one, yet personally distinct, the Father, the Son, and
the Holy Ghost live in eternal covenant friendship
with one another.   And for this same reason, that
reflection of God's life of friendship which is found
in God's covenant with man, was realized when Adam
was created in the image of God, that creaturely likeness of God, which consisted in true knowledge of
God, righteousness, and holiness.   From the very first
moment of his existence, therefore, and by virtue of
his being created after the image of God, Adam stood
in that covenant relation to God, and was conscious of
that living fellowship and friendship which is essential
of that relationship.   He knew God and loved Him and
was conscious of God's love to him.   He enjoyed the
favor of God.   He received the Word of God, walked
with God and talked with Him, and he dwelled in the
house of God in paradise the first.   And as he stood
at the pinnacle of all created things on the earth, the
whole creation through him was comprehended in that
covenant relation of fellowship.   In Adam's heart the
whole creation was united to the heart of God!

In this covenant relation Adam was the friend-
servant and officebearer of God in all creation.   He
was God's co-worker.   And this calling of Adam in
the state of righteousness is to be understood very
concretely and realistically.   His life is not to be
vaporized in our imagination into a sort of mystical
enjoyment of sweet communion with the Lord under
the tree of life.   He had work to do.   He had a very
definite mandate.   God had blessed Adam and Eve
and said to them: "Be fruitful and multiply, and replenish the earth, and subdue it: and have dominion
over the fish of the sea and over the fowl of the air,
and over every living thing that moveth upon the
earth."   Gen. 1:28.   And when the Lord God prepared

for man the garden of Eden and placed him in it, He gave him a specific commandment to dress the garden, i.e. to cultivate it, and to keep it, which probably meant that he had to guard it against the inroads of the devil. He, therefore, had a very definite task to perform. But in all his life and work he was to be busy as the friend-servant of God. Not as a slave that works from the motive of fear for the whip; nor as a wage-earner who puts in his hours merely for his wages; but freely, from the love of God, as His co-worker and being of His party, as the friend of God he was to function as God's superintendent over all the works of God's hands. As such he must replenish and subdue the earth, cultivate and keep the garden, and bring to light all the wonders and powers of the world. And the pure delight of it in the favor of God was his reward.

Thus we may truly say that Adam was God's representative in the earthly creation, His office-bearer, His prophet, priest and king. In general this implies that he had the calling, the mandate, but also the privilege, the right, the ability, but also the will to be the servant of God. The *must,* and the *may,* and the *can,* and the *will* to be God's co-worker were in perfect harmony with one another in him. As God's prophet he knew his God in all the earthly creation and praised Him in a "great congregation." As priest he would dwell in God's house and consecrate himself and all things to Him. And as king he would declare and maintain the will of God in all the earth. All things served him in order that he might serve his God!

IV

The Fall Of Man

"Whence then proceeds this depravity of human nature?" This is the next question that arises after the negative answer given to the sixth question. The instructor reached the conclusion that the human nature is contrary to the law of God. The law demands love and the human nature is inclined to hate. Sin, therefore, is not a matter of a wrong deed only; it is corruption of the human nature. And this corruption of the human nature is the subject of discussion in this third Lord's Day. Whence does this corruption arise? Did God, perhaps, create us so wicked and perverse? This question was answered in the negative. No, God cannot create anything wicked. On the contrary, He created man good and after his own image, in true righteousness and holiness. He was able to know God rightly, and to live with Him in eternal happiness in the covenant of friendship, that he might glorify and praise his Creator. But now the question returns in its direct form: "Whence then proceeds this depravity of human nature?" And the answer directs our attention to the fall and disobedience of our first parents. To that fall must somehow be traced the corruption of the whole nature. There are several questions here that must be answered. First of all, our attention must be directed to that fall of Adam and Eve as such. Of what did their fall and disobedience consist? Secondly, the question arises: how could that one act of disobedience on the part of our first parents corrupt their nature? And, finally, there is the important problem concerning our connection with that fall of Adam and Eve, and concerning the corruption of the whole human nature through them.

The life and calling of our first parents were concentrated in and limited for the time being to the garden of Eden. Dominion was given them over all the earthly creation, and their broader calling was to multiply and fill the earth and subdue it. But it is quite evident that this calling embraced the entire human race, and that the realization of it could hardly be begun as long as all things were still in their primitive state, and our first parents were the only representatives of the race on earth. But God had limited their personal sphere of life and labor. He had prepared for them a special place in the garden of Eden. This garden was for them a house of God. There God dwelled and there they dwelled with God in the covenant of friendship. There God spoke to them as a friend with his friends, and Adam and Eve heard the Word of God. And there God gave them the special mandate to dress or cultivate the garden and to keep it, which probably means that man had to guard and defend it against the inroads of the devil and corruption.

Attention is called to two special trees that were to have a peculiar significance in the life of our first parents. There was first of all the tree of life in the midst of the garden; and near it was the tree of the knowledge of good and evil. Whether these names indicate merely two individual trees or rather a species or group of trees cannot be determined and is rather irrelevant. In the heavenly paradise of God in the new earth the tree of life is, evidently, not one single tree but a group, for it is presented in Rev. 22:2 as standing on either side of the river of life. Of more

importance, however, it is to determine the significance
of the two special trees in the garden of Eden. It
appears that the tree of life, in distinction from all
other trees, produced fruit that had the power to per-
petuate Adam's earthly existence as a living soul. As
long as he might eat of the tree of life he would not
die the physical death. This seems to be the implication of Gen. 3:22: "And the Lord God said, Behold, the
man is become as one of us, to know good and evil: and
now, lest he put forth his hand, and take also of the
tree of life, and eat, and live for ever." But its significance was not limited to this. It was to man also a
token of God's favor, for only in the way of obedience
might he eat of that tree. A sign, a kind of sacrament,
therefore, it was to him of the covenant of God's
friendship. Man was not only a living soul like the
animal; he was created in the image of God. He lived
a higher life, the life of God's covenant in the fellowship of His friendship. He, therefore, could not live
by bread alone, but by every Word that proceedeth
out of the mouth of God. And of that Word of favor
and blessing the tree of life was a visible and tangible
token. As he ate of the tree of life he tasted the lovingkindness of his God over him.

Of this tree of life the tree of the knowledge of
good and evil was the antithesis. Also with it the
Word of God was connected, but it was a word of pro-
hibition. It introduced the "No," God's "No" into
Adam's life, and therefore the calling to respond to
that "No" of God by his own "No." This is evident
from the fact that Adam received command from God
that he might not eat of this tree. But it is also indicated by the name: "the tree of the knowledge of good
and evil." This name does not, of course, express that
the tree was a means to bring Adam to a consciousness

of and discernment between good and evil, to make
him a moral being. Adam was not created a neutral
being, without moral discernment. His moral consciousness was not a blank. He was created in positive
knowledge of God, righteousness and holiness. Yet,
that tree of the knowledge of good and evil introduced
into man's life the possibility of evil in a very concrete
way. Sin was thereby placed concretely before the
consciousness of Adam as something that was to be
condemned and rejected by him as the friend of God.
Apart from this tree there was no "Thou shalt not"
in Adam's life. Nothing in paradise reminded him of
sin. But the tree of knowledge of good and evil, and
the prohibitive command of God connected with it,
introduced the antithesis into Adam's existence. And
his attitude toward that tree certainly would determine
the character of his knowledge of good and evil. For
if he obeyed the commandment of God, he would know
both good and evil in the love of God, so that he de-
lighted in the good and hated evil; while, if he dis-
obeyed he also would know both good and evil, but now
in enmity against God, so that he would hate the good
and love evil. In the latter case he would live from
the motive of the lie that he could for himself, apart
from the revelation of God, determine what should be
good and what should be evil.

And this antithesis was accentuated by the temptation of the devil, who also connected his word with the
tree of knowledge of good and evil, and that in direct
opposition to the Word of God. Sin did not have its
first origin in the world of man, but in that of the
heavenly spirits. Of these heavenly spirits nothing is
told us in the creation narrative. Nor do we read of
them, or of one of them in Gen. 3, in connection with
the temptation of our first parents. Throughout this

chapter we read only of the serpent. But it is evident
from the promise in Gen. 3:15, and from all subsequent
history and revelation, that this serpent was but the
instrument of Satan, although the animal played a
more important part in the temptation than is usually
thought. And in Rev. 12:9 there is a very plain reference to the serpent of the temptation: "And the great
dragon was cast out, that old serpent, called the Devil,
and Satan, which deceiveth the whole world: he was
cast out into the earth, and his angels were cast out
with him." It is very evident, therefore, that there
was a fall of the angels, that part of the angels under
the leadership of Satan rebelled against God, even
before the fall of man and the introduction of sin into
our world. And it is also beyond doubt that the serpent
of Gen. 3 was the instrument of the devil.

From the very beginning, therefore, the Scriptures
point to the connection between sin in our world and
the powers of darkness in heavenly places, and thus
teach us that the battle of the Church is not against
flesh and blood, but against principalities and powers,
against the spiritual forces of evil in high places.
Gathering the data we find in the Bible concerning the
Evil One, our attention is called, first of all, to his
names. He is called the Devil, which means mud-
slinger, calumniator, slanderer, liar; and Satan, the
opponent or adversary. These are his principal names.
They represent him both in his spiritual character as
the one that always speaks the lie, in whom there is no
truth; and in his attitude against God, for he is principally the adversary of God, the one that opposes Him
and slanders Him. All his plans and schemes and
efforts have for their principal object opposition
against God. God he hates above all that is to be
hated, and all other things are the object of his wrath

and fury only as they are related to God. But he is called by other names, that express certain aspects of his diabolical, God-opposing character, such as Destroyer, Deceiver, Evil One, Murderer from the beginning, Tempter, Father of the lie and of liars. Still other names are indicative of his great power and influence both in the realm of spirits and in the world of men. He is the Prince of demons, the Prince of the powers of the air, the Prince of this world, the god of this world. Considering the import of these appellations in the light of all that Scripture reveals to us concerning this Evil One and his work, we may conclude, first of all, that Satan formerly was one of the most wonderful angels, a prince among and over the heavenly spirits, that had great authority. It is not even improbable that he was the chief of all the angels. He was endowed with beautiful gifts and talents and had a position of great authority and power among his fellow angels. This may be gathered from the manifestation of his great power in his present state; from the fact that he is still prince over the angels that fell with him; and from the fact that, according to Scripture, it is such a princely and mighty angel as Michael, to whom is assigned the special task of combatting the devil. Dan. 10:13; Jude 9; Rev. 12:7. In the second place, it is at least suggested that the devil's first sin was pride, dissatisfaction with the position assigned to him and the glory that was given him by his Creator, and aspiration to the very throne of God. He stumbled over his own glory. This is evident from the temptation in paradise, for he holds before the imagination of the woman the possibility of being like God. And in I Tim. 3:6 the apostle Paul suggests that pride is the very characteristic sin of the devil. And Jude speaks of angels that kept not their own estate. And because of his rebellion he and his angels were accursed of God, although they have not yet been consigned to their final place of damnation.

In paradise he came in the form of a serpent. We can imagine a twofold reason for the devil's need of a visible instrument in the temptation of man. First of all, we must remember that man stood in his original integrity, and the devil, therefore, cannot have had direct access to his mind and heart. He had to approach him from without. And secondly, the temptation was connected with and concentrated in the visible and tangible tree of the knowledge of good and evil, and Satan needed a visible instrument to direct the attention of man to this tree. That he assumed the specific form of a serpent, must, no doubt, be ascribed to the fact that the serpent was the most suitable instrument for his purpose. It is evident from Scripture that the serpent was quite different from the reptile we know today. We receive the impression that it was the highest and noblest among animals. For "the serpent was more subtle than any beast of the field." Gen. 3:1. He was the most intelligent of animals. That he is a reptile now, and eats the dust of the ground, is evidently due to the curse that was pronounced upon him. Gen. 3:14. It is certainly true that in the curse upon the serpent also the devil himself is accursed. But the fact remains that also the animal that served as instrument of Satan in the temptation is cursed more than all the rest of the animals. And this certainly implies that the serpent was more than a mere passive instrument of the devil. Somehow it had an active part in the temptation, for that it is cursed definitely implies a measure of guilt. And that he approached the woman rather than Adam cannot be due to her being more susceptible to sin, for both Adam and Eve stood in righteousness before God. It may be that the devil considered the womanly nature more receptive for the appeal to the senses which he made in connection with the tree of knowledge. It certainly is true, that Eve was not the responsible party, that not she but Adam had received the commandment concerning the tree directly from God, and that Adam was more accessible through Eve than by a direct temptation from the devil. All these considerations may have induced Satan to approach the woman rather than the man.

As to the temptation itself, the Scriptural narrative describes it rather in detail, so that its various stages can readily be distinguished. The first stage is expressed in the question of the serpent: "Yea, hath God said, Ye shall not eat of every tree of the garden?" and the answer by the woman: "We may eat of the fruit of the trees of the garden: But of the tree which is in the midst of the garden, God hath said, Ye shall not eat of it, neither shall ye touch it, lest ye die." Gen. 3:1-3. Usually the intent of this first question of the devil is explained as being the confusion of the woman in regard to the real meaning and contents of the commandment of God. But it seems to me, that this explanation gives but little credit to the subtlety of the serpent. Besides, had the woman fallen by this blunt attack, her sin would have been a natural mistake, a fallacy of the memory, not a spiritual-ethical error. I am, therefore, of the opinion that there is a subtle argument in this first question, an argument concerning the sense of the commandment of God. He shrewdly suggests by this question that there is really no sense to the Word of God, that anyone can readily see that the Word of God cannot possibly be true. The argument in full would run thus: "God did not forbid

you to eat of every tree in the garden, did He? There
is no harm, therefore, in eating of all these trees.
How, then, could there possibly be harm in eating of
the one tree?" We must remember that the essence
of the lie is always that there is no harm, that there
is a good in violating God's Word. That is the reason
why the devil is the master deceiver that deceiveth the
whole world. And for the reception and embracing of
this fundamental lie he prepares the heart and mind of
the woman by his introductory question. If this introductory, this preliminary attempt is successful, he
can come out in the open and directly contradict God.
And successful this first attempt was. Notice, that the
woman enters into the argument. And this was the
beginning of her fall for two reasons. First of all,
because she was not the head of the race, and, therefore, not the chief responsible party. Hence, she
should have called her husband to decide this matter.
Instead, she takes it upon herself to debate the question
with the serpent. There is an element of pride and rebellion in this. In the second place, notice that she is
actually tempted to discuss the question proposed by
the devil. And this question was not debatable. God's
Word is only and always true and good, and must be
unconditionally accepted on the simple ground that it
is the Word of God. There can never be a good in
violating the Word of God. But the woman enters
into the discussion. Nor does she quote the Word of
God correctly. From the version she gives of the
commandment of the Lord it is evident that she had
quite well understood the purpose of the devil's question: she was already deliberating upon the question,
whether or not any harm could possibly result from
eating of that one tree. This must be the reason why
she answers: "But of the fruit of the tree which is in

the midst of the garden, God hath said, Ye shall not
eat of it, neither touch it, *lest ye die.*" Now, God had
not said: "lest ye die," as if eating of the tree would
have the natural result of death; but He had very
definitely threatened death as a punishment: "in the
day that thou eatest thereof thou shalt surely die."
Nor must it escape our attention that God had given
the commandment to Adam, even before the creation
of the woman, and had, therefore, definitely spoken in
the singular: *"thou* shalt surely die." But the woman,
taking it upon herself to settle this important matter
alone, for that very reason quotes the commandment
in the plural: "lest ye die." Notice, finally, that she
is very emphatic, in fact, much too emphatic in her
asseveration that the Lord had really spoken of an
evil result being connected with the eating of the fruit
of that one tree. She adds: "neither shall ye touch it."
Now, the Lord had never said such a thing. But the
woman has before her mind the question whether it
would really be such a dangerous thing to eat of that
one tree; and in her exaggeration of the commandment
of God she is really already emphasizing in her own
mind the absurdity of such a commandment. How
could harm come from eating of one tree, while all the
other trees were good for food? But, what is more,
how could anyone die by touching the tree! Surely,
the seed sown by the devil had already struck root!

Thus the way is prepared for the second stage of
the temptation, consisting in this, that the Word of God
is bluntly contradicted, and God Himself is slandered
as one who is not seeking the good for His creatures.
The lie is impressed upon the now receptive heart of
the woman in a twofold way. Negatively, the devil
assures the woman boldly that no harm could possibly
come to her from transgressing the commandment of

God: "Ye shall not surely die." And positively, he
presents the matter as if there would be a great good
in disobedience to God's Word: "For God doth know
that in the day ye eat thereof, then your eyes shall be
opened, and ye shall be as gods (better: as God) knowing good and evil." Gen. 3:4, 5. It is always thus.
The moment you begin to discuss the question whether
or not the Word of God is true, you are already prepared to call it a lie. And you will find many a reason
to support this judgment. God's Word is not debatable. To debate it is already to deny it. And again,
the moment you begin to deliberate upon the advis-
ability of keeping the commandments of God, the
moment you consider the Word of God from a utility
standpoint, i.e. from the viewpoint of the question,
whether it is good *for you* to obey or to disobey, you
have already determined for yourselves to disobey and
cast God's Word to the wind. You have already wist-
fully directed your eye to the forbidden object and in
your heart desired to obtain it. It was thus with our
first mother. And the same is still a matter of every
day experience with sinful men. If we cannot believe
the Word unconditionally because it is the Word of
God, we do not believe it at all: we call it the lie. And
if we will not obey the Word of God unconditionally,
and that for God's sake, regardless of the consequences
(which, however, are always good), we cannot possibly
keep the precepts of our God!

The last stage in the temptation and the fall of the
woman naturally and inevitably followed upon the
woman's acceptance of the word of the serpent by
which he had plainly and boldly contradicted the Word
of God. The lie had been introduced. And it had been
accepted and embraced. It is in the light, or rather,
in the darkness of that lie, that is, with eyes that had

been darkened by the lie, that the woman now looked
at the tree and passed her own judgment upon it. She
saw nothing anymore of the Word of God. On the
contrary, she saw "that the tree was good for food, and
that it was pleasant to the eyes, and a tree to be desired to make one wise." Gen. 3:6. In other words,
already she was filled with lust, the lust of the flesh
and the lust of the eyes and the pride of life. We may
well suppose that part of what the woman saw was,
apart from the Word of God, true. Why should it not
be? There is no reason to believe that the tree was
not good for food, nor that it was not a pleasant tree
to behold, that is, appealing to the natural eye, devoid
of the spiritual light of the knowledge of God. The
only trouble was, that she set aside the Word of God,
and divorced the tree from it. She opposed her own
judgment to the commandment and Word of God, and
considered the tree in the light of her rebellious heart.
And upon that judgment she acted. And she took of
the fruit of the tree and ate.

Did she not, from that very moment experience
the wrath of God and His curse upon her? It would
seem that she must have felt the misery, into which
her act had plunged her, rather keenly and deeply. No
man would ever pass through a similar experience as
that through which she must have passed at that
moment. Ever since, all men are born in sin and under
the wrath of God by nature. But Eve had known what
it meant to walk in the light of God, to live in His
fellowship, to behold His glory, to taste His goodness.
And now her light had changed into complete darkness, her knowledge of God had been corrupted into
spiritual ignorance and love of the lie; she had been
alienated from God, saw the beauty of His revelation
no more, and knew herself to be an object of God's

holy wrath. Her life was changed into death. However, and just because of this corruption of her nature, she immediately went in search of her husband in order to make him her accomplice in sin and her companion in misery. What method she employed to tempt Adam the Bible does not tell us. Very briefly it states: "and gave also unto her husband with her; and he did eat." She had learned the lie in the school of the serpent, and, no doubt, she practised what she had learned upon her husband. But the point is that the truth of what the apostle writes in Rom. 1:32 became immediately manifest in Eve: "Who knowing the judgment of God, that they which commit such things are worthy of death, not only do the same, but have pleasure in them that do them." No longer could she have pleasure in a sinless husband. In fact, by nature she would henceforth hate him, and unless he became her accomplice in sin, she would be ready to persecute and kill him. Such is sin. Hence, it was inevitable that she could have no moment's rest, even though she now very clearly knew by experience the judgment of God, until she had also persuaded Adam to become her companion in disobedience and in death.

Such was the first sin, the one act through which sin entered into the world, and death through sin. The question is often asked, how it was possible that sin could originate in the heart and mind of a creature that had been created good and after God's image, in true knowledge of God, righteousness, and holiness. In the ultimate sense this question must probably remain unanswered, like all questions that concern the beginning of things, and that are not specifically explained in the Word of God. We must remember, of course, that sin is no substance. It has no being in itself. It is the perversion of good powers wherewith God endowed the creature, in this particular case, man. We must also bear in mind that God had created man good, but lapsible. There was no evil in him. But he had not attained to the highest possible state of freedom and goodness, in which he could not sin. Perhaps, we may even say in the light of Scripture, that this state of highest freedom is possible only in Christ, and that too, because He is the Person of the Son of God in human nature. If we bear these various factors in mind, we may approach a solution of the problem, how sin could possibly enter into the heart and mind of a man that was made morally good. God had endowed him with the good and rich gift of imagination. But by this power of his mind he was also able to conceive of the lie, to create for himself another world than that of the Word of God, and to call that world of his imagination reality and truth. And if by an act of his will he embraced that world of his imagination, and acted accordingly, he chose the lie instead of the truth of the Word of God. And that is sin. But even so, while this may explain the first operation of sin in man's heart and mind, it does not give a final and satisfactory answer to the question, how this operation could originate in a sinless nature. Certain it is that also that first sin, though the responsibility of it is entirely man's, and though it was wanton and wilful disobedience, was according to the inscrutable plan and purposes of the Most High, and took place under the controlling guidance of His providence.

V

The Corruption Of The Human Nature

There is another question, one that must and can be answered in the light of Scripture. The Catechism does not merely speak of the fall of our first parents in paradise, but mentions it as the source and cause of the corruption of the human nature. The question is: "whence proceeds this depravity of human nature?" And the answer is: "From the fall and disobedience of our first parents, Adam and Eve, in Paradise; hence, our nature is become so corrupt that we are all conceived and born in sin." The human nature is corrupt. It is the very opposite from what the law demands that it should be. The law demands love; our nature is such that it hates. And this corruption or depravity of the human nature the Catechism traces to the fall and disobedience of Adam and Eve as its source. And this raises the question, first of all, concerning the relation between that first act of disobedience and the corruption of the nature of our first parents. How can one act of sin corrupt the nature, darken the mind, pervert the will, so that henceforth no good can proceed from it any more? This is, evidently, the teaching of the Catechism here. The nature was good. Man was created after the image of God. The sinful deed of disobedience and rebellion against God did, in the case of Adam and Eve, not proceed from a corrupt nature. On the contrary, the deed was first. The corruption of the nature followed. The deed may be traced to its inmost root in the deepest recesses of the heart,—the fact remains that the sinful deed was first. How this was possible remains a mystery, as we have already stated. But the next question is: how could that first deed cause the nature to become depraved? Why could not Adam repent of that first and only deed that had ever been committed, and henceforth walk in obedience and righteousness? That the human nature is corrupt, is evident from all Scripture. For "there is none righteous, no not one: There is none that understandeth, there is none that seeketh after God. They are all gone out of the way, they are together become unprofitable: there is none that doeth good, no, not one. Their throat is an open sepulchre; with their tongues they have used deceit; the poison of asps is under their lips: Whose mouth is full of cursing and bitterness: Their feet are swift to shed blood: Destruction and misery are in their ways: And the way of peace have they not known: There is no fear of God before their eyes." Rom. 3:9-18. Throughout, the Bible speaks the same language. And it is also evident from Scripture that this corruption of the human nature entered into the world through the sin of the one man Adam: "Wherefore, as by one man sin entered into the world, and death by sin; and so death passed upon all men, for that all have sinned." But once more: how must it be explained, that one sinful deed could corrupt the whole nature?

It is this truth that is denied by the Pelagian. According to him, sin is always and only in the act, never in the human nature. A man is righteous only according as he does righteousness; and he is unrighteous only in the measure that he commits sin. But no sinful deed can affect the nature so that it becomes corrupt. It is true, of course, that the sinful deed weakens the will. When one sinful deed is committed, it becomes more difficult to do the right thing the next time. It is also true that certain sins, when repeatedly committed, become habits, so that it appears as if the human nature is completely enslaved to them, and kept in bondage. But in the deepest sense of the word the will of man always remains free to choose either for the good or for the evil. The human nature remains inherently good. The sinful deed cannot possibly corrupt it. And thus the Pelagian denies that by the sin of the first Adam he corrupted his nature so that he became morally depraved.

However, we must not lose sight of the fact, that sin incurs guilt, that guilt is liability to death, and that the death sentence was very really executed upon man when he committed that first sin. By his disobedience Adam became guilty before God. He became delinquent in paying to God what he owed. His calling was to love the Lord his God with all his heart and mind and soul and strength, every moment of his existence and with all he had. Such was his constant obligation. As long as he met this obligation he was in the state of righteousness. Never could he do more than was his obligation. And less he might not do. If he failed even for one moment in this perfect love of God he lapsed into the state of guilt, that is, into the state in which he was worthy of punishment. Debt with God must be paid. It cannot be ignored, forgotten, or simply cancelled. Sin must be atoned. But Adam had nothing wherewith to pay that debt. Hence, he fell hopelessly into the state of guilt as far as he was concerned. And the punishment of sin is death. God had very specifically threatened: "the day thou eatest thereof thou shalt surely die." And that death sentence God executed upon him immediately. Adam died on that very day, yea, the very moment he sinned.

That, according to the eternal counsel of God, Christ
stood behind him, so that as it were he fell on Christ
and was saved; and that, therefore, he did not utterly
perish, is also true. But we may leave this outside of
the scope of consideration for the present. As far
as Adam was concerned, apart from Christ, it can
only be said that he died, because God inflicted the
punishment of death on him. And this punishment
of death certainly included physical death: he was
separated from the tree of life; and corruption and
mortality took hold of his physical frame from that
very moment. But it also implied the spiritual death,
so that: "revolting from God by the instigation of the
devil, and abusing the freedom of his own will, he forfeited these excellent gifts; and on the contrary entailed on himself blindness of mind, horrible darkness,
vanity and perverseness of judgment, became wicked,
rebellious and obdurate in heart and will, and impure
in his affections." Canons III, IV, 2. And thus it is
explained that the deed of that first sin resulted in
the corruption of the human nature in our first parents.
This corruption was not a natural result of his disobedience, but the infliction of God's own sentence of
death upon him.

Thus the disobedience of our first parents was, indeed, a fall, by which man lapsed from the state of
righteousness into that of guilt and condemnation,
from light into darkness, from holiness into corruption, from life into death. If we understand this and,
at the same time, see the reason and cause of this in
the execution of the death sentence upon man, we will
also clearly see the absurdity of the theory that there
was an operation of restraining grace in Paradise,
whereby the process of moral and spiritual corruption
was checked, so that man did not become so depraved

as he would have been without this restraining influence. This is the view of common grace as presented by Dr. A. Kuyper, Sr. According to his conception, death was the natural and inevitable result of
Adam's eating of the forbidden fruit, just as physical
death is the natural result of taking poison. Adam
killed himself. Of course, even so this law of cause
and effect operated according to the ordinance of God,
and in so far death was also punishment. But the fact
remains that for Adam death in all its implications and,
therefore, including moral and spiritual corruption,
was inseparably and naturally connected with that
one deed of disobedience. The word of God: "the
day thou eatest thereof thou shalt surely die," must
be understood, not as a threat which God Himself
would fulfill, but as a prediction of what would happen, and, therefore, as a fair warning. Writes Dr.
Kuyper, *De Gemeene Gratie* I, 209 ff. (I translate):

"Death in connection with man's eating of the tree
of knowledge, can be understood in a twofold way:
either as a punishment that was threatened, or as a
result that would follow therefrom. If death is fixed
as the punishment of high treason, this must be understood as a threat, for one does not die inevitably of
high treason. But when I say: 'Do not take of that
Paris Green, for if you do you shall die,' there is no
question of punishment: all that is expressed is that
this poison is fatal in its effect, and that one who
takes the poison must die. In the last instance, I may,
if one should, contrary to my warning, take the poison
nevertheless, make an attempt to counteract the deadly
effect of the poison by the application of an antidote
to make the patient vomit. Then I certainly spoke
fully in accordance with truth: 'when you take the
poison, you shall die,' and I do not at all come into con-

flict with myself when afterwards I make an attempt
to save the reckless one that took the poison. If this
is clear, then it must also be admitted that the words:
'If you eat of the tree of knowledge, you will surely
die,' are explained in their full implication, when I
understand them as implying nothing else than the
declaration, the warning: 'Know this, that when you
permit yourself to be tempted to eat of that tree, you
will see that death will be the result.' And if this is
the significance, then there is nothing contradictory in
the fact that death was not on that same day fully
inflicted on Adam, because the same God that had
warned them, hastened immediately after their transgression in order to check the results of the evil."

There are many reasons why this entire presentation must be rejected. In the first place, it is not in
harmony with Scripture to explain the words: "the
day thou eatest thereof, thou shalt surely die," as a
warning concerning a natural and inevitable result,
the actual realization of which might then be prevented by God. Everywhere Scripture presents death
as a punishment inflicted by God Himself, and that, too,
in His just wrath. Death is the revelation of God's
displeasure against sin, the execution of His just
sentence, the deliberate infliction of punishment, not a
natural result of the sinful deed. If the corruption of
the human nature must be explained as the natural
result of one sinful deed, the Pelagian is, no doubt,
correct when he maintains that this is spiritually and
ethically impossible. But the inevitableness of this
corruption becomes quite clear if we consider it as the
punishment of death inflicted upon our first parents
for their disobedience. In the second place, sin is no
paris green or any other kind of poison that kills a
man physically and spiritually if he takes it. The sin

of Adam and Eve was a wilful deed of disobedience,
transgression of the commandment of God.   The figure
which Dr. Kuyper employs here, as is the case with
many illustrations in his works, is misleading.   In
the third place, it must be very evident that there is
no golden mean between life and death.   A man is
either alive or dead; he cannot be in some in-between
condition.   To apply Dr. Kuyper's own illustration:
if a man takes paris green he dies; but if an antidote
is administered, and this means is effective and has the
desired result, so that the patient vomits out the poison
he took, he does not die, but lives and will recover
completely.   He certainly is not half dead and half
alive.   The evil results are not "tempered" or checked,
but wholly counteracted and prevented.   Now, if God
warned Adam and Eve when He said: "the day ye eat
thereof, ye shall surely die," so that the sinful deed
was comparable to taking poison; and if thereupon
God administered an antidote of grace, and this means
was effective, our first parents did not die at all; they
certainly lived.   The evil of their deed was not checked,
but entirely prevented.   In no sense of the word could
they be half dead and half alive.   Hence, they lived.
And this means, too, that in paradise the human
nature was not corrupted at all.   It would have been,
if God had not intervened by His common grace.   As
the matter stands, however, Dr. Kuyper's explanation
of what actually happened in paradise, really directs
us to the same view as that of the Pelagians, except
that we arrive there in a round-about way.   But this
is in flat contradiction with the plain testimony of the
Bible, which teaches us that the nature of man became
corrupt through the fall and disobedience of our first
parents in paradise.   The view, therefore, must be
rejected.   Instead we must maintain that in the words:

"the day thou eatest thereof, thou shalt surely die,"
God threatened punishment, the punishment of death
which He Himself would inflict upon the guilty trans-
gressor; and that this sentence was actually carried
out by the righteous Judge of heaven and earth. Only
thus can it be explained, in opposition to the Pelagian
view, how the one deed of disobedience could entail
upon man the corruption of his whole nature.

VI

The Depravity Of The Race

Thus far we discussed the fall of our first parents in Paradise, and we reached the conclusion that it was, indeed, a fall, and not merely an act of sin. By the first act of disobedience, consisting in eating of the forbidden tree, the nature of our first parents was corrupted. It was not merely weakened, but actually debased and ethically corrupted, so that henceforth they could no longer serve the Lord their God in love. They lost the image of God, their knowledge of God became darkness; their righteousness was subverted into rebellion; and their holiness was turned into pollution. Enemies of God they had become. And the reason for this corruption cannot be found in the "natural" effect of that first sin, but must be attributed to the execution of the death sentence which God had threatened upon disobedience. Death was inflicted upon them the moment they transgressed the commandment of God. And death would henceforth have dominion over them, not only physically, but also in the spiritual sense. The carnal mind is death. It is not subject to the law of God, neither indeed can be.

But now we must consider another question. The Catechism is speaking, not merely of the corruption of the nature of our first parents, but of *our* nature. Through the fall and disobedience of our first parents, Adam and Eve, in paradise, *our* nature has become so corrupt that we are all conceived and born in sin. The universality of sin is not only clearly taught in the Holy Scriptures, but is also a matter of universal experience. All men sin and reveal that they are corrupt by nature. That is the testimony of all history, of everyday life, as every issue of our daily papers clearly shows, and as every news broadcast over the radio proclaims; it is the testimony we bear to one another in our social life in the world, for not only do men condemn in others that which they themselves practise, but no man puts confidence in the integrity of his fellows: when any transaction of importance takes place it must be duly sworn and signed and sealed before witnesses; and it is the testimony of every man's conscience, for man not only knows that he is sinful, but he cannot recall that he was ever different. All men are always sinful and corrupt. That is the terrible fact with which the Catechism deals here. The question is: whence is this depravity of the entire human nature?

It cannot escape our notice that the Catechism, in answering this question, emphasizes the organic unity rather than the juridical or legal solidarity of the human race. The question of original guilt is left out of consideration, and the fact of original corruption receives all the emphasis. That the human nature has become *corrupt*, and that, too, through the fall and disobedience of our *first parents*, Adam and Eve, so that we are all *conceived and born in sin*, is the truth that receives all the attention. The organic oneness of the race is stressed. Adam and Eve were our first parents. Both were the bearers of the whole human nature. By their fall and disobedience both became corrupt. And this corrupt human nature, in which it is impossible to do any good, they propagated, and it is continually being propagated in the way of conception and birth. In other parts of our Confessions this same aspect of original sin is emphasized. Thus we read in Art. 15 of the Netherland Confession: "We believe that, through the disobedience of Adam, original sin is extended to all mankind; which is a corruption of the whole nature, and an hereditary disease, wherewith infants themselves are infected even in their mother's womb, and which produceth in man all sorts of sin, being in him as the root thereof; and therefore is so vile and abominable in the sight of God, that it is sufficient to condemn all mankind." And in Canons III, IV, 2, 3, the matter is stated as follows: "Man after the fall begat children in his own likeness. A corrupt stock produced a corrupt offspring. Hence all the posterity of Adam, Christ only excepted, have derived corruption from their original parent, not by imitation as the Pelagians of old asserted, but by the propagation of a vicious nature. Therefore, all men are conceived in sin, and by nature children of wrath, incapable of saving good, prone to evil, dead in sin, and in bondage thereto, and without the regenerating grace of the Holy Spirit, they are neither able nor willing to return to God, to reform the depravity of their nature, nor to dispose themselves to reformation." It is evident that the Confessions consider depravity a moral or ethical disease, a corruption of the human nature that is transmitted from parent to child by the generation of the father and the conception of the mother, and that clings to the nature of the child from the moment of conception, even in the womb.

And this is the explanation of Scripture. The psalmist complains: "Behold, I was shapen in iniquity, and in sin did my mother conceive me." Ps. 51:5. And Job utters the words: "Who can bring a clean thing out of an unclean? Not one." And in Rom. 5:12-14 we read: "Wherefore as by one man sin entered into the world, and death by sin; and so death passed upon all men, for that all have sinned. For until the law sin was in the world; but sin is not imputed where there is no law. Nevertheless death reigned from Adam to Moses, even over them that had not sinned after the similitude of Adam's transgression, who is the figure of him that was to come." In the last passage the apostle is really considering the universality of the reign of death. Nor is there any reason to limit this "death" to the corruption of the body and temporal or physical death only, as some would have it. Sin and death are mentioned in connection with each other, and that entirely in general, without limitation. The death that came through sin certainly includes spiritual death, the corruption of our nature, our being in bondage to sin. The one man Adam is here represented as the one by whom the floodgates of sin and death were opened upon the entire human race. The text makes us think of the dikes that protected the Lowlands in many places against the angry sea. The waves would beat against them sometimes so persistently and powerfully, that they were pierced and the lands behind them were inundated. "Through one man," thus we read literally in the original, sin entered into the world, and death by sin. And this would be quite impossible except for the organic unity of the human race. In the way of propagation the corruption of sin spreads to the very last of men that are born of women. "That which is born of the flesh is flesh." John 3:6.

This raises the question as to the conception and birth of each individual child, particularly of the "soul." The difficult question of the origin of the soul always was a favorite topic of discussion among theologians. In recent years the discussion was re-

vived in the Netherlands, especially by the book of
Dr. Waterink on the "Origin of the Soul," who was
accused of Apollinarianism because of his apparent
identification of the human person with his spirit.
Much was written on the subject, but unanimity of
opinion was not reached. In the past there were three
explanations of this problem. The first is known as
the theory of preexistentianism, and held that all the
souls were actually created in Adam, and that therefore, all human individuals really sinned in our first
father and in him became corrupt. This appears to
have been the view of Augustine, a view that was
really based on a mistaken explanation of the last
part of Rom. 5:12: "for that all have sinned." He
interpreted that clause in the sense that is given to it
in the Dutch translation: "in welken allen gezondigd
hebben." But this cannot possibly be the correct
rendering of the original. It does not justify the
translation "in whom all have sinned"; but very definitely must be rendered: "for that" or "because all
have sinned." But this theory never found much support among theologians, as might be expected. Apart
from the fact that it finds no support in Scripture,
it meets with too many difficulties and is really an
impossible philosophical conception. A second solution of this problem is known under the name of
"traducianism." It, too, proceeded from the distinction of body and soul, and held that the whole man
is born from the parents in each individual instance.
Soul and body constitute the whole man, and soul
and body each individual is conceived and born.
The main objection that was lodged against this conception is that propagation is only applicable to the
body: spirits do not propagate their species. This is
a rather philosophical objection. It seems to me that

a far more weighty objection to this view may be deduced from the incarnation of the Son of God. If the whole man, person and nature, soul and body, is conceived and born from the parents, it seems difficult to escape the dilemma that, either Christ was not a complete man, or He was two persons, a human person as well as a divine. And that would lead us to the error that is known as Nestorianism. A third theory is known as creationism. It holds that the body is born from the parents, while the soul is created by God in birth or conception, or some time between conception and birth of the individual child. Nor is it difficult to raise objections against this theory. Does only part of the human nature propagate itself? How must it be explained that children resemble their parents, not only physically, but also with respect to traits of character? And, more difficult still, how must the language of our Confessions be explained with respect to the propagation of a corrupt offspring by a corrupt stock? If God creates each individual soul, how does that soul become defiled and corrupt? And if the human nature consists of body and soul, did not Christ, then, assume the whole human nature from the virgin Mary?

All these objections would seem to suggest that the distinction of the human being in body and soul cannot serve as a basis for the explanation of the propagation of original corruption. It does not offer us the proper working hypothesis. The reason for this must, perhaps, be found in the fact that it is not clearly defined what is meant by "soul." In Scripture, too, the word for soul has different connotations. Sometimes it is used for the whole man; in other passages it is properly translated by life; while again in other parts of the Bible the meaning

of the term closely approximates that of spirit. It
would seem expedient, then, to proceed from a little
different point of view, and choose another distinction
as our point of procedure. I mean the distinction between person and nature. The whole living nature
of man is propagated through generation, conception,
and birth. But this propagation of the human nature
takes place under the operation of an act of providence
whereby that nature becomes a *personal* nature. This
distinction and explanation has this in its favor, that
it is in accord with what we confess concerning the
incarnation. Also in the incarnation of the Son of
God the whole human nature, we believe, is conceived
in the womb of the virgin Mary and born from her.
But the Son of God assumed an impersonal human
nature: the Person also in this case came from God,
is, in fact, the very second Person of the Holy Trinity
Himself. If, then, the human nature is become corrupt in paradise, and the whole human nature in each
individual child that is born comes from the parents
through conception and birth, we can conceive of the
possibility that a "corrupt stock produces a corrupt
offspring," and that, as the Catechism expresses it:
"our nature is become so corrupt, that we are all
conceived and born in sin."

But this raises another question. Does not the
doctrine that all men are conceived and born in sin,
so that they are incapable of doing any good, exempt
man from all responsibility? I am born corrupt, totally depraved. I came into the world with a nature that
was incapable of doing any good. And this I certainly
cannot help. I never had a chance. To fight against
this corrupt nature is not only hopeless, but also impossible, for the simple reason that I do not even
have the inclination or the desire to reform myself.

I am "by nature" prone to hate God and my neighbor, and I always was, quite without any individual fault of my own. But does it not follow, then, that I cannot be held accountable for my sin? If it is not my fault that my nature is corrupt, how, then, can actual sin that arises from this nature as from a foul fountain, be reckoned to me as guilt? Can God hold me responsible for that which I cannot and never could do? Am I not rather a victim of circumstances, of cruel fate, that is to be pitied rather than condemned? The Catechism does not consider this aspect of original sin in this connection, but only looks at the matter from the organic viewpoint. But unless this question is also asked and answered, the whole subject of the universality of sin and death has not been treated. Hence, what must be our answer, what is the Scriptural answer to this question?

Scripture teaches us, that also from a legal viewpoint God created the human race as a body, a legal corporation, and that the first man Adam was made the head of this body in a representative sense. Even as the human race was created of one blood, so that there is organic unity, so there is in the one legal corporation of mankind legal solidarity. Pelagianism is fundamentally individualism: each individual man stands or falls his own master; there is no communal responsibility and communal guilt. But this is condemned on every side, not only by Scripture, but also by actual experience, and by real life in the State, in society, in the home. It is true, of course, that there is individual responsibility. Scripture emphasizes this very strongly. When the children of Israel complain that the dealings of the Lord are not equal, and attempt to justify themselves in their sins, the Lord says to them through His prophet: "What mean ye, that ye

use this proverb concerning the land of Israel, saying,
The fathers have eaten sour grapes, and the children's
teeth are set on edge? As I live, saith the Lord God,
ye shall not have occasion any more to use this proverb
in Israel. Behold, all souls are mine; as the soul of
the father, so also the soul of the son is mine: the soul
that sinneth, it shall die." The children are not
punished for the sins of their fathers in which they
themselves do not walk. But that does not alter the
fact, that there is also legal solidarity and communal
responsibility and guilt among men. God warns in
His law, that He will visit the sins of the fathers upon
the children, even in the third and fourth generation
of them that hate Him. And this is plainly corroborated in actual life. Individualism stands condemned
everywhere. If our government declares war, it is
the government, and not the individual citizens, that
is responsible for this act. It bears the sword, and it
is responsible for the way in which it uses that sword
also in war. It is only in this light and on this basis
that it can be maintained that the individual soldier
does not commit the sin against the sixth commandment, when he kills the enemy in battle. But this does
not mean that the individual citizens are at liberty to
decide for themselves, whether or not they shall take
an active part in the war. No right minded citizen will
say: let the government, that declared war, fight it
out! On the contrary, the government occupies a
representative place at the head of the State. When
it declares war, every citizen is actually in war. When,
to meet the expenses of the war, a huge debt is accumulated, as is the case in our present time, that debt
is ours, even though we had no part whatever in
its accumulation. And even our children and our
children's children will have to bear the burden of

that debt. Thus it is in the home and in society. Everywhere we see that one must assume responsibility for another. And thus the Bible teaches that the whole human race was created a legal body represented by the first man Adam, so that his first sin is imputed to all, and all men are born under a load of guilt by virtue of their being members of this legal corporation. This also answers the question that was recently debated in circles of the Reformed Church of America, whether infants are guilty before God in Adam. That they are cannot, in the light of Scripture, be regarded as questionable.

This is the meaning of that last clause in Rom. 5:12: "for that all have sinned." We must remember that the apostle is discussing here the problem of universal death. All men are under the dominion of death. Death reigns. But death is no accident. Nor is it the end of a natural process of decay and corruption, the inevitable and natural end of all life. It is punishment for sin. But if it is punishment for sin, how can death be universal? Not all men have sinned after the similitude of Adam's transgression. Death reigned from Adam to Moses, even over those that had no law, no special commandment, and no personal opportunity to keep or to violate that commandment as did Adam. Besides, death evidently reigns over the infants in the cradle. It makes no distinction. But how can this be harmonized with the justice of God if death is punishment? Where is the legal ground for this punishment of death upon all? The answer is: "for that all have sinned." But when and how did all sin? The answer is: in and through the sin of the one man Adam. For through one man sin entered into the world, and death through sin, and death passed upon all men. And vs. 18 of the same chapter of the epistle to the Romans states very specifically, that by the offense of one judgment came upon all men to condemnation. This is a purely legal statement. One man sinned, all are under judgment, all are guilty. This could never be the case, if Pelagianism were true and the human race consisted of a number of individuals without communal responsibility. But this is very clear, if the one man that sinned is accounted as the representative of the entire race, so that all are reckoned in him. This, then, is the Scriptural solution of the problem of original sin. All men are born in sin, with a corrupt nature, that is inclined to hate God and the neighbor. And this original pollution is the punishment of spiritual death, inflicted upon the whole human race, because of the communal guilt of all mankind in the first man Adam.

VII

Total Depravity

The last question and answer of this fourth Lord's Day of the Catechism is concerned with the extent of the depravity of the human nature. Our corruption as a fact was stated in Question 5: "I am prone to hate God and my neighbour." In the following two questions the problem of the origin of this corruption was discussed: it is not to be traced to creation, for God created us good and after His own image; but its cause must be found in the first sin of Adam and Eve in paradise. That sin was a fall. And by that fall not only their own individual natures, but the entire human nature became corrupt, so that we are conceived and born in sin. Now, in Question 8, the Catechism touches upon the matter of the degree or extent of our depravity, and insists that it is *total*. "Are we then so corrupt that we are wholly incapable of doing any good, and inclined to all wickedness? Indeed we are; except we are regenerated by the Spirit of God."

Now, it would seem that this is the only possible position to take, if we would maintain that the human nature became corrupt at all through the fall and disobedience of our first parents in paradise. For by ethical corruption is meant corruption of the heart, and from the heart are all the issues of life. An apple may be rotten in part; you may cut out the rotten spot and eat the rest. But this is quite impossible in an ethical sense. Either the human nature is sound in heart, and in that case it is wholly good; or it is corrupt in heart, and then it is entirely depraved.

151

Total depravity, then, means, first of all, that the
whole man is depraved, and not merely a part of him.
It does not mean that his mind is somewhat darkened,
but that his will is sound; or that the desires are
impure but that the mind is ethically good. But it
implies that the heart is corrupt, and that, therefore,
the whole nature is depraved. And, in the second
place, total depravity signifies that the corruption itself is complete. It is not a certain weakness of character; it is ethical perversity. It is not a moral sickness; it is death. It is not a mere lack of righteousness; it is opposition to the law of God. It is not a
want of love; it is enmity against God. And it is all
this constantly, all the time, unchangeably, unless a
wonder is performed upon that corrupt nature: the
wonder of regeneration. This, I say, is the only possible position one can take, if he would maintain
depravity of the *nature* at all. The only other position
conceivable is that of Pelagianism. According to the
latter, the human nature is never depraved, the heart
is never corrupt, the will is never in bondage: sin
remains a matter of the *act* only; the will, therefore,
must always be free to choose in favor of good or evil.
The nature may be weakened by the sinful deed once
performed, by the temptation to which one has yielded;
the will may be hampered by an evil environment,
so that it would be easier for it to yield to the seduc-
tions of evil than to that which is good, but it always
remains free: man is inherently good. A third position is fundamentally impossible. To speak of *total*
depravity may be expedient for practical purposes, it
is really tautologous because ethical depravity of the
human nature is necessarily total.

It follows that all deviating views, all theories that
deny to any degree the totality of depravity of the

human nature, stand opposed to the doctrine of depravity itself, are Pelagian. This is true of what is known as semi-pelagianism, a term that is really a misnomer. It attempts to attribute some good to man by making a distinction between the "natural" and the "spiritual." These it really separates. Man was created *naturally* good, good "in puris naturalibus." As such he was able to do that which is good in the natural, earthly sense of the word; in these he could walk according to the ordinances of God, his Creator. But without something additional he could not perform "spiritual" good, he could not seek the higher, the heavenly things and attain to them. However, he was endowed originally also with this additional power that enabled him to seek the things above and to perform the spiritual good. That power is the image of God. When he sinned and fell, he lost this image of God, so that he has no longer the power to perform spiritual good. But "in puris naturalibus" he can still do that which is good. It is easy to discern that this is fundamentally Pelagian. After all, though man lost something, his nature is sound and good; and his will and mind, though not capable of seeking the heavenly things, are free to do good with respect to things earthly and temporal.

The "common grace" theory, as developed by Dr. A. Kuyper, and as adopted by the Christian Reformed Churches in 1924, as their official doctrine, reaches the same conclusion, though it travels a different way to arrive at it. It, too, is Pelagian. We must not say that it denies *total* depravity, for partial depravity is a contradiction in terms, by the same token that "total depravity" is a tautology: it denies depravity. It is true, of course, that the official doctrine of the Christian Reformed Churches is still that man is depraved,

for this is the teaching of the "Three Forms of Unity";
it is true, too, that in connection with the question of
the Catechism we are now discussing, preachers in
those churches will proclaim this truth sometimes;
but in as far as they adhere to and preach the truth
of the depravity of the human nature, they deny the
doctrine that was declared in the second and third
points of 1924, and exactly in the measure that they
attempt to maintain the latter they deny the doctrine
of the depravity of the human nature. This flagrant
contradiction also explains the fact that in 1924 they
could condemn and ultimately depose ministers of the
gospel of whom they testified that they were reformed
with respect to the fundamental doctrines of the confessions. All this shows that the doctrine that was
adopted in 1924 stands opposed to what is plainly
taught in the standards of the Reformed Churches:
it is Pelagian. The second and third points of 1924
arrive at the conclusion that the human nature is not
really depraved. It would have been, had not God
administered the preventive of "common grace" as
soon as man fell; and it would be, if God did not continue to administer this antidote of common grace.
By the operation of common grace ethical and spiritual
corruption was and is checked. The result is that man
can still do good "in puris naturalibus." He is not
depraved.

That this is, indeed, the implication of the theory
of "common grace" may be proved by many passages
from *De Gemeene Gratie* of Dr. Kuyper, as well as by
the declarations of the Synod of the Christian Reformed Churches of 1924. From the former we quote
the following:

"The Reformed churches confess in harmony with
Holy Scriptures, that by what happened in Paradise

'our nature is become so corrupt, that we are all conceived and born in sin'; and that, too, in this sense,
'that we are wholly incapable of doing any good and
inclined to all evil.' A condition that cannot be
changed, 'unless we are regenerated by the Spirit of
God.'

"Now, one cannot assert of this confession that it
is in accord with our personal experience, nor even
with much that we read elsewhere in Scripture. *Not*
with our personal experience, for even with people
that are complete strangers to the faith and by whom
we certainly cannot suppose regeneration to exist, we
meet with all sorts of life-manifestations that make
a lovely impression, and that, rather than to be inclined
to evil, oppose it. And similarly, *not* with what we
find elsewhere in Scripture. Abimelech seems to put
to shame even Abraham, the friend of God.—The contradiction implied in this is completely solved by the
confession of common grace. The phrase 'inclined to
all evil and incapable of doing any good' then declares
how every man, apart from regeneration, would
actually reveal himself, if common grace did *not* restrain his evil passion; and experience shows us how
the power of the Lord makes 'the evil nature' largely
harmless behind the bars of common grace. In that
case, the expression 'incapable of doing any good and
inclined to all evil,' does not indicate what we find in
'the regenerated,' nor of what we may discover in the
life of all the unregenerated; but is the acknowledgement of what is hid in the passion of our corrupt
nature, and of what would actually come forth from
it, as soon as God would cease from restraining this
evil inclination by His common grace." II, 49, 50.

It is evident that, according to Kuyper, our confession in the eighth answer of the Heidelberg Cate-

chism does not declare what actually exists, but merely what would be, if there were no common grace. Actually men are not wholly incapable of doing any good and inclined to all evil. What the power of this "common grace" actually accomplishes in fallen man, may become evident from the following:

"If in this spirit we ask concerning the condition of man before regeneration, that is, not of man in general, but of an adult man of integrity, then we learn that he is 'dead in sins and trespasses', but that there are, nevertheless, a few 'remains' or 'sparks' of good left in him, and that he, being supported and strengthened by common grace, is capable, not of doing any saving good, but surely of what is called 'civil righteousness.' This gives rise to numerous questions, of which this is the most important: how anyone that is dead can still be active in works, and how the restraint of common grace can have the result, not merely that sin fails to reveal itself or is decreased, but that he performs something that is *positively good*, even though it be only in the sense of civil righteousness." II, 299, 300.

Here we learn, that the power of common grace does not merely act upon the sinner as a restraint, but enables him to do that which is positively good. It does not merely act as the bars that keep the wild beast in its cage in the zoo, but it positively improves his nature. How far this improving or reformatory influence of common grace goes may be gathered from what Dr. Kuyper writes on p. 306 of the same volume. There he makes a distinction between the *center* of our being, which is our *I* or *Ego*, according to him, and the circumference of our existence: the actual manifestations of our life. And again, he distinguishes between the *Ego* in the narrower sense

on the one hand, and our inclinations, our mind and
our will. And once more he tries to distinguish in the
Ego between the center ("kern") of the *Ego* and its
activity. And then he draws the conclusion that,
apart from regeneration but under the salutary influence of common grace, only the inner center of the
Ego remains corrupt, all the rest is improved. "When
it (common grace) takes hold of the line (of our inner
life) at whatever point that may be, and bends its
further course to the right, the result is a tension or
pressure downward toward the center, which can
never affect the *inner center* of our *Ego*, but which,
nevertheless, exerts its influence on the inclinations,
the consciousness, and the will of man. And thus it
is explained that the unconverted can undergo the
influence of common grace even in his inclinations,
in his consciousness, and in his will."

From this it should be evident, that after common
grace has exerted its influence upon the sinner, he
is no longer depraved. His inclinations, his mind
and will are his nature. And it is that nature that is
improved, regardless of what may become of the
"inner center of the Ego." And, surely, the Heidelberg
Catechism does not teach us, that this "inner center
of the Ego" (whatever that may be) is corrupt, but
that "our nature has become so corrupt that we are
all conceived and born in sin," and that "we are wholly
incapable of doing any good, and inclined to all evil."
Nor does the Catechism here refer to a mere abstraction, to man as he might have been without the influence of common grace, but to the actually existing
man, as he is born of woman, and as he lives and
acts in the present world. It requires considerable
"hocus pocus" of sophistic reasoning to prove that this
philosophy of common grace is in accord with the

teaching of the Reformed Churches as contained in their standards. But one who reads intelligently, and who is acquainted with the Reformed truth, cannot be deceived by this sophistry, but soon discovers that it is the doctrine of Pelagius that is seeking entrance in the Reformed Churches, disguised in the cloak of ambiguity.

And the same is true of the doctrine that was officially adopted by the Christian Reformed Churches in 1924. Point II, and III of the doctrinal declarations of that Synod read as follows:

"II. Regarding the second point, touching the restraint of sin in the life of the individual man and of society, Synod declares that according to Scripture and the Confession there is such a restraint of sin. This appears from the passages of Scripture that were quoted, and from the Netherland Confession, Art. 13 and 36, which teach, how God, by a general operation of His Spirit, without renewing the heart, restrains the unbridled manifestation of sin, through which life in human society remains possible; while quotations from Reformed authors of the best period of Reformed Theology prove moreover, that our fathers in the past maintained this view.

"III. Regarding the third point, touching the performance of so-called civil righteousness by the unregenerated, Synod declares that according to Scripture and the Confession the unregenerated, though incapable of doing any spiritual good (Canons of Dordrecht III, IV, 3) are able to do such civil good. This is evident from the passages of Scripture that are quoted, and from the Canons of Dordrecht, III, IV, 4, and the Netherland Confession, Art. 36, which teach that God, without renewing the heart, exercises such an influence upon man, that he is enabled to perform civil good; while it is moreover evident from the quotations made from Reformed authors of the best period of Reformed Theology, that our Reformed fathers from of old defended this view."

Now, it is at present not our purpose to criticize these declarations and refute their doctrine, nor to expose how utterly incompetent are the references to Scripture and to the Confessions to sustain them. What we do wish to point out is, that these declarations are a denial of the doctrine of depravity, and, therefore, are fundamentally Pelagian. They teach: 1. That, apart from the wonder of regeneration, there is a gracious operation of the Holy Spirit on fallen man restraining the manifestation of sin. 2. That, however, this operation of the Holy Spirit is more than a mere restraint, for it is an influence of God upon man whereby he is able to live a good life in this world. This is the same view of man as that of the so-called semi-pelagians, only arrived at from a different direction. The latter maintain that man has lost only the power to do spiritual good, while his nature remained intact; and so he can do good "in puris naturalibus." The declarations of the Christian Reformed Synod of 1924 teach that man has really become corrupt through the fall, but that his nature is so changed by common grace that he can live a good life in the world, can do good "in puris naturalibus." But what is the difference? In principle there is no difference. Both teach that man's nature is capable of doing good. Both deny the depravity of the human nature. If the natural man does evil "in puris naturalibus," in civil and natural things, he does so, not because by nature he could do no different, but because by an act of his free will (free to perform civil and natural good) he chooses to violate the law of God and to resist the influences of the Holy Spirit. And all the sophistry of those who, after 1924, have exerted their powers to prove that these declarations are in harmony with Reformed doctrine, cannot suffice to deceive the truly Reformed heart and mind. They are Pelagian.

Over against all these Pelagian doctrines and tendencies the Reformed Confessions teach in language that is free from all ambiguity, that man is depraved. This depravity implies that his nature is ethically corrupt. His nature is his heart, his mind, his will, all his desires and inclinations as they function through his present corrupted body, and thus constitute "the members that are upon the earth." Col. 3:5. If his mind is corrupt, i.e. so perverted ethically that it cannot conceive the good; if the will is corrupt, i.e. so in the bondage of sin, that it can never determine to do good; if the desires and inclinations are corrupt, i.e. so defiled and impure that they can only lust after evil; if the heart is perverse, so that it can only hate God and is incapable of loving Him,— then, it is evident even to the most simple that a man who has such a nature, can never perform anything good, either in the saving sense, or "in puris naturalibus." This does not mean, that he cannot do natural things, but it does mean that performing them he cannot do good. And this is the doctrine of the Reformed Confessions. The answer of the Heidelberg Catechism to Question 8 is very plain and specific: "Are we then so corrupt that we are wholly incapable of doing any good, and inclined to all wickedness? Indeed we are; except we are regenerated by the Spirit of God." But the language of the rest of our Confession is no less unambiguous and to the point. Art. 14 of the Netherland Confession teaches the following:

"We believe that God created man out of the dust
of the earth, and made and formed him after his own
image and likeness, good, righteous, and holy, capable
in all things to will agreeably to the will of God. But
being in honor, he understood it not, neither knew his
excellency, but wilfully subjected himself to sin, and
consequently to death and the curse, giving ear to
the words of the devil. For the commandment of life,
which he had received, he transgressed, and by sin
separated himself from God, who was his true life,
having corrupted his whole nature; whereby he made
himself liable to corporal and spiritual death. And
being thus become wicked, perverse, and corrupt in all
his ways, he hath lost all his excellent gifts, which he
had received from God, and only retained a few remains thereof, which, however, are sufficient to leave
man without excuse; for all the light which is in
us is changed into darkness, as the Scriptures teach us,
saying: The light shineth in darkness, and the darkness comprehendeth it not: where St. John calleth men
darkness. Therefore, we reject all that is repugnant
to this, concerning the free will of man, since man is
but a slave to sin; and has nothing of himself, unless
it is given him from heaven. For who may presume
to boast, that he of himself can do any good, since
Christ saith, No man can come to me, except the
Father, which hath sent me, draw him? Who will
glory in his own will, who understands, that to be
carnally minded is enmity against God? Who can
speak of his knowledge, since the natural man receiveth not the things of the spirit of God? In short,
who dare suggest any thought, since he knows that
we are not sufficient of ourselves to think anything as
of ourselves, but that our sufficiency is of God? And
therefore what the apostle saith ought justly to be

held sure and firm, that God worketh in us both to will and to do of his good pleasure. For there is no will nor understanding, conformable to the divine will and understanding, but what Christ hath wrought in man: which he teaches us, when he saith, Without me ye can do nothing."

No less explicit and clear are the Canons of Dordrecht on the truth of the depravity of the natural man. In III, IV, 1, 3 we read: "Man was originally formed after the image of God. His understanding was adorned with a true and saving knowledge of his Creator, and of spiritual things; his heart and will were upright; all his affections pure; and the whole man was holy: but revolting from God by the instigation of the devil, and abusing the freedom of his own will, he forfeited these excellent gifts; and on the contrary entailed on himself blindness of mind, horrible darkness, vanity and perverseness of judgment, became wicked, rebellious, and obdurate in heart and will, and impure in his affections. . . . Therefore all men are conceived in sin, and by nature children of wrath incapable of saving good, prone to evil, dead in sin, and in bondage thereto, and without the regenerating grace of the Holy Spirit, they are neither able nor willing to return to God, to reform the depravity of their nature, nor to dispose themselves to reformation." It is true that in the first half of Art. 4 of the same chapters of the Canons they declare that "There remain, however, in man since the fall the glimmerings of natural light, whereby he retains some knowledge of God, of natural things, and of the difference between good and evil, and discovers some regard for virtue, good order in society, and for maintaining an orderly external deportment." But that the fathers of Dordt did not mean by this declaration to attribute any good whatever to fallen man, may be seen from what immediately follows in the same article: "But so far is this light of nature from being sufficient to bring him to a saving knowledge of God, and to true conversion, that he is incapable of using it aright even in things natural and civil. Nay further, this light, such as it is, man in various ways renders wholly polluted, and holds in unrighteousness, by doing which he becomes inexcusable before God."

This was the doctrine that was developed and defended over against the enemies of the truth by the great men of God throughout the history of the Church. It was this truth that was emphasized by Augustine over against the polished and superficial Pelagius and other opponents. According to him the will of fallen man is free only in the sense that it does not act by compulsion from without. Man still acts as a free agent: he considers, prefers, chooses, and acts according to the choice of his will. But this does not mean that the will is free to choose and to do that which is good. Fallen man is not free to choose both good and evil. We must remember, thus he teaches us, that the will itself is either good or evil, and that the ethical condition of the will determines its choice for good or for evil. Sin or grace determines the condition of the will. And in the natural man it is the sin of Adam that determines his will for evil. Fallen man does not even have a remnant of the original righteousness of Adam in the state of integrity. All righteousness he lost. He is free from righteousness, even as in the state of integrity he was free from sin. He is nothing but a *peccati servus*, a slave of sin. Ench. ch. 30. He does, indeed, serve sin according to the choice of his own will, but never can he choose anything else than evil. He has, therefore, indeed a *liberum arbitrium,* a free will, but only *in malis, ad peccandum,* to evil and to sin, not *ad agendum bonum,* to do the good.

It might be expected that Pelagius c.s. pointed to the virtues and noble deeds of the heathen and ungodly, in opposition to the doctrine of total depravity as defended by Augustine. Highly these virtues of the ungodly were extolled by him, even as is often done today by those that defend the theory of "common grace." But Augustine explained that these virtues were in reality nothing but vices and sins. In the ungodly there is often a conflict of sinful motives and desires, so that one sin restrains another. This is very evident by such men as misers, but may even be discovered among the great Romans. When often they repressed their sinful lusts and accomplished things that are praiseworthy in the estimation of men, they were motivated by their love of honor and sinful ambition. The so-called virtues of natural man may better be called vices. Sin is not checked, *"sed aliis peccatis alia vincuntur,"* some sins are chained by other sins.*

Calvin emphasizes the same truth. It is true that the defenders of the common grace theory often appeal to Calvin for their view that the natural man is able to do good by virtue of the influence of a common, non-regenerating grace. They do this in order to defend their right to the name of Calvinists! And it may readily be granted that the *term* "common grace" is often found in Calvin, while at the same time he explains the so-called virtues of the ungodly in the Augustinian way. The fact that man after the fall retained his reason and the remnants of natural light, he ascribes to the general grace of God. It is true, he

---

*De Predestinatie-leer van Aug. Thom. v. Aquino en Calv. Dr. A. D. R. Polman, p. 77.

writes, that some are born idiots and stupid, but this does not obscure the general grace of God: "Nam quod nascuntur moriones quidam vel stupidi, defectus ille generalem Dei gratiam non obscurat." Inst. II, 2, 17. He even designates as *special grace* the fact that in these natural gifts one is more excellent than another: "Unde enim alius alio praestantior, nisi ut in natura communi emineat specialis Dei gratia, quae multos praeteriens, nemini se obstrictam esse clamat?" He even seems to teach a certain grace whereby corruption in the sinful nature of fallen man is somewhat restrained, so that it does not break forth in all possible sin and violence. He notes that in every age there were some that throughout their life strove to be virtuous. By this they furnished proof that there was an element of purity in their nature: "honestatis studio documentum ediderunt, nonnihil fuisse in natura sua puritatis." But to explain this, we must remember that in the corruption of the human nature there is still a little place for the grace of God, not to remove, but to restrain the corruption: "Sed hic succurrere nobis debet, inter illam naturae corruptionem esse nonnullum gratiae Dei locum, non quae illam purget, sed intus cohibeat." Inst. II, 3, 3. However, we must remember: 1. That Calvin never teaches, that any positive good proceeds from the fallen and corrupt human nature. In this respect his use of the term "common grace" has nothing in common with the modern conception under that name. With Calvin the natural man remains corrupt in all his parts; he is never improved. Man has lost all his excellent gifts. Only of his natural powers he retained a remnant, so that he is still a rational being. But even these natural gifts are corrupted. These natural gifts as such are ascribed by Calvin to the Holy Spirit, who distributes all gifts

and talents even as He will.   But he agrees, nevertheless, with Augustine, that the natural man corrupts
and defiles even these natural gifts, so that he derives
no praise from them for himself: "ita naturalia haec
quae restabant, corrupta fuisse docet (i. e. Augus-
tinus).   Non quod per se inquinari possint, quatenus
a Deo proficiscuntur: sed quia polluto homini pura esse
desierunt, ne quam inde laudem consequatur." Inst.
II, 2, 12-17.   2. That Calvin explains this so-called
restraining grace in a way with which we can heartily
agree, and which makes the *term* grace a misnomer.
For at the end of the same paragraph in which he
speaks of this restraining grace, he explains that some
are restrained by shame, others by fear of the laws
from breaking out in all kinds of corruption, even
though for the most part they do not try to cover up
their pollution (utcunque suam magna ex parte im-
puritatem non dissimulant); some lead an honest life
because they consider it profitable for themselves;
still others rise above the common level in order that
by their majesty they may keep others into subjection.
And thus God by His providence restrains the corruption of the nature, that it does not break out in iniquity.   But He does not purge the nature from within.
Inst. II, 3, 3.   All this quite agrees materially with the
views of Augustine, even though one may object that
the use of the *term* grace is to be condemned as improper in this connection.   For it certainly cannot be
called grace when one is restrained by his own sinful
and selfish motives from breaking out into certain sins.
3. That with Calvin this explanation of the "virtues"
of the ungodly, which he, too, like Augustine, ultimately condemns as vices (see Inst. II, 3, 4: the more excellent one was, the more he was motivated by his carnal
ambition, so that all the so-called virtues of the un-

godly lose their pleasantness before God. Therefore whatever appears praiseworthy in ungodly men must be considered of no worth: pro nihilo ducendum est quicquid laude dignum apparet in hominous profanis.), never occurs as a main doctrine, but only as an appendix to his doctrine of total depravity. Anyone who reads the Institutes will admit that Calvin would never have thought of deposing ministers from their office because they insisted that the natural man is incapable of doing any good, as did the Christian Reformed Church in 1924! 4. That, as far as the employment of the term "grace" by Calvin is concerned (communis, generalis, specialis, specialissima!), we must not forget that our reformer was still in his twenties, and not long out of the Catholic Church, when he wrote his Institutes, and that it is hardly Calvinistic blindly to adopt even the terms which he employed, especially since these terms with him have an entirely different meaning from their present connotation! We conclude, therefore, that Calvin taught the truth of total depravity in all its implications, and that the modern emphasis upon the goodness of natural man is certainly not Calvinistic.

Calvin was not the only reformer who emphasized this doctrine of the total depravity anew in the sixteenth century. Nor are the teachers of this truth at that time limited to his associates. Martin Luther taught the same truth with equal emphasis, and with all the vehemence of his ardent nature defended it against opponents. This may be shown from his polemic against Erasmus' "Diatribe": "The Bondage of the Will." Writes he: "As to the other paradox you mention,—that, 'whatever is done by us, is not done by Free-will but from mere necessity'—Let us briefly consider this, lest we should suffer any thing

most perniciously spoken, to pass by unnoticed. Here
then, I observe, that if it be proved that our salvation
is apart from our own strength and counsel, and depends on the working of God alone (which I hope I
shall clearly prove hereafter, in the course of this discussion), does it not evidently follow, that when God
is not present with us to work in us, everything that
we do is evil, and that we of necessity do those things
which are of no avail unto salvation? For if it is not
we ourselves, but God only, that works salvation in us,
it must follow, whether or no, that we do nothing unto
salvation *before* the working of God in us. But by
necessity I do not mean *compulsion;* but (as they term
it) the *necessity of immutability,* not of *compulsion;*
that is, a man void of the Spirit of God does not evil
against his will as by violence, or as if he were taken
by the neck and forced to it, in the same way as a thief
or cut-throat is dragged to punishment against his will;
but he does it spontaneously, and with desirous willingness. And this willingness and desire of doing evil
he cannot, by his own power, leave off, restrain, or
change; but he goes on still desiring and craving. And
even if he should be compelled by force to do any thing
outwardly to the contrary, yet the craving will *within*
remain averse to, and rises in indignation against
that which forces or resists it. But it would not rise
in indignation, if it were changed, and made willing
to yield to a constraining power. This is what we
mean by the necessity of immutability:—that the will
cannot change itself, nor give itself another bent;
but rather the more it is resisted, the more it is irri-
tated to crave; as is manifest from its indignation.
This would not be the case if it were free, or had a
'Free-will.' Ask experience how hardened against all
persuasion they are, whose inclinations are fixed upon

any one thing. For if they yield at all, they yield through force, or through something attended with greater advantage; they never yield willingly. And if their inclinations be not thus fixed, they let all things pass and go on just as they will." pp. 72, 73.

Or consider the following from the same work: "Where are you now, friend Erasmus! you, who promised 'that you would freely acknowledge that the most excellent faculty of man is flesh, that is, ungodly, if it should be proven from the Scriptures?' Acknowledge now, then, when you hear, that the most excellent faculty of man is not only ungodly, but ignorant of God, existing in the contempt of God, turned to evil, and unable to turn towards good. For what is it to be 'unrighteous,' but for the will (which is one of the most noble faculties in man), to be unrighteous? What is it to understand nothing either of God or of good, but for the reason (which is another of the most noble faculties of man) to be ignorant of God and good, that is, to be blind to the knowledge of godliness? What is it to be 'gone out of the way,' and to have become unprofitable, but for men to have no power in one single faculty, and the least power in their most noble faculties, to turn unto good, but only to turn unto evil! What is it not to fear God, but for men to be in all their faculties, and most of all in their noblest faculties, contemners of all the things of God, of His words, His works, His laws, His precepts, and His will! What then can reason propose that is right, who is thus blind and ignorant? What can the will choose that is good, which is thus evil and impotent? Nay, what can the will pursue, where the reason can propose nothing but the darkness of its own blindness and ignorance? And where the reason is thus erroneous, and the will adverse, what can the man either do or attempt, that is good!" pp. 334, 335.

The same teaching is found in Ursinus' "Schatboek," who under Question 8 of the Catechism discusses various degrees of freedom, and writes of the freedom of the natural man as follows: "The second degree or step of freedom of the will is the will in fallen man, born of corrupt parents, before regeneration. In this state the will acts indeed freely, but is only led to evil and can do nothing but sin. The reason for this is that the fall of man was followed by the loss of the knowledge of God in man's intellect and of the inclination to obedience in the will and in the heart; and that instead he entailed on himself blindness and aversion to God, which man cannot put off unless he is regenerated by the Spirit of God. In short, after the fall there is in man only the capability of choosing evil." p. 82.

Here follows an objection to the doctrine of total depravity, answered by Ursinus:

"*Objection* 1: Nothing is easier, Erasmus says to Luther, than to refrain the hand from theft. Yea, even Socrates, Aristides and others did many virtuous things. Hence, there must have been with them a free will to do good before regeneration. *Answer*: 1. The description of the free will as freedom to do a good work, or the power to exercise obedience well-pleasing to God, is erroneous. This freedom the unregenerate do not possess. Even though they refrain from committing external sinful acts, within them rage the evil passions. 2. God by His providence directs also the hearts of the unregenerate; but from this it does not follow that they can easily perform inner obedience. This cannot be present with them, seeing they were not regenerated." p. 83.

Ursinus, too, discusses the so-called "virtues" of the unregenerate, and in some instances uses language which we would avoid, but he never hesitates to declare that these "virtues" are *sins*. He distinguishes between acts that are as such sinful, and acts that are sinful through "secondary causes." These latter are: "the deeds of the unregenerate and the hypocrites; and they are indeed commanded by God, but they displease Him nevertheless, because they are done without faith and conversion to God; thus also the *adiaphora* that give offense. 'And all that is not of faith is sin,' Rom. 14:23. 'But unto them which are defiled and unbelieving is nothing pure.' Tit. 1:15. 'But without faith it is impossible to please God.' Heb. 11:6. All the virtues, therefore, of the unregenerate, such as the chastity of Scipio, the courage of Julius, the faithfulness of Regulus, the righteousness of Aristides, etc., even though they are in themselves good deeds commanded by God, become sins through something additional and they displease God; both, because the persons that perform them do not please God, and because they are not done in the way and with the purpose required by God, viz., not out of faith and not to the glory of God; and these certainly are the requirements for any good work; without these even the best deeds are sins; so that it is sin when an ungodly man or hypocrite prays, gives alms, offers sacrifices, etc., because he does not do tnese things out of faith and to the glory of God. 'The hypocrites do alms in the synagogues and on the streets, that they may have glory of men. Verily, I say unto you, they have their reward.' Matt. 6:2. 'He that killeth an ox is as if he slew a man; he that sacrificeth a lamb, as if he cut off a dog's neck; he that offereth an oblation, as he that offereth swine's blood; he that burneth incense, as if he blessed an idol. Yea, they have chosen their own

ways, and their soul delighteth in their abominations.'
Isa. 66:3." p. 61.

The most faithful of the leaders and teachers of
the Church, therefore, have always emphasized the
truth that after the fall man is totally depraved. And
when, by way of answering objections, they spoke of
the so-called "virtues" of the ungodly, this part of
their teaching was considered so accidental and un-
important, that no trace of it can be found in the
Reformed Confessions! And it was considered quite
sufficient to declare: "Are we then so corrupt that
we are wholly incapable of doing any good, and inclined to all wickedness? Indeed we are; except we
are regenerated by the Spirit of God."

VIII

Without Restraint

The question arises: what is the meaning of total depravity? The catechism answers: total depravity signifies "that we are wholly incapable of doing any good, and inclined to all evil." But it may be expedient at this point to ask the further question: but what is good and what is evil? It seems a rather severe judgment that all men are wholly incapable of doing any good, and if we look about us in the world and judge of men as we come into contact with them, we are, perhaps, inclined to doubt the truth of this statement. That there is a good deal of corruption among men of every station in life is evident. That men in their relation to one another are often motivated by covetousness, lust, pride, ambition, hatred and envy and the like no one can deny. But that, outside of regeneration, all men are always wicked and perverse, so that they never do anything that is good, is difficult to harmonize with actual experience. It is true that in the lower strata of society one may find men that are so deeply and hopelessly submerged in the mire of sin that one would not hesitate, perhaps, to consider them totally depraved; but is there not also a higher moral level on which one meets with men that give themselves wholly to the pursuit of the happiness and well-being of their fellowmen, and that are characterized by integrity and nobility in all their walk and conversation? And is it not a fact, too, that the same men who on some occasions and in some situations reveal themselves as being actuated by the meanest and most corrupt motives, will at other times perform the noblest and most unselfish deeds? Is, then, one not forced to the conclusion, either that Romans 7 gives us a picture of the natural man, or that there is, besides regenerating grace, some other kind of grace whereby men are somewhat improved, so that in actual life they are not wholly incapable of doing any good and inclined to all evil?

It is not the testimony of Scripture, but that of this apparent conflict between our Confessions on this point and actual experience that led Dr. A. Kuyper to write his work on Common Grace. Writes he: "If one conceives of sin as a cause, indeed, of spiritual and physical deterioration, but not as a deadly and quickly operating poison that, unless it is restrained, leads to spiritual, temporal, and eternal death, there is no room for the restraint of sin, to which Calvin first emphatically called attention, and on which the entire doctrine of *general grace* is based. It is exactly because of this that the Reformed confession has always placed full emphasis on this deadly character of sin, and opposed every attempt to weaken the conception of sin. 'Incapable of doing any good and inclined to all evil' was the formula the Heidelberger used to express this truth. And if you take your position unmoveably in this truth, then it is but natural that you will discover in the narrative of Paradise, and in all the rest of Scripture, and in human life round about you, and in your own heart, evidences of a divine operation, by which the quick and absolutely fatal operation of sin has been and still is restrained in many ways, even there where there is no question of *saving* grace. Or do you not find, even by heathen peoples and by unbelievers in your own environment, many phenomena that bespeak a certain inclination to

good things, and a certain indignation over all kinds
of crime? It is true, there is not found any inclination
to *saving* good, but, nevertheless, a certain attraction
for integrity and things of a good report. Are there
not acts of meanness, dishonesty and perversion of
justice, against which the public conscience, even of
unbelievers, rebels? And can one not relate numerous
deeds of philanthropy and charity, performed by unbelievers, by which they often put to shame the believers? When the daughter of Pharaoh rescued Moses
from the Nile, did she do good or evil? And is it,
then, not evident that the total corruption of our
nature through sin, a truth which we unhesitatingly
confess, is in conflict with reality? And do you, therefore, not clearly see that in such cases you stand before the alternative: either abandon your confession
of the deadly character of sin; or maintain this confession with might and main, but then with the additional confession that there is an operation of general
grace, whereby this deadly operation of sin in numerous cases is restrained." *De Gemeene Gratie*, I, 248,
249.

The question that confronts us, therefore, is
whether the life of the natural, fallen man in this
world, as we observe it, must be explained as being the
result of a certain grace of God, whereby sin within
him is restrained; or whether all its impulses and
manifestations are quite in accord with the statement
of the Heidelberg Catechism that "we are wholly incapable of doing any good and inclined to all evil."
This is not a purely scholastic question, but concerns
the very heart of our Reformed truth on this point.
For, if the life and walk of fallen, unregenerate man
is to be explained as the fruit of grace, this fruit must
certainly be good, the natural man is not wholly de-

praved, and the doctrine of total depravity becomes
an abstraction that does not harmonize with actual
experience.   And again, if this is true, the truth of
total depravity cannot be applied in actual life: a
basis is established for the amalgamation of the Church
and the world, for the cooperation of the believer and
the unbeliever.   In that case there is some concord between Christ and Belial.   That this is the lamentable
result of the doctrine of "common grace" may be seen
in those churches that adopted and glorify this doctrine.   The antithesis is obliterated, and the "sons of
God" are more and more lost in the world.   The question, therefore, is one of great doctrinal and practical
importance.   And this question cannot be decided by
taking our standpoint in experience and by proceeding
from what we see in the world of the life of natural
man, but must be answered solely in the light of the
Word of God, and next, in that of the Reformed Confessions.

And then we may state without fear of contradiction that the Scriptures *never* speak of a *restraining
grace* to explain the activity and development of the
natural man in the world.   Neither the term nor the
idea is found in the Bible.   The life of the regenerated
is, indeed, presented throughout the Word of God as
the fruit of *grace;* the life of the natural man never.
It is true, of course, that also the activity and development of the wicked and of the devils are strictly under
God's control, so that, as Art. 13 of the Netherland
Confession teaches us, "nothing can befall us by chance,
but by the direction of our most gracious and heavenly Father; who watches over us with a paternal care,
keeping all creatures so under His power, that not a
hair of our head (for they are all numbered), nor a
sparrow, can fall to the ground, without the will of our

Father, in whom we do entirely trust; being persuaded
that he so restrains the devil and all our enemies, that
without His will and permission they cannot hurt us."
But this overruling providence of God, whereby He
holds the wicked in His power and controls all their
actions, is quite different from a certain restraining
grace by which the unregenerate are inwardly somewhat improved and enabled to do the good. Of this
the Bible never makes mention.

The passages from the Bible on which this doctrine
is supposed to be based are not to the point. A few
of them we will examine by way of illustration. All
of them are mentioned in Kuyper's *De Gemeene Gratie*.
There is, first of all, the case of Abimelech in relation
to Sarah, Abraham's wife, quoted by Dr. Kuyper as
proof of the proposition that there is a general restraining grace of God operative in all the unregenerate. Let us read the account of it in Scripture: "And
Abraham said of Sarah his wife, She is my sister: and
Abimelech king of Gerar sent, and took Sarah. But
God came to Abimelech in a dream by night, and said
to him, Behold, thou art but a dead man, for the
woman which thou hast taken; for she is a man's wife.
But Abimelech had not come near her: and he said,
Lord, wilt thou slay also a righteous nation? Said he
not unto me, She is my sister? and she, even herself
said, He is my brother: in the integrity of my heart
and innocency of my hands have I done this. And
God said unto him in a dream, Yea, I know that thou
didst this in the integrity of thy heart; for I also with-
held thee from sinning against me: therefore suffered
I thee not to touch her." Gen. 20:2-6. Now Dr. Kuyper
concludes from this passage the following: "mention
is made here, therefore, of a direct operation of God
upon the person of Abimelech, whereby a sinful pas-

sion that was aroused is restrained, an impelling sin
is checked, a premeditated evil is frustrated; and that,
too, of such a direct operation as affected alike his
sensuality and his soul, so that he became sensually a
dead man, and in his soul the passion was broken. It
was necessary to explain this here somewhat elaborately, because Scripture here explains and God Himself
interprets to us the operation of common grace more
broadly than usual." *De Gemeene Gratie*, II, 58.

But is this conclusion of Dr. Kuyper's the true
interpretation of the text as found in Gen. 20? That
it is not will be evident from the following considerations. 1. Whatever may be the correct explanation
of Abimelech's case, it is at all events a very exceptional occurrence, from which no general conclusions may
be drawn with respect to a possible operation of God
restraining sin in all men. Sarah was the covenant
mother of the promised seed, and for her sake God
does not permit Abimelech to touch her. 2. That
Abimelech was an unregenerate man is presupposed
by Dr. Kuyper's interpretation, but is by no means
an established fact. In those days, relatively soon
after the flood, when Shem was still living, when a
God-fearing king like Melchisedec is still found in the
land of Canaan, and when there must have been thousands of children of God outside of Abraham and his
house, a man like Abimelech may very well be classified with those that feared the Lord. In fact, the text
does not at all leave the impression that he was a
wicked person. God speaks to him in a dream, and
with evident reference to himself he answers: wilt
thou slay a righteous nation? Moreover, he says to
God: "in the integrity of my heart and innocency of
my hands have I done this;" and God Himself corroborated this statement. 3. It certainly is quite contrary

to the plain statements of the text when Dr. Kuyper explains that there was in Abimelech's case a direct operation of God "whereby a sinful passion that was aroused is restrained, an impelling sin is checked, a premeditated evil is frustrated." There was no sinful passion, and surely no premeditated evil on the part of Abimelech. He acted on the supposition that Abraham and Sarah spoke the truth, and that he had the perfect right to take Sarah to wife. And God Himself seals the statement of Abimelech that he had done this in the integrity of his heart. It is true, of course, that the act of intercourse with Sarah was prevented by an act of God, but this was no *restraint of sin*, no influence of a certain *grace* whereby Abimelech's nature was somewhat improved, for the simple reason that there was no intention of sin in Abimelech's heart at all. 4. Finally, let us also note, that the act of God whereby the deed of intercourse with Sarah on the part of Abimelech was prevented, was not an operation of *grace*, but such an influence of God upon the body of Abimelech that intercourse with Sarah became a physical impossibility. This is evident from the text itself: "Behold, thou art but a dead man, for the woman which thou hast taken." For all these reasons it may be considered quite evident that Abimelech's case cannot be quoted in proof of the doctrine of a general restraining grace in the nature of all unregenerate men.

The second passage from Scripture to which we must call attention in this connection is Rom. 1:18ff. Especially verses 24, 26 and 28. We read there: "Wherefore God also gave them up unto uncleanness through the lusts of their own hearts, to dishonour their own bodies between themselves." vs. 24. And again: "For this cause God gave them up unto vile affections: for even their women did change the

natural use into that which is against nature." vs. 26.
And once more: "And even as they did not like to retain God in their knowledge, God gave them over
unto a reprobate mind, to do those things which are
not convenient." vs. 28. To understand how the doctrine of a restraining grace is elicited from these
passages, we must let Dr. Kuyper speak. He explains
these passages as follows:

"This fact (that the nations developed from bad
to worse) the apostle attributes to this, that it pleased
God gradually to cause His 'common grace *to shrink*
(*te doen inkrimpen*).' Common grace was extended
after the flood, now again its influence was caused to
shrink, and this shrinking of common grace the apostle
pictures to us in these words, that it pleased God '*to
give them over to a reprobate mind.*' . . . .

"This 'giving over' of the nations by God may not
be understood in the sense of a common hardening.
Obduration and hardening incites to rebellion and
enmity against God, while '*to be given over*' in itself
merely implies that the evil of sin is no longer restrained so forcibly as before, so that as a result the
evil worked through in a most dangerous manner.
Hence, as a result of this 'giving over' the apostle
points as often as three times, not to an audacious
God-provoking presumption as that of Pharaoh, but
constantly to the corruption of morals, i.e. to the being
swallowed up of what is human by bestiality." *De Gemeene Gratie*, II, 412.

The "giving over" of which the apostle speaks in
this passage, therefore, is explained as referring to
such a withholding of the operation of common grace,
that man is left to himself, to his own lust, sin is no
longer restrained, and the world is left to develop in
corruption to its own destruction. And this pre-

supposes that there was a period in which God did restrain the process of corruption and the breaking out of sin by restraining grace. Romans 1:18ff. does not directly teach common grace, but presupposes it. However, against this explanation several objections may be raised. 1. Certainly the text in Romans 1 does not speak of restraining grace, but of the very opposite: of a wrath of God that delivers the ungodly over to their own corruption. "For the wrath of God is revealed from heaven against all ungodliness and unrighteousness of men, who hold the truth in unrighteousness." In these words of the eighteenth verse the theme of the entire section to the end of the chapter is announced. And the apostle explains first of all just how men hold the truth in unrighteousness, in order then to show how God's wrath is revealed from heaven against such ungodliness of men. Their ungodliness and unrighteousness consists in this: a. They know God, for the invisible things of God from the creation of the world are clearly seen, and that which is known of God is manifest in them. b. They glorify Him not as God, neither are thankful. This is their iniquity, and against this is the wrath of God revealed. Now, let us note that the apostle does not write that there was a time when this was different, as Dr. Kuyper presupposes. Always God made Himself known as God; and always men held this truth in unrighteousness. Hence, the wrath of God of which the apostle speaks in this chapter was always revealed. And how was this wrath of God revealed? First of all in this, that God made them foolish, who professed themselves to be wise, so that they bowed themselves before man and beast and creeping things. And secondly in this, that God cast them into the mire of utter moral degradation. The section, therefore, does not speak of restraining grace, but of delivering wrath by which men develop in sin and corruption. 2. The word that is used for "giving over" may not be rendered by the merely passive "letting go," as Kuyper would explain. Three times the apostle uses the word *paredooken*. And that this word has a very positive and active meaning may be gathered from other instances where the same word is employed in Holy Writ. It occurs in Matt. 10:21: "And the brother shall deliver up the brother to death, and the father the child." It is plain that here the meaning is not: "the brother shall let go, or abandon the brother to die," but that a positive act is meant whereby the brother is put to death. In Acts 8:3 we read: "As for Saul, he made havoc of the church, entering into every house, and hailing men and women committed them to prison." The word in the original that is rendered by "committed" in this verse is the same that is translated by "gave over" in Rom. 1. Yet it is plain that the meaning is not that Saul let them go into prison, but that he actively made them prisoners, led them into bonds. In the same sense the word occurs in Matt. 17:22: "The Son of man shall be betrayed (delivered up) into the hands of men." And again in Matt. 24:9: "They shall deliver you up to be afflicted." These examples might easily be multiplied. And they shed light upon the meaning of the word as the apostle employs it in Rom. 1. No more than it can be said that anyone is delivered up into prison or unto death, into the hands of anyone or unto affliction and tribulation, by an act of mere passive abandonment, no more can the words "he gave them up" have that passive denotation in the first chapter of the epistle to the Romans. It denotes a positive act of God, whereby in His holy wrath God cast the ungodly that would

not glorify Him, neither were thankful, deeper into
the mire of sin and corruption. To be sure, this act
of God does not destroy or ignore the moral nature of
man. He gave them up through their own lusts. But
the fact remains that the words "he gave them up"
denote an active delivering up on the part of God. But
if this is true, then it must also be plain that this
term does not at all presuppose a previous period of
restraining grace. Were the meaning of the term
"to let go" it would have sense to say that such a
previous restraint was presupposed. I let go that
which I withhold or restrain first. But now the word
denotes a positive act of delivering up, this divine act
of restraint is not at all presupposed. 3. Besides,
the question arises: why should God cause His common
grace to "shrink"? Dr. Kuyper answers: because men
increased in unrighteousness and ungodliness. The
shrinking of common grace was a punitive measure on
the part of God. But how could men develop in corruption and break out in iniquity, as long as God by
the operation of common grace restrained sin in their
nature? It is evident that thus we are reasoning in
circles: the cause of the shrinking of common grace is
the breaking out into sin on the part of the ungodly,
and the cause of the latter is the shrinking of common
grace. The cause is the effect and the effect is the
cause! But apart from this, it should be quite clear
that Romans 1 cannot be referred to as a proof for
the doctrine of a restraining grace. It teaches the
very opposite.

A third and final passage to which we must call
attention in this connection is Romans 2:14, 15: "For
when the Gentiles, which have not the law, do by
nature the things contained in the law, these, having
not the law, are a law unto themselves: which shew

the work of the law written in their hearts, their
conscience also bearing witness, and their thoughts
the mean while accusing or else excusing one another."
It must be remarked here that the Revised Version
renders verse 14 more correctly, when it translates
"the things of the law" instead of "the things contained in the law." Dr. Kuyper appeals to this passage
in support of his theory of a restraining grace, whereby even the heathen are enabled to do the good. He
finds the following elements in this passage:

1. It teaches that there is a remnant in the hearts
of the heathen of the original divine handwriting of
the law. Writes he: "He (i. e. Paul) explains in so
many words, that the heathen, even in his days, i. e.
forty centuries after the fall really have a remnant
of this divine handwriting in their soul: 'which shew
the work of the law written in their hearts'. Mark
you well, it does not state that they have *the law* itself
written in their hearts, but the *'work* of the law,' as
if to refer to a *practical incentive* rather than to a
clear and pure knowledge. However this may be, it
is plainly stated that there is always in the heart of
the fallen sinner a remnant of this divine handwriting.
Though largely obliterated and having become illegible
in its details, this divine handwriting is nevertheless
left in the fallen sinner to such an extent, that one
can still see that it was originally there, and also can
still make out what was originally written there."
De Gemeene Gratie, II, 14, 15.

2. The passage teaches that the heathen consents
to this remnant of the handwriting of the law of God
in his heart. He consents to it, and responds to it
with an *Amen*. We quote him: "In the second place
it follows from Rom. 2:13, 14 (should be 14, 15) that
this remnant of the law in the heart of the fallen sin-

ner is quickened to a certain extent by divine grace. ('door de Goddelijke genade tot op zekere hoogte levendig in hen wordt gehouden.') For it states 'that their conscience also bears witness in them', i.e. gives testimony to this remnant of the law in their heart, and still responds to it with an Amen. The conscience and the law of God are, therefore, distinguished. The conscience and the law of God are not the same, as many would have it. On the contrary, the conscience bears witness *with* the law. . . . And of this conscience he says that in relation to the remnant of the divine law it is not rebellious, nor silent, but *bearing witness with it*. And since this cannot come out of sin as such, it follows, that God not only left a remnant of His law in the heart of fallen man, but that He also operates into his consciousness and compels him in that consciousness to respond with an Amen to the law." Idem, II, 15, 16.

3. The text teaches that this operation of common grace is not limited to the individual heathen or sinner, but also operates upon his communal life in society. This Dr. Kuyper deduces from the statement: "and their thoughts the mean while accusing or else excusing one another." Although it is by no means certain that this is the correct interpretation of this clause, and though it is not impossible that "one another" refers to "thoughts" rather than to the heathen in their mutual relationship (the Revised Version translates: "and their thoughts one with another accusing or else excusing them") we may let this pass as being of minor importance for our present discussion.

4. Finally, the passage teaches that this common grace enables the fallen sinner to do the good, i.e. to keep the law of God. Writes Dr. Kuyper: "And finally,

in the fourth place, it follows from Rom. 2:13, 14 (should be 14, 15) that this common grace keeps operative in the fallen sinner not merely a sense of what is honorable and dishonorable, of what is just or unjust, good or evil, but also that this common grace furnishes him with power to do the good. For he says: 'If the Gentiles, which have not the law (of Sinai) *by nature do the things of the law.*' They, therefore, not only *know* them, but they also *do* them, and it is precisely from the fact that they do them that the apostle draws the conclusion that they know them. That they do them is for the apostle the point of procedure for his argumentation. And if it is established that even a child of God confesses that he is incapable of himself to think any good, far less to do it, then it follows necessarily that also the Gentiles do not perform this good in their own power, but only because common grace impels them and enables them to do it." Idem, II, 17.

But in reply to this interpretation we may remark the following:

1. That the passage speaks very emphatically of things which the Gentiles do *by nature* (*phusei*) : the Gentiles, which have not the law, do *by nature* the things of the law. Whatever, therefore, may be our interpretation of the rest of the text, whatever may be our conception of just what the Gentiles do, it must be maintained that they do it, *not by grace*, common or special, but *by nature*. *By nature* and *by grace* are terms that are mutually exclusive in Scripture, and on its basis also in our Confessions. *By nature* we are all that which we are by reason of our birth in a fallen human race, from sinful parents and through the fall of our first parents in Paradise. Nothing is added, certainly no grace. For we were "dead in trespasses

and sins; wherein in times past ye walked according to the course of this world, according to the prince of the power of the air, the spirit that now worketh in the children of disobedience: Among whom we all had our conversation in times past in the lusts of our flesh, fulfilling the desires of the flesh and of the mind; and were *by nature* the children of wrath, even as others." Eph. 2:1-3. And the Heidelberg Catechism teaches us that we are *"by nature"* prone to hate God and our neighbor. Q. 5. And it explains that by the fall and disobedience of our first parents in Paradise our *nature* is become so corrupt that we are all conceived and born in sin. Now, surely, even as we are not by grace prone to hate God and the neighbor, and even as we are not by grace corrupt, and even as we are not by grace dead in trespasses and sins, and children of wrath, so the heathen do not by grace the things of the law, seeing that it is plainly stated that they do it *by nature*. When Dr. Kuyper, therefore, introduces into the explanation of the text the idea that the Gentiles do good by common grace, he corrupts the text. Whatever these Gentiles do, they certainly do it *by nature*. If, then, what they do is good (keeping the law), it follows that their *nature* must be good, for only a good tree can bring forth good fruit. But seeing that the whole of Scripture teaches us that we are *by nature* corrupt, dead in trespasses and sins, it must follow that what is said of the Gentiles in Rom. 2:14, 15, cannot be good. For *by a corrupt nature* they cannot do anything that is good.

2. That the text does not state that the Gentiles keep the law of God by nature, nor that the law of God is written in their hearts, nor that there is a remnant of the original handwriting of God in their hearts, but that they do the *things of the law,* and that they show

that *the work of the law* is written in their hearts. And the things of the law and the work of the law are not the same as the law itself. By "the things of the law" I understand *the things which the law does.* Those things which the revealed and written law did for Israel, the Gentiles did themselves. What things did the law do? It distinguished in broad outlines what is good and what is evil, and it prohibited evil and commanded the good. Now, the Gentiles do by nature just that. Fallen man is not such that he does not know the difference between good and evil. He has a certain knowledge of God; he knows that God must be thanked and glorified; he discerns the difference between good and evil: he knows that it is wrong to murder, to steal, to commit adultery, to bear false testimony. The reason for this is, that the *work* of the law, the groundwork, the broad outline of the law is written in his heart. God keeps it there. Fallen man remained a rational-moral being. If he were not, he could not even sin, nor could God condemn him in the day of judgment. But now it is different. That the Gentiles do, indeed, have this groundwork of the law written in their hearts they show not only by doing the things of the law, by distinguishing between good and evil, by making their own laws, but also by the fact that their own conscience bears witness, and that they accuse or excuse either one another or themselves. That this is, indeed, the meaning of the text is also evident from what is added: "these, having not the law, are a law unto themselves."

3. That in all this there is nothing that is not in accord with the truth that *by nature* fallen man is wholly incapable of doing any good and inclined to all evil; nor is there anything in the passage that suggests or requires the theory of a restraining grace. What

do the Gentiles do? Do they have the law of God or a remnant of it written in their hearts? Not at all; but the groundwork of the law, the broad principles of the law are in their hearts, are known to them, so that they discern the difference between good and evil in a broad sense, and are a law unto themselves. What do they do? Do they keep the law? Not at all; but they do *the things* of the law, they announce what is good and what is evil, and show that they are capable of distinguishing between the two. Does this mean that they also do that which they know to be good? Not at all. They may, indeed, show a certain regard for what they know and declare to be virtuous, whenever they consider it advantageous to themselves. But all that Paul has written in the first chapter of this same epistle remains true of them: knowing the judgment of God that they that do such things are worthy of death, they not only commit them, but also have pleasure in them that do them! It is as the Canons of Dordrecht teach us in III, IV, 4: "There remain, however, in man since the fall, the glimmerings of natural light, whereby he retains some knowledge of God, of natural things, and of the difference between good and evil, and discovers some regard for virtue, good order in society, and for maintaining an orderly external deportment. But so far is this light of nature from being sufficient to bring him to a saving knowledge of God and to true conversion, that he is incapable of using it aright even in things natural and civil. Nay further, this light, such as it is, man in various ways renders wholly polluted, and holds it in unrighteousness, by doing which he becomes inexcusable before God."

IX

Enmity Against God

However, if the theory that there is some other kind of grace than that which regenerates a man, must be rejected, the question returns: what is the implication of the doctrine of total depravity? How can the answer of the Heidelberg Catechism to its eighth question be squared with many phenomena in the actual experience and every day life in the world of men that appear to contradict the severe judgment of our instructor: we are incapable of doing any good and inclined to all evil, unless we are regenerated by the Spirit of God? In order to give the correct answer to this question it is paramount that we bear in mind that the Catechism is speaking of ethical good and evil, and to ask ourselves: what is meant by this?

Sin did not and could not change man essentially, i.e. it did not change him into some other kind of being. By the fall he did not change into a devil or demon, nor was he degraded to the level of the animal. It is often alleged that man would have been changed into some kind of a devil immediately when he fell, had not God intervened at once through the operation of His common grace. But all such statements are erroneous. Sin could not change the being of man. It is moral, ethical corruption. Man was created a psychico-physical being, a creature consisting of body and soul, possessing intellect and will. And after the fall he still is such a psychico-physical, rational and moral creature. Sin did not cause mental derangement or intellectual incapacity in man. It is true, that even these natural gifts and powers are greatly marred and weakened through the fall; but they are not lost. Nor has his essential relation to the world about him been changed. It is true that the world bears the curse for his sake: the earth brings forth thorns and thistles, and the creature is in bondage to corruption; it is subject to vanity and it toils and labors in vain. But even so, man is still king of the earthly creation, and exercises dominion over all things. Although he rules in the sphere of vanity, so that no definite goal is to be attained by the "culture" of the world, man, nevertheless, reigns over the earthly creature. He "cultivates" that creation with all its powers and treasures and in every department of its existence and life. The result is that the natural man is able to perform and accomplish many things that are formally correct, and that are well-nigh perfect from a mechanical viewpoint. He makes the world about him, as well as his own existence and life, object of his scientific investigation; he discovers the ordinances of the Creator in all things, and arranges his own life accordingly; he brings to light the hidden wonders of the works of God, and presses them into his service. He can build a good house, and construct a wonderfully perfect machine; he understands the laws of the soil and of the seasons, of summer and winter, of heat and cold, of winds and rain, and he causes the earth to yield the best possible crop. He studies the laws of gravity and gravitation, of steam and electricity, of light rays and sound waves; his searching eye roams through the immensity of the firmament, and he predicts the exact course of the heavenly bodies millions upon millions of miles distant from the earth; and he penetrates into the mysteries of matter, and discovers the ordinances of atoms and molecules. And he invents the telephone

and telegraph, the radio and cinematograph, and
causes his voice to be heard to the ends of the earth.
He speeds along the road in his automobile, he flies
through space in his aeroplane; he swallows up both
space and time, and makes the world very small. He
is able to make terrible instruments of destruction in
the form of guns and tanks, submarines and torpedoes,
bombs and shells; but he also heals the wounds and
fights disease and death, prolonging human life and
alleviating human suffering. And much he can do to
enrich his earthly life and to make it more abundant.
He surrounds himself with means that make his life
both pleasant and comfortable: he eats and drinks, he
plays and dances, and fills his heart with gladness.
All these things the fallen sinner can perform quite
well. In this sense he is not incapable of doing any
good, or prone to do everything wrong. Sin did not
change the being of man, nor his essential relationship
to the world about him.

The natural man is even able to conform his external life and walk in the world to a certain extent
to the moral law of God. He is not morally incompetent in the sense that he can no longer discern the
difference between good and evil. As we have seen
in our discussion of Rom. 2:14, 15, the natural man
does by nature *the things* of the law, and by rather
clearly discerning between good and evil and making
his laws accordingly, he shows that he has the work
of the law written in his heart. And there is even
an attempt on his part to regulate his life and the
life of the community in which he lives according to
the law of God. A complexity of motives such as fear
of punishment, vain glory, ambition, the urge of self-
preservation, shame, and the like, govern him in this
attempt. In general we may state that the natural

man consents to the law that it is good, and that it is salutary for him to keep it, while the wages of sin is always death. Too much adultery and debauchery undermine the body, and have a corrupting effect on society; too much greed and covetousness disrupt economic relations, cause revolutions and wars; too great a laxity in the laws governing marriage and divorce destroys the home and the nation; if the practice of deceit and dishonesty in business is not curbed the result is lack of confidence; the murderer and highway robber are detrimental to society. All this the natural man discerns very clearly. And the love of self and the desire for self-preservation urge him to curb his lust, and to conform his outward life as much as he considers expedient to the precepts of God's moral law. Ultimately he fails in this attempt, for the love of God is not in his heart, and he follows after his sinful lusts. But all this readily explains that in the world of fallen man there is a certain "regard for virtue and external orderly deportment" as the Canons express it.

Yet, in all this the natural man performs no good in the ethical sense of the word. It must still be said of him that he is incapable of doing any good and inclined to all evil. For what is good? It is the perfect keeping of the law of God with all our heart and mind and soul and strength. But what is the law of God? As we have seen in our discussion of question 4 of our Catechism, it is the expression of the living will of God that man shall love Him. To love the Lord our God with all our heart and with all our mind and with all our soul and with all our strength, to love Him in all that we do, to be motivated by that love of God in all our thinking and willing and desires and actions,—that is good, and nothing else is good. All that is not of the love of God, however noble and charitable and beautiful it may appear as far as the outward act is concerned, is certainly evil. And the natural man does not love God, nor is he capable of loving God. On the contrary, he hates Him. For "the carnal mind is enmity against God: for it is not subject to the law of God, neither indeed can be." Rom. 8:7. Hence, all he does is motivated by enmity against God, by love of self apart from God. He seeks his own glory instead of the glory of God. And because of this evil motive and purpose, all he does is always sin. He may be honest in business, he may refrain from drunkenness, he may lead a clean life, he may be charitable to his neighbours, he may be scrupulously correct in his dealings with others, he may even be religious, attend church, give liberally to the poor and to the cause of God's kingdom,—but he is incapable of doing any good and inclined to evil nevertheless. For always he seeks himself and does not love God. If a superintendent of a factory were to expel his employer, and propose to run the shop for his own benefit, he might do so very efficiently, but in all he does he sins against his employer. He may very ably manage the establishment, so that production increases and the work he delivers receives highest praise; he may treat his employees kindly and pay the highest possible wages; but as long as his attitude against his employer is one of rebellion, he sins in all he does. The same is true of man in relation to God. He was created to be God's servant-friend. And he was appointed superintendent over all the works of God's hands, to develop them, to rule over them in the name of God and in love to Him, in order that God might receive all the glory. But he became a rebel, proposed to expel God from his heart, and now intends to run God's establishment as God's enemy and for his own pleasure and glory. He may still be an efficient superintendent, but all he does in that position of rebellion against God is certainly evil. And total depravity means principally that man is incapable of doing anything from the love of God, and that he is always prone to hate Him. In his inmost nature he stands opposed to the law of God.

And this deepest principle of enmity against God also reveals itself in all his life and conversation. For, let us not imagine that man can hate God and love the neighbour, that he can violate the first table of the law and keep the second. He cannot expel God from his life and for the rest live in moral rectitude. God will give His glory to no other. He cannot be mocked. He is terribly displeased with all the ungodliness of wicked men that hold the truth in unrighteousness. And He reveals His wrath from heaven by giving over the ungodly to the lusts of his flesh. And so, ultimately his attempt to show regard for virtue and for an orderly external deportment always fails. Very really the natural man corrupts all life and destroys the earth. The enmity against God that is in his heart becomes a foul fountain of all manner of iniquity. From this corrupt fountain gushes forth spiritual darkness that envelops his mind, so that he loves the lie and pursues it. From that source of enmity against God there issue forth evil desires that corrupt the will, and cause him to pursue after the things of the flesh. From that fountain of evil in his heart proceed not only actual sins against God directly, such as idolatry, profanity, rejection of the Word of God, worship of man's wisdom, ungodly philosophy, cursing and swearing, pride and rebellion, rejection of Christ and hatred of His people; but also those sins that corrupt all of human life in every relationship, such as malice and envy, greed and covetousness, lying and deceit, strife and contention, war and destruction, murder and robbery, fornication, adultery, divorce, love of pleasure, faithlessness, and the like, of all which the world of today is a living testimony.

To be sure, there is difference between one man and another, just as there is difference between one age and another. Not every man commits all sin. Each individual is but a branch in the organism of the human race, and he bears that particular fruit of the root-sin of Adam which is in harmony with his place in the organism. Men differ as to character, power, gifts and talents, means and circumstances. One man is bloodthirsty by nature, another is afraid to see blood; one is a spendthrift, another is a miser; one is weak, another is strong; one has great intellectual capacity, another is dull of mind; one loves pleasure, another loves the honor of men; one is poor while another is rich. And there are coarse sins, but there are also sins that are very refined. Some sins are done in secret, others are openly displayed and extolled on stage and screen. There are individual sins and group sins, social and national sins. There are sins that are punished by the government, and there are sins that are committed by the magistrates. But always the natural man commits iniquity. He is incapable of doing any good and inclined to all evil. Motivated by enmity against God he is corrupt in all his ways. There is no fear of God before his eyes.

Nor is the world improving. On the contrary, there is an organic development of sin, that is, sin develops and increases even as the organism of the race develops. Even as there is no restraint of sin in the heart of the individual sinner, so there is no check on the process and progress of sin in history.

As the race develops in "culture" and civilization, sin grows in proportion. It is for this reason that it is possible that in the day of judgment it will be more tolerable for one generation than for another. More tolerable it will be for Sodom and Gomorrha than for Jerusalem, for Tyrus and Sidon than for Capernaum, for the "world" that crucified Christ the first time than for the "world" that crucifies Him afresh. And thus the development of sin continues until the day of the culmination of the antichristian power. The measure of iniquity must be filled. For sin must become fully manifest as sin in all its horror, that God may be justified when He judgeth, when He casts all the wicked into the pool that burneth with fire and sulphur, where their worm dieth not and the fire is not quenched, and the smoke of their torment ascends forever and ever!

LORD'S DAY IV

Q. 9. Doth not God then do injustice to man, by requiring from him in his law, that which he cannot perform?

A. Not at all; for God made man capable of performing it; but man, by the instigation of the devil, and of his own wilful disobedience, deprived himself and all his posterity of those divine gifts.

Q. 10. Will God suffer such disobedience and rebellion to go unpunished?

A. By no means; but is terribly displeased with our original as well as actual sins; and will punish them in his just judgment temporally and eternally, as he hath declared, "Cursed is every one that continueth not in all things, which are written in the book of the law, to do them."

Q. 11. Is not God then also merciful?

A. God is indeed merciful, but also just; therefore his justice requires, that sin which is committed against the most high majesty of God, be also punished with extreme, that is, with everlasting punishment of body and soul.

I

The Justice Of God's Demand

This Lord's Day is the last chapter of the first part
of our Heidelberg Catechism, whose main theme is
"the Misery of Man." The three questions and answers contained in it are very intimately related.
They are based on a common principle. They have a
common source. All three questions might be expressed in the one query: Is there a way out as far as
sinful man is concerned? Is there a possibility for
man in his fallen state and depraved condition to be
blessed, to escape the wrath of God and punishment?
Considered in this light the three questions represent
a very common attempt on the part of fallen man to
persuade himself that he can maintain himself in his
sin without suffering the consequences. The attempt
is characteristic of unregenerate man. He is not really
sorry for his sin. On the contrary, he has his delight
in iniquity. If only there were no evil consequences
connected with the service of sin, if only he could
sin with impunity, he would not worry about sin at all.
But he is afraid of the results. He dreads the punishment of sin. He would like to escape death and hell.
He likes to feel safe and secure in the service of sin.
It is this fundamental characteristic of the unregenerate man, this urge to escape the dire results of sin for
himself and for society in general, that frequently con-
strains him to curb his lust, and to have a certain regard for virtue and for an external orderly deportment. It is also to this deeply rooted desire that many
a social reformer, who denies Christ and His atoning

blood, who will have nothing of forgiveness based on God's justice and denies the power of regeneration, appeals in his battle against all sorts of crimes and vices. "Crime does not pay" is their slogan, and by a vivid picture of the misery and suffering connected inseparably with a life of dissipation they attempt to frighten men into a life of external virtue. Man loves sin, but he dreads hell. And so he makes an attempt to escape the one while continuing in the other. And it is this possibility that is the subject of discussion in this fourth Lord's Day.

However, there is only one conceivable way in which this attempt to sin with impunity could possibly be successful; or rather, that one imaginary way is really quite inconceivable: God must be changed! And the sinful heart and mind do indeed make the bold attempt to change the living God. It is thus that the sinner tries to entrench and fortify himself in his sin! He makes a god of his own imagination, after his own sinful heart, before whose face he can sin and feel safe. He invents his own god, an idol that is wholly like unto himself. He deprives God of His sterner attributes of righteousness and justice, and speaks of a god of mercy and love that will wink at sin, and make the ungodly the object of His blessing. And thus he tries to quiet the voice of his own conscience, and partly succeeds to create for himself a sense of safety in the way of sin, until he meets the living God in the day of the revelation of His righteous judgment, and discovers that he believed a lie, that he followed after a delusion, and that the eternal God cannot be mocked!

It is this truth which the Catechism expounds in the three questions and answers of this fourth Lord's Day. Can God be changed? Can He be changed in His demand of the law that we love Him with all our heart and mind and soul and strength, so that He comes down to the level of the sinner, and can be satisfied with what sinful man is able and willing to do? We cannot perform the demands of the law. Well, then, if God could be satisfied with the best we can do, all would be well. Or, if that is not possible, cannot God relinquish the strict demands of His justice, so that He does not empty the vials of His wrath upon us, but leaves our sin unpunished? If only we could feel that there were no hell and damnation, our sinful heart would be at rest, and we could safely continue in the way of iniquity. And if, finally, the answer to this second inquiry must be that God's justice is unchangeable, can we not make an appeal to His mercy? Is it not possible to conceive of Him as a God Whose mercy overrules His justice, so that, even though His justice should urge Him to cast us into everlasting hell, His mercy so moves Him with pity and compassion, that He could not possibly behold us in the throes of His wrath? These three inventions of the lying imagination of sinful man the Catechism here investigates, and exposes as so many delusions of the darkened mind of the sinner.

Doth not God then do injustice to man, by requiring from him in His law, that which he cannot perform? This is the first attempt on the part of fallen man to discover a way out of his misery without changing his sinful way and rebellious attitude against the living God. It really represents an attack on God Himself. Man wants to rid himself of the obligation to serve his Creator. He registers a complaint against his divine Employer in order to justify himself in his sin. He tries to justify a strike. His Employer is unjust. The requirements imposed upon him by the Almighty are too severe. The demands of God are far too exacting;

they far exceed his capacity; he can never fulfill them.
And so he refuses to shoulder his obligation. No one,
not even God, has the right to demand of him what he
cannot perform!

Let us notice, first of all, the hopelessness of this
attempt to escape God. Suppose for a moment that
the question that is here asked must be answered in
the affirmative, and that God does indeed do an injustice to man, by requiring of him what he can never
perform; would that change the actual situation at all?
Is it, indeed, possible for man, even then, to escape the
living God? Can man refuse to work in God's world,
and that, too, with God's power and means and tools
and capital? Can he quit work or organize a strike?
Is he at liberty or in a position to leave God's "factory,"
and offer his services to someone else? Among men
this is, of course, quite possible and proper. If an
employer is too exacting and his demands upon his
employees are too severe, or if he does not pay a just
wage and working conditions are bad, his employees
have the right to quit their jobs and seek employment
elsewhere. But with man in relation to God this is
quite different. That he is the servant of the living
God is not the result of a voluntary contract he made
with his Creator. There were no mutual conditions
and stipulations, agreements and demands before man
entered into the service of the Most High. On the
contrary, his employer is GOD! He is the Lord of
heaven and earth, the Creator of all. By an act of His
omnipotent will alone man was called into being,
endowed with his faculties, powers and talents, placed
in God's world and in God's service. In all this there
was nothing of man. By God's sovereign will alone
he was the servant of God. And a privilege and blessing it was that he might thus serve the living God.

However, man did not regard his great distinction. He presumed to rise in rebellion against his Lord. Does this mean that he is actually able to quit work? Can he leave God's "workshop"? Can he cease to be a servant? Of course not. Work he must with all his mind and soul and strength. And work he must with God's gifts, with God's capital, in God's world and with God's tools. Even though because of his rebellion he works in the sphere of death, and though by working he can never do anything else than heap up for himself treasures of wrath in the day of the revelation of the righteous judgment of God, he is, nevertheless, constrained to work. Even though, therefore, this question must be answered in the affirmative, it would not open a way out for man. If God does an injustice to man, the situation does not alter: man is servant by God's sovereign will, and never can he escape from his service.

But does God do an injustice to man? The Catechism speaks of a demand of God which man cannot fulfill. It is important that we bear this in mind. For, what is this demand of God which man cannot perform? The reference here is certainly not to what has sometimes been called the "general mandate," or the "cultural" calling of man. When God had created man the Creator enjoined him to "be fruitful, and multiply, and replenish the earth, and subdue it; and have dominion over the fish of the sea, and over the fowl of the air, and over every living thing that moveth upon the earth." If this were the demand to which the Catechism refers it could hardly be said that man cannot perform it. For, even though all creation is subject to the bondage of corruption, and all things are vanity, and though man works in the sphere of death and is limited by death on every side, yet, even so, he

exerts himself to subdue the earth, and to realize his
kingship over the earth. And as we have seen, in this
he succeeds to a certain extent. If God could be
pleased with modern inventions, with the products of
modern science and industry and art, with the mighty
works of man regardless of their spiritual-ethical content, He might well look with favor upon the accom-
plishments of the modern world. And Dr. Kuyper's
theory might then appear to be correct, that fallen man
is still God's co-worker, and in developing the powers of
creation stands in a covenant-relation of "common
grace" to God, is God's ally against the devil. But
this is not the case. All these mighty works of man
cannot meet with the favor of God as long as man
stands in rebellion against Him. For the demand of
the law of God is that man love Him with all his heart
and mind and soul and strength. And this demand of
the law is not to be divorced from the so-called "cultural" mandate, but, on the contrary, dominates it.
And it is to this demand of the law that the Catechism refers in this ninth question. This demand man
cannot perform. For, as we have learned through our
instructor before: man is prone by nature to hate God
and the neighbor!

There would seem to be reason for the question:
does not God do an injustice to man? For God demands what man cannot perform. God demands that
man love Him; and man is by nature prone to hate
Him. If it were merely a matter of man's will whether
or not he would love God, the situation would be far
different, and the question concerning the injustice
of God's demand would have no point. But man *cannot*
love God. True, he *will* not love Him, but the fact remains that this *will* is subjectively determined by
man's nature, that his nature is such that he is prone

to hate God, and that, therefore, he *cannot* even will to love God. Nor was the nature of the *individual* man ever different. He is born with a nature that is wholly contrary to the law of God. Never was he capable of loving God and thus fulfilling the demand of the law of God. Is, then, the demand not unjust? Justice is equity. In this particular case justice would seem to require perfect equality between the *must* and the *can,* between the demand and the ability to perform it. But the two are wholly unequal. Man is by nature wholly incapable of performing what God demands of him. It would seem, then, that there is reason for the question: does not God do an injustice to man?

But are we, is mere man able to answer this question? Does he have the right to propose this problem, and will he be able to find a solution? It is well for us to consider this question before we proceed. And the answer to this question will certainly have to be negative, if to inquire after the justice or injustice of an act of God would imply that we summon God before the bar of human justice, and that we propose to judge the Most High. For this would mean that we claim to have a criterion or standard of our own which we apply to God, and according to which we express our verdict. But where shall we find such a criterion except with God Himself? Shall we derive our standard of justice from our own intelligence, from our sense of justice, from our conscience, or, perhaps, from the consensus of human opinion as to what is right or wrong? But this is quite impossible. For God is God, and He is the sole Lord of heaven and earth. He is the sole Lawgiver and the sole Judge. There is no law above God; there is no criterion whereby He can be judged; there is no tribunal to which one

can appeal from His verdict. God is the Absolute. He
is His own law. And we are creatures, that are in
every respect dependent upon the Creator, even for
any knowledge of truth and righteousness, for any
criterion of justice we might desire to apply. Besides,
we are sinful creatures, whose mind is darkened,
whose will is perverse, whose verdict about God is
bound to be corrupt. It is evident, then, that the attempt to find an answer to the question, whether God
does an injustice to man, must be abandoned, if the
question implies that man will judge his God, that the
creature will call the Creator before his bar of judgment. Nay, the very question, if thus understood,
must be considered highly presumptuous.

We cannot, therefore, call upon man, upon his intelligence, his sense of justice, his conscience, or upon
the common opinion of men, to answer this question.
There is only one sense in which the question is justified: if it is directed to God. And there is only one
possible way of finding a solution: if we will let God
Himself answer this question. In other words, we
must proceed from the fundamental axiom: God is
just, and He is the sole criterion of all justice. All
His works are justice and truth. The question, therefore, can never be whether God Himself is just, nor
whether His works are righteousness; but whether in
a given case we can understand the justice of God.
And this understanding of the work of God as just
in a concrete case must be determined by God's own
revelation. That this is the correct method of procedure is evident from Scripture. It is applied in
Rom. 9:14-18. There the same question is asked:
"What shall we say then? Is there unrighteousness
with God?" And this question is answered, first of
all, by the familiar and emphatic denial: "God forbid!"

The idea of this denial is: "Let the very thought be far from our minds; let it be established *a priori* that God is just!" Yet, the apostle proceeds to answer it, to demonstrate that in the given case under discussion, that of sovereign election and reprobation, the justice of God cannot be doubted. And he does this by allowing the Word of God to supply the evidence: "For he saith to Moses, I will have mercy on whom I will have mercy, and I will have compassion on whom I will have compassion. So then it is not of him that willeth, nor of him that runneth, but of God that sheweth mercy. For the Scripture saith unto Pharaoh, For this same purpose have I raised thee up, that I might shew my power in thee, and that my name might be declared throughout all the earth. Therefore hath he mercy on whom he will have mercy, and whom he will he hardeneth." We quote this passage, let us bear in mind, only to show that the answer to the question, whether in a given case the work of God is just, must be derived from the Scriptures themselves. And if mere man is not satisfied with this answer from the Word of God, but still raises objections that arise from his own rebellious mind, the apostle answers: "Nay but, O man, who art thou that repliest against God? Shall the thing formed say unto him that formed it, why hast thou made me thus?" Rom. 9:20.

Now, in application to the case in hand, the Heidelberg Catechism fundamentally follows the same method. The case is this: 1. Man is totally depraved. As far as the individual man is concerned, he never was different. He cannot perform the demand of the law. 2. However, God continues to demand of man that he keep his law. 3. Is this demand of God not an unjust one? Does not God in this case do an injustice to man? And the answer of the Catechism is:

"Not at all; for God made man capable of performing it; but man, by the instigation of the devil, and his own wilful disobedience, deprived himself and all his posterity of those divine gifts."

The whole answer is derived from, and based upon, Scripture. God made man capable of performing the demand of the law. The implication of this was discussed in a previous chapter. Man was made good and after God's own image. The "divine gifts" of which the Catechism speaks in this connection are those of true knowledge of God, righteousness, and holiness. Endowed with these gifts, man certainly was able to perform the demand of the law, that is, to love the Lord his God with all his heart, and with all his mind, and with all his soul, and with all his strength. But man was very wilfully disobedient, as we have seen. God's commandment was not grievous. In the midst of the abundance of Paradise he was to refrain from eating of just one tree. And he wantonly violated God's covenant. Upon the instigation of the devil, believing his lie rather than the Word of God, he ate of the forbidden fruit. And the result of this disobedience was that he sank into the darkness of spiritual death, so that he lost all his excellent gifts. And, of course, without these gifts he can no longer keep the law of God. These gifts were changed into their very opposite. His knowledge became darkness, the darkness of the lie; his righteousness became perverseness of heart and will; his holiness became corruption and impurity in all his desires and inclinations. The result is that he now stands by nature in enmity against God. He cannot, in his natural state, perform what God demands of him in His holy law.

Now, it is evident, that the emphasis in this entire answer falls upon the word *man*. *Man* was endowed

with those divine gifts that were necessary to keep the
law; *man* was wilfully disobedient; *man* squandered
those excellent gifts with which he was originally endowed; *man* is still holden by the demand of God to
love Him with all his heart and mind and soul and
strength. And by *man* the Catechism means the whole
race of Adam. All men are reckoned in Adam, and
are organically in him. If this is not true, the whole
argument falls. The point is, that *we*, that you and I,
that each individual man, that all are personally responsible for the squandering of these divine gifts.
We were all originally endowed with these gifts. We
all were disobedient; we all deprived ourselves of these
gifts. And, therefore, God does not do us an injustice
when He still demands that we shall perform His law.
The truth of this juridical solidarity and organic unity
of the whole race in Adam we discussed before. The
point we wish to make now, is that the Catechism turns
to Scripture for its answer to the question: Does not
God do an injustice to man by demanding of him in
his law what he cannot perform? And in the light of
this Scriptural truth of the responsibility of the whole
race and of every individual man for the sin of Adam,
it is very plain that there is no injustice at all in this
demand of God. Suppose that a contractor agrees to
build a home for some party at the cost of ten thousand
dollars. Suppose, further, that the contractor is a
person without means, so that he is not even able to
purchase the necessary material to build the house.
But the party for whom the house is to be built advances the entire sum of ten thousand dollars to the
poor contractor. If now that contractor, instead of
using the money that was advanced to him for the
building of the home, squanders it in drunkenness and
riotous living, so that he is incapable of fulfilling the

terms of the contract, does the party for whom the house is to be built do the contractor an injustice if he still demands of him that he build that home? Of course not. He was supplied with the necessary means. He is obliged to comply with the terms of the contract. This illustration may serve to bring out the point of the answer of our Catechism. God gave man the means to perform the law; man squandered the gifts of God; the demand of the law is still just, though man is now incapable of performing it: love the Lord thy God with all thy heart and mind and soul and strength!

Sinful man may not be satisfied with this answer of Scripture, but that does not alter the matter. He may insist that he will not be responsible for the sin of Adam, that he personally, therefore, never was capable of performing the demand of the law, and that God certainly does an injustice to him if He still demands that he fulfill the law. Or he may grow presumptuous and say that God had no business to create him in Adam. To all this, however, the Word of God replies: "Nay but, O man, who art thou that repliest against God? Shall the thing formed say unto him that formed it, Why hast thou made me thus?" And in the day of the revelation of the righteous judgment of God, God will certainly justify Himself in all His works before the consciousness of all His moral creatures. And no one shall ever again presume to open his mouth against the Lord of heaven and earth! The perfect theodicy will forever silence the rebellious speech of the proud, and cause the righteous to rejoice and to worship Him that sitteth upon the throne!

II

The Justice Of God's Wrath

The second attempt on the part of fallen man to maintain himself in his sinful state and feel safe is expressed in the question: Will God suffer such disobedience and rebellion to go unpunished? This question has been answered affirmatively in various degrees. Some deny altogether that God punishes sin. Others insist that he does not inflict just punishment in time. Still others deny that there is an eternal punishment in hell. While there are also those who are of the opinion that hell is right here in this world, and that all the punishment man will ever suffer he receives in time. However, the Catechism answers: 1. That God is terribly displeased, filled with wrath, both with our original and our actual sins. 2. That this wrath realizes itself in the curse against every one that continueth not in all things that are written in the book of the law to do them. 3. That God, therefore, surely punishes sin in His just judgment, and that, too, in time as well as in eternity.

Let us note here, first of all, that as far as God's attitude over against the rebellious sinners is concerned, the Catechism leaves no room for a distinction between time and eternity. God punishes sin in time as well as in eternity and that, too, in His just judgment. This statement is directly opposed to the theory of common grace on this point, to the first of the famous "Three Points" adopted by the Christian Reformed Church in 1924, as well as to a very general popular notion. God, according to this conception, changes His attitude to the wicked after the latter's death. In time He assumes an attitude of favor and grace to the sinner, and He blesses him with many things; but after death He makes him the object of His fierce wrath. God, therefore, does not apply the sentence of His just judgment in time.

But the Catechism in this tenth question and answer denies that there is such a principal distinction between God's attitude toward the wicked in time and in eternity. God does not change. He is not gracious to the wicked in this world, in order to become filled with wrath against him in the next. His wrath is an ever present reality. His just judgment is executed constantly. God cannot wink at sin even for a moment. He punishes all unrighteousness in perfect justice in time as well as in eternity. God's wrath is even in the prosperity of the wicked. And His just judgment is clearly manifest when in and through their prosperity He prepares them for greater damnation, and that, too, in such a way that they also prepare themselves for eternal destruction. That this is, indeed, in agreement with what the authors of the Catechism had in mind, may become evident from a quotation from Ursinus' "Schatboek": *"Objection* 1: The ungodly often enjoy prosperity here and do many things with impunity. Hence, all sins are not being punished. *Answer*: And yet they shall be punished, yea, they are already being punished here: 1. In the conscience by whose pangs of remorse all are tortured; 2. also in those things which they use with the greatest enjoyment; and that, too, in a greater degree according as they are less conscious of their being punished; 3. often also with other forms of punishment; the heaviest, however, in the future life, where not to be dead will be eternal death." p. 89. And this is quite in accord with Scripture. For the Word of God knows nothing of an attitude of grace on the part of God toward the wicked in this life, but teaches that He is angry with the wicked every day, Ps. 7:11; that He is always in His holy temple to try the children of men, and that His soul hates the wicked, Ps. 11:4, 5; that His wrath is revealed from heaven against all unrighteousness of men, Rom. 1:18; and that His face is against them that do evil, I Pet. 3:12.

This wrath of God against sin as revealed in this present world becomes evident in different ways. There is, first of all, the present death of all men which culminates in the corruption of the body, and all the suffering of this present time connected with it. All men lie in the midst of death, also in the midst of physical death. Death reigns over all men. Rom. 5:12-14. Death encompasses us on all sides. It is the grim spectre that always stands waiting at the end of our earthly way, no matter in which direction we may turn. It is the enemy that relentlessly pursues us, frequently reminding us, by sickness and pain, sorrow and grief, physical and mental agony, of the certainty of its final victory; and dooming all our efforts to ultimate failure: all is vanity! And death is no accident. It is not the natural end of all existence. It is the hand of God that is heavy upon us. Death is the expression of the wrath of God against sin. It is the wrath of God that abideth on us and never gives us even a moment's respite. Looking at man's present existence as such, apart from Christ, it is nothing but a testimony to the truth of what our Catechism declares in this tenth answer: He "is terribly displeased with our original as well as with our actual sins; and will punish them in his just judgment temporally and eternally." The true explanation of our present life

is found in Ps. 90: "For we are consumed by thine
anger, and by thy wrath are we troubled. Thou hast
set our iniquities before thee, our secret sins in the
light of thy countenance. For all our days are passed
away in thy wrath: we spend our years as a tale that
is told. The days of our years are threescore years
and ten; and if by reason of strength they be fourscore years, yet is their strength labor and sorrow;
for it is soon cut off, and we fly away. Who knoweth
the power of thine anger? even according to thy fear,
so is thy wrath." 7-11. The only way out of the
present wrath of God is the cross of Christ, and the
sole ray of light that pierces the darkness of our present death is His resurrection.

Then, too, the wrath of God against sin and His
just judgment become evident in those special miseries
and sufferings that are inseparably connected with
certain particular sins. I have no doubt but that, if
we only could always discern the ways and dealings
of God with men in detail, we would notice that all
sins are met with their own characteristic punishment.
But the truth of this statement appears only in those
grosser and more apparent cases that are plainly manifest to all. If a man practices sexual immorality, God
punishes him in His just judgment with certain diseases and corruption of the body; the drunkard makes
of himself a physical wreck and a mental imbecile;
certain sins of character, such as lying, deceit, pride,
haughtiness, and the like, meet with their own proper
retribution. The ungodly world looks upon these evils
as the natural results of the vices practised, as the
operation of the physical laws of the universe that cannot be changed; but the believer knows that in all these
"results" of sin the hand of God and His righteous
judgment become manifest. And this is true, not only

of individual sins, but of sins committed in and by the family, society, the State, the nations of the world in their relation to one another. Greed and covetousness, pride and vanity, the suppression of the weak by the strong, the ambition to build empires at the expense of smaller nations, love of wealth and of power, malice and envy,—all these meet their just retribution even in this present time in all kinds of unrest and turmoil, revolutions and wars. God in His just judgment leads the world on the way to self-destruction! And this punishment is, indeed, often the more terrible according as the world is less conscious of the fact that the hand of God is heavy upon them in His wrath. It is this, that constitutes the awful character of the present world conflict. The fierce anger of God is upon the nations of the world. It is operative everywhere, on the land, in the sea, and in the air. It is seen in the murderous intent of men killing one another by the thousands on the battlefield; it is heard in the cry or curse of those that are swallowed up into death by the waves of the sea; and in the roar of exploding shells and bombs. It is in the proud decisions of the mighty of the world to destroy either the weak or the equally mighty, as well as in the moaning of the dying on the battlefield, and the lamentations of the bereaved at home. Yet, men continue to speak of chariots and of horses; they gloat over reports of death and destruction; they proudly speak of the new world order they will surely establish; and they know not that the fierce anger of the Most High is consuming them!

Furthermore, there is that peculiar manifestation of the anger of the Most High, according to which He punishes sin with more and greater sin, and thus prepares the vessels of wrath for destruction. When men indulge in the evil passions of their corrupt nature, they play with the dreadful fire of the wrath of God. For God's wrath against sin is operative in and upon those wicked passions and evil lusts, and by means of them He gives men over unto greater sins and fouler deeds, till they become worse than the beasts of the field. It is this fatal process that is described as the manifestation of the wrath of God against all ungodliness of men, in Rom. 1:18ff. It is this wrath of God that makes men foolish, when knowing God "they glorified Him not as God, neither were thankful"; that gives them over "to uncleanness through the lusts of their own hearts, to dishonour their own bodies between themselves"; and that gives them up, through these same lusts, unto "vile affections"; so that, finally, they are utterly given over to "a reprobate mind, to do those things which are not convenient," so that they are filled with all unrighteousness and are hopelessly sunk in the mire of corruption and destruction. vss. 21, 24, 26, 28ff. Let no man imagine that it is possible for him to sin even for a moment with impunity, for God is terribly displeased with all sin, original and actual, and in His just judgment punishes sin in time as well as in eternity.

Of course, temporal and eternal punishment cannot be separated from each other. They are closely related. The wrath of God in time prepares for His wrath in eternity. Existence in the present world cannot be separated from that in the world to come. It is in this light that the prosperity of the wicked must be viewed, in order to understand that even in this the wrath of God is operative. Those who separate the present from the everlasting future may babble of God's favor upon the ungodly and of all the blessings they enjoy in this life, and so deceive themselves and others. But the moment we place the two, time and eternity, in proper relation to each other, we clearly see the folly of this, and realize that the prosperity of the wicked is itself a manifestation of the fierce anger of the Lord, whereby He leads them to greater damnation. It is this truth which the Holy Spirit revealed to us through Asaph, when he entered into the sanctuary of God, and understood the end of the wicked. Then he could view their present prosperity in the light of that end, and discern clearly that in giving them prosperity God set the ungodly upon slippery places, and cast them down into destruction. Ps. 73:17ff. Thus also the author of Ps. 92 was divinely taught to sing of the profound wisdom of God, in that He caused the wicked to flourish and to grow as the grass in order that they might be destroyed forever. Ps. 92:5-7. And thus it is evident that God's government of the universe is always according to justice, and that He always punishes sin in His just judgment. And the day of the revelation of the righteous judgment of God will not set straight all that was left crooked in time, for God never leaves anything crooked; but rather reveal that in all His dealings with the wicked He treated them in justice and righteousness. Surely, God punishes sin temporally as well as eternally. There is no escape even for a moment from this pursuing wrath of God. Only in Christ and Him crucified is the way out. For in Him even the sufferings and death of this present time are made subservient unto our eternal salvation!

Nevertheless, the punishment of sin is not limited to time, but is only a foretaste of eternal desolation in hell. This truth of eternal punishment is opposed and gainsaid by many. Some simply maintain that the punishment of sin in time is sufficient: hell is here.

The grave is the end of the wicked. Others claim that somehow in the end all men will be saved. There will be punishment after death, but also this will come to an end. Ultimately God will deliver all. Many, too, teach that there will be a second probation after death, another chance, which will either result in the salvation of all men, or in the salvation of most of them, while following this second probation the stubbornly wicked will be annihilated. But all have this in common, that they deny the truth of unending punishment in hell. They argue that sin is both temporal and finite, and that it would be gross injustice to inflict eternal punishment upon sin committed by the finite creature in time. Then, too, they deny that Scripture teaches an eternal suffering in hell as punishment for sin. Agents of the Seventh Day Adventists, and of the International Bible Students, followers of Russell and Rutherford, go about teaching and preaching that there is no hell, that "hell" in Scripture means the grave (Sheol, Hades), and that, when the Bible speaks of "eternal" punishment, the word eternal signifies an "age," a long period.

Over against these arguments, we may remark, in the first place, that sin and guilt cannot be measured by the standard of the creature, but must be evaluated in the light of the infinite majesty of God against Whom it was committed. The argument that sin is committed by a finite creature, and that, too, in time; and that, therefore, justice cannot inflict eternal punishment upon the sinner is utterly false. Of this we shall have more to say in our discussion of the next question and answer of the Catechism. Secondly, with respect to the argument that the words often translated "hell" in the Bible do not mean the place of eternal torture, we may begin by admitting that there is an element of truth in this: the words *sheol* and *hades* can often better be translated by "grave," or by "the state of the dead," than by "hell." But this gives no right to the assertion that the Bible does not speak of a hell as the place of eternal punishment. First of all, let it be noted that there is also the word "gehenna" which always denotes the place of eternal desolation, and which surely must be translated by "hell." Thus in Matt. 5:22: "but whosoever shall say, Thou fool, shall be in danger of hell fire." (literally: "shall be obligated into the gehenna of fire.") In vs. 29 of the same chapter we read: "And if thy right eye offend thee, pluck it out, and cast it from thee; for it is profitable for thee that one of thy members should perish, and not that thy whole body should be cast into hell (gehenna)." The same statement occurs in vs. 30. The same word for "hell" occurs in Matt. 10:28: "And fear not them which kill the body, but are not able to kill the soul: but rather fear him which is able to destroy both soul and body in hell." Also in Matt. 18:9: "And if thine eye offend thee, pluck it out, and cast it from thee; it is better for thee to enter life with one eye, rather than having two eyes to be cast into hell fire." In Matt. 23:15 the Lord accuses the hypocritical scribes and Pharisees that they make their proselytes twofold more children of hell (gehenna) than themselves; and in vs. 33 of the same chapter He threatens them: "Ye serpents, ye generation of vipers, how can ye escape the damnation of hell?" Especially decisive against the denial of the truth of an eternal hell is Mark 9:43-48: "And if thy hand offend thee, cut it off: it is better for thee to enter into life maimed, than having two eyes to go into hell (gehenna), *into the fire that never shall be quenched; where their worm dieth not, and the fire is not quenched.* And if thy

foot offend thee, cut it off; it is better for thee to enter
halt into life, than having two feet to be cast into hell
(gehenna), *into the fire that never shall be quenched;
where their worm dieth not, and the fire is not quenched.* And if thine eye offend thee, pluck it out; it is
better for thee to enter into the kingdom of God with
one eye, than having two eyes to be cast into hell fire;
*where their worm dieth not, and the fire is not quench-
ed.*" See also Luke 12:5. Moreover, even though the
words *sheol* and *hades* often refer to the state of the
dead, this is not always the case. Of the rich man we
read in Luke 16:23, 24: "And in hell (hades) he lifted
up his eyes, being in torments, and seeth Abraham afar
off, and Lazarus in his bosom. And he cried and said,
Father Abraham, have mercy on me, and send Lazarus,
that he may dip the tip of his finger in water, and cool
my tongue; for I am tormented in this flame." That
this statement occurs in a parable does not make the
slightest difference, for it is exactly the purpose of the
parable to teach that, while the righteous are blessed,
the wicked are tormented after this life. Note also
such passages as Rev. 14:9-11: "If any man worship
the beast and his image, and receive his mark in his
forehead, or in his right hand, the same shall drink of
the wine of the wrath of God, which is poured out
without mixture into the cup of his indignation; and
he shall be tormented with fire and brimstone in the
presence of the holy angels, and in the presence of the
Lamb. And the smoke of their torment ascendeth up
for ever and ever; and they have no rest day nor night,
who worship the beast and his image, and whosoever
receiveth the mark of his name." And against the
statement that whenever Scripture speaks of everlasting punishment it means a long period of time, may be
quoted as quite sufficient what the Lord states in Matt.

25:46: "And these shall go away into everlasting punishment: but the righteous into life eternal." The point here is that in the original the same word (*aioonion*) is used for "everlasting" and "eternal." Now, if in the first instance (everlasting punishment) the word signifies a long period, it cannot possibly mean anything else in the second instance (eternal life). But we know that "eternal life" in Scripture means life everlasting. It follows, then, that in Matt. 25:46 the phrase "everlasting punishment" signifies punishment without end. The Catechism, therefore, presents the teaching of Scripture, when it declares that God punishes sin temporally and eternally.

The divine motive of this punishment is God's wrath. This is expressed in the words: "He is terribly displeased." The German here has: "Er zürneth schrecklich." The wrath or displeasure of God is not to be compared to human anger. It is not a passing emotion. It is constant. For God's anger is the reaction of the holiness of God against the wicked that tramples under foot the glory of His name and refuses to give Him thanks. God is holy. And His holiness is the divine virtue according to which He always seeks Himself as the only Good. He seeks His own glory also in the creature. And when the creature refuses to give Him the glory that is due unto His name, God's holiness reacts against that creature in wrath. Nor is His wrath directed merely against sin, and not against the sinner. Some like to make this distinction. God is displeased with sin, but he loves the sinner. But this is a pure abstraction, quite contrary to the teaching of Scripture. God's wrath is not directed against sin, but against the workers of iniquity. Punishment is not inflicted upon sin, but upon the sinner.

It is not sin that is cast into hell fire, but the ungodly that commits the sin.

And this wrath of God expresses and realizes itself in the curse. The Catechism quotes: "Cursed is every one that continueth not in all things that are written in the book of the law, to do them." The curse is the opposite of the blessing of God. Both are the almighty Word which God speaks. Blessing is the Word which He speaks in His favor and eternal loving-kindness upon His people. The curse is the Word He pronounces upon the ungodly reprobates in His constant and eternal wrath. It is the Word that brings misery, temporal and eternal misery, upon all that love unrighteousness. And there is no escape. Only in Christ, Who voluntarily bore the wrath of God and the curse on the accursed tree, is there a way out. For in Him there is eternal righteousness, favor of God, and the blessing of life in His fellowship forever.

III

The Justice Of God's Mercy

Is not God then also merciful? In this third and last question of Lord's Day IV is expressed the final attempt on the part of sinful man to find a way out of his misery without satisfaction and without repentance, to change the living God so as to make it quite safe to sin before His face. The first attempt involved an attack on the right of God to demand of the sinner that which he cannot perform. The second denied God's punitive justice. And in this last question the sinful mind makes the foolish attempt to divide, and to divorce from one another the very virtues of God, particularly those of His justice and mercy, and to introduce a conflict between them, such a conflict that God's mercy induces Him to deny His justice. The question is closely related to the preceding one, and implies an objection to the answer our Catechism gave to the latter. God will not leave sin unpunished. His justice demands punishment. He is filled with wrath against all our sin, original and actual. He curses all that do not keep His good commandments. And He punishes them with temporal as well as with eternal punishment. Such is the terrible wrath of God. But now comes the question: is not God then also merciful? The question contains an objection to the conception of God presented in answer to the tenth question. And how common an objection it is! How frequently one meets with it in actual life! The objector that raises this question really means to say that if you insist that God is always filled with

wrath against the sinner, and that He punishes sin
in time and eternity, your conception of God is that
of a cruel tyrant, who knows of no mercy, a Shylock,
that wants his pound of flesh! This indictment is
brought against those who deny that God can be gracious at all to the sinner outside of Christ, as well as
against them that maintain the truth of eternal punishment in hell. God's mercy militates against His
justice, and prevents Him from executing His righteous wrath upon the head of the sinner!

However, the Catechism denies the existence of
such a conflict in God. It readily grants that God is
merciful. But it denies that this mercy of God eliminates the execution of His justice and righteous wrath.
It insists that the blessed mercy of God can reach the
creature only through the channels of His justice.
"God is indeed merciful, but also just; therefore his
justice requires, that sin which is committed against
the most high majesty of God, be also punished with
extreme, that is, with everlasting punishment of body
and soul."

God's justice is that virtue according to which He
maintains Himself as the only Good, as the sovereign
Governor of the universe. God is good. He is a light,
and there is no darkness in Him at all. He is the implication of all infinite perfections. And as the infinitely perfect One He reveals Himself in His relation to,
and His dealings with the moral creature. He will be
glorified. For He made all things for His own name's
sake, even the wicked unto the day of evil. He seeks
His own glory in the righteous and in the wicked
both. And this means that it is His will that all the
moral creatures shall know Him and acknowledge Him
as the infinitely perfect Sovereign of heaven and earth,
for God's glory is the radiation of His divine perfec-

tion. The creature must confess that God is God, that He is the absolute Lord, and that He is the perfection of goodness. Hence, God always reveals Himself to the moral creature as the perfect Sovereign of heaven and earth. He does so by rewarding the good with good, the evil with evil. From this fundamental rule of His government God never departs. From the implications of this rule no creature can ever escape, not even for a moment. God, Who seeks His own glory and would have the creature know that He is infinite perfection, blesses the righteous. He makes the good happy in his goodness, in order that he may taste and acknowledge that the Lord is good. And He makes the evil one miserable. He curses him in the way of his wickedness, in order that the wicked, too, may experience and confess that He is good. "With the merciful thou wilt shew thyself merciful; with an upright man thou wilt shew thyself upright; with the pure thou wilt shew thyself pure, and with the froward thou wilt shew thyself froward. For thou wilt save the afflicted people; but wilt bring down high looks." Ps. 18:25-27. And the Spirit teaches us to pray: "Do good, O Lord, unto those that be good, and to them that are upright in their hearts;" and assures us: "As for such as turn aside unto their crooked ways, the Lord shall lead them forth with the workers of iniquity: but peace shall be upon Israel." Ps. 125:4, 5. This, then, is the justice of God. According to it, He so governs the universe that He becomes known to all His moral creatures as the absolutely good Lord, by rewarding the good with good, the evil with evil.

God's mercy, too, is His infinite goodness. But mercy considers this goodness of God from the viewpoint that He is the infinitely blessed One. With God there is life and light, fulness of joy and gladness;

there are pleasures forevermore at His right hand.
And even as He is blessed in Himself, and that, too,
as the infinitely perfect One, so He is the sole Fount
of all blessing, of all life and joy and delight, for all
His creatures. For the will to glorify Himself implies
that He purposes to reveal Himself as the eternally
blessed God. That God is merciful, therefore, signifies
the will and desire in God to make the creature share
in His own divine blessedness. If, therefore, that
creature is in depths of misery, the mercy of God becomes revealed in the divine act of deliverance. In
relation to the creature, therefore, the mercy of God
is that divine virtue according to which He delivers the
creature from all misery and fills him with life and
joy.

Now, these two perfections in God are often presented as if they are or might be in conflict with each
other. This is the case, according to this conception,
as soon as God's mercy and justice are applied to the
sinner. Then God confronts a dilemma. According to
the justice of God, He must make the sinner miserable;
according to His mercy, however, He desires to deliver
him from all misery and to fill him with blessedness.
If, therefore, God will exercise His justice, He cannot
show His mercy to the sinner. And, on the other hand,
if He would reveal His mercy, He cannot execute His
justice. Now, according to the conception that is implied in this eleventh question of the Catechism, God's
mercy prevails against His justice. This is in the very
nature of mercy, not only among men, but also in God.
A just mercy is a contradiction in terms. If a criminal
receives mercy from the court, justice is set aside in his
case. Justice is overruled; mercy prevails; the criminal is pardoned. The same, according to this view,
must be true of God, if He is merciful. He is just,

to be sure, and according to this virtue He strikes the sinner with the curse in His wrath. But He is also merciful. And in His mercy it is impossible that He can cause suffering and misery to the creature, even though he be worthy of punishment. He yearns for the happiness of the sinner. The result is that He denies His justice, and blesses the sinner even in his sin and guilt. By some this is applied consistently: without satisfaction of His justice, God bestows upon the sinner eternal life and bliss. By others this same error is applied only to this temporal life and existence: without any basis of righteousness God is gracious to and blesses the sinner in His common mercy.

The fundamental error of this conception is apparent: it denies the oneness of God, and presupposes a conflict between the virtues of truth, faithfulness, righteousness, holiness, and justice, on the one hand, and those of love, grace and mercy on the other. Mercy and justice are separated. They are presented as opposed to each other. But this whole conception is false. God is one. It is true, He is revealed to us in many perfections, but all these divine attributes are one in God. We may not separate them, even though they can be distinguished. God *is* His attributes. His mercy *is* His justice, and His justice *is* His mercy. And therefore, His mercy is always a just and righteous mercy; and His justice is always merciful. It is this truth that is denied by the objector that is introduced to us in the eleventh question of the Catechism. And this denial is a very fundamental error, that vitiates all the theology and the whole conception of life of those that present it as the truth. We must emphasize, therefore, that God is one, and that all His attributes are one in Him. The divine virtue of simplicity must be maintained.

If this is clearly understood, it will at once be recognized that unjust mercy is fundamentally no mercy, and that the latter, far from overruling and prevailing against mercy, cannot even be bestowed upon the sinner, except in the way of and with strictest maintenance of justice. This is even true in human life. Suppose that a child has grievously sinned, and that the parent should inflict a severe punishment upon him. However, he cannot bear the very thought of seeing his child suffer, and so he refrains from punishing him. Is the motive on the part of the parent for not chastising the child to be considered mercy? Of course not. It is merely a sinful weakness. And instead of blessing the child and bestowing a good upon him, it hardens him in his sin. Or suppose that a judge, instead of maintaining law and justice, pardons the criminal that is indicted in his court. Is that judge motivated by mercy, or by a "love of humanity," in thus pardoning the criminal, and does he really bestow a blessing upon that criminal? Far from it. Various reasons may motivate the action of the judge, but mercy is not one of them; justice is violated; the criminal is strengthened in his crime; and crime is encouraged in the land. Or again, suppose that a certain governor of a state or country would habitually pardon all criminals in his domain. Would such a governor gain for himself the reputation of being a very merciful and benign sovereign? And would, under his government, even the good be blessed? The answer is evident. His very subjects would condemn such an application of human weakness and gross injustice in the name of mercy. In an infinitely higher sense of the word this is true of God in relation to the sinner. In fact, that all the attempts of men to separate justice from mercy in human life are doomed to failure, has its deepest cause in the fact that these two virtues can never be separated in God. Mercy cannot be bestowed upon the wicked as such. It cannot bless the sinner except on the basis of justice. The guilty sinner cannot be blessed. It is impossible that he should ever be made happy in his sin. Even if he should be taken to heaven, suppose this were possible, there he would be most miserable of all. The wicked would flee far from heaven, because God's presence is there. And, therefore, the question: "Is not God then also merciful?" may in general be answered as follows: "Indeed He is; but this already implies that He is just, for an unjust mercy is fundamentally a contradiction in terms."

This justice, according to the Heidelberg Catechism, "requires, that sin which is committed against the most high majesty of God, be also punished with extreme, that is, with everlasting punishment of body and soul." Justice requires punishment. The wicked is evil, and because God is good and must be known and acknowledged as such, the ethically evil must suffer evil, misery, death. Never may the sinner receive the impression that God blesses him in his sin. Nowhere, in all the wide universe, may the sinner find a place where he can stand and claim that he found rest and peace and life and joy. Not for a moment may he so experience God's government that he can deny that God is good, righteous, holy, and true, too pure of eyes to behold sin. On the contrary, he must taste, even in his way of sin, that God is good; and this he must confess. Hence, he must be made miserable, unspeakably wretched. Punishment must be inflicted upon him. Such is the requirement of the justice of God. He rewards the good with good, the the evil with evil; and that for His own name's sake!

And this punishment must be commensurate with the evil committed. The evil inflicted as punishment upon the sinner must be equivalent to the greatness of the sin. This is the underlying principle of the statement of the Catechism here that "sin which is committed against the most high majesty of God, be also punished with extreme, that is, with everlasting punishment of body and soul." The greatness of sin is not measured by the position and worth of him that commits it, but by the majesty and goodness and sovereignty of Him against whom sin is committed. It is so among men. It makes a world of difference whether one offends against his fellowman on the street or in the shop, or whether his offense is directed at the chief magistrate of the land, be he president or emperor. But sin is committed against God. And God is GOD! He is infinite in majesty and glory, the sole Good and overflowing fountain of good. To sin against Him is to trample infinite majesty and sovereignty under foot. To clench the fist in His face and violate His commandment, is to rise in rebellion against the everlasting Lord of heaven and earth. He is Lord in all the universe; He is Lord in time and in eternity. Always and everywhere and for ever we have to do with Him. Never can we escape Him. There is, therefore, no rest for the sinner. Offense against the infinite majesty of God, than Whom there is no other sovereign, must be punished everywhere and for ever. Extreme, that is, everlasting punishment and that, too, in body and soul, is required by the justice of God!

There is no way out, therefore, as far as man is concerned. Salvation is of the Lord. It is not, it cannot be of man. God is indeed merciful. And it is His everlasting good pleasure that His mercy should be revealed in all the fulness of its glory, even through sin. He does, indeed, lift the sinner from his misery, and reveals the abundance of His mercy by exalting him to the glory of everlasting, heavenly bliss in His tabernacle. And His mercy is revealed, too, as a just mercy. For God revealed His mercy in Christ, His own Christ, in Whom His justice and mercy with relation to the guilty and miserable sinner shine forth in most blessed harmony and sweetest accord. And when that mercy of God revealed in the cross and resurrection of our Lord Jesus Christ is bestowed upon the sinner, he acknowledges by faith that God is abundantly merciful, but also that His mercy is absolutely just!

SECTION II

GOD'S WAY OUT

LORD'S DAY V

Q. 12. Since then, by the righteous judgment of God, we deserve temporal and eternal punishment, is there no way by which we may escape that punishment, and be again received into favor?

A. God will have His justice satisfied: and therefore we must make this full satisfaction either by ourselves, or by another.

Q. 13. Can we of ourselves then make this satisfaction?

A. By no means; but on the contrary we daily increase our debt.

Q. 14. Can there be found anywhere, one, who is a mere creature, able to satisfy for us?

A. None; for, first, God will not punish any other creature for the sin which man hath committed; and further, no mere creature can sustain the burden of God's eternal wrath against sin, so as to deliver others from it.

Q. 15. What sort of a mediator and deliverer then must we seek for?

A. For one who is very man, and perfectly righteous; and yet more powerful than all creatures; that is, one who is also very God.

I

The Necessity Of Satisfaction

This fifth Lord's Day introduces the second part of our Heidelberg Catechism. We recall here that the Catechism, according to its subjective, experiential viewpoint of the truth, divides its subject-material into three main parts: the first treating of sin and misery, the second of redemption and deliverance, the third of Christian gratitude. This second part extends through the eighty-fifth question and answer, and is, therefore, by far the largest of the three divisions of our instructor. It treats of many subjects. After a few introductory questions and answers, setting forth the necessity of a divine-human mediator for the deliverance of the sinner, it follows the line of the so called Apostolic Confession in the discussion of the contents of the Christian faith, which is concluded by a chapter on the justification by faith in Lord's Day 23 followed by a Lord's Day on good works in relation to that justification; and to this is appended a rather elaborate discussion of the means of grace, especially of the sacraments, while the whole is closed by the treatment of the subject of Christian discipline, or the "keys of the kingdom of heaven."

The first main part of the Catechism had left the natural man in an absolutely hopeless state and condition. He is guilty and worthy of damnation. By nature he stands opposed to the law of God, for he is prone to hate God and the neighbor, while the demand of the law is love. He is wholly incapable of doing any good, and inclined to all evil, member of a corrupt race in which he is conceived and born in sin. From the moment of his birth every man lies under guilt and condemnation, and is dead through sin. And there is no way out. In his sinful state he cannot hopefully look to God. God is the terror of the sinner. The living God is unchangeable. He is God—not man. The sinner may seek consolation in his own conception of God, but in this

236

attempt there is no salvation: he cannot change God. He is a Rock in all His virtues. He cannot deny Himself. Upon the rock that is God the sinner and all his vain hopes must needs suffer shipwreck. Unalterably God demands that man shall love Him with all his heart and mind and soul and strength. And this demand is not changed or retracted because the sinner is incapable of meeting the requirements of the law: God once endowed him with all the gifts necessary to keep God's commandments, but man squandered these gifts by his wilful disobedience. And God punishes sin in His just wrath, temporally and eternally, in body and soul. Nor is it effective to appeal to the mercy of God in opposition to His righteousness and justice, for God is one in all His attributes, and even His mercy is forever a righteous mercy. It is exactly because God is as He is that there is no hope for the sinner in his guilty state and corrupt condition. His plight is absolutely desperate.

Such is, in brief, the truth concerning sinful man as expounded in the first part of the Heidelberg Catechism.

And now the second part, which treats of the redemption of man, is introduced. The question still is: Is there no way out? Granted that man's condition is as was described in the first part of the Catechism, and that "by the righteous judgment of God we deserve temporal and eternal punishment," is there no hope even then? How can we escape this punishment and be again received into favor? This question may seem to center around man. It does not appear to be theological in scope or viewpoint. It is concerned with man, or rather, in it man is concerned with himself. It might be objected, as some have done, that the Catechism does not assume a high standpoint. A more exalted and sounder standpoint would have been concerned with the question of the glory of God, rather than with the sinner's desire to escape punishment. However, let us not overlook the fact, first of all, that no matter how strictly theocentric may be the standpoint we assume, the salvation of man remains a very important subject, the fear of death and hell is very real, and the Catechism certainly takes its standpoint foursquare on the basis of this reality, when it asks the question: how can we escape this punish-

ment? We must be careful lest we pretend to be able to assume
the attitude that we are wholly indifferent what becomes of us,
whether we go to heaven or to hell, if God only is glorified.
Secondly, we cannot separate the glory of God from our salvation. The two are inseparably connected. Even though the
question of the Heidelberger here is concerned immediately with
a possible escape from temporal and eternal punishment, it does
not follow that it is not concerned with the glory of God. Certainly the escape from this punishment is only the negative side
of that state in which we will be able to enjoy God's fellowship
and to glorify Him forever. And, thirdly, the Catechism itself
reveals that its view of the matter is quite sound by the addition:
"and again be received into favor." By the escape from punishment it does not refer to a mere escape from temporal suffering
and eternal hell, but to deliverance from the wrath of God and
from the state of being forsaken of Him. And, therefore, the
positive content of the question is: how can we be restored to
the favor of God? And the search and longing after God that is
implied in this question is certainly theocentric. It is the yearn-
ing that is expressed in the well-known words of Ps. 42:1, 2: "As
the hart panteth after the water brooks, so panteth my soul after
thee, O God. My soul thirsteth for God, for the living God;
when shall I come and appear before God?"

The answer of the catechism to this twelfth question may
seem rather disappointing. It is really evasive. Instead of giving
a direct reply to the question the Catechism answers: "God wills
that his justice be satisfied; therefore we must make full satisfaction!" And many a modern preacher would probably grow
somewhat impatient with the Heidelberg Catechism, and complain that it makes no progress at all. Especially if he would
have to preach to his congregation on the basis of one Lord's
Day at a time, as is the custom in Reformed Churches, the
"evangelistically inclined" preacher of today, anxious to "bring
souls to Christ," might conclude that the Catechism is altogether
too slow in its progress of developing the truth, that by this time
we have heard enough about the hopelessness of the sinner's
condition and the unchangeable justice of God, and that it is

high time a full and direct answer were given to the question: is there no way of escape? But one who would so reason would make a serious error. Before the question as to a possible way of escape may be answered, it must become quite clear that as far as man's efforts are concerned to open such a way the matter is quite hopeless. And this truth the Catechism demonstrates and emphasizes by stressing at this point the *necessity of satisfaction*. God will have His justice satisfied! Somehow we must make satisfaction, full satisfaction of the justice of God. Yes, but this means that we can never escape the punishment of sin, for to make satisfaction implies that the punishment be endured to the end. And again, this also implies that on the sinner's side the way is closed forever. He cannot make this full satisfaction. We cannot even see a possible way of escape. If salvation is to come to us, it must come from above, and it must come in the way of a wonder of grace. The way of escape, if there be any, belongs to those things which eye hath not seen, and ear hath not heard, and that have never arisen in the heart of man. It must be opened by Him Who quickeneth the dead, and Who calleth the things that are not as if they were. Salvation does not lie within the scope of humanly conceivable possibilities. And this we must learn to acknowledge, not only as a matter of doctrine, but in true, heartfelt humiliation. We must indeed become nothing; Christ, the revelation of the wonder of God's grace, must become all. We must come to the hearty confession that with us the way of escape is impossible, and that all our works and efforts, all our wisdom and philosophy, even all our piety and religiousness, mean absolutely nothing and are of no value whatever as far as obtaining again the favor of God is concerned. All boasting must be excluded. No flesh must glory in the presence of God. We must cast ourselves unconditionally upon Him Who alone doeth wondrous things. But then we must not speak too lightly of a way of escape. And, surely, we must not speak too superficially of "saving souls." To save a soul is an amazing wonder, higher than the highest heavens, deeper than the abyss. For God will have His justice satisfied, and we must make this satisfaction before we can be restored to God's favor.

Satisfaction is a term that expresses one of the main themes of Holy Scripture. The word denotes the same idea as the Dutch "voldoening," or, better still, "genoegdoening." It means "to do enough," "to make sufficient," to comply with a certain demand, particularly with respect to a debt accumulated or an offense committed. And the truth that God will have His justice satisfied is a theme that runs all through the Word of God from beginning to end. All through history God instructed His people in the truth of the necessity of satisfaction. As soon as they had fallen into sin He taught them that they could be restored into His favor only in the way of satisfaction, for it was He that made for them "coats of skins" presupposing sacrifice and the shedding of blood, instead of the aprons of fig leaves with which they themselves had attempted to cover their nakedness before God and before one another. He it was that taught Abel to bring a sacrifice "of the firstlings of the flock and of the fat thereof," Gen. 4:4, and thus to bring a better sacrifice than Cain, "by which he obtained witness that he was righteous," Heb. 11:4. He plainly taught His people, by means of all the shadows and of the service of the tabernacle and of the temple, that there was no way into His favor, no approach into His presence as He dwelt in the Holiest of all, except by means of perfect satisfaction for sin. And in the New Testament it is the same truth that is emphasized throughout its teaching. Christ gives His life as a ransom for many. He is the propitiation for sin. And as "almost all things are by the law purged with blood; and without shedding of blood is no remission," so Christ, "once in the end of the world hath appeared to put away sin by the sacrifice of himself." Heb. 9:22, 26. Surely, that God will have His justice satisfied, and that there is no other way to be received again into His favor, is one of the fundamental truths of the Bible.

What is this satisfaction of God's justice? In general, satisfaction implies that a person has certain obligations with respect to another, that he has failed to fulfill these obligations, that he is in arrears, that he owes a debt, and that now he makes a full payment of that debt, and so restores the proper relationship between himself and him to whom he was obligated. Applied to our relation to God, this means that we have an unchangeable obligation to love Him. The obligation is a moral, ethical one. It never changes, for God does not change. Always He says to us: "Love Me with all thy heart, and with all thy mind, and with all thy soul, and with all thy strength." Never may we do anything that is not motivated by the love of God. If we love Him we are the objects of His favor. The moment we fail in the payment of this love-debt, we are no longer in His favor, but become the objects of His just wrath. This cannot be emphasized too strongly and repeated too often. Nothing can take the place of this love of God to make us the objects of His favor. Nothing else than this love of God with all our being is righteousness. All our imaginary piety, our Phariseeism, our work-righteousness, our willingness "to do something for God," our humanitarianism, is of no avail to take the place of this one obligation to love God. To love God with our whole heart, to love Him in all that we do, in the very thought of our mind, in every deed we perform, with every step we take on life's pathway, in every relationship of life,—that is our sacred and unchangeable obligation before God. And nothing else can possibly take its place.

In that obligation we have failed and do fail continuously. Hence we are in arrears, we are in debt with God! And let us not be deceived by this word *debt* so that, perhaps, we think of our relation to God in terms of a financial obligation. A man may owe a debt of money and think little of it. He is going to pay it sometime, at his convenience! And as long as his creditor does not trouble him too much, there is little for him to worry about. But with our relation to God this is quite different. We owe a love-debt. And our creditor is not someone who lives far away from us, and occasionally knocks at our door to demand payment, but he is the living God, the Lord of heaven and earth, in Whom we live and move and have our being! He is the Lord of life and of death. In His favor there is light and life and joy; in His displeasure there is darkness and death and everlasting desolation. And He is not far from us. He surrounds us. He encompasses our whole being. And the moment we fail to love Him, that moment He is terribly displeased, filled with holy and

just wrath against us. He makes us feel His just wrath. He
punishes us with death. He makes us unspeakably miserable.
He does this, not in some future state only, but now, at once, the
moment we are in debt and fail to love Him. His hand is heavy
upon us, and by His wrath we pine and die. But let us not forget,
that even so, even while He pursues us and encompasses us in
His wrath, and inflicts the punishment of death upon us, He still
demands: "love Me!" It is quite essential to understand this
clearly, in order that we may comprehend somewhat the terrible
reality of satisfaction. Our obligation is to love God Who is
GOD! We must love Him as He is, because He is good! He is
good when we love Him and He causes us to taste His blessed
favor. But He is good, too, when we fail to love Him and He
causes us to taste His goodness by inflicting upon us the punishment of death, by making us unspeakably miserable! Hence, we
must still love Him, even while He lays His heavy hand upon us!
To love God was our obligation in Paradise, where man was
surrounded by the favor of God. To love God remained his
obligation when God executed the death sentence upon him, and
he was driven out of paradise and from the fellowship of God.
To love God is man's obligation even in the eternal desolation
of hell. Even there God says to man: "Love Me as I reveal Myself to thee here in My righteousness and justice through the
agonies which I cause thee to suffer in outer darkness!" The
love-demand never ceases, never changes. The love-debt remains
forever!

To understand the implication of satisfaction for sin we must
bear in mind this unchangeableness of our love-debt to God.
Not the mere bearing of the punishment for sin, even in hell, is
satisfaction. Surely, the damned in hell fully suffer the punishment for sin in eternal death and desolation. Yet they never
atone, they never make satisfaction for sin; their suffering never
becomes a sacrifice that blots out sin and restores them to the
favor of God. When capital punishment is inflicted upon a
murderer we may often read in our daily papers that the murderer atoned for his crime. But this is not correct. Justice satisfied itself by inflicting the punishment of death on the murderer,

but the murderer did not atone for his crime. He did not offer his life. He did not willingly seek the punishment that he might atone. He probably sought the help of an attorney in order to escape the electric chair. But his life was taken away from him by force, against his will. His death is no satisfaction. So God will surely punish sin even with eternal desolation, and glorify Himself in the damnation of the wicked. But the suffering of hell is no satisfaction, for even there God's demand remains unchanged: "Love Me!" And this demand they cannot fulfill. Hence, the act of satisfaction is the payment of the love-debt to God as He reveals Himself to the sinner in the depth and darkness and unspeakable misery of hell! If there were a sinner that could perform this act of love, that could pass through the woes of eternal desolation, through the darkness of the depth of hell and be motivated by the love of God, that sinner would satisfy the justice of God with respect to sin. Or, to express this truth more vividly still, if there were a man that would be so motivated by the love of God that he would seek that punishment, that for God's name's sake and to fulfill His righteousness would desire to descend into deepest hell, and realize that desire,—that man would make full satisfaction for sin. Such is the sinner's love-debt to God. He is obligated to say to God: "For Thy righteousness' sake let all the billows of Thy wrath pass over me, and even then I shall love Thee!" If he performs this act of love he makes full satisfaction. And in the way of this full satisfaction he will be the object of the favor of God! And this satisfaction is absolutely necessary. The Arminian, who, because of his denial of limited atonement, cannot and does not maintain the truth of satisfaction, may claim that God can accept something else instead of this perfect sacrifice of atonement, a tear, a prayer, a temporal affliction, an example,—but he misleads the sinner. The modernist may make light of this truth and speak of it mockingly as "blood-theology," he only mocks at most dreadful realities. For God cannot deny Himself. He will have His justice satisfied. Satisfaction for sin is the indispensable condition to be restored to the favor of God.

II

The Impossibility Of Satisfaction

In questions and answers 13 and 14 the Heidelberg Catechism demonstrates that, as far as we are concerned, our work, our efforts, our good intentions, the way is absolutely closed: through our own efforts we can never escape punishment and again be received into favor with God. This must become quite clear, before we can even begin to speak of a divinely wrought salvation through our mediator Jesus Christ. God will give His glory to no other. He does not step in to save man as long as there is any possibility that man can merit and bring about his own salvation. His work is always *His* work and must be acknowledged as such. His glory must be revealed, not only in the work of creation, but also, and even on a higher level and to a more marvellous degree in the work of redemption. His work, therefore, is always in the sphere and on the level where it is impossible for man to work. The camel must go through the eye of the needle. That is impossible, indeed, with man, but what is impossible with man is possible with God. And it is exactly through the accomplishment of the humanly and creaturely impossible that He becomes revealed as God who is really GOD, who as Barth would say is the "wholly other." He is the eternal I AM, the infinite, the Almighty, the All-wise, the absolutely independent, self-existent God. "To whom then will ye liken me, or shall I be equal? saith the Holy One . . . Hast thou not known? Hast thou not heard, that the everlasting God, the Lord, the Creator of the ends of the earth, fainteth not, neither is weary? There is no searching of his understanding." Isa. 40:25, 28. "O the depth of the riches, both of the wisdom and knowledge of God! How unsearchable are his judgments, and his ways past finding out! For who hath known the mind of the Lord? Or who hath been his counsellor? Or who hath first given to him, and it shall be recompensed unto him again? For of him, and through him, and to him, are all things: to whom be glory forever. Amen." Rom. 11:33-36. After all, the self-revelation of God and His glory is the purpose of all His works, even also of the work of redemption. And, therefore, it must become fully evident, that it is His work, and that what He performs is impossible with the creature. From this viewpoint questions 13 and 14 occupy a very proper place in this connection. They must not be considered an illustration of scholastic hair splitting or mere mental gymnastics. Presently, in the next Lord's Day, the Catechism will speak of the mediator, the revelation of God in the flesh. But before this can be done, it is quite proper to set forth the impossibility of salvation by your power or wisdom, in order that it may become evident that this mediator of God steps in only to accomplish that which is impossible with man.

"Can we ourselves then make this satisfaction?" And again: "Can there be found anywhere, one, who is a mere creature, able to satisfy for us?" Thus the Catechism asks. And to both these questions it gives a negative answer, and furnishes the reasons for these answers. Of course, there are other elements in the work of salvation, besides satisfaction, that are impossible with man. But satisfaction is basic. Satisfaction must be made before man, the sinner, can even escape eternal damnation, and be again received into the favor of God. All the rest of the work of salvation hinges on this work of satisfaction. If satisfaction cannot be made, it is of no use to investigate further into the possibility of salvation. And, therefore, the Catechism centers on this question of satisfaction, and asserts that it is quite impossible for man to make this satisfaction himself, or for any creature, a mere creature, to make this satisfaction for him. And to appreciate this instruction of our Heidelberger, to see clearly how utterly impossible it is for man or any other creature to make satisfaction for sin, it is necessary that we keep in mind what in the preceding section we said about satisfaction. It is not the mere passive bearing of the punishment. Suffering of the punishment for sin is, of course, quite possible for man. He will suffer that punishment forever, unless he is saved. It were even conceivable that some other creature, or a group of creatures, would suffer that punishment for man, if the demand of God that His justice be satisfied were not so immutable. It is difficult to see, for instance, that salvation could not be through the suffering and death of an animal, if the only reason for such suffering is that God would teach us that we are worthy of such death, and thus would bring us to the acknowledgement of His righteousness and to sincere repentance. But God will have His justice satisfied. And His justice requires that we fulfill His law. And His law is not that we shall do this or that, that we shall bring this or that offering, that we shall do something for Him; it is not even that we shall suffer and die: it is that we shall LOVE HIM! Hence, satisfaction must be an act of love, of the pure and perfect love of God! We must love Him as He is, in His eternal perfections of righteousness and holiness. And since over against us sinners, He reveals Himself in His wrath, and His wrath is expressed in the curse, we must be able to love Him in His wrath, and to bear the curse and the suffering of eternal death in love, in the pure love of God! He who can voluntarily, in the perfect obedience of love, bear the wrath of God and suffer the curse to the very end, fulfills the demands of the law of God and satisfies God's justice with respect to sin. This we must bear in mind in order to understand fully the instruction of our Heidelberger on this point.

Can we ourselves make this satisfaction? This question now has come to mean: can we ourselves actively bear the wrath of God against sin in perfect obedience of the pure love of God? How impossible! The Catechism is most emphatic on this point. *By no means*, it says, can we make this satisfaction. In no wise, by no power of our own, by no conceivable method or means, can we make this satisfaction. We have neither the power nor the will to make this satisfaction. Suppose that a man had the desire to be again received into favor with God. Suppose that in his early childhood, as soon as he came to self-consciousness, he deplored his sinful condition, and was filled with a true sorrow after God. Suppose that in this true sorrow over sin he went in sackcloth and ashes, deploring before God and men his sinful state and condition. Suppose that he wept bitter tears day and night, and that all his life he perfectly kept the law of God and lived in perfection before Him. All this is, of course, for many reasons absolutely impossible, but let us suppose this impossibility. Would this sorrow and these tears, would this life of perfection satisfy the justice of God with respect to a single sin he may have committed even before he came to self-consciousness; or would it atone for the sin in which he was born? Of course not! If a person trades with a certain grocer and for a long time makes his purchases on credit, and accumulates a debt which he cannot pay; and if after a certain period, he begins to buy cash and pays for whatever he purchases; and if, besides, every time he makes a new purchase he bewails and deplores the debt that is still on the grocer's books; does that debtor, by his wailing and by his paying for what he buys of that grocer, pay one single cent to wipe out his debt? Of course not! No more could any sinner by rendering to God what is God's for fifty or sixty years what he owes Him every moment, and by bewailing that he ever refused to love and obey Him with all his heart and mind and soul and strength, satisfy the justice of God with respect to sin. He *owes* that love, that obedience, that perfection, that repentance over sin, that weeping and wailing, that going about in sackcloth and ashes, *every day of the week, every moment of the day.* By all this he could never satisfy God's justice. He would still be under the wrath of God. He still would not be received into God's favor. He still would have to experience the wrath of God in eternal death. And in eternal death, in hell, there is no possibility for mere man to satisfy the justice of God. There God *takes* His own satisfaction, but man has nothing to bring. There all is passivity, a being crushed by the wrath of Him who is a consuming fire!

But how absurd is the above supposition! For where, then, is the sinner that even approximates the likeness presented of him in the preceding paragraph? Where is the sinner who, for a time in his life at least, is sincerely sorry for his sin, and lives in perfection for the rest of his life? There is no such man among them that are born of women. The Catechism cuts off the very possi-

bility of harboring the notion of such a possibility by adding to
its emphatic negative answer to question 13: "but on the contrary we daily increase our debt." Let us remember what we
learned about the sinner from the third Lord's Day. He is so
depraved that he is incapable of doing any good and inclined to
all evil. He does not love God, but is by nature inclined to hate
Him. He is corrupt in heart and mind, darkened in his understanding so that he cannot know what is good, and perverse in
his will so that he is incapable ever to will that which is in accord
with the will of God. He will not, he cannot, he cannot will to
love God. He chose against God in paradise, where he was surrounded by the abundance of God's goodness every day; he does
not love God in this world, in which things have not yet reached
their final and eternal consummation, in which he still eats and
drinks and is merry. How, then, shall he ever be able to bring
the sacrifice of love to the living God, and satisfy His justice?
How shall he be able even to conceive of the possibility of willingly offering himself up to the eternal wrath of God? You see
how impossible it is. He does the very opposite: daily he increases
his guilt. Every step he takes on life's path (and he must take
that step, he cannot stop!) defiles his way; every word he speaks
(and he must speak that word, he cannot be silent!) testifies
against him; every work of his hand (and work he must, he
cannot be idle) is to his condemnation, every thought of his mind,
every desire of his heart, every secret inclination in his inmost
soul (and he can never stop thinking and desiring) makes him
increasingly guilty before God. If (say this were possible) God
would blot out all his sins up to a certain moment and give him
complete forgiveness, the next moment he would surely have
plunged himself once more hopelessly into the state of utter
condemnation. How, then, shall that sinner ever bring the perfect sacrifice of love to God, that he may satisfy His unchangeable justice? It is impossible. As far as man is concerned the way
is closed.

We daily increase our debt! What does that mean? It means
that our life in this world is never anything else, and never can
be anything else than a piling up of treasures of wrath for our-

selves! For every day, and every hour, and every beat of our heart, we are working, thinking, willing, choosing, deciding, speaking, acting. And with all this inner and outward activity we stand in the midst of the world, God's world, in which we find the means to live and move and act. And with all these powers and means, with all this activity of our soul and body, our mind and will, we constantly face the demand of God's living law: love Me! And a thousand times an hour we say: I will not! We increase our debt, each one of us individually, so that, if a man live and act eighty years he piled up for himself much greater treasures of wrath than if he had been taken away in infancy. But we also increase our debt daily collectively, organically, as a human race. For six thousand years men have increased their debt with God, and the treasures of wrath are piled astoundingly, alarmingly high in our present time. That is why it will be more tolerable for Sodom and Gomorrah in the day of judgment than for Jerusalem and for Capernaum; and it will be more tolerable for the latter in that day than for the final antichristian world. For we increase our debt through the centuries! And as the debt increases the wrath of God increases, even the wrath of God that is revealed from heaven upon our present world; and as the wrath of God increases we are given over into greater sin and corruption! Terrible, you say? O, but indeed, it is terrible to fall into the hands of the living God! But the point is that this dreadful condition is hopeless. For, before we even have the right to be delivered from it, satisfaction must be made. And we can never bring the required satisfaction ourselves. The way is closed!

But how about the possibility of substituting some other creature to satisfy the justice of God in our stead? The Catechism had referred to this possibility in the answer to the twelfth question: "we must make this full satisfaction either by ourselves, *or by another.*" And in the fourteenth question it investigates this possibility of making full satisfaction by another: "Can there be found anywhere, one, who is a mere creature, able to satisfy for us?" Ursinus in his "Schatboek" explains that the reference in the question to one, "who is a *mere* creature," is intentional. "In the question there is added: '*mere* creature,' in

order that the answer may be completely negative. A creature
must satisfy for the sin of the creature; but not necessarily such
a one who is nothing else than creature, for such a one could
not possibly satisfy, as will be shown." We face here a threefold
question: 1. Can *we* satisfy the justice of God by substituting
another creature? 2. Can another *creature,* who is not man,
satisfy for the sin of man? 3. Can a *mere* creature, one who is
nothing else than creature, bring such satisfaction as is required
to deliver us? The first of these three questions is not directly
answered by the Catechism, but the question is suggested by the
answer to question 12: "*we* must make this satisfaction either by
ourselves, *or another.*" We, therefore, make the satisfaction,
even though it be through another. If, then, that "other" is a
mere creature, it must be a creature that we bring to God, that
we substitute. Now, again it must be emphasized that this is
unthinkable as far as man's willingness and spiritual capability
to bring such a substitute are concerned. For such a substitute
he must bring to God in perfect love and in true repentance.
One who daily increases his guilt is incapable of substituting
any creature as a sacrifice of love. But, secondly, *we* cannot substitute any other creature, for the simple reason that we have no
creature to substitute. Where in all the wide creation shall we
find a creature we can so call our own that we can offer it to God
in our stead? I may owe a man five thousand dollars, and if I
have not the money but own a house, I may offer him the house
as a substitute. But what shall I bring to God? Shall I offer
Him all my goods? But what goods have I that are not His? All
the silver and gold are His! And, besides, I am worthy of hell!
Shall I kill a lamb or bullock and ask Him to accept it as a substitute for my life? But the cattle on a thousand hills are His!
I have no creature that I can substitute to make satisfaction for
my sin. And, thirdly, I have not the *right* to determine upon a
substitution. This is even true among men. If I owe a man one
hundred dollars, I have no right to decide that he shall take my
old car instead. And surely, man has no right to determine that
God shall be satisfied with another creature, even if there could
be found such a creature, to atone for man's sin.

And do not say that all this is mere abstract reasoning, quite out of touch with real life, for the very opposite is true. Always sinful man attempts to impose a substitute upon God to satisfy for his sins, to take the place of mercy and truth and righteousness. The old Pharisees felt that they did God a favor when they brought their bulls and goats to the temple, and when they gave tithes of all they possessed. And the fundamentally corrupt notion that *we* can bring something to God is still very general. A man gives a million dollars to some charitable institution, and in his heart he tries to feel that by this deed he is giving something to God that will make up for many a sin he may have committed in the past. He is trying to make God accept a substitute of his own. Or he will give large sums to missions to bring the gospel to the poor distant heathen, and probably attempt to smooth his conscience and feel that God may accept this sacrifice as a substitute for the evil he does to his neighbor next door, or for the hire of his employees whose wages are kept back by him through fraud. Yes, indeed, this notion of substituting another creature, even though it be not by killing bulls and goats, is a very popular one with sinful men. Missions have been established, hospitals have been built, theological schools have been endowed with large sums, in order that men might make satisfaction to God through another creature! The heart in man is deceitful more than anything! It is desperately wicked! For if it were not, man would understand that such a sacrifice of the wicked is an abomination to the Lord of heaven and earth. If a man is in debt to the amount of one thousand dollars, which he never cares to, nor is able to pay; and if, then, on Christmas he brings to his creditor a dollar necktie, at the same time revealing in his entire attitude that he feels that his creditor ought to be ever so pleased with him, is he not a fool? And will not his creditor utterly despise him? How abominable, then, must man be in the sight of God, the sinner, who owes to God the infinite debt of love, who is worthy of eternal damnation, and who tries to substitute some of God's own silver and gold to make satisfaction for his sin! If, therefore, the question is put in this form: can *we* bring a substitute to God to make full satisfaction for

252 LORD'S DAY V

sin? the answer must be negative. We cannot and will not make such a substitution in the love of God; we have no creature that we can possibly substitute and bring to God, for all things are His; and we do not have the right to determine upon our own substitute and expect that God will accept it.

The second question that must be answered in this connection is: "Can *another* creature, a creature that is *not man,* satisfy for our sin?" The Catechism answers: "God will not punish any other creature for the sin which man committed." This will of God to punish only the creature that sinned and no other creature is not arbitrary. God's will is always in accord with His justice, and justice and righteousness belong to His very Being. And God cannot deny Himself. And He certainly would deny Himself if He would punish another creature for man's sin. This statement does not exclude the possibility of a substitute. For a substitute is not another *creature,* but another *person,* and the relation of one person to another or to others may be such that he is permitted according to justice to take the place of the others in judgment. But here it is the question of *another creature.* It is a creature that has not the same kind of nature as man. It is different. It has not the same body, mind, will, experience, life as man. It does not live a *human* life, and it cannot die a *human* death. Now, whether that creature is animal or angel, it could never receive man's punishment for man's sin in his stead. For if the justice of God demands that an evil be inflicted upon the sinner which is commensurate with or equivalent to the sin committed, "an eye for an eye, a tooth for a tooth," then it is evident that only *human death,* i.e. the suffering of death in and by human nature can be the proper punishment for the sin of a human being. Hence, God will not punish the sin which man committed in any other nature than that of man. Besides, it must not be forgotten, that the ultimate purpose of punishment is that the sinner must acknowledge that God is good. Sin is really an attempt to deny the goodness, i.e. the holiness, righteousness and truth of God. It is transgression of the law. It is the realization of the intention to set up another standard of goodness than the will of God. And God maintains His goodness, and compels the sinner to acknowledge that He is the only good by inflicting the punishment of death upon him, by thus causing him to experience the unspeakable misery of departing from and rising in rebellion against the living God. But this purpose could not be attained by punishing another creature, a creature that exists and lives outside of the scope of man's experience, for the sin of man. It is in the experience of human nature, of the human body and the human soul, of the human mind and will, that God's holy wrath must be felt, and that He must make Himself known, even in opposition to sin, as the sole Good. Hence, the same creature that sinned must receive the punishment for sin. For it is not possible that the blood of bulls and of goats should take away sins. Heb. 10:4.

The third question is closely related to the second: can a *mere* creature substitute for us? At first blush it may appear as if this question had really already been answered. If man cannot satisfy for himself, and if another creature cannot take his place, then it stands to reason that there is no mere creature anywhere that is able to satisfy the justice of God with respect to sin. Yet, this last question considers the matter from a different viewpoint. The question now is, not whether another kind of creature is able to take our place, but whether a mere creature, one that is nothing but a creature, one that is no more than a creature, even if it were permitted to substitute for us, would be able to bear our punishment and to restore us to the favor of God. And to this question the Heidelberg Catechism gives a double answer: (1) no mere creature can sustain the burden of God's eternal wrath against sin; and (2) no mere creature could deliver us from that wrath of God. All emphasis should be placed here on the word "sustain." One could not substitute a term like "suffer" here. The German uses the term "ertragen." The word conveys especially two ideas: that of actively bearing any burden, and that of bearing such a burden to the very end. In our discussion of the implications of satisfaction we stressed the fact that the wrath of God must be endured as an act, in the obedience of the love of God. To satisfy the justice of God one must not merely suffer, passively bear, the punishment for sin. That is done by the damned in hell, too. Yet they never bring a sacrifice for sin, and they never atone for their guilt, for the simple reason that in suffering the wrath of God they never perform an act of love. God *inflicts* punishment, He *takes* payment from them, but they never willingly *give* it. Now, no *mere* creature can ever so sustain the wrath of God that he performs a willing act of obedience in the love of God. For the punishment of sin is death, utter death, physical and spiritual death, eternal death. In order to be active in death, *to perform the act of death,* one must have a life that he has the power to lay down. And that is not true of any creature. The creature's life is given to it. It is never its own. He may forfeit that life, and he does, if with it he does not constantly consecrate himself to God in the obedience of love. And if he forfeits it, his life is taken away from him and he suffers death. But never can he have the right and the power to lay it down so as to bring a sacrifice to God. He has the right to consecrate that life to God *in life*; he cannot possibly make it a gift in death. One must be more than a mere creature in order to lay down his life and to perform the atoning act of death. But to sustain, "ertragen," also expresses the notion of *endurance to the end.* In order to satisfy the justice of God, one must be able to *finish* the act of bearing the punishment against sin. He must get through with it. If he does not finish it, he must be crushed under the burden of the wrath of God, and there is no deliverance. In other words, he must have the authority so to lay down his life, that by this act he obtains the right to take it again. And he must also have the power, the ability, the capacity, so to lay down his life that through death he will live. He must be able to live and act even while he is dying, and so performing the act of death he must emerge from all death as the living one. And it is evident that no mere creature can ever emerge from death in his own power. He has no life in himself to overcome death. It is evident, then, that no one who is not more than a creature could ever *sustain* the wrath of God.

Besides, the Catechism reminds us, that a substitute must so bear and sustain the burden of the wrath of God, that he delivers others from it. And this implies, first of all, that by the act of laying down his life, such a creature must obtain the *right,* according to the justice of God, to deliver many from that wrath and to restore them to God's favor. And how could a mere creature ever so perform the act of death? Suppose there were a creature that had a life to offer, and that was able to offer it to God in sacrifice; and suppose such a creature was in a position to offer it as a substitute; how could the sacrifice of that one life ever serve as a substitute except for only one other life similar to the life that was offered? A mere creature is never capable of bringing a sacrifice for many. But it implies, secondly, that after the creature has sacrificed his life, he must have the power to actually deliver us from death and impart new life to us. We *are* in death. We are not like prisoners that have been condemned to death and still await the execution of that sentence; we are already in the power of death. We must be delivered. We must be quickened. And one that is to save us, must have the power so to deliver us that the shackles of death are broken and we are quickened unto new life. But to speak of the possibility that a mere creature, that has no life in himself, would have the power to deliver us after he laid down his life as a sacrifice for sin, is absurd.

The conclusion, therefore, is that as far as we are concerned the way is closed. There is no possibility of satisfaction. Our case is strictly hopeless. We can sin, but we can never atone. We could fall from a state of righteousness by wilfull disobedience, but we can never return to that state. We can make ourselves worthy of God's wrath and of His just sentence of eternal damnation, but we can never do anything or bring anything to God that will again make us worthy of His favor. We can cast ourselves into the prison of sin and death, as we did through the fall and disobedience of our first parents in paradise, but after we do so the door is locked and we can never unlock it: the justice of God keeps it securely barred. And not only is there no power or possibility in and with us to deliver us, but in all creation there is no hope. Wherever we turn, there is no possibility of satisfaction. There is no way out!

III

The Possibility of Satisfaction

Where, then, must we look for salvation? If there is no hope
in self, and if in all the universe there cannot be found a creature
that is able to bring satisfaction for sin and to deliver us from
the guilt and power of sin and death, whither shall we turn?
That is the next question asked by the instructor in our Heidelberg Catechism. What sort of a mediator and deliverer then
must we seek for? It would seem that there is no longer room
for a question such as this. The way has been closed. It would
appear that all possibilities have been considered and thoroughly
investigated. We must satisfy the justice of God, and we cannot.
Unless that justice of God is fully satisfied we cannot be received
again into the favor of God. We have no right to be delivered
from the power of sin and death, no right to life, unless the
justice of God be first completely satisfied. But it seems that this
is an impossible demand. The condition of satisfaction, so we
have seen, we can never meet. Nor is there another creature, a
mere creature that can take our place in the judgment of God and
satisfy in our stead and in our behalf. Must we, then, not give up
all hope? And is it not absurd at this point to ask the question:
what sort of a mediator must we then look for? It certainly would
be, if the question meant that we should investigate once more
the possibility of salvation on our part. But this is not the intent
of the question. It is not the natural man, but the believer that
asks this question concerning a possible mediator and deliverer
after all creaturely possibilities have been exhausted. It is a
question of faith. And faith is an evidence of things unseen, the
substance of things hoped for. It regards not the things that are
seen, but the things that are not seen. It clings to God as seeing
the Invisible. It is not desperate, it does not hopelessly give up
the search after salvation when it is proved that there is no

hope in the creature. It knows that with God all things are possible. It understands that it is the glory of God to reveal His power and wisdom exactly there where human power is utterly inadequate. And so, it is not dismayed, but rises from the creature to the almighty God. And it is that faith that continues the search for salvation and asks: what sort of a mediator and deliverer must we then seek for?

We must understand that the Catechism here does not yet speak of the real, but only of the possible mediator. It intends to demonstrate in the next Lord's Day the necessity of the incarnation. It would give an answer to the question of Anselm: *Cur Deus homo?* why must God become man? This answer is supplied in the first two questions of the next Lord's Day. It might appear as if logically this question should have been the first question of Lord's Day VI. Yet, this is not the case. The question as it appears here, at the end of Lord's Day V is a summary and conclusion. The instructor of our Heidelberg considers, as it were, once more the condition of the sinner with a view to possible salvation. It measures carefully the gap caused by the fall of man, in order to ask the question what kind of a deliverer would be able to fill that gap. And it reaches the conclusion that only a mediator that is real and righteous man, and that is at the same time very God, would be able to fulfill all the conditions of a deliverer from sin and death. We must look: "for one who is very man, and perfectly righteous; and yet more powerful than all creatures; that is, one who is also very God."

This, then, is the conclusion after careful consideration of the condition of the sinner in the light of God's demand for satisfaction of His justice, and after investigation of all possible creaturely mediators and deliverers. For, as we consider our condition and measure the gap made by our fall into sin and our rebellion against the living God, we find that we must have a mediator, one who mediates in our behalf, who takes our place in judgment and makes satisfaction in our stead, for we ourselves could never bring that satisfaction. He must, therefore, be a representative person, for otherwise he had not the right to substitute himself for us. We found, too, that he must be a man, for only in the human nature will God punish the sin man committed. He must be very man, flesh of our flesh, blood of our blood, living our human life, and entering into our human experience. He must be able to bring the sacrifice of his life and enter into all the suffering of death *willingly,* and make of death an act of love. He must, therefore, not be a sinner, but a perfectly righteous man. However, we found, too, that a mere creature is not sufficient, for he must be able to deliver many, and his sacrifice must have infinite value. Besides, he must be able to die and live, to lay down his life and to take it again, and to deliver us from the power of death and impart eternal life to us. He must, therefore, be more than mere creature, that is, he must be very God. And so the Catechism draws the conclusion that our condition is such, that, if we are to be saved, there is only one "sort of mediator" that can meet all the requirements and fulfill all the conditions: Immanuel, God with us, the Son of God in the flesh!

The reasons for the necessity of the incarnation with a view to our salvation we need not now discuss in detail, for the Catechism considers them in the next Lord's Day. But surely, the question forces itself upon our minds and hearts: how must it be explained that the condition of fallen man is such that his salvation requires the incarnation of the Son of God? Here we meet with a striking phenomenon! The state of fallen man is exactly such that only a divine-human mediator can save him! The gap which he caused by his fall and disobedience is exactly of such size and shape that the incarnated Son and He alone fits in it! How must this be explained? Surely, one cannot be so blind as to attribute this striking fact to mere accident or coincidence? There must be a plan and purpose behind all this. The one must be adapted to the other. When you see a large building erected, and you notice that as the walls are being built by the masons large rectangular gaps are left therein; and as you continue watching the construction of that edifice you discover that in those holes left in the walls window frames are placed that fit exactly in the gaps to fill them, you do not conclude that it is a happy accident that those windows exactly fill those holes in the walls, but you know that the latter were intentionally built into the wall, in order that there might be room for the former. There is purpose, there is design in the work of the builders. Well, here you behold a condition of fallen man that requires the incarnation of the Son of God, if man is to be saved. Would you conclude that this is a mere coincidence? Or shall we say, that the incarnation of the Son of God is an afterthought of the Most High, and that it is *determined* by the fall and disobedience of man? Would you say that the shape and size of the windows in the edifice of our illustration were determined by the shape and size of the holes that were left in the walls by the builders? You reply, of course, that exactly the opposite is true: the latter are determined by the former; the architect has designed exactly those particular windows for that building, and the holes were left in the walls accordingly. But would you, then, speak differently of the work of the Most High? Would you say that it is a terrible accident that man by his disobedience caused the gap of sin and death, and that afterwards the incarnation of the Son of God was designed to fill that gap? You know better. How then could God be GOD? Rather, when you examine the condition of man from every aspect from the viewpoint of the question of his salvation; and when you discover that there is one and only one possibility of his salvation: the coming of the Son of God in the flesh; you draw the conclusion that the former must serve the latter: the fall and disobedience of man, the temptation of the devil, and all the work of darkness must serve the purpose of opening the way for the coming of Immanuel. For, He is the Firstborn of every creature. And by him were all things created, that are in heaven, and that are in earth, visible and invisible, whether they be thrones, or dominions, or principalities, or powers: all things were created by him, and for him. And he is before all things, and by him all things consist. And he is the head of the body, the church: who is the beginning, the firstborn from the dead; that in all things he might have the pre-eminence. For it pleased the Father that in him should all fulness dwell. Col. 1:15-19. And, therefore, as we stand by the gap caused by the fall and disobedience of man, and discover that only Immanuel fits into the gap to save us, we know that divine wisdom so designed all things that even our sin must serve the purpose of opening the way for the coming of the Son of God in the flesh. O the depth of riches both of the wisdom and knowledge of God! how unsearchable are his judgments, and his ways past finding out!

LORD'S DAY VI

Q. 16. Why must he be very man, and also perfectly righteous?

A. Because the justice of God requires that the same human nature which hath sinned, should likewise make satisfaction for sin; and one, who is himself a sinner, cannot satisfy for others.

Q. 17. Why must he in one person be also very God?

A. That he might, by the power of his Godhead sustain in his human nature, the burden of God's wrath; and might obtain for, and restore to us, righteousness and life.

Q. 18. Who then is that Mediator, who is in one person both very God, and a real righteous man?

A. Our Lord Jesus Christ: "who of God is made unto us wisdom and righteousness, and sanctification, and redemption."

Q. 19. Whence knowest thou this?

A. From the holy gospel, which God himself first revealed in Paradise; and afterwards published by the patriarchs and prophets, and represented by the sacrifices and and other ceremonies of the law, and lastly, has fulfilled it by his only begotten Son.

I

The Necessity Of The Incarnation

There is some difference between the original German text of
the answer to question eighteen, and our translation of it. The
German reads: "Unser Herr Jesus Christus, der uns zu vollkom-
menen Erlösing und Gerechtigkeit geschenkt ist." In English the
correct rendering would be: "Our Lord Jesus Christ, who is
given unto us for complete redemption and righteousness." Our
translation follows the Latin text, which in turn, evidently followed the text of I Cor. 1:30: "But of him are ye in Christ Jesus,
who of God is made unto us wisdom, and righteousness, and sanctification, and redemption." To the sense, however it makes no
real difference, whether the one or the other translation is
adopted, though it must be remembered that the one that follows
the German text, which is the original, is the more correct one.

As to the contents of this sixth Lord's Day, the first two questions are still concerned with the question of a possible mediator,
and, particularly, with the necessity of his being both very God
and real righteous man in unity of person; the third question
places us at once before the real Mediator, our Lord Jesus Christ,
in all the fulness of His saving riches and power; and the last
question points to the holy gospel as the source of our knowledge
of this Mediator.

As we consider the first two questions of this sixth Lord's Day,
we are once more impressed by the fact that our instructor takes
his time about the matter. We are even inclined to remark that
he is rather slow in coming to the point. After investigating the
possibility of salvation, and insisting on the necessity of satisfaction; and after having pointed out the impossibility of satisfaction by man himself, or by any other, mere creature; the
Catechism had, in the previous Lord's Day, reached the conclusion, that if ever we are to be saved it must be through a mediator

that is at once very God, and real righteous man. And now, in the sixth Lord's Day, instead of immediately pointing to the only Mediator of God and man, the instructor first devotes two more questions to a *possible* mediator, and to the reasons why he must meet some very definite requirements. Ministers that are required to preach on the Catechism must often have the feeling, when they reach this sixth Lord's Day, that it is difficult to avoid repetition of what was already treated in connection with the preceding Lord's Day. And, in fact, there is a measure of repetition here. What is stated negatively in Lord's Day V, to make plain that it is impossible for man or for a mere creature to bring the required satisfaction, is here stated positively. There it is explained that God will not punish any other creature for the sin man committed; here it is stated that God requires that the same human nature that has sinned shall make satisfaction for sin. There we were taught that we ourselves cannot make the required satisfaction, because we are sinners, and can only increase our debt; here we are told that one who is himself a sinner cannot satisfy for others. There the reason why no mere creature can deliver us was found in the fact that a mere creature cannot sustain the wrath of God and deliver others from it; here we are taught that a possible mediator must be very God, in order that, by the power of his Godhead, he might be able to sustain the wrath of God, and that he might be able to obtain for us, and to restore to us righteousness and life. There can be no question about the fact, therefore, that there is a measure of repetition of what was treated before in this sixth Lord's Day. The same arguments are used. Only, while in the previous Lord's Day the instructor adduced these arguments to demonstrate the impossibility of salvation by man or any other, mere, creature; in this Lord's Day the same elements are brought forward in order to give reasons for the necessity of the incarnation. This, therefore, must be borne in mind when we explain the first two questions of Lord's Day VI. And when we consider them from this viewpoint, we can appreciate the fact that the instructor is rather slow in coming to the point, and that he demonstrates the necessity of the real manhood, the righteous manhood, the very God-

head, and the unity of the person of the mediator that is to deliver us from sin and death.

We must remember that, at a very early date in the history of
the New Testament Church, all these different elements of the
truth concerning the Saviour were denied, one after another, by
false teachers. It was denied that Christ possessed a real and
complete human nature. There were some who taught that His
human nature was only such in appearance, not in reality, not
of our flesh and blood; even as angels can and often did assume
the appearance of men for a time, so the Son of God assumed
the resemblance of a human nature. There were others, who
insisted that Christ assumed only a partial, not a whole or complete human nature: the Son of God, the divine nature, took
upon Himself a human body and a human soul, but no human
"mind," or "spirit." The divine nature took the place of the
human *nous* or mind. Then, too, at an early date of our era, the
real and essential Godhead of Christ was attacked and denied:
Christ was a highly gifted and exalted man, who, according to
His exalted position and office, is worthy of the title "Son of
God," but who is not one in essence and co-eternal with the
Father and the Holy Ghost. Again, by some, both the real Godhead and the real manhood of Christ were denied, when they explained that through the incarnation the human and divine
natures had merged or fused into one nature. They preferred
to speak of the Lord Jesus Christ as the Godman, the "Theanthropos." And, on the other hand, by others the unity of the
two natures in the one person was denied; and they so separated
the two natures that Christ really became two persons. This
controversy about the person of the Mediator was brought to a
close, as far as the Church was concerned, by the decisions of the
council of Chalcedon, in 381, which declared that Christ is very
God and real righteous man, and that the two natures of Christ
subsist in unity of divine Person, without change, without mixture, without division, and without separation.

When one considers these early attacks upon the truth concerning the Saviour, His person and natures, and is aware of the
fact that all or most of these heresies repeatedly arise in the

Church on earth, and attempt to destroy the true Christian doctrine concerning Christ and salvation, he will be able to appreciate properly the efforts put forth by the Heidelberg Catechism to demonstrate the *necessity* of the two natures, and of the unity of the person of Christ. For by so doing, it emphasizes the importance and preciousness of the truth, and it impresses upon believers the urgency of the calling to maintain and defend the true faith in all its purity of doctrine. It shows that there is an inseparable relation between our salvation and true doctrine. Salvation cannot be accomplished except by exactly such a mediator as is described in these two questions and answers with respect to his chief requirements. Deny them, and you deny salvation. Deny that Christ is eternal God, the second person of the Holy Trinity, and you have no Saviour left. Deny that He is very man, flesh of our flesh, and blood of our blood, and you lose the Christ of God. Deny that these two natures are never separated, nor ever mixed, but that they subsist in unity of the divine person of the Son of God, and you deny all possibility of salvation. By demonstrating this, the Catechism certainly impresses upon our minds and hearts the necessity of being indoctrinated thoroughly in the truth of the Word of God. And it warns us that we shall not assume a sympathetic attitude toward those that would introduce false doctrine into the Church of Christ in the world.

The Catechism considers the necessity of the incarnation only from the viewpoint of its relation to our salvation. This is wholly in accord with its practical character. It is possible, of course, to view this necessity from a different aspect, and to consider it from a higher, a theological point of view. The ultimate reason for all necessity, for every "must," is the eternal counsel and good pleasure of God. It was God's eternal purpose that in Christ as the incarnated, crucified, raised and glorified Son of God, all the fulness of God should dwell bodily. And as we stressed before, this is not an afterthought of God, so that Christ is appointed only to repair what has been marred and destroyed by sin and the devil; but it is God's first and only final purpose. He purposed to reveal Himself, and to realize His everlasting covenant, and thus to glorify His holy name, in the highest possible degree. And this revelation is to be realized in Christ, the Son in the flesh, crucified and raised from the dead. Thus it is God's good pleasure. And it is for this reason that Christ is called the firstborn of every creature, i.e. the firstborn in and according to the eternal counsel of God, for whom and through whom, and unto whom all things are created. If we consider the necessity of the incarnation from this higher viewpoint, even sin and death, the devil and all the powers of darkness, are but means unto an end: they are subservient to God's purpose of bringing His Son into the world, and of realizing in and through Him all His good pleasure. However, our instructor does not consider the necessity of the incarnation in its relation to God and His eternal good pleasure, but in its soteriological relation to sin and salvation.

Why, then, must our mediator be very man, real man, and also perfectly righteous? The Catechism answers that he must be very man because satisfaction must be made in the human nature, the same human nature that has sinned; and that he must be righteous man, because no sinner could satisfy for the sin of others. He must be *very*, i.e. real man. And a real man is one that partakes of our human nature. He must not assume a temporary appearance of a human being, for then he is not related to us. He must not come in a specially created human nature, for then he stands outside of the scope of our race. He must be of us. He must subsist in the very human nature that was created in the beginning, and as far as his humanity is concerned, he must have been with us in the loins of Adam. He must be a very real "son of man." This is necessary, for otherwise He cannot make the required satisfaction. As we have seen before, God will not punish the sin of man in another creature. This same truth is now positively stated: "the justice of God requires that the same human nature which hath sinned, should likewise make satisfaction for sin." The punishment inflicted must be equivalent to the sin committed; the evil suffered must be commensurate to the evil done. Such is God's justice. Human sin is sin committed in and through human nature, the human soul, the human mind and will and heart, the human body, the human eye and ear and mouth and hand and foot; such sin can be atoned for only by suffering human punishment, i.e. death in the human nature. A cow or a dog could not possibly receive the punishment for sin committed in the human nature. We may add here, that Christ must also be very man, and actually subsist in our nature, because as mediator He must be able to deliver us from death, and impart His own new resurrection-life to us, and this is possible only if He is organically related to us, if He partakes of our human nature. It would be quite impossible to transfuse the blood of a horse into the veins of a human body; and similarly, the resurrected Lord could never transfuse His own life into our hearts, if He were not related to us. A mediator that is to save us, i.e. who is to make the required satisfaction, and who is also able to deliver us from the power of sin and the dominion of death, and give us new life, must be very man.

But he must also be perfectly righteous. This means, first of all, that he must not fall under the imputation of Adam's first transgression. Though, according to his nature, he is like us in all respects, and was with us in the loins of Adam, yet he must not personally stand in the same relation to the first man Adam as we. He must have no original guilt. Secondly, this also implies that he must be free from original pollution. Even though he is a son of man, born of woman, blood of our blood, and flesh of our flesh, yet the defilement and pollution that adheres to all men, to the whole human nature, may not cleave to him. He must be perfectly righteous. And the reason which the Heidelberg Catechism here gives is, that "one, who is himself a sinner, cannot satisfy for others." The underlying thought here seems to be that one, who is himself a sinner, would have to satisfy for himself, and could never apply his satisfaction to others. And this is self evident. But we may go a step further, and say that no sinner can bring the required satisfaction at all, not even for himself. This truth we have repeatedly tried to make plain. Let it suffice now, therefore, to remind ourselves that to satisfy the justice of God with respect to sin, one must be able to bring the perfect sacrifice of love. Nothing else will do. And one, who is himself a sinner, is wholly incapable to bring that sacrifice. A mediator, that is to save us, therefore, must be perfectly righteous; he must have neither original guilt, nor original pollution; and all his life and death must be perfectly consecrated to the living God.

But why must our mediator also be very God? In the conclusion of the previous Lord's Day it was stated that the "sort of a mediator" we need must be "more powerful than all creatures, that is, one who is also very God." Let us take note of this, lest we receive a wrong conception of what this name "mediator" indicates. Often it is presented as if a mediator is someone, who stands in between God and man. They, i.e. God and man, are at variance. They are separated from each other. And now a third party interposes himself between them to bring them together. He reconciles God to man, and man to God. But let us notice here, that the Catechism knows nothing of intermediary beings between God and man. A mere creature, so it is taught us, cannot sustain the wrath of God and deliver others. Very well; a mediator must, therefore, be more powerful than any mere creature. Does that mean that we must look for a third, a kind of intermediate being, that is greater than all creatures, yet is not very God? But no; if mere creature is incapable of sustaining the wrath of God, there is only one other possibility: that God does it Himself! O, indeed, the mediator we need must also be very man. He must be God and man united. But do not make the mistake that for this reason you consider this mediator a sort of intermediate being, standing between God and man. For such a mediator, who is real man and very God, could not possibly come into being by an act of God and man both, by each coming half way to meet the other; but the very idea of such a mediator implies that God Himself comes down, reaches down all the way to man's low estate, to become His own mediator in our behalf!

Very God the mediator must be. That means that He must be of the divine essence. He must be the eternal One Himself, the I AM, the infinite God, Who exists in Himself, and has life in

Himself, Who is the almighty, the allwise, the omniscient, the Lord of all! The mediator must not be a god, but he must be very God! For, first of all, the Catechism reminds us, he must sustain, "ertagen," bear completely, bear through, and bear to the end, the wrath of God against sin; and this no mere creature can do. There must be divine power to bear to the end, and to bear away, to bear and live through divine wrath. Hence, the mediator we need must be very God. And there must be a very intimate relation, a close union between the divine and the human nature of this mediator. For, although the mere human nature could never sustain the wrath of God and live, yet, it must be in that human nature that the wrath of God must be borne! The divine nature could not be the object of the divine wrath. Nor can the divine nature suffer and die. The relation between the real manhood and true Godhead of this mediator, therefore, must be such, that in the human nature the divine nature sustains the infinite wrath of God, that God bears the punishment for sin in the human nature! He must, therefore, not only be real man and very God, but be man and God in one person! Only then can he sustain the wrath of God to the end and live. Only then can he give infinite value to His atoning sacrifice. And only then can he deliver us from the power of sin and death, and restore to us righteousness and life! Indeed, the incarnation is necessary. Without it there is no possible salvation.

II

The Mediator Of God And Man

Who then is that Mediator, who is in one person both very
God, and a real righteous man? For this question we, perhaps,
had been looking for some time. We probably grew impatient
with the Catechism as it discussed the hopelessness of our condition, the impossibility of salvation on our part, and the question
of a possible Mediator, the necessity of His being true and
eternal God and real righteous man in one person. And all the
while we were left groping in the darkness of our sin and misery.
Yet, we saw how essential it is for the maintenance of the true
doctrine concerning our salvation that these matters be emphasized, and not lightly passed over. For, on the one hand, it must
be clearly and fully understood, before we can even begin to
speak of a Saviour and salvation, that with us the matter is
strictly without hope. In no sense can we accomplish our own
salvation, or any part of it. And, on the other hand, we must
see sharply and clearly that no other Mediator than the Christ
of the Scriptures can possibly help us, so that to falsify this
Christ, to adulterate the truth concerning Him as revealed to us
in the holy gospel, is to shut out all possibility of salvation. The
questions the Heidelberg Catechism thus far discussed may appear abstract and academic, they are, nevertheless, intensely
practical, questions of life and death. However, now it has been
clearly demonstrated and firmly established that we need just
such a Mediator, who is both God and man, and that, too, a
righteous man, the Catechism all of a sudden unveils before our
longing eyes the complete figure of a real and only Mediator of
God and man, in all the fulness of His glory and blessings of
salvation! For in answer to the question: "Who then is that
Mediator?" it declares: "Our Lord Jesus Christ: 'who of God

is made unto us wisdom, and righteousness, and sanctification, and redemption.' "

In this procedure of the Catechism, according to which it now places us at once before the Christ in all His fulness and significance, before it explains Him in the details of His blessedness, there is an underlying truth to which we may well call attention. It is this, that faith receives and embraces Christ Himself, before it can possibly appropriate any of the blessings of salvation, yea, even before it fully understands the significance of His Person and work. Christ Himself is the fulness of our salvation. It is Himself we receive. Himself He imparts to us through faith by His Spirit. We do not receive Him piecemeal, bit by bit; we do not receive the blessings of salvation one by one until gradually we have appropriated the whole Christ and all His benefits: we receive Him! Into Him we are ingrafted by a true faith. Members of His body we do become, both legally and organically by that same faith. And when thus we have become His possession, one plant with Him, we possess Him in all His fulness. We say: "Our Lord Jesus Christ!" And that is our salvation. We may grow in the knowledge of Him through the Holy Scriptures. And growing in knowledge we may attain to a fuller understanding of the confession expressed in the words: our Lord Jesus Christ. But although we may, and actually do, thus grow in grace and in the enjoyment of the liberty we have in Christ, from the very first moment of our being grafted into Him, our faith lays hold on Him, on the whole of Him. To say "*our* Lord Jesus Christ," is, indeed, to be saved! To say that Jesus is Lord, *our* Lord, is to possess *Him*, all at once, in all the fulness of His grace! For that reason the method followed by the Catechism is quite correct. It will explain all the implications of the answer it here gives in future chapters. But here it confronts the faith of the Christian with the full Christ, in order that from the depths of our misery we may at once rise to the heights of complete salvation by appropriating Him, and confessing in spiritual joy: "Our Lord Jesus Christ!"

To expound this answer in all its implications this is not the place. It would mean to explain all the details of the doctrine concerning our salvation. And this is to be done in succeeding chapters. Here we must be satisfied with the main features of this Christ as they are drawn before the eyes of our faith by the Catechism in a few bold strokes. The answer here given is literally taken from I Cor. 1:30: "But of him are ye in Christ Jesus, who of God is made unto us wisdom, and righteousness, and sanctification, and redemption." The general meaning of this text is plain: Christ is our all, our complete redemption. There is a question, however, as to the relation between the various concepts occurring in the text: wisdom, righteousness, sanctification, redemption. The question is especially whether *wisdom* is to be regarded as the main concept, so that the other three: *righteousness, sanctification, redemption,* are explanations of this one term. The Revised Version suggests this meaning in a marginal note that would translate the text thus: "But of him are ye in Christ Jesus, who was made unto us wisdom from God, both righteousness and sanctification and redemption." And there is something in favor of this interpretation. For, first of all, in the context the apostle had emphasized this notion of wisdom, in fact, it may be said to be the main theme of the chapter from verse eighteen to the end. The wisdom of the world is contrasted with the wisdom of God in the "foolishness" of preaching. "God hath made foolish the wisdom of the world. For seeing that in the wisdom of God the world through (its) wisdom knew not God, it was God's good pleasure through the foolishness of preaching to save them that believe." vss. 20, 21. Moreover, this wisdom of God is power, power to save, which seems to favor the idea that in vs. 30 also wisdom is looked upon as a power of righteousness, sanctification, and redemption, "Seeing that the Jews ask for signs, and Greeks seek after wisdom: but we preach Christ crucified, unto the Jews a stumbling-block, and unto the Gentiles foolishness; but unto them that are called, both Jews and Greeks, Christ the power of God, and the wisdom of God. Because the foolishness of God is wiser than men, and the weakness of God is stronger than men." vss. 22-25. And the order in the original of verse 30 seems to favor somewhat the translation as suggested by the marginal note of the Revised

Version. However, these arguments are not conclusive. In fact, if the apostle had meant to give the last three terms as explanations of the term *sophia,* wisdom, he could, and in all probability would have expressed himself more clearly and precisely. However, in the original the terms *righteousness* and *sanctification* are certainly more closely connected with each other than with either *wisdom* or *redemption.* And, therefore, we would favor the translation: "But of him are ye in Christ Jesus, who of God is made unto us wisdom, also both righteousness and sanctification, and redemption."

One more remark we must make about the relative position and value of the various terms in the text. It cannot but draw our attention that the word *redemption* stands at the end of the series. However, in the work of salvation redemption is not last, but first. Christ is first our redemption, and because He is our redemption He is our wisdom, righteousness, and sanctification. For redemption is the purchasing free of one that is in bondage, the effecting of one's release by paying the price, the ransom. Now, it is clear from all Scripture that this is first, and basic for all the other blessings of grace. Redemption presupposes that we are guilty, and that we are legally in the bondage of sin and death. We have no right to be delivered from that bondage. We are legally shut up in the prison of the lie, unrighteousness and corruption. If, then, we are to be liberated, the price, the ransom must be paid for us. Before we even can have the right to become partakers of wisdom, righteousness, and sanctification, we must be redeemed. This price of our redemption was paid for us by Christ on the accursed tree, where He bore the punishment of our sin in most perfect obedience to the Father. And because of this, on the basis of this, He is also become our wisdom, our righteousness, and our sanctification. That the word redemption has the last place in the series of terms, therefore, is not because it is actually last, but because it has the emphasis. Christ is become our wisdom, and righteousness, and sanctification, because He is our redemption.

A more beautiful passage of Scripture the Heidelberg Catechism could not very well have selected for its present purpose than the text from First Corinthians. For, as we have stated, it is the purpose of our instructor to place before us all at once the fulness of the Christ in all the riches of His salvation. And for this the text from Corinthians is eminently fit. For notice that the text does not state merely what Jesus *did* for us, or still *does* for us, nor even what He *gives* unto us, but what He *is* to us. He is made or become unto us wisdom, righteousness and sanctification, and redemption. He *is* all this for us. The Christ of the Scriptures, the Son of God come into the flesh, born of a virgin, Who sojourned among us and revealed the Father unto us, Who suffered under Pontius Pilate, was crucified on Golgotha, buried in the sepulchre of Joseph of Arimathea, was raised on the third day, ascended into the highest heavens from the Mount of Olives, and was exalted by the mighty power of God on the right hand of the Majesty in heaven, far above all principalities and powers, and every name that is named both in this world and in the world to come,—that Christ *is* unto us wisdom from God, righteousness and sanctification, and redemption. O, indeed, He merited this all for us by His work of perfect obedience; He revealed it all to us both personally and through the prophets and apostles; He gives all this to us, making us partakers of it all through the Spirit that was given unto Him and that was poured out into the Church. But even this does not fully explain what is expressed in the text: He was made, He became unto us wisdom, righteousness and sanctification, and redemption. He *is* our all! To lay hold on Him by faith is to appropriate wisdom, righteousness and sanctification, and redemption. To see ourselves by faith in Him, is to see ourselves filled with wisdom, perfectly liberated from the bondage of sin, righteous and holy. To know Him is to know the wisdom of God; to trust in Him is to be righteous, and holy, and free. To possess Him is to possess salvation, righteousness, and eternal life and glory!

And the terms employed here do, indeed, express a fulness of salvation. Our Lord Jesus Christ is truly the Mediator we need, and beyond Him we need none other. For we are guilty, and to blot out our guilt by complete satisfaction of the justice of God is absolutely required in order to be restored to the favor of

God. And this we could never do in ourselves. We need, therefore, one that is our redemption. And this is our Lord Jesus Christ, who was delivered for our transgressions, and raised for our justification. To believe in Him is to be liberated from the dominion of sin according to God's own justice. But redemption is not enough. We are actually in the prison of sin, dead through trespasses, and we must be delivered. We are blind, and our mind is in darkness. We are slaves of the lie, in bondage to the foolishness of spiritual ignorance. We grope in darkness, we hate the good, we hold the truth under in unrighteousness. And moreover, we exist in a world in which the wrath of God is revealed from heaven, and from the testimony of that wrath there is no escape. There is no way out. No philosophy of man can help us. "The world by its wisdom knew not God." But Christ is our wisdom! Not only did He reveal the Father unto us, and did He make known the full counsel of salvation, but He Himself, in His Person and work, *is* the wisdom of God; and by His Spirit and grace through faith He is our wisdom. He is the light in our darkness, the solution of all mysteries, the way out of sin and death into the light of life! He is our righteousness and sanctification. In the judgment of God we stand condemned in ourselves, both because of our original and our actual sins. But Christ *is* our righteousness, and, therefore, our eternal life. For in Him there is a righteousness that far transcends the righteousness of the first Adam before the fall. He Himself, the Christ of the Scriptures, is that righteousness that is worthy of glory and immortality. And in ourselves we are dead in sin, polluted and defiled, hating God and hating one another, seeking the things of the flesh rather than the things that are above. But Christ *is* our sanctification, our complete purification, and our consecration to the living God. No, indeed, if the instructor of our Catechism purposed to bring before us all at once the image or revelation of the full Christ in all His glory and power of salvation, it could not do better than quote this significant passage from First Corinthians.

We must note, too, that in this answer of the Heidelberg Catechism it is emphasized that this Mediator is all of God. In fact, this is one of the main thoughts in the text as it is found in Corinthians. O, indeed, it is our salvation that is accomplished through this "Lord Jesus Christ." But even that salvation is not the chief purpose of this Mediator and His revelation. On the contrary, the wisdom of the world must be made foolish, and the power of the world must be put to nought. It must be revealed that the foolishness of God is wiser than men, and the weakness of God is stronger than men. And, therefore, God chose the foolish things of the world, that he might put to shame them that are wise; and God chose the weak things of the world, that he might put to shame the things that are strong; and the base things of the world, and the things that are despised, did God choose, yea, and the things that are not, that he might bring to nought the things that are, vss. 27, 28. For no flesh may ever glory before God, but he that glorieth must glory in the Lord. Hence, this Mediator is made unto us all that He is from God. He is *Mediator,* indeed, but not one whom we interposed between God and ourselves, or whom we appointed or requested or even desired and sought that He might act in our behalf with the Most High. He *mediates* in our behalf, but not as a *third party* that places himself between two contending parties in order to reconcile them. He is from God! There is nothing in Him that is to be attributed to us. God's Mediator is He, made of God, and wholly commissioned by God in order to accomplish the things of God, even in behalf of us.

For notice that He *became,* or *was made* unto us wisdom, and righteousness and sanctification, and redemption, and that this is all from God. He became all this unto us by a wonder of the Triune God, Father, Son, and Holy Ghost, and according to His eternal good pleasure. For it was determined from before the foundation of the world that the Son should be the revelation of all the fulness of God, the first born of every creature, and the first begotten of the dead. And to Him was given the Church, for we are chosen in Him (Eph. 1:4), that He might redeem that Church unto Himself and to God, and through the deep way of death might justify, and purify, and glorify that Church, in order that the fulness of God's glory, dwelling in Him, might be revealed in manifold reflections of grace and beauty through the millions upon millions of the members of His body. And thus He was, from before the foundation of the world, made wisdom, and righteousness and sanctification, and redemption, and that, too, *unto us* that are chosen in Him. And all this was realized in time. From God He became or was made the fulness of salvation, righteousness, and eternal life. He became all this from the manger of Bethlehem to the cross of Golgotha, and *through* the death of the cross into the highest glory of his position at the right hand of the Most High. And all this was the work of God. The incarnation of the Word, the work of Jesus' ministry, the death of the Son of God, the resurrection of Jesus Christ from the dead, His ascension into heaven and His exaltation far above all principalities and powers,—all this belongs to His *becoming* or *being made* unto us wisdom, and righteousness and sanctification, and redemption. Not until He travelled the way from the incarnation through death to glory is "Our Lord Jesus Christ" perfected, completed, fully made, as the revelation of the God of our salvation. And not until this glorious Lord has received the Spirit of promise, and poured out that Spirit into the Church, is He become salvation *unto us.* And all this is of God, of the triune God. Of the Father, through the Son, in the Holy Spirit, are all the works of God, both in creation and in redemption. And of the Father, through the Son, in the Spirit, i.e. of the one God and Father of our Lord Jesus Christ, are the incarnation, and the ministry, the death and resurrection, the ascension and the exaltation and the outpouring of the Spirit, of "our Lord Jesus Christ." And so it is all of God, even also that we are in Him. For "*of him* are ye in Christ Jesus, who was made unto us wisdom *from God,* and righteousness and sanctification, and redemption." He that glorieth, let him glory in the Lord!

III

The Holy Gospel

"Whence knowest thou this?" Whence knowest thou that our
Lord Jesus Christ is "that Mediator, who is in one person both
very God, and a real righteous man?" And whence knowest thou
that this Mediator is "of God made unto us wisdom, and righteousness, and sanctification, and redemption?" To this question
the Catechism gives one of the finest answers in the whole book
of instruction: "From the holy gospel, which God Himself first
revealed in Paradise; and afterwards published by the patriarchs
and prophets, and represented by the sacrifices and other ceremonies of the law; and lastly has fulfilled it by His only begotten
Son." This is a remarkable answer, indeed. We might, perhaps,
have expected that our instructor would have answered "I know
this from the Holy Scriptures, which are the infallible Word of
God, and my only rule for faith and life." But the Catechism,
evidently, had in mind the saints of all ages, and remembered,
that all the saints, both of the old and new dispensation, from
the very beginning of history, were saved through that same
Mediator, and must have possessed the same promise of salvation,
the same source of knowledge concerning this Mediator of God
and man, although they certainly did not possess the Holy Scriptures, from which we of the new dispensation derive the knowledge of the Christ. And, therefore, it calls our attention to the
holy gospel, and emphasizes that as long as there were heirs of
the promise in the world this holy gospel was delivered unto
them. And it also reminds us that this "holy gospel" is not merely
something that was preached from the beginning of the world,
but that it was also fulfilled in God's only begotten Son.

Very often we read of the "gospel" in Holy Writ. It is called
"the gospel of God" to emphasize its exclusively divine origin
and authorship. Rom. 1:1; II Cor. 11:7; I Thess. 2:8, 9; I Pet.

4:17. The gospel is not ours but God's. In no sense is it of human origin. God conceived of the gospel. He realized it, and He proclaims it. With a view to its contents this gospel of God is called the "gospel concerning His Son Jesus Christ our Lord," or simply "the gospel of His Son." Rom. 1:3, 9; Mk. 1:1. The contents of this gospel is, therefore, the revelation of the Son of God in the person of Jesus Christ our Lord. It is the "gospel of Christ," the Anointed of God, or "the gospel of Jesus Christ," the Anointed Saviour, "who shall save His people from their sins." Rom. 15:19; I Cor. 9:12; II Cor. 2:12; 9:13; 10:14; Gal. 1:17. It is defined as "the glorious gospel of the blessed God," and as "the gospel of the Kingdom"; or as "the gospel of the grace of God," and "the gospel of your salvation," "the gospel of peace." I Tim. 1:11; Matt. 4:23; 9:34; 24:14; Acts 20:24; Eph. 1:13; 6:15. All these terms describe "the holy gospel" as something **divine,** something that concerns the Son of God and our salvation, something that is not of this world, neither concerned with this world, but with things which "eye hath not seen, and ear hath not heard, neither have entered into the heart of man." It is concerning this "holy gospel" that the Catechism instructs us in its nineteenth answer.

It is evident from this answer of the Heidelberger that it conceives of a very intimate and close relationship between the gospel and the promise. For when it speaks of "the holy gospel" as being fulfilled in God's only begotten Son, it is thinking of the gospel as the promise of God. And this is quite in accord with the teachings of Scripture. In the Bible the words *epangelia* (promise), and *euangelion* (gospel) are synonyms. In the usage of the Church the two are often combined in the phrase: "the promise of the gospel." Thus our Heidelberger uses the term in its answer to the question: "What are sacraments?" The answer reads: "The sacraments are holy visible signs and seals, appointed of God for this end, that by the use thereof, He may more fully declare and seal to us the *promise of the gospel.*" And also in its answer to the question concerning the preaching of the Word as one of the keys of the kingdom, it employs the same term: "Thus: when according to the command of Christ, it is declared and publicly testified to all and every believer that, whenever they receive *the promise of the gospel* by a true faith, all their sins are really forgiven them of God, for the sake of Christ's merits," etc. Qu. 84. To denote the real nature of the gospel, however, it were better to turn this phrase about, and to speak of *the gospel of the promise.* The idea of the gospel is that it is good news concerning the promise. One that has some news to bring, in the name of God, concerning the promise, preaches the gospel. This idea is clearly expressed in Gal. 3:8: "And the Scripture, foreseeing that God would justify the heathen through faith, preached before the gospel unto Abraham, saying, In thee shall all nations be blessed." This last clause: "In thee shall all nations be blessed," is, of course, simply the promise. And the text declares that when God makes an announcement of this promise to Abraham, the gospel is preached to him. The gospel is, therefore, identified with the promise. It is the announcement of the promise. The same truth is expressed in Acts 13:32, 33: "And we declare unto you glad tidings (*euangelidzometha,* we preach the gospel), how that the promise which was made unto the fathers, God hath fulfilled the same unto us their children, in that He hath raised up Jesus again; as it is also written in the second psalm, 'Thou art my Son, this day have I begotten thee.'" It is evident that the promise here mentioned as being "made unto the fathers," is the same as the one mentioned in Gal. 3:8. The promise: "In thee shall all nations be blessed," is fulfilled in the resurrection of Jesus Christ from the dead. And also in the text from Acts the promise and the gospel are simply identified. When the apostles preached the gospel, they announced glad tidings concerning the fulfillment of the promise. If, therefore, we would understand what is meant by the gospel, we must inquire into the nature of the promise of God.

Very frequently the Bible speaks of the promise of God. Sometimes the plural, *promises,* is used to denote the manifold riches of the grace of God, in other passages the singular is employed to remind us that the promise of the gospel is essentially one. In Heb. 11:13 we read: "These all died in faith, not having received

the promises, but having seen them afar off, and were persuaded
of them, and embraced them, and confessed that they were
strangers and pilgrims on the earth." And at the close of that
marvellous chapter it is said with a view to all the saints of the
old dispensation: "And these all, having obtained a good report,
through faith, received not the promise: God having provided
some better thing for us, that they without us should not be made
perfect." These passages teach plainly that all through the old
dispensation there was *the* Promise, which was always the same.
As the Catechism teaches us, the gospel certainly was preached
to the saints from the very beginning. And the essence of that
gospel was *the* Promise. This promise was not yet fulfilled: they
did not receive the promise. But through the grace of God they
embraced the promise by faith, and they saw it afar off. Because
of that promise they lived in hope, and confessed that they were
strangers on the earth. So glorious was that promise even then,
that for the sake of it the saints of the old dispensation were
willing to forsake all rather than lose their hold on the promise.
They "subdued kingdoms, wrought righteousness, obtained
promises, stopped the mouths of lions, quenched the violence of
fire, escaped the edge of the sword, out of weakness were made
strong, waxed valiant in fight, turned to flight the armies of
the aliens. Women received their dead raised to life again; and
others were tortured, not accepting deliverance, that they might
obtain a better resurrection. And others had trials of cruel
mockings and scourgings, yea, moreover, of bonds and imprison-
ment: They were stoned, they were sawn asunder, they were
tempted, were slain with the sword: they wandered about in
sheepskins and goatskins; being destitute, afflicted, tormented:
(Of whom the world was not worthy) : they wandered in deserts,
and in mountains, and in dens, and in caves of the earth." How
glorious was the promise of the gospel, if even the distant view
of it could fill them with such zeal of faith, and endurance of
hope!

Of this promise also the epistle of Paul to the Galatians speaks.
For to Abraham and his seed were the promises made. 3:16. And
although the promise was temporarily placed under the law, yet

the law could not possibly make the promise of none effect. In fact, the promise remained the essential thing, even under the law. Gal. 3:17. For never was the inheritance of the law; always it was given to Abraham unconditionally by promise. And seeing that the true seed of the promise is Christ, we also are Abraham's seed if we are of Christ, and heirs according to the promise. 3:29. As to the contents of this promise, Scripture speaks of it as "the promise of the Holy Ghost," the exalted Christ received and poured out into the Church. And this promise of the Holy Ghost, which is the realization of the gospel that was preached to Abraham, and by which all the nations of the earth should be blessed, we also receive. Gal. 3:15. It is a promise "of the life that now is, and of that which is to come." I Tim. 4:8. "And this is the promise that He hath promised us, even eternal life." I John 2:25. It is the promise of His coming, II Pet. 3:4; the promise to enter into His rest, Heb. 4:1; the promise to be heir of the world, "for the promise, that he should be heir of the world, was not to Abraham, or to his seed, through the law, but through the righteousness of faith." Rom. 4:13. For this reason, Scripture speaks of "the Holy Spirit of promise": Eph. 1:13; and of "the children of the promise" that is of those children that, in distinction from mere children according to the flesh, are born in virtue of and through the power of the promise, Rom. 9:8; and of the heirs of the Promise, unto whom the Lord seals the riches of the promise and the inheritance with an oath, Heb. 6:17; 11:9. Hence, when the apostle Peter on the day of Pentecost, standing on the threshold of the new dispensation, preaches the gospel, he declares: "For unto you is the promise, and unto your children, and to all that are afar off, as many as the Lord our God shall call." Acts 2:39. The gospel, therefore, is the glad news concerning the promise that was given to Abraham and his seed, the heirs of the promise, chosen before the foundation of the world, as they walk in the midst of darkness of this sin-cursed world.

And this promise is sure. It can never fail. The Word of God can never be made of none effect. The "gospel of the promise" is, therefore, not to be changed into a vague, general, "well meaning offer of grace to all." For between "the gospel of the promise" and a "well meaning offer" there is as much difference as between day and night. The two have nothing in common. He that preaches a well meaning offer cannot preach the glad tidings of the promise. A well meaning offer depends for its realization, in part at least, on the will of him to whom the offer is made; a promise is as sure as the truth and integrity of him by whom the promise is made. Preach a "well meaning offer" and all certainty is gone, for the realization of this well meaning offer of grace and salvation is contingent on the will of man, of a man that is dead through trespasses and sins, and that will always despise the offer of grace. And if this is the case, salvation is a completely lost cause. But the promise rests in God alone, in the truth and faithfulness of the eternal, unchangeable God. The promise of the gospel signifies that the eternal God, Who can never deny Himself, bound Himself to give to the heirs of the promise, that is, to the elect, eternal life and all things. For also in this do the promise of the gospel and a well meaning offer of salvation differ: the latter is general and undefined, it can be made to all men without distinction; the former is particular and clearly defined: it concerns only those whom God in His eternal good pleasure ordained unto salvation.

And how could it be different? Is not God GOD? Is He not the only One, and there is none beside Him? And is He not the all-sufficient God in Himself, and the absolutely sovereign Potentate? Where, then, would be the party to whom God would promise anything or offer something, unless He Himself in His sovereign good pleasure ordained and formed that "party?" Indeed, if there is a promise of the gospel, it must follow that this promise is entirely His, conceived by Him, given by Him, realized by Him, bestowed by Him, and also the heirs of the promise are sovereignly determined by Him alone. Then God has sovereignly foreknown and foreordained the heirs of the promise in His everlasting counsel. For whom He hath foreknown, them He also did predestinate to be conformed according to the image of His Son; and whom He did predestinate, them He also called, and whom He called them He also justified, and whom He justified them He also glorified, Rom. 8:29, 30. The promise of the gospel is sure, but it is sure to the heirs of the promise alone. One may, therefore, preach the gospel promiscuously to all men without distinction, but a gospel without distinction he may preach to no one in the name of God. If he does, he makes God a liar, Christ powerless to save, the gospel of none effect, and the assurance of the believer groundless. But, according to Holy Scripture, God's promise is sure, and the heirs of the promise are determined by His sovereign foreordination. For, first of all, the Chief Heir of the promise is Christ Himself. For "to Abraham and his seed are the promises made," but, mark you well, "He saith not, And to seeds, as of many; but as of one, And to thy seed, which is Christ." Gal. 3:16. And no one dare deny that Christ is of God, sovereignly ordained by Him to be *the* heir of the promise. But if the Chief Heir of the promise is ordained of God, so they that are His. And only thus could God swear by Himself that He would surely fulfill the promise to Abraham and his seed. "For when God made promise to Abraham, because he could swear by no greater, he sware by himself, saying, Surely blessing I will bless thee, and multiplying I will multiply thee. And so, after he had patiently endured, he obtained the promise. For men verily swear by the greater: and an oath for confirmation is to them the end of all strife. Wherein God, willing to shew more abundantly unto the heirs of the promise the immutability of His counsel, confirmed it by an oath: That by two immutable things, wherein it was impossible for God to lie, we might have a strong consolation, who have fled for refuge to lay hold on the hope set before us." Heb. 6:13-18. To the heirs of the promise the promise is sure, because it is based on and rooted in the immutable counsel of the eternal God!

Now, the announcement of this promise is the gospel. It is *euangelion*, good tidings, good news, because it is the sure promise of light in the midst of darkness, of righteousness in the midst of sin, of eternal life to them that lie in the midst of death. For, by nature the heirs of the promise lie with all the world under the curse, in the darkness of sin and death. In and with that world

they are of the first Adam, born in sin, children of wrath, even
as also "the others." And the promise, and that, too, exactly
because it is the promise of God, causes the glad light of hope to
dawn in their hearts the hope of redemption and deliverance out
of the night of misery through the which they walk. Good news
the announcement of this promise of the gospel is to them,
especially because that promise speaks of things which "eye hath
not seen, and ear hath not heard, and that never entered into the
heart of man." The promise does not merely bring to them the
prospect of redemption from their sin, and the deliverance from
their present death, and of a return to a former state of integrity,
but it holds before them the glorious hope of eternal life, the life
of immortality and incorruption, the hope of the inheritance
incorruptible and undefiled, and that fadeth not away. And the
glory and blessedness of that state that is assured them by the
unchangeable promise of God, is as highly exalted above the
original state in the first Paradise, as the Lord of heaven is
exalted above the man that is of the earth earthy. The news of
the gospel, therefore, is unspeakably good news. It is *euangelion*
indeed. And it is news. For the gospel is not of this world. It
never did, and it never could arise in the heart of man. Philosophy could never invent this news. The princes of this world could
never conceive of it. It is the gospel of God concerning things
that are wholly new. It is, therefore, God Himself that announces
the promise, and that proclaims the gospel of His Son. Or, as
the Heidelberg Catechism reminds us: "From the holy gospel,
which God Himself revealed." To the heirs of the promise the
gospel comes *by revelation* even though it is proclaimed by men.
No mere word of man is sufficient for this. The heirs of the promise must hear the Word of God. Hence, the Catechism certainly
touched upon the heart of the matter, when, in answer to the
question: "whence knowest thou this?" it called attention to "the
holy gospel, which God Himself first revealed in Paradise; and
afterwards published by the patriarchs and prophets, and represented by the sacrifices, and other ceremonies of the law; and
lastly has fulfilled it by His only begotten Son." Always it is of
God. Always there were pilgrims of the night that were heirs of

the promise in this world, from its very beginning. And always they longed for the *euangelion,* for some glad news concerning the promise. And again, always it was none other than God Himself that satisfied their earnest longing by publishing to them the gospel concerning His Son, our Lord Jesus Christ!

That the holy gospel, according to the Heidelberg Catechism, is essentially good news concerning the promise, may be gathered from the statement: "and lastly, has fulfilled it by his only begotten Son." The gospel was fulfilled in the fulness of time in Jesus Christ our Lord. But this is possible only if the gospel is essentially a promise. And also the fact that the gospel was always proclaimed and received by the heirs of the promise, from the very beginning of history, is plainly taught by the Catechism in this nineteenth answer. The holy gospel is not the same as the Bible. For the Bible did not always exist, in fact, in its present form it exists only a comparatively short time. More than twenty centuries elapsed of the world's history before there was even a part of the holy Scriptures written, another two thousand years became history before the entire canon of the Bible could be adopted by the Church; and even then and long after, copies of Holy Writ were scarce and expensive. That every believer may rejoice in the possession of a Bible for himself, and may daily read the Scriptures, is of relatively recent date. But although the Bible was not always in existence, there never was a time when the heirs of the promise were without the holy gospel. And let us understand this clearly: they did not have *a part* of the gospel, but they possessed the *entire* gospel of the promise from the very beginning of history. It is true that the riches of the gospel were only gradually displayed, proclaimed and understood as the centuries rolled by and the time of the fulfillment approached. All the implications of this glorious gospel of the promise could not all at once be explained and comprehended. But this does not alter the fact that the *whole* gospel was revealed from the beginning of the world, and not only a part of it. When the seed of a maple tree has sown itself in my garden, and the following year a small plant appears with a slender stem and a couple of small leaves, that little sprout is not a part of a maple tree, but

is just as complete a tree as the tall maples that stand forty or
fifty feet tall in our front lawn. The same is true of the holy
gospel. It was revealed in early times in a simple form, adapted
to the needs of the hearers, and it gradually grew in riches of
contents, but also that gospel in its simple form was nevertheless,
the entire gospel. And wholly in harmony with this, the Catechism teaches us that God Himself first revealed the holy gospel
in Paradise; afterwards published it by the patriarchs and prophets, and represented it by the sacrifices and other ceremonies
of the law; and lastly, has fulfilled it by His only begotten Son.

In the light of this proper conception of the holy gospel
throughout the ages of history, we can understand why the
promise of Gen. 3:15 was always called the *protevangel*, the
moederbelofte (mother of promises). It is the first revelation
of the entire holy gospel immediately after the fall of our first
parents, Adam and Eve, in Paradise. The first man Adam was
an image of Him that was to come. He had been created in
earthly glory, in covenant friendship with the living God, king
over all earthly creation, and servant of the Lord of all. All
creatures served him that he might serve his God. But "being in
honor, he understood it not, neither knew his excellency, but
willfully subjected himself to sin, and consequently to death,
and the curse, giving ear to the words of the devil. For the commandment of life, which he had received, he transgressed; and
by sin separated himself from God, who was his true life, having
corrupted his whole nature; whereby he made himself liable to
corporal and spiritual death. And being thus become wicked,
perverse, and corrupt in all his ways, he hath lost all his excellent
gifts, which he had received from God, and only retained a few
remains thereof, which, however, are sufficient to leave man
without excuse; for all the light which is in us is changed into
darkness." Conf. Belg. XIV. By violating the covenant and
eating of the forbidden fruit, man had plunged himself into the
night of sin and death, from which he could see no way out.
And in Adam the whole human race, including also the seed of
the promise, the heirs of eternal salvation according to God's
sovereign purpose of election, was carried into the abyss of cor-

ruption and death. But God has provided some better things for
these heirs of salvation. And although he causes the whole creation to bear henceforth the curse of His wrath, vanity and death,
toil and suffering, yet He maintains His covenant, and at once
begins the work of salvation and grace in Christ the Lord. And
He proclaims at the same time to the heirs of the promise the
holy gospel in the words that announce the utter defeat of the
devil: "I will put enmity between thee and the woman, and
between thy seed and her seed; it shall bruise thy head, and thou
shalt bruise its heel." That promise is the whole gospel. Nothing is ever added to this first revelation of the gospel of the
promise that is not, in principle, implied in it. And the entire
revelation of the holy gospel that follows in succeeding centuries
is but the unfolding of the riches of this mother of promises, this
protevangel.

And since that time the gospel is always preached, and revealed
in ever increasing clarity and fulness of riches. And in the light
of this holy gospel the heirs of the promise walk through the
darkness of the present night of sin and corruption and death.
The way is dark, indeed, and the battle with the children of
darkness in this world is often hard and fierce, but God fulfills
His promise, works His work of grace and deliverance, and
causes the light of the gospel of the promise to strike an ever
clearer path through the darkness of the night. He proclaimed
the gospel concerning His Son through patriarchs and prophets.
He revealed the gospel to them, directly through His Spirit, indirectly through visions and dreams, through angels and by the
revelation of the Angel of Jehovah, and through many signs and
wonders. Thus the gospel was revealed and proclaimed in the
awful world of prediluvian times. The night of suffering and
toil, "because of the ground which the Lord hath cursed," was
oppressive; and the struggle with the generation of the children
of this world was a bitter one. But in that dark night the heirs
of the promise carried the gospel of the promise revealed in
paradise with them, and the patriarchs of those days proclaimed
what they had heard from above of the glad news concerning
the promise. In the days of Enos, the son of Seth, men began to

call upon the name of the Lord. Enoch walked with God, and
already spoke of the coming day of the Lord, and of the redemption of His saints, when he prophesied: "Behold, the Lord
cometh with ten thousand of his saints, to execute judgment upon all, and to convince all that are ungodly among them of all
their ungodly deeds which they have ungodly committed, and
of all their hard speeches which ungodly sinners have spoken
against him." The seed of the serpent was to suffer defeat, the
promise of the gospel was to be fulfilled! Lamech called his son
Noah, convinced that in him Jehovah had given them a seed that
would comfort them over their work and toil. And, indeed, in
Noah God continues and establishes His work of grace. He
becomes a preacher of righteousness in the midst of the ungodly
world of his days. In his days the seed of the serpent is crushed,
and the seed of the woman is saved in the ark. Noah becomes
heir of the world through faith. With him God establishes His
everlasting covenant, and the sign of this covenant He establishes
in the clouds when He sets His bow in the expanse of the firmament, a silent but mighty witness of the holy gospel of promise!

But also through the patriarchs and prophets after the flood
God continues to reveal the gospel of the promise in ever brighter
rays of light. The attempt of the seed of the serpent to establish
itself as all powerful in the world is frustrated in the confusion
of tongues at Babel. And God calls Abraham from Ur of the
Chaldees and out of Haran, in order that He might show him
the land of promise, make a great nation out of him, and establish with him and with his generations for ever His everlasting
covenant. And God proclaimed the gospel unto Abraham, saying: In thee shall nations be blessed. Gal. 3:8. And He showed
him the realization of the promise, not only in Isaac, in whom
his seed would be called, and who was the seed of the promise,
but also in the land of Canaan, which He promised to him and
to his seed for an everlasting possession. And although in all
these things the patriarch could only see the beginning of the
promise, and though with Isaac and Jacob he lived in tents and
confessed that he was a stranger and sojourner in this world,

yet he understood and received the promise, saw the fulfillment afar off, even saw the day of Christ, and died in faith.

Thus the light of the gospel continued to shine with ever increasing brightness and clarity in the thickening darkness of the world. Dark, indeed, was the night when the children of Israel, the heirs of the promise, were in bondage in the land of Egypt, groaning under the oppressive hand of a haughty world-power, and threatened with extinction. But Jehovah realizes the promise of the gospel afore preached to Abraham. With a mighty hand He delivers His people Israel from the house of bondage and leads them out to liberty. The seed of the serpent is crushed, indeed, when Pharaoh and his host are destroyed in the Red Sea, and the seed of the woman is given the complete victory. He realizes His promise unto them, receives them into His covenant, forms of them a people peculiar unto Himself, and leads them through the desert into the land of promise. Even in the desert He constantly reveals the gospel of the promise unto them by word and deed, through His mediator Moses, and by mighty signs and wonders. For He feeds them daily with the Bread from heaven, a promise of the true Bread from heaven that was to come; and He quenches their thirst by water that gushed from the rock in the desert, and they drank from the spiritual rock that followed them, and that rock was Christ. And thus He performed His work of grace and salvation for them, constantly causing them to walk in the light of the gospel, and finally leading them into the "Rest" He had promised unto them, that there He might dwell among them, and He might be their God, and they might be His people!

It is true that at Sinai, and from that moment until the fulfillment of the promise in the fulness of time, the law was imposed upon the promise. Yet, it was never the purpose of the law to make the holy gospel of the promise of none effect. For the apostle writes: "Brethren, I speak after the manner of men; Though it be but a man's covenant, yet if it be confirmed, no man disannulleth, or addeth thereto. Now to Abraham and his seed were the promises made. He saith not, And to his seeds, as of many; but as of one, And to thy seed, which is Christ. And this I say, that the covenant, that was confirmed before of God in Christ, the law, which was four hundred and thirty years after, cannot disannul, that it should make the promise of none effect. For if the inheritance be of the law, it is no more of promise: but God gave it to Abraham by promise. Wherefore then serveth the law? It was added because of transgressions, till the seed should come to whom the promise was made; and it was ordained by angels into the hand of a mediator. . . Wherefore the law was our schoolmaster (to bring us) unto Christ, that we might be justified by faith." Gal. 3:15-24. In fact, although the law was super-imposed, as it were, upon the promise, for a time, yet the law itself plainly revealed that it was never meant to replace the promise of the gospel, as if from Sinai on the way to the inheritance was that of the righteousness of the works of the law. The glory of the light of the gospel clearly shone through the law. In fact, the very law was a medium for the revelation of the gospel. For Christ is the end, the *telos,* of the law, and the finger of the law clearly pointed forward to Him. Beautifully this was witnessed in the face of Moses when, with the tables of the law in his hands, he came down from the mount. For the light of the glory of the holy gospel was reflected in his face. Without that light, there was, indeed, nothing but the law, and the mount that could be touched, and thunder and lightning and smoke and darkness; and there was the terrible sentence: "Cursed is every one that continueth not in all that is written in the law." But the light that shone in the face of the mediator of the old dispensation was a reflection of "the light of the knowledge of the glory of God in the face of Jesus Christ." II Cor. 4:6. And it was typical of the attitude of all carnal Israel that "the children of Israel could not look stedfastly to the end of that which is abolished," II Cor. 3:13; and that, therefore, they asked Moses to cover his face with a veil, thus extinguishing the light of the gospel in the law, and having nothing left but the righteousness which is through the law, and the resulting curse. For "their minds were blinded: for until this day remains the same veil untaken away in the reading of the Old Testament; which veil is done away in Christ.

But even unto this day, when Moses is read, the veil is upon their heart." II Cor. 3:14, 15.

Indeed, God proclaimed the gospel of the promise through the law. It is to this fact that the Heidelberg Catechism calls attention by stating that God also "represented (the holy gospel) by the sacrifices and other ceremonies of the law." In two ways God revealed the holy gospel through the law. In the first place by making the ordinances of the law shadows and symbols of things to come. Heb. 10:1. The entire tabernacle, with its ark of the covenant, and the mercy seat; with its holy of holies, and holy place; its altar of incense and altar of burntoffering; its candlestick and table of shewbread; was an "example and shadow of heavenly things, as Moses was admonished of God when he was about to make the tabernacle: for, See, saith he, that thou make all things according to the pattern shewed to thee in the mount." Heb. 8:5. And in the entire service of the tabernacle, with its priests and sacrifices, its washings and shedding of blood, the gospel of the promise was clearly proclaimed to the heirs of the promise. And, in the second place, these ordinances of the law, these shadows and types and examples of heavenly things, plainly bore the testimony of their own unreality and imperfection, and thus pointed forward to the fulfillment of the holy gospel in Christ. "For the law made nothing perfect, but the bringing in of a better hope did." Heb. 7:19. "And truly they were many priests, because they were not suffered to continue by reason of death." Heb. 7:23. And "the law maketh men high priests which have infirmity," and they needed daily "to offer up sacrifice, first for their own sins, and then for the people's." Heb. 7:27, 28. And again: "when these things were thus ordained, the priests went always into the first tabernacle, accomplishing the service of God. But into the second went the high priest alone once every year, not without blood, which he offered for himself, and for the errors of the people. The Holy Ghost thus signifying, that the way into the holiest of all was not yet made manifest, while as the first tabernacle was yet standing. Which was a figure for the time then present, in which were offered both gifts and sacrifices, that could not make him that did the service perfect, as pertaining to the conscience." Heb. 9:6-9. "For the law having a shadow of good things to come, and not the very image of the things, can never with those sacrifices which they offered year by year continually make the comers thereunto perfect. For then would they not have ceased to be offered? because that the worshippers once purged should have had no more conscience of sins. But in those sacrifices there is a remembrance again made of sins every year. For it is not possible that the blood of bulls and of goats should take away sins." Heb. 10:1-4. On the one hand, therefore, there was a rather clear shadow of things to come in the ordinances of the law; on the other hand, these ordinances clearly testified by their very imperfection that they were not the things themselves; and thus they pointed to Christ as the end of the law and proclaimed the holy gospel to the heirs of the promise of the old dispensation.

"And lastly, has fulfilled it by his only begotten Son." It is remarkable that, as the time of fulfillment approaches, the shadows gradually grow dimmer, but at the same time, the direct word of prophecy, the holy gospel as proclaimed through the prophets, becomes more distinct. The tree of David is cut down: nothing remains of it but a root in a dry ground. The sceptre is, outwardly at least, departed from Judah. The glory of Mount Sion is extinguished. The temple is demolished. And although it is rebuilt after the captivity, the ark of the covenant never returns: a stone must take its place in the holy of holies. At the time of the cruel type of Antichrist, Antiochus Epiphanes, the holy place is defiled, and the people "are killed all the day long. " But as the light of the gospel in the law grows dim, the direct proclamation of the gospel through the prophets becomes clearer, more definite, fuller and richer. And in the fulness of time, the holy gospel is fulfilled in God's only begotten Son, Jesus Christ, our Lord. It is fulfilled in the incarnation, the cross and resurrection of the Son of God, His ascension and exaltation at the right hand of God, and the outpouring of His Spirit upon all flesh. And while the gospel is being fulfilled, it is also revealed and proclaimed more fully and clearly than ever before. For not only *is* Christ, as the fulfillment of the holy gospel, Himself the revelation of the promise in all its riches, but He also preached the gospel during the years of His public ministry, as it never had been proclaimed before. For "God who at sundry times and in divers manners spake in time past unto the fathers by the prophets, hath in these last days spoken unto us by His Son." Heb. 1:1, 2. And having ascended into glory, and having received and poured out the promise of the Holy Ghost, He still revealed the riches of the holy gospel and proclaimed them through the apostles. And He guided them through that same Spirit, even in committing the fulness of the holy gospel to writing, so that the Church of the new dispensation may possess the infallible record of the revelation of the gospel in the holy gospel. But still, it is always He, the only begotten Son, come in the flesh, crucified, dead, and buried, raised on the third day, exalted into highest glory, Who not only is the fulfillment of the holy gospel, but Who also reveals it, and proclaims it by His Spirit and Word, gathering His Church, and causing men to know everywhere that the Mediator, Who in one person is both very God, and real righteous man, is our Lord Jesus Christ, who of God is made unto us wisdom, and righteousness, and sanctification, and redemption.

LORD'S DAY VII

Q. 20. Are all men then, as they perished in Adam, saved by Christ?

A. No; only those who are ingrafted into him, and receive all his benefits by a true faith.

Q. 21. What is true faith?

A. True faith is not only a certain knowledge, whereby I hold for truth all that God has revealed to us in his word, but also an assured confidence, which the Holy Ghost works by the gospel, in my heart; that not only to others, but to me also, remission of sin, everlasting righteousness and salvation, are freely given by God, merely of grace, only for the sake of Christ's merits.

Q. 22. What is then necessary for a Christian to believe?

A. All things promised us in the gospel, which the articles of our apostolic undoubted Christian faith briefly teach us.

Q. 23. What are these articles?

A. I. I believe in God the Father, Almighty, Maker of heaven and earth:

II. And in Jesus Christ, his only begotten Son, our Lord:

III. Who was conceived by the Holy Ghost, born of the Virgin Mary:

IV. Suffered under Pontius Pilate; was crucified, dead and buried: He descended into hell:

V. The third day he rose again from the dead:

VI. He ascended into heaven, and sitteth at the right hand of God the Father Almighty:

VII. From thence he shall come to judge the quick and the dead:

VIII. I believe in the Holy Ghost:

IX. I believe an holy Catholic church: the communion of saints:

X. The forgiveness of sins:

XI. The resurrection of the body.

XII. And the life everlasting. AMEN.

I

Salvation For Believers Only

In the chapter that now follows, through Lord's Day 24, the Heidelberg Catechism discusses the essence and nature, the contents and significance of saving faith. And it approaches and introduces this discussion with the question: "Are all men then, as they perished in Adam, saved by Christ?" And we realize immediately that this peculiar approach of the subject is due to the subjective and experiential method followed throughout by our instructor. In a dogmatic exposition of the truth, the order and arrangement of the different parts of the truth discussed would be quite different. Such a discussion would begin with the knowledge of God, to answer the question what He is, Who He is, and what He does. It would continue with a treatise on creation, man, and the fall. It would then expound the truth concerning Christ, His person and nature, His offices and work of salvation, His power and glory. And having finished this part of the truth, it would call attention to the Holy Spirit and His work in applying Christ and all His benefits to the elect. And as part of the work of the Holy Spirit it would discuss the important subject of saving faith. But how different is the order in the Heidelberg Catechism! In the preceding Lord's Day mention was made of the Mediator, "Our Lord Jesus Christ: who of God is made unto us wisdom, and righteousness, and sanctification and redemption." And the source of the knowledge of this Mediator was pointed out as "the holy gospel." And now, instead of developing the doctrine of this Mediator, our instructor turns to the question of faith. The result of this is that in the following chapters all the main doctrines of the Church, such as the trinity, creation and providence, the incarnation, the atonement, the resurrection and exaltation of

296

Christ, the return of the Lord and judgment, the Holy Spirit and the Church, forgiveness of sins, the resurrection of the dead, and everlasting life,—all these are considered and explained from the viewpoint of their being the object of the Christian's faith. And since the catechism views the whole truth from the standpoint of the Christian comfort, and, therefore, of salvation, it introduces all this with the question: "Are all men then, as they perished in Adam, saved by Christ?"

This question is a very important one, and should be taken very seriously. We would do well, perhaps, to look closely at the question, and to assure ourselves that we understand it in all its implications before we attempt to answer it. Are all men saved? Even this part of the question, taken by itself, is of tremendous import. It is hardly to be treated as if it were a mathematical problem, the solution of which is interesting, indeed, but which, for the rest does not cause us any grave concern. One cannot really do justice to a question of this kind by making it the subject of a round table discussion in a philosophical club. It is of very grave importance. It concerns men. It is interested in the reality of life and death, of everlasting bliss and desolation. Yes, but that is not the most important element in the question. For it really concerns God. The question, what may become of all men, is, indeed, sufficiently serious, and becomes more serious according as one considers men in their concrete existence and relations in this world. But a far more important question is, nevertheless, that which concerns God and His dealings with the children of men. And it is, evidently, from this aspect that the Catechism considers the matter of the salvation of all men. Are all men saved? is an inquiry that concerns God as the Subject, man as the object of salvation. The question is not, whether somehow it happens that, fortunately, all men are saved, as it might be reported of the crew and passengers of a shipwrecked ocean steamer, some of which save their lives in lifeboats, others with life-preservers or on rafts, and all of which are ultimately picked up and rescued. Nor does the question: "Are all men saved?" mean to inquire unto the success of a determined attempt to save all men. Nor does it mean: are all men willing to be saved? or: do all men have a chance of salvation? or: is salvation offered to all men? On the contrary, the question wholly concerns God. For salvation is of the Lord. And, therefore, as the Catechism puts the question, it must certainly mean: does God save all men?

And because this inquiry concerns God, we should be very careful that *we* do not answer, that we do not offer *our* answer to this question. Probably we would feel inclined to answer the question in the affirmative, either if we solve this problem rationally, or if we let our emotions determine the answer. As to the latter, we must remember that the question concerns, not abstract conceptions of men, but men in their concrete existence and relationships. The question concerns the child that is your flesh and blood, the wife of your love, the brother that grew up in the same home with you, the friend of your bosom, with whom you take sweet counsel, your fellowman that lives and struggles and dies in the same world with you, your own flesh and blood. If, then, you let your own flesh and blood determine the answer to this question, you will probably seek an affirmative reply. Did not Paul's flesh and blood declare once that he could wish to be accursed from Christ for his brethren, his kinsmen according to the flesh? By all means, then, take this question seriously, and if you must answer negatively, let it be "with great heaviness and continual sorrow" as long as you, too, are still in the flesh! But also a logical or rational solution of this problem would seem to point in the same direction: the salvation of all men. Especially is this true if we consider the entire question as proposed by the Catechism: "Are all men then, *as they perished in Adam,* saved by Christ?" All men perished *in Adam!* Is it not quite rational, then, to suppose that God will also save them all? Does not the fact that all men perished in Adam imply that they are all one, one in a legal sense, and one in an organic sense? And, granted that all men also bear individual responsibility for their sin, does not the fact remain that the first beginning of their sin and death lies beyond their individual existence, and that they are born in guilt and damnation? If *we,* then, must give an answer to this question, would it not be most rational to conclude that God will certainly save the entire corporation and organism, and every individual of the human race?

And *men* have given and still do often give their own answer to this tremendous question. But even so they did not and do not agree. Very few are they who have the courage to give an affirmative answer without qualification to the question of the Catechism. Yet, from the earliest period of the history of the church there were those who taught that in the end all will be saved. Already such early church fathers as Clemens of Alexandria and Origen favored the universalistic view. And in our day all shades of universalists defend the same theory. They usually argue, not directly from Scripture, but from the fact that salvation is through Christ, and that there are a large number of men who, in this life, never had an opportunity to come into contact with Him. The majority of men die without ever having heard of the Saviour. And so, there must be another opportunity to accept Christ, after death, or even after the final day of judgment. And in this way, according to some, all men will gradually obey the gospel and be saved; or, according to others, the majority will repent, while the stubbornly impenitent will be annihilated.

However, like all teachers of false doctrines, these universalists also appeal to Scripture, and have their texts to support their doctrine. They point to such passages as Matt. 10:15: "Verily I say unto you, It shall be more tolerable for the land of Sodom and Gomorrah in the day of judgment than for that city." Matt. 11:20-24: "Then began he to upbraid the cities wherein most of his mighty works were done, because they repented not: Woe unto thee, Chorazin! woe unto thee, Bethsaida! for if the mighty works, which were done in you, had been done in Tyre and Sidon, they would have repented long ago in sackcloth and ashes. But I say unto you, it shall be more tolerable for Tyre and Sidon at the day of judgment than for you. And thou, Capernaum, which art exalted unto heaven, shalt be brought down to hell: for if the mighty works, which have been done in thee, had been done in Sodom, it would have remained until this day. But I say unto you, That it shall be more tolerable for the land of Sodom in the day of judgment than for thee." Lu. 12:47,48, where the Lord makes a distinction between the servant that shall be beaten with many, and he that shall be beaten with few stripes. But it is evident that no universal salvation is taught in these passages. They merely make a distinction of degree in the measure of punishment that is to be inflicted upon the wicked.

Besides, they appeal to John 15:22-24: "If I had not come and spoken unto them, they had not had sin, but now they have no cloke for their sin. He that hateth me hateth my Father also. If I had not done among them the works which none other man did, they had not had sin, but now they have both seen and hated both me and my Father." From these words the general conclusion is drawn, that one has no sin and, therefore cannot be condemned unless he had come in contact with Christ first. But it is evident that this is not the meaning of the Saviour's words. For if such were the meaning, it had been better if the Saviour had never come into the world. And the Word of God teaches everywhere that sin and death have come upon all men through the first man Adam. The Saviour, therefore, means, not that the Jews would have had no sin at all, that they would have been righteous, if Christ had not come and spoken and showed His mighty works unto them, but that the special sin of hating Him and His Father would not have become manifest in them. For it is this manifestation of sin that renders them wholly worthy of rejection.

More difficult to explain, perhaps, is a passage like that in I Pet. 3:18-20: "For Christ also hath once suffered for sins, the just for the unjust, that he might bring us to God, being put to death in the flesh, but quickened by the Spirit: By which also he went and preached unto the spirits in prison; Which sometime were disobedient, when once the longsuffering of God waited in the days of Noah, while the ark was a preparing, wherein few, that is, eight souls were saved by water." The universalists use this text to prove that there is another opportunity after death to hear the gospel. Roman Catholics and Lutherans find proof here for a personal descension of Christ into hell, although they differ with respect to the purpose of this descension. Reformed interpreters usually explain that Jesus did not preach to the spirits in prison after His death, but at the time of Noah and through the Spirit of prophecy. It was then that God's Spirit strove with men, and that through the prophets the gospel was preached to the prediluvian ungodly. However, it seems to us: 1. That the text speaks of a preaching to the spirits in prison, not at the time before the flood, but after the resurrection of Christ. Jesus was put to death in the flesh, quickened by the Spirit, and then, in that Spirit He went and preached. 2. That He preached, not to men in the flesh, not to the disobedient when they were on earth, but to disembodied spirits, to the prediluvian wicked after they had gone into "prison." This is plainly stated: he "preached to the spirits in prison." And to this is added that they were "sometime disobedient." This, of course, refers to the time when "the long-suffering of God waited in the days of Noah." But the point is that this refers to a period before the preaching took place of which the text speaks. 3. That the text does not speak of a personal descension of Christ into hell in order to preach to these spirits in prison. He went in the Spirit. 4. That the text gives no ground for the contention that the Lord preached *the gospel* to them. The word that is used here in the Greek is the mere formal term for preaching, without informing us as to the contents of the preaching. It means "to herald", loudly to proclaim. Hence, the text expresses no more than that Christ in the Spirit after His resurrection, proclaimed **something to** the spirits of prediluvian ungodly in prison. Now, if we consider that this prediluvian race of ungodly men had been extremely wicked, had, in fact, filled the measure of iniquity for that time, so that God executed final judgment in the destruction of the first world; and if we recall that the saints of that period had proclaimed to that wicked world that the Lord would come to execute judgment, and that, although they witnessed the judgment of God upon them in the flood, yet did not see the justification of the saints they had persecuted and killed; we can at least conjecture why the Lord should preach to these particular spirits of the prediluvian world, and what must have been His message. He, through whose death and resurrection the world was judged and the prince of this world had been cast out, through the Spirit convicted the spirits of the ungodly in prison of their own utter condemnation and defeat, and of the justification and victory of Himself and His people. For let us not forget that before Him, Whom God exalted at His right hand, "every knee should bow, of things in heaven, and things in earth, and things under the earth, and that every tongue should confess that Jesus Christ is Lord, to the glory of God the Father." And this is the result of this preaching of the exalted Lord through the Spirit, even in them that are in hell.

One more text to which universalists often appeal to sustain their view that there will be another opportunity to come to Christ and be saved after death, must be briefly considered here. I refer to I Pet. 4:6: "For this cause was the gospel preached also to them that are dead, that they might be judged according to men in the flesh, but live according to God in the spirit." Now, it may be said at once that this text, whatever may be the correct explanation of it, certainly does not speak of a preaching of the gospel after death, for the simple reason that the preaching here spoken of is presented as antecedent to the death of those to whom it was preached: the gospel *was* preached to them that *are* dead, or simply to the "dead" (nekrois). For this same reason, I cannot agree with the interpretation that explains the "dead" as referring to spiritual death. Rather do I think that the apostle has in mind a special class of dead: those of the church that had died in martyrdom. This seems clearly expressed in the text, for they were those that had been "judged according to men in the flesh," but they had been justified, for they lived "according to God in the spirit." And this also is suggested by the context. To those martyrs the gospel had been preached exactly in order that they might suffer according to men, be condemned and killed by them; *"for this cause,"* i.e., in order that the wicked world may be condemned in the day when they shall "give account to him that is ready to judge the quick and the dead." vs. 5.

But it is not only those that are known as universalists, who answer the question: "Are all men saved?" affirmatively, at least with certain qualifications, and as far as God is concerned in the work of salvation. The Pelagians held that there are several degrees of salvation, and, accordingly, different ways to be saved. Man can be saved from condemnation if he obeys the "law of nature." The Israelite could be saved by keeping the law of Moses. And the believer is saved thru obedience to the faith, the "law of Christ." And the Arminian proposes that, as far as God is concerned, all men are saved. For in God's intention, Christ died for all men. It is true that some men are not saved, but this is not due to any limitation God places upon salvation, but to the will of man that rejects the well meaning offer of salvation in Christ Jesus. It is evident that it follows from this, not only that salvation as a work of God is universal, and that it is man that limits this universal work of God; but also that salvation must be extended to all those that never come into contact with the preaching of the gospel, such as all the little children that die before they come to years of discretion, and all the heathen to whom the gospel was never proclaimed. Surely, if it be true that God wills all men to be saved, it must follow that there be other ways of salvation than the one that is prepared through the death and resurrection of Jesus Christ our Lord. It is evident that, underlying all these universalistic errors, are two main errors. The one is, that one can be damned only for the sin of rejecting Christ and the proffered salvation: original as well as actual sin in itself is not a sufficient ground for damnation. And the other is, that salvation depends for its realization upon the will of man, who can either accept or reject the salvation which, as far as God is concerned, is universal.

Radically opposed to all these universalistic and semi-universalistic theories of salvation stands the answer of the Catechism: "No; only those who are ingrafted into him, and receive all his benefits by a true faith." This answer is worthy of our closest consideration especially for two reasons. First of all, by the expression "ingrafted into him" it presents faith, not as an act on the part of man, but as a gift of God, a means whereby God saves the sinner through Christ. And secondly, by the same expression, as well as by the clause "and receive all his benefits by a true faith" the Catechism opposes all intellectualistic and philosophic conceptions of saving faith, and presents it as the spiritual bond by which the believer is united with Christ.

As to the first point of interest mentioned above, the rather precise and exact expression "ingrafted into him," was, no doubt, intentionally employed by the authors of the Catechism, in order to convey accurately their conception of the importance of saving faith. How easily might the answer be cast into a different form, which apparently would express the very same truth, but which would actually deprive it of its real meaning and force! In answer to the question: "are all men saved?" the majority of evangelical Christians of our own day would most probably say: "No; all men are not saved; but only those that believe in Jesus Christ, and accept Him as their personal Saviour." To many a Christian, unskilled in the discernment of the true doctrine and the detection of errors, it would seem as if this answer, though different in form, expresses exactly the same truth as that of the Heidelberger. And the advantage of this form is that it is very popular, and if you say no more, all orthodox Christians will agree with you. In fact, you may go a step further, and insist that faith is a gift of God, without causing any serious disagreement. Nay more, in answer to the further question: to whom does God give this faith? you may even appear to be very Scriptural and Reformed, and maintain that this gift of grace is bestowed only upon God's elect, and no Arminian will differ with your statement, as long as you only leave room for the answer to the original question: "Only those are saved that believe in Christ, and that accept Him as their personal Saviour." For the Arminian would say that the elect are those that are willing to believe in Christ and to accept Him, and upon those that so reveal their willingness God bestows the gift of faith. O, it is granted, it is even emphasized that salvation is only of grace. But whether the sinner will receive this grace depends in last analysis upon himself. All men are not saved, but God is willing to save all. And you must leave room for the well-meaning offer of salvation to all, for the "altar call" from pulpit and radio. Faith, therefore, though it is a gift of God, must be presented as an act of man, an act whereby the sinner accepts Christ. But notice, now, that the Catechism uses an entirely different terminology in its answer, a terminology that leaves the sinner entirely passive in the hand of God: "No, but only those that *are ingrafted* into him." One must be ingrafted into Christ before he can accept Him, even before he can be willing to accept Him. And the ingrafting into Christ is an act of God, never of man. As long as the sinner is not ingrafted into Him, he is dead in trespasses and sins. And he cannot, he will not, and cannot will to come to Christ. As sinner, indeed, he is very active. He will resist and reject the gospel in unbelief. But with a view to salvation he is wholly passive. Christ must come to him, before he can come to Christ. Salvation is of the Lord. It is not of him that willeth, nor of him that runneth, but of God that sheweth mercy. Rom. 9:16.

Viewed in this light, this question of the Catechism and its answer becomes very serious. They speak, not of man, but of God. Are all men saved? No; but only such as it pleases God, and that in absolutely sovereign grace, to graft into Christ by a true and living faith.

As to the second point of importance mentioned in the beginning of this chapter, the Catechism here offers a profound spiritual conception of saving faith: it is the means whereby we are united with Christ, the spiritual bond whereby we are made one body, one plant with Him, so that by faith we may live from Him, draw our all from Him, and thus receive all His benefits. We shall have more to say about the character of faith in the next chapter. But here we must briefly call attention to this essential nature of faith as our union with Christ.

Faith is not another work by performing which we become worthy of salvation. All the work that makes us worthy of righteousness and eternal life and glory has been performed and completely finished by Christ. Even the gift of faith He merited for us by His perfect obedience. Nor is faith a condition upon our fulfillment of which God is willing to give us the salvation merited for us by Christ. There are no conditions whatsoever unto salvation. It is free and sovereign. Nor is it the hand by which we on our part accept the proffered salvation. Often it is presented thus. Salvation is compared to a beautiful gold watch which I freely offer to someone. I hold it in my extended hand and beg the person upon whom I would bestow this gift to take it. It is his for the accepting. But he will never actually possess that watch unless he will extend his own hand to take it from mine. Thus, it is alleged, faith is the hand whereby we take hold of the salvation proffered in the gospel. But also this is not true. For, first of all, the reception and appropriation of the benefits of Christ is by no means such a mechanical and external transaction as taking a watch from a man's hand. It is a profound spiritual activity of the entire soul. And, secondly, the natural man has no hand whereby he is able to accept the salvation of God in Christ, were it merely offered him. No, but faith is a bond, a spiritual bond, whereby we are so united with Christ that by it we live out of Him.

That is the meaning of the figure that underlies the expression: "ingrafted into Him." It is the figure of a twig or scion of one tree that is ingrafted upon another. That ingrafted branch becomes one organism with the tree upon which it is grafted, so that from it it receives all its life-sap. The figure is thoroughly Scriptural. The Saviour compares the relation between Himself and believers to that between the vine and the branches. "I am the true vine, and my Father is the husbandman. Every branch in me that beareth not fruit he taketh away; and every branch that beareth fruit . . . . I am the vine, ye are the branches: He that abideth in me, and I in him, the same bringeth forth much fruit: for without me ye can do nothing." John 15:1-5. The apostle speaks of the olive tree and of branches that are grafted into it. Rom. 11. And he speaks of being planted together in the likeness of Christ's death, and in the likeness of His resurrection. And the spiritual bond that so makes us one plant with Christ that we live out of Him, is faith.

One might use other figures to illustrate this same truth. You can put a dead stick in the ground, but it will never show signs of life, nor do you expect it to sprout into foliage and bear fruit. On the contrary, it will rot. And the richer the soil, the faster will be the process of decay. But plant a little tree in that same soil, and it will strike its roots into it and draw its nourishment from the soil, and grow and bear fruit. This may illustrate the difference between the unbeliever and the believer. You may bring the former into contact with the Christ through the preaching of the gospel: it will only harden him in his unbelief. And the richer and stronger the gospel that is preached to him, the more he will hate it and rebel against it. But let the wonder of grace be performed upon a sinner and let the power of faith be implanted in his heart, and he will strike the roots of his soul into the Christ that is presented to him in the gospel, and from that Christ he will draw his life. A more mechanical, and for that reason less suitable figure, is that of the relation of your lighted home to the central power plant in your city. In that central power plant there is, so to speak, the power that is able to light your home at night. But if your home is not properly wired and connected with that central plant, so that the current is carried right into your home, your rooms will remain dark. So there must be a living connection between Christ and your heart, if you are to partake of the light of life. And that connection is saving faith.

The truth is, that all our salvation is in Christ. In Him is our redemption, the forgiveness of sin, the adoption unto children, eternal and perfect righteousness, knowledge of God and wisdom, freedom from the dominion of sin and sanctification, eternal life and light and joy,—all the blessings of salvation are not only merited by Him, but they are in Him. He *is* our wisdom and knowledge, our righteousness and holiness, our eternal life and peace. In order, therefore, to obtain these blessings of salvation, we must first become one plant with Him. We must be united with Him in a spiritual-organic sense of the word. And the bond whereby we are united with Him is faith, a gift of God, a means whereby God joins us forever to Christ. And when we are so united with Him by the power of faith, we become active, and by that faith we receive Him and all His benefits. By that faith whereby we are ingrafted into Christ, we appropriate Him unto ourselves so that His righteousness and holiness, His life and peace become our own, and we rejoice in the God of our salvation!

II

The Nature Of Faith

In the preceding chapter we already touched upon the character and significance of saving faith and its relation to salvation through Christ. The believer is saved through faith. Without faith he is not saved for a moment. If it were conceivable or possible that he should ever, even for a moment, lose his faith, that moment he would be lost, and again he would be dead in trespasses and sins. For all his life and salvation are in the Lord Jesus Christ, and by faith he is joined to that Christ, ingrafted into Him, and receives all His benefits.

But now the Catechism calls special attention to the nature of true, saving faith. In answer to the question: "What is true faith?" it points to the following elements: 1. Faith is both a certain knowledge and a hearty confidence. 2. This knowledge concerns all that God has revealed to us in His word. 3. The confidence of faith is trust concerning my personal salvation as being freely given me of God by grace, and that only for the sake of Christ's merits. 4. With respect to this confidence of faith, it is said that it is wrought in the heart by the Holy Ghost through the Gospel.

The answer places all the emphasis on the element of confidence. It is the peculiar property of saving faith, that distinguishes it from all other kinds of faith. All other kinds of faith are also a "certain knowledge," but saving faith is *not only* this, but also a hearty confidence that I have a personal part in the salvation God has wrought in Christ. In fact, the answer leaves the impression that not the element of a "certain knowledge," but only this hearty trust is wrought in our hearts by the Holy Ghost through the gospel. The "certain knowledge" of faith is not the special work of grace that is wrought in our hearts through the gospel by the Spirit of Christ.

That this is, indeed, the meaning of the answer is corroborated by the explanation Ursinus gives of this part of the Catechism. We read: "The *justifying faith* is described in the Catechism. In this description of faith 'knowledge and holding for truth' are mentioned as characteristics of faith in general. Faith does not exist in a doctrine which is not known; one must necessarily know the doctrine before he can believe it. For this reason, we reject the 'implicit faith' of the Romish Church (i. e. believing what the church teaches, regardless of the question whether or not one is acquainted with it). This description of faith differs from the general definition in that it speaks in addition of confidence, and of application of the forgiveness of sins through and for the sake of Christ. The peculiar characteristic of faith is: to rest and to rejoice in God on account of so great salvation. The efficient cause of it is the Holy Ghost. The means whereby He works this: the gospel, implied in which is also the use of the sacraments. And it is the will and the heart of man that experiences this operation.

"This justifying or saving faith differs from the other kinds of faith in this, that it is a firm confidence, whereby we appropriate to ourselves the merits of Christ, i. e. are firmly convinced that the righteousness of Christ is given and imputed also to us. Now, confidence is an inclination of the heart and of the will; this inclination has regard to some good, rejoices in it and relies on it; also in our language (German) it denotes 'a complete reliance on something.' The Greek word for faith is derived from a root which implies the idea of confidence. In this sense even profane authors, like Phocylides and Demosthenes, already used the word." 1, 147.

It is plain, then, that according to Ursinus, the knowledge of saving faith is the same as that of all other kinds of faith. It is simply the intellectual apprehension and assurance of a certain truth or doctrine. There is knowledge in so-called historical faith. All men believe in their deepest heart that God is. Even the devils believe that God is one, and they tremble in this knowledge. Jas. 2:19. There is knowledge in the general faith in the objectivity of the world according to the testimony of our senses. The same is true of "miraculous faith," or the assurance that some wonder will be performed by us or upon us. And even what is called "temporary faith," and which is nothing but a temporary stir of the emotions, is not possible without knowledge. Now, this element of knowledge these other kinds of faith according to Ursinus, have in common with true, saving faith. And it is also wrought by the Holy Ghost, but not by the Spirit of Christ, and not necessarily through the gospel. There is a general revelation of God, and there is also a general operation of the Holy Spirit, whereby every man is assured of certain truths, e. g. of the existence of God. But it is the element of confidence that distinguishes saving faith from all other kinds. And this confidence of saving faith it is that is wrought by the Spirit of Christ, and through the gospel, as a special work of grace.

We call special attention to this part of the answer of the Catechism, and to its explanation by Ursinus, because we cannot accept this exclusive emphasis on the confidence of faith, as if it alone were the work of grace by the Spirit through the gospel. And no one does. Not only the confidence of saving faith, but also its certain knowledge is peculiar to itself, and is wrought by the Spirit through the gospel. Even though usually attention is not called to the somewhat strange separation between the knowledge and the confidence of faith the Catechism makes, the answer is always explained as if it presented both elements as the fruit of the special operation of the Spirit of God in Christ. Dr. A. Kuyper Sr. writes (E Voto, 1, 129, 130):

"This 'certain, secure knowledge' does not consist in a further development of a knowledge which in part we already possessed, nor in an unfolding of a knowledge that was hid within us. One does not make any headway in this knowledge, though he would finish the courses in all the schools. Even if one would do nothing else all his life long than read the Bible, and compare Scripture with Scripture, he would not even advance one step toward the knowledge that is here meant. No, here a *new* knowledge is meant, which you did not possess as a sinner, and of which you received the power in regeneration. Another *kind* of knowledge this is, comparable to the original knowledge which Adam received in Paradise, and which is given us of God in Christ 'our wisdom.' He that receives this knowledge, *knows* differently, *sees* differently, *touches* differently. That which before he could not discern, he now perceives, and it becomes life to him. 'Enlightened eyes of the understanding' the apostle therefore calls this knowledge; and they are eyes too, that gaze with such uncommon accuracy, that they afford immediate and complete certainty and assurance concerning those things that are perceived by them: so clearly, so lucidly, so sharply this knowledge defines the things before your consciousness. The natural man does not see anything of this, but the spiritual man that has the gift of faith discerns *all* things. On the other hand, if one is not born again, he cannot even *see* the kingdom of God.

"Without the implanting of this saving faith, one may, therefore, indeed, commit the Bible to memory, and accept its contents historically, but this does not help him. He may also work himself into it by the spur of the emotions, and for a time rejoice in it, but neither this 'historical' nor this 'temporary' faith has anything in common with the faith whereby we are ingrafted into Jesus. Even 'miraculous' faith has nothing in common with saving faith, for although you had a 'faith to remove mountains' (and that is miraculous faith) and love was not infused into your heart, you still would be nothing.

"Disputations, therefore, do not help. We must have *testimony,* the Word must be administered, because usually it pleases God to use the Word as a means for implanting of faith; but even though you talk day and night to someone, as long as his soul cannot see through the eye of faith, you cannot show him the glories of God."

Calvin treats the subject of faith elaborately in his Institutes, Book III, chapter 2. Also according to him faith is both knowledge and confidence, and both are of a special, a higher kind than the knowledge and assurance of faith in general. Writes he: "Knowledge, as we call faith, we do not understand in the sense of comprehension, such as we have of those things that fall within the scope of human sensation. For this knowledge is even so far superior, that the mind of man must exceed and surpass itself, in order to attain to it. And even when he has attained to it, he does not understand that which he discerns; but while he has a persuasion of what he does not grasp, he apprehends more by the very certainty of this persuasion than he would by perceiving something human by its own capacity." (1). And again: "This also the words of Paul indicate: whilst we are at home in the body, we are absent from the Lord: for we walk by faith, not by sight, (II Cor. 5:6,7), whereby he shows that those things which we understand by faith, are, nevertheless, remote from us, and hid from our view. Whence we conclude that the knowledge of faith consists in certainty rather than in apprehension." (2). It appears that, according to Calvin's view, the confidence of faith is the result of this special and higher knowledge that consists in certainty rather than in comprehension. For he writes: "This is the principal hinge on which faith turns, not that we consider the promises of God's mercy to be entirely apart from ourselves, and not at all within us, but rather that, by embracing them from within, we make them our own. And out of this is born at last that confidence which elsewhere he calls peace (Rom. 5:1), unless one would rather derive peace from thence."

---

(1) Cognitionem, dum vocamus, non intelligimus comprehensionem, qualis esse solet earum rerum, quae sub humanum sensum cadunt. Adeo enim superior est, ut mentem hominis se ipsam excedere et superare oporteat, quo ad illam pertingat, Neque etiam ubi pertigit, quod sentit, assequitur; sed dum persuasum habet quod non capit, plus ipsa persuasionis certitudine intelligit, quam si humanum aliquid sua capacitate perciperet. Lib. III, cap. 2; 14.

(2) Id indicant et Pauli verba, nos in hoc corpore habitantes, a Domino peregrinari: qua per fidem ambulamus, non per aspectum (II Cor. 5:6): quibus ostendit, ea quae per fidem intelligimus, a nobis tamen abesse, et aspectum nostrum latere. Unde statuimus, fidei notitiam certitudine magis quam apprehensione contineri. Lib. III, cap. 2; 14.

(3). And again he writes: "Let this be the sum of the matter. When even the smallest drop of faith is instilled into our minds, we begin at once to contemplate the face of God as peaceable, serene and kind toward us, and that, indeed, far off and remote from us, but nevertheless by so certain an intuition that we know that we are not at all mistaken." (4).

According to Calvin, then, the knowledge of saving faith is not a general certainty of the truth of the Word of God, while the real and chief element of faith is the hearty confidence that my sins are forgiven, but it is quite a special kind of knowledge, far beyond the capacity of the human intellect, whereby the believer contemplates the face of God as being kind and merciful toward him. And, according to the reformer, it is even the chief element of faith, at least in this sense that it is first, and that confidence is based on it, and follows from it. This scriptural knowledge of faith clings to the Word of God as contained in the Scriptures, particularly, so Calvin teaches us, to the promises of God. And since these promises of God are all concentrated in Christ, since Christ is the realization of all the promises of God, the knowledge of faith looks to Him, and the confidence of faith relies on Him as the revelation of the God of our salvation. And not only the confidence, but also the knowledge of faith is a special gift of the Holy Spirit, enlightening our minds so as to be able to apprehend the spiritual things of the Word of God. It is true, so he writes in paragraph 33 of chapter 2, book III of the Institutes, that the mere and external demonstration of the Word ought to be abundantly sufficient to work faith in us, if it were not that our natural blindness and stubborn perversity makes this impossible. For the inclination of

---

(3) His praecipuus fidei card vertitur, ne quas Dominus offert misericordiae promissiones, extra nos tantum veras esse arbitremur, in nobis minime: sed ut potius eas intus complectendo nostras faciamus. Hinc demun nascitur fiducia illa, quam alibi pacem idem vocat (Rom. 5:1), nisi qui pacem derivare inde malit.

(4) Summa haec sit. Ubi primum vel minima fidei gutta mentibus nostris instillata est, iam faciem Dei placidam et serenam nobisque propitiam contemplari incipimus: procul id quidem et eminus, sed ita certo intuitu, ut sciamus nos minime hallucinari.

our mind to vanity is such that it will never adhere to the truth of God, it is so dull that it is always blind to His light. And from this it follows that without the illumination of the Holy Spirit, the Word avails nothing. (Sine Spiritus sancti illuminatione, verbo nihil agitur). Whence it is evident that faith is far superior to the mere human intellect. Nor will it be sufficient that the mind is enlightened by the Spirit of God, by His power the heart must also be strengthened and sustained. And he concludes that in both aspects faith is a special gift of God: as a purification of the mind to taste the truth of God, and as the strengthening of his spirit in that truth. (Ergo singulare Dei donum utroque modo est fides, et quod mens hominis ad degustandam Dei veritatem purgatur, et quod animus in ea stabilitur).

A good deal was written on the important subject of saving faith, its nature, object, and activity by A. Comrie (A. B. C. des Geloofs, Eigenschappen des Zaligmakenden Geloofs, Verklaring van den Heidelbergschen Cathechismus), to whom also Dr. Kuyper refers in his work "The Work Of The Holy Spirit." We cannot refrain from offering our readers part of a quotation from Comrie occurring in the last named work of Kuyper on the subject of faith:

"We will shortly enumerate the objects of this knowledge of faith.

"First, this knowledge is a divine light of the Holy Ghost, through the Word, by which I become acquainted, to some extent, with the contents of the Gospel of salvation, which hitherto was to me a sealed book; which, although I understood it after the letter and its connections, I could not apply to myself, to direct and support my soul in the great distress, conflict, and anguish which the knowledge of God and of myself had brought upon me. But it now became plain and knowable to me. Now I learn by the inshining of the Holy Spirit the contents of the Gospel, so that I can deal and commune with it. And so I suck from these breasts of consolation the pure, rational, and unadulterated milk of the everlasting Word of God . . . . And

in this way, by means of the heavenly light, which pours in
upon the inwrought faith, the soul obtains knowledge of the
secret of the Lord in Christ, who is revealed to her . . . .

"Second, this knowledge is a divine light of the Holy Spirit
in, from and through the Gospel, by which I know Christ, who
is its Alpha and Omega, as the glorious, precious, excellent, and
soul-rejoicing Pearl and Treasure hid in this field. Although I
knew all things, and I did not know Jesus by the light of the
Spirit, my soul would be a shop full of miseries; a sepulchre
appearing beautiful without, but within full of dead men's
bones. And this knowledge of Christ, imparted to the soul by
the inshining of divine light, through the Gospel, can never
from itself give any light to the soul as long as it is not ac-
companied by the immediate inworking and illumination of
the Holy Spirit. For it is not the letter which is effectually
working in the soul, but the direct working of the Holy Spirit
by means of the letter.

"And now you may ask, In what respect must I know Jesus?
We will confine ourselves to the following matters: This
knowledge of faith, the object of which is Christ in the Gospel,
is a knowledge by which I know, through the divine light of the
Holy Spirit, my absolute need of Christ. I see that I owe ten
thousand talents, and that I have not a farthing to pay; and
that I must have a surety to pay my debts. I see that I am a
lost sinner, who am in need of a Savior. I see that I am dead
and impotent in myself and that I need Him who is able to
quicken me and to save me. I see that before God I cannot
stand, and that I need Him as a go-between. I see that I go
astray and that He must seek after me. Oh! the more this
necessity of Christ presses me, from this true knowledge of faith,
the more earnest, intense, heartmelting, and persevering the
outgoings of my soul are from the inwrought faith, and attended with greater conflict. . . .

"Third, it is through this knowledge that I, by the light of
the Spirit, know Jesus in the Gospel, as adapted in every respect
to my need. It is the very conviction of the fitness of a thing
which persuades the affections to choose that thing above every

other; which makes one resolute and persevering in spite of
every obstacle, never abandon the determination to secure to
himself the thing or person chosen for this fitness to his need
. . . . But when the divine light of the Holy Spirit in the Gospel
illuminates my soul, and I receive this knowledge of faith
from Jesus, oh! then I see in Him such fitness as a Surety, a
Mediator, a Prophet, Priest, and King that my soul is touched
in such a measure that I judge it impossible to live another
happy hour, except this Jesus becomes my Jesus. My affections
are inclined, taken up, directed, and settled upon this object,
and my resolution is so great, so determined, so immovable,
that if it required the loss of life and property, of father and
mother, sister, brother, wife and child, right eye or right hand,
yea, though I were condemned to die at the stake, I would
lightly esteem all this, and would suffer it with joy, to have this
wonderfully fit Savior to be my Savior and my Jesus. . . .

"Fourth, this knowledge of faith is a divine light of the Holy
Spirit whereby I know Christ in the Gospel in all His sufficient
fulness. By this I see not only that He is well disposed to
poor sinners such as myself—for a man might be favorably disposed toward another to assist him in his misery, but he might
lack the power and the means to do so, and the best that he
could do is to pity the wretch and say, 'I pity your misery, but
I cannot help you'—but this divine light teaches me that Christ
can save to the uttermost; that though my sins are as scarlet
and crimson, heavier than the mountains, greater in number
than the hairs of my head and the sands of the seashore, there
is such abundance of satisfaction and merits in the satisfaction,
by virtue of His Person, that though I had the sins of the human
race, they would be compared to the satisfaction of Christ,
which has by virtue of His Person an infinite value, as a drop
to a bucket, and as a small dust in the balance. And this con-
vinces my soul that my sin, instead of being an obstacle, much
rather adds to the glory of the redemption, that sovereign grace
was pleased to make me an everlasting monument of infinite
compassion. Formerly, I always confessed my sin reluctantly;
it was wrung from my lips against my will only because I was

driven to it by my anguish, for I always thought, the more I confess my sin, the farther I will be from salvation and the nearer my approach to eternal condemnation; and, fool that I was, I disguised my guilt. But since I know that Jesus is so all-sufficient, now I cry out, and much more with my heart than with my lips, 'Though I were a blasphemer and a persecutor and all that is wicked, this is a faithful saying, and worthy of all acceptation, that Jesus Christ has come into the world to save sinners, of which I am chief.' And if need be, I am ready to sign this with my blood, to the glory of sovereign grace. In this way every believer, if he stands in this attitude, will feel inclined to testify with me.

"Fifth, it is this knowledge by which I know in the light of the Holy Spirit shining into my soul through the Gospel Jesus Christ, as the most willing and most ready Savior, who not only has the power to save and to reconcile my soul to God, but who is exceedingly willing to save me. 'My God, what is it that has brought about such a change in my soul? I am dumb and ashamed, Lord Jesus, to stand before Thee, by reason of the wrong I have done Thee, and of the hard thoughts which I entertained concerning Thee, O precious Jesus! I thought that Thou wast unwilling and I willing; I thought that the fault lay with Thee and not with me; I thought that I was a willing sinner and that Thou hadst to be entreated with much crying and praying and tears to make of Thee, unwilling Jesus, a willing Christ; and I could not believe the fault lay with me . . . '

"The believing knowledge of the willingness of Jesus, in the light of the Holy Spirit through the Gospel, makes me see my former unwillingness. But as soon as this light arises in my soul the will is immediately bent over and submissive. They who say that Jesus is willing, but that I remain unwilling, speak from mere theory; but they lack the knowledge of faith, and have not discovered this truth. For as the shadow follows the body, and the effect the cause, so is the believing knowledge of the willingness of Christ toward me immediately followed by my willingness toward Him, with perfect abandonment of myself

to Him. 'Thy people shall be willing in the day of Thy power'
(Psalm CX, 3).

"Lastly, by this knowledge through the promise of the
Gospel, and by the light of the Holy Spirit, I learn to know the
Person of the Mediator in His personal glory, being so near to
Him that I can deal with Him. I say, 'in the promise of the
Gospel,' to show the difference between a vision of ecstasy like
that of Stephen and the conceited knowledge of which heretics
speak outside of and against the Word. The Word is the only
mirror in which Christ can be seen and known by saving faith.
And herein I see Him in His personal glory with the eye of
faith, so near as I have ever seen any object with the bodily
eye. For this inwrought faith and the light of the Holy
Spirit shining thereon brings the Person Himself in substantial
form to the soul, so that he falls in love with Him, and so
enchanted with Him that he exclaims: 'My Beloved is white and
ruddy, the chiefest among ten thousand. For His love is stronger than death; jealousy is more cruel than the grave; the coals
thereof are coals of fire, flames of the Lord. Many waters cannot quench that love; if a man would give all the substance of
his house for love, it would be utterly contemned' (Cant. III,
10; VIII, 6, 7)." (A. Kuyper, *The Work Of The Holy Spirit*,
422-427).

I made the above quotations, which could easily be multiplied, to show that, according to Calvin and Reformed theologians, knowledge is a very essential part of saving faith, and that
it is a very special kind of knowledge, by which a man discerns
and appropriates spiritual things. To be sure, it is a certain
knowledge whereby I hold for truth all that God has revealed
to us in His Word. Without the Word of God we know nothing
of the things of the Spirit. Faith, the knowledge of saving faith
is not a certain "inner light" that can do without and despises
the letter of the Word. It is in the Holy Scriptures that the
Christ is mirrored. And faith is *certain* knowledge. It holds
for truth and it assents to all that is revealed in the Scriptures.
It is not necessary, therefore, to discover three elements in saving faith, and to speak of *assent* as the third element. For this

assent is, in part at least, implied in the certainty of the knowledge of saving faith; while, in as far as assent means personal
application of and reliance on the truth of the Word, it is included in the confidence of faith.

But this does not mean that the knowledge of faith is mere
intellectual certainty and assent to the truth. Saving faith is
not historical faith plus a hearty confidence. The knowledge
of faith is more than this intellectual apprehension and assurance of the truth. It is different. It is not at all like the
knowledge a natural man may have of the truth of the Word
of God. For the natural man does not discern and receive the
things of the Spirit. The knowledge of saving faith is spiritual.
It is experiential. It is not a theoretical knowledge *about* God
in Christ, but it is knowledge *of* Him. There is a wide difference between knowing all about a thing or person, and
knowing that thing or person. In the former instance, my
knowledge is purely theoretical, and my relation to the thing or
person known is external and superficial. I place myself above
the object of my knowledge, investigate it, feel rather superior
to it, criticize it, analyze it minutely and describe it. But in the
latter case, my knowledge is experiential, it is a knowledge of
love and fellowship, and my relation to its object is profound
and spiritual. A dietician may be able to analyze thoroughly
every item on a menu, and inform you exactly as to the number and kinds of vitamins each offered dish contains, but if he
has cancer of the stomach he cannot taste the food and enjoy
it, neither is he able to digest it, and derive the necessary
strength from it. On the other hand, the man with the hungry
stomach may sit at the table with him, know absolutely nothing
about vitamins, but he will order his meal, relish his food, and
appropriate it to himself in such a way that he is refreshed and
strengthened. Thus a man may be a keen theologian, so that
he can ably and thoroughly discuss all kinds of dogmatical subjects; he may be thoroughly versed in Christology, and deliver
learned discourses on the incarnation, the person and the
natures of Christ, the atonement and the resurrection, and His
exaltation at the right hand of God, but if he is a mere natural

man, he is like that scholarly dietician with his stomach full
of cancer. He knows all about Christ with his natural mind,
yet he does not know Him, neither can he appropriate Him.
In reality he does not even see Christ, nor does he hear His
voice, for Christ is spiritually discerned. He does not feel need
of Him, for though he has a head full of theories about sin,
he does not know his sin; and though he knows all about the
atonement, he does not flee to it; and though he probably delivered a lecture on the bread of life, he does not hunger after
it and can not eat it. He has knowledge, but it is not the
knowledge of faith. On the other hand, a person may be far
inferior to this able theologian in intellectual capacity, and
his knowledge of the Gospel may be very simple, if he has the
knowledge of saving faith, he will be like the hungry man that
relishes and digests his food. He will know himself in all his
misery and emptiness, as a damnable and guilty sinner, void of
light and wisdom and righteousness, full of darkness, foolishness and iniquity, and he will deplore all this before God. He
will know Christ as the Bread of life, as the fulness of his own
void, as the righteousness in his guilt, the holiness in his corruption, the light in his darkness, the life in his death. And he
will hunger and thirst in this knowledge of faith for the Bread
and Water of life, take it, eat it, relish it, appropriate it, make
it part and parcel of himself, and live! The knowledge of
saving faith is the kind of knowledge of which Jesus speaks
in John 17:3: "And this is life eternal, that they might know
thee the only true God, and Jesus Christ, whom thou hast
sent."

Saving faith, however, is also hearty confidence. The Catechism teaches us that true faith is not only a certain knowledge,
"but also an assured confidence, which the Holy Ghost works
by the gospel in my heart; that not only to others, but to me
also remission of sin, everlasting righteousness and salvation,
are freely given by God, merely of grace, only for the sake of
Christ's merits." After the emphasis we placed upon the knowledge of faith as a spiritual apprehension of the God of our
salvation in Christ, and of all the spiritual blessings in Him, it

would seem that there is but little room left for this confidence
as a distinct element of true, saving faith. And, indeed, the
two elements of faith, knowledge and confidence, although
they may be distinguished from each other, can never be separated as if they were two distinct spiritual dispositions, and
two separate acts of the saved soul. They are two aspects of
one and the same spiritual power, but faith is one, and the activity of saving faith is one. The reason for this is that the human soul, as the seat of life, is one, and the human personality
is indivisible. One may distinguish various so-called faculties
in the human soul, but these may never be presented as if they
were separate powers or functions. Man is an intellectual-
volitional being. He has a mind and a will. And from interac-
tion of these two arise the emotions. But although we may distinguish in the soul of man the faculty of the intellect, and the
faculty of volition, these two do not exist, or ever act, apart
from each other. There is never a mere or pure thought, a
separate functioning of the intellect: all man's thinking is volitional and emotional thinking. Nor could there possibly be a
pure act of volition, apart from the intellect: all man's willing
is rational, intellectual willing. Man is one, and as one being,
he lives a physical and psychical, an intellectual and volitional
life. And all his actions involve all his powers and faculties,
cooperating and interacting most intimately.

This may explain the reason why, when we speak of the
elements of true faith, we can never speak of the one without,
in part, also entering into a discussion of the other. Faith is
one. It is a spiritual *habitus,* disposition, function, power and
act of the entire soul of man, of his whole personality. Hence,
there is never "pure" knowledge of faith without confidence;
nor is there ever mere confidence without true knowledge.
Knowledge without confidence would be blind, would have no
object in which to trust, and would, therefore, be impossible.
And so, when one defines the true spiritual knowledge of saving faith, he cannot avoid to speak of confidence at the same
time. Nevertheless, the two may be distinguished. The knowledge of faith is strictly a spiritual disposition and act of the

intellect, confidence belongs to the domain of the will. Knowledge presents to the believing soul the object of confidence, the God of our salvation in Christ as revealed in the Scriptures; confidence clings to that Object, and by the act of confidence the soul surrenders itself to, and wholly relies on Christ revealed. Confidence is the immediate result of the true knowledge of saving faith.

It is not true, as the answer of the Catechism would seem to suggest, that only the confidence of faith is wrought in our hearts by the Holy Ghost and through the gospel: this holds for the knowledge of faith as well. One dare not say that only the confidence of faith is *personal,* so that through its activity I come for the first time into a personal possession of the blessings of salvation: even by the knowledge of true faith I apprehend the God of my salvation in Christ as *my* God. The knowledge of faith as well as its confidence is assurance that my sins are forgiven me. But confidence is an act of friendship whereby I draw unto Him without fear, make known to Him the secrets of my heart, flee to Him for refuge in all my miseries, cast myself upon Him laying hold upon His promises, assured of His good will toward me, and of His power to save me to the uttermost. The knowledge of God's favorable attitude to me personally is the indispensable ground of confidence. I must be assured of someone's good will in regard to me before I can have confidence in him. A simple but good illustration of confidence is the squirrel that approaches me to be fed out of my hand in my backyard. At first it dared not come near me. As I would hold out my hand and show it the nut I intended to let it feast on, it would sit up straight and in various ways reveal its eagerness for the delicious morsel I offered it, but it would remain at a safe distance. It was not assured of my good will. It feared that the delicacy in my hand might be a trap. I had to devise means to assure it of my real and honest intention to feed it, by throwing out bits of nut-meat, first at a safe distance, gradually a little closer in, till finally I had gained its full confidence, and it would approach me without fear to take the nut out of my hand.

Thus it is with the confidence of faith. The sinner is afraid of God. He looks upon God as his enemy. And he has abundance of reasons to be filled with terror at the thought of God. Everything warns him that he should beware of the living God. For "the wrath of God is revealed from heaven," and in that consuming wrath he pines and dies. And his own conscience, i. e., the handwriting of God in his own moral consciousness, witnesses against him, and accuses him before the Judge of heaven and earth. God intends to kill him! God will for ever consume him in His fierce anger! Such is the testimony that reaches the sinner from every side, from without and from within. And, therefore, he is afraid of God, dreadfully afraid! He tries to hide himself, to cover his own nakedness before the face of God. He would flee far away from Him. But God assures that sinner of His eternal good will toward him. He reveals Himself to that sinner in the face of Jesus Christ, His only begotten Son. In the cross and resurrection of the Christ, and in His exaltation at the right hand of God, He reveals His exceeding great power to save to the uttermost, and His eternal good will and covenant friendship and love to the elect sinner. And He speaks of His boundless grace and mighty power unto salvation in the gospel. But this is not sufficient. A "general offer" is of no avail to fill the sinner with confidence in that God of Whom he is dreadfully afraid. It is not sufficient for him to know that God loves sinners: he must know "that not only to others, but also to him" personally, God is gracious and filled with eternal good will. And this "assured confidence" God works through the Holy Ghost by the gospel in the sinner's heart. It is the confidence of faith, and by it the sinner wholly casts himself upon the eternal mercies of the living God in Christ, expecting from Him every good thing.

The Catechism expresses the matter very correctly and beautifully, therefore, when it teaches us that this confidence of faith implies the assurance "that not only to others, but to me also, remission of sin, everlasting righteousness and salvation, are freely given by God, merely of grace, only for the sake of Christ's merits." Indeed, the sinner must know that his sins are blotted out, removed for ever, forgiven him freely, and that he is clothed with an everlasting righteousness, if he is to approach God with boldness and confidence. It is God's righteousness and his own sin that fill him with terror and that are an impassable barrier between God and himself. If he may be assured that there is forgiveness with God, that God justifies the ungodly, that the Judge of heaven and earth loves him as a redeemed and justified sinner, then, and then only, can he have boldness to enter into the sanctuary. The confidence of faith is assured of this. It is peace with God through our Lord Jesus Christ. Even in the midst of this world, and while the sinner is still in the flesh and lies in the midst of death, the believing sinner has this peace and flees to the God of his salvation for refuge. While all his experience in this world bears the testimony to him that he is a damnable sinner, by the strong confidence of faith he clings to the God of his salvation, assured that he is righteous. In the midst of death he lays hold upon life in Christ, and with fear of hell all about him he clings to the mighty God of his salvation, and looks forward to eternal salvation in heavenly glory. God is able to save. It is God's eternal purpose to save. And God knows how to save. Upon that God of perfect salvation the confidence of faith relies for time and eternity!

———————

The question is often asked, in what sense, from what viewpoint the Christian defines true faith in its twenty-first answer. Is our instructor speaking of the power of faith or of its activity? Does he have in mind the being or the well-being of saving faith? Yet, it appears rather plain that the Heidelberger, at least in answer twenty-one, is not thinking of this distinction, and is simply speaking of the activity of a conscious faith. This should be evident from the fact that it ascribes the work of faith to the Holy Ghost *through the Gospel.* And it is not the power or *habitus,* but the activity of saving faith that is wrought in our hearts by the gospel. If the Catechism may at all be said to speak of faith as a power, it must be found in the twentieth answer where it speaks of those "who are ingrafted into him by a true faith." But in the answer to question twenty-one it has in mind the activity of a conscious faith.

However, the distinction may be made between the gift or power of faith as such and its activity. Nor is the distinction merely one of scholastic interest. On the contrary, it has its practical importance and value. The conscious activity of saving faith is not always equally strong and clear; in fact, it is not always present in the life of the believer in this world. It may seem lost sometimes. And in the case of very small infants, who can have no contact with the gospel as yet, this activity of saving faith is not consciously present at all. But the gift and power of faith is always the same and can never be lost. It is present when, in the humdrum of our daily life, we are not conscious of spiritual things whatever, and seem to be wholly occupied with the things that are seen; or when tempted by the allurements of the world and the evil inclinations of our own flesh, our soul appears to lose its hold upon Christ, and we are enveloped in spiritual darkness. And it is certainly present in those elect infants whom God regenerates from their mother's womb, and who know nothing of Christ and the Gospel, but who are saved by faith nevertheless. These too are ingrafted into Christ by a true faith. The distinction between the power and the activity of saving faith, therefore, is rooted in experience, and is of practical importance for our life as believers in the world.

Faith is, first of all, a gift, a power, a spiritual *habitus*, a new disposition or aptitude to apprehend and appropriate Christ and all His benefits, the things which "eye hath not seen, nor ear heard, neither have entered into the heart of man, the things which God hath prepared for them that love him." I Cor. 2:9. It is not another natural faculty of the soul, in addition to those of intellect and will. It is rather a new disposition of the entire soul, a spiritual aptitude which makes the whole soul of man, with mind and will and all the inclinations of the heart, peculiarly fit to apprehend spiritual things. It is the fitness to believe in distinction from the act of believing itself. Analogies of this distinction may be found in natural life. When a child is born it has all the faculties and powers and gifts it will ever have, even though they do not as yet actively function. The infant in the cradle has the faculty to think, to will, to perceive, to understand the world about him, to walk and to act in general, even though at that time it does not actually think and will, perceive and understand, speak and walk. If later in life the child develops into a great mathematician or skillful musician, this mathematical bent of mind or artistic tendency was not added to the child's talents after it was born, but they were all given with birth. The same may be said of saving faith. As a spiritual aptitude, it is given with our spiritual birth, i. e., in regeneration, while it develops into the conscious activity of believing through contact with the gospel applied to the heart by the Spirit of Christ.

Now, it is about this *habitus* or spiritual aptitude of faith that we must make a few remarks. First of all, it may be said of this power or disposition of faith, as well as of active and conscious faith, that it is both knowledge and confidence. Only, as a power it is the *capability* to know, and *capability* to confide in the God of our salvation in Christ. Without this spiritual aptitude it is impossible for a man to believe in Christ. If a child is born blind he cannot be taught to see; if he is born dumb, he will never speak; if he is born deaf, the activity of hearing will never develop. The same is true spiritually. By nature the sinner is born blind and deaf and dumb with regard to spiritual things. As such no one can possibly teach him to see and hear and confess the God of his salvation in Christ. Even though you would instruct him in the knowledge of Christ from infancy, and preach the gospel to him all his life, there would never be any other response than that of contempt and rejection. For "the natural man receiveth not the things of the Spirit of God: for they are foolishness to him: neither can he know them, because they are spiritually discerned." 1 Cor. 2:14. But when the power of faith is implanted in the heart, the sinner thereby receives the necessary aptitude to discern spiritual things: it is a power of spiritual knowledge and confidence.

Secondly, we may observe that this aptitude of saving faith may be and is implanted in the heart by the Holy Spirit regardless of age. It is wrought in the heart immediately by the Spirit of Christ, without the preaching of the gospel. Hence, the power of faith may be in the heart of the smallest infant as well as in the adult. And what is more, we may, no doubt, assume that in the sphere of the historical realization of God's covenant God usually gives this power of faith to the elect of the covenant in their infancy. For, not only does He continue His eternal covenant in the line of the generation of believers, but it is also His will that one generation of His people shall instruct the next in the things of the kingdom of heaven, and declare unto them the marvellous works of God. He places His people in the very sphere of the Church, where the Spirit of Christ operates, and the gospel is preached, from their infancy, in order that from earliest childhood they may become acquainted with the Word of God concerning their salvation. But why should the allwise God place His elect within the sphere of His covenant and of the preaching of the Word, as deaf and blind and dumb? He certainly would never do anything so incongruous. Although, then, we cannot establish a general rule in this matter, it is safe to say that *usually* God bestows the gift of the power of faith on His elect covenant children in their infancy. And it is in this confidence that the Church instructs the covenant seed, and preaches the gospel of Christ unto them as early as possible, that they may gradually become active believers, and appropriate Christ and all His benefits consciously.

Thirdly, we wish to remark that the activity of saving faith, as well as its *habitus* or power, is the fruit of the work of the Holy Ghost. It is true that the power of faith becomes active belief only through the gospel. Without that gospel, faith has no Christ to apprehend or cling to, and can, for that reason, never become active belief. But we must not make the mistake of presenting the matter of saving faith as if its *habitus* or power were implanted, wrought in the heart by the Holy Spirit, while its activity is caused by the gospel without the operation of the Holy Spirit. This is not true. Both, the power and the activity of faith, are wrought through the Spirit of Christ only. It is the Spirit that applies the preaching of the gospel to the heart of the sinner in whom the aptitude of faith was wrought, and it is, therefore, the Spirit of the Lord that calls and awakens the power of faith into the conscious activity of belief.

Finally, it may be said that this spiritual power or aptitude of faith can never be lost. As we have remarked above, the activity of saving faith may be very weak at times, may seem to have died out and disappeared, so that we seem to have no hold on Christ and the precious promises of Christ, and the soul is enveloped in darkness. But the power of faith can never be lost. Once a believer is always a believer. But that this is true is not due to any inherent virtue in the aptitude of faith, but only to the abiding indwelling and continued operation of the Holy Spirit in the innermost recesses of our hearts. Without that Spirit, dwelling within us, saving faith could not exist and maintain itself even for a moment. But the Spirit never leaves us. The bond with Christ is never broken, because it is constantly preserved by His Spirit. And so, the ultimate ground of the statement that the power of faith is never lost, is the fact that faith is most absolutely a gift of God, which He bestows on the elect only. And "the gifts and calling of God are without repentance." Rom. 11:29. He that glorieth, let him glory in the Lord!

III

The Object Of Faith

At the close of the important seventh Lord's Day the Catechism introduces the object or contents of the Christian's faith, which then, in subsequent chapters it expounds in detail. In Question and Answer 22 it briefly defines that which "is necessary for a Christian to believe" as "All things promised us in the gospel, which the articles of our apostolic undoubted christian faith briefly teach us." And in answer to Question 23 it quotes the so-called Apostles' Creed.

It draws our attention that the Catechism defines the object of saving faith, not as "the Word of God," nor as "all that God has revealed to us in his Word," as was stated in Answer 21, nor even as "all things contained in the holy gospel," but very definitely as "all things *promised* us in the gospel." The promises of the gospel, therefore, are the object of saving faith, according to the Catechism. The question arises: how must this be understood? It is possible, of course, to take this expression in a perfectly sound sense. In that case it does not intend to exclude the rest of the Word of God in any sense of the word from the object of saving faith, but merely intends to emphasize that to true faith, as *saving* faith, that embraces Christ and all His benefits, the holy gospel is the gospel of the promise, the *Euangelion* of the *euangelia,* and the promises of God, therefore, stand in the foreground. Or one could express it in this way: just as in Scripture the entire Word of God is sometimes called *law,* or *law and prophets,* or *testimonies, statutes, precepts,* etc., so it may also be designated by the term *the holy gospel,* and the heart of that gospel are the promises of God realized in Christ; and saving faith naturally looks upon the Word of God especially from the viewpoint of its being the gospel of Christ, the good tidings concerning the promise of God. But it is also quite possible to offer a different interpretation of the statement in Answer 22. The promises of the gospel

330

may be taken in the strict sense, as referring to only part of the Word of God. The meaning of the answer then would be that, while *faith in general* holds for truth and assents to all that is revealed in the Scriptures, *saving* faith appropriates particularly the promises of the gospel.

The former interpretation must undoubtedly be considered as conveying the truth, regardless now of the question whether it was the intention of the authors of the Catechism to express this meaning. Saving faith is assured of and relies on the entire Word of God as revealed in the Scriptures, and it does not have the promises of the gospel only for its object. All that the Scriptures teach concerning God and creation, man and sin, Christ and salvation, the Holy Spirit and sanctification, the Church and means of grace, the coming of Christ and things eternal, is included in what is necessary for a Christian to believe. That this is true, is evident even from the fact that the Catechism refers to the Apostles' Creed as the brief expression of the object of saving faith. For in that catholic confession the Church does not declare itself with regard to the promises of the gospel only, but speaks concerning all the main doctrines of Scripture. And, therefore, when the Catechism here answers to the question what is necessary for the Christian to believe, "All things promised us in the gospel," we will have to take the statement in the broadest sense, so that it includes all the knowledge of God, His Will and precepts, and the whole counsel concerning our salvation and all things revealed in the Holy Scriptures.

When we insist on this we assume the stand that agreement with the Heidelberg Catechism does not necessarily always imply agreement with the meaning and interpretation of its authors. For Ursinus in his explanation of the Catechism makes it quite plain that he intended to convey the sense set forth in the second interpretation mentioned above. As we explained in a previous chapter, in the answer to question 21 he distinguished between the knowledge of *faith in general*, which holds for truth all that God has revealed in the holy Scriptures, and *saving* or *justifying faith*, consisting in a hearty and assured confidence that the blessings of salvation are freely given me of God, for the sake of Christ's merits. That this presentation of the authors' meaning in Ans. 21 was correct, is corroborated by Ursinus' own commentary on the answer to Qu. 22. Writes he: "After our treatment of the subject of faith, the question now follows concerning the contents of what must be believed or the object of faith. Faith in general, as became evident from our description of it, embraces the entire Word of God, and assents to it fully. But justifying faith in particular respects the promises of the gospel or the preaching of grace through Christ. The gospel is therefore particularly the object of justifying faith. For this reason the gospel is also called the doctrine of those things which are to be believed, in distinction from the law which is the doctrine of those things that must be done." p. 155. Here Ursinus makes it very plain that, according to him, the whole Word of God is the object of the knowledge of *faith in general,* while *justifying* or *saving faith* deals exclusively with the promises of the gospel. And these distinctions are, in our opinion, untenable. Faith is one. And that one faith is both a true spiritual knowledge and a hearty confidence. And it has for its object the one and entire Word of God, revealing the God of our salvation in Jesus Christ our Lord. And the knowledge of this Word of God is briefly expressed in "the articles of our catholic, undoubted Christian faith."

––––––––

A word must here be said about these "articles of our catholic, undoubted christian faith," generally known as the Apostles' Creed. Its exact origin is unknown. The tradition that gave rise to its name, as if the apostles themselves were the authors of this confession, must be rejected as false. For not only is there no shred of evidence for this tradition, nor even for the contention that this symbol in its present form existed in the time of the apostles, but it did not belong to the proper calling of the apostles as such to prepare confessions of faith for the Church. Their proper task it was to lay the foundation of the Church, other than which no man can lay, and their infallible writings belong to the Canon of the Scriptures. The confession of the

Church is based on their word. This does not mean that there can be any serious objection to maintain the name by which these articles of our faith are universally known. But the name expresses that the contents of this confession are truly apostolic, in fact they are almost verbally taken from the New Testament Scriptures. It is, however, one of the most ancient symbols of the Church. And even though in its present form it cannot be traced farther back than the sixth or fifth century of our era, parts of it date from the immediate post-apostolic time. It was not composed at once in its present form. The general opinion is that it gradually developed from the instruction that was given by the church to catechumens before their being baptized, and from the confession they were required to make at baptism. Writes Schaff, *Creeds of Christendom*, Vol. 1, p. 16ff.: "As to the origin of the Apostles' Creed, it no doubt gradually grew out of the confession of Peter, Matt. 16:16, which furnished its *nucleus* (the article on Jesus Christ), and out of the baptismal formula, which determined the trinitarian order and arrangement. It cannot be traced to an individual author. It is the product of the Western Catholic Church (as the Nicene Creed is that of the Eastern Church) within the first four centuries. It is not of primary, apostolic, but of secondary, ecclesiastical inspiration. It is not a Word of God to men, but a word of men to God, in response to his revelation. It was originally and essentially a *baptismal confession,* growing out of the inner life and practical needs of Christianity. It was explained to the catechumens at the last stage of their preparation, professed by them at baptism, often repeated with the Lord's Prayer, for private devotion, and afterwards introduced into public service. It was called by the ante-Nicene fathers 'the rule of faith,' 'the rule of truth,' 'the apostolic tradition,' 'the apostolic preaching,' afterwards 'the symbol of faith.' But this baptismal creed was at first not precisely the same. It assumed different shapes and forms in different congregations. Some were longer, some shorter; some declarative, some interrogative in the form of questions and answers. Each of the larger churches adapted the nucleus of the apostolic faith to its peculiar circumstances and wants; but they all agreed in the essential articles of faith, in the general order of arrangement on the basis of the baptismal formula, and the prominence given to Christ's death and resurrection. . . . .

"The most complete or most popular forms of the baptismal creed in use from that time in the West were those of the churches of Rome, Aquileja, Milan, Ravenna, Carthage, and Hippo. They differ but little. Among these again, the Roman formula gradually gained the acceptance in the West for its intrinsic excellence, and on account of the commanding position of the Church of Rome. We know the Latin text from Rufinus (390) and the Greek from Marcellus of Ancyra (336-341). The Greek text is usually regarded as a translation, but is probably older than the Latin, and may date from the second century, when the Greek language prevailed in the Roman congregation.

"The Roman creed was gradually enlarged by several clauses from older and contemporaneous forms, viz., the article 'descended into Hades' (taken from the creed of Aquileja), the predicate 'catholic' or 'general' in the article on the Church (borrowed from Oriental creeds), 'the communion of saints' (from Gallican sources), and the concluding 'life everlasting' (probably from the symbols of the churches of Ravenna and Antioch). These additional clauses were no doubt part of the general faith, since they are taught in the Scriptures, but they were first expressed in local creeds, and it was some time before they found a place in the authorized formula.

"If we regard, then, the *present* text of the Apostles' Creed as a complete whole, we can hardly trace it beyond the sixth, certainly not beyond the close of the fifth century, and its triumph over all the other forms in the Latin Church was not completed till the eighth century, or about the time when the bishops of Rome strenuously endeavored to conform the liturgies of the Western churches to the Roman order. But if we look at the several articles of the Creed separately, they are all of Nicene or ante-Nicene origin, while its kernel goes back to the apostolic age. All the facts and doctrines which it contains are in entire agreement with the New Testament. And this is true even of those articles which have been most assailed in recent times, as the

supernatural conception of our Lord (cf. Matt. 1:18; Luke 1:35),
the descent into Hades (Comp. Luke 23:43; Acts 2:31; 1 Pet.
3:19; 4:6), and the resurrection of the body (1 Cor. 15:20 sqq.,
and other places)."

There is something charming in the simple beauty of the
structure and contents of this creed of the whole Christian
Church. It is very brief, yet quite comprehensive, giving expression to all the main truths of revelation that are "necessary for
a christian to believe." Its form is wholly positive, not controver-
sial: in it the Church professes her faith, apparently without
considering the possibility of its being gainsaid, or the necessity
of defending the truth over against heretics. It is a declaration
of the historical facts of the gospel, rather than an abstract statement of doctrines. It professes faith in the triune God, yet it does
not expressly mention the trinity, far less declare any specific
doctrine concerning the relation of the Persons of the trinity
to the divine Essence. All the salient doctrines of Christology are
professed in this *Credo,* the divinity of Christ, His virgin birth,
the humiliation and exaltation of our Lord, and His expected
return, but they are all stated simply as so many facts of the
gospel, without as much as suggesting their dogmatic implications. And the same is true of the articles concerning the Holy
Spirit, the Church and the benefits of Christ's work such as the
forgiveness of sins, the resurrection of the body, and everlasting
life. Schaff truly gives the following evaluation of this creed:
"It is not a logical statement of abstract doctrines, but a profession of living facts and saving truths. It is a liturgical poem and
an act of worship. Like the Lord's Prayer, it loses none of its
charms and effect by frequent use, although, by vain and thought-
less repetition, it may be made a martyr and an empty form of
words. It is intelligible and edifying to a child, and fresh and
rich to the profoundest Christian scholar, who, as he advances
in age, delights to go back to primitive foundations and first
principles. It has the fragrance of antiquity and the inestimable
weight of universal consent. It is a bond of union between all
ages and sections of Christendom. It can never be superseded
for popular use in church and school." (Creeds of Christendom,

1, p. 15). Indeed, one can conceive of the wish that this *Credo* of our catholic undoubted christian faith might have proved sufficient for all times, and that the Church of Christ in the world could have remained united on its basis!

However, as the Church developed and advanced in the knowledge of the truth a brief statement of the object of faith like the Apostles' Creed must needs prove inadequate as a bond of union; and it would be quite impossible for the Church of today to turn the clock of history back, and return to this ancient creed as the sole basis of agreement for the whole church in the world. For, first of all, many doctrines whose maintenance is quite essential to the Church on earth, are not even mentioned in this symbol. The fundamentalists of our time may, in this respect, be satisfied with the declaration of the Apostles' Creed, for the four truths on which they lay emphasis as essential to Christianity, the virgin birth of the Saviour, vicarious atonement, the resurrection of Christ, and His return for judgment, are at least mentioned here, although this can hardly be said of the doctrine of substitutional atonement. But they are in error when they think that the defense of these general doctrines is sufficient to safeguard the faith of the Church over against the attack of the enemy. They may be compared to a certain extent to a gardener that weeds his vegetable plot, but is satisfied by pulling off the tops of the weeds, leaving their roots in the soil. There are fundamental doctrines without whose maintenance even truths such as the vicarious atonement of our Lord cannot be successfully defended. The great doctrines of sovereign predestination, with election and reprobation, of sin and grace, of preservation and perseverance, are not even mentioned in the Apostolic Confession. And yet it is quite essential that they be defined in the standards of the Church of today.

But, in the second place, such a summary and factual statement of the great truths of the gospel as is contained in the Apostles' Creed can hardly be considered adequate as a clear and unambiguous expression of the faith of the Church. And this is especially true in our times. It is a well-known fact that those that seek to undermine the foundation of the truth upon which the Church is built, and to introduce false doctrines, hardly ever reveal their evil intention by openly declaring their opposition to the doctrines as they have been formulated by the Church in the past. On the contrary, they prefer to employ the very same terms the Church has always used to express her faith, although they give them a new and entirely strange content. If they mean to deprive the Church of the truth of sovereign grace, and to introduce the false doctrine of free-will, they employ the Scriptural terms of predestination, election, and reprobation nonetheless; only they declare that God has chosen them that believe, and rejected those that remain in their unbelief. Or they speak of a "double track" and insist that, while they firmly believe in the truth of absolute predestination, they also hold the very opposite, viz., that God will have all men to be saved. And thus they do with regard to every fundamental truth of the Bible. Even present day modernism, though it rejects and opposes all the fundamental doctrines of historical Christendom, is often very efficient in the employment of practically all the terms used to express the object of the Christian faith. They, too, speak of Christ as the Son of God, but in their mouth the term is completely emptied of its true significance so that it does not express at all the essential divinity of the Saviour. And they love to speak of the kingdom of God and its righteousness, while they refer to a kingdom of mere man, and of this world. And so we might go on. It shows, that as the Church advances in the knowledge of the truth, it will not only need a more elaborate confession to express its faith positively, but it must also more definitely and fully define its doctrines, lest they be open to the attack of gainsayers because of their ambiguity. And, therefore, though the Apostles' Creed will certainly always remain the basis of unity for all that understand its declarations in their historic and biblical sense, it cannot possibly serve as the *sole* basis of unity for the Church in the world. And for this reason, the Heidelberg Catechism proceeds from the correct standpoint, when it does, indeed, declare that these articles contain all that is necessary for a Christian to believe, but at the same time offers a rather elaborate exposition of these articles in the chapters that follow.

LORD'S DAY VIII

Q. 24. How are these articles divided?

A. Into three parts; the first is of God the Father, and our creation; the second of God the Son and our redemption; the third of God the Holy Ghost, and our sanctification.

Q. 25. Since there is but one divine essence, why speakest thou of Father, Son, and Holy Ghost?

A. Because God hath so revealed himself in his word, that these three distinct persons are the one only true and eternal God.

I

Faith In God

In Lord's Days eight to twenty-two inclusive we are really dealing with two symbols or creeds: the Apostolic Confession and the Heidelberg Catechism, and the latter appears here as an exposition of the former. And yet, these chapters of our Heidelberger offer us much more than a mere exposition of the twelve articles of faith formulated by the early church, if by mere exposition is meant nothing more than a setting forth of the truths that are plainly and directly expressed in the *Apostolicum*. All that is developed in the following chapters of the Catechism cannot possibly have been in the mind of the early church, and clearly before the consciousness of her faith, when she confessed the truth as expressed in the twelve articles of faith. We must bear in mind that a period of several centuries intervenes between the time of the *Apostolicum* and the composition of the Heidelberg Catechism and its adoption as part of our Reformed confessions. During those intervening centuries, the truth as it is in Christ had been the object of study and contemplation, and had been developed in detail; many heresies had arisen regarding the very truths declared in the *Apostolicum,* not only in the Romish church, but also within the bosom of the churches of the Reformation, false doctrines concerning the birth of Christ and the virgin Mary, the suffering and death of the Saviour, the atonement and good works, justification, the ascension of the Lord, the Church, and the doctrine concerning the "last things." A mere exegesis of the words of the Apostolic Confession, a symbol claimed by all the different groups of Western Christendom, Romish or Protestant, would not suffice therefore, to set forth the faith of the Reformed Churches of the sixteenth century. The great truths of the *Apostolicum* had to be developed in all their implications, in the light of Scripture, and to be defined clearly

339

over against the false doctrines that had arisen. And it is this we must expect to find in the ensuing chapters of the Heidelberg Catechism. This must not be understood as if the Catechism arbitrarily imposes its own views upon the words of the Apostolic Confession. On the contrary, it faithfully adheres to their simple meaning. But at the same time, it gives fuller and richer development to the truths expressed. Taking the twelve articles of faith, the symbol of the early church, for its basis, the Catechism builds at the superstructure of the truth that must needs be raised on such a foundation. And it was the conviction of our Reformed fathers that the positive line of the faith of the true Church in the world runs from the confessions of the early church, not over the declarations of the Council of Trent, but over the Reformation of the sixteenth century, and that, too, as its principles are most purely set forth in the Reformed symbols. And this is still the conviction of every Reformed believer worthy of the name.

In the present Lord's Day, the Catechism calls our attention to the threefold division of the *Apostolicum*, and makes it the occasion to insert a question and answer concerning the doctrine of the holy trinity. In Lord's Days nine and ten, our instructor explains the meaning of the article concerning "God the Father, and our creation." The second part of the Apostolic Confession, that which concerns "God the Son, and our redemption," is explained in Lord's Days eleven to nineteen inclusive. And the part that treats of "God the Holy Ghost, and our sanctification" is treated in Lord's Days twenty to twenty-two.

The answer to question twenty-four: "How are these articles divided?" seems rather simple, and might easily give rise to misunderstanding: "Into three parts; the first is of God the Father and our creation; the second of God the Son, and our redemption; the third of God the Holy Ghost, and our sanctification." That this threefold division is actually found in the *Apostolicum* is evident. The first article speaks of God the Father, Who is almighty, and the Creator of heaven and earth. Articles two to seven set forth the truth concerning Jesus Christ, God's only begotten Son, His Person and work. And the last five articles are devoted to the truth concerning the Holy Ghost, and the application of salvation to us. Yet, we all feel at once that the twenty-fourth answer of the Catechism needs careful explanation, if we are to avoid the error of tritheism. The statement of answer twenty-four might easily be understood as meaning that the First Person of the holy trinity is our Creator, the Second our Redemptor, and the Third our Sanctifier. And such a division of the work of the three Persons of the trinity was, of course, not in the minds of the authors of our Catechism. This is evident from the "Schatboek" I, 159, 160. Ursinus here meets the following objection: "Creation is here ascribed to the Father, redemption to the Son, sanctification to the Holy Ghost. Therefore the Son and the Holy Ghost did not create heaven and earth; neither did the Father and the Holy Ghost redeem the human race; nor do the Father and the Son sanctify the believers." And he answers as follows: "We deny the consequence which is here deduced, for creation is ascribed to the Father, redemption to the Son, sanctification to the Holy Ghost, not exclusively, i.e. in such a manner that these works do not properly belong to all persons. . . . By this distinction is merely indicated the order of operation proper to the persons of the Godhead. To the Father is ascribed the work of creation, not exclusively or to Him alone, but because He is the source of the Godhead, and of all the divine works, and therefore also of creation. For all things He did, indeed, create out of Himself through the Son and the Holy Ghost. Redemption is ascribed to the Son, not exclusively or to Him alone, but because it is the Son who immediately performs the work of redemption. For the Son only is become a ransom for our sins, He alone paid the price for us at His cross, not the Father, nor the Holy Ghost. Sanctification is ascribed to the Holy Ghost, not exclusively or to Him alone, but because it is the Holy Ghost who sanctifies us immediately or through Whom our sanctification is immediately effected." And in reply to a similar objection he writes: "The divine works are indivisible, but the order and manner of operation or working proper to each of the three persons must be maintained. For all the divine persons perform the *outgoing* works of God; but the following order must be maintained: the Father does all things of himself through the Son and the Holy Ghost, the Son does all things of the Father and through the Holy Ghost, the Holy Ghost does all things of the Father and the Son through himself. It follows therefore that all the persons create, redeem, and sanctify: the Father mediately through the Son and the Holy Ghost; the Son mediately through the Holy Ghost; the Holy Ghost immediately through himself, mediately through the Son, in so far as the latter is mediator."

Similarly Dr. A. Kuyper, in *E Voto,* I, p. 168, explains the answer of our Heidelberger to question twenty-four as follows: "Consequently, only and exclusively in this sense must be understood what the Catechism refers to in the familiar distinctions: of God the Father and our *Creation,* of God the Son and our *Redemption,* of God the Holy Ghost and our *Sanctification.* By this the Catechism does not at all intend to express that each of these three Persons operates *in turn*: first the Father to create you, then the Son to redeem you, and finally the Holy Ghost to sanctify you; but on the contrary that He Who created you is the Triune God, and that He Who redeemed you is the Triune God, and that He Who sanctified you is the Triune God, so that you as a creature from your first coming into existence until your eternal state of glory, never have to do with the Father separately without the Son, or with the Son without the Father, but that you always have to do with the Lord Jehovah, with the living God, with the Eternal Being, and thus with Father, Son, and Holy Ghost. However, whereas these operations of God affect you as being *creative,* and *redemptive,* and *sanctifying,* the Catechism makes a distinction, and that of such a nature, that in all the operations that concern *Creation* the *Father* is the chief worker with whom the Son and the Holy Spirit coöperate; in all that concerns *Redemption* the *Son* is the chief worker with whom the Father and the Holy Spirit coöperate; and in all that concerns your personal *sanctification* the *Holy Ghost* is the chief worker and the Father and the Son coöperate."

The above quotation may serve to show how difficult it is properly to define the truth concerning the relation of the three Persons of the holy trinity, as soon as the attempt is made to proceed beyond the simple declarations of the Apostolicum. They agree in this that the twenty-fourth answer of the Catechism may not be understood to teach that the outgoing works of God are divided, apportioned among the three Persons of the Godhead, so that the Father creates, the Son redeems, the Holy Ghost sanctifies. God triune is the author of all His works, and that in such a way that the relation of the three Persons to one another within the divine Being is maintained and revealed in the works of God *ad extra*. Yet even so, it may be regarded as questionable whether justice is done to the meaning of the Apostolic Confession. Especially might one hesitate to explain with Dr. Kuyper that in each of the works of God, creation, redemption, and sanctification, one of the three Persons functions as the chief actor, while the other two coöperate. This would appear to introduce a relation of subordination into the trinity in violation of the essential co-equality of the three Persons, as well as a change into their mutual relationship with respect to the outgoing works of God. Even as it would be a serious error to teach that to the Father alone belongs the work of creation, to the Son that of redemption, and to the Holy Ghost that of sanctification, so it must be regarded as fallacious to say that the Father is chief in the work of creation, the Son in that of redemption, the Holy Ghost in that of sanctification. The truth is that, while all the works of God are the works of one God, in them the First Person is always operating as Father, the Second Person as Son, the Third Person as Holy Ghost. While, therefore, the three Persons appear as essentially co-equal in all the outgoing works of God, their personal relation to one another never alters.

If we return again to the wording of the *Apostolicum*, it certainly is evident that the doctrine of the trinity is its underlying groundwork, due, no doubt, to the fact that it gradually grew out of the baptism formula, and the instruction that was based on it. Yet, it is equally evident that it does not offer an abstract confession of the truth of the trinity as such, in such a way that the first article speaks only of the first Person, articles two to seven of the second Person as such, and articles eight to twelve of the third Person in the Godhead. This should be evident at once from the first article: *Credo in DEUM PATREM omnipotentem; Creatorem coeli et terrae.* I believe in GOD FATHER almighty (Pisteuoo eis THEON PATERA panktokratora); Creator of heaven and earth. We feel at once that we could not possibly substitute here: I believe in the *First Person* of the Holy Trinity, the Father, almighty, creator of heaven and earth. This is impossible because of the close connection between GOD and FATHER (written in all capital letters both in the Greek and Latin versions, and in the former without the definite article), but also because the attribute of omnipotence is not peculiar to the first Person, but is an essential property of the Godhead, while, besides, the work of creation must be ascribed to all the three Persons of the Holy Trinity. Nor could we begin the second part of the *Apostolicum,* treating of the Son, by substituting: "And in the *Second Person* of the Godhead, the only begotten Son." For the subject of this second part, articles two to seven, is not the eternal Word as he subsists in the Godhead, but JESUS CHRIST. And it is these two names that are emphasized in the original versions both Greek and Latin, by being all capitalized. To be sure, it is affirmed of this JESUS CHRIST that He is the only (*unicum*), or only begotten (*monogenee*) Son of the FATHER GOD, yet the entire section speaks of this Son of God as He revealed Himself in human nature and tabernacled among us, suffered and died and was buried, rose the third day, and was exalted at the right hand of God. And although it is not so directly evident that the last part of the Apostolic Confession does not treat of the Holy Ghost merely as the *Third Person* in the trinity, but as the Spirit of Christ Who realizes the salvation acquired by the Mediator, yet the articles that follow article eight are limited wholly to the realization of the work of Christ: the church, the communion of saints, the forgiveness of sins, the resurrection, and eternal life. Notice, too that the words "in GOD" occur only in the first article: they are not repeated in articles two and eight.

For all these reasons, it would seem quite in harmony with the original meaning the early church attached to the *Apostoli-*

cum to say that it speaks of the triune God, not in the abstract, but as the God of our salvation and in relation to the believing church. The first article does not refer merely to the ontological Fatherhood of the First Person in relation to the Second, but also to the Fatherhood of the one true and living God in relation to: 1. Jesus Christ, the Mediator, our Lord. (According to Scripture, He is the *God* and Father of our Lord Jesus Christ). 2. Creation, called forth by His omnipotent will. 3. Believers for Christ's sake. The second part of the Apostolic Confession, does not simply speak of God the Son, in His relation to the First Person of the trinity, but of Jesus Christ, the Incarnated Word. And the third part speaks of the Holy Spirit as the Spirit of Christ, realizing the salvation accomplished for us unto all the elect. There is, according to this conception, a certain relation of subordination of the entire contents of the Confession to the First article, and particularly to the words: I believe in GOD. And we would paraphrase its meaning briefly as follows: I believe in GOD: Who revealed Himself as FATHER, and as omnipotent, in the work of creation; Who revealed Himself as REDEEMER in JESUS CHRIST, His only Son, our Lord; and Who revealed Himself as SANCTIFIER in the HOLY GHOST, as the Spirit of Christ.

––––––––

Credo in Deum! The Church believes in God! It is the Church, and the individual believer that is a member of that Church, that is here speaking, and that is the only possible, the only conceivable subject of this *Credo*. The believer in Christ alone is able to say: "I believe in God," and know what he is saying. For by *faith he knows the only, true and living God, Who is GOD, as He revealed Himself in Jesus Christ, the revelation that is contained in the Holy Scriptures, and in the light of which he hears and interprets the speech of God in all His works*: and knowing this only true God, he trusts in Him as the God of his salvation. In his Römerbrief, p. 18, Barth exclaims: "Gott! Wir wissen nicht, was wir damit sagen. Wer glaubt, der weiss, dass wir es nicht wissen." (God! We know not what we express by this. He that believes knows that we do not know this). But this is cer-

tainly not in accord with the faith of the Church expressed in
this: *Credo in DEUM PATREM!* The believer does not mean
to say: "I believe in some Unknown One, and I know not what
I say when I say *God.*" On the contrary, in the words *Credo in
Deum,* he takes the stand that God is known, because He has
revealed Himself.

In this confession, "I believe in God," the Church and the individual believer declare that God is GOD. He is the transcendent One, Who dwelleth in the light no man can approach
unto. He is Holy One of Israel, the Incomparable, that cannot
be likened to any creature. He cannot be classified or defined.
Human logic can never reach Him. In this sense, all the so-called
"proofs" for the existence of God must be considered failures.
No syllogism can reach out beyond its own premises, and no
human premise can postulate God who is GOD. Whatever man
may say about God, mere man, of himself, is sure to be a lie.
Always he will make a god like unto himself, and that which he
calls God is only an idol. For God is the Infinite, He transcends
the finite; He is the Eternal, He transcends time; He is the Invisible, He transcends the whole world of our experience; He
is the Immutable, He transcends all the flux of existence; He is
not the First Cause, nor the Cause of causes, as philosophy has
called its God, but He is simple Being: He transcends all causes.
He is GOD.

But by this confession, *Credo in Deum,* the Church and the
believer also express that He is the Immanent. He is not far from
any of us, for in Him we live and move, and have our being.
Were He merely the transcendent One, it would forever be impossible to say "I believe in God," or, at least, if we did say it,
we would have to add with Barth: "Gott! Wir wissen nicht, was
wir damit sagen." He would be the Unknowable of Herbert
Spencer, the One Whom we must needs seek but can never find.
Then we would not even be able to say, "that there is one only
simple and spiritual Being, which we call God; and that he is
eternal, incomprehensible, invisible, immutable, infinite, almighty, perfectly wise, just, good, and the overflowing fountain of
all good." (Conf. Belg. Art. 1). In that case all that we would say

about the transcendence of God would be a mere negation. But
although by its *Credo in Deum* the Church confesses that her
God is not the proud conception of *Pantheism*, but that He is
infinitely transcendent above all that is called creature, she does
not thereby postulate an infinite chasm between God and us, so
that, after the fashion of Deism, the transcendent God remains
for ever outside of the world. Nor is it thus that this *Deus
absconditus* occasionally speaks to us, in the "moment" when
the vertical line of His Word bisects the horizontal line of our
existence, and that the Church now speaks of God in the memory
of that Word of God. On the contrary, *Credo in Deum,* presupposes that the transcendent One is also immanent in all
things, and through all the works of His hands He speaks concerning Himself constantly, while He speaks of Himself as the
God of our salvation through Jesus Christ our Lord, in the
Holy Gospel, and through the Spirit of Christ He *dwells* in the
Church and establishes His everlasting covenant with us.

And thus it is only the believer that is able to say: I believe in
God. Philosophy cannot find Him. "Natural Theology," in the
sense that the natural man, either from "nature" or from himself,
can present the knowledge of the true God, who is GOD, does
not exist. This must be attributed, however, not to the fact that
God leaves Himself without witness, even apart from the revelation of the Holy Gospel. It is certainly true that even now "the
heavens declare the glory of God; and the firmament sheweth
his handiwork; day unto day uttereth speech, and night unto
night sheweth knowledge." Ps. 19:1, 2. And "the invisible things
of him from the creation of the world are clearly seen, being
understood by the things that are made, even his eternal power
and Godhead." Rom. 1:20. Nor dare it be said that this speech
of God in no sense of the word penetrates the consciousness of
the natural man. For by his "natural light" he retains "some
knowledge of God." And there is, no doubt, a general testimony
of the Spirit, corresponding to this speech of God in the works
of His hands, and writing indelibly upon every conscience that
He is, and that He is God! For "that which is known of God
(*to gnooston tou Theou*) is manifest in them, for God mani-

fested it unto them (*ho Theos gar autois ephaneroosen*). Rom.
1:19. Agnosticism and atheism are not the result of a certain
natural fallacy of the human mind. On the contrary, they are
the results of sin. The trouble is not "natural," but spiritual,
ethical. "The fool *saith in his heart,* There is no God." Ps. 14:1.
And the ungodliness and unrighteousness of men become revealed in this, that they "hold the truth in unrighteousness."
Rom. 1:18. Man contradicts the Word of God. He holds it under
in unrighteousness. He prefers to make his own God. And
making his own God in the foolishness of his vain imagination
and darkened heart, he makes him altogether like unto himself,
or even unto birds, and fourfooted beasts, and creeping things.
Rom. 1:23. Hence, it is only in the Church, the sphere of the
indwelling Spirit of Christ, that the Word of God concerning
Himself is heard and received by faith, and that the confession
is possible: Credo in Deum!

II

Of The Holy Trinity

Very sober and brief is the Heidelberg Catechism on the doctrine of the Holy Trinity. Strictly speaking, it expresses all it has to say on this important subject in one question and answer, the twenty-fifth: "Since there is but one only divine essence, why speakest thou of Father, Son, and Holy Ghost? Because God has so revealed himself in his word, that these three distinct persons are the one only true and eternal God." But although very brief, the answer may be considered quite complete. It reminds us that we can speak of the trinity only "because God has so revealed himself in his word." It teaches that God is *one*: there is only one divine essence, hypostatically distinct but essentially one, for they are "three distinct persons," but they are "the one only true and eternal God." But although all the essential elements of the doctrine of the trinity are present in this answer of our Catechism, these several elements need further explanation and development, if we are to understand what the Church means by her confession that God is one in essence and three in persons. And this we must understand. Even though it is true that the triune God far transcends our understanding, the *doctrine* of the Church concerning the mystery is, of course not *contrary* to our reason, and is capable of being expounded and understood.

Thus, at least, the early Church conceived of the matter, as is evident from what her greatest minds have written on the subject. The truth that God, one in essence, subsists in threeness of persons, was one of the first dogmas established by the Church. And as is usually the case, the final formulation and adoption of this doctrine was attained only in the way of a struggle with opposing and heretical views. The controversy centered around the question as to the proper *deity* and *distinct personality* of the Son. Even before the Church was disturbed by the Arian controversies, there were those who denied any hypostatical distinction in the Godhead. The so-called *Patropassians* held that God is one, the Father. This one God is Father in His invisible essence, but He is Son in His revelation. In the incarnation this Father-God animated a human body, and in that body He suffered and died on the cross. Hence, their name *Patropassians,* which denotes their peculiar view that the Father suffered. Others are known as *Nominal Trinitarians.* They, too, denied the personal subsistence of the Son and of the Holy Spirit. From one God, the Father, emanate two powers or effluences: the illuminating power, Wisdom or the Logos, and the quickening or enlivening power, called the Spirit. Both these heretical conceptions, however, still ascribed a certain *divinity* to Christ, though they denied His proper deity. Arius, however, denied both. According to him, Christ is a mere man, not divine in any sense, although He is the first and highest of all creatures. It was especially the Arian controversies that finally led, first to the convocation of the Council of Alexandria in 321, where the Arian heresies were condemned, and soon after, to the Council of Nicea (325), where the positive doctrine concerning the trinity was established, and officially adopted in a creed, the Symbol of Nicea.

From this Nicene Creed, it is very evident that theological thinking of that time was concentrated on the person of Christ, and His relation to the Godhead. And it was from that viewpoint that the doctrine of the trinity was discussed and established. On the one hand, it must be maintained that the Son was not a mere emanation or impersonal effluence from the Godhead, but a distinct hypostasis or person. And the same truth must be held with respect to the Holy Ghost. On the other hand, equal emphasis had to be placed upon the truth, that the Son (and also the Holy Spirit) was *not created,* but so begotten of the Father that He is very God, of the same essence as the Father, having His personal subsistence within the divine Being through *eternal generation.* Hence the Nicene Creed declares:

"We believe . . . in Jesus Christ, born of the Father, the only begotten, that is of the essence of the Father (*genethenta ek tou patros monogenee, toutestin ek tees ousias tou patros*), God of God, Light of Light, very God of very God, begotten, not made, of the same essence (*homoousion*) with the Father." And after this symbol has spoken very briefly of the Holy Ghost, it returns once more to the subject of the essential divinity or *deity* of Christ, and the eternal generation of the Son, when it condemns those "who say: There was a time when he was not; and: He was not before he was made; and: He was made out of nothing, or: He is of another substance, or essence, or: The Son of God is created, or: changeable, or: alterable."

It is, perhaps, partly due to this strong concentration upon the question of the deity of Christ, and His personal relation to the Godhead, that the Nicene Creed is remarkably silent on the deity and personality of the Holy Ghost, and His relation to the Father and to the Son. It simply declares: "And we believe in the Holy Ghost." But of course, the Arians were just as heretical in their views on the Holy Spirit as they were in their teachings respecting the Son. And soon after the Council of Nicea, some of the Semi-Arians, who were willing to concede a certain divinity (not deity) to Christ, (*homoiousion*, not *homoousion*), openly denied the divinity of the Holy Spirit. After their leader, a certain bishop Macedonius, these Semi-Arians were called *Macedonians*. According to them the Holy Spirit is not co-equal with the Father and the Son, but rather a minister or servant. They argued that, if the Holy Spirit were *begotten*, He must be begotten either of the Father or of the Son. If the former, there are two Sons in the Godhead, and they are brothers; if the latter, the Holy Spirit is a grandson of the Father. Superficial and profane though this form of reasoning was, it was evident that the brief declaration concerning the Holy Spirit made by the Council of Nicea was not sufficient. Also the deity and personal subsistence of the third person of the trinity must be established. And it was this that was accomplished by the Council of Constantinople in 381. It enlarged upon the article concerning the Holy Ghost as follows: "And in the Holy Ghost, the Lord and Giver of life; Who proceedeth from the Father; Who with the Father and the Son together is worshipped and glorified; Who spake by the prophets." We may notice, that although in this elaboration upon this doctrine of the Holy Ghost the essential deity and personal relation of the third person to the Father are clearly established, it is silent with respect to His relation to the Son. It does neither affirm nor deny the procession of the Holy Ghost from the Son. This gave rise to the controversy concerning the "filioque" (and from the Son), the question concerning the double procession of the Spirit. And it was the Western Church, perhaps under the powerful influence of Augustine, that inserted this phrase in the creed adopted at Constantinople, thus separating itself principally from the Eastern Church, that refused to confess the double procession of the third person of the trinity.

Somewhat dialectic in form and, perhaps, on that very account beautiful, is the *Symbolum Quicunque* (The Symbol "Whosoever" so called after its first word), often, though no doubt erroneously, ascribed to Athanasius. We quote it here: "1. Whosoever will be saved: before all things it is necessary that he holds the Catholic Faith: 2. Which Faith except everyone do keep whole and undefiled: without doubt he shall perish everlastingly. 3. And the Catholic Faith is this: That we worship one God in Trinity, and Trinity in Unity; 4. Neither confounding the Persons: nor dividing the Substance (Essence). 5. For there is one Person of the Father: another of the Son: and another of the Holy Ghost. 6. But the Godhead of the Father, of the Son, and of the Holy Ghost, is all one: the Glory equal, the Majesty coeternal. 7. Such as the Father is: such is the Son: and such is the Holy Ghost. 8. The Father uncreate (uncreated): the Son uncreate (uncreated): the Holy Ghost uncreate (uncreated). 9. The Father incomprehensible (unlimited): the Son incomprehensible (unlimited): the Holy Ghost incomprehensible (unlimited, or infinite). (The Latin here has: *Immensus* Pater, etc). 10. The Father eternal: and the Son eternal: and the Holy Ghost eternal. 11. And yet they are not three eternals: but one eternal. 12. And also there are not three uncreated: nor three incomprehensibles (infinites), but one uncreated: and one incomprehensible (infinite). 13. So likewise is the Father Almighty: the Son Almighty: and the Holy Ghost Almighty. 14. And yet there are not three Almighties: but one Almighty. 15. So the Father is God: the Son is God: and the Holy Ghost is God. 16. And yet they are not three Gods: but one God. 17. So likewise the Father is Lord: the Son is Lord: and the Holy Ghost is Lord. 18. And yet not three Lords: but one Lord. 19. For like as we are compelled by the Christian verity: to acknowledge every Person by himself to be God and Lord. 20. So are we forbidden by the Catholic Religion: to say, There be (are) three Gods, or three Lords. 21. The Father is made of none: neither created, nor begotten. 22. The Son of the Father alone: not made, not created: but begotten. 23. The Holy Ghost is of the Father and of the Son: neither made, nor created, nor begotten: but proceeding. 24. So there is one Father, not three Fathers: one Son, not three Sons: one Holy Ghost, not three Holy Ghosts. 25. And in this Trinity none is afore, or after another: none is greater, or less than another (there is nothing before, or after: nothing greater or less). 26. But the whole three Persons are co-eternal and co-equal. 27. So that in all things, as aforesaid: the Unity in Trinity, and the Trinity in Unity, is to be worshipped. 28. He therefore that will be saved, must (let him) thus think of the Trinity."

Essentially nothing has been changed in or added to the doctrine of the trinity as adopted by the early Church. The Nicene Creed is still the expression of the faith of the entire Church of Christ in the world. There were controversies and re-statements of doctrine with respect to other parts of the truth, but the dogma of the trinity remained the same since its adoption by the Council of Nicea. The Church of the Middle Ages adopted this truth, and the great minds of Scholasticism did not alter it either in form or in content. It is true that there were always individual thinkers that departed from the line of this fundamental doctrine. Old heresies were revived and appeared sometimes in a new form. Some presented views that reminded of *Nominal Trinitarianism,* like Scotus Erigena and Abelard; others separated the Persons of the Godhead, and were inclined to tritheism, or even to tetratheism. But all such deviations were regarded by the Church as heretical, and never was she seriously disturbed by any of them. And the same is true of the period of the Reformation. The Reformers taught the same doctrine on this score as did Athanasius, Hilary, and Augustine before them. Calvin writes extensively on this subject in his Institutes, I, 13. He insists that the Word of God teaches us that there are in God three substances, subsistences, hypostases, a concept which is properly expressed by the Latin Church in the word *personae,* persons. "We certainly conclude from the words of the apostle (in Heb. 1:3) that the Father has a subsistence of His own (propriam esse in Patre hypostasin), which is reflected in the Son. Whence again may easily be deduced the subsistence of the Son, which distinguishes him from the Father. The same is true in respect to the Holy Spirit: because we shall at once prove that he is God, and nevertheless it is necessary to consider him another distinct from the Father. Moreover, this distinction is not one of the Essence, which may not be made manifold. If therefore the testimony of the apostle demands belief, it follows that there are in God three subsistences (sequitur tres in Deo esse hypostases). And since the Latins expressed this by the word Person, it is a proof of too much haughtiness and obstinacy to squabble about so clear a matter. Verbally translated one would render it subsistence. Nor, in truth, was the use of the word Person peculiar to the Latins alone, but also the Greeks, probably to express their agreement, taught that there are three *prosopa* in God. But whoever, whether Greeks or Latins, differ among one another as to the term, they certainly agree in the main thing." Inst. I, 13, par. 2.

It draws the attention that Calvin here appears to use the words Person, Prosopa, Hypostasis, Subsistence promiscuously, as referring to the same thing. He is aware of the fact that, especially by the use of the term *subsistence* or *substance,* he exposes himself to the indictment of teaching tritheism. But he refuses to strive about mere words, if only it is established that

Father, Son, and Holy Ghost are the one true God, yet so that they are distinguished in respect to their personal properties. The Latins, he writes, translated the term *homoousios* by *consubstantialis*, and therefore used the word *substance* to denote *being*. And Jerome considered it blasphemy to say that there are three substances or subsistences in God. And yet one will find that Hilary, for instance, declares more than a hundred times that there are three substances in God! But even though the terms employed may not be above reproach, Calvin reminds us that it is necessary to employ these terms, because the truth of the trinity must be maintained over against such heretics as Arius and Sabellius. As for himself, however, by *Person* he understands "a subsistence in the divine essence which related to the others, is distinguished from them by an incommunicable property. By the term subsistence we wish to be understood something different from essence. For if the Word would simply be God, and would not have a peculiar property, John would have spoken rashly when he said that he was always with God. When immediately after, he adds that the Word also is Himself God, he reminds us of the unity of the Essence. But because he could not be with God without being in the Father, there arises hence that subsistence, which, although connected with the essence by an unbreakable bond, nor can be separated from it, has nevertheless a special mark, by which it is distinguished from it. Now I say that each of these three subsistences stands related to the others by a distinct property. The word *relation* is here expressly used, because when mention is made simply and without further definition of God, the reference is no less to the Son and to the Spirit than to the Father. But whenever the Father is compared with the Son, his own property distinguishes each from the other. Thirdly, I assert, that whatever is the peculiar property of each, is incommunicable, because whatever is attributed to the Father as a mark of distinction, cannot be applied or transferred to the Son. And truly, the definition of Tertullian does not displease me, provided it be rightly understood: that there is in God a certain disposition or economy which changes nothing in the unity of the Essence."

This doctrine of the trinity has found a place in all the main creeds of the Protestant Churches, nor dared the Roman Catholic Church differ from them in this respect, although the declarations of the Council of Trent take issue with the Protestant faith on many other points. As has been pointed out, the Heidelberger is very sober and brief on this point. But the *Confessio Belgica* teaches that "According to this truth and this Word of God, we believe in one only God, who is the one single essence, in which are three persons, really, truly, and eternally distinct, according to their incommunicable properties; namely, the Father, and the Son, and the Holy Ghost. The Father is the cause, origin and beginning of all things visible and invisible; the Son is the word, wisdom, and image of the Father; the Holy Ghost is the eternal power and might, proceeding from the Father and the Son. Nevertheless God is not by this distinction divided into three, since the Holy Scriptures teach us, that the Father, and the Son, and the Holy Ghost, have each his personality distinguished by their properties; but in such wise that these three persons are but one only God. Hence then, it is evident, that the Father is not the Son, nor the Son the Father, and likewise the Holy Ghost is neither the Father nor the Son. Nevertheless these persons thus distinguished are not divided, nor intermixed: for the Father hath not assumed flesh, nor hath the Holy Ghost, but the Son only. The Father hath never been without the Son, or without his Holy Ghost. For they are all three coeternal and coessential. There is neither first nor last: for they are all three one, in truth, in power, in goodness, and in mercy."

The overwhelming testimony of the Church, therefore, brands the Unitarians as heretics, outside of the Christian Church. Servetus launched a violent and blasphemous attack upon this most fundamental of Christian truths, and it cost him his life. But the fathers of modern Unitarianism, and of modern Rationalism, are the two brothers Laelius and Faustus Socinus. They agreed in denying the trinity, and they succeeded where Servetus failed, in founding a sect of their own. They found an asylum in one of the Polish Palatines, produced a number of theologians, and formulated a creed of their own. From there it made inroads into other parts of the world, especially in England and America, while on the continent it found a powerful ally in rationalistic philosophy. But in its Anti-trinitarian position it stands condemned by the entire Church of all ages, for the Spirit that leads into all the truth constantly taught her, through the Holy Scriptures, to confess that God is one essence, distinct in three persons, and that these three persons are the one, only, eternal God, Whom to know is eternal life!

III

The Revelation Of The Living God

The Catechism emphasizes that the doctrine of the holy trinity is known only from revelation. The Church and the individual believer speak of Father, Son, and Holy Ghost, as three persons in the divine essence, only "because God hath so revealed himself in his word, that these three distinct persons are the one only true and eternal God." This does not mean that the doctrine of the trinity as such, as a dogma, can be found in the Bible. The Scriptures do not speak of the trinity, of three persons in one essence, nor explain the relation of the three persons to one another. It is not a system of doctrine from which one may simply quote literally in order to prove the truth of a certain dogma adopted by the Church. It is the revelation of the living God. God came down to us to speak to us, on our own level, in language we could understand, concerning Himself. And when He thus reveals Himself, speaking of His glorious majesty, His works and virtues, He stands before us as the triune God, Who is one, yet also three, and Who through His threeness makes Himself known as the one, true, and eternal God. And the written record of that revelation of the living God we have in the Holy Scriptures. Hence, even though the ready made dogma of the trinity is not to be looked for in the Bible, it should not be difficult to demonstrate that "God hath so revealed himself in his word, that these three distinct persons are the one only true and eternal God."

Abundantly the Scriptures witness that God is *one*. In distinction from, and in opposition to the polytheism of the heathen nations, Israel must know and confess that there is only one God, and that He is one Lord: "Hear, O Israel: the Lord our God is one Lord." Deut. 6:4. His name is Jehovah, the I AM, the One Who exists of and by Himself, the Being of beings, the

Unchangeable, the Eternal, the infinite God, the incomparable Holy One of Israel. He, therefore, is God alone, for two or more independent Beings, possessing infinite properties, would imply a contradiction in terms. Hence, without expressly declaring the unity of God, the Scriptures deeply impress the oneness of God upon our minds whenever they speak of the infinite attributes or virtues of God. Hence, He is the one God, beside Whom there is none other, and Who alone is worthy of all praise and adoration, Whose name is excellent in all the earth, and Who set His glory in the heavens, Ps. 8:1; Whose glory the heavens declare, Ps. 19:1; and Who reveals His eternal power and Godhead, in order that men should glorify Him as God, and be thankful to Him, Rom. 1:20, 21. As the one only true God He speaks to us in the singular, and insists that there is no other God beside Him. "I am the Lord thy God" are the introductory words of the Decalogue, and hence, heading all the commandments stands the first: "Thou shalt have no other gods before me." In the prophecy of Isaiah the first personal pronoun with reference to God often occurs with great emphasis. "I have called thee by thy name; thou art mine. When thou passest through the waters, I will be with thee . . . For I am the Lord thy God, the Holy One of Israel, thy Saviour: I gave Egypt for thy ransom, Ethiopia and Seba for thee. Since thou wast precious in my sight, thou hast been honorable, and I have loved thee: therefore will I give men for thee, and people for thy life. Fear not: for I am with thee: I will bring thy seed from the east, and gather thee from the west; I will say to the north, Give up, and to the south, Keep not back . . . for I have created him for my glory, I have formed him, yea, I have made him . . . Ye are my witnesses, saith the Lord, and my servant whom I have chosen: that ye may know and believe me, and understand that I am he: before me there was no God formed, neither shall there be after me. I, even I, am the Lord; and beside me there is no saviour. I have declared, and have saved, and I have shewed, when there was no strange god among you: therefore ye are my witnesses, saith the Lord, that I am God. Yea, before the day was I am he: and there is none that can deliver out of my hand:

I will work, and who shall let it? . . . I am the Lord, your Holy One, the creator of Israel, your King." Isa. 43:1-14. God is one, Gal. 3:20; and there is one God and Father of all, who is above all, and through all, and in you all, Eph. 4:6.

There is, therefore, "one only simple spiritual Being, which we call God," and to this one Being belong all the essential divine attributes. This one Being is self-existent, infinite, eternal, immutable, transcendent and omnipresent, omniscient, all-wise, good, righteous, holy, gracious, merciful, infinitely glorious and blessed, all powerful, the one sovereign Lord. And He is one in Himself, so that all His virtues, although reflected and revealed to us in their manifold riches, are one in Him. He *is* His virtues. He *is* love and truth, knowledge and wisdom and power, righteousness and holiness, mercy and grace. Nor is there any division or conflict between these various divine virtues. They are absolutely one, so that His righteousness *is* His love, and His mercy *is* His holiness, and His grace *is* His truth. And this one only simple spiritual Essence, "which we call God," and Who is the Incomprehensible, Who dwelleth in the light no man can approach unto, revealed Himself as the *one* Lord, in order that He might be glorified as God, and be the sole object of all our adoration and worship, of all our confidence and hope, that we might know Him, have fellowship with Him, and in that fellowship and adoration of the living God be blessed for ever!

Yet, it is equally true that Scripture everywhere reveals that there is a plurality, a threeness, in this one simple spiritual Being, a threeness that never eliminates or destroys the essential oneness. Even on the very first page of Scripture this plurality in the oneness is plainly indicated: "And *God* said, Let *us* make man in *our* image, after *our* likeness." Gen. 1:26. Here, let it be noted: 1. God is addressing Himself, as is evident from the very contents of His speech: to no one beside Himself could He ascribe the work of man's creation or any participation in that work; 2. He is the *one* God speaking: God said; to which it dare not be objected that the plural form for God in the Hebrew (Elohim) implies a plurality of Gods, for the Hebrew form of the verb *said* (wajomer) is in the singular; 3. That, nevertheless, a plurality is ascribed as subsisting in the one divine essence by the plural pronouns *us* and *our*. God is one, and His image and likeness are one; yet, He is, in some sense more than one, and that, too, in such a manner that He is able to speak to Himself, suggesting a plurality of *personal* subsistences.

And thus the Word of God throughout reveals that the one God is also more than one, is three in persons. The "Angel of the Lord" is Himself God, even though He is also distinct from Him. For this Angel speaks as God to Hagar in the wilderness: "I will multiply thy seed exceedingly, that it shall not be numbered for multitude," Gen. 16:10; and Hagar recognized Him as God, for she "called the name of the Lord that spake unto her, Thou God seest me." Gen. 16:13. It is, no doubt, with reference to this same Angel of the Lord that we read: "Then *the Lord* rained upon Sodom and upon Gomorrah brimstone and fire from the Lord out of heaven." Gen. 19:24. Moreover, we learn from the Scriptures that in all His works God reveals Himself as acting in threeness of persons. For "by the Word of the Lord were the heavens made, and all the host of them by the Spirit of His mouth," Ps. 33:6. In calling the things that are not as if they were, God speaks creatively, and in the Gospel according to John Scripture comments upon this divine work as follows: "In the beginning was the Word, and the Word was with God, and the Word was God. The same was in the beginning with God. All things were made by him; and without him was not anything made that was made." And, besides, we read in Gen. 1:2, that the Spirit of God moved upon the face of the waters. Ps. 110:1 puts the following words in the mouth of the inspired author: "The Lord said unto my Lord, sit thou at my right hand," where David calls the Christ his Lord, Matt. 12:41-45. In the synagogue of Nazareth the Saviour quotes the words of Isaiah 61:1 with application to Himself: "The Spirit of the Lord God is upon me." It is the same Spirit of the Lord that renews the face of the earth. Ps. 104:30.

In the New Testament this threeness in God is much more clearly and distinctly revealed, for the Son of God is sent into the flesh, and the Spirit is poured out into the Church. And this Son of God is very God Himself, for "the Word was made flesh, and dwelt among us, and we beheld his glory, the glory as of the only begotten of the Father, full of grace and truth," John 1:14. And He is "the only begotten God (monogenees theos), which is in the bosom of the Father," John 1:18; "the true God, and eternal life," I John 5:18. And He declares of Himself that He is one in essence with the Father: "I and my Father are one (hen, essence)," John 10:30. And throughout divine names, virtues, works, and honors are ascribed to Him. And the same is true of the Holy Spirit. He is called God, Acts 5:3, 4, 9; He searches all things, even the deep things of God, I Cor. 2:10; and He alone knows the things of God, I Cor. 2:11. He participates in creation, Gen. 1:2, Ps. 33:6; is the Spirit of life, and of the resurrection, Rom. 8:2, 11; and of the adoption, Rom. 8:15; the Spirit in whose name, as well as in the name of the Father and of the Son, we are baptized, Matt. 28:19, and through Whom the blessings of grace are bestowed upon the Church, II Cor. 13:13. Moreover, He is not an impersonal power, but everywhere He appears as a person, Who comforts, John 14:16; teaches all things, and brings to remembrance the words of Christ, John 14:26; reproves the world of sin, righteousness, and judgment, John 16:8; speaks not of Himself, but speaks whatsoever He hears, and shews things to come, John 16:13; and He works all the several gifts of grace, dividing unto every man severally as He will, I Cor. 12:11. Indeed, "three there are that bear record in heaven, the Father, the Word, and the Holy Ghost, and these three are one," I John 5:7 (A. V.).

A profound mystery is this truth of the trinity. And this need not surprise us, for God Himself is the Mystery of mysteries. We may know Him as He has revealed Himself to us, but behind or beyond that revelation we cannot possibly penetrate. The infinite depths of His being we can never fathom, the immensity of His essence we can never comprehend, the secrets of His nature we can never scrutinize. But this does not mean that the *doctrine* of the trinity is an absurdity, or that the revelation of the trinity is contrary to our understanding. We must give ourselves account, therefore, of what we mean when we say that

God is one, and that He is yet three. In what sense is God one, and in what sense is He three? For that He cannot be one and also three in the same sense is evident. And this question the Heidelberg Catechism answers by stating that "there is but one only divine essence," and that yet the three *Persons* are distinct in that divine essence, so that Father, Son, and Holy Ghost are the one only true and eternal God.

There is, then, one divine essence: God is one with respect to His Being. There are not three Gods, there is only one God. There are not three divine natures, there is only one divine nature. There are not three divine minds, there is only one divine mind. There are not three divine wills, there is only one divine will. And it is in that one divine essence and nature that all the divine attributes subsist: the one divine essence is the implication of all infinite perfections. But in that one divine being there are three subsistences, hypostases, persons. And here three questions arise that require an answer in order somewhat to understand the doctrine of the trinity, viz., 1. What is meant by *person?* 2. What is the relation of the three persons of the Trinity to the divine Essence? 3. And what is the relation of the three persons of the Trinity to one another?

What is a *person?* In man his person is that which he calls his Ego, his *I.* It is the subject of all his actions, and it remains the same through whatever changes he may pass, in life or in death. *I* think, *I* desire, *I* will, *I* speak, *I* see, *I* hear, *I* eat and drink, *I* rejoice and sorrow, *I* love and hate, *I* sing and weep, *I* suffer and die, and *I* am raised from the dead. In all these actions and experiences my *person* is the subject that performs and experiences, and that remains the same throughout. From infancy to old age we pass through many changes, yet we know quite well that we remained the same individual subjects. In death the earthly house of this tabernacle is dissolved, yet it is the same person that passes through death, and into his eternal home. A person, then, is the subject of all actions and experiences in a rational, moral nature. A tree may be an individual tree, and a cow may be an individual cow, but neither the tree nor the cow is a person: they possess no rational-moral natures. But the human nature is rational-ethical. And the individual in that nature is a self-conscious person, a rational-moral subject acting through mind and will. When, therefore, we assert that there are three persons in the Godhead, we mean that in the one spiritual nature of God there are three subjects, three that say *I*, distinct from one another in personal properties, but subsisting in the same divine essence, and eternally remaining the same in their distinct subsistence. These distinct personal properties are indicated by their names: Father, Son, and Holy Ghost. The Father is eternally and distinctively Father: He generates the Son. The Son is eternally Son: He is generated by the Father. The Spirit is eternally Spirit: He proceeds from the Father, and from the Son. The Father is subject of all the divine essential properties, and of all the divine works, as Father: He thinks, wills, loves, counsels, decrees, creates, saves, as Father, never as Son, nor as Holy Spirit. The Son is subject of all the essential divine attributes, and of all the divine works, as Son, never as Father, nor as Holy Spirit. And the Holy Spirit is subject of all the essential virtues of the Godhead, and of all the divine works, as Spirit, never as Father, nor as Son. One divine essence, one divine nature, one divine mind and will, one divine life we confess; but in that one divine essence and nature there are three that think, will, love, and live, each in His own distinct personal manner. The Holy Trinity is a threeness of persons in unity of essence.

As to the relation of these three persons to the essence of the Godhead, we must emphasize that there is no division, no separation, no subordination between the three persons, but that all are equally God in the one Being. It is not so, that the divine essence is divided among the three persons, that each of the three persons subsists in part of the divine essence, or that the three persons are of different rank, subordinated to one another. That would lead to tritheism, to the doctrine of three Gods. On the contrary, all the three persons of the trinity subsist in the whole divine essence, and equally possess all the essential properties of the Godhead. All are equally infinite, eternal, immutable, almighty, wise, and good. If I may express myself thus humanly, all the three persons live and act on the same plane of the infinitely perfect Being of God. The Father is not the chief God, the Son God in a secondary sense, and the Holy Spirit in a still more subordinated sense of the word. These three distinct persons are equally the one true and eternal God!

And so, the relationship of the three persons of the Holy Trinity to one another is such that He is the living God, and that He lives the life of infinitely perfect friendship: He is the covenant God in Himself, and His own covenant life of friendship is the infinite archetype and basis of our covenant relation to, and covenant fellowship with Him.

The doctrine of the trinity implies that God is the living God! He is Life, and He lives in and through Himself. Life is energy expressing itself in activity. And it presupposes relationship, harmonious relationship. To live is to act and react normally in that relationship. Life cannot be in solitude. It always is some kind of communion, of fellowship. Now, God is the implication of infinite energy. In Him there is an infinite depth of divine power, of *dunamis,* of wisdom and righteousness and holiness and goodness and love and mercy and truth, incessantly active. And in the triune God there is also the infinitely perfect relationship and harmony for this energy to express itself into constant activity. For He is one, and this oneness is the eternal basis of the divine unity and harmony: in God there is no discord, no conflict, no dissonance, no disagreement; He is eternally in harmony with Himself. Yet, He is not alone, though He be one. Were He alone, He could not be the living God in Himself. But now the one God subsists in threeness of persons, Father, Son, and Holy Spirit, that sustain the relationship of perfect harmony to one another, and that react upon one another with all the energy of the divine nature, in knowledge and wisdom, in righteousness and holiness, in infinitely perfect love. And so there is a continuous current of divine energy, of infinitely perfect divine self-consciousness and joy, a glorious stream of life from the Father, to and through the Son, and in the Holy Spirit. God is life. He lives in Himself. And as the living God He is perfectly self-sufficient. He is in need of none beside Himself.

Of the Father, through the Son, in the Spirit, He knows and is known, He loves and is loved, He adores and is adored, He glorifies and is glorified in Himself. The truth of the trinity means that God is the living God!

And He is the covenant God. For the idea of the covenant is not that of an agreement, pact, or alliance: it is a bond of friendship and living fellowship. Friendship is that bond of fellowship between persons according to which and by which they enter into one another's life in perfect knowledge and love, so that mind is knit to mind, will to will, heart to heart, and each has no secrets for the other. It presupposes a basis of likeness, of equality, for only like knows like; and on that basis of equality it requires personal distinction, for without this there is only sameness, there can be no fellowship. And both, the equality and the personal distinction are in God. For He is the triune! The most absolute equality exist between Father, Son, and Holy Spirit, for these three are one in essence. And in Him there is the personal distinction between the three persons subsisting in the one Essence. And so, the three persons of the Holy Trinity completely and perfectly enter into one another's life. Their fellowship is infinitely perfect. They have no secrets from one another. There is no conflict between them. Their relationship is one of perfect harmony. The Father knows and loves the Son in the Spirit; the Son knows and loves the Father in the Spirit; the Spirit knows and loves the Father through the Son in Himself. The living God is the covenant God! That is the great significance of the truth that God is triune, and that these three distinct persons are the one only true and eternal God!

LORD'S DAY IX

Q. 26. What believest thou when thou sayest, "I believe in God the Father, Almighty, Maker of heaven and earth?"

A. That the eternal Father of our Lord Jesus Christ, who of nothing made heaven and earth, with all that is in them; who likewise upholds and governs the same by his eternal counsel and providence, is for the sake of Christ his Son, my God and my Father; on whom I rely so entirely, that I have no doubt, but he will provide me with all things necessary for soul and body: and further, that he will make whatever evils he sends upon me in this valley of tears turn out to my advantage: for he is able to do it, being Almighty God, and willing, being a faithful Father.

I

The Father Of Our Lord Jesus Christ

Only one Lord's Day, strictly speaking, the Heidelberg Catechism devotes to the discussion of the first article of the *Apostolic Confession*: "I believe in God the Father, Almighty, Creator of heaven and earth." It is true that also Lord's Day X is arranged under this head, but it occurs as an appendix to the present Lord's Day, and as an elaboration of the statement already found concerning the providence of God in this ninth chapter. And let us note that this entire answer consists of one sentence. Yet, this one answer is both beautiful and very significant. It is beautiful, for it is not a mere dogmatic explanation of the article of the Confession: it is the expression of a living faith. The Catechism would have us bear in mind that it is discussing the truth from the viewpoint of the faith of the Church, and that, too, as the expression of a living, saving faith, which is both a true spiritual knowledge and a hearty confidence. Ursinus, in his *Schatboek*, reminds us that the first article of the *Apostolic Confession* speaks of faith *in* God. And: *"I believe in* God signifies: I believe that He is my God, that whatever He is and has, He is and has unto my salvation. *To believe God* is, strictly speaking, to believe that there is a God in accord with all His perfections. *To believe in God* is: to accept that God causes all that is ascribed to Him, for His Son's sake, to work together unto my salvation." I, p. 186. And this is clearly and beautifully expressed and emphasized in this ninth Lord's Day: the eternal Father of our Lord Jesus Christ . . . is my God and Father for Christ's sake, and I rely completely on Him, in prosperity and adversity, knowing that He is both able and willing to turn all things unto my advantage and salvation.

But not only is this ninth Lord's Day, brief though it be, beautiful and rich as the expression of a living faith, it is also highly significant from a doctrinal viewpoint. One cannot but wonder, when considering this twenty-sixth answer of our Heidelberger, at the ability of its authors to crowd so much important doctrine into a single sentence. Let us note that this Lord's Day speaks of: 1. The eternal Fatherhood of God with relation to our Lord Jesus Christ. 2. Of the work of creation out of nothing. 3. Of God's providence. 4. Of his eternal counsel. 5. Of his Fatherhood in relation to the believer for Christ's sake. 6. Of his omnipotence. 7. Of his power and willingness to cause all things to work together for good. And let us notice, too, that all these truths are set forth in their proper order and relation to one another: It is *the God and Father of our Lord Jesus Christ* Who as such, i.e. precisely as *God and Father of our Lord Jesus Christ,* created all things, and upholds and governs all things; and Who, being for Christ's sake also my God and Father, from the very beginning adapted all things, and still adapts all things, according to His eternal counsel, to my salvation; so that I may, indeed, completely confide in His almighty power, and eternal love!

The main theme of this Lord's Day is plainly the Fatherhood of God. A mistake do they make who, instead of emphasizing this Fatherhood of God in their explanation of the Catechism in speech or print, present an elaborate discussion of creation. It is not creation but the Creator that is the chief subject of the first article of the *Apostolic Confession.* Faith in *God* is expressed there. And it speaks of this God as Father Almighty, Who is revealed as such in His divine work of creating heaven and earth. The Catechism has discerned this quite clearly, and while speaking of the work of creation and of providence only in passing as it were, places all the emphasis on the Fatherhood of God. And we may distinguish here at once a threefold divine fatherhood, viz. the fatherhood of God with relation to our Lord Jesus Christ, His fatherhood as the Creator, with relation to all things, and His fatherhood with relation to His people in Jesus Christ and for His sake. It is this first fatherhood of God, His father-relation to our Lord Jesus Christ, that is the subject of our discussion in the present chapter.

But here we must at once make an important distinction, that, namely, between the eternal fatherhood of the First Person in relation to the Son in the divine nature, and the fatherhood of the triune God in relation to Christ as the Mediator, in His human nature. This distinction is frequently overlooked, and in some instances even expressly and consciously denied, but it is very important that it be clearly discerned and maintained. In *Sermons on the Apostles' Creed,* edited by H. J. Kuiper, we read on p. 27: "After this general description we must now direct our attention to the fact that, in harmony with what Holy Scripture reveals about God, the ninth Lord's Day of our Catechism speaks of God's fatherhood in more than one sense. To be father is to be the root, the cause of things or persons to whom that fatherhood pertains. To be the Alpha, the origin, of all that is and lives can be said only of the Creator in an absolute sense, and not of any creature. But to God that fatherhood is attributed in different ways, for God is not the first cause of all beings in exactly the same sense, or by the same activities. Scripture clearly distinguishes between three kinds of fatherhood which are ascribed to God. *Of course, when speaking here of three different kinds of divine fatherhood, we have reference to the first person of the Trinity.* (Italics are mine.) He is the Father of the second person, the eternal Son, by his act of eternal generation. But in his Word He is also revealed as the Father of the entire universe. And, lastly, we honor Him as the Father of believers, whom He has adopted as his beloved children. He is the father of Christ, of all the creatures in general, and of his spiritual children in Christ. Thus we should think and speak of Him as we meditate on the first Article of the Apostles' Creed: 'I believe in God the Father, Almighty, Maker of heaven and earth.' "

I do not know, of course, whether and in how far the author of this sermon was fully conscious of the implication of these sentences; but it seems to me that, on second thought, he will discern that they present a serious error. For they imply that in the first article of the *Apostolic Confession* the believer speaks of the first person of the Holy Trinity only, that only the first person is the Creator of the heavens and the earth, and that only the first person is the Father of believers, so that, when they address God in the Lord's Prayer as "Our Father, who art in heaven," they are praying to the first person only, to the exclusion of the Son, and of the Holy Spirit. It is evident that this cannot be the meaning of the *Apostles' Creed*, and that this is not the correct presentation of the sense of the ninth Lord's Day.

That it was not the conception of Ursinus is plain from his *Schatboek*. In explanation of the words "I believe in God," he writes: *"In God.* The name God is here to be taken as denoting the being in the place of God the Father, the Son, and the Holy Spirit; because the verb *to believe* connected with the preposition *in* has reference in the same manner to all the three persons of the Godhead. For we do no less believe in the Son and in the Holy Ghost than in the Father." p. 186. And on the term Father in the first article of the *Apostolic Confession* he writes as follows: *"The Father.* The word *Father* here stands over against Son to denote the person and signifies the first person of the Godhead; *when He is compared with the creatures, one understands by this word the being of God, and thus the word Father refers to the whole divine essence,* (Italics are mine.) as in the Lord's Prayer: 'Our Father, who art in heaven.' " idem p. 186.

And the same distinction is presented by Dr. A. Kuyper in his *E Voto*, I, p. 186: "Speaking on this point, we must meanwhile remark that the name *Father* may be used by the creature, either in the narrower sense of the First Person of the Trinity, or likewise of the Divine Being without distinction of persons. Over against the creature, Father, Son and Holy Ghost is the Creator and the Fountain of all good; and we call upon the Triune Being as our Father in heaven. But if we inquire further, in which of these three Persons this Fatherhood in the Eternal Divine Essence is found more particularly (that is, economically), this Fatherhood in the narrower sense must be ascribed to the First Person."

We must, then, make a distinction between the unique fatherhood of the first person of the Holy Trinity with relation to the essential and eternal Son of God, and the fatherhood of God with relation to all creatures. The former is a relation within the economy of the Trinity, the latter a relation of the Triune God to the creature outside of Him. The former is a relation between two persons of the Trinity, the latter is a relation between the Being of God, as subsisting in three persons, and the creature formed by His will and power. The former is an eternal relation, the latter is called into being in time. The former may be called a natural, necessary relation in God, the latter is rooted in God's sovereign counsel and will.

And for the same reason we must make a distinction between the relation between the Father and the Son within the Holy Trinity, and the relation between the "God and Father of our Lord Jesus Christ," and the Mediator in His human nature. The author of the sermon from which we quoted above ostensibly denies this expressly. He writes: "God is our Father for Christ's sake. By that very expression we also state that God's Fatherhood over us is essentially different from his relation to the eternal Son. In the present humanistic tendencies of our American churches we must not suffer ourselves to be led into modernistic vagueness and confusion. Remember how carefully our Savior expressed himself when he instructed the disciples about the Father and his Fatherhood. He never confused the relations but spoke distinctly about 'my Father' and 'your Father.' Never did he draw human beings, even if they were his beloved friends, into that unique relationship between the Father and Himself. He never spoke about *our* God and *our* Father, but always clearly distinguished between 'my' and 'your' Father. Only once did He use the expression: 'Our Father, who art in heaven.' But we know that was to be the disciples' prayer, not his own." pp. 31, 32.

The truth in the above quotation is, that there is an eternal distinction between Christ's Sonship as the "only begotten God," and our sonship of adoption and regeneration. As condemnation of modernism to draw the essential Sonship of Christ as the second person of the Trinity down to the level of man's sonship, or, pantheistically, to raise our sonship to that of the second person of the Holy Trinity, the distinction made is quite true. But when the author insists that *in no sense* Christ could say *our* God and *our* Father together with His *brethren,* i.e. according to, and in and through His human nature, he is in error. And even to successfully defend the distinct essential Sonship of Christ in His divine nature, it is necessary to point out that He was also the Son in His human nature, the "holy Child Jesus," and that, although the two are related so that the latter is rooted in the former, even as the two natures are united in the one divine Person, yet they must be distinguished. This is evident even from the very words of the Lord to which the above quotation seems to refer, the words of Jesus to Mary Magdalene: "But go to my brethren, and say unto them, I ascend unto my Father, and your Father; *and to my God, and to your God."* John 20:17. For how could the Son in His divine nature call the Father *His God?* As the essential Son He is very God Himself, and in the divine nature He could no more call the Father His God than the Father could call Him His God. Or how could the second person of the holy trinity *ascend* to the first person? It is plain, then, that the Saviour in these words speaks as the Mediator, the Brother among many brethren, in His human nature; and that as such He speaks of "my Father and your Father" in one sense, in the same sense in which God is also "my God and your God." It is not the second person in the divine nature that here speaks of His relation to the first person, but the divine Son in and through His human nature, that here calls, not the first person, but *God* His Father. This is corroborated by the well known expression "the God and Father of our Lord Jesus Christ," Rom. 15:6; I Cor. 15:24; II Cor. 11:31; Eph. 1:3; I Pet. 1:3. It is true that some interpreters claim that the genitive "of our Lord Jesus Christ" (tou Kuriou heemoon Jesou Christou) must be understood as modifying only the name Father, and not also God. But not only have they no exegetical reason for this construction, and not only is it much more natural to connect the genitive with both, God and Father; but besides, we find the expression "The God of our Lord Jesus Christ," Eph. 1:17; and the Savior calls Him *his* God, Matt. 27:

46; John 20:17; Rev. 3:12. All this, and many other evidences in
Scripture of the same truth, plainly show that we must make
a distinction between the essential and eternal Sonship of Christ
in relation to the Father as the First person in the Holy Trinity,
and the assumed sonship of the Saviour in His human nature
in relation to God as His Father.

We must bear this in mind, even when we would quote proof
texts for the doctrine of *eternal generation*. There is no doubt
that Scripture teaches this truth. But we must be careful when
we quote texts in support of this doctrine, lest we do violence to
Scripture. Thus, to mention just one example, Ps. 2:7 is often
offered as direct proof of the eternal generation of the Son of
God: "I will declare the decree: the Lord hath said unto me,
Thou art my Son: this day have I begotten thee." But if we are
not careful we will, by quoting this text as referring directly
to the generation of the Son of God, fall into the error of modernism, or, at least, into that of the theory that the Son is subordinate to the Father. Let us notice, in the first place, that there
is mention here of the *decree*. It is, therefore, according to the
decree of God that the one that is here speaking is God's Son.
But surely, the second person is not Son by virtue of a decree
of the Triune God, but by virtue of the act of eternal generation
by the first person. We must, therefore, at once conclude that
these words do not refer exclusively, and not even in the first
place, to the eternal generation of the Son of God. And the context of the second psalm bears this out. For it is evident that the
psalm has its historical background in David as the theocratic
king of Israel, and that the words of vs. 7 must be applied to
him in the first place. It is against him that the "heathen rage,
and the people imagine a vain thing." He is the anointed of the
Lord against whom "the kings of the earth set themselves, and
the rulers take counsel together." It is of him, first of all, that
the Lord declares: "I have set my king upon my holy hill of
Zion." And it is he, too, as far as the historical background of
the psalm is concerned, to whom the words refer: "Thou art my
Son, this day have I begotten thee." In this historical back-

ground of the Psalm, therefore, we must take our startingpoint, would we do justice to the meaning of Holy Scripture.

Yet, we must immediately add that it is only in a comparatively small way that the words of Psalm 2 can be applied to David. They are spoken of him only as a type, as a faint prefiguration of Another. This is evident from the words of the Psalm itself. It would be the height of presumption to apply all the words of this inspired prophecy to a mere man. This is evident if we only consider the last verse: "Kiss the Son, lest he be angry, and ye perish from the way, when his wrath is kindled but a little. Blessed are all they that put their trust in him." But this is very plain if we consult the passages in the New Testament that quote the second Psalm. By these it is raised beyond all doubt that David spoke prophetically of the Christ, the Son of God in human nature, the Anointed *par excellence,* who is made heir of all things, and to whom indeed the ends of the earth are given for His possession. But even so, the words of Psalm 2:7 may not even in the second place be directly applied to the eternal generation of the Son: they refer directly to the fact that according to the *decree God begot Christ,* His Servant, the Anointed, the King over Zion, against whom all the kings of the earth set themselves, and the nations rage and imagine a vain thing, but who is victorious and made heir of all things. This is evident from that beautiful prayer the Church uttered upon the return to them of Peter and John: "Lord, thou art God, which hast made heaven, and earth, and the sea, and all that in them is. Who by the mouth of thy servant David hast said, Why did the heathen rage, and the people imagine vain things? The kings of the earth stood up, and the rulers were gathered together against the Lord, and against his Christ. For of a truth against thy holy child Jesus, whom thou hast anointed, both Herod, and Pontius Pilate, with the Gentiles, and the people of Israel, were gathered together, For to do whatsoever thy hand and thy counsel determined before to be done." Acts 4:24-28. It is evident that here the words of Psalm 2 are applied to the "holy child Jesus," the Anointed of God, Christ in His human nature. And more specifically, the words of Psalm 2:7 are applied to the resurrection of Christ in Acts 13:32, 33: "And we declare unto you glad tidings, how that the promise which was made unto the fathers, God hath fulfilled the same unto us their children, in that he hath raised up Jesus again; as it is also written in the second Psalm, Thou art my Son, this day have I begotten thee." It was, therefore, in the resurrection of Jesus Christ from the dead that the decree was fulfilled: "Thou art my Son, this day have I begotten thee." It was then that God begat Him to be for ever King over Zion. It was in the resurrection that we find the beginning of that exaltation that was completed when He was placed at the right hand of God in glory. "This day" of Psalm 2:7, therefore, refers, first of all, to the moment of David's anointing as king of Israel; and, secondly, to the moment of Christ's resurrection from the dead. From all this it is evident that, when we speak of Fatherhood of God with relation to Christ, we must make a distinction between the Fatherhood of the first person of the Holy Trinity with relation to the second person, and the Fatherhood of the Triune God with relation to Christ in the flesh. The first is by eternal generation, as we hope to explain in the next chapter, the second is according to the *decree* by which the Son was anointed Mediator, and heir of all things. And according to the last relation the "holy child Jesus" is subordinate to the Father, His servant, and the Father is also the God of our Lord Jesus Christ.

II

The Eternal Father Of The Son

Even though passages like Ps. 2:7 cannot be directly quoted to prove the doctrine of the eternal Fatherhood of the first person of the Holy Trinity, and of eternal generation; and even though they refer also to David, and to the resurrection of Christ, yet there can be no doubt about the fact that in last analysis they do speak of that eternal Fatherhood. The Church is not in error when she quotes these words as proof of the eternal generation of the Son. The fatherhood of God with relation to the "holy child Jesus" has its root and basis in the eternal fatherhood of the first person in relation to the second. This may, first of all, be considered as following from the fact that God by His relation to the creature does not *become* what He is not eternally in Himself. That would make God dependent on His own creation. He is the absolutely self-sufficient One. He has no need of the creature in any sense. Whatever He is in relation to the creature, He is first and eternally in Himself. This is also true of His fatherhood. He did not *become* Father through His relation to Christ as the Mediator, nor through His relation to creation in general, nor through His relation to His people in Christ Jesus. He is Father, eternally, perfectly, within His own being, and all other fatherhood of God is only a reflection of His own divine and eternal fatherhood. It is this truth which the Church has sought to maintain and to express, when she spoke of *eternal generation*.

But this truth is also abundantly evident from other parts of Holy Writ. Thus Scripture calls the second person of the Holy Trinity *the Word* of God. "In the beginning was the Word, and the Word was with God, and the Word was God. The same was in the beginning with God. All things were made by him; and without him was not anything made that was made." John 1:1-3.

This term itself, *the Word,* is significant. With us *speech* is the expression of what we *conceive* in our mind. Only, with us speech: (1) Consists of many words; (2) We speak of many things; (3) Our speech is but for a moment; (4) And our speech is not causative, it does not bring forth anything; it expresses what is, it never causes to be what is not. However, with God this is different. For with Him: (1) Is *the Word,* the one expression of the infinite fulness of all that is in God. God conceives His own glorious, infinite fulness, and that divine conception is expressed in *the Word.* (2) Is the speech concerning *Himself.* Of whom shall the eternal, self-sufficient God speak but of Himself? Even creation is God's manifold speech concerning Himself. But the Son of God is His eternal, Infinite Word, which God speaks *of Himself and unto Himself.* That one, eternal Word is the Word which God addresses to Himself, and which only He can hear and understand. This latter idea is beautifully expressed in the text from John quoted above. For the Word was *with God,* He was eternally toward God, He is the Word that *faces* God (pros ton Theon). (3) Is the eternal speech. The Word is spoken within the divine Being, for the Word was God. It is, therefore, spoken eternally and it is the Word exactly by virtue of its being spoken constantly. It is eternally perfect, full, complete, yet never so that it subsists apart from the Speaker. (4) Is the causative Word, the Word that brings forth, that gives subsistence, life. He so speaks that the Word is also God, and, moreover, a subsistence, a hypostasis, a person, Who Himself speaks, creates, lives. John 1:3, 4. In this term, *the Word,* therefore, we have an indication of an act that is performed within the divine being, an eternal act, that is always perfect and complete, yet never ceases to be performed, and through which Someone receives subsistence *as God, and with God.* And this is exactly what is meant by the eternal Fatherhood of the first person of the Holy Trinity, *generating the Son eternally.*

Moreover, the Bible speaks of Christ as the *only begotten Son.* For "the Word was made flesh, and dwelt among us, and we beheld his glory, the glory as of the only begotten of the Father, full of grace and truth (mongenous para Patros). For God so loved the world, that he gave his only begotten Son (ton Huion ton monogenee), that whosoever believeth in him should not perish, but have everlasting life." John 1:14; 3:16. And it is even very probable that John 1:18 should be read as follows: "No man hath seen God at any time; *the only begotten God,* which is in the bosom of the Father, he hath declared him." And in John 4:18: "He that believeth on him is not condemned: but he that believeth not is condemned already, because he hath not believed in the name of the only begotten Son of God." Many other passages might be quoted to prove this unique Sonship of Christ. The devil does not speak of a general and creaturely sonship when he tempts the Christ, and says to Him: "If thou art the Son of God," for on the assumption that this is true he expects Him to be able to command the very stones that they become bread. The hostile Jews understand very well that when Christ speaks of God as His Father He does so in an altogether unique sense of the word, for they accuse Him of blasphemy, because He makes Himself equal with God. And the disciples confess Him to be the Son of God in such a way that they plainly witness of His essential divinity. But we are not now speaking of the unique Sonship of the historical Jesus, or of Christ, but of the Fatherhood of the first person of the Holy Trinity with relation to the only begotten Son. And for this the terms "the only begotten Son," and "the only begotten God," are very significant. For they teach us: (1) That in distinction from all other sonship there is one Son that is "begotten" by a unique act of the Father. What is it to beget? It is to bring forth a being like unto oneself. Adam was the son of God (Lu. 3:38) by reason of the fact that God begat him, i. e., He created him after His own image: there was a creaturely likeness of God in man. And of Adam we read: "And Adam lived an hundred and thirty years, and begat a son in his own likeness, after his image, and called his name Seth." This, then, is the idea of generation. It is an act of love whereby one, as it were, reproduces himself in another, begets an individual like unto himself, in his own image.   Now there is an

infinite difference between God's act of begetting or generation
and that of man. Fatherhood among men cannot function alone:
it requires motherhood; but the Fatherhood of the eternal
Father of our Lord Jesus Christ is perfect in itself: the Father
begets or generates the Son of Himself. With us the act of generation is but for a moment, and the son we beget does not receive his continued subsistence by a continued act of generation
on our part. But God is eternally Father: He generates the Son
by an act of infinite love from everlasting to everlasting. Not
for one moment does the first person of the Holy Trinity cease
to be Father. With us the likeness of the being which we give
subsistence through generation is very imperfect, and very much
in part. But the likeness produced through God's act of eternal
generation is complete and absolutely perfect. For, finally,
with us generation means not only that we produce another
person, but that person is also a separate *being;* but with God
the act of generation takes place *within the divine Being,* and
the person of the Son is essentially one with the Father, and
never separated from Him. He is in the bosom of the Father.
He is the only begotten God! And (2) that in the act of the
generation of this only begotten Son the whole infinite Being
of God is active, the first person is Father in the whole divine
nature with all its infinite perfections: *God is wholly Father,*
just as He is wholly Son, and wholly Spirit; yet so that God
the Father is never God the Son, nor God the Spirit.

In the same direction point all those passages that speak of
Christ as the *image,* the express image of His person, the brightness of His glory. In the introductory verses of the epistle to
the Hebrews this is especially clear and emphatic: "God, who at
sundry times and in divers manners spake in time past unto
the fathers by the prophets, hath in these last times spoken unto
us by His Son, whom he hath appointed heir of all things, by
whom also he made the worlds; Who being the brightness of
his glory (apaugasma tees doxees), and the express image of
his person (charakteer tees hupostaseoos autou), and upholding all things by the word of his power, when he had himself
purged our sins, sat down on the right hand of the Majesty

on high. Being made so much better than the angels, as he hath by inheritance obtained a more excellent name than they. For unto which of the angels said he at any time, Thou art my son, this day have I begotten thee? And again, I will be to him a Father, and he shall be to me a Son? And again, when he bringeth in the firstbegotten into the world, he saith, And let all the angels of God worship him." It is true that even these words must be read and explained with discrimination. They do not merely speak of the glory of the eternal Son of the Father; they also speak of the unique glory of the Mediator in His human nature. For, to be sure, it was in His human nature that He purged our sins, that He sat down on the right hand of the Majesty on high, and that He was so much better than the angels as He obtained a more excellent name than they. But all this has its root and eternal background in the glory of the eternal Son of God. For only of the divine Son it could be said that He upholds all things by the word of His power, that by Him the worlds are made, and that all the angels of God must worship Him. Especially this last is significant, not only because worship is a divine prerogative, God only may be worshipped, but also because these words really identify this Son with God. They are quotations from Deut. 32:43, and Ps. 97:7, as they are translated in the Septuagint. We need not enter into the somewhat difficult question in how far they may be considered literal quotations. The point is, that the Old Testament passages refer to God; and what is there predicated of God is here applied directly to the Son.

Now, this Son is called: "the brightness of his glory," and "the express image of his person." It is especially these terms that are of significance for the doctrine of the Fatherhood of God, and of eternal generation. The Son is the brightness of the glory of God. Now, the glory of God is the radiance of all His infinite virtues. God is good. He is infinitely good. He is the implication of all infinite perfections. Of this perfection, and that, too, exactly because it is *infinite*, the radiance is called glory. Of this glory, and hence of all the divine perfections, Christ is said to be the "brightness." The original word used here is *apaugasma*.

The word may mean either the emitting of light or brightness, as the rays of the sun are the brightness of the sun, or it may signify the *reflection* caused by that emitted light, effulgence or refulgence, radiance or reflection. The latter is probably the correct interpretation of the term. For our present purpose it makes no difference, however, which of these two meanings is accepted as the correct one, for in both instances it suggests the act of eternal generation. With respect to the Son the term expresses: (1) the idea of distinct personal subsistence: the Son subsists as the reflection of the Father's glory; (2) the idea of perfect and complete resemblance: the Son is the reflection of the *glory* of God, all the divine perfections are reflected in Him; and (3) the idea of constant derivation, for the reflection is caused by the constant emittance of the light it reflects. But especially this latter notion signifies with respect to the Father, that from Him proceeds this constant radiance that is reflected in the Son. Just as the light radiates constantly from the sun, and reflects itself in many objects, so the glory of God radiates eternally from the Father and causes the perfect and infinite reflection which is the Son. The Son, therefore, with relation to the Father, is Light of Light, and the shining forth of that Light within the divine essence that gives subsistence to the Reflection in the person of the Son is called eternal generation.

Somewhat different is the notion expressed by the words: "the express image of his person." It is probably better to translate: "the express image of his essence." The word *hypostasis* assumed the meaning of *person,* or subsistence in the language of the Church in later ages, but it is at least doubtful whether it had this connotation in the usage of the apostles. The meaning, therefore, is that Christ is the express image of the Being of God. The word used for "express image" is *charakteer,* an impress made in wax. And although this term does not suggest as beautifully as that of "the reflected brightness of his glory," the act of eternal generation on the part of the Father, yet it expresses: (1) that the Son is the full and exact image of the Father; (2) that He derives His personal subsistence as the image of God within the divine Essence from the Father, Who makes the impress. God, therefore, is the eternal Father, apart from any relation to the creature, and from everlasting to everlasting He beholds His own image and reflection in the person of the Son.

In this connection we cannot refrain from calling attention to one more passage of Scripture. We mean that profound and glorious description of the immense contrast between the eternal and essential glory of the Son of God in divine nature, and the deep and exhaustive humiliation of that same Son in human nature, which is found in Phil. 2:6-8: "Who being in the form of God, thought it not robbery to be equal with God: but made himself of no reputation, and took upon him the form of a servant, and was made in the likeness of men: and being found in fashion as a man, he humbled himself, and became obedient unto death, even the death of the cross." We now have to do only with the first part: "Who being in the form of God." But how could one, dealing with this passage at all, refrain from remarking upon the tremendous contrast that is here pictured, the amazing humiliation that is here described, the utter self-negation of a perfect obedience that is here mentioned. Being in the form of God! O, in order to visualize a little of the awful self-humiliation of Christ described in these verses, we must not carry any time element into this particular expression, as if Christ once *was* in the form of God, and then, at His incarnation discarded that form. No, Christ *is*, eternally subsists in the form of God in the divine nature, and He did not cease to be in that form of God at the moment of His incarnation, even though then He also appeared in the form of man. He is, according to the divine nature in the form of God, when as a little babe He lies in Bethlehem's manger, when He walks about in the form of a servant, when He is seen in the likeness of man, when He is abused, mocked, maltreated, spit upon, captured, scourged, condemned, crucified. Being in the form of God in the divine nature, eternally being in the bosom of the Father, He emptied Himself completely in the human nature, and became obedient unto the death of the cross! He is in the form of God. That form of God expresses approximately the same as the *apaugasma*, the reflection, and the *charakteer*, the express image, of Heb. 1:3. *It is the Being reflected.* It is the form that presupposes the Being, that is the expression of the Being. As Being and Form belong together, as the one is the expression of the other, so the Father and the Son belong together, as two subsistences in the same essence. The Father is He that eternally *forms*, the Son is He that eternally is formed. Yet, although the Father forms eternally, the act of formation is eternally perfect and complete. And although the Son is eternally formed, yet the form of the Son is eternally finished by the eternal act of the Father's formation. God is the eternal, the infinitely perfect Father in Himself with relation to the eternal, only begotten God!

Finally, we must call attention to John 5:26: "For as the Father hath life in himself, so hath he given to the Son to have life in himself." Also these words have reference to an eternal act of the Father with relation to the Son within the divine essence. It is true that some have denied this, and explain the words as if they had reference to God's giving life to the Mediator in His human nature. They point especially to the following verse, which speaks of the Father's having given Christ, and that, too, as the Son of man, authority to execute judgment. But, although it may be granted that vs. 27 refers to Christ in His human nature, this cannot possibly be adduced as a ground to interpret vs. 26 as also referring to "the Son of man." The two verses yield a very natural sense when vs. 26 is understood as referring to the act of the Father whereby He eternally gives life to the Son, while vs. 27 is explained as referring to God's gift of authority to execute judgment bestowed upon Christ in the flesh. The one is the eternal background of the other. What decides, however, in favor of the explanation that in vs. 26 there is mention, not of bestowing creaturely life upon the human nature of Christ, but of imparting divine life to the Son of God, is the expression: "to have life in Himself." The creature has life, but never in himself. God only has life in Himself, for He is life. The text, therefore, speaks of a bestowal of life by the Father upon the Son, the result of which is that the Son is equal with the Father, has life in Himself, i. e., in the divine essence.

And so, everywhere, and in many ways, Scripture reveals to us that God is an eternal Father with relation to the Son. The Father is the Begetter, the Son the Begotten; the Father is the radiating light of glory, the Son is the light reflected; the Father is God forming, the Son is God formed; the Father is God Expresser, the Son is the Impress; the Father is God effulgent, the Son is God refulgent. The Father is the eternal Subject, the Speaker, the Son is the eternal Predicate, the Word of God! And God is the all sufficient One in Himself, that has no need of the creature even to rejoice in His glorious and eternal Fatherhood. He loves the Son forever!

III

The Eternal Father Creator

Very properly and beautifully the Heidelberg Catechism, speaking of God's fatherhood with respect to all things, as the Creator of heaven and earth, mentions God's eternal counsel. It is true that it introduces this counsel here, strictly speaking, not in connection with creation, but as the power whereby God still upholds and governs all things; but this necessarily implies that the same universe that is thus upheld by God's counsel was also created according to and by the same eternal decree.

And let it be understood from the very outset that it is of utmost importance to speak of this eternal purpose and counsel of God as logically preceding the act of creation, and to present the whole universe, all that exists in space and time, as the revelation and unfolding of this eternal counsel. For only in this way can we maintain a clear and correct conception of God's relation to the world as its Creator. Only then can we maintain and somewhat understand, that God, as the Catechism expresses it, "out of nothing made heaven and earth," and that creation reveals Him as the One Who "calleth the things that be not as though they were," or again, "that the worlds were framed by the word of God, so that things which are seen were not made of things which do appear." Rom. 4:17; Heb. 11:3. And understanding this, we will be in no danger to exchange the teaching of Scripture on this point for the philosophy of man with regard to the origin of the world, and, therefore, also with respect to God. Then we will have no inclination whatever to compromise with the theory of evolution, nor admit that it is capable of offering a solution of the problem it claims to solve, for it can never understand that "things which are seen are not made of things which do appear." Nor will we be in danger of the

386

pantheistic conception that the world emanates from the divine essence, as light from the sun, or as water from a fountain. And although we may figuratively speak of God as the "overflowing Fountain of all good," when we wish to speak accurately we will even refuse to adopt the language of philosophy which prefers to speak of God as the Cause of all things, or the First Cause, or the *Causa causarum*, or the ultimate Source of the universe. A cause, even though it be the ultimate and first cause, belongs to its effect by the law of necessity. If God is the First Cause of the universe He is not transcendent above the world. But God is not the Cause, nor the Source, but the Creator of the world. And that implies that He called all things into exist- ence by an act of intelligent and omnipotent will. The finite does not emanate from the Infinite, the temporal does not evolve from the Eternal, but the world in time and space is called into being by and according to the eternal counsel of the living God. In the beginning God created the heavens and the earth.

But there is another reason why it is paramount to speak of the counsel of God in this connection. When, on the basis of Scripture, we confess that we believe in "God the Father, Almighty, maker of heaven and earth," we are stating some- thing about *God*. The first article of the *Apostles' Creed* is not concerned about the universe, but about the knowledge of its Creator. Creation is revelation. The question is: what does the act of creation reveal to us about the invisible things of the Most High? And then it appears that, unless we would make creation itself co-eternal with God, we confront two very serious difficulties here. The first is that the creation of the universe in time would necessarily seem to postulate a change in God. Creation is an act of God in time. When we read in Gen. 1:1: "In the beginning God created the heavens and the earth," the meaning is, no doubt, not that there *was* a begin- ning, but that God created time in the very first act of the formation of the chaos. Time is created together with the world, just as well as space. And this means that Scripture would give us to understand at once, that God, the eternal and infinite One, places creation in time and space, outside of and in distinction from His own essence. But we ask: does not this act of creation presuppose a change in God? Did He not *become* the Creator of the world *in the beginning?* Did He not do something "in the beginning," and ever since, which He did not do before? Yet, we know from Scripture that the answer to this question must be negative, for with God there is no variableness neither shadow of turning. How, then, can the immutability of God be maintained in the light of the *bereshith* (in the beginning) of Gen. 1:1? And the second difficulty we confront here concerns God's absolute self-existence, independence, and self-sufficiency. God is in Himself the implication of all infinite perfections. He is self-sufficient. He has no need of the creature. Nor can the creature add anything to God's infinite greatness. Yet, when we consider Gen. 1:1 we are inclined to ask: but did not creation enhance God's glory and greatness? Was not God "before" the beginning of Gen. 1 without the world? And is not God *plus* the world greater than God *without* the world? Again, we answer immediately: God forbid! For we know from Scripture that He is the self-sufficient One. But the question arises: how can we harmonize this self-sufficiency of God with the act of His creating the world in time?

Now, in attempting to approach a solution of these problems, we may do well to recall that here, indeed, we ultimately face unfathomable mysteries, for the simple reason that we deal here with the relation of the Eternal to that which exists in time, of the Absolute to the relative, of the Infinite to the finite. God is incomprehensible. In Himself He is infinitely above and beyond our puny understanding. "Behold, God is great, and we know Him not, neither can the number of his years be searched out," Job 37:26. For over against all that is relative He is the Absolute, in comparison with the finite He is the Infinite, over against all limited existence He stands as the Limitless, the unfathomable Deep; over against the multifariousness of the creature He is pure Being, the one, simple incomparable Essence. God *is,* the creature *exists.* God is from everlasting the same, the creature *becomes* in time, is in a constant state of flux, increasing and decreasing, appearing and disappearing, growing and decaying, never remaining the same, existing but for a moment. How then shall we ever find Him out? The Lord is great, and his greatness is unsearchable, Ps. 145:3. "Behold, the nations are as a drop of the bucket, and are counted as the small dust of the balance: behold, he taketh up the isles as a very little thing. And Lebanon is not sufficient to burn, nor the beasts thereof sufficient for a burnt offering. All nations before him are as nothing; and they are counted to him less than nothing and vanity. To whom then will ye liken God? or what likeness will ye compare him? . . . There is no searching of his understanding." Isa. 40:15-18; 28. And how then shall we comprehend His work? Can the caused find out the Uncaused? Can existence find out pure Being, or follow Him in His unsearchable ways? Can the meandering brook swallow up the deep ocean? Can the faint light of the candle surpass the glory of the sun? Even though this were possible, yet it would be absurd to imagine for a moment that little man could search out the living God. "Canst thou by searching find out God? Canst thou find out the Almighty unto perfection? It is as high as heaven; what canst thou do? deeper than hell; what canst thou know? The measure thereof is longer than the earth, and broader than the sea." Job 11:7-9. Contemplating the revelation of the glory of God's infinite majesty, the child of God can only prostrate himself before Him in humble adoration, and cry out: "O the depths of riches, both of wisdom and knowledge of God! how unsearchable are his judgments, and his ways past finding out! For who hath known the mind of the Lord? or who hath been his counsellor? Or who hath first given to him, and it shall be recompensed unto him again? For of him, and through him, and to him, are all things: to whom be glory for ever. Amen." Rom. 11:33-36.

However, all this does not mean that our mind can cease from contemplating upon the marvellous works of God to reach out as far as possible for the knowledge of Him. And this means for the believer that he turns to His own revelation for an answer to the questions that arise. And if we do so, we shall find at least an approximate solution of the two problems raised above in the Scriptural teaching concerning the counsel, the eternal decree and purpose of God with regard to all things in time and space. This counsel or eternal plan and will of the Almighty, this "good pleasure of his will," Eph. 1:5, or "good pleasure which he hath purposed in himself," Eph. 1:9, or "purpose of him who worketh all things after the counsel of his own will," Eph. 1:11, is eternal and absolutely all-comprehensive. For our present purpose it is sufficient to bear this in mind.

God's counsel is eternal. Let us try to understand the implication of this Scriptural teaching. It means, negatively, that we may not conceive of the eternal purpose of God under the image of a blueprint of plans and specifications, such as an architect makes of an edifice that is to be erected. We are apt to do just this, when we contemplate the counsel of the Most High. The reason is that we think of eternity in terms of endless time. The Bible itself often does this, when it speaks of God's eternal purpose as having been formed "before the foundation of the world." But we must not forget, first of all, that Scripture usually speaks anthropomorphistically, i. e., in terms derived from our own existence; and, secondly, that in this and similar terms in Scripture it is often a logical, rather than a temporal, relation that is expressed. If we forget this we will conceive of eternity as endless time. And in this conception the eternal purpose of God is a certain plan of the world which God made at some point of time before the "beginning" of Gen. 1:1. But this is a serious error. Eternity is not time, not even time *ad infinitum*. There is a qualitative difference between eternity and time. Time is not a part of eternity: it is outside of eternity, essentially distinct from it, as creation is distinct from God. Hence, when the Word of God teaches us that God's counsel is eternal, we must understand that it is not some kind of plan of the world, that once was not, then was made in some point of time before "the beginning," and that is no longer of real value when it is realized in the actually finished world, but that it is the eternal and living and almighty will and mind of God Himself with respect to all things created, in time and in space. Not inaptly this was often expressed by saying that "the decree of God is the decreeing God." God never was, never will be, never is, without His counsel. *He is eternally decreeing.* God's counsel is the living conception of all things that is eternally before His mind.

And to this must be added that His decree is all-comprehensive. It embraces all things that are, that ever were, that ever will be, in their proper meaning and significance, their interrelation to one another, their movement and their development, their beginning and their end, their inception and their destination. We see and experience only a small part of "the world" at any moment. For we are children of time. We see the world in its "present moment." That moment comes, is, and is gone. The world of the past is no more, the world of the future is not yet, the world of the present is constantly moving from the past into the future, or out of the future into the past, on that indivisible moment of the present. But with God this is different: *He has eternally the whole world in space and in time before His divine mind!* And that, too: not by experience derived from the existing world, or from foreknowledge of the future world, *but by the sovereign decree of His own will!* Eternally He conceives of the whole world, from beginning to end, yea, unto everlasting time. All things that ever were and are and shall be are ever before Him. The first creation, and the first paradise, the first man in his state of righteousness and in his fall into sin, Cain and Abel, the flood and its little church in the ark, Abraham and Moses, David and his seed, Christ in His incarnation, His death, His resurrection and exaltation, the Church as it develops in the new dispensation, the angels and demons and all their activity, the wicked and their fury culminating in the Antichrist of the latter days,—all these moments of the world in time, in their exact relationship as decreed by God with perfect wisdom, are eternally before the mind of God by His own will and sovereign conception. In God's counsel the first paradise stands eternally in its proper relation to the second, the first man Adam eternally appears in his righteousness and fall, sin and death do their work eternally, Cain kills Abel for ever, Christ is killed and sacrifices Himself, is raised and exalted for evermore! Christ and His glorified Church, and the new creation, but also all that leads up to their realization and perfection in glory, are for ever in and before God's mind. In His decree God creates and upholds and governs all things eternally! That is the meaning of God's eternal purpose!

On the basis of Scripture, we may make one more observation concerning this eternal purpose and counsel of God's will. All the individual moments in that counsel are conceived and arranged in their relation to one another according to infinite divine wisdom and logic. And this means that in God's mind all these individual moments are so conceived that all in their own position serve the one purpose: the highest possible revelation of God in the glory of His majesty and the beauty of His triune covenant life. In this sense, I would never hesitate to maintain that the supralapsarian view of the counsel of God is the only true, and biblical, conception. There is, of course, no time element in God's decree. It is eternal. We cannot properly speak of *before* and *after* when referring to the eternal good pleasure. But there is perfect subordination of means to ends, and of all means to the one end: the glory of God. And this means that in God's counsel Christ, and that, too, as the incarnated Son of God, as the crucified One that rose again, as the first-begotten of the dead, is in that sense "the firstborn of every creature." Of Him God conceived "first." In Him He purposed to reveal all the fulness of His glory. And unto Him, i. e., in order that the glory of His grace might become fully manifest in all its manifold riches, the Church is given as His body by the decree of election. And all the rest, the counsel of reprobation and the counsel of creation, the counsel concerning the fall and the counsel of providence occupy in God's eternal purpose the place of means unto the end of the realization of the glorious Christ and His glorious body dwelling in the tabernacle of God in the new creation. All things exist for the Church, the Church exists for Christ, and Christ exists for God!

This conception of the eternal, all-comprehensive, living and infinitely wise counsel of the Most High we obtain from Scripture. It is of this decree as the eternally decreeing God that Prov. 8 speaks in language of incomparable beauty. I quote from vs. 22 on: "The Lord possessed me in the beginning of his way (certainly more correctly, as suggested in the margin of the R.V.: "The Lord formed me *as* the beginning of his way." The original has *reshith,* a predicate objective, not *bereshith,* in the beginning), before his works of old. I was set up from everlasting, from the beginning, or ever the earth was (or: from the foundation of the earth). When there were no depths, I was brought forth; when there were no fountains abounding with water. Before the mountains were settled, before the hills was I brought forth; while as yet he had not made the earth, nor the fields, nor the highest part (or: the beginning) of the dust of the world. When he prepared the heavens, I was there: when he set a compass (measured out a circle) upon the face of the depth: when he established the clouds above (better: the sky or ether, the firmament), when he strengthened (or: restrained) the fountains of the deep: When he appointed the foundations of the earth: Then I was by him, as one brought up with him (better: as a director of the work): and I was daily his delight, rejoicing always before him; Rejoicing in the habitable part of his earth; and my delights were with the sons of men." It is not our purpose now to give a complete exegesis of this most profound and rich portion of Scripture. For our present purpose it may suffice to observe the following: 1. On the one hand, it should be plain that Wisdom in this section is not identical with the Logos (the Word) of John 1:1-3. For the Logos is the infinite Word God speaks, the personal Image of the Father, and is *begotten* of the Father. But in this passage Wisdom is distinguished from God, the Lord, and is created, or formed, i. e., conceived in God's mind (*Canani,* in the LXX: ektise). 2. On the other hand, the language forbids us to think of a mere figure of speech, when throughout Wisdom is presented as having personal subsistence. This Wisdom, then, though not itself the eternal Word, has its personal subsistence in the Logos. In other words, it is the whole implication of God's eternal counsel with respect to all things, the decree of God as the living and eternal conception of God, conceived by the Triune God "before the world was," and that, too, of the Father, through the Son, and in the Spirit. The eternal Son of God, Who is the perfect and express image of the Father, is also the "Mediator of the decree of God," in the sense that in Him, in Whom the Father beholds the infinite perfections of the Godhead, He now also eternally conceives the reflection and revelation of those perfections in the created world. Wisdom, then, is the "world-idea" as eternally conceived by the Father, through the Son, and in the Holy Spirit.

This same truth, that in God's eternal good pleasure Christ is first, and all other things are conceived in Him and unto Him, is also taught in other passages of Holy Writ. We have in mind especially that glorious and profound part of the epistle to the Colossians that expresses the theme of the whole letter: "Who is the image of the invisible God, the firstborn of every creature: For by him were all things created, that are in heaven, and that are in earth, visible and invisible, whether they be thrones or dominions, or principalities, or powers: all things were created by him, and for him: And he is before all things, and by him all things consist. And he is the head of the body, the church: who is the beginning, the firstborn from the dead; that in all things he might have the preëminence. For it pleased the Father that in him all the fulness should dwell; And having made peace through the blood of his cross, by him to reconcile all things unto himself; by him, I say, whether they be things in earth, or things in heaven." Col. 1:15-20. To be sure, He of whom the apostle here speaks has His personal subsistence in the Son of God, the second Person of the Holy Trinity. And yet, even as was the case with Wisdom in Proverbs 8, it is evident that all that is predicated here of this Firstborn cannot be said of the Son of God in the divine nature. Whatever attempts have been made to explain the expression "the firstborn of every creature" so that it might be applicable to the divine Son of God, it is very clear that this phrase does not apply to the second Person of the Trinity. He is not the "firstborn of every creature," for He is neither born nor a creature: He is the eternally begotten God! Nor is the Son as such the head of the body, or the first begotten from the dead; nor even can it be said of the Son of God in the divine nature, that He has the preëminence in all things, or that by the good pleasure of the Father all the fulness dwells in Him. But all these predicates are readily understood if we apply them to Christ, and that, too, as He appears in God's eternal conception of all things, that is, in the counsel of God. In that counsel Christ, and that as the firstborn from the dead, the glorified Christ, in whom all the fulness should dwell, is the beginning (the *archee*; the *reshith* of Prov. 8), and the firstborn of every creature, Who, in the counsel of God is not only logically first, but Who as the firstborn, also opens the womb of creation, and prepares the way for all creatures; and again, Who as such holds the preëminence above them all. The eternal Son of God, the Word that is with God in eternity, and Who is the express image of His substance, is, as it were, the infinite pattern according to which all things are conceived, and in Whom as the Christ exalted all the fulness must dwell. God is first the "Father of our Lord Jesus Christ," and as such He is also the Creator of heaven and earth. As the Catechism expresses it: "The eternal Father of our Lord Jesus Christ" made of nothing the heaven and the earth and all things that are therein, and still upholds them by His eternal counsel and providence!

Now, all this may not completely dispel the mists that hide the deep things of God from our searching eye, but it shows us the direction in which, could we only see far enough, we would find the solution of the two problems we mentioned before: that of God's immutability, and that of God's self-sufficiency in relation to the "beginning" of Gen. 1:1. It is true, even so we cannot fathom the relation of the "beginning" to eternity, because in all our thinking we are strictly subject to and limited by time, and for evermore we are inclined to ask: and what was before the beginning? Nor can we fathom the relation of space to the Infinite, and always we postulate more space beyond space. When we say that God created heaven and earth out of nothing, we speak in mysteries, for we cannot conceive of "creation," but neither can we conceive of "nothing," except as empty space, which is not *nothing*, but itself a creature. But we can at least begin to see that God in Himself, by virtue of His *eternal* counsel, is the Eternal Father Creator, and that the "beginning" and all things in time are eternally in Him, so that they do not postulate a change in God. And, secondly, we can also obtain a glimpse of the truth that God remains the self-sufficient One, and that creation does not add anything to His infinite greatness. The world as it is eternally with God in His eternal conception and decree is far more immense than it can ever be in any moment of its existence in time. Our world of the moment is but a small reflection of the fulness of the world in God's eternal conception!

Thus we can begin to understand the significance of the confession: *I believe in God the Father, Almighty, Maker of heaven and earth.* Creation is revelation. It does, indeed, reveal God to us as the *omnipotent One.* The act of creation is an act of omnipotent will! The catechism tells us that God "of nothing made heaven and earth, with all that is in them." This is hardly meant as a *definition* of the act of creation. As such it would be very defective. It may have value from a pedagogical viewpoint to teach our children that "creation is to make something out of nothing," but as soon as they begin to reflect they should be shown the inadequacy of such a definition or description of the act of creation. For, to be sure, "nothing" is not the source of creation, nor is creation always out of nothing: the plants are called out of the ground, so are the animals, and man is formed out of the dust of the earth. Nevertheless, it may serve to emphasize that apart from God's creative act there is absolutely nothing: God was not limited in His act of creation by some kind of material that existed, and upon which He wrought creatively; and it brings out emphatically that all things are the product of His omnipotent will alone. He called the things that are not as if they were! And by faith we understand that the worlds were framed by the Word of God, so that the things which are seen are not made of things that do appear! And thus the act of creation reveals God as the absolute Sovereign of all, and as the Father Omnipotent. Only, we must not conceive of omnipotence merely in the vague sense of infinite power, but rather in the concrete sense that there is no power, never was any power, and never will be any power, whether within God or in all the universe, except the power of God. His is *the* power for ever!

Secondly, in this first article of the *Apostolic Confession* we confess that the world is exactly as God willed it. The truth of creation teaches us that God's will and counsel are the only *raison d' être* of the whole universe. There was nothing that limited the will of God. When man makes something, he is limited and determined on every side by the material out of which the proposed article must be fashioned. When an architect draws plans and specifications of an edifice that is to be constructed, he is subject to, and must figure with all kinds of existing laws; and he is limited by the means at hand. Not so with God. Creation means that the universe is solely the product of His omnipotent will, and this will is limited by nothing. He is above all laws, and Himself the sovereign Creator even of them. He proposes the end, and He creates the means; He conceives of the idea, and He calls into being the material of His world. The world is exactly as He willed it to be. Creation is an act of absolute freedom and sovereignty.

This also means that the world, as it was called forth in the beginning, as it develops in time, and as it will be perfected in the "age of ages," is the revelation of perfect divine wisdom, the highest possible revelation of the glory of God. I think we may even say, on the basis of Scripture, that it is a *complete* revelation of God, and in that sense adequate, even though it is true, of course, that the measure of this revelation is creaturely. For it pleased the Father that in Christ, as the firstborn of every creature *and* the firstborn from the dead, all the fulness should dwell. We may say, therefore, that even though God's works are a *creaturely* revelation of Himself, so that He Himself for ever remains the Incomprehensible One, they are not a *partial*, but a full revelation of the living God, through which all His glorious virtues will shine forth and be declared for ever. And it is, no doubt, the highest possible revelation of that glory. You understand, I am not now referring merely to the world as it was formed in the beginning, but to the world as it is in God's counsel. Hence, we must also maintain that this is the best possible world, and for that very reason the only world God could create. In the abstract it may be granted, perhaps, that God could have created an infinite number of worlds. And often this is asserted and considered a statement of great piety and reverence. But if *this* world is the revelation of the highest purpose of God, adapted to the reflection of His greatest glory, this is the only world God, Who can only make that which is characterized by highest perfection, could conceive of: the greatest and fullest revelation of His own excellent virtues.

Further, conceived of as the realization in time and space of God's eternal good pleasure, the end of which is that in Christ, crucified and raised, all things should be reconciled and united, so that in Him all the fulness should dwell, the world in the "beginning" was adapted to the end with perfect wisdom, i. e., was so created that, through the deep way of sin and death, it could be raised to the highest possible glory by the power of grace in Christ. God knows the end from the beginning, and the latter is adapted to the former. When He created the world, He had that end in view: the highest realization and revelation of His tabernacle with men in Christ Jesus our Lord! When God in the beginning saw that all things were good, the meaning is not simply that they were perfect and flawless, without defect, as they had come forth from His hands, but also that they were perfectly adapted to the end He had in view. And that end is the Kingdom of heaven, the heavenly tabernacle of God with men in Christ. It is because of this that the things as they were made in the beginning are an image of things to come, and that things *are done* or take place in parables. It is true, of course, that without God's revelation in Christ as we have it in the Holy Scriptures, we could never see this reflection of things to come in the things that are made; and that Christ only could point out the parables that take place round about us; but the fact remains that the earthy creation reflects the things of the kingdom of heaven, is an image of things heavenly. Adam is an image of Him that was to come, and Christ is the last Adam. The First Paradise is an earthly picture of the Paradise of God in the new creation, and the original tree of life is to be fully realized in its heavenly beauty when all things are made new. The seed that falls in the earth and dies and is quickened again is a parable of the resurrection, both in its spiritual, and its physical sense. The sun that dispels the darkness of the night is an image of the Sun of righteousness, and the moon that floods the night with its mellow light, and assures us that the sun is still there, though we do not see her, is a silent preacher of the promise of God that the Sun will rise again in all its glory in the Day of the Lord. And so all creation, the lion and the lamb, the soaring eagle and the strong ox, the tall cedar and the sturdy oak, the mighty mountain and the barren desert, the flashing lightning and the rolling thunder, storm and zephyr, earthquake and eruption, color and number, as well as man in all the relations of man and wife, brother and sister, father and son, king and subject,—all speak the language of redemption to us, if our ear is only attuned and made receptive by the Word of God in Christ Jesus our Lord. And so, all the works of God are one, even as He is One. They were one in the beginning. For God did not create a mere number of creatures, but a kosmos, rising by His creative power from the darkness of the chaos in a succession of creatures higher and higher, until they reached their pinnacle in man, in whose heart the whole kosmos was united with the heart of God; a kingdom, in which all creatures must serve man, that man might serve his God. But they are also one, in that the beginning is connected with and adapted to the end: the new creation that will for ever be united with God in the heart of Immanuel, God with us!

And thus, finally, we can fully appreciate and understand the language of the Catechism in this ninth Lord's Day, and that, too, as a firm ground for our only comfort in life and death.

"What believest thou when thou sayest, 'I believe in God the Father, Almighty, Maker of heaven and earth?' That the eternal Father of our Lord Jesus Christ, who of nothing made heaven and earth, with all that is in them; who likewise upholds and governs the same by his eternal counsel and providence, is for the sake of Christ, his Son, my God and my Father; on whom I rely so entirely, that I have no doubt, but he will provide me with all things necessary for soul and body: and further, that he will make whatever evils he sends upon me, in this valley of tears turn out to my advantage; for he is able to do it, being almighty God, and willing, being a faithful Father."

What does it all mean? This is not the place to discuss every element of this glorious confession with respect to God's Fatherhood and our sonship, and the practical implications of this relationship, in detail. For we shall have occasion to speak of our sonship for Christ's sake in a different connection; and much of what the Catechism here mentions must be discussed as we explain the next Lord's Day. But the central idea the Catechism here expresses must be grasped clearly: it is the God and Father of our Lord Jesus Christ, and that, too, not only as the eternal Father of the eternal Son, but also as the Father of Jesus Christ, that created all things according to His eternal counsel; and Who as such is my God and Father for Christ's sake; hence, by faith I may put the present evil moment in God's perfect counsel of wisdom and love, and believe that all is well!

God is the eternal Father of the elect. O, it is true, He is the Father of all in the sense that He brought them forth, created them. But in the true, spiritual sense, He is the Father only of His own, whom He gave to Christ in His eternal counsel. For through sin men became the children of their father the devil, and do his will. They neither have the right nor the power to be children of God. We must not follow modernism in its boast of a universal fatherhood of God. But in Christ, and for His sake, we obtain the right to be called children of God, and by His grace we are also conformed according to the image of His Son. And all this is realized according to God's eternal purpose, that same purpose and good pleasure, according to which He created all things, and governs all things. What then? Knowing that He is my Father for Christ's sake, I know that in His eternal wisdom He so arranged all things that all things must coöperate unto the final revelation of Christ, and the salvation of all that are in Him! Knowing that He is almighty, I am assured that He will surely accomplish all His good pleasure, so that nothing can betide me but by His will. And knowing that He loves me, and that, too, with an eternal and immutable love, manifested in the death of His Son, I trust that He will surely cause all things to work together unto my salvation. And so, the believer in Christ relies on Him entirely, confident that all things always work together for good to them that love God! The eternal Father of our Lord Jesus Christ, the Creator omnipotent, the only Potentate of potentates, the God of our salvation, is my God and Father!

LORD'S DAY X

Q. 27. What dost thou mean by the providence of God?

A. The almighty and everywhere present power of God; whereby, as it were by his hand, he upholds and governs heaven, earth, and all creatures; so that herbs and grass, rain and drought, fruitful and barren years, meat and drink, health and sickness, riches and poverty, yea, and all things come, not by chance, but by his fatherly hand.

Q. 28. What advantage is it to us to know that God has created, and by his providence still upholds all things?

A. That we may be patient in adversity; thankful in prosperity; and that in all things, which may hereafter befall us, we place our firm trust in our faithful God and Father, that nothing shall separate us from his love: since all creatures are so in his hand, that without his will they cannot so much as move.

I

The Idea Of God's Providence

The doctrine of creation postulates that of divine providence. If you open your window to fill your room with the golden light of the sun, that sunlight in your room is constantly dependent for its continued existence on its connection with its source. Draw your shades, shut off the light in your room from its source, and there is no light left in the room. And thus it is with all creation in relation to God. If God *created* all things, if He called them by His omnipotent will, if they were framed by the Word of God, then He remains the Author of their continued existence. That they came into existence was due only to His sovereign will; that same will is the ultimate and only ground of their continued existence. For creation can never mean that God gave independent being to a creature outside of Himself. An independent creature is impossible. To speak of it is a contradiction in terms. If, therefore, after all things were created, they would have been separated from the will and power of God, they would at that very moment have sunk back into nothingness. The world did not develop of itself; it cannot exist by itself. It is from moment to moment dependent on "the almighty and everywhere present power of God." Creation postulates providence.

Hence, the Heidelberger is quite correct in appending to the chapter on the Father-Creator, a Lord's Day on the providence of God. The first article of the *Apostolic Confession* does not speak of this upholding and governing power of God, but only of God the Father, Almighty, Creator of heaven and earth. But realizing that the doctrine of creation postulates, even implies that of providence, our instructor, in explaining the first article of our holy catholic faith, appends a chapter on this important point of doctrine.

403

The word *providence* is not a very accurate term to express what it is meant to denote. From the term itself the idea cannot be deduced. In the sense in which it is used in this connection it does not occur in Scripture at all. Literally, according to its derivation, the word means *foresight*. And it has acquired the added meaning, which it now commonly has, of fulfilling a need, of making provision beforehand. We see that winter is coming, and we provide for it by filling our coal bin. So one provides for the needs of his family, a traveler provides himself with money for the journey, a ship is provided with supplies for the voyage, etc. It is, perhaps, because the word is usually employed in this sense, that even in modern circles, that have long forgotten the Scriptural teaching about God Who is really GOD, He is preferably spoken of as Providence, as if God were nothing but some good and beneficent Power, Who really exists to help us in our need, and more especially to be called in when we perceive that we can no longer help ourselves, or when we are in trouble. And on thanksgiving day we remember this Providence for the abundance of worldly prosperity in which we may rejoice. But this is certainly not the teaching of the Word of God concerning the "providence" of God, nor is it in this sense that the Church employs the term. And it may, therefore, be well to remember that Scripture never uses the word at all. It is a theological, not a biblical term.

The Heidelberg Catechism defines the providence of God as "the almighty and omnipresent power of God; whereby, as it were by his hand, he upholds and governs heaven, earth, and all creatures." The basic idea, therefore, of God's providence is His omnipresence. And we will do well to give ourselves account of what is really meant by the omnipresence of the Almighty. For even of this marvellous virtue of God we are very apt to form a wrong conception.

By the confession of God's omnipresence the Church really expresses two ideas, that may never be separated from each other, those of God's immanence, and His transcendence; by which she opposes two very serious errors, that of Deism on the one hand, and that of Pantheism on the other. These two heretical views are usually so distinguished that Deism denies God's immanence, His presence in the world, and only believes in His transcendence; while Pantheism teaches that God is only immanent, and denies His transcendence. For practical purposes this distinction may be adopted, although, strictly speaking, it does not accurately describe these heresies. For, although Deism certainly will have nothing of an immanent God, it neither has a correct conception of His transcendence; and although Pantheism knows nothing of a transcendent God, it can neither speak of an immanent God, for it identifies God with the world. According to Deism God is not in the world, neither is He really transcendent in relation to the world, but He exists outside of the world, and has nothing to do with it. Just as man builds a house, but when the house is finished has really nothing to do with its continued existence except to keep it in repair whenever necessary; or just as the mechanic constructs an automobile that can function and run without him when it is ready; so God formed the world, gave it its laws and inherent powers, and now the universe runs by its own power and by virtue of its own laws. God is not transcendent, still less immanent in the world, but He is outside of the universe He created. And according to Pantheism, God is not transcendent in relation to the world, neither can it be said that He is immanent in all things, but He *is* the world. The essence of God and the essence of the world are identified. Everything is God, and God is everything. All things are a part of God's being, and especially in man God reaches His supreme self-expression, and self-consciousness.

We may remark here in passing, that while Pantheism is the ultimate expression of man's sinful pride, instilled into his heart through his acceptance of the word of the devil: "Ye shall be as God"; every day thinking and life are rather Deistic, so that men either rule out God from their own and the world's affairs, or are reminded of Him only on special and striking occasions. Even our language is usually Deistic. Are we not accustomed to replace the name of God by the impersonal pronoun "it?" We say that *it* rains, *it* snows, *it* thunders, *it* freezes, etc. How different is the language of Scripture in this respect! It is God, who "sendeth the springs into the valleys, which run among the hills . . . He watereth the hills from his chambers; the earth is satisfied with the fruit of thy works. He causeth the grass to grow for the cattle, the herb for the service of man: that he may bring forth food out of the earth . . . He appointed the moon for seasons: the sun knoweth his going down. Thou makest darkness, and it is night: wherein all the beasts of the forest do creep forth." Ps. 104:10, 13, 14, 19, 20. Or again: "He sendeth forth his commandment upon the earth: his word runneth very swiftly. He giveth snow like wool: he scattereth the hoar frost like ashes. He casteth forth his ice like morsels: who can stand before his cold? He sendeth out his word and melteth them: he causeth his wind to blow, and the waters flow." Ps. 147:13-18. According to Scripture God is very near, He is in all things, and they all reveal His wonders.

However, over against the Deistic and Pantheistic philosophies the Church confesses that God is omnipresent, that He is both immanent in, and transcendent above the world. By the latter is meant that God is essentially different from, and infinitely greater than all creation; by the former is expressed that with His infinite and transcendent being He is in all creation, and in every creature. We must beware, lest we conceive of this transcendence of God in terms of space, or in terms of time. We are very apt to do this. Not only is our thinking necessarily bound to the laws of space and time, but Scripture itself often speaks of God anthropomorphistically in the same language. "Behold, the heaven and heaven of heavens cannot contain thee; how much less this house which I have builded." I Ki. 2:27. And then we conceive of God as being endlessly extended in space, or as being infinitely extended in time. God's omnipresence, according to this conception, simply means, that He fills all space (His immanence), but that He also infinitely is extended beyond the limits of our space (His transcendence). But this is not correct. God is infinitely exalted above all creation essentially. He is the simple, infinite, absolute, eternal, independent, and immutable essence. There is an infinite chasm between the being of God, and the essence of the creature. He is infinite in His being and nature, in all His virtues and wonders. The creature exists in time, and time is change, succession of moments, constant flux. On that indivisible moment that constantly moves from the future into the past, the creature is carried on, and in that moment he exists only in part. He never is what he was, nor will he be what he is. But God is the eternal One: He is transcendent above all time. To be sure, this also signifies that He is without beginning and without end. But eternity is not time, not even time conceived as endlessly extended into the past and into the future. There is no time in and for God. Paradoxically the Bible expresses this by saying "that one day is with the Lord as a thousand years, and a thousand years as one day," II Pet. 3:8. He is the I AM, Jehovah is His name. There is no change or becoming, no flux or succession of moments in God. Constant, infinite fulness is He. God is transcendent above all time, and above all that exists in time. And the same is true of His relation to space. The creature exists in space, and he occupies space. And space is distance from one point to another, extent, limitation, form. But God is immense, immeasurable. There is no space for God, nor does He exist in space essentially, although no point of space excludes Him. You cannot measure the distance from God to the world, nor is there distance or extent in Him. And to conceive of Him under any form is to create an idol instead of the living God. He is God, the Lord of heaven and earth, essentially and infinitely exalted above all that is called creature! The transcendent One is He.

But this transcendent God is also immanent in the world, in every creature, and in every point of all that exists, and that, too, as the transcendent One. Let us make no mistake. God's transcendence and His immanence may not be divorced from each other in our conception of Him. As the immanent One He is transcendent; and as the transcendent One He is in all creation. We are apt to conceive of God's immanence as consisting in this, that His divine essence is distributed through space, so that He is everywhere in extent. Just as the ether fills all space, so God is everywhere present. But this is an erroneous conception. Nor may we conceive of God's immanence as referring merely to His *power*. It is true, the Heidelberg Catechism speaks of God's providence as being "the almighty and omnipresent power of God; whereby, as with his hand, he upholds and governs heaven, earth, and all creatures." But this may not be understood as implying a denial of the omnipresence of God's essence. God's power cannot be separated from His essence. For He is a simple Being. His essence *is* His attributes, and His attributes *are* His essence. Wherever God's power is, there He is Himself, the almighty and ever living God. But God's immanence does mean that with His essence, and that, too, with His whole infinite, transcendent essence, He is in all creation, in every creature according to the nature of that creature, and in every atom of the universe. Nothing can contain God, yet He is in all things. Eternally He is transcendent, yet, as the transcendent One He is immanent. For "the heaven and heaven of heavens cannot contain Him," I Ki. 8:27; and He, the "Lord of heaven and earth, dwelleth not in temples made with hands," Acts 17:24; yet, He is "not far from every one of us: For in him we live, and move, and have our being." Acts 17:27, 28. "Thou hast beset me behind and before, and laid thine hand upon me . . . Whither shall I go from thy spirit? or whither shall I flee from thy presence? If I ascend up into heaven, thou art there: if I make my bed in hell, behold, thou art there." Ps. 139:5, 6-8.

This, then, that God is essentially present in the universe, and in all things, in every creature, in every part of every creature, in the material and spiritual world, in all the sense and meaning, in all the movement and relations of the universe, must be strictly maintained in order to understand the idea of the providence of God. The existence of the creature is in contiguity, in constant touch with the essence of God. Nowhere is there separation between God and the world. As the Catechism expresses it: he upholds *as it were by his hand,* all things in heaven and earth. This essential immanence of God must not be confused with the covenant idea of God's dwelling with us. For this means that God is near to His people in His blessed favor, grace, friendship, so that He takes them to His heart, reveals to them His secrets, has most intimate communion with them, and they with Him, so that they taste that the Lord is good. In this sense, He is near unto His people in Christ Jesus only, while He is far from the ungodly, is present to them in His fierce wrath, as a consuming fire. Not His covenant nearness and fellowship, but His essential contiguity in all created things is meant when we speak of God's immanence in the world. He is in everything visible and invisible. He is in space and time, and in all that exists and moves in them. He is in the light and in the darkness, in the flower of the field and in the trees of the forest, in the lightning and in the thunder, in sea and land, in storm and earthquake, in man and beast, in color and form, in every relationship and movement, in matter and force. And He is in every creature and all its component parts according to the nature of that creature, and according to its meaning and relation to all the rest of creation.

In the second place, we must remember that God is present in all creation and in every creature as the living, almighty, ever active, sovereign Lord. God's providence is not mere contiguity of God and the creature, it is such a presence that there is a continuous action of God upon the creature, whereby the creature continues to exist. God is the living God. He is almighty power. And this almighty power is constantly active. With this almighty power God is present in, and reacts upon the whole world in all its parts and relations. He is and remains the sovereign Lord of the universe. Not for one moment does anything exist without this act of God's almighty power. God alone exists in and of Himself. The creature has no independent existence, it receives its being from God constantly. This does not mean that God's providence is the same as a continuous act of creation, as Ursinus asserts (I, 196). For creation is the act of God whereby He called the things that are not as if they were. And the heavens and the earth were finished on the sixth day. Nothing is added to them by God's providence. But it does mean that ever since the end of the sixth day there is a constant influx of the activity of God's almighty power into the world

He created and into all things, and that it is only by this continued activity of God that all things exist and continue to be
what they are. When you turn the electric switch in your living
room there is light in the bulb of your lamp that illuminates
the entire room. Does that light now exist independently in the
electric bulb, so that you can cut the electric current and still
have light? Of course not. There must be a constant current
of electricity into that bulb in order to keep it lit. The same is
true of God's relation to all creation. He is the almighty God,
the living Lord. And as such He created all things in the beginning, calling the things that are not as if they were. And through
this act of creation the world received existence in distinction
from God. Does that mean that henceforth that world can exist
by itself, and that God can cease to act upon the world He
created? Not for one moment. If God does not uphold all things
constantly they sink back into *nihil*.

This, then, is the meaning of the Catechism when it states
that God, as it were by His hand, upholds heaven, earth, and all
things. Let us not be misled by the anthropomorphism of the
expression "he upholds, as it were by his hand." For then we
might still entertain the idea that the thing that is upheld has
existence in itself. When I carry a book in my hand, I may be
said to uphold it. But the book that I thus carry and uphold
does not receive its continuous existence through my act of upholding it. It exists apart from my power. I may put it on the
table, or drop it to the floor, but it still exists. But if God would
not uphold the creature it would not simply drop somewhere, it
would be nowhere, it could not possibly exist even for one
moment. By omnipotent, infinitely intelligent will all things
were called into being, and by that same omnipotent will they
are kept where and what they are. By the Word of God they
were called into being, and by that same Word they are caused
to continue in existence. He is "upholding all things by the
word of his power." Heb. 1:3. Of Him, but for that very reason
also *through* Him, are all things. Rom. 11:36. Providence is
not an act of continuous creation, but it is the continuation of
the Word God spoke in the beginning. He does not continue to

speak new words, but He does continue to speak the Word He spake in the beginning. When God says: "Let there be light," light springs into existence. And only when He continues to speak that same word, can light continue to exist. If God would recall that word "light," or cease to speak it, that moment the light would exist no more. It is thus that God upholds all things, "as it were by his hand." And thus we can also understand that all things in heaven and earth are a revelation of the living Word of God concerning Himself, so that "the heavens declare the glory of God; and the firmament sheweth his handiwork. Day unto day uttereth speech, and night unto night sheweth knowledge." Ps. 19:1, 2.

II

The Scope Of God's Providence

This, then, that God, the Creator of the universe, is omnipresent, not only in His power, but also in His essence; that as the transcendent One He is immanent in all things, and that, too, as the living and ever active God, Who continues to speak the Word that once creatively proceeds out of His mouth, and Who thus upholds all things by the Word of His power, is the basic idea of the providence of God.

From moment to moment, therefore, God is the Lord, and remains strictly and absolutely sovereign with relation to the world He created, not only because He created all things, but also because they are in His hand, and they exist only by His will. This is to be understood in the most absolute and unlimited sense of the word. The sun, and moon, and stars, the sea and the dry land, the mountains and the hills, forest and plain, trees and flowers, corn and wheat, rain and sunshine, gold and silver; the bread we eat, and the water we drink, and the air we breathe; the light and the eye, the sound and the ear; our power of mind and will, the strength to labor and toil, — all things exist and continue to exist, each in their own sphere and according to their own nature, only by the will and word of God "in whom we live, and move, and have our being." God is the Lord. Without Him nothing could have had being at all; and without His will nothing would continue to exist even for a moment.

And this providence of God implies, too, that He is the absolute Ruler of the universe, and that He governs all things according to His decree and eternal purpose. This signifies, in the first place, that in the world He created, the Lord maintains and executes His own ordinances, and strictly and sovereignly controls and directs the movement of every creature. The universe is not a dead, inactive thing, or combination of motionless beings: it is a living, organic whole. It is the creation and reflection of the living Word of God, of God of Whom it may be said that He is *actus purissimus*, i.e., activity in the absolute sense of the word. And so, everything lives and moves in all the rich and wonderful creation of God. The planets move around the sun in the firmament, even as they rotate around their own axes, and so the sun rises every morning to drive away the night, and sets every evening at its appointed time; the moon glides through the silent night, flooding it with its mellow, silvery light; and the planets, comets, and stars roam with incredible speed through the immensity of space, each keeping to their appointed course. Light, it is said, moves with a rapidity of one hundred and eighty-six thousand miles a second; and though with far less speed, sound also travels: the reverberation of thunder, the howling of the wind, the whisper of the zephyr, the song of the lark, the cry of the young raven, the roar of the lion, the spoken word, the prayer that leaves your lips, — all these, and thousands upon thousands of other sounds that constantly fill the universe, have wings, and fly into space. The color of the lily and of the rose, as well as their fragrance, the lingering glow of the setting sun in the western sky, the silvery path struck by the moon across the lake, the reflection of your face in the mirror, the beautiful span of the rainbow in the heavens, — they all live and move according to their own nature and laws. The clouds gather, the flash of lightning zigzags through the darkness, the rain descends, rivers and brooks restlessly meander to their destination, tides rise and fall, the seed falls into the earth and dies to rise again, the seasons follow one another in regular succession, your heart beats and the blood courses through your veins, — everything is constantly in motion. And then there is the movement of the living creature, of animals and men, of holy angels and wicked demons: the worm crawls along in its path, the sparrow takes off on its wings, the wild beast roams through the forest, man thinks and plans, desires and chooses, speaks and acts, the angels sing and attend to the Word of their Lord, and the devils believe and tremble! In all the wide creation there is nothing motionless or dead. And even if we could penetrate with our perception into the existence of a grain of sand, we would detect life and movement similar to that of the stars in the firmament!

The doctrine of God's providence teaches us that God controls and directs all these movements and actions of the creature. As the Catechism expresses it: He "governs heaven and earth, and all creatures," and that "as it were by his hand." God is the Lord. He remains absolutely sovereign in relation to the world. When we contemplate the manifold movements and activities of the various creatures, we notice that they are not all of the same kind. Some are involuntary and automatic: their organic functions are unconscious, determined by what we are accustomed to call "law"; others are deliberate and voluntary, determined by the inner instincts and choice of the creatures themselves. And again, the former may be distinguished into two classes: those that occur regularly, so that their movements may be predicted accurately both as to time and space; and those that take place without such regularity of recurrence. The sun rises and sets each day of the year exactly at the appointed moment, so that the length of each day for a certain part of the globe can be predicted with absolute certainty; but the weatherman often fails even when he prepares his forecast one day ahead. And who is able to predict "rain and drought, fruitful and barren years?" Again, the deliberate or voluntary movements and acts of the creature may be distinguished into those that are the result of the limited instinct of the animals, and those that are the expression of intelligent will, the acts of men and angels. All these acts and movements are under the government and direction of the Sovereign of heaven and earth, and there is nothing that moves or stirs apart from or against His will.

This means that we may not distinguish, either deliberately or thoughtlessly, between events that are "providential," and others that have nothing to do with the providence of God, or between the "natural" and the "super-natural." All things are providential, and all things are alike natural and supernatural.

The unbelieving man of science takes delight in the discovery of laws, and in speaking of them as if they were something apart from God, forces inherent in the universe by virtue of which the world runs by itself. For the Christian a "law of nature" is nothing but God's regular and orderly mode of operation. There are laws of gravity and gravitation, laws of contraction and expansion, of attraction and repulsion, principles of chemistry and physics, but they are all governed constantly, and that, too, "as it were by his hand," by the living God. Even those "laws" that can be expressed in exact mathematical formulas reveal but the orderly way in which God works and rules the universe. God works harmoniously, and in an orderly fashion. The universe is no chaos. It is exactly because of this fact that man can be a "co-worker" with God, and that he can order his own life and activity according to God's ordinances and times. How impossible this would be, if God's mode of working were arbitrary! How impossible it would be for man to order his life, if the sun would rise at three o'clock in the morning one day, and at noon the next; or if he could not depend on the regular recurrence of the seasons; or if a stone thrown in the air would come down at a certain velocity today, at a different speed tomorrow, and would remain suspended aloft at other times! However, God is a God of order, and His orderly way of operation in the universe man discovers in order that he may arrange his own life and work accordingly. "Doth the plowman plow all day to sow? doth he open and break the clods of the ground? When he hath made plain the face thereof, doth he not cast abroad the fitches, and scatter the cummin, and cast in the principal wheat and the appointed barley and the rye in their place? *For his God doth instruct him to discretion, and doth teach him.* For the fitches are not threshed with a threshing instrument, neither is a cartwheel turned about upon the cummin; but the fitches are beaten out with a staff, and the cummin with a rod. Bread corn is bruised: because he will not ever be threshing it, nor break it with the wheel of his cart, nor bruise it with his horsemen. *This also cometh forth from the Lord of hosts, which is wonderful in counsel, and excellent in working.*" Isa. 28:24-29.

But the fact that God works in a regular and orderly fashion may not tempt us so to speak of "laws" as if these operated by themselves, independently from the living God. When lightning strikes your house or barn, it is His hand that directs it, and when the sun rises and sets at appointed times, it is again His hand that moves the solar system. When a tornado suddenly tears across a stretch of country, along a very arbitrary and unpredictable path, destroying everything in its way, it is the Sovereign of heaven and earth that guides the tornado "as it were by his hand"; and when a stone falls to the ground according to an exact mathematical formula, it is by His hand that the stone is pulled down.

But this is true also of the movement and acts of the living creatures, that move by an impulse from within. The sparrow that takes to its wings is directed in its course by the hand of the Lord of all: "Are not two sparrows sold for a farthing? and one of them shall not fall to the ground without your Father," Matt. 10:29. Swarms of beetles fly down to settle on your bean crop, and they devour the plants in a single night, but the course of every one of them is determined by the same sovereign Lord: He directs their course "as it were by his hand." Millions of invisible germs creep and multiply in your lungs, dragging you down into the grave; mosquitoes carry the malaria germ into your blood, prostrating you on your bed with a burning fever; the worm crawls along the ground, apparently without purpose; millions upon millions of fishes, small and great sweep through rivers and lakes and oceans; the eagle soars into the sky, and the hawk glides in circles above its prey; the lion roams through the forest; and all the millions upon millions of living creatures move about on land and in the sea, in meadows and forests, on mountains, in deserts, or in the sky, swarming and creeping, flying and running, leaping and jumping; they sing and chirp, they cry and roar, they seek their food and rejoice, — all directed collectively and individually by the hand of the Sovereign of heaven and earth. Not one of them is ever forgotten. "These wait all upon thee; that thou mayest give them their meat in due season. That thou givest them they gather: thou openest thine hand, they are filled with good. Thou hidest thy face, they are troubled: thou takest away their breath, they die, and return to their dust. Thou sendest forth thy spirit, they are created: and thou renewest the face of the earth." Ps. 104:27-30.

And with equal force this is applicable to all the acts of God's moral, rational creatures, men and angels. God is the Lord even in relation to the thoughts and intents, the desires and aspirations, the imaginations and determinations of the heart of man, and in relation to all his acts. Here, at least, the Pelagian insists, there is a limit to the sovereignty of the Most High. Man is a free, moral, rational creature. He has an intelligent will. He makes his own determinations, and that, too, by free choice, either for good or evil. Hence, his determinations of will are beyond the control of God. He is a free agent. And he alone is responsible for his acts. It is quite impossible, therefore, that the thoughts of his heart and his deeds, which he performs as the result of his free determinations, can be predetermined, or that they can be controlled and governed by God. The freedom of God's moral and rational creatures constitutes a limit to God's sovereignty. Others are less radical, but, hesitant to confess God's absolute sovereignty over the acts of men and angels, and fearful lest the latter's responsibility is denied, rather describe God's relation to these acts by the word *permission*. Especially with application to the evil acts of men, they prefer to say that God permits them. Or the term *coöperation* is used to define God's relation to the moral acts of God's rational creatures. We make a threefold distinction in the concept of God's providence, and speak of His preservation, coöperation, and government. In respect to the acts of His moral creatures, it is said that God coöperates with them and in them.

Now, it is undoubtedly true that man is a moral being, and that as such he may be said to be a free agent in a certain sense. He is endowed with intelligence and will. Accordingly, he acts with conscious choice and determination from within. He is a person, the subject of his own actions, and responsible for them. Even in his lowest state, he retains some knowledge of God, and acts in relation to Him. The work of the law is inscribed in his heart, and his conscience either excuses or accuses him. And God will surely bring him into judgment, that he may receive according to his work. But all this does not alter the truth that God remains sovereign also with respect to man's moral acts. He controls them, governs them, and through them fulfills His own will, and realizes His own counsel. One dare not say that God *permits* the acts of His moral creatures, either good or evil, for that would postulate an agent capable of operating in independence from Him, and imply a denial of His absolute sovereignty over men and angels. Nor does the term *coöperation* precisely denote the relation between God's sovereignty and man's acts as a moral agent, for this suggests a relation of equality. Reformed theologians are wont to define the relation by the terms *primary cause,* and *secondary causes.* And this distinction has a good deal in its favor. It avoids the danger of destroying man's moral nature, and of presenting God as the *Author* of man's moral actions; and yet, it leaves man utterly dependent upon God. Certain it is that the relation between God's providence and man's moral acts is such that on God's part it is one of absolute sovereignty, on man's part it is one of dependence. His freedom is never sovereign. It is a creaturely freedom, and, therefore, dependent. God is immanent, too, in the hearts and minds, the thoughts and inclinations, the desires and determinations of men, as the living Lord, governing them according to His will, so that, even though man remains the conscious and willing author of his own acts, it is God that brings them about, and thus accomplishes His eternal purpose.

This is the clear teaching of Scripture. The sons of Jacob certainly acted as moral agents, following the inclination of their own evil hearts, and seeking to accomplish their own purpose, when they sold their brother Joseph to the Midianites; yet God so controlled and sovereignly governed their every intention, that His purpose was accomplished, as Joseph later explains: "But as for you, ye thought evil against me; but God meant it unto good, to bring to pass, as it is this day, to save much people alive." Gen. 50:20. The sons of Eli certainly did wickedly, and "the sin of the young men was very great before the Lord,"

I Sam. 2:17; and deliberately they refused to hearken unto the voice of their father; "notwithstanding they hearkened not unto the voice of their father, *because the Lord would slay them.*" God so governed their sinful way, that in the way of their sin they should be slain according to His purpose. I Sam. 2:25. Sovereignly God hardens Pharaoh's heart, and the Word of God must even be proclaimed to him: "And in very deed, for this cause have I raised thee up, for to shew in thee my power; and that my name may be declared in all the earth." Ex. 9:16. Nor dare it be said that Pharaoh was *first* in hardening his own heart, and that God's hardening of the king's heart was merely an act of retribution, as is frequently alleged, for before Moses even reaches Egypt the Lord informs him that He will harden Pharaoh's heart, so that he will not let the people go. Ex. 4:21. The haughty ruler of the world-power boasts of his own strength, and intends to accomplish his own evil purpose: to destroy Jerusalem and the people of God; and he is not at all conscious of the fact that God uses him to cut off "nations not a few"; yet, he is only the axe that boasts against the hand that heweth therewith, and the saw that magnifies itself against the hand that draws it. Isa. 10:5ff. There is no doubt about it, that Judas, and the Sanhedrin, and all the powers that rose against the Lord Jesus to slay Him, acted as moral agents, when they fulfilled their evil will upon the Savior, yet they crucified Him through the determinate counsel of God. Acts 2:23. And so the Church confesses, when Peter and John return to them, being released by the rulers of the Jews: "Lord, thou art God, which hast made heaven and earth, and the sea and all that in them is; Who by the mouth of thy servant David hast said, why did the heathen rage, and the people imagine vain things? The kings of the earth stood up and the rulers were gathered together against the Lord and against his Christ. For of a truth against thy holy child Jesus, whom thou hast anointed, both Herod, and Pontius Pilate, with the Gentiles, and the people of Israel, were gathered together, For to do whatsoever thy hand and thy counsel determined before to be done," Acts 4:24-28. Indeed, "the king's heart is in the hand of the Lord as rivers of water: he turneth it whithersoever he will." Prov. 21:1. In the light of all these passages, there can be no question about the Scriptural teaching on this point: God is the Lord, and He sovereignly governs and controls to His own purpose all the purposes and acts of men and angels, both good and evil. He sits enthroned on high in the heavens, and accomplishes whatsoever He pleases. And there is no power in heaven or on earth that can even for a moment take the reins out of His hand, or thwart His sovereign purpose.

III

The Goal Of Providence

Thus far we spoke of God's providential government only with respect to the world as it exists and moves. He controls and directs every movement and all the activity of the creature, inorganic and organic, brute and rational, good and evil. But God's government of the world also implies that He directs the course of its history and development, from its beginning to its end, and that according to His eternal good pleasure, and unto the end He has in mind and determined upon before the foundation of the world. When a big ocean liner leaves the harbor and plows through the waves of the Atlantic, there is within the ship itself a veritable world of activity and movement, of men and machines, of passengers and crew, all under the direction of the captain; but with all its life and activity aboard, the ship also makes progress from the point of its departure toward its destination, and this, too, is under the government of its chief officer. The same is true of God's providence with relation to the world. Creation is teeming with life and activity, and all its movement is directed as by the very hand of God; but it also makes history. Like the ocean liner, the world God finished on the sixth day of creation week was destined to make progress, to pass through a certain course of development. It was designed to cross the ocean of time, and to advance from its beginning in creation to the destination God determined for it in His eternal good pleasure. It proceeds through the ages from the *alpha* of creation to the *omega* of its consummation. And when we speak of God's providential government we also mean that it is He Who directs this entire course of the world throughout the ages of history. He is the Captain aboard this ocean liner of the universe, and so governs its course, that it advances along a straight path, without ever deviating from it, toward its final destination.

It is an important question, the answer to which determines for us the meaning of history, as well as the proper "world and life view" of the believer in regard to the present world and his own position and calling in it, what may be the end, the destination of our universe according to God's eternal purpose. What is the meaning of this present age? What is the pattern of all things? Whither are we drifting, and what is the proper evaluation of all the labor and toil of the creature, particularly of man? Is there really such a thing as progress, and is man, with all his strife and effort, with his toil and suffering, his culture and civilization, his war and bloodshed and destruction, really accomplishing something, attaining a certain goal? If so, what is the goal toward which he is advancing? What is the final purpose of all things in our present world, and what may be the proper position of the Christian and his calling with respect to this world?

And here we may at once discard as false the answer of evolutionistic philosophy to the question regarding the direction in which the world is moving, and the end that is to be attained. Its answer is that the world is constantly moving in the direction of the highest possible perfection by way of gradual development. It is evident to all, even to the unbelieving philosopher, that the present world, such as it is, with all its suffering and death, with all its hatred and strife, with all its corruption and crimes, with its war and bloodshed, cannot be the final, the ideal, certainly is not the perfect world. There is something, there is a good deal that is wrong. But we are making progress in the direction of the perfect world. And when we reflect whence we started, and consider the aboriginal state of the savage whence we ascend step by step the steep and difficult road of advancement and improvement, of culture and civilization, of social and political as well as moral reform, we have good reason to congratulate ourselves, and to be filled with hope for the future that the end shall be attained, the world of social and political prosperity and peace, from which all hatred and strife shall be banished, and in which suffering, perhaps, even death, shall be overcome, and all men shall enjoy the more abundant life. He that believes the Word of God cannot for a moment agree with this philosophy of evolutionism. For it ignores the fact of the fall of man, and all its consequences. The meaning of history is certainly not that of gradual progress toward the highest possible perfection of the present world. The goal and direction of God's providential government is not that of evolutionistic philosophy. And the Christian cannot possibly coöperate toward the attainment of its ideal.

The same holds true for modern post-millennialism. We are not thinking now of this conception as opposed to that of premillennialism, still less must we be understood as declaring ourselves in favor of the latter. We are not at present concerned with the unbiblical teachings of post-millennialism concerning the second coming of Christ, the final judgment and the resurrection of the body. It is rather the post-millennial view of God's providence, of His government of the present world, with relation to the kingdom of God, and, therefore, its conception of the meaning of history, that concerns us here. For, according to it, this relation of God's providential government to the coming of the kingdom of God is such that, if they are not identical, the former at least supplies the basis and forms for the latter: in the development of the present world and of human culture and civilization the kingdom of God is gradually coming, until the kingdoms of this world shall have become the kingdoms of our God and His Christ.

"God has not confined himself to distinctively religious and Christian agencies in building his kingdom in the world. 'The earth is Jehovah's and the fulness thereof; the world and they that dwell therein' (Ps. 24:1), and therefore all facts and forces are at his disposal in his works of providence and grace. Our whole expanding, progressive civilization, therefore, may be viewed as a means of extending his kingdom. Though this civilization is not the kingdom itself, yet more and more as it is progressively Christianized will it be merged into the kingdom, and the two may finally become practically identical when 'The kingdom of the world is become the kingdom of our Lord, and of his Christ' (Rev. 11:15).

"Civil government, from this point of view, is an instrument of God for protecting and extending his kingdom (Rom. 13:1). Commerce is a powerful means of knitting the world into unity and brotherhood. All trains and ships are shuttles weaving the world into one web. Great inventions readily lend themselves to this service. The first book printed on the printing press was the Bible, and the press has been a powerful gospelizer ever since. Every inventor practically lays his machine at the feet of Jesus Christ as the wise men laid their gold and frankincense and myrrh at the feet of the infant Jesus. Steam and electricity are turning the wheels and flashing the currents of the world for him, railways are speeding their trains across the continents and steamships are plowing the seas for him, the airship spreads its wings for him, the sewing machine sews for him, the typewriter writes its messages, telephone and telegraph have enmeshed the globe in a network of wires that is the great nervous system of humanity and flashes everywhere its truth and grace, and wireless telegraphy shoots his messages through the ether around the earth. Even swords and guns and all our mighty modern engines of destruction, as we have already seen, may fight for his kingdom and help to bring in its universal peace.

"Our developing science and art are contributions to his kingdom. All truth is religious and comes from God, as all our light shoots from the sun. The kingdom of God is enthroned in the intelligence of the mind as well as in the loyalty of the heart and we are to love the Lord our God with all our mind. This means that we are to be open and hospitable to all truth from whatever source it comes and use it in unveiling God's glory and furthering his kingdom. So, all true art is religious, for it discloses the beauty of God. God is beautiful, and so he has built a beautiful world and is building a beautiful kingdom. There should be no unfriendliness between our science and our theology, and between our art and our worship. The beauty of the Lord our God should be upon us in all that we think with our minds and do with our hands.

"The growing social sense of the world, leveling artificial and unjust distinctions and privileges, letting all men out to liberty and brotherhood, and earnestly endeavoring to build a social order that will give the means of a worthy and beautiful life to every human being, is a long step towards the kingdom of God on earth, a highway along which the redeemed shall come to Zion with songs and everlasting joy upon their heads."[1]

This beautiful post-millennial idealism, then, finds the meaning of history in the gradual development of all things in the direction of the kingdom of God on earth. God's government of this world is such that it leads directly to the goal of the perfected kingdom of God. But the following objections must be raised against this view: 1. It is quite contrary to the picture Scripture everywhere gives us of the trend of development we must expect of this world, as well as of its end. Iniquity will abound, the means and forces of this world will be pressed into the service of ungodliness, the faithful will be few, and will have no standing room in the world. 2. It closes its eyes to the fact that all creation is under the curse, and that the creature is in the bondage of corruption, and subject to vanity. There is in this world no material for a perfected kingdom of God. 3. It denies the antithesis, according to which God works out His counsel in this world along the lines of election and reprobation. 4. It forgets that all the forces and institutions of this world are also, and especially, used by the forces of evil for the realization of the kingdom of antichrist, and is in grave danger of looking upon the latter as the kingdom of God. 5. It seeks the kingdom of God in outward forms and institutions, rather than in the power of grace and regeneration, and forgets that in this world the scope of the kingdom is limited to the sphere in which the Spirit of Christ dwells. 6. And to this we may add that it closes its eyes to reality and actual experience, for with all its boasted culture and civilization the world is characterized by corruption, apostasy, hatred, war and destruction more than ever before.

A peculiar view is offered by those who present God's providential government of this world as a matter of common grace. According to this view, the goal of God's government of the present world is the realization of His original creation ordi-

---

(1). *The Coming of the Lord,* James H. Snowden, pp. 112-114

nance, through man as His covenant-friend and co-worker, and
to the glory of His name. Man's calling was to "cultivate" the
earth and its fulness, to employ all his powers and gifts and
talents as the servant of God to explore and develop and bring
to light the hidden wonders and forces of the universe, and thus
to bring the world to its highest possible perfection. This was
the original creation ordinance of God. But Satan, intending
to deprive God of the glory of His name, makes an attempt to
frustrate this plan of God, and to ruin the present world, by
tempting man, causing him to fall into sin and death, and making him an enemy of God. In this attempt he is apparently successful, for the friend of God, who was king of creation, heeds
the word of the devil, rejects the Word of God, and falls into
sin and death. And Satan would have been completely successful, had God not intervened by His common grace. Adam and
Eve would have perished right there and then in Paradise, would
probably have been cast into hell at once, the beautiful creation
of God would have turned into a chaos, and God's original
ordinance of creation would never have been realized. But God
immediately intervened by His common grace. He restrained
the process of sin, of death, and of the curse. The result is, not
only that man did not die on the day he ate of the forbidden
tree, but also that creation was preserved against sinking into a
chaotic state. Moreover, man did not become as totally and absolutely depraved as he undoubtedly would have become, if
this common grace of God had not intervened. And this operation of restraining grace continues throughout the history of
this present world. On its basis and by virtue of its power, God
could enter into a covenant with all men, outside of Christ, the
sign of which He gave in the rainbow that spans the heavens.
And in this covenant man is God's partner and co-worker over
against Satan, for the purpose of realizing the original creation
ordinance of the Most High and frustrating the attempt of the
devil to rob God of His glory. Thus man is able, apart from
Christ and regeneration, to accomplish much good in the present
world, to cultivate the earth and all its powers, press them into
his service in science and art, industry and commerce, and build

the proud structure of culture and civilization through the common grace of God. At the same time God carries out His purpose of salvation in Christ, gathers His Church, and establishes His kingdom in the world that is thus preserved and developed through this power of common grace, and the latter is therefore subservient to the former. The fruits of common grace shall even be carried into the New Jerusalem. However, toward the end God will withdraw the restraining influence of common grace, the world will rush headlong into corruption and destruction, and the man of sin, whom Christ will consume by the brightness of His coming, will be destroyed to make room for the new heavens and the new earth, in which righteousness shall dwell for ever. The meaning of history, and the goal of God's providential government with respect to the present world, according to this view, is the realization of the original creation ordinance of God.

Many objections may be raised against this thoroughly dualistic conception of history, but for our present purpose the following may suffice. 1. There is no original ordinance of creation which Satan attempted to frustrate. God's eternal purpose with all things is never any other than that which is actually attained. When He created the world His purpose surely cannot have been, and was not, that the earth and its fulness should be brought to its highest possible perfection and development under the first man Adam, and without sin. He had in mind the higher realization of His glory and of His eternal covenant in and through the second Adam. And this purpose He realizes even through the temptation of the devil and the fall, death and the curse, through the wonder of His grace. 2. Sin is ethical, and could not possibly have resulted in the reduction of the world to a chaotic state. Even though the spiritual-ethical relation of man to God was radically changed, so that, instead of being the friend of God, he became his enemy and the ally of Satan, there is no reason why God should not sustain and preserve him, together with all the world and its powers, in essentially the same relationship as before the fall. 3. Satan certainly intended to deprive God of His glory through the temptation of man, but not by reducing the world to a chaos, but rather by subject-

ing man and all the earthly creation to himself, and causing
man to develop all the powers of creation in the service of sin
and iniquity. And this is, indeed, the purpose of fallen man,
and the spiritual character of the kingdom he is establishing,
and of the cultural structure he is building. 4. Sin is not a process of corruption in the human nature that can be checked in
its course, so that man is only half depraved: it is the total corruption of the whole nature, the subversion of the image of
God, the radical change from light to darkness, from righteousness to unrighteousness, from life to death. This corruption
the first man, and all men in him, suffered the day he ate of the
forbidden tree, according to the testimony of all Scripture.
5. Death and the curse are not powers that operate in themselves,
apart from God, so that God must restrain them in their course
of operation, as is the dualistic presentation of the theory of
common grace. They are inflicted by God Himself. 6. Even if
there were an original creation ordinance, i.e., a purpose of God
to bring the present world to its highest possible perfection, God
Himself has rendered this for ever impossible by laying the curse
upon the whole creation, so that the creature is in bondage of
corruption and subject to vanity, and man moves within the
limits of his death cell from which he can never escape except
through Christ. It is true that with the limited natural light
and power left to him he still cultivates the earth and performs
many wonderful things, but it is all subject to vanity: to build
a perfect world he neither has the power nor the materials after
the fall. 7. Even in as far as fallen man cultivates the earth and
builds his house of culture, of science and art, of industry and
commerce, he is not a co-worker with God, nor is the house he
is trying to build to the glory of God. The contrary is true. He
employs God's powers and talents and means and all the riches
of God's world in the service of sin and Satan, to oppose God
and His Christ, and to glorify himself. And so he increases his
guilt daily, and also very really works out his own destruction.
8. Nor does the Bible teach us that God restrains the power and
manifestation of sin in the course of the organic development
of the human race by a certain gracious operation of His Spirit.

The very contrary is true. "For the wrath of God is revealed from heaven against all ungodliness and unrighteousness of men, who hold the truth in unrighteousness," Rom. 1:18. And in His wrath He gives them over, so that they become "vain in their imaginations," and their foolish heart is darkened, Rom. 1:21. "Wherefore God also gave them up to uncleanness through the lusts of their own hearts," vs. 24; and unto "vile affections," vs. 26; and "unto a reprobate mind, to do those things which are not convenient," vs. 28. And so they become "filled with all unrighteousness, fornication, wickedness, covetousness, maliciousness; full of envy, murder, debate, deceit, whisperers, backbiters, haters of God, despiteful, proud, boasters, inventors of evil things, disobedient to parents, without understanding, covenant breakers, without natural affection, implacable, unmerciful: who knowing the judgment of God, that they which commit such things are worthy of death, not only do the same, but have pleasure in them that do them." vss. 29-32. The goal of God's providential government, and the meaning of history, cannot be the realization of a supposed original creation ordinance, with the natural man as co-worker to God's glory through His common grace.

The consummation of all things will certainly usher in the perfect world, the New Jerusalem in the new creation in which righteousness shall dwell, and in which the tabernacle of God shall be with men. But that state of eternal perfection and heavenly glory, it must be remembered, does not lie in direct line of development and progress with this present world. It is the kingdom of heaven. It is the world in which all things shall be for ever united in Christ, as the Head of all, the First-born of every creature, through Whom and unto Whom all things were created. From our present world it differs, not only in that sin and death, suffering and sorrow shall be no more, but also in its heavenly character. It is elevated to a plane of existence as much higher than our present earthly universe as Christ is higher than the first man Adam. The first Paradise was an image of that eternal state of heavenly perfection, but it was not its beginning in the sense that the latter is the final development of the former. And, therefore, it is not the direct goal of the

providential government of God as it is discussed by this tenth
Lord's Day of the Heidelberg Catechism: it will be realized
only through the wonder of God's grace. To be sure, the general
providence of God, according to which "as it were by his hand,
he upholds and governs heaven and earth, and all creatures;
so that herbs and grass, rain and drought, fruitful and barren
years, meat and drink, health and sickness, riches and poverty,
yea, and all things, come not by chance, but by his fatherly
hand," — this general providence may not be separated from
the wonder of God's grace, whereby He raises all things to the
higher level of heavenly perfection, and that, too, through the
deep way of sin and death and the final catastrophe. The counsel of predestination and the counsel of providence, though they
may be distinguished, are one counsel. God's providential government is such that all things in the present world are subservient to the realization of His eternal covenant and kingdom.
But this may not be understood as if the providence of God as
such leads up to the world that is to come. Between our world
and the eternal world of heavenly perfection stands the Christ,
the incarnation, the cross, and the resurrection. And even as the
Church must pass through death into the glorious resurrection,
so the present world must pass through the destruction of the
final catastrophe, in which the very elements shall burn, into
the perfection of the new heavens and earth, in which righteousness shall dwell.

Hence, the meaning of history is not that all things tend and
make progress in the direction of the perfect world, as evolutionistic philosophy would have us believe. Nor is the end of God's
providence the realization of the original creation ordinance,
the full development of the original paradise, in spite of the
opposition of Satan, and through a certain power of common
grace. Again the meaning of history is not that this world develops in the direction of the kingdom of heaven, so that it will
finally merge into the glorified creation. But it certainly is the
proper stage that is set for the realization of God's purpose of
predestination, election and reprobation, the revelation of the
Son of God, the cross and the resurrection, the cause of God's

covenant, the bringing forth and the gathering of the Church, the wonder of grace; and that, too, in antithesis to sin and darkness, the devil and his host, the man of sin culminating in the antichrist of the latter days; and through it all for the highest possible revelation of God's own covenant of friendship, the glory of the life of the triune God. That all things in their cosmical unity and organic development may be subservient to this purpose of the antithetical revelation of the wonder of God's blessed covenant of friendship, and shall have served that purpose, when the fulness of Israel and of the Gentiles shall have come in, the measure of the suffering of Christ shall have been fulfilled, and sin shall have become fully manifest as sin,— that is the end of God's providence, and the meaning of history. When that end is attained, the fashion of this world may pass away, the glorious liberty of the children of God may be revealed, and also the creature may be delivered from the bondage of corruption to which it is subjected in order to participate in the glory of the saints in the new heavens and earth.

Unto this end the world was adapted from the beginning, and is preserved and governed by the hand of the Almighty ever since.

For in the beginning the God and Father of our Lord Jesus Christ created all things with a view to Him, Christ, and to the realization of the wonder of His grace and His everlasting covenant, through the way of sin and death, and along the antithetical lines of election and reprobation. For Christ "is the image of the invisible God, the firstborn of every creature: For by him were all things created, that are in heaven, and that are in the earth, visible and invisible, whether they be thrones, or dominions, or principalities, or powers: all things were created by him, and for him: And he is before all things, and by him all things consist. And he is the head of the body, the church: who is the beginning, the firstborn from the dead; that in all things he might have the preëminence. For it pleased the Father that in him all fulness should dwell." Col. 1:15-19. And it was "the mystery of his will, according to his good pleasure, which he hath purposed in himself: That in the dispensation of the fulness of times he might gather together in one all things in Christ, both which are in heaven, and which are on earth." Eph. 1:9, 10. He created the world a kosmos, not a mere aggregate of many separate creatures, but one organic whole, interrelated and interdependent, rising in an ascending scale from the inorganic to the organic, the brute to the rational creature, and with its center in man, who was created after the image of God, and in whom the whole creation was united to the heart of God. For man, thus formed after God's image, stood in covenant-relation of friendship to his Creator. In his heart was the spiritual-ethical center of the *kosmos*, and through him all creatures were comprehended in the covenant of God. They found in man their priest-king, and all must serve him, that he might serve his God. (Netherland Confession, Art. XII).

But this original state of earthly perfection was not destined to continue. A breach was struck into the harmonious relation of the kosmos to God by sin. We say that it was not *destined* to continue, by which we mean that it was not the purpose of the good pleasure of God. For, to be sure, even though Adam fell by his own willful disobedience, he fell according to the eternal purpose of God, and under the all controlling direction of God's providential government. If it be confessed that God, "as it were by his hand," upholds and governs all things, it dare not be denied that He did so from the beginning, and that it was by His providence that the breach of sin was struck into the original relation of creation to Himself. This does not deny man's responsibility, but it does make him, even in his ethical life and choice, dependent upon God. Even when the devil beguiled the woman, and she ate of the forbidden fruit, and she gave to Adam, and he fell, God was governing all things "as it were by his hand." However, we must remember that the breach was of an ethical nature; it was struck in the heart of man. Sin did not, and could not possibly destroy the essential, organic relation and unity of all creatures. Even though man violated the covenant of friendship with his God, and became an enemy of God, loving the lie, perverse of will, unclean in all his desires and inclinations, God still continued to uphold and to govern "as it were by his hand," the universe as a *kosmos,* and that, too, in such a way that man stands at the head of the earthly creation even in his sin, and all creatures must serve him.

However, quite in harmony with the altered spiritual-ethical relation of man to God, he and the whole creation with him were placed under the curse. God's government of the world in sin is such that all things are "vanity and vexation of spirit." And also through this governmental act of God's providence the present world becomes the stage for the enactment and revelation of the wonder of God's grace, and the realization of His purpose of predestination, election and reprobation. The judgments of God upon the fallen world that are pronounced immediately after the fall, may not be considered as merely punishments for sin. For, first of all, *the* punishment of sin is eternal death in hell, not mere temporal suffering. And hell could not be prepared immediately after the fall: God's counsel of salvation must first be realized, and the root-sin of Adam must have become fully manifest in all the horror of its iniquity in the ripened fruit borne by the whole human race. Besides, it must not be forgotten, that the temporal punishments mentioned in Gen. 3:15ff. are announced after the promise of redemption, the protevangel, had been proclaimed: "I will put enmity between thee and the woman, and between thy seed and her seed; it shall bruise thy head, and thou shalt bruise his heel." Adam fell upon Christ, and the covenant that was violated by the first man, is maintained, established, and raised to a higher level in the second Man. For Him and His revelation the stage of the present, fallen world is set. All things become vanity, but even in their vanity, or rather *exactly in their vanity,* they must serve the purpose of God's counsel of predestination in Christ, the firstborn of every creature. Temporal death, the return of his physical nature to the dust, is inflicted upon man, in order that generation after generation may disappear from the stage, after they have served God's purpose. The "sorrow and conception" of the woman are made very great, which (if the expression is taken literally, and not as a hendiadys) means that the repro-

ductive capacity of the race is greatly increased, so that all things
hasten to the end. And the "sorrow" of the woman does, indeed,
witness of the fact that we can only bring forth children of wrath
by nature, yet, for the believing woman this sorrow is not without hope, for she is still blessed in bringing forth children when
she bears her sorrow with her eye on the promise. Even the relationship between the man and the woman is placed under a
curse, for while the woman's desire shall always be to her husband, the latter shall rule over her. Gen. 3:16. This sentence
can hardly have reference to the fact that man is the head of
the woman, for this is not due to the curse, but to creation:
"For Adam was first formed and then Eve," I Tim. 2:13. But
this original relationship is now placed under a curse, so that
man's rule becomes one of pride and boastful cruelty and
tyranny. While the woman violated the proper relation to her
husband by deciding the matter of the forbidden fruit by herself, and by tempting and deceiving him, everything that concerns her relation to him after the fall is now subjected to
suffering and humiliation. Her desire shall be to her husband
even in her sorrow and subjection. And, quite in accord with
the sinful and cursed condition of fallen man, all creation is put
under the bondage of corruption. The ground is cursed. And
this implies that it shall henceforth bring forth thorns and
thistles, representative of all obnoxious weeds, so that the toil
of man in eliciting the necessary sustenance from the soil is
greatly increased. Man shall eat thereof only in the sweat of
his face, and in "sorrow all the days of his life." Gen. 3:17, 18.
The cursed earth shall henceforth produce corruptible food for
his corruptible body, so that in the sphere of corruption he eats
and drinks corruption unto death. But this also refers to all the
suffering of the groaning creation, to earthquakes and volcanoes,
hail and fire, destructive winds and floods, scorching heat and
drought, locusts and other pests that destroy all the toil of the
husbandman in one day. And the creature is made subject to
vanity, not willingly, but by reason of him who hath subjected
the same, i.e., by the will of God, Rom. 8:20. Thus creation is
sustained and governed by God, in its cosmical coherence and

unity, and directed in its course of organic development, in the sphere of vanity, and bearing the curse. And thus the Heidelberg Catechism rightly speaks of this present world as "this valley of tears," and in describing the government of God in the present Lord's Day mentions rain, but also drought; fruitful, but also barren years; health, but also sickness, as coming "not by chance but by his fatherly hand."

And thus the stage is set for the antithetical revelation of the wonder of grace in Christ, and of the covenant of God's friendship. God reveals Himself, not only as the Creator, Who calls the things that are not as if they were; but also as the Redeemer, Who quickens the dead. He calls the light out of darkness, righteousness out of corruption, life out of death, heavenly glory out of the desolation of hell. And all this He realizes through Christ, the cross and the resurrection, the exaltation at the right hand of God, and the coming again in power; and in the elect Church, chosen unto everlasting life, that they might be to the praise of the glory of His grace in the Beloved. With His elect He realizes His eternal covenant of friendship. But at the same time there is upon that world in sin and vanity an operation of God's anger and fierce wrath, along the line of reprobation, whereby the ungodly are given over unto foolishness and ungodliness, unto religious and moral degradation, and the vessels of wrath are fitted unto destruction. And thus arises the antithesis, not of nature and grace, but of sin and grace, of light and darkness, of Christ and Belial, of righteousness and unrighteousness. For the creatures are upheld and governed by God in their cosmical coherence and unity, elect and reprobate are of one blood, and they have all natural things in common. But they differ fundamentally in their spiritual-ethical relation to God. And while the ungodly develop and live and act from the spiritual-ethical principle of sin, using all things as means to give expression to that principle, and creating a world full of the lust of the flesh, and the lust of the eyes, and the pride of life, they that are called fight the good fight of faith, living from the principle of regeneration, representing the cause of the Son of God in the world, strangers and pilgrims by virtue of their heavenly calling, and seeking the things that are above, where Christ sitteth at the right hand of God. This is the meaning of history. And thus the twofold harvest of the world grows and ripens: the tares and the wheat must grow up together. And when the harvest is ripe, the Lord of the harvest will come and reap, will gather the wheat into his barn, and destroy the tares with unquenchable fire. Then the stage may also disappear, in order to make room for the eternal House of God in the new creation! Such is the end of God's providence.

And thus the believer may place his firm trust in the God and Father of our Lord Jesus Christ, fully confident that nothing shall separate him from His love, "since all creatures are so in his hand, that without his will they cannot so much as move." For he knows that all things in the present world, all things literally, in heaven and on earth, and more especially also the things that appear evil, must work together for his eternal salvation. For he knows that the eternal Father of our Lord Jesus Christ, and that, too, *as* the eternal Father of Christ our Lord, made all things out of nothing, and according to His sovereign good pleasure; and that *as* the Father of our Lord Jesus Christ, with a view to Him and His Church, and with a view to the antithetical revelation of His covenant of friendship, He upheld and governed the universe from the very beginning, so that nothing ever thwarted or frustrated the realization of His eternal counsel; and that He still upholds and governs the same by His almighty and omnipresent power. He understands that the world to come is not the final development of the present world but the final revelation of the wonder of grace; and refusing to be deceived by any theory of common grace, as if some kind of a perfected paradise, the realization of the original creation ordinance, were still to be expected, he will have nothing of the idealistic philosophy of the world, loves not the world, neither the things that are in the world, but seeks the things that are above, where Christ sitteth at the right hand of God. In the meantime, he understands his calling, and by grace he is willing to serve God's purpose even in this world, that he may represent the cause of the Son of God to the praise of the glory of His grace in the beloved, and that, too, over against a world that lieth in darkness. And unto this purpose he makes all things subservient, in Church and State, in home and school and society. He does not go out of the world, but in the world he serves the Lord Christ.

In this attempt and purpose it is sometimes given him to prosper. He may live as a believer in his home, with his wife and children. He may establish his own school, where his children are educated according to the principles of the Word of God. He may promote the proclamation of the true gospel. He may even exert some influence in society and in State. God gives him the means and the power to realize the purpose of his calling. And in this prosperity he is thankful. More often, however, he shall meet with the power of opposition, and he shall have to fight the battle of faith, suffering with Christ in that battle. Moreover, he, too, partakes of the suffering of this present time in general, of drought and barren years, of sickness and sorrow and death, of war and destruction, of famine and pestilence. But in all these things he may be patient, and give thanks in all things, confident that "all things come, not by chance, but by his fatherly hand," that "nothing shall separate us from his love," that "all creatures are so in his hand, that without his will they cannot so much as move," and that further "he will make whatever evils he sends upon me in this valley of tears turn out to my advantage; for he is able to do it, being Almighty God, and willing, being a faithful Father." That is the comfort and victorious power of faith in God, the Father, Almighty, Maker of heaven and earth!

THE DEATH OF THE SON OF GOD

LORD'S DAY XI

Q. 29. Why is the Son of God called Jesus, that is a Saviour?

A. Because he saveth us, and delivereth us from our sins; and likewise, because we ought not to seek, neither can find salvation in any other.

Q. 30. Do such then believe in Jesus the only Saviour, who seek their salvation and welfare of saints, of themselves, or anywhere else?

A. They do not; for though they boast of him in words, yet in deeds they deny Jesus the only deliverer and Saviour; for one of these two things must be true, that either Jesus is not a complete Saviour; or that they, who by a true faith receive this Saviour, must find all things in him necessary to their salvation.

I

The Only Name

In this eleventh Lord's Day the Heidelberg Catechism begins
the discussion of the second article of the *Apostolicum*, and
thereby introduces the discussion of the second main part of
that Confession of faith, the part containing the profession of
what the Church of old believed concerning "God the Son,"
but not now as the second Person of the Holy Trinity, but as
the Mediator of God and men. This second main division
covers articles two to seven inclusive. And although it is very
brief, it is remarkable for its fulness of expression, mentioning
as it does all the chief points of doctrine concerning our Lord
Jesus Christ. It speaks of His person and work, of His divine
and of His human nature, of His conception by the Holy Ghost
and of His virgin birth, of His humiliation, His suffering, crucifixion, death, burial and descension into hell, and of His
exaltation, resurrection, ascension, sitting at the right hand of
God, and return to judgment; and it mentions His names:
Jesus, Christ, Lord, Son of God. In general, we may say that
this part of the *Apostolicum* speaks of our Lord's names, His
natures, and His states, while under the name Christ the Heidelberg Catechism naturally explains the offices of the Mediator.
Three Lord's Days are devoted to a discussion of the names of
our Lord, as contained in the second article of the *Credo;* three
Lord's Days cover the state of humiliation as described in articles
three and four; and, finally, three Lord's Days discuss the state
of exaltation of the Saviour, mentioned in articles five to seven
of the Apostles' Creed. In the present Lord's Day, the eleventh,
of the Catechism a beginning is made with the explanation of
the second article: "And in Jesus Christ, his only begotten Son,
our Lord."

"Why is the Son of God called Jesus, that is Saviour?" With this question the Catechism introduces its explanation of the names of Christ. The question, and that, too, exactly in this form, is significant, and may well demand a moment of our attention. Especially in modern times it is important to put the question concerning the Saviour precisely thus, and before any other question. One may also ask: "Why is Jesus called the Son of God?" And in the thirteenth Lord's Day we may find the answer to this question. But before we can properly discuss why Jesus, the historical Jesus of Nazareth, the man Jesus, is called the Son of God, we must ask this: "Why is the Son of God called Jesus, that is Saviour?" To ask this question first, and to put it in these words, is the method of faith. Philosophy, and modern theology, would strenuously object to this method. They would refuse to begin with this question. They would object that it is guilty of begging the question. They would have no objection to beginning with the problem of Jesus' being called the Son of God. For then, thus they would argue, we take our startingpoint in a historical fact. Jesus was a historical person, as we may learn from the gospel narratives. And it is certain, too, that he was called the Son of God. Now, we must first of all investigate the meaning of this fact not that He is, but that He *was called* the Son of God, and determine just in how far this claim is true, and what is the exact meaning of this claim. And having thus investigated the meaning of, and given definite content to the name Son of God, we may, perhaps, also ask why this Son of God is called Jesus. But to ask first of all "Why is the Son of God called Jesus?" is begging the main question and proceeds from the supposition that He really is the Son of God, and that, too, even before He is Jesus. However, the Catechism is not proposing a philosophical question, but discussing the *Credo* of the Church. It does not employ the language, neither follow the method of rationalism, but speaks from faith. And for the faith of the Church it is an indubitable truth that Jesus is the true, essential, only begotten Son of God. He is this first. He is not first Jesus, a man who somehow was called Son of God. On the contrary, He is first Son of God. In fact, unless He is first Son of God, the eternal God begotten of the Father, we are in no wise interested in His name Jesus. Son of God He is in eternity; the name Jesus brings Him to us in time, but still as Son of God. The question, therefore, is not at all how it came about that Jesus was called the Son of God, but is very really this: "Why is the Son of God called Jesus?"

Besides, we must understand that the Catechism in asking this question does not express a certain curiosity as to the reason why *men* called this Son of God Jesus, for then the question would have no significance whatever. We are dealing here with the contents of the Christian faith, with one of those matters that are "necessary for a Christian to believe." The Heidelberger would instruct us in the knowledge of the holy gospel, of the Mediator that can and does save us from our sin and deliver us from all our misery. That is the reason why this question is asked. It is based on the assumption that the answer to this question will inform us about the Saviour, that His name answers the question Who He is. Modern theology would probably smile somewhat sympathetically at this obsolete method of attempting to elicit knowledge about the Christ from a study of His name. It would consider this method altogether inadequate. How can you find out anything about a man by asking for his name? And what good does it do to make a study of the names of Christ? We must gather all the facts we can about this Jesus of Nazareth, compare them and study them critically, learn to know what He did, what was His teaching, how He reacted toward His contemporaries, and then write His biography, a "Life of Jesus," especially also in order that we may bring out His "character." Then we have something. The result of such a thorough study will be the knowledge of a real Christ, Whose teachings may be to our advantage, and Whose example may be followed! But to study His names is vain and fruitless.

However, faith is not at all interested in a "Life of Jesus." And what is more, the Scriptures do not furnish us with the necessary material to construe a biography of our Lord, nor do they offer us a sketch of His character. In the Bible we have four gospel narratives, and they together record the gospel of Jesus Christ, but in all of them together we have no "life of Jesus," and as far as they are concerned our Lord may have had no "character" at all. If you read these gospel narratives with a view to finding out what sort of man Jesus of Nazareth was in regard to His physical stature and psychological inclinations, whether He was tall and powerful or weak and of a frail frame, whether he had blue eyes or brown, was strikingly beautiful or common in appearance, whether he was of a phlegmatic or sanguinous temperament, whether He was an accomplished student and profound thinker, or a man of average mentality; or even with the end in view to discover what He accomplished to make this world better, and to advance civilization, — you will not only search in vain, and find the gospel narratives very inadequate, but you will also be deeply disappointed at every step of your investigation. What they narrate about His birth is so strange, that you can deduce nothing from His descent with a view to His character. Of the first thirty years of His life they tell you next to nothing. What influence His early training had upon His life and career seems to be of no concern to these gospel writers. His birth, three years of activity and teaching, His death and His resurrection, — this appears to be all that matters. And any attempt to construe a "life of Jesus" from these gospel narratives, or to determine His character, must needs fail. He does not appear as a mere man among men, but as *the* Son of man. This does not mean that He was no specific individual, and that He had a sort of "general human nature," but it does mean that the Scriptures are not interested in His individual life and character, but give us the *revelation of Jesus Christ,* the Son of God in the flesh, the God of our salvation. And if this is understood, it will also be plain that we are not concerned with what *men called Him,* but with what *God revealed to us of Him.* God called Him Jesus. And if God called Him Jesus, there is significance in the name, and there is real sense in the question: "Why is the Son of God called Jesus, that is Saviour?"

Great significance is attached to a name in Scripture. In fact, the name of anything is its real essence, its sense, its meaning, the denotation of that which it is in itself and with relation to everything else. With us this is different. A name of a person or thing is hardly more than a sign by which we distinguish one person or thing from others. It is one of the effects of sin that we no longer discern the real nature and meaning of things, and are no longer able to express the true sense of anything in a name. We see some external phenomena, and from these we deduce some characteristics of the objects to which these phenomena belong. We discern the difference between one object and another, between a bird and a tree, a lake and a river, between one star and another, between a sheep and a lion, an animal and a man. But we do not intuitively discern the essence and nature of anything, even though we bring it within the range of our telescope, or minutely examine and analyze it under the microscope. And so, our names at the very most express some external characteristics of the object named. But originally this was different. Adam in the state of rectitude intuitively looked in the essence of things, saw their real meaning, and was able to express this sense of all things in their proper names. This is very evident from the fact that God brought the animals to him, to see how he would name them, "and whatsoever Adam called every living creature, that was the name thereof." And the real Scriptural meaning of a name is exactly that it is the denotation of the true nature of the thing named.

The underlying reason for this is evident. For all things were called into existence by the Word of God. God, Who calls the things that are not as if they were, spoke creatively, and by that creative Word of God all things received being. And when God speaks, even when He speaks creatively, He always speaks concerning Himself, so that His Word is His self-revelation. It follows that the real essence of any creature is that Word of God by which it was called into being, and through which it continues to exist. Not its outward form, not its material substance, not its chemical composition, not its biological structure, but the Word of God in the creature is its real nature. Its sense, its meaning, is its essence. And that meaning it derives only from the Word of God, through which every creature is but an integral part of the speech of God concerning Himself in all the universe, and all creatures together unite in spelling the Name of God. That Word of God in every creature is its real name. And that name man in his original state of righteousness could read, in order that thus he might read the Name of the Lord his God in creation, and glorify Him in adoration. In this light we can understand what the Scriptures declare in such passages as Eph. 3:14, 15: "For this cause I bow my knees unto the Father of our Lord Jesus Christ, of whom the whole family in heaven and earth is named." All things are names, because God has put His Word in them. And originally all these names were interpreted intuitively by man, that he might behold and declare the glory of the Name of his God. But this power is lost through sin. Nor can it be regained even by means of telescope or microscope. However, though in the world of our very dim understanding the "name" has no longer its original significance, the Bible still speaks of the name in that sense. This is especially evident from the way in which it speaks of the Name of God. God's Name is Himself as He is revealed to us. By His name He came down to us, is near us, surrounds us on all sides. His name is in all the works of His hands as the psalmist sings in Ps. 8:1-9. And that His name is near, His wondrous works declare. Ps. 75:1. To fear His name is to fear Him, to glorify His name is to glorify Him, to trust in His name is to trust in Him, to believe on His name is to believe on Him. The Name of God is revealed. Besides, that the Scriptures use "name" in its original sense, may also be gathered from the fact that names are sometimes changed intentionally so as to have proper meaning. Abram is changed to Abraham, Sarai to Sarah, Oshea to Jehoshua. The name denotes the essence. And it is on the ground of this truth that the Catechism asks the question concerning the Christ: "Why is the Son of God called Jesus, that is Saviour?"

The meaning of this question, therefore, is, that God called His Son Jesus, and that because God called Him thus, Jesus is

His name. We may, and by grace do also call Him Jesus, when by the intuitive knowledge of faith we discern Him in His real significance. And when we do so that Name becomes to us the only name given under heaven whereby we may be and are saved. Then we believe in that Name, trust on that Name, find our only comfort in life and in death in that Name, have all our salvation in that Name, love, worship, and adore it. But all this is only true and has sense only if it be true that God called His name Jesus. If God did not call His only begotten Son Jesus, our faith and trust and adoration have no basis, no sense, are vain. And that God called His Son Jesus, signifies that from all eternity the triune God so called Him. It means that the name Jesus, revealed in time, has its roots in eternity, that it is eternal, that the Son of God is eternally called Jesus. It signifies that the Son of God is called Jesus by a free act of the sovereign God, and by the determination of the good pleasure of God "who worketh all things after the counsel of His own will." Even as the act of creation is not the necessary effluence of God's being, but the free and determinate act of His sovereign will, rooted in His counsel, so also this naming of the Son of God as Jesus is the eternal act of God's good pleasure. And as all God's works are acts of the triune God, so also this naming of the Son of God. We may not so present the matter as if the first Person of the Holy Trinity called the second Person Jesus, for all God's works are of the Father, through the Son, and in the Holy Spirit. All the three Persons of the Godhead, each according to His own place and relation in the economy of the Holy Trinity, willed from eternity that the Son should be called Jesus! "Why is the Son of God called Jesus, that is Saviour?" Because from all eternity He was so called according to a free and sovereign determination of God triune! And on the basis of the revelation of that eternal act of God, we, too, may call Him Jesus!

That this is true is evident not only from Scripture in general, and from the revelation of this Jesus in the old dispensation, but also very specifically from the testimony of Holy Writ concerning the way in which the Saviour received His name in time.

Exactly because the child Jesus had a name before He was conceived in the womb of the virgin Mary, the giving of His name to Him in time may not be left to the determination of Joseph and Mary: His eternal name must be revealed, and by that name He must be known to men. And so, when Joseph, naturally misinterpreting the condition of his espoused wife, contemplated putting her away privily, "the angel of the Lord appeared unto him in a dream, saying, Joseph, thou son of David, fear not to take unto thee Mary thy wife; for that which is conceived in her is of the Holy Ghost. And she shall bring forth a son, and thou shalt call his name Jesus: for he shall save his people from their sins." And mark you well, "all this was done, that it might be fulfilled which was spoken of the Lord by the prophet, saying, Behold, a virgin shall be with child, and shall bring forth a son, and they shall call his name Emmanuel which being interpreted is God with us." And so, Joseph "did as the angel had bidden him, and took unto him his wife: And knew her not till she had brought forth her firstborn son: and he called his name Jesus." Matt. 1:19-25. And also the gospel according to Luke refers to this revelation of the name in ch. 2:21: "And when eight days were accomplished for the circumcising of the child, his name was called Jesus, which was so named of the angel before he was conceived in the womb." For not only to Joseph, but also to Mary, who preferred to keep things "pondering them in her heart," it was revealed by the angel Gabriel that the name of the Son, whom she should bring forth, must be called Jesus. Luke 1:31. And so the apostles can preach that "neither is there salvation in any other: for there is none other name under heaven given among men, whereby we must be saved." Acts 4:12. The name Jesus is of divine origin, and is the revelation of an eternal purpose and act of God. The question is, therefore, a perfectly proper one: "Why is the Son of God called Jesus, that is Saviour?" And the true answer to this question is indeed the gospel of God concerning His Son. He is called Jesus because He *is* Jesus, the God of our salvation reaching down to us in our misery, to redeem us, and to deliver us from death!

II

The Perfect Saviour

The name Jesus, a Greek rendering of the Hebrew name
Joshua or Jehoshua, is explained by the Catechism as briefly
meaning Saviour: "why is the Son of God called Jesus, *that is
Saviour?*" Of old there has been and still is difference of opinion
among scholars as to the proper derivation of the name Jehoshua.
According to some it is supposed to be a simple verbal noun,
and in that case the meaning is *salvation*. According to others,
the name is composed of two parts, *Jeho*, an abbreviation of
Jehovah, and *shua*, salvation or saves, and according to this
derivation the name means Jehovah-salvation or Jehovah saves.
We cannot, of course, enter more deeply into the merits of this
controversy. Let it suffice to state that, in our opinion, the
analogy of many similar names in the Old Testament is de-
cidedly in favor of the latter view. Thus the name Jehohanan
is composed of *Jeho* and *hanan,* and means Jehovah-gracious
or Jehovah granted; Jehoiada is composed of *Jeho* and *iada,*
meaning Jehovah knows; Jehoiachin consists of *Jeho* and *iachin,*
signifying Jehovah appoints; Jehoiakim is composed of *Jeho*
and *iakim,* and means Jehovah sets up; Jonathan (Jehonathan)
is *Jeho-nathan,* meaning Jehovah gives, etc. It is quite in line
with these and many other examples in Scripture to explain the
name Jehoshua or Joshua as being composed of *Jeho* and *Shua*
and as meaning Jehovah-salvation. This, then, is the full meaning of the name Jesus. And thus explained, the name has a
profound and rich significance. It signifies that Jesus is the
revelation of the God of our salvation, or rather that He *is*
Jehovah-salvation. In Him we see Jehovah, the EHJEH ASHER
EHJEH, the I AM THAT I AM, the eternal, self-existent, immutable God, Who is eternal and immutable in Himself, and

450

eternal and unchangeable also in relation to His people and covenant, come down to us in our misery and death, reaching down with His mighty arm to save us. Creation is the revelation of the Almighty, Who calleth the things that are not as if they were. But Jesus, i.e. the Christ of the Scriptures, the Son of God come into the flesh, bearing our iniquities, crucified and slain, raised on the third day, gone into the heavens and exalted at the right hand of the Most High,—this Jesus is the revelation of Jehovah our salvation, Who calls light out of darkness, righteousness out of sin, life out of death, heavenly glory out of the desolation of corruption and hell.

It is noteworthy that the Catechism in this eleventh Lord's Day lays stress on the truth that the name Jesus implies that He is a complete Saviour, a perfect Saviour, in Whom we must find everything that is necessary to our salvation; and that for this reason He is also the only Saviour, so that we "ought not to seek, neither can find salvation in any other," and that they, "who seek their salvation or welfare of saints, of themselves, or anywhere else," do not believe in Jesus, "for though they boast of him in words, yet in deeds they deny Jesus the only deliverer and Saviour." The reason for this emphasis on the part of the Heidelberger is, of course, that the Roman Catholic church does, indeed, teach men to seek salvation also in Mary, in the saints and in men. And although our controversy is no longer so directly with the Roman Catholic church as it was in the days when our Heidelberger was composed, even in this respect and with a view to this controversy the Catechism is not quite so obsolete as is sometimes supposed, witness the following replies in recent years broadcast over the radio: "What is her (Mary's) place in the Christian religion? Mary's place in the Christian religion should be obvious. She is the morning star preceding the Light of the world, Christ. The only difference is that all her light is received from the Son she heralds. By God's eternal decree Mary has been associated with the highest mysteries of the Christian religion, being the very instrument of the Incarnation of the Eternal Son of God, and, therefore, of our redemption. We have devotion to her because of our admiration of her, and because of her interest in our eternal welfare . . . In what way did Mary take her part in the redemptive work of mankind which was accomplished by Christ alone? Christ was the principal Author of our redemption, but there were many secondary cooperators in the work. We even find St. Paul saying that we are to fill up what is wanting to the sufferings of Christ. The explanation of this, however, would demand a treatise on the mystical body of Christ as comprising all the members of the Church, and I can scarcely do justice to it now. All I can say is that Mary cooperated in the redemptive work in a way quite special to herself. As Jesus is the second Adam, so Mary is the second Eve. As our first Mother Eve brought us forth to misery and suffering, so our second Mother Mary, in bringing forth our Saviour, brought us forth to happiness and salvation. Mary's consent was asked by God when the time for the Incarnation was at hand: she consented to the full work of Christ from the cave of Bethlehem to the cross of Calvary. She provided the very blood that was shed for us. In union with Christ she had her own passion, and Simeon rightly predicted to her, under the inspiration of the Holy Ghost, 'Thy own soul a sword shall pierce.' With, in, and through the work of Christ her sufferings also contributed secondarily towards our redemption. And she was given to us from the cross as a mother for a mother's work. To all of us Christ said in the person of St. John, 'Son, behold thy mother.' We catholics, therefore, regard Mary as our spiritual Mother, entertaining towards her the devotion of children. Every Christian woman above all, should regard Mary, the Mother of Christ, as the glory of her sex." Radio Replies, III, by Dr. Leslie Rumble. Or note this by the same author in answer to another question: "Essentially that work was accomplished on Calvary by the death of Jesus on the cross. And Mary was there, standing at the foot of the cross, identifying herself with the offering of her Son. By man and woman came death. Both sexes cooperated in our downfall, and both sexes cooperated in our redemption . . . Mary is the second Eve as Christ is the second Adam. And both repaired the evil of our first parents,

Christ principally and Mary secondarily and subordinately to Christ. . . . Mary's work was to be our co-redemptress, and to mediate for us together with Christ, but of course in subordination to Him. . . . She is our spiritual Mother in heaven, and she fulfills the duties of a Mother, winning for us by her intercession that grace of Christ which is life to our souls and which, please God, will mean eternal life in the end." idem, II, p. 162.

Nor has the Roman Catholic doctrine changed with regard to prayers to Mary and to the saints in heaven, and with respect to looking for help and salvation from them, and even through their relics. "Why do Catholics believe that Mary prays for them and helps them? Because they believe that she is their spiritual Mother, and that she has not lost her interest in those for whom her Son died, merely because she is in heaven. . . . We do not pray to Mary instead of to God, but we do pray to her as well as to God. . . . Two prayers are better than one, above all when the other whom I have asked to join in my petition is the very Mother of Christ." idem, p. 161. And as to worshiping the saints, note the following: "Why pray to Saints? Is it not better to pray to God directly? Not always. The same answer applies here as in the case of prayers to the Virgin Mary, who after all is the greatest of the Saints. God may wish to give certain favors through the intercession of some given Saint. In such a case it is better to seek the intercession of that Saint as God wishes." And as to worshiping the relics of the saints, the same author has this to say: "Why do Catholics worship relics of Saints? They do not worship relics as they worship God, by adoration. If you mean worship in the sense of honor or veneration, then Catholics certainly venerate the relics of the saints." And when one objects to the Roman Catholic practice of expecting help or favors through relics, the same writer answers: "No real difficulty arises in this matter. No one holds that material relics of themselves possess any innate or talismanic value. But God Himself can certainly grant favors even of a temporal nature through the relics of Saints, thus honoring His Saints, and rewarding the faith and piety of some given Catholic." idem, I, p. 289, 291. These quotations may suffice to demonstrate that the emphasis of the Catechism on the absolutely sole sufficiency of Jesus as Saviour is, ever in opposition to the present Roman Catholic doctrine, not out of date.

Yet, our immediate concern today is not so much with the errors of the Roman Catholic church as with those who, while they loudly and emphatically proclaim that "Jesus saves," yet deprive Him of all power to save unless the sinner gives his consent. This is a great evil, and a very general and prevalent one in our day, all the more dangerous because those that thus preach Jesus ostensibly emphasize strongly exactly that which they, nevertheless, deny: that Jesus saves. The name of Jesus is on the lips of many a preacher today, who, nevertheless, proclaims a Jesus that is impotent to save. And the words "Jesus saves" may be read on billboards and auto licenses, as well as above entrances to church buildings, but if you should inquire of those that are responsible for these advertisements just what they mean by that winged slogan, you would discover that they attach a meaning to it quite different from what the words actually express. For they do not mean that Jesus actually saves, but that He is willing to save, provided the sinner gives his consent, will let himself be saved by Jesus; if not, their Jesus is powerless to save. In other words, they do not find in their Jesus absolutely all things necessary to save a sinner, and that, too, not a willing, but an unwilling sinner that is dead through trespasses and sins. And, therefore, it is not only proper, but urgently necessary for the church that prizes and would preserve the truth as it is in Christ, to emphasize that Christ is a complete, a perfect and only Saviour, and that He is not only willing, but powerful to save even unto the end. His name is called Jesus, "because he shall save His people from their sins."

The Heidelberger instructs us that "the Son of God is called Jesus, that is a Saviour, because he *saveth us and delivereth us* from our sins." Mark you well, He is called Jesus, not because He *is willing* to save and to deliver us, nor even because He *is able* to save and to deliver us from our sins, but because *He actually does save and deliver us.* And again, the Catechism declares that "they who by a true faith receive this Saviour, must find all things in him necessary to their salvation." Now, salvation is that marvelous work of God's grace whereby the sinner, loaded with a burden of guilt that renders him damnable before God, chained from within with shackles of corruption and death, which he can never break, standing in enmity against God, loving the darkness rather than the light, wholly incapable to save himself, or to contribute even the least to his salvation, impotent and unwilling to turn to God to be saved, is redeemed from his guilt, is liberated from his bondage of sin and corruption, is delivered from the dominion of death, and is raised to the status of a free son of God translated from darkness into light, and from death to eternal life in fellowship with God and in heavenly glory. And when we say that Jesus is a complete Saviour we mean that He alone accomplishes absolutely all that is implied in this marvelous work of grace. Let us consider this a little more in detail.

We may distinguish here between that part of the work of salvation which Jesus accomplished *for* us, *in our behalf,* and that other part which He performs *upon* us and *within* us. The first part is the work of redemption, whereby Christ purchased us free from the guilt of sin and from the bondage of death, and merited for us the *right* to be delivered, and to receive all the blessings of salvation. This is first. It is basic. For we must recall that we are guilty and damnable before God, and that our being in the bondage of sin is the result of God's just sentence of death upon us. We are born in original guilt because of Adam's transgression, and we increase our guilt daily by our actual sin. And guilt is liability to punishment. And the punishment of sin is death. That punishment is not something that will be inflicted upon us in the future, after physical death only, but that is also upon us now. And to that just punishment belongs our spiritual death, our totally undone and depraved condition. Hence, before all things, before we can even have the right to be saved and delivered from the bondage and power of sin, it is necessary that our guilt be removed, and that we become juridically or forensically righteous before

God. To use an illustration, as our just punishment for our
sin God shut us up in the prison of corruption and death, and
securely locked the door of our prison. He that would deliver
us from our bondage cannot simply break into our prison by
main force. On the contrary, he must receive the key to our
prison door from God Himself, that he may set us free. But
to obtain that key, he must make us worthy of liberation, he
must remove from our heads the sentence of damnation, satisfy
the justice of God and remove our guilt, and obtain for us
everlasting righteousness. And this is what Christ did for us.
He did so by His perfect obedience, His suffering and death
on the accursed tree, whereby He atoned for all our sins, and
obtained for us that righteousness according to which we are
worthy of eternal life and glory.

Why, then, is the Son of God called Jesus? First of all because
He redeemed us. In Him God reconciled us unto Himself, not
imputing our trespasses unto us. In the death and resurrection
of Jesus Jehovah is revealed to us as the God of our salvation,
Who justifies the ungodly. That is the meaning of the name
Jesus!

But this is not all. In fact, if it were all, He would not be
Jesus. He must not only accomplish that part of salvation that
must be done for us, in our behalf, but also that other part that
is to be realized within us. Not only our state, our legal status
before God, must be changed from one of guilt into one of
perfect and everlasting righteousness, also our actual condition
must undergo a complete and radical change, such a change
as is nothing less than a resurrection from the dead. We must
not only be redeemed, but we must also be *delivered* from sin.
We must be changed from death into life, from darkness into
light, from rebellious and cursing children of the devil into dear
children of God, from the misery and desolation of our natural
state into the glory of heavenly perfection. Our whole nature
must be radically turned about, so that the image of God is
restored in us, and instead of loving the lie we love and do the
truth, instead of being slaves of the devil and yielding ourselves
as servants of iniquity unto unrighteousness, we follow after

righteousness, and instead of being corrupt and rebellious of will and inclination we are consecrated to God. We must receive spiritual eyes to see the things of the kingdom of God, and to recognize Jesus as the revelation of the God of our salvation; and spiritual ears to hear spiritual things, and a spiritual heart to obey the Word of God. And we must receive all these spiritual blessings, not in such manner that after having once received them we now possess them in ourselves, but constantly. We must be united with Christ, that from Him we may live as the branches live out of the vine, as the members live only in organic union with the body. And so we must be preserved even unto the end, and that, too, in the midst of a world in which everything stands opposed to us, and in which the devil, the world, and our flesh constantly try to destroy us. And, finally, we must be glorified. Through death we must pass into heavenly glory, into the "first resurrection" of the building of God, not made with hands, eternal in the heavens. And through the grave we must pass into glory of the final resurrection, that we may inherit the kingdom of God, which flesh and blood cannot inherit. This corruptible must put on incorruption, and this mortal must put on immortality, and the image of the earthy which we now bear must be replaced by the image of the heavenly, that in the new heavens and the new earth we may be fit inhabitants of the tabernacle of God that shall be with men!

And when we say that Jesus is a complete Saviour, we mean that He alone accomplishes all this marvelous work in us, and that they, who by a true faith receive this Saviour, find all these glorious blessings of grace in Him, and in Him only. He not only obtained the right of our deliverance, He also received the key to our prison of sin and death, and the commission to liberate us and to lead us on to eternal glory. For He is raised from the dead, and in Him is life and immortality. And He went into the highest heavens, and is exalted at the right hand of God, endowed with all power in heaven and on earth. And being exalted at the right hand of the Majesty in the heavens, He received the promise of the Holy Spirit, in order that through that Spirit He might return to us, dwell in us, and make us partakers of the blessings of grace He merited for us by His perfect obedience. And by the power of that Spirit, and through His Word, He delivers us, and saves us even unto the end. It is He that regenerates us, imparting unto us His own resurrection life; it is He that calls us, so that we come to Him and embrace Him by a true faith; it is He that unites us with Himself, that lives in us, that cleanses us from the pollution of sin, that sanctifies us unto God, that preserves us in the midst of the opposing forces of this world, so that nothing can pluck us out of His hand. And it is He that is the resurrection and the life, and that will lead us through death into glory, through the resurrection into the heavenly tabernacle of God. All this is in Jesus only, nor ought we to seek any part of this in ourselves, or in any other. The Son of God is called Jesus, Jehovah-salvation, because He is a perfect Saviour!

III

The Effectual Saviour

In the previous chapter we emphasize the truth that Jesus is a perfect and complete Saviour, i.e. that He perfectly accomplishes all that belongs to and is implied in the work of salvation from beginning to end. He not only performs that part of the work of salvation that must be accomplished for us, in behalf of us, our redemption; but He also is the Author of the wonder of salvation that must be wrought within us and upon us to lead us out of sin and death and shame to everlasting life and righteousness and glory. Now, this really implies that He must be an effectual Saviour, i.e. one that is wholly capable and powerful to save. For if He alone accomplishes *all* the work of salvation, if we really find in Him only *all* that is necessary unto our salvation, it follows that His alone is all the power to save, and that He is in no need of help on the part of man. Hence, it would seem to be somewhat superfluous to write a special chapter on the absolute efficacy, the sureness, the unfailing power of Jesus as Saviour.

Yet, to cut off all possibility of misunderstanding on this point, and with a view to the prevailing and pernicious spirit of Arminianism in circles that profess to believe in Jesus the Saviour, it may be expedient to emphasize for a moment the truth that Jesus actually and effectually saves, and, that, too, without the will or consent of the natural man, yea, in spite of the fact that the latter will never give his consent to be saved, and will exert himself to the utmost to oppose this Jesus that saves him from his sin and death.

O, the difference between sound doctrine and the Arminian error on this point often appears to be so slight and insignificant, that it would not seem worth the effort to explain it! When

459

you insist that Jesus is a complete Saviour, and that one must find in Him all that is necessary unto salvation, the Arminian seems to agree fully and wholeheartedly with you. Salvation is all of Christ, in no respect or degree of man, he will say. It is not of works, it is all of grace! Christ alone merited our redemption for us by His perfect sacrifice on the cross, and that, too, while we were yet enemies. And in Him are all the spiritual blessings of salvation. He bestows them upon us. He regenerates us and gives us faith whereby we may appropriate Him and all the blessings of grace. There is nothing of man in it. Of ourselves we can do nothing. We cannot believe, we cannot accept Him, we cannot fight the good fight and persevere to the end. Always His grace is first. And the Arminian will not even object if you insist that Christ bestows these blessings of salvation only upon the elect! Surely God has chosen them that believe in Christ, and that will inherit eternal life, from before the foundation of the world, and these are surely and infallibly and powerfully saved. Jesus saves!

You say, perhaps, that all this is sound doctrine, purely Reformed, and that no man confessing these truths can possibly be an Arminian?

But what about the Arminian document that was composed in Gouda, the Netherlands, in 1610, known as the *Remonstrantie?* That document begins with an article on the doctrine of predestination as follows: *"Wij gelooven, dat God, door een eeuwig en onveranderlijk besluit, in Jezus Christus Zijnen Zoon, eer 's werelds grond gelegd was, besloten heeft uit het gevallen menschelijk geslacht diegenen in Christus, en om Christus' wil en door Christus zalig te maken, die door de genade des Heiligen Geestes in Jezus gelooven en in dat geloof en in de gehoorzaamheid des geloofs door diezelfde genade ten einde toe volharden zouden."* After all, does not this article plainly and explicitly teach that only the elect shall be saved, and that election is an eternal and immutable decree? You object, perhaps, that this article teaches election of believers and of those that will persevere, but does not the article also definitely state that one can believe only through the grace of the Holy Spirit? Or consider the third article of this same document, and see whether you can find anything in it that is not sound doctrine: *"Wij gelooven, dat de mensch het zaligmakend geloof van zichzelven niet heeft, noch uit kracht van zijnen vrijen wil, alzoo hij in den staat der afwijking en der zonde niets goeds, dat waarlijk goed is (gelijk inzonderheid het zaligmakend geloof) uit en van zich zelven kan denken, willen of doen, maar dat het noodig is, dat hij van God in Christus door zijn Heiligen Geest worde herboren en vernieuwd in zijn verstand, genegenheden, wil, en alle krachten, opdat hij het ware goed recht moge verstaan, bedenken, willen en volbrengen."* Would you suspect that men, who did not hesitate to express themselves so strongly on the total incapability of man to do any good, and on the absolute necessity of regeneration by the Spirit, could teach the doctrine of universal atonement and of the free will of man in the matter of salvation?

This would seem impossible.

Yet, this is exactly the truth. In the second article of the same *Remonstrantie* the Arminians declared: *"dat krachtens Gods eeuwig besluit Jezus Christus, de Zaligmaker der wereld, voor ieder mensch gestorven is, alzoo dat Hij voor allen door den kruisdood de verzoening en de vergeving der zonden verworven heeft, alzoo nochtans dat niemand de vergeving der zonden werkelijk geniet dan de geloovige."* Here they teach the error of general atonement. Christ died for all. Yet, only believers actually enjoy the forgiveness of sins which the Saviour merited for all. And in the fourth article of this document, after they emphasized strongly that the grace of God is the beginning and end of all good, so that without it man does absolutely nothing, they declare that this grace is not irresistible: *"Maar wat de manier van de werking dier genade aangaat, die is niet onweerstaanlijk; want daar staat van velen geschreven: dat zij den Heiligen Geest wederstaan hebben. Hand. 7 en elders op vele plaatsen."*

In this last statement may be found the reason why the Arminian can often use language that leaves the impression that he is perfectly sound, that he believes in an effectual Jesus

and in sovereign grace, while, nevertheless, he rejects both. O
yes, it is all of and through grace, but whether a man shall receive this grace or not depends on himself! For grace is not
irresistible! And this means that it can be efficacious only if
man consents. If the sinner resists, the Saviour can do nothing
with him. Jesus is not an effectual Saviour. And because He
is not an effectual Saviour, He is really not a Saviour at all.
The slogan which the Arminian loves to write on billboards
and over the doors of his church, *Jesus Saves,* does not represent
what he actually teaches. For his Jesus, the Arminian Saviour,
is capable of saving only those sinners that are willing to be
saved. And such there are not! *The Arminian Jesus does not
save!*

And that is why it is so extremely important that we understand the difference between this Arminian error and the truth
of the Word of God on this point. It appears so insignificant,
but it is very fundamental. It is not merely a question as to
whether all men or only the elect are saved: it is a question
that concerns salvation itself. For in order to be able to present
atonement as universal, and salvation as an opportunity for all
men, the Arminian must deny the efficacy of grace; in order to
be able to teach that Jesus is willing to save all, he must deny
that He effectually saves any!

Let us clearly understand this.

Christ died for all men, the Arminian teaches. By His death
on the cross He obtained the forgiveness of sins and reconciliation for every man. But did He really, according to Arminian
doctrine? Did Christ by His perfect sacrifice really obtain salvation for all men in the sense that through His death all men
were brought into a state of reconciliation and eternal righteousness before God? Or let us put the question thus: did Christ
then, actually pay for the sins of all men by His atoning death?
Not at all! The Arminian dare not teach this. He understands
full well that, if Christ had actually and effectually paid by His
blood for the sins of all men, all must be saved. For then the
sins of all would be blotted out, forgiven for ever, and all men
would be justified. And not only does actual experience as well

as Scripture condemn such universalism, but such a doctrine would indeed make men careless and profane, seeing that their salvation and justification have absolutely nothing to do with their own attitude toward sin and righteousness, and toward the Christ of God. And, therefore, in order to be able to maintain the universality of the cross, the Arminian denies its *effectualness*. Christ did not pay for the sins of all, actually and effectually, but only as to His *intention*. *Effectually* He atoned for *no one*. As to His *intention* He atoned for *all*. In the death of Christ there is the *possibility* of forgiveness for *all men*. *Actually* there is forgiveness in that death for *no one*. And so it comes about that Arminianism is principally a denial of the blood of Christ and of vicarious atonement. A man that preaches salvation depending on the free will of man and a Christ for all, may not be conscious of this, and he may not intentionally deny the atonement through the blood emphatically; it is nevertheless the truth that he denies the truth of vicarious atonement. For vicarious atonement means that Jesus actually and effectually blotted out the guilt of sin for those for whom He died. Arminianism teaches that Christ did this for *no one*, but that *in His intention* He did it for *all men*. Jesus is not an effectual Saviour. For the majority of men He died in vain.

And the same is true of the Arminian error with application to the work of salvation as it is wrought upon us and within us. As we have learned from the quotations made above from the *Remonstrantie*, the Arminian emphatically teaches that grace must do it all. Man can of himself do nothing. It is only through the grace of the Spirit of Christ that he is regenerated and that he can believe in Jesus. And so it is to the end. Grace must not only save the sinner: it must also preserve him. Of himself he can do nothing to fight the good fight even unto the end, and to be faithful. But through the power of grace he is able to stand and to persevere. And all this grace is in Jesus. Is He then, according to this Arminian doctrine, an effectual Deliverer from the power and dominion of sin and death, and does He really liberate the sinner from the shackles of corruption? This the Arminian could never maintain, and at the same

time defend the universality of salvation. For it is evident that
if Christ would thus effectually and powerfully deliver all men
from sin and death, no one could possibly be lost. And this i
contrary to all experience. All men are not actually saved. The
majority of men are lost. Even the majority of men that come
into contact with Jesus through the preaching of the gospel
must have nothing of Him. And so, as we have seen, the
Arminian introduces his doctrine of resistible grace. Christ died
for all, not actually, but in His intention. And now, Christ is
the Deliverer of all men, not effectually, but again in His in
tention! He is *willing* to save all men, if they will only let Him
He is ready to bestow His saving grace upon them all, if only
they do not resist Him. He would like to enter the hearts of
all men, if they will only open their hearts to Him, but if they
refuse to open when He knocks, He is powerless to save them
He *offers* salvation to all men, well meaningly, earnestly, but
He *effectually* saves *no one!*

And thus it is with respect to preservation and perseverance.
To the end the Arminian Christ is the *willing* but *powerless*
Saviour, powerless, that is, to overcome the resistance of the
sinner. When once the sinner has consented to be saved, and
Christ has come into his heart, it is by no means sure that he
will be saved in the end. To be sure, Christ must preserve him
if he is to be saved. And Christ is *willing* to keep him. But
grace is never irresistible, and if the believer is not willing to
let Christ continue to work in his heart and to preserve him by
the grace of His Spirit, he will fall away and be lost. The
Arminian Jesus is not an effectual Saviour. As they preach
Him, the slogan *Jesus saves* does not apply to Him, is utterly
false! A Christ *pro omnibus* is a Jesus for *no one*. To maintain
the universality of salvation the Arminian must change the cer
tainty of salvation into a mere chance dependent upon the will
of man. To preach a *universal* Christ he must present a *power
less* Jesus.

Let us see this clearly.

A universal Christ must needs be an impotent Jesus. And
the converse is equally true: *a mighty and effectual Jesus must*

needs be particular. Either you *offer* a Jesus that is *willing* to save *all men* but cannot, or you *preach* a Jesus that *effectually* saves *His people only.* And we may go a step further, and say: Christ either actually and effectually saves or He does not save at all! But the name *Jesus* means that He is an *effectual* Saviour of *His people,* not that He is a *possible* Saviour of *all men.* For thus even the angel interprets the name: "Thou shalt call his name Jesus: for he *shall* save *his people* from their sins." Matt. 1:21.

And this is the teaching of Scripture throughout.

The name Jesus expresses that Christ is an effectual Saviour, because there is *election* in that name. He shall save His people! And this means that it is the eternal will and immutable decree of God that Jesus shall surely and infallibly save all those, and those only, whom the Father has given Him. "For I came down from heaven, not to do mine own will, but the will of him that sent me. And this is the Father's will which hath sent me, that of all which he hath given me I should lose nothing, but should raise it up again at the last day." John 6:38, 39. That is the reason why the Lord can assert so positively in the face of the unbelief and apostasy from Him of the Jews in Capernaum: "All that the Father giveth unto me shall come to me; and him that cometh to me I will in no wise cast out." John 6:37. He is the good shepherd that lays down his life for *the sheep,* and that, too, according to the commandment He received from the Father, John 10:11-18. He knows His sheep and is known of them, John 10:14. And His sheep are those whom the Father gave Him, John 10:29. They also hear His voice, and He knows them, and they follow Him, and He surely gives unto them eternal life, and they can never perish. Their ultimate salvation is absolutely sure, because He is an effectual Saviour, that holds His own in His hand, and no one can pluck them out of that mighty hand. John 10:27-30.

And thus this name of Jesus is preached and explained by the apostles after the resurrection. "For whom he did foreknow, he also did predestinate to be conformed to the image of his Son, that he might be the firstborn among many brethren.

Moreover whom he did predestinate them he also called, and whom he called, them he also justified: and whom he justified, them he also glorified." Rom. 8:29, 30. The purpose of election must stand, not of works, but of him that calleth, even as it is written: "Jacob have I loved but Esau have I hated." Rom. 9:13. "For he saith to Moses, I will have mercy on whom I will have mercy, and I will have compassion on whom I will have compassion. So then it is not of him that willeth, nor of him that runneth, but of God that sheweth mercy." Rom. 9:15, 16. Salvation is not a chance, or a possibility, but an absolute certainty, for the God and Father of our Lord Jesus Christ "hath blessed us with all spiritual blessings in heavenly places in Christ: *according as he hath chosen us in him* before the foundation of the world." Eph. 1:3, 4.

Consider what this means. It is according to the pattern, and strictly within the scope of election that all the spiritual blessings of grace come upon us. These blessings are sure because they have their source in God's eternal election: they are certain because they are particular. This means that God has *reconciled* us in Christ, according as he hath chosen us, that He prepared the atonement of Christ for us, according as He has chosen us in Him; that He blotted out our sins, according as He has chosen us in Him; that He called us, bestowed faith on us, justified us, delivered us, sanctified us, according as He has chosen us in Him; and that He will surely preserve and keep us, and glorify us in the end, all according to the pattern and within the scope of His eternal election of us in Christ!

And so, Christ is an effectual Saviour, not of all men, but of His people, those whom the Father hath given Him: He *shall* save *His people* from their sins! His death on the cross is effectual redemption, i.e. by His perfect obedience Jesus actually paid for all the sins of all His own, and He effectually obtained for them all true and everlasting righteousness, and the right to eternal life and glory. Atonement is not a mere intention for all, but a certainty for the elect. Their sins are blotted out, and they cannot be imputed to them any more. God *has* blessed them with the blessing of forgiveness, not because they *willed* o receive it, for they did not will, neither could they possibly will to receive righteousness, but solely because on the accursed tree Christ truly represented the elect, and He really brought the perfect sacrifice of atonement for them. And He is an effectual Deliverer, that is not only willing, but perfectly able and powerful to bestow all the blessings of salvation upon us, and that not because we will or desire or pray Him to give us these blessings of salvation, but in spite of the fact that we do not and cannot will to receive His grace, and because He is the mighty and effectual Saviour, able to save whomsoever He will, and willing to save whomsoever He received of His Father, i.e. the elect. He enters into their hearts, the door of which they would keep shut against Him. He establishes His throne in those hearts of His own, breaks the shackles of sin and death, rules over them by His grace, justifies and sanctifies them, preserves them even unto the end, without fail, and without any possibility of failure, till He shall raise them at the last day, and lead them into the glory prepared for them before the foundation of the world. Yes, indeed, Jesus is willing to save, but He is also powerful to save whom He will. He is an infallibly effectual Saviour!

LORD'S DAY XII

Q. 31. Why is he called Christ, that is anointed?

A. Because he is ordained of God the Father, and anointed with the Holy Ghost, to be our chief Prophet and teacher, who has fully revealed to us the secret counsel and will of God concerning our redemption; and to be our only High Priest, who by the one sacrifice of his body has redeemed us, and makes continual intercession with the Father for us; and also to be our eternal King, who governs us by his word and Spirit, and who defends and preserves us in (the enjoyment of) that salvation, he has purchased for us.

Q. 32. But why art thou called a Christian?

A. Because I am a member of Christ by faith, and thus am partaker of his anointing; so that I may confess his name, and present myself a living sacrifice of thankfulness to him: and also that with a free and good conscience I may fight against sin and Satan in this life: and afterwards reign with him eternally over all creatures.

I

Jesus Is The Christ

The above text of this twelfth Lord's Day does not offer a
very correct rendering of the original German. Instead of the
perfect tense: *"has fully revealed* the secret counsel and will of
God concerning our redemption," the German uses the present:
"der uns den heimlichen Rath und Willen Gottes von unseren
Erlösung vollkommen offenbaret." The words that are placed
in parentheses, "the enjoyment of," do not occur in the original,
and should be eliminated, especially because they certainly do
not improve the sense. And instead of "he has *purchased* for us,"
it is more in harmony with the original to translate "he has
obtained for us." In question and answer 32 the adjective
"good" should be eliminated before "conscience," for the German simply reads: "mit freiem Gewissen"; and instead of "Satan"
the original has *Teufel*, the devil.

In this Lord's Day the Catechism explains the significance of
the name Christ, and treats of the offices of the Saviour. We
may notice that, quite in harmony with the general character
of the Heidelberger, and, more particularly, with this second
part which treats of our redemption, our instructor considers
the name Christ, and the offices of the Lord, only from the viewpoint of their significance for us and our salvation. The name
Christ signifies that Jesus is *our* chief Prophet, who *reveals to us*
the secret counsel and will of God concerning our redemption;
that He is *our* only High Priest, who *redeemed us* and *intercedes
for us;* and that He is *our* eternal King, who *governs us,* and
defends and *preserves us* to the end. Yet, an exposition of the
soteriological aspect of the work of Christ as God's Anointed,
as His officebearer in the world, hardly exhausts the meaning of
the name Christ. For that name has a far wider, a universal

significance. It signifies that Jesus is the Firstborn of every creature, by Whom and unto Whom all things in heaven and on earth are created, Who is from all eternity ordained to be the Head over all things, God's official Representative in all the visible universe in the new creation, the Heir of the world, and that, too, as the Firstborn of the dead, and as the Head of the Church, the glorious Lord of lords and King of kings for ever! It is only in the very last part of the thirty-second question that the Catechism refers to this eternal and universal aspect of Christ as God's officebearer in the words: "and afterwards reign with Him eternally over all creatures."

Strongly the Scriptures emphasize the importance of the confession that Jesus is the Christ. "Whosoever believeth that Jesus is the Christ is born of God," I John 5:1. The faith that the historical Jesus, Who was born in Bethlehem, walked among us, suffered and died on Calvary, is the Christ, is here presented as a sure proof that one is born of God. Without being reborn it is impossible to believe that Jesus is the Christ. The disciples, by mouth of Peter, confess that Jesus is the Christ, the Son of the living God. And the Lord replies that flesh and blood did not reveal this unto Peter, but His Father who is in heaven. And upon the rock of this truth Christ will build His Church. Matt. 16:16-18. When the bread-seeking multitude in Capernaum have become offended in Jesus, and He turns to His twelve disciples with the question: "Will ye also go away?" they answer, once more through Simon Peter: "Lord to whom shall we go? thou hast the words of eternal life. And we believe and are sure that thou art that Christ, the Son of the living God." John 6:67-69. The Samaritan woman reports to the men of Sychar that she has met the Christ; and after Jesus had taught two days in that city the men of Sychar themselves believed "that this is indeed the Christ, the Saviour of the world." John 4:29, 42. Gradually, during Jesus' public ministry, as He taught and performed His marvelous works, it became the urgent and pressing question whether He were indeed the Christ. And there were many that believed He was. On the other hand, the more it became evident that Jesus of Nazareth claimed to be the Christ, the more the carnal Jews and their leaders hated, opposed, and persecuted Him. And it was, no doubt, because, on the one hand, the Jews refused to acknowledge Him as such, that they finally conspired to kill Him. They looked for a Christ, but for one altogether different from this Jesus of Nazareth. And it was ultimately because of His confession under oath that He was the Christ, the Son of the living God, that the Sanhedrin declared Him worthy of death. And when the apostles have been endowed with the power of the Spirit, they preach: "Therefore let all the house of Israel know assuredly, that God hath made this same Jesus, whom ye have crucified, both Lord and Christ."

In a sense, the whole epistle to the Hebrews may be said to be a treatise on the theme that Jesus is the Christ, the High Priest, to be sure, but then according to the order of Melchisedec, the glorious royal Priest. He is appointed heir of all things, 1:2; and He has obtained a more excellent name than the angels, 1:4; to Him it was said: "Thy throne, O God, is for ever and ever: a sceptre of righteousness is the sceptre of thy kingdom. Thou hast loved righteousness, and hated iniquity; therefore God, even thy God, hath anointed thee with the oil of gladness above thy fellows," 1:8, 9. His excellency above the angels is evident from the Word of God to Him: "Sit on my right hand, until I make thine enemies thy footstool," 1:13; in Him is fulfilled the testimony of the eighth psalm: "What is man that thou art mindful of him? or the son of man that thou visitest him? Thou madest him a little lower than the angels; thou crownest him with glory and honor, and didst set him over the works of thy hands: Thou hast put all things in subjection under his feet," 2:6-8. He it is that is set over the whole house of God, and that was counted worthy of more honor than Moses, as the builder is worthy of greater honor than the building, 3:3-6. And from God He received this honor, for he "glorified not himself to be made an high priest; but he that said unto him, Thou art my Son, today have I begotten thee. As he saith also in another place, Thou art a priest for ever after the order of Melchisedec," 5:5, 6. All that was prefigured in Melchisedec, the priest of the most high God, king of righteousness, king of peace, without beginning or end of days, a priest continually and for ever, is fulfilled in Christ, chapter 7. And He is not entered into holy places made with hands, but into heaven itself, now to appear in the presence of God for us, 9:24. And after He had offered one sacrifice for sins for ever, He sat down at the right hand of God, from henceforth expecting till his enemies be made his footstool, 10:12, 13. He is, indeed, the one that was promised all through the old dispensation, the expected One, the Messiah, and all the shadows are completely fulfilled in Him. Jesus is the Christ.

The name Christ is the same as the Old Testament name Messiah even as Jesus is the New Testament form of Jehoshua. It signifies the Anointed. It is, therefore, a title rather than a name, indicative of His official dignity rather than of His person and nature. In the old dispensation there were many anointed ones, types and shadows of Him that was to come. Those that were called to hold office in the kingdom of God as it existed in the old dispensation among Israel were anointed. Holy anointing oil, specially prepared for that purpose, was poured out over the head of the one that was called by God to function officially in the kingdom of God, as prophet, priest or king. This ceremony of anointing had symbolical meaning. The oil used for anointing, fragrant and glittering, was symbol of the Holy Spirit. This is evident from several passages of Holy Writ. It is the meaning of the oil in the seven lamps of the golden candlestick that stood in the holy place of the tabernacle and the temple. The seven-armed lamp was, no doubt, a symbol of the people of God as the light of the world, shining before the face of God, called out of darkness into His marvelous light, to declare His praises and reflect His glorious virtues. But the lamps were in themselves nothing. Without the oil they could not burn, and had no light. And thus the people were reminded that without the grace of God's Spirit they were not, and could not be the people of God.

This is evident, too, from the wonderful vision recorded in Zech. 4:1-6. The prophet beholds a golden candlestick, with a bowl containing oil above it, and pipes leading from the bowl to the seven lamps of the candlesticks. The idea is, evidently, that the lamps are constantly supplied with oil from the bowl through the seven pipes that lead to each of the lamps. And the angel interprets the vision to the wondering prophet in the words: "This is the word of the Lord unto Zerubbabel, saying, Not by might, nor by power, but by my Spirit, saith the Lord of hosts." Without entering into a detailed explanation of this vision, it will be evident that the oil in the bowl constantly flowing into the seven lamps is symbol of the Holy Spirit by Whom alone the House of God, the true spiritual temple of the Most High can be built and maintained. And the same applies to the oil that was used for anointing. The holy ointment was fragrant and shining, a picture of life and light, and as such a symbol of the Holy Spirit. That this is, indeed, the meaning which Scripture attributes to the holy oil of anointing is plain from Isa. 61:1, where the gift of the Spirit is directly connected with the idea of anointing: "The Spirit of the Lord God is upon me; because the Lord hath anointed me to preach good tidings unto the meek; he hath sent me to bind up the broken-hearted, to proclaim liberty to the captives, and the opening of the prison to them that are bound."

And even as the anointing oil was symbol of the Holy Spirit, so the ceremony of anointing was designed to express that the anointed one received the Spirit of God to qualify him for a certain office. Two ideas, therefore, were expressed or implied in the act of anointing, viz. those of ordination or appointment unto a certain office, and of qualification for that office. That Jesus is the Christ signifies, therefore, that He is God's office-bearer, ordained and qualified by God Himself to function in behalf of God's covenant and kingdom in the world. As the Catechism reminds us, He is called Christ, that is anointed, "because he is ordained of God the Father, and anointed with the Holy Ghost," to be our Prophet, Priest, and King. Jesus is the Christ, the Messiah, the Anointed, i.e. He is officially ordained and qualified for the "things pertaining to God." And as all the officebearers of the old dispensation were but

types and shadows of Him that was to come and all officebearers of the new dispensation are but reflections of Him, and
function through Him, He is the Anointed *par excellence,* the
"Son over his own house," the High Priest, the Prophet of all
prophets, the Lord of lords, the King of kings.

Two questions arise here. First of all: what is the idea of
an office, and what is an officebearer? And, secondly: what is
the office unto which Christ was ordained and qualified?

As to the first question, we may remark that the office is
essentially one, not three. We may, indeed, distinguish the one
office into the three aspects of it that are denoted by the terms
prophet, priest and king, but these may never be separated.
They are not three separate offices, but rather three different
aspects or functions of the one office. There is one fundamental
thought in them all, one idea lies at the basis of all three. And
this fundamental notion may briefly be expressed by saying that
by office is meant the position of servant-king in relation to
God. We might also express the same idea by describing an
officebearer as the official representative of the invisible God in
the visible world. More fully defined, by office is meant the
position in which man is authorized and qualified to function
in the name of God and in His behalf in God's covenant and
kingdom, to serve Him and to rule under Him. There are,
therefore, two sides to the office. With relation to God the
officebearer is servant. He may not act upon his own authority,
and according to the imagination of his own heart. Nor does he
function in his own behalf. On the contrary, he is a servant of
the living God. In relation to God he is clothed with humility,
prostrates himself in the dust, and always asks: "Lord, what
wilt thou have me to do?" It is his calling to know the will of
God, to love that will, and to have his delight in performing it.
He must love the Lord his God with all his heart, and with all
his mind, and with all his soul, and with all his strength. He
is the servant of Jehovah. But, on the other hand, with relation
to the creaturely sphere in which he functions, the kingdom
of God in the visible world, the officebearer is king. He is clothed
with authority and power to represent the sovereign God in the

world. All creatures must serve him, in order that he may serve his God.

Thus the first man Adam was God's officebearer in the earthly creation. In the covenant-relation he was God's friend-servant, and as such dominion was given him over all the earthly creation. He was king under God. For this position he was ordained and qualified. For he was created after the image of God, in true knowledge of God, righteousness, and holiness. He knew his Creator in love, had his delight in doing the will of God, and consecrated himself and all things to the Lord of all. And he was placed at the head of the earthly creation. All creatures served him, that he might serve his God.

And in this he was the image of Him that was to come. However, he was no more than His image. For as the heavens are higher than the earth, so far is Christ, the last Adam, exalted above the first Adam. We must not proceed from the idea that Christ's office consisted merely in this that, after Adam is fallen into sin, and with him the whole creation is made to bear the curse, He redeems His own, and delivers them from sin and death, in order to restore the original relationship and the first state of rectitude in Paradise. It is certainly true that this work of redemption and deliverance belongs to His work as God's Anointed. He is, indeed, our chief Prophet to make known unto us, who are by nature in darkness, the whole secret counsel and will of God concerning our redemption. As our only High Priest, He does intercede for us with the Father after He has obtained redemption for us by His perfect sacrifice on the accursed tree. And as our eternal King, He fought the battle for us against sin and death and all the powers of darkness, and gained the complete victory over them; and He preserves us unto the salvation He obtained for us. But this is not the whole of His work as God's Officebearer. If this were true, His work as God's Anointed would be finished, and He would cease to function in His office, as soon as the work of redemption were completed. But we know that this is not the truth. The Word of God emphasizes everywhere that Christ's office is without end, that His dominion is an everlasting dominion, that He must reign for ever, that He is Priest for ever after the order of Melchisedec. The last Adam does not appear simply as a Restorer of what the first Adam spoiled and destroyed by his disobedience. He is not ordained simply to repair the damage done by the powers of darkness. Nor dare we present the matter as if Christ were so to speak an afterthought of God, occasioned merely by the fact that sin came into the world. It is to be feared that some such conception is in the minds of many. Adam is the real and original officebearer of God, according to this view. And God's original purpose surely was that he should be the head of all His works, and that under him creation should normally develop to its highest possible state of glory. But sin entered. The first officebearer became unfaithful. And now God ordains Christ, His Son in the flesh, to take the place of the first Adam, and to restore righteousness and peace and lead all things to that perfection which Adam failed to attain.

Instead of all such erroneous notions, we must proceed from the correct and Scriptural viewpoint, that in His eternal counsel God decreed to unite all things in Christ, and to make Him the Head over all things, not only in the earth, but also in heaven. The last Adam in history is the first in God's counsel. He is not an afterthought. He does not occupy the second place. He is strictly first. For God purposed in His eternal good pleasure to reveal and glorify Himself in the realization of His everlasting kingdom and covenant, not in the first Adam, but in Christ, the firstborn of every creature, and that, too, *as the firstbegotten of the dead,* and, therefore, in the way of sin and grace. In the new creation, the new heavens and the new earth, in which the tabernacle of God shall be with men for ever and in heavenly beauty and glory, the covenant of God's friendship shall be perfected, God's House shall be finished, and His kingdom shall be established. Christ shall everlastingly be the Head over all, the visible representative of the invisible God, the glorious

Servant King, the Lord of lords, and the King of kings. King over all, He shall subject Himself unto the Father, that God may be all in all. Even angels and principalities shall for ever be subject unto Him. And in that glorious reign the Church shall participate. Such is the glorious office unto which Christ is anointed from before the foundation of the world.

II

The Prophetic Office And The Fall

The central idea of an officebearer is that he is God's friend-servant, authorized to function as God's representative, as His vice-regent, in the visible world.

In this general sense of the word Adam in the state of rectitude was very really an officebearer, for in virtue of the covenant relation in which he was placed by his Creator, he was God's friend-servant. For, as we have seen before, the covenant of God with Adam in Paradise was not a sort of pact or agreement, did not consist in "a condition, a promise, and a penalty," but was a living relationship and fellowship between God and him. Adam was the friend of God. And since Adam, even in that relation of friendship with God, remained, nevertheless, a creature, in subjection to his Creator as the Sovereign of heaven and earth, he was also servant of the Lord. Friend-servant he was. He was not a slave in the house of God. Nor was he a wage-earner who served God for the remuneration connected with such service. He was free, and served his God in voluntary friendship. It was his delight to do God's will. And as God's friend-servant he stood at the head of all the earthy creation, authorized and empowered to have dominion over all creatures, and in the midst of them all to represent his God. True, he was not the head and king of the entire creation. He was made a little lower than the angels. But all earthly creatures found their focus, their climax, their head and representative in him, and he was their lord. For he was created after the very image of God, in true knowledge, righteousness, and holiness, and in his heart the whole creation was united with the heart of God. Hence, Adam, the friend of God, was servant of the Lord, not only in as far as he himself was concerned, but as the head of

478

the visible world. He was chief steward in the house of God's creation, with the calling to keep and tend to that house before the face of God, cultivate it, and bring the glory of it all in loving service to his Creator.

Such was Adam's office.

And this office, although essentially one, was threefold, presented three aspects. For man was God's friend-servant with his whole being, with all his heart, and mind, and soul, and strength. He was God's officebearer in his entire life and with relation to the whole creation. He was God's friend-servant with the intellectual side of his nature, to know his God and declare His praises; with the volitional side of his life, to will the will of God and consecrate himself and all things to Him; and with all his power and might over all the earthly creation, to subject himself and all things to the living God and to rule over the visible world in the name of God. His one office of servant of the Lord was differentiated according to these three aspects as the prophetic, the priestly, and the royal office. He was prophet, priest, and king.

In the light of these general observations we must try to understand the significance of the prophetic office. In the popular mind, a prophet is one that is capable of foretelling future events. The idea of predicting the future is regarded as essential to the prophetic office. However, this is hardly correct. It is true that it belongs to the work of a prophet to speak of things to come with relation to the kingdom of God, but this is quite different from saying that foretelling the future is the main and one calling and task of a prophet. In general, a prophet is one that has the knowledge of God, speaks in His name, and thus declares His praises. The Hebrew word for prophet is picturesque, and rich in meaning. It is derived from a word meaning to overflow, to boil over. The idea seems to be that a prophet is one that is so filled with the true knowledge of God that his mouth overflows, that he is impelled to speak of Him, and to show forth His glorious praises. God reveals Himself to him. He puts His mighty Word in the prophet's heart, and this Word of God becomes a fire in his bones, urging him to speak of that God Who revealed Himself to him. Thus the matter is presented repeatedly in the prophetical books of the Old Testament. The Word of God overpowers the prophets. They eat His Word and fill their whole being with it. They are wholly in subjection to that Word, so that they cannot keep silent, but must speak of Him, His covenant, His will, whether the revelation they thus received had reference to the past, the present, or the future. A prophet is one who knows God, and speaks in His name and of Him, as the friend-servant of the Most High.

In this general sense, Adam was prophet of God in the original state of rectitude. He was created after the image of God. This implies that also in his intellectual life he stood entirely in the service of God. He was capable of knowing God with a true knowledge, that is, with the knowledge of love, and thus to enter into His intimate fellowship. And not only was he capable of receiving this true knowledge of God, but from the very first moment of his existence he was filled with the light of this knowledge. It is true that this knowledge of God in the first man Adam functioned on a lower plane than that which is in Christ Jesus our Lord, and is not to be compared to the glorious knowledge that is the heritage of the elect in the final realization of God's covenant, when His tabernacle shall be with men in heavenly perfection. For Adam was of the earth earthy, and his knowledge of God was the reflection of God's glory in his consciousness through the mirror of the earthly creation. He did not as yet see face to face. But the fact remains that Adam possessed the true knowledge of God as soon as he opened his eyes upon the wonder of God's creation round about him. God revealed Himself to him. And Adam's receptivity was perfect. There was a perfect contact between the Word of God that spoke to him through the things that were made, and his own consciousness. For all things were made through the Word of God, and as such they were God's revelation of Himself. Creation was God's speech concerning Himself. Every creature had its own name. That name was its essence. And that essence of every creature was the Word of God. And all these creatures together spelled the Name, the glorious Name of Him that had called the things that were not as if they were. And in the midst of this speech of God, addressing him on every side, day and night, stood Adam, hearing this Word of God, and receiving it in his pure consciousness, and through his consciousness into his heart, filled and moved by the love of God. Besides, God revealed Himself to Adam in the garden, and spoke to him as a friend with his friend. And as Adam was the recipient of this true knowledge of God, hearing and interpreting the speech of God through all creation, he would prostrate himself in the dust before his Creator, and in loving adoration declare His wonderful virtues. Adam was in the true sense God's prophet.

The fall of man caused a radical change. The knowledge of God was completely lost not only, but was subverted into its very opposite: darkness, the love of the lie. Man became by nature the false prophet, a prophet in the service of the devil.

For, on the one hand, we must certainly maintain, that in a certain sense man remained a prophet. His light was not changed into darkness in the sense that he ceased to be an intellectual and volitional, a rational and moral being. Even though also from a natural viewpoint the light of his knowledge does not shine any more in its original brilliancy, he does retain some remnants of natural light, by which he has some knowledge of God and of the difference between good and evil, remnants of light that are sufficient to leave him without excuse. Even though he does no longer clearly discern the Word of God in creation, by the light of the remnants of his natural knowledge, he knows that God is, and that He must be thanked and glorified, and that man is called to declare the praises of the Most High. For, on the other hand, creation remained a medium of revelation of the glorious power and wisdom of God. The invisible things of God are clearly seen, being understood through the things that are made. The light shines in the darkness, even though the darkness comprehendeth it not. God does not leave Himself without witness, even in the conscience of the natural man. Because of this continued speech of God concerning Himself in the works of His hands, and this work of the law written in man's heart, and the remnants of natural light, man is still a prophet, even though through sin he became a false prophet.

But it may not be forgotten, that with all his natural light fallen man has become a servant of sin. From a spiritual-ethical viewpoint all the light that is in him is very really darkness. He is no longer a prophet of the living God in the true sense of the word. He has forfeited the privilege, he has neither the ability nor the will and desire, he is no longer authorized to appear as the representative of God in the visible world, to know Him and to speak in His name and in His behalf. For he is guilty before God, the object of His wrath and condemnation, an exile from the house and fellowship of God. He is darkened in his understanding, so that he loves the lie, and prefers the word of the devil to the knowledge of God. And he is perverse of will and obdurate in heart, so that he stands in enmity against God, and always holds the truth under in unrighteousness. In as far as he still has knowledge of God through the remnants of natural light, and the speech of God through the things that are made, he does not know God in love, but hates Him, opposes Him, contradicts Him, and makes gods after his own imagination. For the carnal mind is enmity against God. It is not subject to the law of God, neither indeed can be. Rom. 8:5-7. God is not in all his thoughts, and being foolish in the spiritual-ethical sense of the word, he always says within his heart that there is no God. Although, therefore, he is still a prophet, he is in no sense of the word a prophet of God. Through sin he has become a false prophet, who lies about the living God.

This cannot be too strongly emphasized, lest, as is frequently done in our day, we ascribe the remnants of natural light to the operation of a certain common grace of God, even as did the old Remonstrants. They that thus philosophize about fallen man's natural knowledge enlarge upon these remnants until they are presented as possessing true spiritual-ethical value, so that the natural man in virtue of these "sparks" from the hearth of his original righteousness, does actually seek after God. Even the old and well-known heresy of the Arminians that these remnants of natural light are a kind of seed of religion, which, even though in itself not pure, are capable of leading him on to the true and spiritual knowledge of God if they are only used aright, is being revived by those that are supposed to be Reformed in their thinking and convictions. On this basis one dare no longer evaluate the philosophy of the world for what it truly is: foolishness with God. On the contrary, it is presented as true wisdom, and regarded with profound respect and admiration. And this lack of proper distinction and discernment, this confusion of darkness and light, more and more threatens with destruction the whole system of what is supposedly Christian education, higher and lower. It is this fundamental error, this pernicious fallacy of presenting as true wisdom what is essentially nothing but foolishness, that makes many in our day loudly proclaim and enthusiastically worship as Calvinism what is principally nothing but modernism. That all philosophy is false prophecy is no longer understood. That all the wisdom of the world is foolishness with God is often laughed to scorn, even by those that present themselves as advocates of Christian education. That Christ is the only true prophet, and that all that is not of Him is only darkness, is no longer recognized. And, therefore, the theory that through a certain operation of common grace man's natural light represents a remnant of his original wisdom and knowledge, is not only a theoretical error, but from a practical viewpoint a damnable heresy and pernicious fallacy. Over against this error one cannot stress too strongly that through sin man is become a liar, a false prophet, that holds the truth in unrighteousness. He is not a fool in a natural sense. He has the light of reason. He is often possessed of a keen mind. But in a spiritual-ethical sense he is a fool. He is an enemy of God. And he presses the remnants of natural light into the service of sin. Man, having rejected the Word of God, is become a prophet of the devil.

If we bear this in mind, we can also understand that in the world, and throughout history, there is a development of the lie in the direction of, and culminating in the false prophet that is pictured to us in the book of Revelation. For the natural man that stands in enmity against God works out his own philosophy, the wisdom of the world, which, according to James, is from below, is natural, earthly, devilish, and is foolishness with God. This philosophy of the world, although in the wisdom of God it does not know God, and does not want to know Him, develops its own conception of God, of man, of the world and its origin, of religion and ethics, of society and the State; and it is always chiefly characterized by the fact that it rejects and opposes God's revelation. It speaks of itself and closes its ears to the speech of God. The line of this philosophy in the pagan world of the old dispensation is clearly traced in the first chapter of the epistle to the Romans. For there we are taught that the invisible things of God are, indeed, clearly seen from the beginning of the world, being understood from the things that are made; and that what is known of God is manifest in the natural man. But man deliberately opposes this revelation of God. He holds the truth of God's eternal power and divinity in unrighteousness. Knowing God, he does not want to acknowledge Him as God, neither glorify Him. He revealed that he loved the darkness rather than the light. Rejecting the Word of God, he followed his own philosophy of the Most High, and changed the glory of the incorruptible One into the image of a corruptible creature, and bowed himself before man and beast and creeping things. Thus man's philosophy gave birth, first of all, to the pagan religion and its polytheism. And, secondly, this false philosophy and pagan religion, operating under the wrath of God that was revealed from heaven, proved its destructive character in the demoralization and degradation of all life in the pagan world, its corruption and bestiality. For God gave them up through the lust of their own wicked heart unto uncleanness and vile affections, unto a reprobate mind, to do those things which are not convenient. It is true, of course, that this false prophecy in the pagan world appeared in different forms, according as the nations moved on different levels of culture and civilization. But even in its most polished and cultural form, as in that of Greek philosophy at the time of Plato and Aristotle, it was false prophecy nevertheless, the wisdom of the world that is foolishness with God. There is none that seeketh after God, no not one!

It stands to reason that this spirit of false prophecy reveals itself, not only in the pagan world, but also in the line of the generations of the people of God, with whom God establishes His covenant, and to whom He reveals His counsel of redemption. In fact, within the scope of the historical realization of God's covenant in the world, the false prophet expresses himself much more boldly and directly. For there the Word of God is heard much more distinctly, and, accordingly, is contradicted by the flesh much more sharply and vehemently. There shines, not only the light of revelation as it radiates through the things that are made, but as it shines in the face of Christ Jesus. In the pagan world the light of the *Logos* shines in the darkness, and the darkness comprehendeth it not; in the sphere of the covenant the judgment applies that He came unto His own, and His own received Him not. It is Israel that gives rise to the false prophets in their worst form, in their most hateful opposition of the truth of God. It is Israel that, accordingly, commits more idolatry than any nation under the sun, that tramples God's covenant under foot, despises His precepts, kills the prophets and stones them that are sent to them by God. It is Israel that finally develops a false conception of the Messiah that was to come, and that rejects and crucifies the Christ of God. It is among the people in whose true prophets the Spirit of Christ dwells and operates, that the false prophets appear in their most determined and wicked opposition to the Word of God.

Thus it was in the old dispensation.

And in the new dispensation it is no different. Even today there still is the pagan world, whose millions upon millions prefer the darkness of their own philosophy and false prophecy to the light of the gospel, and who fast become prepared to play their own part in the final scene of the drama of God's program for the world's history. But also in the days of the new dispensation it is true that the false prophet must not be sought primarily in the heathen world, but rather within the scope of what is known as Christendom. There he reveals and expresses himself in the more refined forms of culture and civilization, of science and philosophy, of religion and philanthropy; there he appears as an angel of light, as the true Christ Himself; but there he exerts his most profound and pernicious influence. It is within the scope of Christendom that the antichrist is developing, and that the false prophet, the combination and culmination of all false religion and false science and false philosophy must be expected to appear. Let no one be deceived by his marvelous display of intellect and power, nor by his deceitful appearance of religiousness and piety. For he already does great things, and will do greater and mightier works in the future. And, no doubt, he will deceive many. But it should not be difficult to know and distinguish him as the false prophet in spite of his glittering display of culture and power. For he lies about God, and about His Anointed. He opposes the word of the true Prophet of God. He denies that Jesus Christ is come into the flesh. And "hereby know ye the Spirit of God: Every spirit that confesseth that Jesus Christ is come into the flesh is of God: and every spirit that confesseth not that Jesus Christ is come into the flesh is not of God: and this is that spirit of antichrist, whereof ye have heard that it should come; and even now is already in the world." And the spirit of antichrist is the false prophet, that will speak great things and blasphemies, and perform signs and wonders, but whom Christ will cast alive into the lake of fire burning with brimstone. Rev. 19:20.

III

Christ Our Chief Prophet

Thus far we saw that the Lord God had formed the first man Adam in such a way, and placed him in such a relation to Himself, that he could function as God's officebearer, as His friend-servant in the midst of the earthly creation. We called attention, too, to the threefold implication of this office of man: he was prophet to know his God rightly, and to glorify Him in all things and before all creation; he was priest, in order that he might consecrate himself and all things in love to the Most High; and he was king, in order that all things might serve him, and he might serve his God. God's Name must be glorified, God's will must be done, God's kingdom must be established on earth, and His sovereignty must be acknowledged, also through the first Adam. Finally, we paid more particular attention to man's calling as God's prophet, noticed that through his disobedience and fall he became nothing but a prophet of the devil, loving the darkness and hating the light, and demonstrated that a continuous line of false prophets developed from fallen man, a line that will culminate in the false prophet pictured in the book of Revelation.

However, all this does not destroy or frustrate the counsel of the Most High, but must serve its realization. It is true, by wilful disobedience man violated God's covenant, and fell away from his high estate of rectitude, so that he, and not God, is the author of sin. But this must not tempt us to deny that God is the Most High, and that He does whatsoever He pleases, even when the first man falls, violates the covenant, and becomes a servant of Satan. For even though it was, no doubt, the purpose of the devil to silence for ever the voice of true prophecy, to change the truth into the lie, and the praise of God from man's

mouth into blasphemy, yet God's purpose was the revelation of
His greater glory, and His counsel must stand. He had anointed
His own prophet from before the foundation of the world.
The Son was ordained from eternity to become flesh, that He
might stand at the head of a great congregation, and declare
unto us the Father, and reveal His glory, in such fulness and
beauty as the first Adam would never have been able to conceive. He was anointed to do this antithetically, over against
a world that loves the lie and walks in darkness, saving out of
that world a people that in eternal glory would with Him and
through Him declare the glory of Him that called them out of
darkness into His marvelous light. The work of the devil and
the rebellion of the first man do not frustrate the purpose of
God, but must serve His good pleasure to make room for the
coming of the Messiah, the anointed of God, as the chief Prophet.

The confession of the Church, as expressed in the twelfth
Lord's Day of our Heidelberger, that Christ is "ordained of
God the Father, and anointed with the Holy Ghost, to be our
chief Prophet and Teacher," is based on Holy Writ. As such
He was announced in the old dispensation by Moses in Deut.
18:15-22: "The Lord thy God will raise up unto thee a Prophet
from the midst of thee, of thy brethren like unto me, unto him
shall ye hearken, according to all that thou desiredst of the Lord
thy God in Horeb in the day of the assembly, saying, Let me not
hear again the voice of the Lord my God, neither let me see this
great fire any more, that I die not. And the Lord said unto me,
They have well spoken that which they have spoken. I will
raise them up a Prophet from among their brethren, like unto
thee, and will put my words in his mouth; and he shall speak
unto them all that I shall command him. And it shall come
to pass that whosoever will not hearken unto my words which
he shall speak in my name, I will require it of him. But the
prophet which shall presume to speak a word in my name,
which I have not commanded him to speak, or that shall speak
in the name of other gods, even that prophet shall die. And
if thou shalt say in thine heart, How shall we know the word
which the Lord hath not spoken? When a prophet speaketh in

the name of the Lord, If the thing follow not, nor come to pass, that is the thing which the Lord hath not spoken, but the prophet hath spoken it presumptuously: thou shalt not be afraid of him."

It was necessary to quote the entire passage from Deuteronomy, in order to make plain that this passage does not speak of Christ as the chief prophet exclusively, but rather refers to the entire line of prophets that, in the old dispensation, declared the Word of God unto the people of Israel. This is evident, first of all from the context of this passage. The people are warned that, when they have come into the land of promise, they shall not do after the abominations of the heathen, with their divinations, observers of times, enchanters, witches, charmers, consulters of familiar spirits, wizards and necromancers. They shall not turn to these in order curiously to inquire into secret things. For the secret things are for the Lord their God, but the revealed things are for them and for their children. And these the Lord will declare unto them through His prophet. And although it is true that the text speaks in the singular of the Prophet, and that, therefore, ultimately the reference is to the Christ, we would make a mistake if we would apply it exclusively to Him, and failed to include the entire succession of prophets that preceded Him. This is evident, too, from the last part of this passage, in which the people are taught to distinguish between the true and the false prophet. For false prophets will arise among them, men that pretend to speak in the name of the Lord, but who have not been anointed by the Most High, and in whose mouth the word of the Lord is not found; and they shall speak the lie, and tempt the people to apostatize from the living God. They must, therefore, distinguish between the true and the false prophet. And they may do this by applying this test, that the word of the Lord, spoken through His prophet, will surely come to pass, while the word of the false prophet shall fail. The latter they must not heed, neither need they be afraid of him.

Yet, on the other hand, there can be no doubt that these words of Moses refer also, have reference chiefly and centrally to Christ. For Christ is not only the culmination of the whole line of Old Testament prophets, the One to Whom they all point, but He it is also that spoke the Word of God in them and through them to the people of God of the old dispensation. Without Him they could not have been prophets. They spoke because His Spirit was in them. I Pet. 1:12. All through the old dispensation, from Abel to the last of the prophets, it was He who "fully revealed unto us the secret counsel and will of God concerning our redemption." True, the Word had as yet not become flesh, and did not yet speak to us of heavenly things in personal union with our nature. This had to wait until the fulness of time. But He was anointed to be our chief Prophet from before the foundation of the world, and he began to function in that capacity from the beginning of history.

He functioned as such through visions and dreams, through types and shadows, through Moses and all the prophets, as well as directly in the revelation of the Angel of the Lord. In all the prophets He was the speaking Subject, the faithful Witness in all the witnesses, the Servant of Jehovah in all the servants. Always He is our chief Prophet. This is the reason why Deut. 18, though having reference also to all the prophets of the old dispensation, nevertheless speaks of Him. This is the reason, too, why the prophets of the Old Testament frequently speak as if they identify themselves with the person of the Christ. This is true, no doubt, of many of the psalms. It is emphatically true of Isaiah. Note the following: "Listen, O isles, unto me; and hearken, ye people, from far; The Lord hath called me from the womb; from the bowels of my mother hath he made mention of my name. And he math made my mouth like a sharp sword; in the shadow of his hand hath he hid me, and made me a polished shaft; in his quiver hath he hid me; And said unto me, Thou art my servant, O Israel, in whom I will be glorified. Then I said, I have labored in vain, I have spent my strength for nought; and in vain: yet surely my judgment is with the Lord, and my work with my God.

And now, saith the Lord that formed me from the womb to be his servant, to bring Jacob again to him, Though Israel be not gathered, yet shall I be glorious in the eyes of the Lord, and my God shall be my strength. And he said, Is it a light thing that thou shouldest be my servant to raise up the tribes of Jacob, and to restore the preserved of Israel: I will also give thee for a light to the Gentiles, that thou mayest be my salvation unto the ends of the earth. Thus saith the Lord, the Redeemer of Israel, and His Holy One, to him whom man despiseth, to him whom the nation abhorreth, to a servant of rulers, Kings shall see thee and arise, princes also shall worship, because of the Lord that is faithful, and the Holy One of Israel, and he shall choose thee." Isa. 49:1-7.

Or attend to the following passage: "The Lord God hath given me the tongue of the learned, that I should know how to speak a word in season to him that is weary: he wakeneth me morning by morning, he wakeneth mine ear to hear as the learned. The Lord God hath opened mine ear, and I was not rebellious, neither turned away back. I gave my back to the smiters, and my cheeks to them that plucked off the hair: I hid not my face from shame and spitting. For the Lord God will help me; therefore shall I not be confounded: therefore have I set my face like a flint, and I know that I shall not be ashamed. He is near that justifieth me; who will contend with me? let us stand together: who is mine adversary? let him come near to me. Behold, the Lord God will help me; who is he that shall condemn me?" Isa. 50:5-9.

Evidently, passages like the above are not applicable in all their implication to the prophet. He speaks as he does, only because it is Christ speaking in and through him.

Nor need there be any doubt about this frequent identification of Christ with the subject of the Old Testament prophet. That it is the Christ that speaks in Isa. 61:1-3, for instance, is directly proved in the New Testament. We read there: "The Spirit of the Lord God is upon me; because the Lord hath anointed me to preach good tidings to the meek; he hath sent me to bind up the broken hearted, to proclaim liberty to the

captives, and the opening of the prison to them that are bound:
to proclaim the acceptable year of the Lord, and the day of
vengeance of our God; to comfort all that mourn; To appoint
to them that mourn in Zion, to give unto them beauty for ashes,
the oil of joy for mourning, the garment of praise for the spirit
of heaviness; that they might be called trees of righteousness,
the planting of the Lord, that he might be glorified." To be
sure these words also refer to the prophet himself. But they
were not fulfilled in him. Their fulfillment must be found in
Christ. And in Lu. 4:16-21 we find the direct proof of this
statement. For there we read that the Lord Jesus in the synagogue of Nazareth read this passage from the book of Isaiah,
or part of it, "and closed the book, and he gave it again to the
minister, and sat down. And the eyes of all them that were in
the synagogue were fastened on him. And he began to say unto
them, This day is this scripture fulfilled in your ears." When
the Lord had read these words, they were fulfilled, not before.
For He, and not Isaiah, was the real Subject that spoke in them.

The same is evident from a comparison of Isa. 8:18 and Heb.
2:13. In the former passage the prophet is speaking concerning
himself. He appears in the midst of wicked Jerusalem together
with his family and a few disciples, and declares: "Behold, I
and the children whom the Lord hath given me are for signs
and for wonders in Israel from the Lord of hosts which dwelleth
in mount Zion." But from Heb. 2:13 we learn that it was not
Isaiah, but the Lord Himself to Whom these words of the
prophet have reference in their final meaning. He it is that is
represented as having spoken them.

In the same chapter of the Hebrews, as a proof that Christ
is not ashamed to call His people brethren, the words of Ps.
22:22 are quoted as being spoken directly by the Lord: "Saying,
I will declare thy name unto my brethren, in the midst of the
church will I sing praise unto thee." Heb. 2:12. Many more
quotations might be offered to show that the real Subject in
all the prophets of the old dispensation was the Christ, the chief
Prophet of God. All this corroborates the statement that the

Prophet referred to in Deut. 18 is centrally none other than the promised Messiah.

And the New Testament clearly proves that this position is correct. For, first of all, we read several times in the gospel narratives that Moses spoke of the Christ. And this was generally known and admitted. When Philip informs Nathanael about the Christ, he says: "We have found him of whom Moses in the law, and the prophets did write, Jesus of Nazareth, the son of Joseph." John 1:46. To the unbelieving Jews the Lord says: "Do not think that I will accuse you to the Father: there is one that accuseth you, even Moses, in whom ye trust. For had ye believed Moses, ye would have believed me: for he wrote of me." John 5:45, 46. Hence, the Jews expected the great Prophet. The Samaritan woman knew "that Messias cometh which is called Christ: when he is come, he will tell us all things." John 4:25. The carnal Jews of Galilee, when they had seen the miracle of the feeding of the five thousand, want to take Jesus by force to make Him a king, saying: "This is of a truth that prophet that should come into the world." John 6:14. The sojourners to Emmaus speak "concerning Jesus of Nazareth, which was a prophet mighty in deed and word before God and all the people." Lu. 24:19. And when the Lord would explain to them the necessity of the suffering of this Christ concerning whom they were having their discourse, He begins "at Moses and all the prophets," and expounds unto them in all the scriptures the things concerning himself.

But the words of Deut. 18 are also directly quoted and applied to the Lord as the chief Prophet. Thus in Acts 3:22, 23: "For Moses truly said unto the fathers, A prophet shall the Lord your God raise up unto you of your brethren, like unto me; him shall ye hear in all things whatsoever he shall say unto you. And it shall come to pass, that every soul which will not hear that prophet, shall be destroyed from among the people." And Stephen, too, quotes this passage before the Jewish council: "This is that Moses which said unto the children of Israel, A prophet shall the Lord your God raise up unto you of your brethren, like unto me; him shall ye hear." Acts 7:37.

Christ, therefore, according to the testimony of all Scripture, is, indeed, our chief Prophet and Teacher, the true Subject in all the prophets, the One that declares the name of God unto His brethren, and reveals unto us the full counsel of redemption. He is the same as that Wisdom that is speaking in Prov. 8, Who was "set up from everlasting, from the beginning, or ever the earth was." He is identical with that Wisdom who "hath builded her house, she hath hewn out her seven pillars: she hath killed her beasts; she hath mingled her wine; she also furnished her table. She hath sent forth her maidens: she crieth upon the highest places of the city, Whoso is simple, let him turn in hither: as for him that wanteth understanding, she saith to him, Come, eat of my bread, and drink of the wine which I have mingled. Forsake the foolish and live; and go in the way of understanding." Prov. 9:1-6.

And as He functioned in the old dispensation speaking through and in the prophets, so He came personally in the fulness of time, to dwell among us, and speak to us face to face and mouth to mouth. For "the Word was made flesh, and dwelt among us (and we beheld his glory, the glory as of the only begotten *of the Father,) full of grace and truth.*" John 1:14. *And "no man hath seen God at any time; the only begotten* Son, which is in the bosom of the Father, he hath declared him." John 1:18. He speaks, and is able to speak, of heavenly things, for he is the one "that came down from heaven, even the Son of man, which is in heaven." He is the light of the world, that shines in the darkness, and they that follow him shall not walk in darkness, but shall have the light of life. John 3:19; 8:12; 12:35, 36, 46. He is the true and faithful witness, who receives not testimony from men, but whom the Father Himself bears witness as being sent from Him. John 5:32 ff. He speaks the words of eternal life, and His words are spirit and are life. John 6:63, 68. His doctrine is not His own, but the Father's Who sent Him, and if any man will do the will of God, he will surely acknowledge that Christ's doctrine is of God. For "he that speaketh of himself seeketh his own glory, but he that seeketh his glory that sent him, the same is true, and no unrighteousness is in him." John 7:16-18. And he speaks the things which He has seen with the Father. John 8:38. And He always glorifies, not Himself, but the Father. John 17:4. Indeed, "God, who at sundry times and in divers manners spake in time past unto the fathers by the prophets, hath in these last days spoken unto us by his Son, whom he hath appointed heir of all things, by whom also he made the worlds." Heb. 1:1, 2.

As God's prophet, Christ is far more excellent than the first man Adam in paradise. For He is the Person of the Son of God, Who is eternally in the bosom of the Father, the eternal Word, the express image of His substance, the effulgence of the Father's glory, God of God, Who knows the Father with an infinitely perfect knowledge. It is this Person of the Son of God, Who from eternity to eternity is essentially and truly God, assumed the flesh and blood of the children, took upon Himself our nature, and united that human nature with the divine in His own Person. In Him, therefore, there is the closest possible union of God and man, the most intimate communion between the divine and the human natures. In Him the Person of the Son, very God, lived with us, walked with us, talked with us, thought in our mind, willed with our will, had human desires and passions, human love and human sympathies, spoke to us by human mouth and in human language. Is not He the most perfect Prophet conceivable? Who could be more excellently equipped to be our "chief Prophet and Teacher," and who could be more able than He to reveal unto us "the secret counsel and will of God concerning our redemption?" He knows the Father as none other could know Him. His human consciousness is enlightened and filled with the knowledge of God from within. Because of the union of the divine and human natures the knowledge of God in Christ is direct, and in the highest sense of the word perfect. In the darkness of the world He is the light. Over against the lie of the false prophet He is the truth, the faithful witness. He glorifies the Father over against a blaspheming world of sin. And to His own He imparts the knowledge of the God of their salvation.

Thus He functioned in the old dispensation through the prophets and shadows.

As our Prophet He spoke to us face to face in the days of His flesh, and in His public ministry He revealed the Father through His person, His word, and His work.

But His prophetic office does not terminate with His death and resurrection, is not limited to His ministry among us in the flesh. On the contrary, He is our eternal Prophet. For He died and was raised from the dead; and He was exalted at the right hand of God, and received the promise of the Holy Spirit, and in that Spirit He returned to us on the day of Pentecost to dwell in the Church, and abide with her for ever. And He is with us as our chief Prophet, our Teacher, Who instructs us by His Spirit and Word. For a time after His exaltation at the right hand of God, He gave to His Church apostles, that through them He might more fully reveal unto us the secret counsel and will of God concerning our redemption. Then, when His revelation is complete, He functions as our chief Prophet in and through the Church, by His Spirit and in and through the Word preached according to the Holy Scriptures. There is no instruction, there is no preaching of the Word, there is no exhortation or consolation, except of Him, our only and chief Prophet. And even unto all ages of ages it will be of Him and through Him as our Prophet that we shall receive and rejoice in the perfect knowledge of the God of our salvation.

IV

Melchisedec

The Catechism continues to expound for us the meaning of the name Christ by calling our attention to the priesthood of our Lord. He is not only our chief Prophet and Teacher, but also "our only High Priest, who by the one sacrifice of his body, has redeemed us, and makes continual intercession with the Father for us." Here again, we notice that the Heidelberger views the priesthood of Christ exclusively from the viewpoint of His work of redemption. As such Christ was priest according to the order of Aaron, for also the high priest of the old dispensation sacrificed and made intercession for the people. And this view is perfectly correct. Only, the priesthood of Christ was not limited to the order of Aaron. He was more than Israel's high priest. And this greater excellency of Christ's priesthood is expressed in the Scriptural statement that He was a priest "after the order of Melchizedek." Even though the Catechism does not directly refer to this aspect of the priesthood of Christ, we will do well to ask ourselves the question: what is the meaning of this statement?

That this is an important question should be evident from the repeated emphasis of Scripture on this excellency of the priesthood of Christ. That the Messiah would be a priest after the order of Melchisedec was already revealed in the old dispensation. For David spoke concerning Him: "The Lord said unto my Lord, Sit thou at my right hand, until I make thine enemies thy footstool. The Lord shall send the rod of thy strength out of Zion: rule thou in the midst of thine enemies. Thy people shall be willing in the day of thy power, in the beauties of holiness from the womb of the morning: thou hast the dew of thy youth. The Lord hath sworn and will not repent, Thou art a priest for ever after the order of Melchizedek." Ps. 110:1-4. We may notice at once that the priesthood of Christ is here presented as an everlasting priesthood, and that it is closely connected with His royal exaltation to power and glory.

This higher and more glorious aspect of the priesthood of our Lord is emphasized, too, in the Word of God through the writer of the epistle to the Hebrews. For he writes: "For every high priest taken from among men is ordained for men in things pertaining to God, that he may offer both gifts and sacrifices for sins. Who can have compassion on the ignorant, and on them that are out of the way; for that he himself also is compassed with infirmity. And by reason thereof he ought, as for the people, so also for himself, to offer for sins. And no man taketh this honour unto himself, but he that is called of God, as was Aaron. So also Christ glorified not himself to be made an high priest; but he that said unto him, Thou art my Son, today I have begotten thee. As he saith also in another place, Thou art a priest for ever after the order of Melchisedec." Heb. 5:1-6. In these words the divine ordination of Christ as priest is evidently emphasized. The same is true of vs. 10 of the same chapter: "Called of God an high priest after the order of Melchisedec." He is our forerunner, Who has entered into the inner sanctuary in heaven, "made an high priest for ever after the order of Melchisedec." Heb. 6:20. For perfection did not come through the Levitical priesthood. If it had, there would have been no need "that another priest should arise after the order of Melchisedec, and not be called after the order of Aaron." 7:11. It is, moreover, evident that Christ, of whom these things are spoken, is not from the tribe of Levi, as was a requisite for the Aaronitic priesthood, but from another tribe, of which no man served at the altar. "For it is evident that our Lord sprang out of Juda; of which tribe Moses spake nothing concerning priesthood. And it is far more evident: for that after the similitude of Melchisedec there ariseth another priest, who is made, not after the law of a carnal commandment, but after the power of an endless life. For he testifieth, Thou art a priest for ever after the order of Melchisedec." Here again, the idea receives emphasis that the priesthood after the order of Melchisedec is everlasting. Besides, in distinction from other priests, Christ was made high priest with an oath, by which it is manifest that He was made surety of a better covenant. "And inasmuch as not without an oath he was made priest: (For those priests were made without an oath; but this with an oath by him that said unto him, The Lord sware and will not repent, Thou art a priest for ever after the order of Melchisedec:) By so much Jesus was made a surety of a better testament." 7:20-22.

The fact, therefore, that Christ was a priest, not after the Aaronitic order, but after the similitude of Melchisedec, is strongly emphasized in Scripture.

Before we try to answer the question just what is implied in this for the priesthood of Christ, it may help us to ask: who was this Melchisedec, and how must his excellent and peculiar priesthood be explained?

In the Hebrews we are told many things may be said of this Melchisedec, things that are hard to be uttered. For he was king of Salem, priest of the most high God, and he blessed Abraham as the latter returned from the slaughter of the kings. And Abraham acknowledged his superior priesthood by giving him tithes of all. Moreover, it is explained that his name denotes him as a king of righteousness, while the fact that he was king of Salem designates that he was king of peace. Stranger still, we are told that he was "without father, without mother, without descent, having neither beginning of days, nor end of life; but made like unto the Son of God; abideth a priest continually." Heb. 5:11; 7:1-3. In view of all this, we need not be surprised that the person of Melchisedec as he appears in Gen. 14 has been variously explained. One theory has it that this Melchisedec is the son of Cainan (Gen. 5:11), who guarded the hill Golgotha, where Adam was buried who died in the days of Cainan. According to others he is the same as Shem, the son of Noah, who certainly was living in the days of Abraham. Still others dare not make of Melchisedec, of whom such wonderful things are written, a mere man. They make him an angel, or some sort of incarnation of the Holy Ghost, or of the

Word, or some higher God. All these allegorical interpretations and conjectures, however, have no sound basis in Holy Writ. There can be no question about the fact that Scripture in Gen. 14 pictures Melchisedec as a real man of flesh and blood, who lived in the days of Abraham, was king of Salem, and a priest of the most high God.

But how to explain this priest-king and his priesthood, in view of the fact that he appears outside of the line of Abraham in the land of Canaan, among what we probably would be inclined to consider wicked nations and tribes?

Dr. Kuyper Sr. (*Dictaten Dogmatiek*, III, *Locus de Christo*, 92; and *De Gemeene Gratie*, I, 332 ff.) explains the priesthood of the historical Melchisedec as a remnant of the original priesthood of Adam in the state of rectitude. Adam, too, was priest of God. His priesthood was, of course, not that of redemption, and had nothing to do with atoning sacrifices for sin. It simply consisted in Adam's calling and ability to love God, and to consecrate himself and the whole creation to the living God. Now, this priesthood, according to Kuyper, was not at once completely lost through sin. A remnant of it remained, and continued to reveal and express itself even unto the days of Melchisedec, in whom there is an especially glorious manifestation of this priestly office and function. And the fact that such a wonderful manifestation of the original priesthood of man could be preserved till so late a date, Kuyper explains from the restraining and preserving power and influence of common grace. This marvelous power commenced to assert itself immediately after the fall of Adam, to check the corrupting influence of sin in human nature, so that man did not become so totally corrupt as without this influence of grace he would have been. And so, even of his original priesthood, according to which he consecrated himself in love to the Most High, man retained a remnant. Much of it was lost, indeed, but a glittering of the original glory remained. And a beautiful manifestation and expression of this priesthood of creation we find in Melchisedec.

With this explanation of the historical appearance of Melchisedec and his priesthood we cannot possibly agree.

First of all, the proposition that such a priesthood of creation existed, or can possibly have existed at the time of Melchisedec, or even immediately after the fall, must, in the light of all that Scripture teaches us concerning the state of fallen man, be regarded as utterly false, a mere myth.

True, as we have stated before, in his original state of rectitude man was certainly a priest of the most high God. He was God's officebearer, His friend-servant, and lived in covenant fellowship with God. And as such it was his calling, not only to know and to glorify the name of his God in the midst of all the earthly creation as God's prophet; but also as priest to offer himself and all things a living sacrifice to the Most High. There is no dispute about this. There was an original priesthood of creation. But through sin this whole relation to God was turned into reverse. He not merely lost the image of God, but his knowledge of God changed into darkness, his righteousness into perversion, his holiness into pollution and love of sin and corruption. And even as through sin he became the false prophet, loving the lie, so he became the false priest. Instead of consecrating himself and all things unto God in love, he became an enemy of God, and devotes himself to the service of sin and the devil.

Such is the clear teaching of Scripture concerning natural man. There is no remnant of his original priesthood left in him.

Nor is it historically correct to maintain that after the fall there was a manifestation of this priesthood of creation in the line of fallen man, that this beautiful after-glow of man's original glory disappeared only slowly and gradually, and that in the priesthood of Melchisedec we find a final and marvelous reflection of this priesthood. On the contrary, history as revealed in Scripture plainly traces another line of development after the fall with respect to this original priesthood of creation, the line of a false and wholly corrupt priesthood, that has its commencement with Cain, continues in his generations, reaches a climax in the vainly boasting Lamech, and perishes in the flood. And after the deluge there is the same line of development. In the world of heathendom, outside of the covenant line that runs through the generations of Abraham, men turn away from the living God, corrupt the glory of the invisible One, make themselves gods after their own hearts, and consecrate themselves, through their idolatrous priests and shrines, to gods of wood and stone, worship sun, moon, and stars, man, beasts, and creeping things, corrupting themselves in the lust of their flesh, in immorality and bestiality of every imaginable sort. It would seem quite impossible to find room for a figure like that of Melchisedec in this line of development.

But also among Israel there is found, alongside of the central line of the covenant and of the true priesthood, a continuous line of this carnal and wicked priesthood, represented by a veritable multitude of official priests that defile the sanctuary, make of God's house a den of robbers, lead the people in their worship of golden calves, and introduce into the holy land literally all the gods of the nations round about Israel. And when, in the fulness of time the true High Priest comes to His temple, it is this line of false and corrupt priests that hates Him, rejects Him, and ultimately nails Him to the accursed tree.

And as it was in the old dispensation, so it still is in the new. Always the great majority of mankind still makes its own gods. Paganism is polytheism. But also in the midst of nominal Christendom the line of the false priests continues. The Christ of the Scriptures is rejected openly, or transformed into the modern Jesus; the blood of atonement is despised and trampled under foot. And although the man of modern culture does not make his gods of wood and stone, or literally bow himself before calves and oxen, he is, nevertheless, an idolater, whose carnal mind is enmity against the true and living God, and prefers to corrupt himself in the worship and service of the gods of his own imagination and philosophy. And we are told in the book of Revelation that this modern idolater, this false priest, will ultimately even make an image for men to worship, and persecute to the death all that refuse to bow down before it. The false prophet of the antichristian dominion is also, and that, too, necessarily so, a false priest.

In this entire historical line of development, from the fall in
paradise to the final manifestation of the man of sin in the
antichristian dominion, there is no room for the priesthood of
Melchisedec.

But how could one even expect to find Melchisedec in this
line and among the representatives of the false priesthood? Does
not the epistle to the Hebrews plainly teach us, and does not
already Ps. 110 presuppose, that this man Melchisedec, as he
appears in history according to Gen. 14, must be regarded a
type of Christ, and that, too, one of the most glorious types that
ever appeared? How, then, could he be found, or expected to be
found, in the line of the generations of Cain, of Ham, of Babylon, of the Antichrist? Type and antitype, shadow and reality,
belong together, are inseparably connected, and occur on the
same line in history. Cain is no type of Christ. Sodom and
Gomorrha are not shadows of Jerusalem. Babylon is the antithesis of the city of God that comes down out of heaven. The
one cannot be a picture of the other. Type and antitype are
one. The latter bears the former, receives its *raison d'etre,* and
the very possibility of its being from the former. If Melchisedec
does not stand on the line of grace, but on that of sin, and
the development of fallen man, he cannot possibly point forward to the Christ as the High Priest that is to come. Then he
points very really in the opposite direction. It surely cannot be
said that, in that case, Christ is priest after the order of Melchisedec, for that would be tantamount to saying that the
Christ of God is priest after the order of Antichrist! And to
say this is blasphemy!

Besides, if in the priesthood of Melchisedec we must see a
small remnant, a faint glittering of Adam's original priesthood,
and if Christ is priest after the order of Melchisedec, it follows
that also the priesthood of the Saviour, in distinction from that
of Aaron, is only a restoration of the original priesthood of man
in the state of righteousness. And against this presentation of
the matter we have grave objections. It is rooted in the false
conception that salvation is nothing but the reparation and
restoration of creation. What Adam failed to do, Christ accom-

plishes. If Adam had not fallen, he would have attained to eternal life, and the human race would have attained to heavenly glory in and through him. But since he fell into sin and death, Christ must take his place, and obtain for us the eternal righteousness and life. Salvation is repair work. Sin and the devil really marred the work of God and prevented Him from realizing His original creation-purpose. But this entire view is contrary to Scripture, and unworthy of God, Who is the Lord and hath done whatsoever He hath pleased. There never was any other purpose in the eternal mind of God than that which is now attained in Christ, the anointed Servant of Jehovah. That purpose was to lead the Church and all things to their heavenly destination and perfection in Christ. Not the first, but the second Paradise of God is the end that must be attained. Not the covenant as it was established in the first Adam, but the tabernacle of God as it rests in the last Adam, the incarnated Word, the Lord from heaven, is the purpose God had in mind from before the foundation of the world. Not the priesthood of the first Adam, but the far more exalted priesthood of the Son of God in the flesh, is the divine ideal. Unto the attainment of that priesthood, which is as far more glorious than the original priesthood of creation as the Son of God in the flesh, raised and exalted at the right hand of God, is more glorious than the first man Adam, all things are subservient, and must serve the counsel of the Most High, even the fall, sin, the devil, and death. And Adam's original priesthood was only a faint image of that glorious priesthood of the Son of God. But if this is borne in mind, it should be evident that the priesthood of the historical Melchisedec, which was typical of the glorious priesthood of Christ, cannot have been a weak afterglow of Adam's priesthood.

The place of Melchisedec and his priesthood will have to be found in the line of grace.

His historical origin must be traced, not to paradise and the state of original righteousness, but to the ark, and to the grace Noah and his seed had found in the eyes of the Lord.

Not in the line of reprobation, in which by the power of a certain common grace a remnant of the original integrity is preserved, but in the line of election, in the generations of the people of God, saved by sovereign grace, the priest-king Melchisedec, as Abraham met him after his victory over the allied kings, must be placed. Historically, he was a real man of flesh and blood, and all the strange things that are written of him in the epistle of the Hebrews dare not be applied to his person, but have reference to his peculiar priesthood as typical of the priesthood of Christ. As priest he stands without father or mother, without genealogy, but as a person he has his descent in the generations of the sons of God.

In the abstract it were quite conceivable that Melchisedec even as a person was called forth by a wonder of God's grace, simply for the purpose of creating an altogether unique type of Christ, so that even as a historical person he appeared suddenly and inexplicably, without any historical connection with his contemporaries, as a priest of the Most High. There are those that prefer this explanation of his exalted figure. In that case he simply appears as a wonder of God's grace. He cannot be explained in connection with the history of his time. There is no relation between him and the world of his day and environment. As a unique individual, as a marvelous exception, he appears in the midst of a wicked and perverse nation. And in the midst of a world full of iniquity, he appears as a priest of the most high God, a wonderful manifestation of the wonder of God's grace.

But there is no need of such an interpretation, and the sober narrative of Genesis 14 leaves a different impression. He was a real historical person. He certainly was king of Salem, and he must have ruled over a real people. And as king he was also priest of God in the midst of his people, and in a sense, the people over which he ruled as king-priest must have been a priestly people, consecrated to God. The narrative of Genesis 14 leads to the conclusion that at the time when Abraham sojourned in the land of Canaan, there still was a group of people, a small nation, that knew Jehovah, that served and worshipped the Most High, and that, through Melchisedec as their high priest, brought their sacrifices to the God of Shem. Indeed, the Canaanite, too, was in the land, and the Canaanite was accursed, and had long trampled the covenant of Jehovah, established with Noah and his seed, under foot. But in the midst of a wicked generation there was also a remnant of God's people, according to the election of grace, a people that knew and served the Lord, and that were headed and represented by the priest-king Melchisedec. But if this is true, it is but natural to look for a historical explanation of this marvelous priest-king and his people. Only, this explanation must not be sought in the line of the wicked reprobates, but in the line of the generations of the people of God, in which, even outside of Abraham, God still preserved His covenant in those days.

Nor can this present any special difficulties, if we bear in mind the organic development of God's covenant and its continuation in the line of generations. Then it is at once evident that Melchisedec as a priest of the most high God, together with the people over which he rules, has his origin in the ark. In the ark and through the flood the Church of God had been saved out of and from the wicked world. And with Noah and his seed God had established His covenant, not a certain covenant of common grace with all men, but His covenant in Christ in the line of election. But as always, so also from the loins of Noah there developed the twofold seed, the seed of the promise and the carnal seed. The main line of the covenant according to election ran through Shem, and was afterwards more specifically limited to the generations of Abraham. But this may not be understood as if with the calling of Abraham God's covenant was strictly limited to him and his family, so that the father of believers was a lonely remnant of those that knew Jehovah, and called upon the name of the Lord. He who would thus explain the situation at the time of Abraham's calling, would fail to reckon with the organic development of the covenant-line in history. Not at once and all of a sudden was the fear of the Lord limited to the generations of Abraham. For, first of all, during Abraham's life many of the old patriarchs from the generations of Shem that culminated in Terah, the father of Abraham, were still alive, and even Shem was still living when the father of believers was called. Even though the immediate ancestors of Abraham apostatized and turned to idols, there must have been thousands of others in the earlier generations that kept the covenant of Jehovah. Besides, although the generations of Shem had been mentioned as those that were destined to receive the covenant blessing in the special sense, for a long time the fear of the Lord must have been preserved also in the generations of Japheth, and it is not even improbable that also in the line of Ham there were found those that called upon the name of Jehovah. In view of all these data, it is by no means strange that even in the land of Canaan, at the time of Abraham's sojourn in the land, a group of people is found that have the knowledge of the true God, and that are ruled and represented by a priest-king like Melchisedec. Some four centuries later we meet with a similar figure in the person of Jethro, the father-in-law of Moses. He, too, was a priest of the Most High among his people, although the line of the covenant in the narrower sense of the word did not run over the children of Keturah, but over Isaac, for "in Isaac shall thy seed be called." Hence, if only we bear in mind the organic development of the covenant in the line of generations, we will have no need of explaining Melchisedec as a product of common grace. Nor is it necessary to interpret his appearance as priest of the Most High through an exceptional wonder of God's grace. Although he stands outside of the generations of Abraham, and, perhaps, even of Shem, Melchisedec as a historical person must be explained as belonging to the generations of those that fear the Lord, and with whom God still continued His covenant.

He was a priest of the Most High by grace.

And as such he was a type of Christ.

V

After The Order Of Melchisedec

Interesting as may be the historical appearance of Melchisedec as a king-priest, Scripture is chiefly concerned with his typical significance. Emphatically the Bible teaches that Christ is a priest after the order of Melchisedec. This is the teaching of that beautiful, prophetico-Messianic Psalm 110 as further interpreted in the epistle to the Hebrews. Distinction is made between the priesthood of Aaron and that of Melchisedec, and with this distinction in view Christ is said to be a priest according to the similitude of the latter. This does not mean that there is an antithesis between the two orders of priesthood, and that the two exclude each other. It is evident that in certain respects they were alike. Also the priesthood of Aaron foreshadowed that of the great High Priest that was to come: Aaron, too, was a type of Christ. The situation is rather thus that, while the priesthood according to the order of Melchisedec included that of Aaron, the former is of a far more exalted character than the latter, was much richer in significance, of a wider scope, of far greater power and authority. And while the priesthood of Aaron found its final fulfillment in Christ, and in some respect also its termination, that of Melchisedec was so realized in the Lord that in Him it is perfect and remains for ever.

The question, therefore, is: what is the distinction between the two orders of priesthood? In what respects was the priesthood of Melchisedec of a higher order than that of Aaron? Scripture emphasizes especially two points of difference. The first is that, while among Israel the priestly and the royal offices were separated, so that one and the same person could not function in both offices, they were combined in Melchisedec:

he was a royal priest. And the second point of difference is that, while the priesthood of Aaron in its specific meaning was temporal, and must come to an end as soon as the perfect sacrifice was made, that of Melchisedec is everlasting. In both these respects Christ was a priest according to the similitude of Melchisedec.

This is emphasized, first of all, in Psalm 110. This Psalm is peculiar in that it is directly Messianic. By this we mean that, while in other Messianic Psalms David speaks first of himself, and only in last instance of the Christ that was to come, this cannot be said of the one hundred and tenth Psalm. Usually there was a historic occasion for the Messianic prophecies in the psalms in the person and circumstances and experiences of the human author of these psalms, especially of the psalms of David. David was a type of Christ as the theocratic king of Israel, and his experiences, his battles, his victories, and his sufferings foreshadowed the suffering, victory and exaltation of the Messiah that was to come. And when in those circumstances David, inspired and guided by the Spirit of Christ, expressed his experiences in the psalms, whether in lamentation and wailing because of his suffering and reproach, in deprecation against the enemies of God and His Anointed, or in triumph over his foes, he spoke, indeed, of himself, but thus speaking, he prophesied at the same time of Christ. The Spirit of Christ in the psalmist made use of his personal experiences and circumstances to draw a prophetic picture of the Messiah. But this is not the case with Psalm 110. It is directly Messianic. Its contents cannot refer to the Psalmist.

That this is true is evident, first of all, from the very first verse of the Psalm: "The Lord said unto my Lord, Sit thou at my right hand, until I make thine enemies thy footstool." In His controversy with the Pharisees the Lord refers to these words as proof that Christ is the Son of God: "While the Pharisees were gathered together, Jesus asked them, saying, What think ye of the Christ, whose son is he? They say unto him, The son of David. He saith unto them, How then doth David in spirit call him Lord, saying, The Lord said unto my Lord,

Sit thou at my right hand, till I make thine enemies thy foot-stool? If David then call him Lord, how is he his son?" and we read that the Pharisees were not able to answer him a word. Matt. 22:41-46. Cf. Mk. 12:35-37; Luke 20:41-44. From the first verse of the Psalm, and from the application made of it by Christ, it is evident, therefore, that David is not at all speaking of himself, but refers consciously and objectively to the Messiah. Him he calls his Lord. And to Him Jehovah said: "Sit thou at my right hand until I make thine enemies thy footstool."

But this is true also of vs. 4: "The Lord hath sworn, and will not repent, Thou art a priest for ever after the order of Melchisedec." It is true that, according to some interpreters, these words are interpreted as being spoken by the people, and addressed to David. But, first of all, this explanation is contrary to the tenor of the whole psalm, which, as has been shown, speaks of the Messiah directly. It is quite in harmony with the context to say that also these words are addressed to Christ. And, secondly, they could not have been spoken of David. For the offices of priest and king were not combined in him. He was king of Israel, but the priesthood was found in the generations of Aaron, not in those of Judah and David. Hence, these words cannot have reference to him. Nor can the interpretation be accepted that one of the priest-kings of the time of the Maccabees is the author of this psalm, and that the reference is to him. It is true that in some of the Maccabees the two offices of priest and king were combined in the same person. But the one great objection to this interpretation is that the psalm is Davidic, as is sufficiently proved by the Lord's own reference to it in the words quoted above. Hence, there is only one possibility, and that is, that the words concerning the priest-hood after the order of Melchisedec are immediately and directly Messianic. And this is corroborated by the reference to them in the epistle to the Hebrews.

Now, even from these words in their context it is evident that the priesthood after the order of Melchisedec was distinct from that of Aaron in two respects. First of all, it is a royal priesthood. The kingship is combined with the priesthood. For in the context we have a description of Christ in His royal glory, of the King going to battle at the head of His people, and victorious over His enemies. It is to Christ in His royal power and exaltation that it is said: "Sit thou at my right hand, until I make thine enemies thy footstool." And to this victorious and exalted King it is promised by oath "Thou art a priest for ever after the order of Melchisedec." Even as Melchisedec was a royal priest, or a priestly king, so also Christ will combine in Himself the kingly and priestly office, and that, too, in final and highest perfection, at the right hand of God. And, secondly, in close connection with this combination of the royal and priestly offices, the priesthood after the order of Melchisedec is distinct in that it is for ever: "thou art a priest *for ever.*" The priesthood of Aaron would come to an end; that of Melchisedec as realized in Christ is everlasting.

This interpretation of the priesthood according to the similitude of Melchisedec with its special element in the combination of the royal and priestly offices, is quite in harmony with the prophecy of Zechariah in chapter 6:9 ff. The prophet is enjoined to take silver and gold of them that of the captivity have come from Babylon to Jerusalem, and to make crowns of the precious metal thus acquired. These crowns he is to set upon the head of Joshua, the high priest, thus indicating prophetically that the priest shall be crowned king. However, this is to be fulfilled, not in Joshua, but in the BRANCH, for the prophet must explain his prophetic act by saying to Joshua: "Thus speaketh the Lord of hosts, saying, Behold, the man whose name is The BRANCH; and he shall grow up out of this place, and he shall build the temple of the Lord: Even he shall build the temple of the Lord; and he shall bear the glory, and shall sit and rule upon his throne: and the counsel of peace shall be between them both." It is evident that in this prophecy we have a further prediction of what was already promised in Psalm 110, and that the last words have no reference whatever to any alleged covenant of redemption in the eternal decree of God, but to the harmonious union between the king and the priest, united in the one person of the BRANCH, that is, of the Messiah.

And this is rather elaborately developed in the epistle to the Hebrews. Of Melchisedec as a type of Christ the author of this epistle is speaking. And calling attention to his name, and to the place of his reign, he explains that as a typical figure Melchisedec was both king of righteousness and king of peace. The name *Melchi- sedec* signifies *king of righteousness,* and as *Salem* means peace, king of Salem signifies *king of peace.* And concerning his priesthood the author of the epistle to the Hebrews reminds us, first of all, that Melchisedec was a priest of the most high God, and, further, he describes him as appearing "without father, without mother, without descent, having neither beginning of days, nor end of life; but made like unto the Son of God; abiding a priest continually." Heb. 7:1-3. You understand that all this is applicable to Melchisedec, not as a historical person, but as a type of Christ, and with reference only to his priesthood. He appears in Genesis 14 as priest without any reference to his descent or genealogy. Nor is anything said about his end, or about the continuation of his priesthood in his generations. He had no need, as did the Aaronitic priest, to prove that he descended from the priestly family. And in all this he is typically, not personally, made like unto the Son of God, the Christ, in Whom all these typical traits are realized in highest perfection. And here again, the same two elements of the priesthood of Melchisedec that were mentioned in Psalm 110 appear on the foreground: he was a priest-king, and his priesthood is everlasting.

In both these respects, that the priestly office and the kingship were combined in one person, and that he was a priest for ever, Melchisedec is a type of Christ. Christ is the real Melchisedec, the royal priest, the king of righteousness, and the king of peace. He functions in both the royal and the priestly office.

From this viewpoint it may be said, indeed, that there was a figure or image of this priesthood in that of the first Adam in paradise in the state of rectitude. He was an earthly image of the eternal, heavenly priest-king. For Adam was very really priest of the Most High. This we cannot understand as long as we see the essence of the priesthood and of the priestly function in the offering up of bloody sacrifices. For this there was no room in the original state of righteousness. This was added after the fall, and became necessary because of sin. But bloody sacrifices are not an essential element of the priesthood. Even as the prediction of future events, though belonging to the office of the prophet among Israel, cannot be considered essential to the prophetic office, so the offering up of bloody sacrifices, though for a time necessary on account of sin, is not the essence of the priesthood. The central idea of the priestly office is that of consecration of oneself and all things to the living God. A priest is a servant of God. He loves God. He consecrates himself to the Holy One. He serves in God's tabernacle, in His house. In this sense, Adam was surely priest of the most high God in the midst of the earthly creation. All things must serve him, that he might serve his God, and be consecrated to Him with all his heart and mind and soul and strength. And as priest he was also king. Dominion was given him over all the earthly creation. The royal and the priestly offices were harmoniously united in his person. And this was but proper. Only the servant of God has the right to have dominion, for only as long as he stands in the right relation to the Creator of all things, that is, in subjection and obedience, can he properly rule over all things in the name of the Lord, and according to His will. Prostrating himself in the dust before the Sovereign of heaven and earth, and consecrating himself and all his power, together with the whole earthly creation, to the living God, Adam in the state of rectitude might have dominion and sway the royal sceptre over all creatures. He was priest-king, servant-king, king under God.

Among Israel this was different. Aaron was priest, but he did not sway the sceptre. The two offices were strictly separated in Israel's theocracy. The king might not minister at the altar, the priest could not occupy the throne. Hence, Aaron, though prefiguring a phase of the priestly office of Christ, was not His perfect type. The perfect type is found in the figure of Melchisedec, king of Salem, and priest of the Most High. His priesthood is realized in Christ. For Christ is the perfect Priest, the perfect Servant of Jehovah, Whose meat it is to do the Father's will, and Who, as the Son of God in human nature, is consecrated to Him with His whole being. He is the only High Priest over His brethren, and is set over the whole house of God, to accomplish all things pertaining to God. And having accomplished all, and having become revealed as the perfect Servant of Jehovah, Who became obedient unto death, even unto the death of the cross, He is exalted at the right hand of the Majesty in the heavens, henceforth expecting till all things shall be put under His feet. Hence, the priesthood of Melchisedec is fulfilled in Him. He entered in the sanctuary above, not made with hands, and constantly consecrates Himself and all things to the Father; and He has all power and authority in heaven and on earth, and sits in His Father's throne. As the perfect High Priest, He is also King of righteousness, and on the basis of God's own everlasting righteousness He is King of peace!

And His priesthood is without end. It is everlasting. This was not, and could not be true of the priesthood of Aaron. It represented but a phase of the priestly calling of Christ, that phase which had become necessary on account of sin. And this phase could not be everlasting. It belonged to the way the High Priest must travel to realize His everlasting priesthood; it was part of the work that must be performed to build the House of God. It was accomplished in the perfect sacrifice of Christ on the cross, and there it came to an end. Of this phase of the priesthood of Christ that of Aaron was a shadow. Hence, while the eternal priesthood of Christ could be typified in just one figure, that of Melchisedec, the priesthood of Aaron must be spread over a long line of generations. For the blood of bulls and of goats could never blot out sin. It must ever be repeated until the perfect sacrifice of reconciliation had been offered in the blood of the cross. But it could not last for ever. Not only must there come an end to the sacrificing of bulls and goats, but also the perfect sacrifice of the High Priest Himself could never be repeated. This phase of the priesthood of Christ was finished when the High Priest laid down His life as a ransom for many. But the priesthood of Christ did not reach its end on Golgotha. It is everlasting. He is a priest after the order of Melchisedec. For ever He consecrates Himself, and His people, and all things, in perfect love to the Father. And presently He will come again to perfect the work the Father gave Him to do, to finish the House of God, and establish it in heavenly beauty in the new Jerusalem. Then the tabernacle of God will be with men. In that tabernacle all things will be sanctified to God. And in that everlasting House of God Christ will for ever be the perfect King-Priest, the King of righteousness and the King of peace, after the order of Melchisedec!

VI

The One Sacrifice

The Heidelberg Catechism, as we stated before, does not discuss the priesthood of Christ after the order of Melchisedec, but considers it solely from the viewpoint of the work of redemption He was and is to accomplish for His people. We would almost feel inclined to apologize for having gone off on a tangent as far as we did in our previous discussion, were it not true that for a full understanding of the significance of Christ as the Anointed of God it is quite essential to consider Him in this wider connection. Now, however, we may return to the Catechism, which teaches us that to the work of Christ as Priest belong especially two elements: 1. That "by the one sacrifice of His body He has redeemed us," and 2. That "he makes continual intercession with the Father for us."

The way into the sanctuary of God, and into the glory of His priesthood after the order of Melchisedec, lay for Christ over the accursed tree. To His perfect obedience and consecration to the Father belonged "the one sacrifice of His body." For He was appointed High Priest at the head of a people that were by nature sinful, guilty and damnable before God, "that he might redeem us from all iniquity, and purify unto himself a peculiar people, zealous of good works." Tit. 2:14. "Wherefore in all things it behooved him to be made like unto his brethren, that he might be a merciful and faithful high priest in things pertaining to God, to make reconciliation for the sins of the people." Heb. 2:17. For it pleased God to make reconciliation through Him. For, "God was in Christ reconciling the world unto himself, not imputing their trespasses unto them; and hath committed unto us the word of reconciliation." Hence, this faithful and merciful High Priest is authorized to send out the word of reconciliation: "Be ye reconciled to God." II Cor. 5:19, 20. For "when we were enemies, we were reconciled to God by the death of his Son." Rom. 5:10. The High Priest according to the order of Melchisedec, standing at the head of a people in sin, estranged from God, and children of wrath, must bring "the one sacrifice of his body" to make reconciliation for the sins of His people.

Reconciliation is a covenant idea. It presupposes a relation existing between the parties that are to be reconciled, whether of friendship or of love or of obligation. Perfect strangers are not reconciled. One can speak of reconciliation between man and wife, between friend and friend, between a subject and his king, between father and son. With respect to divine reconciliation, the relation that is presupposed is the eternal covenant of God with His people. When God, through Christ, reconciled us unto Himself He revealed His eternal covenant love and friendship toward us. Reconciliation presupposes, however, also that the relation between the parties to be reconciled has been violated, so that it cannot function, and the parties are at variance with each other. With respect to divine reconciliation the cause of this separation and variance lies wholly with man. By his wilful disobedience he violated the covenant of God, and became an object of wrath by nature. As such all men come into the world, also God's own elect. They are enemies of God, and have forfeited all right and claim to God's favor. And the act of reconciliation consists in the removal of the cause of the separation and variance. It is that act of God whereby he changes the state of the sinner from one of guilt, in which he is the proper object of God's wrath, into one of righteousness, in which he is the object of God's love and favor.

These main elements of divine reconciliation must be clearly understood and borne in mind, lest we misrepresent this fundamental truth of salvation. God is the Reconciler. Never may we represent the matter as if God were the One that is reconciled. This error is often committed. According to this presentation of the matter, God and the sinner are at variance, and Christ steps in between, intervenes with His sacrifice, in order to bring the two parties together. But Scripture never supports this view. It never speaks of God and the sinner being mutually reconciled. Nowhere do we read that God reconciled Himself to us, or that Christ reconciled God to His people. But always it represents God as the Reconciler, and His people as those that are reconciled to Him by His gracious act. Christ is not a third party intervening between God and us, but He is the revelation of God the Reconciler. For God was in Christ reconciling not Himself, but the world unto Himself, not imputing their trespasses unto them. We are in a state of guilt and under wrath by nature, and God removes the guilt, and translates us into a state of favor and friendship.

The way of this reconciliation is that of satisfaction. Men may be reconciled to one another by merely "forgetting and forgiving" whatever may be the cause of their separation. But this is impossible with God. The cause of our alienation from God *must be removed*. And a basis of reconciliation must be established in the righteousness of God. This cause of our separation from God is our sin, the sin that is ours in connection with the whole human race in Adam, and which we can only increase daily. For it is because of the guilt of sin that we lie under the judgment of damnation, and are the objects of the wrath of God. By nature we lie in the midst of death. If, therefore, reconciliation is to be established, the guilt of sin must be removed, blotted out, and righteousness must be established. But how is it possible to remove sin? Only by the satisfaction, the perfect satisfaction of the justice of God against sin. There is no other way. Whatever a supercilious modernism may mockingly object to this truth when it speaks of "blood-theology," and whatever it may try to offer instead about a God that is all love, and that is so merciful that He is ready to overlook sin, to wink at it, simply to act as if it had never been committed, the truth of satisfaction for sin is emphasized throughout Scripture, and must be strongly maintained as belonging to the fundamentals of the Christian faith. God cannot deny Himself. And He is righteous and just. Hence, there can be no reconciliation without satisfaction.

But what is satisfaction? How can the justice of God against sin be satisfied? Only by a perfect sacrifice. And what is a perfect sacrifice? It is the offering up of oneself, with an act of perfect obedience and in the love of God, to God's perfect justice against sin. The punishment of sin is death. One, therefore, who would satisfy the justice of God and make an atonement for sin, must suffer this punishment. He must taste death in all its implications, eternal death. The vials of God's wrath must be poured out over him, and must be emptied. But in suffering this agony of the wrath of God, these torments of hell, in dying this death, he must not be merely passive, still less dare he be rebellious against the heavy hand of God upon him: he must perform an act in suffering, he must be obedient in dying, he must still love God when His heavy hand oppresses him. Mere passive suffering is no sacrifice. Even the damned in hell suffer the wrath of God, without ever atoning for their sin. To satisfy the justice of God one must perform an act that is the perfect antithesis of the act of willful disobedience of man in the first paradise. His act must be the perfect *Yes* over against the sinner's *No*. He must will to die for God's righteousness. He must *offer himself*.

And that is the meaning of the cross!

On Golgotha our only High Priest offered the "one sacrifice of his body" to satisfy the justice of God against sin. And this sacrifice was vicarious, substitutional. Voluntarily He entered into death, and suffered the deepest agonies of hell, not for His own sins, but for the sins of those whom the Father had given Him. And thus our only High Priest "by the one sacrifice of his body, has redeemed us," purchased us free from the bondage of sin in which we were held, obtained eternal and perfect righteousness for us, and merited for us the favor of God. Thus His sacrifice is the offering of reconciliation. God was in Christ reconciling us unto Himself.

He was able and authorized to make this perfect sacrifice, and to make it instead of all His own. For, as to the first, He is without sin. He had no original sin, for He is the person of the Son of God in human nature, so that the guilt of Adam's transgression could not be imputed unto Him; and He was conceived of the Holy Spirit, so that His nature was undefiled. "For such a high priest became us, who is holy, harmless, undefiled, separate from sinners, and made higher than the heavens." Heb. 7:26. He is the Lamb without blemish. He was able to become perfectly obedient, even unto the death of the cross. He could offer to God the perfect *Yes* over against the terrible and wanton *No* of sin. And He could lay down His life, that He might take it again, for voluntarily He had assumed human life, and from the Father He had received commandment and authority to lay it down. And, as to the second, namely, that He was able and authorized to bring that perfect sacrifice for His own, we must remember, first of all, that He represented them all in virtue of His eternal anointing. God had chosen His elect in Him, and He was the head of all His own. Election is the basis of vicarious atonement. Without eternal, sovereign election, substitutional atonement is impossible. Either Christ represented His elect on the cross, and died in their stead; or He represented no one, and His death is in vain. And because He is the person of the Son of God that died, He could suffer death for all His own so as to satisfy for them all, and redeem them unto life. All the vials of God's wrath, under which we all would have had to perish everlastingly, were poured out on Him in the moment of the cross, and in perfect obedience He bore that wrath even unto the end. For "Christ being come an high priest of good things to come, by a greater and more perfect tabernacle, not made with hands, that is to say, not of this building; neither by the blood of goats and calves, but by his own blood he entered in once into the holy place, having obtained eternal redemption for us." It is finished!

———

Some of the elements of this doctrine of vicarious atonement by the one sacrifice of Jesus on the cross will have to be discussed more elaborately in connection with other parts of the Heidelberg Catechism. But even here they had to be briefly touched upon, in order to set forth the meaning of this sacrifice of our

High Priest in our stead and in our behalf, and to maintain the truth of vicarious atonement over against several false theories that have been developed to explain the death of Christ.

First of all, there is the so-called *moral theory* of the suffering of Christ. It denies that the death of Christ was a sacrifice for sin in the proper sense of the word, and, of course, also that He died in our stead. Christ's death was no satisfaction of the justice of God in respect to sin. According to this theory, the true purpose of the death of Christ is to exert a salutary, reformatory influence upon the moral condition of man. Christ left us a worthy example, when He willingly sacrificed His life for the truth. Or, He revealed that God will suffer with us, and that He entered into all our afflictions and death, in order that He might be able to sympathize with us. But in whatever way this theory may try to explain the real character and purpose of the death of Christ, it denies that it is an offering for sin, and that He died in our stead to satisfy the justice of God; and it insists that Christ's suffering meant to make a moral impression upon us, and to exert an improving influence upon mankind. To consider the suffering Man of sorrows tends to the moral uplift of men.

It is hardly necessary to point out that this theory stands in direct contradiction to the testimony of Scripture.

The *moral theory* of the suffering of Christ stands condemned, first of all, in the light of all that Scripture teaches us concerning the state and condition of the natural man, and the character of sin.

For, according to Scripture, sin is guilt, and the sinner is liable to punishment, worthy of damnation, wholly unworthy of God's favor, a child of wrath. Sin is not only, and not in the first place, an inherent weakness or defilement of the human nature, some moral imperfection that may be removed by the influence of some sound moral example: it is guilt. And this means that the sinner, as the object of God's just condemnation, lies in the midst of death, and has no right to life. This also implies his spiritual death, according to which he is incapable of doing any good and inclined to all evil. He is legally a slave of sin. His moral depravity is the punishment that is inflicted upon him by the righteous judgment of God. Hence, suppose even that it were possible to reform man, to deliver him from his moral depravity by a mere example or moral influence, the natural man would not even have the right to such deliverance from the slavery of sin. Before he may be delivered the justice of God against sin must be satisfied. And, as we have repeatedly emphasized, this satisfaction of God's justice can be accomplished only through such a voluntary bearing of the wrath of God and of the punishment of sin that constitutes an act of the perfect obedience of love. There is no deliverance from sin without atonement for sin. There is no possibility of sanctification without justification. If the death of Christ is not the sacrifice of vicarious atonement, it certainly cannot have the power of moral improvement or reformation.

Besides, this *moral theory* of the atonement really proceeds from the supposition that man is inherently good, though his nature is weakened and morally incapacitated somewhat. If only he considers how infinitely good and loving and merciful God is, he will, by the contemplation of this good and loving Father, be persuaded to love Him too, and strive for improvement that he may be pleasing in God's sight. And that he may be able to understand and contemplate this great love of God, the Most High enters into our deepest woe through the death of His Son. However, Scripture teaches us, not that man is morally weak by nature, but that he is dead through trespasses and sins. He is not in need of reformation, but of regeneration, and unless he is born again, he cannot even see the kingdom of God. No amount of moral influence will do him a particle of good. The very contrary is true. The more the love of God is demonstrated, provided it is truly the love of GOD that is shown, the more he will hate God and hold the truth in unrighteousness. The very cross of Christ, that is supposed to exert this salutary moral influence upon the sinner, is sufficient proof of this. Let us not be oblivious of that fact, that, although God delivered His only begotten Son to the death of the cross, he was taken and slain by the hands of wicked men. And rather than being morally improved by the sight of the suffering of the righteous Son of God, they jeered and mocked and blasphemed as long as they dared at the spectacle of Golgotha! Apart from God's act of reconciliation through the atoning death of His Son, the cross reveals nothing but wrath and judgment. It is the condemnation of the world.

Further, what demonstration of God's love could one possibly discern in the cross of Jesus, considered as an act of God, if the death of Christ is not an atoning sacrifice for sin? If Christ did not bear our sins upon the accursed tree, He did not represent us. And if He did not represent us, He could not justly enter into our death, and God could not justly send Him into our death and hell. Surely, it is quite impossible to discern how such an unjust and quite superfluous infliction of suffering on the righteous Son of God, which apart from the idea of atonement and suffering for sin can be little more than an empty, though terrible show, could be a revelation of God's love, and a power for the moral improvement of the sinner.

Lastly, it is quite true that the Bible holds before us the sufferings of Christ as an example, which we must follow. But, let it be noted, first of all, that this example of Christ's suffering is held, not before the natural man and for his moral improvement, but before those that have been redeemed by the death of Christ, called by His grace out of darkness into the light, and in principle delivered from the power and dominion of sin and death, that they might be to the praise of the glory of God's grace in the Beloved. And, secondly, though the Scriptures certainly present the suffering of Christ as an example for us to follow, it never does so except after it has first proclaimed the death of Christ as an atoning sacrifice for the sins of His own. Jesus Christ, the righteous, is a propitiation for our sins, I John 2:2. He is the faithful and merciful High Priest, that makes reconciliation for the sins of the people, Heb. 2:17. He Himself bare our sins in his own body on the tree, that we, being dead to sins, should live unto righteousness, I Pet. 2:24. The Church is bought with a price, I Cor. 6:20; 7:23. And all the sacrifices of the old dispensation point to the same truth: Christ's death is the vicarious atonement, whereby the justice of God is for ever satisfied against the sins of His people, and through which they are reconciled to Him.

A second theory of the significance of the death of Christ that denies the Scriptural truth of satisfaction and vicarious atonement, is known as the *governmental theory*. It denies that it was necessary that God's justice be satisfied. Christ did not have to suffer and die in order to bear the sins of many, and thus to atone for them. God's mercy is exactly that He forgives sin, that He cancels the debt without payment. However, it would be a dangerous, a morally impossible thing to forgive the sinner, and to treat him as if he had never committed any sin, without first causing him to acknowledge the righteousness and justice of God. He would get the impression that God is indifferent to sin, that He is not terribly displeased with the workers and work of iniquity. Even though God forgives the sinner, and receives him again into His favor, He must maintain the moral order of the universe, and the sinner must repent and acknowledge that God is holy and righteous. And to bring him to the acknowledgment of God's righteousness, and to true repentance, God gives a demonstration of His wrath and justice in the death of His Son. In delivering up His own Son He clearly reveals to the sinner what He might righteously do to every sinner. Just as a general might court-martial and sentence to death every soldier of a regiment that committed mutiny, but singles out only one, the ringleader, perhaps, and hangs him in the sight of all the rebels, so God demonstrated His righteousness and displeasure against sin by sending Christ into death that we might go free. And the sinner, looking by faith at that demonstration of the justice and wrath of God, will confess his sins, acknowledge that God is righteous, and thus assume the position in which God, while maintaining His moral government of the universe, may forgive him, and treat him as if he had never had or committed any sin.

That also this theory must be rejected as contrary to the plain teachings of Holy Writ, and, besides, as inherently absurd and impossible, is not difficult to see. All the Scriptural passages that speak of the death of Christ as a sacrifice for sins, a ransom, as a price that was paid for our redemption, as a propitiation for sin, as an atonement and reconciliation through blood, condemn this presentation of the significance of Christ's death and of the redemption of the Church as contrary to the revealed Word of God. To be sure, the death of Christ is a setting forth, a demonstration, a declaration of the righteousness of God in justifying the ungodly, but only and exactly because it is a payment of the debt, a satisfying of the justice of God, a "propitiation through faith in His blood," Rom. 3:25, 26. Only because Christ represented His people in the hour of the righteous judgment of God, and as their Representative took upon Himself the guilt of their sins, so that He could justly bear the wrath of God in their stead and in their behalf, was the death of Christ indeed a demonstration of God's unchangeable righteousness.

How otherwise could it possibly be such a demonstration? Even if, according to the illustration used above, the general of an army selects one of the guilty mutineers to punish him in the sight of all the rebels, and lets the others go free, this can hardly be considered a demonstration of righteousness and justice, for all were guilty and deserved punishment. However, in such a case it is, at least, one of the guilty ones that is selected to receive the punishment as an example to all the rest. An innocent outsider could not possibly serve such a purpose. But with Christ this is different. He knew no sin. Unless the guilt of His people could be and was imputed to Him, so that He could suffer their punishment in their stead, there was no sin and guilt upon His head for the which He could justly be made to suffer death. If, therefore, our Lord suffered merely as a demonstration of the justice and righteousness of God against sin, in order to impress us sinners with the truth that God might justly damn us all to eternal death, the demonstration misses the point entirely. To make the just suffer as an example for the unjust is not a show of righteousness and of justice, but of the grossest injustice. Such a demonstration, even though this method would be sufficient to satisfy and maintain the justice of God, would be quite devoid of power to bring men to an acknowledgment of the justice of God, and to true repentance and sorrow over sin, simply because it is no demonstration of justice, but of injustice.

And finally, such a demonstration of the righteousness of God could never accomplish the reconciliation of men with God. Sin is not merely a denial of the justice of God in the consciences and consciousness of men, it is also in the objective sense a violation of God's law. It is rebellion against the Most High. It is guilt. It must be blotted out. And it can be blotted out only through satisfaction, that is, through an act of obedience that is the complete antithesis of the act of sin committed. Not the mere acknowledgment that God could justly punish every sinner with eternal death, not the most earnest and heartfelt repentance can satisfy the justice of God. But only such an act of obedience, whereby the sinner voluntarily and from the love of God suffers the punishment for sin to the end, is capable of blotting out the guilt of sin. This act of loving obedience in the suffering of eternal death the sinner could never perform, still less accomplish perfectly to the end. But God's own eternal Son in our flesh, ordained to be the Head of all His elect, was authorized and capable to bring this willing sacrifice instead of His guilty people. This, and not a mere demonstration of the justice of God, is the meaning of the cross of Christ. And this is also its power unto salvation unto every one that believes.

Finally, we must briefly review in this connection what is known as the *mystical theory* of the death of Christ. This theory, in common with the two presentations of the meaning of Christ's suffering which we already discussed, also denies that Christ's death is substitutional. It must have nothing of what is often called "blood theology." Those who support this view scoff at the idea of the necessity of satisfaction. They will not hear of guilt and punishment, but rather emphasize that the sinner is morally weak and sick, and must be delivered from the power of sin. To this end Christ entered into our nature, and on the cross He actually bore our sinful nature and delivered it up unto death. On the cross our sinful nature died principally.

And in the resurrection He arose with a new, glorified, holy nature, wholly free from sin and death. Now, through faith we become mystically one with that Christ, who led to death and buried our sinful nature, and who arose in glory and righteousness. Through this mystical union also their sinful nature is crucified, and also they rise unto newness of life. And so they become reconciled to God.

There is, of course, an element of truth in this mystical theory, provided it is left in its proper connection, and viewed in the proper light. The Word of God teaches us, indeed, that by grace we become one plant with Christ, so that our old nature is crucified with Him, and with Him we are raised to newness of life. We are crucified with Christ, and we are raised with Him, and we are set with Him in heavenly places. Scripture teaches, indeed, that in and through the suffering and death of Christ, sin itself was condemned in the flesh, so that it has no longer the right and the power to have dominion over us. Rom. 8:3. And thus there is surely power in the cross to deliver us from the power and corruption of sin through our union with Christ. But we must not overlook the fact that the Word of God always presents this power of deliverance from the dominion and defilement of sin as the fruit of the cross, never as the ground of our reconciliation and justification. The latter is found only in the vicarious suffering of our Lord, in His perfect sacrifice for sin, never in our being crucified with Christ in mystical union with Him. And, secondly, this spiritual fruit of the death of Christ is given us only on the ground of His perfect satisfaction, and of our being justified by faith in Him. We are not justified because we die and rise with Christ in the mystical sense, but we are delivered and sanctified because we are justified through His blood. Justification is ever the ground of our sanctification.

All these theories of the meaning and power of the death of Christ must be rejected. They are a denial of the one sacrifice of Christ accomplished on the cross. They deprive us of the sure ground of our salvation, and of the only comfort in life and death, that we are not our own, but belong to our faithful

Saviour Jesus Christ, who fully satisfied for all our sins, and delivered us from all the power of the devil. For this sure ground can only be the righteousness of God, realized in the perfect obedience and satisfaction of Christ, imputed to us freely by grace, and given unto us and appropriated by us through faith. All these theories somehow substitute a righteousness of man for the righteousness of God; and the former can never be the ground of our salvation. God was in Christ reconciling the world unto Himself, not imputing their trespasses unto them. For He hath made Him sin that knew no sin, that we might become the righteousness of God in Him. All this was actually accomplished nineteen hundred years ago. It is purely of God, in no wise of us. Not our goodness, not our faith, not our religion or piety, not anything that is of us can possibly be the ground of our salvation. But the righteousness of God through Jesus Christ, and that righteousness absolutely alone, is the ground of our hope in God, the sure basis of all our salvation, our eternal peace!

VII

Atoned For The Elect

Christ is the High Priest of His people. And His people are they whom the Father hath given Him before the foundation of the world. And these are the elect, chosen and ordained unto eternal life out of free and sovereign grace. And His sacrifice to atone for the sins of sinful men, was brought, not for all men head for head, but only for those whom the Father had sovereignly ordained unto eternal life, and chosen in Him. That this is true is abundantly testified by all the Scriptures. Christ Himself frequently speaks of this. To the Jews in Capernaum He declares: "For I came down from heaven, not to do mine own will, but the will of him that sent me. And this is the Father's will which hath sent me, that of all *which he hath given me* I should lose nothing, but should raise it up again at the last day." John 6:38, 39. Hence, the Lord is never discouraged, even though under His preaching the things of the kingdom of heaven are hid from the wise and prudent, and revealed only to the babes, for He knows that this is the good pleasure of the Father, Matt. 11:26. And "all that the Father giveth me shall come to me." John 6:37. He is the good shepherd, and He knows His sheep, and is known of His. And He lays down His life, not for all men, but for His sheep. It is not the free will of man that determines who shall belong to His sheep, for the Saviour knows His sheep as those whom the Father gave Him, even before they know Him. Hence, he can declare: "And other sheep I have, which are not of this fold: them also must I bring, and they shall hear my voice; and there shall be one fold, and one shepherd." John 10:14-16. To the opposing and murmuring Jews he says: "But ye believe not, because ye are not of my sheep, as I said unto you." Let us take note of this remarkable word. Many may be inclined to turn this saying of the Lord about, so that it would read: "Ye are not of my sheep, because ye believe not." Nevertheless, the Lord emphatically declares the very opposite: because they are not His sheep, i.e. because they do not belong to His God-given flock, therefore they do not believe. His sheep surely hear His voice, and He knows them, and they follow Him, and He gives them eternal life. And no one is ever able to pluck them out of His hand. His Father Who gave Him the sheep is stronger than all, and no one can pluck them out of His Father's hand. John 10:26-29. Only those, then, whom the Father ordained to life and gave to Jesus, belong to His sheep. And for them He gave His life, and offered the perfect sacrifice on the cross.

It is for the elect, too, that the Lord prays in His sacerdotal intercession. Very clear this is from the Lord's high priestly prayer as it is preserved for us in John 17. Expressly He declares there: "I pray for them: I pray not for the world, but for them which thou hast given me; for they are thine." It is true, that in the narrowest sense and in the first instance these words have reference to the disciples. But this does not alter the fact that, according to Jesus' own words "the world" is excluded from His prayer. This is evident, not only from vs. 9, but also from the whole chapter. In the entire chapter the term "world" stands in sharp antithesis to those whom the Father has given to the Saviour, and must, therefore, be interpreted as referring to the reprobate ungodly. To His own Christ gave His word, and the world hated them, because they are not of the world even as He is not of the world, vs. 14. Besides, He does not limit His prayer to those that were with Him in the world at that moment, but extends it to all that will believe on Him through their word, vs. 20. Yet, even so, all that will ever believe are those whom the Father gave Him, the elect, and for them He prays: "Father, I will, that they also, whom thou hast given me, be with me where I am; that they may behold my glory which thou hast given me; for thou lovedst me before the foundation of the world." vs. 24. For the elect, then, the Saviour prays, and that, too, for them in distinction from the world for whom He does not pray. But since this sacerdotal intercessory prayer is based on His redemptive work on the cross, on His perfect sacrifice of atonement, it follows that the latter is as limited as the former, and that He shed His lifeblood for the elect alone.

Besides, the doctrine of limited atonement is in harmony with the whole Word of God. It is those He hath foreknown, and predestined to be conformed according to the image of His Son, that He might be the firstborn among many brethren, whom He hath also called, and justified, and glorified. Rom. 8:29, 30. But surely, this implies that it was also for them that Christ offered Himself on the cross, for their calling and justification and glorification rest in the atonement. Accordingly, He hath blessed us with all spiritual blessings in heavenly places in Christ, and these blessings all have their ground in the perfect sacrifice and obedience of Christ, *according as He hath chosen us* before the foundation of the world. Eph. 1:3, 4. If the elect alone receive the spiritual blessings, it is because they alone are in Christ from before the foundation of the world, they alone were in Him on the cross, and for them alone Christ atoned. He predestinated the elect unto the adoption of children by Jesus Christ to Himself, according to the good pleasure of His will, to the praise of the glory of His grace, whereby He has made us acceptable in the beloved, and, therefore, these elect have the redemption in His blood, the forgiveness of sins. Eph. 1:5-7. The blessing of forgiveness, though appropriated by faith, does not rest on faith, but solely on the atoning sacrifice of Christ. And while this spiritual blessing flows from the eternal good pleasure of God to the elect, it follows that also the atonement was accomplished for them alone. Hence, these also have become an inheritance, being predestinated according to the purpose of Him Who worketh all things according to the counsel of His own will, Eph. 1:11. Many more passages of Scripture might be added to these to prove that the Word of God does, indeed, clearly teach the truth of limited atonement, the doctrine that Christ died, as far as His intention and the purpose of the Father are concerned, not for all men, but for the elect only.

And even though this truth is bitterly opposed by many, and, especially in our day, the preaching runs generally along bold Arminian lines, the opponents cannot successfully appeal to Scripture for their view that Christ died for all men.

This does not mean that they do not make the attempt to support their theory of universal atonement by passages from Holy Writ. On the contrary, they point to many texts that, considered apart from their context, and without application to them of the *regula Scripturae,* seem to teach that Jesus died for all.

They reveal special preference for passages that contain the term "world," or the word "all," in connection with God's purpose of salvation. God so loved *the world* that He gave His only begotten Son, that whosoever believeth in Him should not perish, but have everlasting life. God was in Christ, reconciling *the world* unto Himself, not imputing their trespasses unto them. And He is a propitiation, not only for our sins, but also for the sins of the whole world. John 3:16; II Cor. 5:19; I John 2:2. And the contention is that *the world* denotes all men and every man. And so they point out, Scripture frequently speaks of *all men,* or simply of *all.* As by the offense of one judgment came to all men to condemnation, so by the righteousness of one the free gift came upon *all men* to justification of life. Rom. 5:18. Sound exegesis, they claim, demands that, seeing that the term *all men* occurs twice in this passage, they must be interpreted as having the same implication. And seeing that there can be no doubt about the fact that the first *all men* refers to every member of the human race, the same term must have the same comprehensive meaning in the second part of this passage. And there are many similar passages. God wills that *all men* shall be saved, and come to the knowledge of the truth, I Tim. 2:4. The grace of God that bringeth salvation hath appeared to *all men,* Tit. 2:11. And He is not willing that any should perish, but that *all* should come to repentance. II Pet. 3:9. On the basis of these and similar passages they attempt to gainsay the doctrine of limited atonement, and to maintain that Christ died for every man.

It would require too much space, were we to examine all these passages in detail. Nor is this necessary. Rather do we point the reader to some fundamental errors in exegesis that must be, and are actually committed by those who elicit from them the doctrine of universal atonement.

The first, and most important, of these is the violation of the rule that words may not be lifted out of their context, but must be interpreted as defined by the context in which they occur.

Thus, with respect to the term "world," it should be plain from a comparison of a few passages of Holy Writ: (1) That it does not denote the same concept wherever it occurs in Scripture, and (2) That it never means the same as *all men*. Compare, for instance, John 3:16 with John 17:9, and with I John 2:15-17, and you will see this at once. God loved the world, to be sure; but Jesus prays not for the world; and in I John 2:15-17 we are told that we must not love the world, neither the things that are in the world; that all that is in the world is the lust of the flesh, and the lust of the eyes, and the pride of life; that this is not of the Father, but of the world; and that the world passeth away, and the lust thereof. Who does not see that in these passages the same term refers to two entirely different concepts, and that, therefore, you cannot explain the word *world* at random as simply meaning *all men?* Who, moreover, cannot for himself draw the conclusion, that, since both these "worlds" are in our present world as we see it, so that each is but a part of it, neither can possibly refer to all men, but in one instance it refers to the world of the ungodly, in the other instance to the world of the godly according to God's election? John 3:16 refers to God's world, to the world as it is the object of His everlasting love; and the world for the which Christ refuses to pray is excluded from this world of God's love. For the latter God sent His Son, and for the latter He died.

The same is true of the term *all men,* or *all,* or even *every.* These terms dare not be interpreted as referring to all men that ever lived, and shall live, or even to all men that lived in the whole world at a certain period of time. Their content and scope must be determined from the context in which they occur. A few examples ought to make this plain. In I Tim. 4:4 the apostle writes: "For every creature of God is good, and nothing to be refused, if it be received with thanksgiving." The context, as well as the text, plainly shows that the meaning is: "every creature of God is good to eat." But who would be so foolish as to insist that the apostle here teaches that every existing thing, stone and wood, iron and steel, rats and mice, etc., is good for man's consumption? No one has any objection to limit the term "every creature" to *every eatable creature*. In I Tim. 5:20 we read: "Them that sin rebuke before all, that others also may fear." Is there anyone that has any objection to limit the word *all* in this text to a very limited group? Does anyone insist that the apostle means all men head for head? Or would anyone understand the words of the apostle as meaning that the church ought to call a meeting of the whole town and all the citizens on the public marketplace, in order there to rebuke the offending church member? Of course not! We understand without difficulty that at most the whole church is meant, or, perhaps, all that are involved in the offense committed. Or consider the text in II Tim. 1:15: "This thou knowest, that all they which are in Asia be turned away from me." Does the apostle refer to all the inhabitants of Asia? Or has he in mind, perhaps, all the saints in Asia? No one understands the words in that sense. He refers to a very limited group of men, of coworkers, perhaps. But why, then, should we insist that when the matter of salvation is the subject *all*, or *every*, or *all men*, must needs refer to every individual in the world? Is it not very evident that this cannot possibly be the meaning in Tit. 2:11: "For the grace of God that bringeth salvation hath appeared to all men?" Mark you well, that the apostle here asserts that saving grace had at that time, at the time when he wrote his epistle to Titus, already appeared to all men, which certainly implies that the gospel of salvation had already been preached to all. But could the apostle possibly mean that in his own day there was not a single living man that had not heard the gospel? We know better.

Thousands upon thousands had never been reached by the preaching as yet. And we have no difficulty to understand the words of the apostle, considered in the light of the context, as meaning that the grace of God that bringeth salvation had appeared to all classes of men, to aged men and women, as well as to young men and young women, to servants as well as to masters. And thus the context must determine the meaning of *all*, or *all men*, wherever it occurs.

But insistence upon finding proof for the doctrine of universal atonement in such passages that contain the word *world*, or the terms *all men*, or *all*, implies another exegetical error, the error, namely, that justice is not and cannot be done to the rest of the texts in which such words occur.

Take, for example, the text in II Cor. 5:19: "To wit, that God was in Christ, reconciling the world unto himself, not imputing their trespasses unto them." Suppose that we understand the term "world" in this passage as meaning "all men" in the strict sense of that word. Then what does the text teach? Evidently this, that all men are saved. If all men are reconciled to God, so that God does not impute their trespasses unto them, it follows that all men are saved. Their sins were atoned for nineteen hundred years ago, and they are blotted out for ever. But the Arminian understands very well that this would prove too much, for as a matter of fact all men are not saved. And so he is compelled to weaken the meaning of reconciliation, and to explain the text as teaching that in the cross of Christ there is a way, a chance, an opportunity of reconciliation, which is to be realized through man's consent to be reconciled. That this is a corruption of the text is evident. For in the cross of Christ, God actually did blot out the sin of "the world," He actually did reconcile "the world" unto Himself, and He nevermore imputes the sins unto that world. It should be evident, then, that by "world" in this text is meant the same as by that term in John 3:16: God's elect world.

The same applies to Rom. 5:18: "Therefore as by the offense of one judgment came upon all men to condemnation; even so by the righteousness of one the free gift came upon all men to justification of life." As we already mentioned, those who find the doctrine of universal atonement in this passage insist that the term *all men* must be given the same content and scope in both members of the text. Suppose we give that meaning to this term in both instances, and see what is the result. The second part of the passage would, in that case, signify that the gift of grace unto justification is actually bestowed upon every man that ever lived and will live, which means that all men are actually saved. Now, again, this would prove too much even for the Arminian, seeing that all men are not saved. Hence, the attempt is made to explain the text as meaning that, as far as God's intention is concerned, the gift of grace came upon all men, but that the actual reception of this gift of grace depends upon the free will of men. Even if this interpretation were possible, the concept "all men" would still have to be limited, unless it may be supposed that there will be an opportunity to accept this gift after death, for, in the first place, the knowledge of this gift in the old dispensation was limited to a very few, and, in the second place, even in the new dispensation millions die without ever coming into contact with the gospel. But apart from this consideration, the text does not allow such an interpretation. We must not overlook that there is a comparison here: "*as* by the offense of one judgment came upon all men to condemnation, *even so* by the righteousness of one the free gift came upon all men to justification of life." The question, therefore, must be asked: how, in what way, did by the offense of one judgment unto condemnation come to all men? With their consent? By their own free will? Not at all, but only by God's imputation of the sin of Adam to all. No choice of their free will can undo this fact. But then must the same truth be applied to the second member of the passage: the fact that the free gift unto justification of life comes upon men does not depend upon their own choice, but is an objective fact: those for whom the gift is intended are surely saved, and that, too, by an act of God alone. If this is true, however, the term *all men* in both members of the text can only mean: all men in Adam . . . all men in Christ. And the passage cannot be quoted in support of the doctrine of unlimited atonement.

We will examine one more passage that is frequently quoted by those who teach that Christ died for all men, and that God intends all men to be saved. It is the well-known text from II Peter 3:9: "The Lord is not slack concerning his promise, as some men count slackness; but he is longsuffering to usward, not willing that any should perish, but that all should come to repentance." The general meaning of the text is plain. God's people had to endure much suffering for Christ's sake. And in their suffering they looked forward to the realization of the promise, i.e. to the speedy return of Christ their Lord in glory. However, it appeared to them that he delayed His coming, that God was slack in the fulfillment of His promise. The apostle, however, explains that God is not slack concerning His promise. He is longsuffering over His people in tribulation, that is, He longs to deliver them, and, no doubt, will deliver them as soon as possible, but, speaking from a human viewpoint, He waits until the time is ripe. And when is the time ripe for the final coming of the Saviour from heaven and the perfect redemption? This is indicated in the last part of the text: God will not that any should perish, but that all come to repentance. The meaning of the text is, therefore, that God's longsuffering must and will endure until this condition is fulfilled, until no one shall have perished, and all shall have come to repentance. For this the realization of the promise and the coming of Christ must wait. But if this is understood, is there any possibility left of interpreting the *all* in the text as referring to every individual man? There is not, for that would mean that the final salvation would never be revealed, that the promise would never be fulfilled, that Christ would never return. Always there are many that perish. All men never come to repentance. That, therefore, cannot be the will of God, nor the meaning of the text. But the text is perfectly plain if to *all* is given the meaning of all the elect, the whole Church, the fulness of the Body of Christ. Then the meaning is: God is longsuffering to usward, i.e. to His chosen Church in the world, for He is not willing that any of us, that is, of His elect Church, shall perish; the coming of Christ, and the realization of the promise must wait until the last one of the elect shall have come to repentance.

These examples may suffice to teach us that we must be on our guard when the Arminian quotes texts at random in support of his contention that Christ died for all men, according to His and God's intention. Superficially considered such passages may leave the the impression that they can serve as a basis for the doctrine of universal atonement. However, when they are studied somewhat more closely, and in the light of their context, it soon becomes evident that this superficial impression is erroneous. Scripture teaches plainly that our Saviour brought the sacrifice of atonement for the elect alone, and there are no passages in Holy Writ that contradict this truth.

We will close this chapter by adding to what has been said about Christ's dying and making satisfaction for the elect only, a few remarks concerning the Arminian presentation of this matter.

First of all, it should be evident that the Arminian view of election can be of no value or help to him in the defense of a *Christus pro omnibus,* a Christ for all. The former cannot really serve as a basis for the latter.

Also the Arminian professes to believe in the truth of election. It is too plainly taught in the Scriptures to be denied altogether. No one who believes the Bible, and claims to derive his doctrine from the Scriptures, can simply ignore the truth that God has chosen His people from before the foundation of the world. But the Arminian offers his own explanation of this truth. He has his own conception of sovereign election unto salvation. According to him, eternal election is based on God's prescience, His foreknowledge of those that would believe in Christ, and that would persevere unto the end. He did not choose sovereignly, without respect to works. He chose them that, in His foreknowledge or prevision, He knew would accept Christ as their Saviour.

But let us suppose for a moment that this view is correct. Can the doctrine of universal atonement be made to rest upon this view of election as its basis?

Plainly, this is impossible.

If God foreknew from eternity the number of them that will believe in Christ, and accept Him as their Saviour, it is evident that this number is fixed. It cannot be changed. No one can add to it, nor can anyone ever subtract from it. For, either God foreknew this number with divine certainty, and then the number of the foreknown elect is unchangeably determined; or the number of them that are saved is undetermined, contingent upon the mind and will of man, but then even God does not foreknow it. But again, if God foreknew with absolute certainty the number of them that would be saved in Christ, if He had written all their names in the book of His foreknowledge from before the foundation of the world, He has that number in His mind and heart eternally, and eternally, with an unchangeable love, He loves them. He knew them as such in the hour of Christ's suffering on the accursed tree. And Christ as the Son of God knew them. What is more, if He foreknew all that would believe and be saved through the blood of Christ, He also knew with the same divine, unchangeable certainty, all that would reject the Christ and hate Him, and crucify Him afresh. And even as He knew His own in love, so He foreknew the enemies of Christ in divine hatred. Foreknowing this, and knowing this, i.e. being unchangeably mindful of this foreknowledge in love and foreknowledge of hatred, is it even conceivable that God gave His Son unto the death of the cross for those whom He foreknew as His everlasting enemies in wrath and hatred? And is it conceivable that Christ, also foreknowing all that would not believe in Him, would, nevertheless, pay the price of their redemption for them?

It should be evident that the doctrine of an election based on the foreknowledge of God cannot possibly serve as the ground of the theory that Christ shed His lifeblood for all.

He necessarily atoned only for the elect.

Finally, it must be pointed out that the Arminian doctrine of a *Christus pro omnibus,* of universal atonement, is, in principle, a denial of vicarious atonement.

If Christ died for all, *He died instead of no one!*

And if the Arminian will only be consistent, and carry out his doctrine to its utmost consequences, he will prove to be a modernist. History, the history of dogma, clearly proves this statement. No church can with impunity deny the doctrine of sovereign election and of particular atonement.

That is the grave danger for the church of the Arminian view.

Let us make plain the intrinsic necessity of the movement from Arminianism to modernism, from the doctrine that Christ died for all to the denial that He atoned at all, i.e. that He fully satisfied for all our sins.

What is the implication of the doctrine of vicarious atonement and satisfaction? It means: 1. That sin is guilt, liability to punishment, worthiness of God's wrath and damnation. 2. That the justice of God must be satisfied if the sinner is ever to be received by God in favor, be freed from the power of death, and be made worthy of life. 3. That the justice of God can only be satisfied by a payment that is made for sin, and that this payment must consist in bearing the wrath of God and the punishment for sin by an act of perfect obedience in love. 4. That, while the sinner can never perform this act of perfect obedience and satisfy the justice of God, God ordained His only begotten Son to represent them as the Christ, and to perform the act of obedience unto and in death *for* them, *in their stead.* 5. That Christ did just this on the cross. He represented us. He was our Vicar. And because He was legally before God our Vicar, He was able to take our sins, the guilt and responsibility for them, upon Himself. And He suffered and died in our stead. He fully paid for all our sins. This is simply an objective fact. All the guilt of sin of those for whom Christ died on the tree is for ever blotted out. Objectively, they whom Christ represented on the cross are justified and worthy of eternal life. They can never be condemned.

Let us clearly understand this, for the truth of vicarious atonement means exactly this.

Suppose that one hundred people owe a debt of one thousand dollars each to a certain creditor. And imagine that some millionaire, loving those people and understanding that they have nothing to pay their debt, approaches their creditor and pays him one hundred thousand dollars to cancel the debt of the one hundred. Are not all the one hundred debtors debt-free? Can the creditor ever exact another payment from him? You agree: their debt is paid once for all; no payment can be demanded of them anymore. Suppose their benefactor announces to the one hundred debtors that he fully paid all they owed their creditors; and suppose again that they do not believe him; does that make any difference as to their debt-free state? You say: of course not, for their being free from all debt does not depend upon their believing the fact of its having been paid, but simply upon the act of their benefactor by which he satisfied the demands of the creditor. Their benefactor vicariously satisfied the righteous demand of their creditor, and for ever paid all their debt in their stead. Suppose that the law of the land is that any debtor that does not pay his debts can be sentenced to jail; can the one hundred for whom their benefactor paid, ever be so sentenced, whether they believe or disbelieve that their debt is paid? Of course not. They are free from punishment.

Now let us apply this illustration to the vicarious atonement and satisfaction of Christ according to the Arminian view that Christ died for all. What follows? You answer: if Christ really satisfied for the sins of all men, if He really paid the debt for all, it must follow that all are objectively justified before God, and that all are saved. And you are right. For their justification, the cancelling of their debt with God and their eternal righteousness does not at all depend upon their faith in this objective justification, but only on the objective fact of the vicarious satisfaction of Christ, their benefactor. Suppose they do not believe that Christ's sacrifice atoned for their sins; does that make the fact of none effect? Of course not. Can God justly demand payment for their sins from them? No; the punishment for sin is borne once for all, and all are free and worthy of life.

Vicarious atonement necessarily implies that all for whom Christ atoned are absolutely, objectively, for ever free from the guilt of sin, and worthy of eternal life.

If, then, Christ vicariously atoned for all men, all are saved, and all will have eternal life.

But the fact is, and even the Arminian must face it, that all men are not actually saved.

The Arminian proposition, therefore, must be, and actually is: Christ died for all men, but all men are not justified and saved.

What follows from this Arminian proposition as to the value and power of the death of Christ? This, that although He died for all men, He did not vicariously atone for all, for if He had all men would be justified before God and be worthy of eternal life.

And, therefore, the man who teaches that Christ died for all men must deny that His death has the power of vicarious satisfaction. He must invent other theories of the death of Christ, such as the governmental, the moral, the mystical conception, which we already discussed, and exposed as false and contrary to Scripture.

And thus, Arminianism is, in principle, nothing but modernism.

The doctrine of universal atonement is very dangerous for the Church of Christ in the world.

And this also holds for the camouflaged Arminianism that professes to believe in sovereign election, and in particular atonement, but presents the gospel as a well-meaning offer of salvation on the part of God to all men without distinction. God's well-meaning "offer" of salvation cannot possibly be wider in scope than the objective satisfaction and justification of the cross of Christ. And those that preach a well-meaning offer of God to all men, must and will ultimately embrace the doctrine of universal atonement also.

Let us contend for the true faith, and by God's grace keep ourselves far from all these Arminian corruptions!

VIII

Christ Our Intercessor

In the eighth chapter of his epistle to the Romans, the apostle Paul writes: "Who is he that condemneth? It is Christ that died, yea rather, that is risen again, who is even at the right hand of God, who also maketh intercession for us." vs. 34.

Yea rather!

The meaning is, that however important it may be that Christ died, and that, therefore, there is no power anywhere in the universe that is able to condemn us, it still is of greater importance that He is risen again, that He is exalted at the right hand of God, and that in heaven He makes intercession for His people with the Father. In fact, His death would be of no avail, could be of no benefit to us, had He not also risen again, for His resurrection is God's own seal upon His vicarious sacrifice and perfect obedience. And again, the power of His resurrection would never become a power of salvation for us, had not the risen Christ also ascended up to heaven, and were He not at the right hand of God, ever living to make inter-cession for us. What we need is the living Christ to save us. We do need the Christ crucified, Who was delivered for our transgressions, the *Jesus for us*. But no less do we need the Christ exalted, the living Christ Who has the power to deliver us from the bondage of sin and death, and to make us actual partakers of eternal life, the *Christ in us*. Even as it belonged to the office of the typical high priest of the old dispensation to sacrifice in behalf of the people, but also to pray for them, and to bless them with the blessing of Jehovah their God, so it belongs to the high-priestly office of our Saviour, not only that He bring the perfect sacrifice in their stead and in their behalf, but also that He intercede for them, and make them partaker of all the spiritual blessings of grace.

The work of Christ is not finished on the cross.

It is true that just before He died the Saviour cried out: "It is finished." But this next to the last cross utterance dare not be interpreted as signifying that all that pertains to the work of salvation, as far as our Lord was concerned in it, was now accomplished, and that henceforth He can rest and wait for the fruit upon His labors. The outcry must rather be understood as having reference to His suffering, to the perfect sacrifice which He was to bring on the cross. In His flesh He must suffer death in all its horrible darkness. He must taste the depth of death before He gave up the ghost. He must bear the full burden of the wrath of God against the sin of His people. There was, therefore, a measure for His suffering. And that measure was now filled. Whatever He had to suffer in the flesh had been borne to the end. Obediently He had entered into the nethermost parts of the earth. Of this He is conscious even at the cross. The head of the serpent had been crushed. He may now give up the ghost, confident that He shall presently enter into the glory of His resurrection. And with a view to this accomplished sacrifice He cried out: "It is finished."

But His work as Saviour is not ended with His death on the cross.

He arose, and He entered into the glory of the Father, not merely in order to enjoy His own glory, but that the salvation He merited for His people by His perfect obedience might become the possession of all the Father had given Him.

Nor do the blessings of righteousness and life come into the possession of sinners merely by His being proclaimed and preached in all the world, and by men's accepting this Christ as their personal Saviour.

Nor again may the matter of salvation be presented as if Christ is the mediator of atonement and reconciliation, on the basis of Whose perfect sacrifice we obtained the right to righteousness and life, and that now it is God, *apart from Christ,* Who makes us partakers of the benefits of Christ.

On the contrary, all the work of salvation is accomplished and perfected through Christ as the Mediator. Out of God and through Christ we receive all the blessings of grace. He is not only the Mediator of reconciliation, but also the Mediator of the application of this salvation to us, of our actual deliverance from the dominion of sin and death, of our regeneration and calling, our faith and justification, our sanctification and perseverance, our perfection and glorification. This truth is expressed in the confession that Christ is our intercessor with the Father. As the High Priest of His people He is ascended into heaven, entered into the true holy of holies, ever lives to make intercession for them, in order that He may bless them with all the spiritual blessings in heavenly places which He merited for them by His perfect sacrifice and obedience.

Thus the Heidelberg Catechism teaches us.

Speaking of Christ as our only High Priest, the instructor not only mentions the perfect sacrifice of His body, whereas He has redeemed us, but also emphasizes that He "makes continual intercession with the Father for us." And to this continual intercession of our only High Priest we must now pay particular attention.

Scripture very frequently refers to this prayer of Christ in our behalf.

It teaches us that we *have* a great high priest, that is passed into the heavens, Jesus the Son of God, and that He is not an high priest that cannot be touched with the feeling of our infirmities, but Who was in all points tempted even as we are, though without sin. And it is exactly because of the presence of this great high priest in the inner sanctuary of God that we may come boldly unto the throne of grace, confident that we will obtain mercy, and find grace to help in time of need. Heb. 4:14-16. He is the forerunner, Who entered into the holies for us, there to remain an high priest for ever after the order of Melchisedec. Heb. 6:20. In distinction from all priests that were before Him, "this man, because he continueth ever, hath an unchangeable priesthood. Wherefore he is able to save them to the uttermost that come unto God by him, seeing he ever liveth to make intercession for them." Heb. 7:24, 25. And "we have an high priest, who is set on the right hand of the throne of the Majesty in the heavens; a minister of the sanctuary, and of the true tabernacle, which the Lord pitched, and not man." Heb. 8:1, 2. "For Christ is not entered into the holy places made with hands, which are the figures of the true; but into heaven itself, now to appear in the presence of God for us." Heb. 9:24. While, therefore, we have boldness to enter into the holiest by the blood of Jesus, by a new and living way, which He has consecrated for us, through the veil, that is to say, His flesh, and while, moreover, we have in that holiest an high priest over the house of God, we may surely draw near, and ourselves enter into the sanctuary, with a true heart, and in full assurance of faith. Heb. 10:19-22. "And if any man sin, we have an advocate with the Father, Jesus Christ the righteous." I John 2:1. Who then is he that condemneth? Christ has not only died, He is also risen, He is also at the right hand of God, He also makes intercession for us. Rom. 8:34.

Hence, according to Scripture, Christ is not only our High Priest in that He redeemed us by the one sacrifice of His body, but also in His continual intercession, which has its answer in His blessing us with all spiritual blessings in heavenly places.

The question is: how must we conceive of this intercessory prayer of our Lord as our High Priest in the heavenly sanctuary? How does He intercede for us at the throne of grace?

In answer to this question, we must, on the one hand, eliminate from our conception of this heavenly mystery all that is earthy, temporal, and imperfect. Even though Scripture necessarily employs figurative language, and speaks in earthly language, to aid our understanding of the heavenly realities, yet we must never forget that all these terms and symbols have a deeper, spiritual, heavenly meaning. There is, of course, no material throne in heaven, on the which there is seated a visible manifestation of the invisible God, and before which our Saviour appears occasionally to utter a prayer in behalf of His redeemed people. Christ, let us remember, is Himself the person of the Son of God, the second Person of the Holy

Trinity, God of God, in His divine nature one in essence with the Father and the Holy Ghost, eternally dwelling in the Father's bosom. And in His glorified human nature He has the most intimate fellowship with the Father. He took our human nature into the most intimate communion with God that is possible, and the union of the divine and human natures in Him is rooted in and rests in the divine Person. It is, therefore, not partial but perfect and complete; not temporal and occasional, but everlasting and constant; not mediate but immediate. Hence, all that is imperfect, temporal, earthy, mediate, must be eliminated from this communion of Christ with the Father, and from its expression in the intercessory prayer of our Lord in our behalf. And, on the other hand, we dare not speak about this sacerdotal intercession as if it were a mere figure of speech, without a corresponding reality, but we must rather insist that it is highest and deepest reality: as a petition it is the most perfect and highest possible realization of true prayer; and as intercession it is the richest and ultimate expression and function of His mediatorial office of High Priest.

Two aspects, therefore, there are to this intercessory prayer.

As *prayer* it is directed to God. And it is highest reality. Even as with us prayer signifies that we seek and find the Father, that we exercise fellowship with Him, that we speak to Him in adoration and petition, that we open our hearts and pour them out before Him, and that we approach Him as the overflowing Fount of all good, in order that we may drink from that Fountain and be satisfied, that we may receive His grace and Spirit: so the prayer of Christ as our High Priest in the heavenly sanctuary is a real seeking and finding of the Most Blessed, fellowship with Him, a pouring out of His Mediator's heart before Him, to receive from Him and out of Him all the fulness of the blessings of salvation for His people. Only, while with us this fellowship with God, this drinking out of the eternal and overflowing Fount of all good, is very much in part and imperfect, with Christ it is perfect and constant. Constantly He stands in the attitude and relation of prayer to God, and constantly He receives from the Father the full answer to His prayer.

And as *intercession* it is directed to the salvation of His people as its end. In this prayer the Lord is ever conscious of His inseparable union with the elect. Not for one moment is this prayer concerned with Himself alone. He prays for His own, for those whom the Father has given Him. He prays as the High Priest over the whole house of God, as the representative of all those for whom He shed His lifeblood on the accursed tree, as the Head of the Church, which is His body. And He prays in order that He may bestow the fulness of grace and blessings He receives from the Father upon His people.

It is strictly a mediatorial prayer.

We must remember the relation which He sustains to His people, and the relation in which He, with His people, stands to the Father.

He and His people are inseparably united. They are one. He is their Head, they are members of His body.

And this unity is both legal and spiritual, forensic and organic.

His people are, so to speak, a legal corporation of which Christ is the Head in the representative sense of the word.

But they are also a living spiritual body, united with Christ as their Head in the organic sense.

Only when we bear this in mind can we somewhat understand the necessity and significance of Christ's intercession with the Father in behalf of His people.

As their Head in the representative sense of the word He was authorized to accomplish all the work of salvation for them, in their stead, and in their behalf, and with it to appear before the Father as the ground of His intercessory prayer. In this capacity, our only High Priest took upon Himself the guilt of our sins, and in the hour of wrath and judgment bore them away on the accursed tree. As such He could enter into death in their stead, and blot out all their sins, yea, obtain for them eternal righteousness, the right to all the blessedness of salvation, eternal life and glory. Our righteousness, our right to redemption and liberation from the power of sin and death, and to the glory of God's eternal tabernacle, is never in us, it is always and only in Him. We lie in the midst of death. Apart from Christ, we are not righteous for one moment. On the contrary, we are guilty, and worthy of eternal damnation. We must never overlook or distort this truth. Perhaps, we are inclined to imagine that, when once we are justified by faith, we have a certain ground of righteousness in ourselves. But it is never so. Christ is and remains our only righteousness for ever. If it were possible that we could even for one moment be separated from Christ as our Head in the judicial sense of the word, that moment we would be damnable in our sin and guilt. However, this is for ever impossible, because this relationship between Christ and His people is rooted in sovereign election. Christ's perfect obedience, therefore, is our only righteousness. Hence, on the basis of that obedience He also represents us as our Intercessor with the Father. On the ground of His perfect righteousness, merited for us, He can say: "Father, I will that they also, whom thou hast given me, be with me where I am; that they may behold my glory, which thou hast given me: for thou lovedst me before the foundation of the world." John 17:24. And this implies that on the basis of His merits He prays the Father for all those spiritual blessings that are indispensable to bring them where He is, and to place them in a position to behold His glory.

It is true, this prayer also becomes our own, but this is possible only through Him, in His name, and on the basis of His perfect right to intercede for us.

But even so all is not said.

If we do not say more we create the impression that Christ's intercession simply means that He petitions the Father to bestow all the blessings of salvation upon us, but that with the actual bestowal of these blessings our High Priest has nothing to do. Upon His prayer God makes us partakers of His grace without Christ. The river of the water of life flows directly from the throne of God, apart from Christ, into the New Jerusalem.

But this is not according to Scripture.

It belonged to the calling of the high priest under the old dispensation, not only to sacrifice and pray for the people, but also to bless them.

The river of the water of life flows from the throne of God *and of the Lamb.* It is true, indeed, that Christ promised that He would pray the Father, and He would send us another Comforter, that He might abide with us for ever, John 14:16. It is equally true, however, that He said that He Himself would send the Comforter, the Spirit of truth, unto us, John 16:7. And on the day of Pentecost it is, indeed, He, the exalted Christ, that pours out the Spirit, Acts 2:33. He *is* the water of life, which we must drink; the bread of life, which we must eat unto eternal life. He is made unto us wisdom from God, righteousness, sanctification, and redemption.

Hence, we receive all the blessings of salvation out of Him.

He bestows them upon us.

He imparts Himself to all the elect. For He is their Head, not only in the juridical sense of the word, but also in the spiritual, organic sense. He is the vine, they are the branches. He is the Head, they are the members of His body. There is a spiritual bond that unites them to Him. Hence, they live out of Him, and He, as the quickening Spirit, lives in them. All the spiritual blessings they need as sinners, guilty and damnable, corrupt and defiled, dead through trespasses and sins in themselves, to become living children of God, liberated, justified, sanctified, and glorified, flow from Him unto them. He is ascended up on high, leading captivity captive, to give gifts unto men, Eph. 4:8. He it is that gives to His Church in the world "some apostles; and some, prophets; and some, evangelists; and some, pastors and teachers; For the perfecting of the saints, for the work of the ministry, for the edifying of the body of Christ." Eph. 4:11, 12. For he "fills all things." Eph. 4:10. And He it is, too, out of Whom we receive "even grace for grace." John 1:16. And "as many as received him, to them gave he power to

become the sons of God, even to them that believe on his name."
John 1:12. And so, the grace of salvation in all its implications,
redemption and forgiveness of sins, adoption unto children and
eternal righteousness, sanctification and preservation, perseverance and glorification, reaches us, flows unto us from the
Christ, the Son of God come into the flesh, crucified and slain,
raised from the dead, and exalted in the highest heavens; Christ,
the resurrection and the life, our Intercessor with the Father!

But they come unto us from Him *as the Mediator.*

The only and deepest Fount of all the blessings of salvation
is the triune God. Out of God, but through Christ as the
Mediator, the stream of the water of life reaches us.

God is the limitless Ocean of life and bliss; Christ is the
reservoir that is constantly filled from the divine Ocean; and
out of the reservoir Christ, the river of the water of life flows
into the Church. "I in them, and thou in me, that they may be
made perfect in one."

Of God, through Him, and unto Him, are all things, also the
Christ in all the riches of His salvation.

In the light of all this, we can somewhat understand the
intercessory prayer of Christ. He prays the Father, and upon His
prayer He receives the Spirit and the power to send His Spirit
into the Church. He prays the Father, He, as the Son of God
in the exalted human nature; and upon His prayer He Himself
receives all the spiritual blessings from God, "the God and
Father of our Lord Jesus Christ," in order that He may bestow
the blessings of salvation upon His people, and "fill all things."

Thus it is constantly.

And thus it will be for ever. The living stream of the water
of life flows out of God, through Christ, into the Church.

Thus the intercessory prayer is very real.

It is the perfect prayer. It is characterized by none of the
imperfections that cleave unto our prayers. We know not what
we should pray for as we ought; Christ knows all our needs.

It is a constant prayer. Constantly, Christ stands in the attitude of prayer before the Father, that out of Him as the Fount He may receive all the blessings of grace to bestow them upon His people.

It is a prayer that is based on strictest justice and perfect righteousness, the righteousness of His own perfect sacrifice.

And it is always, and constantly heard!

Our Eternal King

In its explanation of the name Christ, "that is anointed," the Heidelberg Catechism finally points to Christ's eternal kingship. He is not only our chief Prophet and Teacher, and our only High Priest, but "also our eternal King, who governs us by his word and Spirit, and who defends and preserves us in (the enjoyment of) that salvation, he has purchased for us."

The words in parentheses do not belong in the text. The original reads: "und bei der erworbenen Erlösung schutzet und erhält," that is: "and defends and preserves us in the redemption obtained for us."

Christ, then, according to this confession, is the King of His Church. As such He rules over her and in her by His Word and Spirit, preserves and defends her in the midst of the world over against all the forces of darkness, and leads her unto the glory prepared for her before the foundation of the world. Unto this end, He is also King over all things, even over all the powers of evil, all principalities and powers are made subject unto Him. He has received a name above all names, and all power in heaven and in earth. And He uses His mighty power for the preservation of the elect, and unto the coming of the day of His return and the establishment of His eternal kingdom in glory.

He is King over His Church by grace.

But He is also the Lord of lords, and the King of kings by His power.

This glorious and comforting truth is denied by the Chiliasts, or Premillennialists.

According to them, Christ is not the King of the Church, but merely her Head in the organic sense. He is the king of the Jews, of the nation of Israel, and as such He must still be

revealed in the future. This national Israel, the Kingdom-
people proper, rejected Him in His first advent. He came unto
His own, but His own received Him not. On the contrary, they
crucified the Lord of glory, their King. Because of this the Jews
are for the time being rejected. They are in captivity, in exile,
in the diaspora, scattered over the face of the earth among all
nations. And during this period that the kingdom-people are
in the diaspora and God does not deal with them unto salvation, He gathers another people out of the Gentiles. This other
people, gathered in the interim of Israel's captivity, is the
Church, the body of Christ, the Bride of the Lamb, that will
be taken up in heavenly glory when it is complete. This Church
is not the kingdom of Christ. On the contrary, the Jews are and
remain forever the royal people of Christ, and Christ is their
anointed King. And when the Church shall have been gathered,
and the fulness of the Gentiles shall have come in, Christ shall
once more turn to His own, gather them out of all nations,
cause them to return to their own land, the Old Testament land
of Canaan, and rule over the house of Jacob and on the throne
of David for ever.

We cannot in this connection refute this theory in detail.
Fact is that it is based on a fundamentally wrong conception of
the relation between the old and the new dispensation, between
the Old and the New Testament, between the Church and
the kingdom of heaven. As to this last, there can be no question
about the fact that the only kingdom of which the New Testament ever speaks is the kingdom of heaven. And that the
relation between this kingdom and the Church is such that the
members of the latter are also the citizens of the former, cannot
be subject to doubt. Concerning the kingdom of heaven the
Lord taught the people in parables. Thus He explains that the
kingdom of heaven is likened unto a man who sowed good seed
in his field, but while men slept an enemy came and sowed
tares among the wheat. And He interprets that the field is the
world, the good seed are the children of the kingdom, and the
tares are the children of the wicked one. Surely, according to
this, the children of the kingdom are not the Jews, but the be-

lievers out of all nations, for "the field is the world." The enemy that sowed the tares is the devil; the harvest is the end of the world, so that nothing can be expected after that harvest; and the reapers are the angels. And when the time for the harvest is ripe, "the Son of man shall gather out of his kingdom (established in all the world) all things that offend and them which do iniquity; And shall cast them into a furnace of fire: there shall be wailing and gnashing of teeth. Then shall the righteous shine as the sun in the kingdom of their Father." Matt. 13:37-43. Surely, these righteous, these children of the kingdom, are not the Jews, but the elect gathered by Christ's word and Spirit out of all the nations of the world. The Church is also His kingdom, and He is our eternal King!

Now, as we discuss the kingship of Christ in connection with the twelfth Lord's Day of our Heidelberg Catechism, we must needs limit ourselves to a consideration of this function of our Saviour as an aspect of His office in general. If we fail to do this, we will be tempted also to treat of Christ's exaltation at the right hand of God, whereby He is raised to the glory of His present dominion over all things. The two are, of course, closely connected. Yet, of the latter we must not speak here, for of this the Catechism speaks in the nineteenth Lord's Day, in connection with the sixth article of the *Apostolicum*. Here, therefore, we must consider the kingship of our Lord in connection with His name *Christ, Messiah,* the Anointed of God. He is the Servant of Jehovah, God's officebearer, "ordained of God the Father, and anointed with the Holy Ghost." And this office, threefold though it be, is one. In a sense, it may be said to culminate in His kingship. For the Servant of Jehovah, Who as prophet reveals and glorifies the Father, as Priest consecrates Himself to God and fulfills all righteousness, is as such also king, authorized to be over the whole house of God, and to have dominion over all the works of God in His Name. Christ is priest after the order of Melchisedec, and, hence, He is priest-king.

Also in His royal office, let it be remembered, He is our Mediator, Who takes our place, Who redeems man as the fallen king, and delivering him from the power and dominion of the devil, restores him to his office as priest-king, at the same time raising him in that office to the highest possible level of royalty and glory. In general, we already referred to all this in the first chapter under this twelfth Lord's Day. We must now draw the line somewhat more definitely with respect to the royal office of Christ.

Also of this royal office of Christ, then, there was a reflection in Adam in the state of rectitude in Paradise. For the first man, too, was king under God, expressly ordained by God to that position in the earthly creation. For God gave him dominion over the beasts of the field, over the fowls of the air, and over the fish of the sea. It must be emphasized, however, that man's original dominion was limited to the earthly creation. We dare not say without qualification that he was king of the world, over all creation. Adam was of the earth, earthy. He was not the Lord from heaven. All things, in heaven and on earth, were not, and could not possibly be, united in him, and did not belong to his dominion. It was, indeed, God's counsel and eternal purpose to raise man to that exalted position in which all things would be subjected under his feet. That this is true is evident from a comparison of Psalm 8 with Heb. 2. The psalmist exclaims in wonderment: "What is man, that thou art mindful of him? and the son of man, that thou visitest him? For thou hast made him a little lower than the angels, and hast crowned him with glory and honor. Thou madest him to have dominion over the works of thy hands; thou hast put all things under his feet." 4-6. It is true that the psalmist, evidently, still considers man in his original position, and in his dominion over the earthly creation: sheep and oxen, the beasts of the field, the fowl of the air, and the fish of the sea. But in the epistle to the Hebrews the Holy Spirit interprets this dominion as having reference to all things. There the psalm is interpreted as meaning that originally man was, indeed, made a little lower than the angels, that his original dominion was limited to earthly things, but that he was destined to reign over all the works of God's hands: "But one in a certain place testified, saying, What is

man, that thou art mindful of him? or the son of man, that thou
visitest him? Thou madest him a little lower than the angels;
thou crownedst him with glory and honour, and didst set him
over the works of thy hands: Thou hast put all things in subjec-
jection under his feet. For in that he put all things in subjection
under him, he left nothing that is not put under him." Heb.
2:6-8.

But this highest form of universal dominion was not destined
to be realized in the first Adam. He was, indeed, an image of
Him that was to come. And of the kingship of the latter there
was a reflection in that of the former. But himself was not king
over all the works of God's hands. He was made a little lower
than the angels, though destined, in the last Adam, to rule even
over them. His dominion was limited to the earthly creation.
But even so, he was king. He was king, as servant of God. As
the friend of God in His covenant, it was His calling to acknowledge the Most High as His Lord, to love and to serve Him with
all his heart, and mind, and soul, and strength, and thus, as
friend-servant of the Lord, he was to rule over all the earthly
creation.

The first servant of the Lord, however, rebelled against his
sovereign Lord, rejected His Word, preferred the lie of the
devil, and became the latter's servant. And with his dominion
he is made subject to God's curse and to the power of death.
There are, indeed, remnants of his original royal power and
dominion. And these are plainly visible in the mighty works
he still accomplishes, and in all his attempts to subject all things
under him. Man constantly struggles, even in the present world,
burdened by the curse, to regain and maintain his royal dominion, and though in the attempt he is often overcome, he
despises death in the struggle to attain to the end he has in
view. He makes the world about him the object of his scientific
investigation. He discovers God's ordinances in creation, and
arranges his own life accordingly. He brings to light the hidden
powers and wonders of the world, and presses them into his
service. He understands the laws of the seasons, of winds and
rains, of seeds and of the soil, and he makes the earth produce

the best possible crop. He studies the laws of gravity and gravitation, of steam and electricity, of light waves and sound waves, and he invents many wonderful things: telephone and telegraph, radio and television. He plows through the depth of the sea, and flies through space. He studies the structure and laws of the human body, fights disease and death, alleviates human suffering, and prolongs human life. And he surrounds himself with means to enhance and enrich his life in the world. It is true, that all this is but a faint afterglow of man's original glory. It is also true that in reality he accomplishes nothing, for the creature is made subject to vanity; and that in the ultimate sense he is always defeated, for he dies like the beasts that perish. But this does not alter the fact, that there is a certain remnant of man's original kingship. And it is exactly because of this remnant that there is a *kingdom* of darkness. For in the spiritual-ethical sense of the word, man became an enemy of God, and a slave of the devil. And thus there develops in this world a kingdom of the devil, that will culminate in the world-power of the Antichrist, in which all the powers of creation shall have been exploited and pressed into the service of man, but in which, at the same time the measure of iniquity shall be filled, and the root-sin of the first man Adam shall have become completely revealed in the fully ripened fruit of iniquity.

All this, however, stands strictly in the service of God, and of His eternal good pleasure. For He had provided some better thing for us. And before the foundation of the world, He had ordained His Servant to be King over all the works of God's hands. Even though it remains true that the first man plunged himself and all his posterity into the abyss of misery and death by an act of willful disobedience, and that for this he is responsible to his Lord; nevertheless, also his fall is no accident from God's viewpoint, but must serve to prepare the way for God's bringing "the firstbegotten into the world." Heb. 1:6. For God is the Lord. He is in the heavens and performs all His good pleasure. His counsel was never frustrated; His purpose was never thwarted. Always He accomplished all His good pleasure, even through the devil's temptation, and through the fall of man. There never was a power on earth, in heaven, or in the abyss of darkness that really opposed Him, or that forced Him to change His plan. Though the powers of darkness, as far as their own intention is concerned, set themselves against Him, and vainly take counsel to dethrone the Almighty, and though in this attempt and purpose they become guilty and worthy of damnation, the fact remains that they can only serve the realization of God's eternal purpose, and that God, without deviation from the straight line of His counsel, attains to His purpose.

This truth must be established.

Nor need we fear to emphasize this truth, especially in our age with its mighty emphasis on man.

God is God!

And always He is the Lord!

His counsel shall stand, and He shall do all His good pleasure.

Salvation is no repair work, by which God mends His handiwork marred and destroyed by the devil and the powers of darkness. It is the realization of His eternal purpose in a straight line. And all things, all creatures, also the devil, also the fall of man, must be subservient to the accomplishment of His purpose.

Hence, although through willful disobedience, the first man, the king of the earthly creation, falls according to the determinate counsel of the Most High, and in order that this counsel may stand. He fell, in order that He Whom God had ordained from before the foundation of the world to be king over all, His Servant *par excellence,* the firstborn of every creature, and the firstbegotten of the dead, the Head of the Church, might come into the world, and might be revealed in all the glory of His righteousness, truth, and grace.

For that was God's eternal purpose. Not to perfect things in the first man Adam, the earthy king, but to unite them all under the kingship of the last man, the last Adam, the Lord from heaven, was the end of God's counsel. His own Son, the only Begotten, had been ordained, is eternally ordained to be the Firstborn of every creature, King over all things, in order that as the Lord of His elect brethren, and with them, He might for ever reign over all the works of God's hands.

Unto this end He comes in the flesh.

And in the flesh He fights the battle against the powers of darkness in the way of obedience, and He enters into the strong-holds of the devil, sin, and death, fighting His way as the King of His Church even into the depth of hell, "that through death he might destroy him that had the power of death, that is, the devil; and deliver them who through fear of death were all their lifetime subject to bondage." Heb. 2:14, 15. And He is victorious. Perfect and everlasting righteousness He establishes as the foundation of His kingdom. Through the darkness of death He breaks into the glory of His resurrection. And He is exalted into highest glory, in order that, at the right hand of the Father, clothed with all power in heaven and on earth, He may reign over all things even in the present dispensation, until all God's counsel is fulfilled, His Church shall have been gathered, His kingdom shall be perfected, and He shall subject Himself with His kingdom, as the eternal Servant-King, to the Father, that God may be all in all.

This mighty King is Lord of lords, and King of kings.

By grace He reigns over His Church. The Catechism instructs us that "he governs us by his word and Spirit." He is King of His Church, but then as the Head of the body. Surely, He alone has all legislative, judicial, and executive power in the Church. He reigns over believers individually, and over the Church as a whole, organically and institutionally. His will is the only law. And to that will all are subject, also those that are ordained to be officebearers in the Church on earth. But He rules by His Word and Spirit, and, therefore, by grace. Not only by the Word, but by the Spirit, His own Spirit, and the Word He reigns. For even as He fought the battle for them, and in their behalf, even unto death, so He also delivers them from all the power and dominion of the devil. By His Spirit He enters into their hearts, dethrones the powers of darkness in that heart, enthrones Himself by the power of His grace, and from the heart He reigns over them. He makes them His willing

subjects by His Spirit and Word. He calls them out of darkness
into His marvelous light. He writes His law in their inmost
hearts, so that it becomes their delight to do His will. And by
His Spirit He remains in them, and abides with them forever.
The result of that spiritual reign of Christ over His own is that
they repent of sin, and hearing His Word follow Him whithersoever He leads. And they fight the good fight, even unto death,
that no one take their crown.

But as the King of His Church, He also defends and preserves
His own in the redemption and salvation He obtained for us.

For the present the Church, though redeemed and victorious
in her Lord, is in the midst of a hostile world, and is surrounded
by enemies that always aim at her destruction. And though
she has life, eternal life, in her King, she still lies in the midst
of death. The final victory, eternal glory in the tabernacle of
God and in the new creation, has not yet been reached. And,
therefore, the battle must still be fought by the Church of
Christ in the world. She has her battle, not against flesh and
blood, but against principalities and power, against the rulers
of the darkness of this world, against spiritual wickedness in
high places, Eph. 6:12. Besides, believers are not yet delivered
from the body of this death. Sin and the motions of sin are
still in their flesh. And always that enemy within the gates
seeks an alliance with the powers of darkness in the world. In
the midst of, and over against all these powers of darkness the
Church as a whole, and believers individually, must be preserved and defended, and through them all they must be led
on to eternal glory and victory. Yea, they must be more than
victors, for even their enemies must, in spite of themselves, cooperate unto their salvation, and the very devil may only serve
the purpose of being the watchdog of the Good Shepherd.

And also this work of defending and preserving His Church
in the midst of and through a hostile world, belongs to the
office of Christ as King. In themselves, in their own power, they
are nothing. They could never stand and remain faithful to
the end. They would be quite helpless in the midst of the
powers of darkness. But Christ preserves them. And this, too,

He does, as far as their spiritual preservation is concerned, through His Spirit and Word. Never He leaves them. Always He abides with them, and in them. And never can they finally fall away. No one can possibly pluck them out of His hand. Even as He is at the right hand of God, and intercedes for them, so He constantly blesses them with all spiritual blessings in heavenly places, and preserves them in the salvation He obtained for them. He strengthens them in the battle. He keeps them in temptation. When they stumble He raises them up. And He fills them with the hope of eternal joy in the midst of the suffering of this present time.

But He also defends them by His power, and causes all things in this present world to work together unto their salvation. For He is King, not only by grace over His Church, but also by His mighty power over all things, even over principalities and powers, over the rulers of this world, over all the forces of darkness, and all things are subjected under His feet even now. For although the word of the eighth psalm is not yet completely realized, and although "now we see not yet all things put under him," we do "see Jesus, who was made a little lower than the angels, for the suffering of death crowned with glory and honor." Heb. 2:8, 9. And even now God has set Him "at His own right hand in heavenly places, far above all principality, and power, and might, and dominion, and every name that is named, not only in this world, but also in that which is to come." Of this we must speak further in connection with the nineteenth Lord's Day of the Catechism. But even now it must be pointed out that Christ uses this mighty power, that has been given Him as the Anointed of the Father for the benefit of His Church, to defend and preserve her against all enemies, to cause all things to work together for her salvation, and to lead His own to final glory.

And thus Christ will reign for ever.

For when all things shall have been accomplished, the last of the elect shall have been called, the measure of iniquity shall be filled, He will come again in great power and glory, establish His eternal Kingdom in the new creation, that He may reign everlastingly over His Church, and with all His people as the royal priesthood over all the works of God's hands. For Christ is an eternal King. His dominion is an everlasting dominion. And although it is true that He, as the perfect Servant of the Lord, will also subject Himself to the Father, this does not mean that He will ever abdicate and cease to be King. On the contrary, He is King for ever, even as He is an eternal Priest after the order of Melchisedec. And in the eternal kingdom of glory, all things shall serve Christ and His people, that they may serve their God, and He may be all and in all for ever!

X

Partakers Of His Anointing

To the exposition of the name Christ and the offices of the Saviour, the Catechism appends a discussion of the name Christian, and that, too, with personal application to the confessing believer who throughout the Heidelberger is the respondent to the questions. "But why art thou called a Christian? Because I am a member of Christ by faith, and thus am partaker of his anointing; that so I may confess his name, and present myself a living sacrifice of thankfulness to him: and also that with a free and good conscience I may fight against sin and Satan in this life: and afterwards reign with him eternally, over all creatures."

It must be evident from the outset that the question *Why art thou called a Christian?* cannot be taken in the same significance as the preceding questions concerning the names of Christ: "Why is the Son of God called Jesus, that is a Savior?" and: "Why is he called Christ, that is anointed?" For the latter two questions are concerned with names that are directly from God, which cannot be said of the name *Christian* at all. The Son of God is called Jesus, not by man's invention, not even by His human parents, but in God's counsel, and by direct revelation. And He is called the Christ because He is the promised Messiah, the One that was ordained from eternity, and anointed with the Holy Ghost to be the Servant of Jehovah over His whole house, and, therefore, again by divine appointment. But this is not the case with the name Christian. In Scripture believers are never addressed as Christians, even though once they are referred to by that name. Their common designations are "believers," "saints," "brethren," "elect of God," "the faithful," "servants" of God or of Christ, "beloved," "children of God."

It is plain, then, that the question *Why art thou called a Christian?* cannot be placed on a par with the questions that precede it about the name of the Saviour.

Scripture informs us that believers were called Christians first in Antioch. We read in Acts 11:26: "And when he had found him, he brought him unto Antioch. And it came to pass, that a whole year they assembled themselves with the church, and taught much people. And the disciples were called Christians first in Antioch." It is evident, therefore, that the name did not originate with believers themselves. They did not of their own accord call themselves and one another Christians, as, for instance, the Society of Jesus call themselves Jesuits. On the contrary, the name was invented by the people in Antioch. They called the disciples Christians. It must also be evident that it was not the Jewish element of the population of Antioch that thought of applying this name to the followers of Jesus. They would rather designate them by the term of contempt *Nazarenes,* or the sect of the Nazarenes. It was the heathen element of the people there that invented the name. And in their parlance, the name denoted simply an adherent of Christ, Whom the apostles preached, and Whom the disciples followed and confessed as their Lord. In popular slang the name was intended to denote members of a certain party or sect. In this sense, it is, no doubt, also employed by King Agrippa, and that, perhaps, with a touch of sarcasm, in the well-known words: "Almost thou persuadest me to be a Christian." Acts 26:28. There was, therefore, from the beginning a certain reproach attached to the name. And, perhaps, there is a reference to this reproach in the use of the name by the apostle in I Pet. 4:16: "Yet if any man suffer as a Christian, let him not be ashamed, but let him glorify God on this behalf." For to suffer as a Christian meant to "be reproached for the name of Christ." I Pet. 4:14.

Before long, however, the name was adopted and appropriated by believers themselves. If this had not been the case, the thirty-second question of the Catechism could never have been asked, or, at least, if it had been given a place in the Instructor, the answer would have been entirely different from the one here given. And for this adoption of a name, which had its origin in the heathen world, there must have been a good reason. Believers must have considered that it was in God's providence that they should be called Christians by the world. And as they contemplated the meaning of the name, they also discovered that it was not at all improper as an appellative of the disciples of Christ, that, in fact, as a name by which they might be known in the midst of the world, and in distinction from unbelievers, it was very fitting. The name Nazarenes they could not adopt, not only because it was too expressive of the hatred and contempt on the part of their enemies against them and against their Lord, but also because it had no sense. As disciples of Christ, they could not call themselves after the name Jesus, for that name is altogether too unique and belongs exclusively to the Saviour. He alone is Jehovah-salvation, and in the work which He accomplished under that name they could not possibly share in any sense. That the well-known Romish Society call themselves Jesuits is nothing less than presumption. But with the name Christ this was different. Christ meant Anointed, and by His grace they, too, that believed on His name, became anointed ones. It signified that He was God's Servant *par excellence,* and through His name they, too, were servants of the Lord. And so they soon adopted the name, that was at first imposed on them by popular slang, as their own. They called themselves Christian, their religion became known as the Christian religion, and their faith as the Christian faith.

And so there is a special meaning to the pointed, personal question of the Heidelberger in this connection.

Fact is, of course, that the reason why believers of today are called Christians is that even in the days of the apostles the heathen population of Antioch applied that appellative to them, and, soon after, they themselves adopted it. Hence, one is called a Christian because he is born in the Church visible in the world, or incorporated into this gathering of professing believers and their children. It follows that one need not necessarily *be* a Christian, that the meaning of the name Christian does not have to be applicable to one, in order to be *called* by that name. Fact is, that there are thousands upon thousands that are Christians only nominally, without having a personal part in the spiritual reality denoted by the name. In the light of all this, the question of the Catechism receives a new significance: why art *thou* called a Christian?

Are you called a Christian merely because you happen to belong to that group of people that years ago were called by that name, and ever since were known by it, in distinction from the heathen? Or does the name, in its true spiritual significance, apply to you personally? Do you know the meaning of that name, and knowing it, can you claim the right to bear it?

The heart of the answer to this question which our Instructor places on the lips of the professing believer is contained in the words: "Because I am a member of Christ by faith, and thus am partaker of his anointing."

All that follows in the answer is implied in this.

I am a Christian when I share in His anointing, and that, too, in utter dependence upon Him, by faith, and through His grace. Also this dependency is implied in the name. For I am not another Christ, but a Christian. He is the Head, I am member of His body, and as the member is nothing apart from the Head, or as the branch is nothing apart from the vine, so I am nothing apart from Christ. The anointing is always His, and I partake of it. To be a Christian, therefore, I must abide in Him. "Abide in me, and I in you. As the branch cannot bear fruit of itself, except it abide in the vine; no more can ye, except ye abide in me. I am the vine, ye are the branches: He that abideth in me, and I in him, the same bringeth forth much fruit: for without me ye can do nothing. If a man abide not in me, he is cast forth as a branch, and is withered; and men gather them, and cast them into the fire, and they are burned. If ye abide in me, and my words abide in you, ye shall ask what ye will, and it shall be done unto you." John 15:4-7. And again: "But ye have an unction from the Holy One, and ye know all things . . . . But the anointing which ye have received of him abideth in you, and ye need not that any man teach you; but as the same anointing teacheth you of all things, and is truth, and is no lie, and even as it hath taught you, ye shall abide in him." I John 2:20, 27.

The spiritual reality, therefore, of our partaking of Christ's anointing is the fruit of Christ's imparting Himself to us through His Spirit, and of our partaking of Him, and appropriating Him by faith, of our drawing out of Him "even grace for grace." Christ, the Anointed of God, Who was obedient unto death, and merited for us an eternal righteousness, Who was raised on the third day in glory, Who ascended up on high, leading captivity captive, and is exalted at the right hand of the Father, received the promise of the Holy Spirit, and in that Spirit returned unto His own, that He might impart Himself to them, and fill us with His blessings. And thus we receive His anointing, through the means of faith, which He works in us, and whereby we are united with Him and appropriate Him.

But just what is the specific implication of this participation by faith in Christ's anointing?

We recall that Christ's anointing signifies that He was ordained from eternity by God the Father, and qualified by the Holy Ghost to be God's officebearer, the Servant of Jehovah, representing His cause in the world, that He might reveal unto us the full counsel of God concerning our salvation, fight the battle against sin and death, and having overcome all the powers of darkness, might occupy His place as the Firstborn of every creature in all the universe. That exalted position, according to which He has a name above all names, and is King over all, He now occupies. He is made Christ and Lord.

Of His anointing we partake.

This means, therefore, that through Him believers, too, are ordained and qualified by His Spirit to be officebearers, servants of the living God. It means that in Christ they have the privilege and the calling, the will and the power to be and to function in this world, and for ever, as God's friend-servants. By nature, they have none of this. The *must* is, indeed, upon them, for God will not relinquish His demand upon man, that he love Him with all his heart, and mind, and soul, and strength. But by his wilful disobedience, man has lost the right and the privilege, as well as the will and power, and all the qualifications to be the servant of God. Christ, however, as the Servant of God *par excellence,* and that, too, as the Head of those whom the Father gave Him, by His perfect obedience even unto the death of the cross, blotted out all their sins, obtained for them perfect righteousness, and thus He merited for them the *right* to be received again in God's service. To partake of Christ's anointing, therefore, means that in Him we have once more the right to stand as servants in the house of our God. In Him is our ordination as God's officebearers, as representatives of His cause. But, in the second place, that we by faith partake of Christ's anointing also implies that in and through Him we are qualified to function as servants of the Most High. The *will* and the *power* to fulfill our calling as Jehovah's servants we also receive from Him, by His Spirit, and through the activity of true faith. Christ not only took our place as the Servant of Jehovah, fulfilling all in our stead, but He also delivers us from the slavery of sin and the devil, and renews us unto willing servants of God.

And as the office of our Lord is threefold, that of prophet, priest, and king, so through our partaking of His anointing we also become servants of God in that threefold sense. Christ is our chief Prophet, and as such He is the fulness of all the knowledge and wisdom of God. At the head of His people He glorifies the Father, and declares His righteousness in the great congregation. But as such He also changes us into true prophets of God. For He revealed the Father unto us, He instructs us by His Spirit and Word, He delivers us from the darkness of our understanding and the perversion of our mind, and by His grace we are called out of darkness into the marvelous light of God, so that we have the true knowledge of God. Here this knowledge is still in part, for we see as in a glass darkly, but presently it will be perfected, and then appear on a plane of heavenly glory, unspeakably higher than that of the knowledge of God Adam possessed in the state of rectitude in the first paradise. For then we shall see face to face, and know even as we are known, and walk in the light of God's countenance for ever.

Christ is our only High Priest. And as such He represented us in His humiliation, and offered Himself as the perfect sacrifice for our sins. As such He still represents us with the Father, and intercedes for us. But as our High Priest He also makes us partaker of His anointing, and forms His Church into a holy priesthood. He makes us priests of God. He removes the enmity against God that is the motivating power of our flesh, and instils into our hearts the love of God, dwelling in us by His Spirit, and cleansing us from the defilement of sin, so that we may become living sanctuaries of God, consecrated to Him in true holiness. Also this is as yet true only in principle. But in the perfection of God's tabernacle this shall be perfected on the plane of heavenly glory. In the New Jerusalem there is no special temple, for the simple reason that the entire glorified Church is become a perfect sanctuary of God.

And so He is our eternal King. And as such He fought and finished the battle for us and in our behalf, against all the powers of darkness, the devil, sin, and death. He crushed the head of the serpent, and is seated at the right hand of the Majesty in the heavens. And He reigns over us, and leads us to the everlasting glory. But also as King He causes us to partake of His anointing, so that by His grace we also become kings with Him under God, and are formed into a *royal* priesthood. He delivers us from all unrighteousness and perversion of our will, according to which we desire to do the will of our father the devil, and instils into us a new righteousness, according to which it is our delight to do the will of God. He gives us the right to reign over all things, enables us to fight the battle of faith, and makes us partakers, even in the midst of battle, of His own victory. And especially with a view to our royal office as believers, it is evident that our partaking of Christ's anointing still is imperfect, and that we have but a small beginning of the new obedience, the firstfruits of the Spirit. For not only have we not as yet entered into the glory of our royal dominion with Christ, and not only are we engaged in a daily struggle against sin and Satan, but outwardly we suffer defeat, and in the world we have tribulation. Yet, we may be of good cheer, for we are more than victors. And when Christ shall be revealed, and we shall be manifested with Him in glory, it shall appear that we always had the victory, and we shall reign with and through Christ, as servant-kings of God, over all the works of His hands in the new creation.

This threefold aspect of our partaking of the anointing of Christ is plainly indicated in the answer of our Heidelberger to the question: "But why art thou called a Christian?" For it points to a threefold calling of believers in this world, which follows from their partaking of Christ's anointing.

First of all, their calling is to confess His name. This is their calling and privilege in virtue of their prophetic office. They are made prophets, in order that they may confess the name of Christ as the revelation of the God of their salvation. They are to the praise of the glory of His grace in the beloved. They must show forth the praises and marvelous virtues of Him that called them out of darkness into His marvelous light. And they must do this in the midst of the world, antithetically, holding forth the word of life over against the lie of sin, and in the midst of a crooked and perverse nation.

Secondly, the Catechism describes the calling of believers as consisting in this, that they present themselves a living sacrifice of thankfulness to Him. This evidently refers to their priestly office. To consecrate themselves, with soul and body, with all their heart, and mind, and soul, and strength; with all things, and in every department of life, in home, and school, and shop, and office, to the living God, — such is their calling as priests of the Most High, and that, too, in opposition to a world that devotes itself to the service of the devil and unrighteousness.

And so, finally, the Catechism refers to the royal office of believers in the words: "and also that with a free and good conscience I may fight against sin and Satan in this life: and afterwards reign with him eternally over all creatures." O, indeed, in this battle, and in this warfare alone, one may fight with a "free and good conscience," for fighting they have the assurance that they represent the cause of the Son of God in the world, and that they are more than victors through Him that loved them. And although in this world this cause must often appear as suffering defeat, they have the blessed assurance that in the day of Christ their God will vindicate their cause, and cause them to enter into the glorious victory of their Lord!

LORD'S DAY XIII

Q. 33. Why is Christ called the only begotten Son of God, since we are also the children of God?

A. Because Christ alone is the eternal and natural Son of God; but we are children adopted of God, by grace, for his sake.

Q. 34. Wherefore callest thou him our Lord?

A. Because he hath redeemed us, both soul and body, from all our sins, not with gold or silver, but with his precious blood, and hath delivered us from all the power of the devil; and thus hath made us his own property.

I

This Jesus Is Very God

The thirty-fourth answer is a somewhat free translation of the original German, which reads as follows: "Weil er uns mit Leib und Seele von der Sunde und aus aller Gewalt des Teufels nicht mit Gold oder Silber, sondern mit seinem theuren Blut ihm zum Eigenthum erlöset und erkaufet hat." And this may be translated: "Because he redeemed and purchased us, with body and soul, not with gold or silver, but with his own precious blood, from sin and out of all the power of the devil, to be his own property." The sense remains essentially the same, except that in the original our salvation, both from sin and from the power of the devil, is presented as having been accomplished through both, the redemption and purchasing by Christ through His precious blood.

We must clearly understand just what truth is the subject of the thirty-third question and answer, lest we repeat what was already explained in connection with the eighth and ninth Lord's Day of our Instructor. There we discussed the doctrine of the Holy Trinity, and paid more particular attention to the eternal Fatherhood of God in relation to the Son, and to the Sonship of the second Person of the Godhead. In question thirty-three the subject is also "the only begotten Son," and it is explained that Christ is "the eternal and natural Son of God." We might, therefore, easily be tempted to treat once more of the Son of God as He appears in the trinity, and of the doctrine of eternal generation.* Yet, this would be a mistake. The subject in question and answer thirty-three is not the second Person of the Godhead as such, but Jesus Christ. The Catechism, following the *Apostolicum*, is explaining the words: "And in Jesus Christ,

---

*Cf. Section II, *God's Way Out*, pp. 349-385.

575

his only begotten Son, our Lord." The main point of our discussion in this connection, therefore, is expressed in the proposition: *Jesus Christ is very God.* That the Son of man, the
historical Jesus, Who was born in Bethlehem in the fulness of
time, Who grew up in the home of Joseph and Mary in Nazareth
as an ordinary child, Who sojourned among us, taught the
people and performed His mighty works during the three years
of His public ministry, and Who finally was crucified and slain
by His enemies, nailed to the accursed tree, but Who, according
the Scriptures, was raised on the third day and exalted on the
right hand of the Majesty in the heavens, — that this Jesus is
very God, not born but eternally begotten, God of God, and
Light of Light, is the subject of discussion in the thirty-third
question and answer of our Heidelberger.

The truth of the Godhead of Jesus Christ is clearly defined
and strongly maintained in the confessions of the Church from
earliest times, and to the present day, and that, too, in opposition
to every form of heresy that arose to undermine it. The Nicaeno-
Constantinopolitan Creed, 381, states this truth in the following
words: "And in one Lord Jesus Christ, the only begotten Son
of God, begotten of the Father before all the worlds, God of
God, Light of Light, very God of very God, begotten, not made,
being of one substance with the Father; by whom all things were
made." The Symbol of Chalcedon, 451, declares: "We, then,
following the holy Fathers, all with one consent, teach men to
confess one and the same Son, our Lord Jesus Christ, the same
perfect in Godhead and also perfect in manhood; truly God
and truly man, of a rational soul and body; consubstantial with
the Father according to the Godhead, and consubstantial with
us according to the Manhood; in all things like unto us, without sin; begotten before all ages of the Father according to the
Godhead, and in these latter days, for us and for our salvation,
born of the Virgin Mary, the Mother of God, according to the
Manhood; one and the same Christ, Lord, Only-begotten, to be
acknowledged in two natures, inconfusedly, unchangeably, indivisibly, inseparably; the distinction of natures by no means
being taken away by the union, but rather the property of each

nature being preserved, and concurring in one Person and one Subsistence, not parted or divided into two persons, but one and the same Son, and only begotten, God the Word, the Lord Jesus Christ; as the prophets from the beginning have declared concerning him, and the Lord Jesus Christ himself has taught us, and the Creed of the holy Fathers has handed down to us." And the so-called Athanasian Creed has the following: "Furthermore it is necessary to everlasting salvation: that he also believe rightly the Incarnation of our Lord Jesus Christ. For the right Faith is, that we believe and confess: that our Lord Jesus Christ, the Son of God, is God and Man; God of the Substance of the Father; begotten before the worlds: and Man, of the substance of His Mother, born in the world. Perfect God: and perfect Man, of a reasonable soul and human flesh subsisting. Equal to the Father as touching his Godhead: and inferior to the Father as touching his Manhood. Who although he is God and Man; yet he is not two, but one Christ. One; not by conversion of the Godhead into flesh: but by taking of the Manhood into God. One altogether; not by confusion of the Substance: but by unity of Person. For as the reasonable soul and flesh is one man: so God and Man is one Christ."

The same teaching is found in the later Creeds.

The Augsburg Confession declares in Article III: "Also they teach that the Word, that is, the Son of God, took unto him man's nature in the womb of the blessed Virgin Mary, so that there are two natures, the divine and the human, inseparably joined together in unity of person; one Christ, true God and man." The Formula of Concord, Article VIII teaches: "That the divine and the human nature in Christ are personally united, and so completely that there are not two Christs — one the Son of God, the other the Son of man — but that one and the same is Son of God and Son of man." And the attributes of the divine nature of Christ are said to be omnipotence, eternity, omnipresence, etc.

The Second Helvetic Confession, Article XI, has this to say: "Moreover, we believe and teach that the Son of God, our Lord Jesus Christ, was from all eternity predestinated and fore-

ordained of the Father to be the Saviour of the world. And
we believe that he was begotten, not only then, when he took
flesh of the Virgin Mary, nor yet a little before the foundations
of the world were laid; but before all eternity, and that of the
Father after an unspeakable manner . . . . Therefore the Son
is coequal and consubstantial with the Father, as touching his
divinity: true God, not by name only, or by adoption, or by
special favor, but in substance and nature . . . . We acknowledge,
therefore, that there be in one and the same Jesus Christ our
Lord two natures, the divine and the human nature."

The French Confession of Faith states in Article XV: "We
believe that in one person, that is Jesus Christ, the two natures
are actually and inseparably joined and united, and yet each
remains in its proper character: so that in this union the divine
nature, retaining its attributes, remained uncreated, infinite,
and all-pervading."

Likewise our own Netherland or Belgic Confession declares:
"We confess, therefore, that God did fulfill the promise which
he made to the fathers by the mouth of his holy prophets when
he sent into the world, at the time appointed by him, his own
only-begotten and eternal Son, who took upon him the form
of a servant, and became like unto men . . . . so that he is in
truth our Immanuel, that is to say, God with us." Article XVIII.
And again: "We believe that by this conception the person of
the Son is inseparably united and connected with the human
nature; so that there are not two Sons of God, nor two persons,
but two natures united in one single person; yet each nature
retains its own distinct properties. As then the divine nature has
always remained uncreated, without beginning of days or end of
life, filling heaven and earth, so also hath the human nature not
lost its properties, but remained a creature . . . . But these two
natures are so closely united in one person, that they were not
separated even by his death. Therefore, that which he, when
dying, commended into the hands of the Father, was a real
human spirit, departing from his body. But in the meantime
the divine nature always remained united with the human
nature, even when he lay in the grave; and the God-head did not

cease to be in him, any more than it did when he was an infant, though it did not so clearly manifest itself for a while." Art. XIX.

Article II of the Thirty-nine Articles of the Church of England expresses this truth as follows: "The Son, which is the Word of the Father, begotten from everlasting of the Father, the very and eternal God, and of one substance with the Father, took man's nature in the womb of the blessed Virgin, of her substance: so that the whole and perfect natures, that is to say, the Godhead and Manhood, were joined together in one Person, never to be divided, whereof is one Christ, very God, and very Man."

Likewise the Westminster Confession, VIII, 2: "The Son of God, the second person in the Trinity, being very and eternal God, of one substance, and equal with the Father, did, when the fulness of time was come, take upon him man's nature, with all the essential properties and common infirmities thereof, yet without sin: being conceived by the power of the Holy Ghost in the womb of the Virgin Mary, of her substance. So that two whole, perfect, and distinct natures, the Godhead and the manhood, were inseparably joined together in one person, without conversion, composition, or confusion. Which person is very God and very man, yet one Christ, the only mediator between God and man."

The Church throughout the centuries, therefore, confesses that the man Jesus Christ is the eternal, essential, only begotten Son of God.

And this is the clear teaching of Scripture.

Before the Church made this confession, even during Christ's sojourn in the flesh of His humiliation, the apostles confessed that He is the Son of God. Thus Nathanael, the Israelite in whom there was no guile, exclaimed at the very beginning of Jesus' public ministry: "Rabbi, thou art the Son of God; thou art the King of Israel." John 1:49. When Jesus was with His disciples in the coasts of Caesarea Philippi, after having inquired of them as to men's opinions about Him, He placed them before the personal question: "But whom do ye say that I am?"

And Peter replied with the well-known confession: "Thou art the Christ, the Son of the living God." And the Saviour sealed this confession, both as to its truth and with respect to its fundamental importance, when He said: "Blessed art thou, Simon Bar-Jona: for flesh and blood hath not revealed it unto thee, but my Father which is in heaven. And I say unto thee, That thou art Peter, and upon this rock will I build my church; and the gates of hell shall not prevail against it." Matt. 16:15-18. And Thomas, who would not believe, unless he put his finger in the print of the nails, overcome by the glory of the risen Lord, cried out in adoration: "My Lord, and my God!"

And this is the teaching of Holy Writ throughout.

For "in the beginning was the Word, and the Word was with God, and the Word was God. The same was in the beginning with God. All things were made by him; and without him was not any thing made that was made .... And the Word was made flesh, and dwelt among us, and we beheld his glory, the glory as of the only begotten of the Father, full of grace and truth .... No man hath seen God at any time; the only begotten Son, which is in the bosom of the Father, he hath declared him." John 1:1-3; 14, 18. "And without controversy great is the mystery of godliness: God was manifest in the flesh, justified in the Spirit, seen of angels, preached unto the Gentiles, believed on in the world, received up into glory." And "who is he that overcometh the world, but he that believeth that Jesus is the Son of God?" I John 5:5. And again, "we know that the Son of God is come, and hath given us an understanding, that we may know him that is true, and we are in him that is true, even in his Son Jesus Christ. This is the true God and eternal life." I John 5:20. The apostle Paul writes: "Whose are the fathers, and of whom as concerning the flesh Christ came, who is over all, God blessed for ever." Rom. 9:5. Moreover, attributes that are only divine, such as eternity, omniscience, omnipotence, are ascribed to this Jesus, Micah 5:1, John 21:17, Rev. 1:8; 22:13. And he performs divine works. He creates, sustains all things, forgives men's sins, raises the dead, etc. John 1:3; Col.

1:17; Heb. 1:3; Lu. 5:20, 24; John 5:21. And he and the Father are one, i.e. one in essence. John 10:30.

And so, the Heidelberg Catechism stands on the basis of Holy Writ, and its teaching is in harmony with that of the Church of all ages, when it maintains in the thirty-third question and answer the true, essential, and distinct divinity of Jesus Christ.

We say: the *distinct divinity of our Lord.*

For this it is, indeed, that the Catechism emphasizes. Both in Scripture, and in the Apostolic Confession, Christ is called "the only begotten Son of God." And the Catechism calls special attention to this exclusive and distinctive term *only begotten.* Why should Christ be called thus? What is the meaning of the term? What does it teach us? Scripture calls angels also the sons of God. Moreover, believers are called by that name. And even Adam is so called. If there are more sons of God, then, if Christ is not the only Son of God, how can He be called the *only begotten?* What does this exclusive term express? And in the answer the Heidelberger distinguishes between the Sonship of Christ, and that of believers. It is true, that believers are also called the children of God, yet Christ is the Son in an altogether special and unique sense of the word. Christ's sonship belongs not to time, but in eternity; ours has a beginning, belongs to time: we are adopted. And the Sonship of Christ is *natural;* He is by *nature,* essentially, the Son of God; we become children of God only through grace.

And it is well, that this distinction is made, and that thus the unique Sonship of Christ, and His true divinity is maintained.

For, first of all, this is necessary in opposition to all kinds of heresies that have arisen, and always do arise against this doctrine of the true and essential Godhead of Christ.

And the Church must instruct her children clearly and definitely in this doctrine, in order that they may not be tossed to and fro by every wind of doctrine, but stand in the faith once delivered unto the saints.

The matter would not be so serious, if those that deny this fundamental truth would only speak in plain language, and unambiguously declare that Jesus is not the Son of God. But this they do not. Those who desire to instil the poison of their false doctrine into the minds and hearts of believers, and thus to destroy the Church of Christ, never proclaim their heresies boldly and openly. On the contrary, they try to hide the real meaning of their views by preserving and speaking in the same terms as the Church. And so, they try to deceive the people of God, and make them believe that their heresies are harmless, that they are, in fact, fundamentally in harmony with the faith of the Church, and with the teaching of Holy Writ.

This is also true with regard to heresies concerning the doctrine of the divinity of Christ. Old Arius did not deny that Jesus is the Son of God, but he pointed out that the name *Son of God* is a *title* that is given to Christ, that is applicable to Him especially after the resurrection, and that denotes Him as a very exalted human being. He is not essentially and eternally God, but God bestowed upon Him the unique honor of being called His only begotten Son. The Nominal Trinitarians did not teach that Jesus is not the Son of God, but they insisted that the name *Son of God* denotes an effluence or power of the Father, not a distinct person in the trinity, and that this power or effluence of the Father was especially strong in Christ. Hence, it is in virtue of this strong presence and power of God in Him, and not because He is essentially God, that He is called the only begotten of the Father. The Socinians and the Moderns of today have no objection to the doctrine that Jesus is the Son of God; He may even be called the only begotten; but to them this does not mean that He is very God, the second person in the trinity. Rather does it mean that He was so truly divine because He was so truly and really human. We are all children of God, for we all are made in God's image. The distinction of Christ is that He was so deeply and clearly conscious of His Sonship, and that He lived so perfectly as a child of God. The God-consciousness was strong in Him!

It is, then, quite necessary that believers are instructed in the truth of Christ's unique, distinctive, essential Sonship.

For, secondly, with this fundamental truth stands or falls the whole truth concerning our salvation. If Christ is not very God, there is no Immanuel, no Incarnation, no union of God and man, no tabernacle of God with men, no covenant of friendship, no revelation of the Father. If He, Who died on Calvary, was a mere man, was not the Son of God in the flesh, there was no perfect sacrifice for sin on that accursed tree, there is no atonement, God did not reconcile us unto Himself in the blood of His Son. If Christ is not very God His own resurrection is but a beautiful legend, and He cannot be the resurrection and the life for us. In one word, if Christ is not essentially and eternally God, our faith is vain, we are still in our sins, and we are still without God in the world.

And no beautiful philosophy of the Man of Galilee can take the place of the Christ of the Scriptures.

But, thanks be to God, God sent His only begotten Son into the world, that He might represent His own, lay down His life for His sheep, bring to light life and immortality, reconcile us unto Himself, and unite us with Him for ever in the blessed fellowship of His eternal tabernacle!

For this Jesus is very God!

II

Christ's Sonship And Ours

To avoid repetition, we must clearly distinguish just what subject the Heidelberg Catechism is discussing in the thirteenth Lord's Day.

We must not, in this connection, speak of the mystery of the incarnation as such, the doctrine that the Son of God assumed our flesh and blood from the Virgin Mary. For this is treated in the following Lord's Day.

Nor is it the purpose of this part of the Catechism to discuss the mystery of the sonship of the second Person in the Holy Trinity, for this was treated in the eighth and ninth Lord's Day of our Instructor.

But the Catechism is here explaining the words of the Apostolic Confession: "And in Jesus Christ, *the only begotten Son of God.*" That Jesus Christ is the eternal and essential Son of God, that the Man Jesus, Who was born in Bethlehem, and Who left His life on the bloody tree of Golgotha, is very God Himself, — that is the definite point of discussion in this thirteenth Lord's Day. It is true, of course, that, to bring out this specific truth in bold relief, it cannot be avoided to say something about the *eternal Sonship* of this Jesus. But this is necessary only in so far as it is required to distinguish this man Jesus from all other men, to maintain and exhibit the infinite chasm there exists between His Sonship and that of all other children of God, especially that of His brethren.

Let us clearly understand the importance and the necessity of this distinction.

The importance lies in the fact that the Church confesses: "*I believe* in Jesus Christ." Now, if in this confession she does not also clearly and definitely maintain that this Jesus Christ is *very God,* her faith is nothing but hero-worship, faith in Man, in Self. Then Jesus is not the revelation of the Father, the God of our salvation reaching out to us from the mysterious depths of eternity and infinity, but merely the noblest product of the human race, the revelation of the wonderful possibilities that lie hid in the human nature. Then the confession: "I believe in Jesus Christ," means: "I believe in the man of Galilee, in his goodness, nobility, teaching, example, and that I have all the requirements necessary to follow him, and to make myself like him." Then Jesus is not the revelation of the righteousness, and wisdom, and sanctification, and redemption of God, but of the righteousness, and wisdom, and holiness, and redemption of man.

Such is the Christ of modern philosophy.

It is this Christ upon whom the proud but hopeless structure of modernism is built. The keystone of this structure, that which makes it so hopelessly weak, is a mere denial: the denial that this Jesus is very God.

But the faith and hope of the Church cannot rest in man. When the Church says: "I believe," the object of that faith is always GOD, the only God, the One that dwells in the light no man can approach unto, the Eternal, the Infinite, Who is not comprehended by time or space, but Who Himself spanned the chasm that separates Him from us by His revelation. He is the One Whom no one knows save the Son, and those to whom the Son will reveal Him.

Therein lies the importance of the distinction the Catechism here makes.

Deny that this Jesus is very God, and the article of our faith by which we confess that we believe in Jesus Christ means: "I believe in Man."

Confess, however, with the Church of all ages, that Jesus Christ is the only begotten Son of God in an altogether unique sense of the word, and your faith and hope are still in the only true God.

And necessary this distinction is, necessary it is always again to insist on, to emphasize this distinction, and to set it in bold relief, because in the revelation of Jesus Christ God approached us so closely, He came so dangerously near unto us, that He, as it were, challenged sinful men to deny that He is very God.

In creation He reveals His eternal power and Godhead, and sinful men refuse to glorify Him, and to give Him thanks. The heavens declare the glory of God, and the firmament sheweth His handiwork. In the theophany of the first Paradise, when Adam apprehended the approach of God in the cool of day, there was a clear revelation of His majesty, before which Adam hid himself. Even when He revealed Himself through the speech of angels, there always was some manifestation of divine glory that made men fear and tremble. Sinai is hid in smoke and darkness, it quakes and trembles at the approach of the Most High, and from its summit roars the voice of the Almighty as the voice of thunder, striking terror into the hearts of men. But in Jesus the chasm between the infinite Majesty and mere men, even sinful men, between the Creator and the creature, the Eternal and time, the infinite God and finite dust, the only Lord and His servants, appears to be completely abridged, eliminated. In the revelation of Jesus Christ GOD seems hid! In the manger He is a babe, helpless and dependent. In Nazareth He grows up as any other child: He increases in wisdom and stature. He dwells among us, eats and drinks, speaks and works, is tired and sleeps, is troubled and weeps. Men can see Him, hear Him, understand Him, touch Him; even contradict Him, oppose Him, mock Him, take hold of Him and bind Him, judge Him and condemn Him, kill Him and bury Him!

GOD in the flesh, yea, in the likeness of sinful flesh!

O, how easy it is to deny that He is God at all! And this is exactly what mere men always did. They denied it when, in the days of His flesh, He walked and tabernacled among us, and they even killed Him because He confessed that He was the Son of the living God. And they denied it from Arius to the present time. They admitted that He was a wonderful man, a good man, a man that was more deeply God-conscious than any other before Him, a man that was entitled to the name

Son of God, that was *appointed* to be Son of God, but they denied that He is GOD. And they still deny it.

And, therefore, it is very necessary that the Church jealously guard this truth, this Rock upon which she is built, and insist that when she confesses that she believes in Jesus Christ she means nothing else than what she began to confess in the first article of the *Apostolicum*: *Credo in Deum*. And because in the revelation of Jesus Christ, God is also man, there is no more effective way to preserve the truth of the unique Sonship of Christ, than by drawing clear and sharp lines of demarcation between the sonship of the only Begotten and that of the mere creature, particularly that of believers. Such lines the Catechism draws in question and answer 33: "Why is Christ called the only begotten Son of God, since we are also the children of God? Because Christ alone is the eternal and natural Son of God; but we are children adopted of God, by grace, for his sake."

Christ, according to His divine nature, is *begotten* of God. He is the *only* begotten. Another Son that is *begotten* there is not. Other sons of God may be *created*, or they may be children by reason of a gracious act of *adoption*, they may even be *born* of God, but they are not *begotten*. But Christ is *begotten* of God. He is not created, i.e. He is not the Son of God through an act of God's omnipotent will, in virtue of which He calls the things that are not as if they were; nor is He adopted, i.e. the right and privilege of being called Son of God are not bestowed upon Him by grace; nor is He born of God, i.e. He is not made a being outside of God endowed with a creaturely reflection of God's virtues; He is begotten. True, He is also born. He is the firstborn among many brethren, the firstborn of every creature, the firstborn of the dead, but all this is true only of the Son of God in human nature. In His divine nature He is begotten, the only begotten. He does not have His origin in the divine conception, in the divine will, in the eternal counsel. On the contrary, with the Father and the Holy Ghost, He is the Subject of that counsel. He is begotten by an act of the Father in the divine *Essence*.

Hence, Christ is the *eternal* Son of God. And this means, to be sure, that as Son of God He has no beginning and no end. There is no distinction of time between the Father and the only begotten Son, as if the Father were first, and thereupon He gave being to the Son. The Father was never without the Son, the Son was never without the Father, the Father and the Son were never without the Holy Spirit. But it also implies that the divine act within the divine Essence, whereby the Father begets the Son, takes place in eternity, not in time at all. Eternity is not time, even as God is not the creature; and time is not eternity, even as the world is not God. There is a chasm between eternity and time that can never be bridged, even as there is such a chasm between God and the world, between the Creator and the creature, between the divine and the human. Time is change, flux, becoming, succession of moments; eternity is the unchangeable, infinite fulness of being and activity. That Christ is the *eternal* Son of God means that He IS Son in virtue of an unchangeable act of the Father within the divine Essence, in which the Father is active with all the infinite fulness of the Godhead. Incessantly, eternally, with infinite perfection of activity of the whole divine Essence, the Father gives life to the Son. This unfathomably deep mystery the Church tried to express by the term *eternal generation*.

And so, as the Catechism expresses it, Christ is, according to His divine nature, the *natural* Son of God. In virtue of the fact that He is *begotten,* and that, too, by an eternal act of the Father within the divine Essence, *the Son is essentially God. Having His origin as Son in the divine Essence, He is of the divine Essence,* God of God, Light of Light, Eternity of Eternity, Infinity of Infinity. The act of generation being an eternal activity of the whole divine Being proceeding from the Father, the Son is Himself God, possessing in and of Himself all the divine perfections. He is Almighty, All-wise, Omniscient, Omnipresent, Eternal, Independent, Self-existent, Incomprehensible, the implication of all infinite perfections, and the overflowing Fount of all good. He is the *natural* Son of God!

And, mark you well, *Jesus* is that only begotten, that eternal, that natural Son of God. He, the eternal Son, at His incarnation, did not change into man. We must not speak of a pre-existent Christ in the sense that before His incarnation He *was* in the form of God, but now *changed* into the form of man. His incarnation did not mean that He *left* the bosom of the Father, in order to become mere man. No, this Jesus, this Christ, this Babe in the manger, this Child of Nazareth, this Man of Galilee, this Sufferer on the cross, IS very God. More must be said about this in connection with the next Lord's Day. But even now it must be remembered that we are speaking of the historical Jesus, when we confess that He is the only begotten, the eternal, the natural Son of God. "For unto us a child is born, unto us a son is given: and the government shall be upon his shoulder: and his name shall be called Wonderful, Counsellor, the mighty God, the everlasting Father, the Prince of Peace." Isa. 9:6.

"I believe in Jesus Christ," means: "I believe in the God of my salvation."

How different, how infinitely different from this eternal Sonship of the Christ, is our sonship as believers!

He is begotten, we are adopted, and born of God.

He is the eternal Son, our sonship belongs to time.

He is the natural Son of God, we are children of God by grace, for His sake.

He is the essential image of the Father, we are but creaturely reflections of His image.

He is Son within the divine Essence, we are children without the Essence of God.

He is God, we are creatures.

Adam, too, was the son of God. He was such by reason of his creation, by an act of God whereby He called the things that are not as if they were. It pleased Him to create a son. Hence, He made Adam after His own image, so that in his very nature he was adapted to reflect the virtues of God, was endowed with true knowledge of God, righteousness, and holiness, and stood in the relation of a son to God, his Creator-Father. He was known of God, and knew Him; he was loved of God, and loved Him; he had the right to dwell in God's house, and enjoyed His fellowship; and he served the Father in the freedom of a son. But he became disobedient. He rebelled. And he lost his sonship. He forfeited all his rights as a son, and became guilty, damnable, worthy of God's wrath, an exile from God's house with no right to return, worse than a stranger. And he also became in his very nature an enemy of God. The image of God in him was perverted into the very image of his father the devil. He became darkness, unrighteousness, unholiness, a lover of iniquity. Man by nature is no longer the son of God.

But it pleased God, nevertheless, to have many sons, and to lead them to a higher glory of sonship than Adam could ever have attained. He adopted us, i.e. He gave us the right to be his sons, and all the privileges of children of God. Us, who by nature are no children of God, but children of the devil, exiles from His house, enemies of God, He adopted, gave the right to His love, to His care, to His blessings, and to the blessed fellowship of His tabernacle. Just as a human father may adopt a strange child, that is not of his flesh and blood, that is, give it the legal status of his child and heir, so God adopted us, who were no children, and thereby made us legal heirs of all the blessings of salvation.

This adoption is an act of pure grace.

And we may distinguish various aspects of, or, if you please, stages in this gracious act of adoption.

It has its source in God's eternal counsel. For in that counsel He ordained His only begotten Son to be the firstborn of every creature, the firstborn of the dead, and the firstborn among many brethren, the Head of the Church; and in Him and unto Him He adopted all the elect to become sons of God. For He "predestinated us unto the adoption of children by Jesus Christ unto himself, according to the good pleasure of his will, to the praise of the glory of his grace, wherewith he hath made us accepted in the beloved." Eph. 1:5, 6. And Christ "is the image of the invisible God, the firstborn of every creature . . . . and he is the head of the body, the church: who is the beginning, the firstborn from the dead; that in all things he might have the pre-eminence." Col. 1:15, 18. "For whom he did foreknow, he also did predestinate to be conformed to the image of his Son, that he might be the firstborn among many brethren." Rom. 8:29. In sovereign grace, therefore, He adopted us from before the foundation of the world, and that, too, in Christ, the firstborn from the dead.

And this adoption is realized in time, and will be perfected in the day of Christ, through the resurrection, and by the revelation of the righteous judgment of God.

It is realized through the cross, the perfect sacrifice of Christ. For in ourselves, as we come into the world in Adam, we are children of wrath, with no right to sonship whatsoever, guilty and worthy of eternal desolation. But the only begotten Son assumed the flesh and blood of the children, came in the likeness of sinful flesh, and for sin, took His ordained position at the head of all the elect, took the whole burden of their guilt and sin upon His mighty shoulders, and with that burden of sin upon Him took the place of God's judgment and wrath in their stead, and in their behalf, offered the perfect sacrifice for sin, obtained for His own perfect and everlasting righteousness, the right to be restored to God's favor, to become the sons of God, and to dwell in His house forever. God realized our adoption unto children and heirs through the death of His only begotten. And in the resurrection of Christ from the dead, this adoption received His own official seal. For He was raised for our justification. Rom. 4:25. Christ, crucified and raised, is the ground of our adoption. We are children for His sake.

This adoption is bestowed upon us, and realized in us, through the Spirit of Christ, and by faith. For the Spirit of Christ is the Spirit of adoption through Whom we cry Abba, Father. And: "because ye are sons, God hath sent forth the Spirit of his Son into your hearts, crying, Abba, Father." Gal. 4:6. He makes us partakers of the adoption unto children by the faith He works in our hearts, through the gospel, by which we embrace Christ and all His benefits, are confident that we are justified, and that for the sake of Christ we are the sons of God with all the rights of children. Besides, this Spirit witnesses with our Spirit that we are the sons of God, Rom. 8:16. And the same Spirit also realizes the adoption by causing us to be born of God, by restoring within us the image of God, and making us like the image of the Son as the firstborn from the dead. For what an earthly father is impotent to do, i.e. to make of his adopted child a son of his own flesh and blood, God performs by the wonder of His grace in Christ. He regenerates us, calls us out of darkness into His marvelous light, makes us partaker of His own life and love, and thus bestows upon us the grace of actual sonship.

All this is true only in principle as long as we are in the body of this death. But this adoption unto sons of God awaits its final perfection in the day of Christ. For we "ourselves also, which have the firstfruits of the Spirit, even we ourselves groan within ourselves, waiting for the adoption, to wit, the redemption of our body." In that day we shall be publicly and before all the world justified and manifested as sons of God, and the image of God shall be raised in us to the highest possible glory of a creaturely likeness, for then we shall be perfectly conformed to the image of God's only begotten Son in the glorified Christ.

But for ever Christ remains the only Begotten, the eternal, the natural Son of God, Whom we can never approach, but Who reached out for us in the flesh; while we are for ever children adopted, by grace, for His sake, highly favored, yet always creaturely reflections of the divine image.

III

Our Lord

In the Apostolic Confession, the confession that Jesus Christ is our Lord follows upon the declaration that He is the only begotten Son of God. And this sequence must not be broken or lost sight of in the explanation of the phrase *nostrum dominum,* our Lord. The lordship of Jesus Christ over His Church as a whole, and over believers individually, is the lordship of the only begotten Son of God. It is true that in the way of sin and grace this lordship receives a new and deeper meaning. For the only begotten Son of God, as we shall learn subsequently, was also conceived by the Holy Ghost, and born of the virgin Mary; He suffered under Pontius Pilate, was crucified, dead, and buried, and descended into hell. He was raised on the third day, and is exalted in the highest heavens at the right hand of God. And in this way He became our Lord in a new, a deeper, a richer sense than could ever have been revealed in His lordship as the Creator of all things. It is to this that the Catechism refers in its answer to the question: "Wherefore callest thou him our Lord?" For it gives the following reply: "Because he hath redeemed us, both soul and body, from all our sins, not with gold and silver, but with his precious blood, and hath delivered us from all the power of the devil; and thus hath made us his own property." Yet even so, it dare not be forgotten, that this Jesus, crucified and raised, exalted at the right hand of God, is the only begotten Son of God, the same by Whom all things are created, and that as such, even while He is our Mediator in human nature, we call Him our Lord.

This is evidently the meaning of the confession: the *only begotten Son our Lord.*

If we do not bear in mind that Christ is the "natural and eternal Son of God," very God, like unto the Father and the Holy Spirit, or deny it, the confession that He is our Lord is emptied completely of all its real significance. For then He is Lord as mere man, a lord among other lords, more powerful, perhaps, than all, yet strictly limited in His authority and might, both with regard to its scope and with respect to its intrinsic power. Then His lordship becomes a matter of relative significance. He really is Lord because we call Him so, just as other religious groups in the world might call their leader lord. The act of calling Him lord is really a matter of hero-worship. We are, in that case, only a group of religious enthusiasts, among many others in the world, who reverence the founder of their religion by calling him their lord. And we may, perhaps, claim that, comparatively, he is worthy to become lord of all the world, because the religion he founded is much purer and nobler than any other religion, such as Confucianism, Brahmism, Mohammedanism, and whatever religions there may be found anywhere. Or, to stay a little nearer at home, by calling Jesus Christ *nostrum Dominum,* "our Lord," we probably express a feeling of sentimental piety: we consider that He has done so much for us that we feel we ought to do something for Him. He is our Lord because we are willing to serve Him, to further His cause, to crown Him king, and to win souls for Him. And failing to understand the real lordship of the only begotten Son of God, we feel rather "religious" and self-righteous.

Over against all these inventions of our sinful heart, we must clearly understand, and emphatically maintain, that by calling Jesus Christ "our Lord" we do not place Him in a class, in a category of lords such as we know many in the world, but that we acknowledge Him as the sole Lord over us and over all. We do not understand the term in a relative, comparative, but in the absolute sense of the word. The expression *nostrum Dominum* in the confession of the Church does not refer to a limited, but to an unlimited lordship. It does not tolerate other, perhaps inferior, lordships next to or even under the lordship of Jesus Christ, but it is strictly exclusive of them, and wholly intolerant. His lordship is not contingent or dependent upon anything we may do: He is not and does not become Lord, nor even *our* Lord, because we acknowledge Him as such, and are willing to serve Him, but on the contrary, our acknowledgment of Him as our Lord is strictly dependent on the sovereign exercise of His lordship over us. Even the marvelous fact that we are able to say: *"Credo . . . . in Dominum nostrum,"* I believe . . . . in our Lord, is only a manifestation of His mighty and sovereign lordship. For "no man can say that Jesus is the Lord, but by the Holy Ghost," which is the same as saying that no one can acknowledge His lordship but by the power of His own lordship over him.

But to maintain this we must not remove the expression "our Lord" from its proper place as it appears in the *Apostolic Confession,* i.e. in immediate connection with "his only begotten Son." We must not even make the mistake of treating, at this point, the exaltation of our Lord Jesus Christ at the right hand of God, as if His lordship had its deepest origin in the power that was conferred upon Him at this glorification of His human nature. All this comes later, and is not discussed till the nineteenth Lord's Day of the Catechism. We are now dealing with the lordship of the only begotten Son of God, not, indeed, as He created us, but as "He redeemed us, body and soul, from all our sins, not with gold and silver, but with his precious blood, and delivered us from all the power of the devil; and thus made us his own property." The only begotten Son, always the revelation of the Father, i.e. of the triune God, is our Lord, not only now as our Creator, but also as our Redeemer and Deliverer. With Thomas the Church confesses: "My Lord, and my God." John 20:28. It is He of Whom the apostle Paul writes: "for the same Lord over all is rich unto all that call upon him. For whosoever shall call upon the name of the Lord shall be saved." Rom. 10:12, 13. The only begotten Son, God of God, and Light of Light, Who, to be sure was manifested in the flesh, Who died and was raised, and Who is exalted at the right hand of God, but Who is still very God Himself, — Him we call *nostrum Dominum,* our Lord. And in Him we call our Lord, and now in a deeper sense than ever before, Him, Whom in our natural state we refuse to acknowledge as such: the God of our salvation!

You see, the only begotten Son is also Lord as our Creator, as the eternal Word, through Whom all things were made. For "in the beginning was the Word, and the Word was with God, and the Word was God. The same was in the beginning with God. All things were made by him; and without him was not anything made that was made." This same Jesus Christ, Whom we now call our Lord, is also the Son, by Whom God made the worlds, Who is the brightness of His glory, and the express image of His person, and Who upholds all things by the Word of His power, Heb. 1:2, 3. He is the image of the invisible God, and by Him were all things created, that are in heaven, and that are in earth, visible and invisible, whether they be thrones, or dominions, or principalities, or powers: all things were created by Him and for Him, Col. 1:15, 16. He is, therefore, the Creator, the sole Proprietor, the absolute Lord of all things, also of you and me, and with body and soul we belong to Him. Also in creation He is the revelation of the only sovereign God, the Lord of all, Whom we are bound to love with all our heart and mind and soul and strength, to glorify, to serve, to adore, and to give thanks.

But we rebelled against this Lord.

We refused to acknowledge Him as our Lord. We turned away from Him, rejected His word, and gave heed to the word of the devil in preference to His. And thus we became slaves of Satan, and were held in the bondage of sin and of corruption.

Not, you understand, as if this affected the Lordship of our God, or as if we really succeeded to dethrone the Lord of heaven and earth, the Creator, the Word by Whom all things were made. He is and remains sovereign, the sole Lord of all. Even the fact that by our rebellion we became slaves of the devil, lost in sin, guilty and damnable, so that we were incapable of doing any good and inclined to all evil, dead through trespasses and sins, unspeakably miserable, is but a manifestation of His Lordship, the execution of His sentence upon us. But although He is and ever remains Lord, ethically we choose the lordship of the devil, and our rightful Lord, Whom to know and to serve in love is life, we hated in our unspeakable folly. And although "the invisible things of him from the creation of the world are clearly seen, being understood by the things that are made, even his eternal power and Godhead," yet we held, and do hold, "the truth in unrighteousness," and we "glorified him not as God, neither were thankful; but became vain in our imaginations, and our foolish heart was darkened," Rom. 1:19-21.

But what happens?

God will give His glory to no other. Before the foundation of the world, He had determined to reveal His Lordship, and to be known and acknowledged as the sole Lord, and to be served and glorified as Lord, in a far higher and deeper, a far more intimate and glorious sense than in creation. Accordingly, He had ordained His only begotten Son, the image of the invisible God, the Word of creation, to be the Firstborn of every creature, and that, too, *as* the Firstborn from the dead, and *as* the Firstborn among many brethren, the Head of the elect Church. And according to this eternal good pleasure of God, the only begotten Son of God, the eternal Word, in the fulness of time was manifested in the flesh. Our Lord, Whom we had rejected, and against Whom we had rebelled, came very near us, spoke to us face to face and mouth to mouth, united Himself with us in an inseparable union. What is more, He reached down into our misery, into our darkness of sin and death, where in our folly, and by divine sentence of this same Lord, we were held in the slavery of the devil, and He redeemed us. He purchased us free from the bondage of Satan, not as if He paid the price of redemption to the devil, for he had no other right over us than that which was implied in the divine sentence of death, but to the Father Whose revelation He is, and, therefore, — O wonder of wonders! — to Himself. And He did not pay a mere external price, He did not dig into the treasures of His own creation, for all the gold and silver in the world would not have been sufficient unto our redemption, but He redeemed us with His own precious blood, the price of an eternal love! And thus He obtained for Himself, i.e. at the bar of divine justice, the right to make us His property, not, you understand, as a mere possession with which He may do as He pleases (for this we are even in our sin), but a precious property of love! He obtained for Himself the right of that lordship according to which we may once more, and now in a deeper sense than ever before, love Him, trust in Him, and serve Him, as our Lord!

But what then?

Does the devil, seeing that the justice of God is satisfied, and that the price of their redemption is paid, now willingly surrender the elect to their rightful Lord? Or, perhaps, does this *only begotten Son our Lord* now send men to us to tell us how He loved us, to offer us His lordship, and are we thus persuaded of our own free will to forsake the service of the devil, and to enter His service? Do we, of ourselves, seeing how great a price He paid for our redemption, now say: "this hath He done for me, now I will do something for Him?"

God forbid!

No, but having redeemed us, He also *delivers* us from the dominion of sin, and from all the power of the devil. His lordship is always *His* lordship, whether in creation or in redemption. We never make Him our Lord. And no man can say that Jesus is Lord except by His own Spirit. And if anyone hath not the Spirit of Christ, he is none of His. He exercises His lordship over us. He, the only begotten Son of God, the eternal Word, our rightful Lord against Whom we had rebelled, and Whose enemies we are by nature, and Who became flesh, was crucified and raised, exalted at the right hand of God, and is become the quickening Spirit; He Himself, having destroyed him that had the power of death, that is the devil, now comes to visit us in our prison of sin and death, and *delivers* us, "who through fear of death were all their lifetime subject to bondage." Heb. 2:14, 15. He dethrones the devil and sin from our heart, He breaks the shackles of corruption and death in which we are held, He removes the enmity against our rightful Lord from our inmost mind, He dispels the darkness of our folly, He enlightens us, sheds abroad the love of God in our hearts; and then He calls us by His own mighty and sovereign Word, through the gospel. And then we come. Then we see the folly of our sin, the unspeakable foolishness of ever having wanted to rebel against His blessed lordship, the unspeakable wretchedness of the slavery of the devil. Then we begin to love Him, our Creator-Lord, now as our Lord-Redeemer, and to long for Him, to cry out to Him from the depths. Then we trust in Him, surrender ourselves to Him, and fall down before Him in adoration with the words of glad worship on our lips: "My Lord, and my God!"

Thus we come to the confession: *Credo* . . . . *in Dominum nostrum*, "I believe . . . . in our Lord." The confession is but the fruit of the exercise of His lordship. It is but the expression of our experience of the lordship of the only begotten Son of God, our Redeemer and Deliverer, the God of our salvation.

All boasting is excluded!

No flesh can ever glory in His presence. His lordship is always known and experienced as strictly *His*, and as absolute. Hence, we can only meet it with a *credo*, that is itself the fruit of His dominion over us!

And since He exercises this particular lordship by the one Spirit, and in the one Body, His Church, therefore, we say emphatically "Dominum *nostrum*," *our* Lord. For now "there is one body, and one Spirit, even as ye are called in one hope of your calling. One Lord, one faith, one baptism, one God and Father of all, who is above all, and through all, and in you all." Eph. 4:4-6.

The only begotten Son, the eternal Word, the Creator-Redeemer, Jesus Christ our Lord!

And do you not see now, how serious this confession is? Do you not understand that the lordship of Jesus, which we confess with the Church of all ages, is all-comprehensive, strictly exclusive, absolutely intolerant, and it dare never be mentioned in the same breath with any other lordship? Can you not see the reason why the saints of the early Church preferred the stake and the scaffold, preferred to be cast before the wild beasts, or into a caldron of boiling oil, rather than say: "Jesus is Lord, and Caesar is also Lord." Do you not discern now, that this was, ultimately, not a matter of their own choice, but the exercise of Jesus' lordship in them and over them? Next to Jesus, no Caesar is ever lord!

That Jesus is our Lord means that He is our Proprietor, He alone, and that we are His property, His alone and completely. We are His with body and soul, with heart and mind and will, with wife and children, and brothers and sisters, with all our life and possessions. It means that our heart and all its issues are His, that our thoughts and desires, our intentions and our motives are His. It means that the sight of our eyes, the hearing of our ears, the speech of our mouth, the actions of our members belong to Him. They are His alone. They belong to no one else.

That Jesus is our Lord implies that He is responsible for us, and for all that we are, with body and soul, in life and in death, for time and all the ages of eternity, to keep us, to love us, to defend us, and to lead us on to the final victory, to the glory of God's everlasting tabernacle. And it means that He alone can bear that responsibility, that no one else can possibly share it with Him. And the confession that He is our Lord implies that we completely trust in Him, and surrender ourselves to His responsibility, that we trust in no other lordship, neither are fearful of, and terrorized by any other. Under His lordship there is freedom from fear!

That Jesus is our Lord means that He rules over us, not by force and compulsion, but by grace and the impelling power of His love. It signifies that His mind is our mind, that His will is our will, that His Word is our law, and that His law is our delight. It is He alone that determines, not only what we shall do, but also what we shall think, and feel, and desire, and by what motives we shall be governed. It means that He has dominion over the life of our body and of our soul, and over all our relationships in the midst of this present world, in the home and in the shop, in labor and industry, in the school and on the street, in the Church and in the State, in peace and in war, in prosperity and in adversity. And the confession that He is our Lord implies that we gladly and willingly acknowledge

His lordship, and that it is our earnest desire and endeavor to know His will, and to obey no other Word than His in any department of our life in the world, no matter what may be the cost, yea, though we should lose our very life in His service.

For, let us make no mistake, the confession that Jesus is Lord is limited to the Church. It does not mean that you can gain the world for Christ, or that you can crown Him King in every domain of this present world. He alone exercises His lordship of grace; and He limits it to His elect Church. And the world hates His lordship, and hates those that consistently confess it. Hence, if you represent the cause of the Son of God in the world, you must expect tribulation. Only by compromising the strictly intolerant lordship of Jesus Christ can you escape this. We must suffer with Him. But even so, we are of good cheer. For we know that He is responsible for us, and that He has overcome the world. And if we suffer with Him, we shall also be glorified together!

LORD'S DAY XIV

Q. 35. What is the meaning of these words—"He was conceived by the Holy Ghost, born of the virgin Mary?"

A. That God's eternal Son, who is and continueth true and eternal God, took upon him the nature of man, of the flesh and blood of the Virgin Mary, by the operation of the Holy Ghost; that he might also be the true seed of David, like unto his brethren in all things, sin excepted.

Q. 36. What profit dost thou receive by Christ's holy conception and nativity?

A. That he is our Mediator; and with innocence and perfect holiness, covers in the sight of God, my sins, wherein I was conceived and brought forth.

I

Without The Will Of Man

Except for the adjective "true" or "real" modifying "nature of man" in the thirty-fifth answer (*wahre menschliche Natur*), our text is a correct translation of the original German.

This Lord's Day offers a brief exposition of the words of the *Apostolicum*: "conceived by the Holy Ghost, born of the virgin Mary." While in the preceding Lord's Day the subject was that the man Jesus is the true and eternal Son of God, in the present chapter of the Heidelberg Catechism the emphasis falls on His humanity: the Son of God is become man, the Word is become flesh. We are confronting two questions here: 1. that concerning the mystery of the two natures of Christ, or the union of the human nature with the divine in Him; and 2. that of the origin of His human nature, or the mode of the accomplishment of this union of the divine and human nature. Strictly speaking, the Apostolic Confession speaks only of the latter: the Church confesses that Jesus, the only begotten Son of God our Lord, was conceived by the Holy Ghost, born of the virgin Mary. This would seem to refer only to the origin of the human nature of the Saviour, to the way in which the Word became flesh. Yet, this "historical" statement certainly implies the entire mystery of the incarnation, and of the union of the two natures in the Person of the Son of God. And once again we marvel at the comprehensiveness of the comparatively brief explanation by the Catechism of this statement of the *Apostolicum*. In its answer to the thirty-fifth question our Instructor explains: 1. That the assumption of the human nature of Christ is strictly a work of God, wholly and immediately, i.e., without the will and instrumentality of man. God alone is the Father of our Lord Jesus Christ, also according to His human nature: the

Son of God, the second Person of the Holy Trinity, Who as Son is never to be separated from the Father, by the operation of the Holy Spirit, the Spirit that proceeds from the Father and the Son, took upon Him the nature of man. 2. That by this divine act the nature of the Godhead did not change: the Son is and continueth true and eternal God. 3. That through the act of the incarnation the human nature retained its own identity, and was not merged into the Godhead: he took the true or real human nature upon Himself, and that, too, from the flesh and blood of a woman. 4. That this woman, who through the wonder of God's omnipotence was chosen and "graced" to become the mother of Jesus Christ, was a virgin. 5. That through the birth of this Son of God in the flesh from the virgin Mary, He was the true seed of David, born in the line of the promise. 6. And that thus He, the incarnated Son of God, became like unto His brethren in all things, except that also in His human nature He was without sin.

These various elements, therefore, are now the subject of our further exposition.

And these truths must be maintained by the Church in opposition to every form of false doctrine, both of the early centuries of the history of the Church, and of modern times.

Even in very early times several false doctrines developed in regard to the humanity of Christ, as well as in respect to His true divinity. There were those who taught that the Son of God assumed merely the appearance of a human nature. Even as angels occasionally appeared in the form of man, so Christ was not really flesh of our flesh and bone of our bone, but appeared in the form of a man. Others presented the view that Christ assumed only a partial human nature: He took upon Himself a human body, and a human soul, but not a human "mind" or spirit; the place of the latter was taken by the divine nature. Still others erred in regard to the union of the two natures, some speaking of two persons as well as two natures in Christ, only one of whom was crucified and raised from the dead; others presenting this union as a merging of the two natures into one "theanthropos," a God-man. In modern times the incarnation is denied as purely and exclusively a wonder of God: God did not come down to man in the incarnation of the Son, but man is reaching out for God, becomes God-conscious.

Over against all these old and new errors the Church must hold fast to the truth concerning the mystery of the incarnation. She lives, not by human philosophy, but by faith in revelation. And by that faith she confesses, that Christ assumed a real human nature, body and soul, from the flesh and blood of the virgin Mary; that in His human nature He is of the seed of David, in every respect like unto His brethren, sin excepted; that the human nature through the wonder of the incarnation did not merge with the divine, nor was ever separated from the divine nature, but is and remains for ever united with Christ's deity in the unity of the Person of the Son of God. And in the same faith she confesses that the incarnation is in no sense an act of man, but solely of God. Man did not reach out for God, or develop to new heights of God-consciousness, but God came down to us, ever to remain with us and dwell with us. The incarnation is the revelation of the living God! The Creator united Himself most intimately with the creature; the Lord also became servant; the Eternal One came into time, the Infinite One into space. Great is the mystery of godliness: God is manifest in the flesh!

This truth it is which the Church meant to express in the words of the *Apostolicum*: "conceived by the Holy Ghost, born of the virgin Mary."

The two parts of this confession are intimately related. They constitute one whole. They are only aspects of one and the same truth: that God alone is the Father of our Lord Jesus Christ, even according to His human nature, although He was not created but had a human mother, and was born of us. It is the truth that the birth of the Son of God is a human impossibility, a revelation of the God of our salvation. Christ was born without the will of man.

That this is the testimony of Scripture cannot be doubted.

Even in the old dispensation the sign of the virgin that would conceive and bear a son was given: "Therefore the Lord himself

shall give you a sign; Behold a virgin shall conceive, and bear
a son, and shall call his name Immanuel." It is true that those
who deny the virgin birth of Christ point out that the Hebrew
word used in this text for "virgin" may also refer to a young
woman recently married. Fact is, however, first of all, that the
word signifies the age of puberty, a person of marriageable age
but not yet married; and secondly, that the text speaks definitely
of a *sign*. Now a sign is a phenomenon that draws the attention
of men by its extraordinary character, its being radically different
from the facts of experience, a wonder of grace. But there certainly would be nothing extraordinary in the fact that a young
woman would conceive and bear a son. We maintain, therefore,
that the prophecy in Isa. 7:14 ultimately looks forward to the
wonder of the birth of our Lord from the virgin Mary.

This is, moreover, corroborated by the passage in Matt.
1:18-25. In the twenty-second and twenty-third verses we read:
"Now all this was done, that it might be fulfilled which was
spoken of the Lord by the prophet, saying, Behold, a virgin
shall be with child, and shall bring forth a son, and they shall
call his name Emmanuel, which being interpreted is, God with
us." The "word of the Lord by the prophet" is, evidently a
reference to Isa. 7:14. And "all this was done" refers to what
is narrated in the preceding verses. Joseph, having noticed
Mary's condition, had been minded to leave his espoused wife
secretly, but the Lord had revealed to him in a dream that she
was quite innocent of the sin he had suspected her to have committed, "for that which is conceived in her is of the Holy Ghost."
vs. 20. This passage, therefore, is not only in itself a clear proof
for the virgin birth of the Saviour, but also corroborates the
view that in Isa. 7:14 this amazing wonder was predicted.

Moreover, that the Scriptures plainly teach the virgin birth
is also evident from the annunciation of the birth of Christ by
the angel Gabriel to Mary in Nazareth, the narrative of which
we find in Luke 1:26-38. We may note here especially the question of Mary: "How shall this be, seeing I know not a man?"
There is more implied in this question than what may appear
on the surface. The angel had saluted Mary with the words:

"Hail, thou that art highly favored, the Lord is with thee: blessed art thou among women." vs. 28. And when Mary was evidently troubled at this strange salutation, the angel continued: "Fear not, Mary: for thou hast found favor with God. And, behold, thou shalt conceive in thy womb, and bring forth a son, and shalt call his name Jesus. He shall be great, and shall be called the Son of the Highest: and the Lord God shall give unto him the throne of his father David: And he shall reign over the house of Jacob for ever: and of his kingdom there shall be no end." And it is then that Mary asks her question of astonishment: "How shall this be, seeing that I know not a man?"

Now there is reason to ask: what induced Mary to ask this question? The mere fact that, at the moment, Mary was still a virgin, would hardly seem sufficient to explain this. It is true, of course, that she was not as yet married. But it is also a fact that she "was espoused to a man named Joseph." She was, therefore, about to be married. How, then, could she be so absolutely certain that she would "not know a man?" Certainly there was nothing in the words of the angel that would suggest this, far less raise it beyond a doubt that she would become pregnant without the normal intercourse to cause such a condition. Why could she not interpret the words of the angel as meaning that she would get married to Joseph as soon as possible, and that then, in the normal way she would become with child? Would not that have been the most natural conclusion for her to draw from the announcement of the angel, rather than at once think of the astounding possibility that she would conceive without knowing a man? Yet, of this one thing she appears absolutely sure. She will not know a man. And because of this, the words of the angel appear to her to be humanly impossible of realization. How must this certainty on the part of Mary be explained?

It seems to me that there can only be one answer to this question: there was no man for her to know, i.e., there was no man left in the royal line of the promise that could beget the promised Messiah. That Davidic generation of royal seed that, according to the promise, was expected to bring forth the

Christ, had ended in a virgin! The realization of the promise
had become an impossibility from a human viewpoint. Long
before Gabriel visited Mary in Nazareth the glorious tree of
David had been cut down to the ground, and never it had
flourished again since the Babylonian captivity. But at the
moment of the annunciation all that was left of it was a "root
in a dry ground." There was no male descendant in the line
of the generations of the promise. Only a virgin was left. And,
therefore, when the angel came to announce to her that she
would become the mother of Him that would reign over the
house of Jacob for ever, the question arose immediately: But
how shall this be, seeing I do not know a man?

This explanation is based on the conviction that in Matt.
1:1-17 the evangelist gives us very really "the book of the generation of Jesus Christ," that is, not the legal line of Christ's
fathers according to the flesh, but the organic line. In other
words, in this "book of generation" we have the genealogy, not
of Joseph, but of Mary. If this is true, the sixteenth verse of the
first chapter of Matthew must mean that Jacob had no male
children, that Mary was the only heir, and that, when Joseph
married Mary he was received and inscribed legally in the
registers of generations that ran from David over Jacob (vs. 16)
to the mother of Jesus. In this legal sense Joseph was of the
house and lineage of David. Whether he was also of the generations of David in the organic sense, is a question that depends
on the other question whether or not in the third chapter of the
gospel according to Luke we have the genealogy of Joseph.
There is good ground to believe that also in Luke we meet with
the genealogy of Mary, although legally it is that of Joseph.
However this may be, if our interpretation of Matt. 1:16 be
correct, Joseph was not of that line of generations, that continued line of Davidic kings (II Sam. 7:12 ff.; Ps. 89:19 ff.), that
would culminate in the Messiah. Mary alone was left. It is not
improbable that she often "pondered this in her heart," before the
angel came to visit her with his amazing message, and that the
question that had frequently troubled her soul arose to her

mind at once as she listened to the angel's words: But how shall this be? How shall the promise be fulfilled, seeing there is not a man, and I am the only one left of the royal generations of David?

If this is correct, we can understand why denial of the virgin birth of Christ usually implies or leads to the denial of the incarnation of the Son of God, the truth that Jesus Christ *came into* the flesh. There are those who would maintain the truth of the incarnation and of the real divinity of Christ, but who deny that He was born of a virgin, and claim that Christ's assuming our human nature did not necessarily require His birth of a virgin. The Son of God could just as well unite Himself with our nature as it is normally conceived and born from a human mother and by the will of man. Now, this is, to say the least, a proposition that is difficult to prove, if not impossible. We know very little about the mystery of the conception and birth of a normal child, much less about the birth of the Son of God in the flesh. Even though we may not be able to demonstrate the truth of this proposition, we much rather assume, on the basis of Scripture, that the virgin birth of Christ was also ontologically necessary, that is, that the Son of God could assume the human nature only by way of elimination of the will of man. But whether this be so or not, certain it is that God purposely creates the *sign* of the virgin birth to make known unto us that Jesus Christ's coming into the flesh is His act exclusively, and that Christ is born, not by the will of man, but by the conception of the Holy Spirit. God reveals Himself where all human possibilities have come to an end. The incarnation does not take place until the generations from which He was to be born according to the promise have ended in a virgin, that is, until an impossible situation has been created, in order that He may be revealed as the Lord, Who not only calls the things that are not as if they were, but Who also quickens the dead. Only when we are forced to ask the question: "how shall this be?" does God give us the answer: What is impossible with men, is possible with God. The virgin birth is a *sign*, a revelation of the mystery of the conception by the Holy Ghost. The two are inseparably connected.

And this is quite in harmony with the answer Mary receives through the angel to her perplexing problem. For the angel replied: "The Holy Ghost shall come upon thee, and the power of the Highest shall overshadow thee: therefore also that holy thing which shall be born of thee shall be called the Son of God." The answer to Mary's question: how shall a virgin conceive and bear a child? is, therefore, *through the conception by the Holy Ghost.* We refrain, of course, from any attempt to explain this profound mystery. All we can say about it is that it signifies that the Son of God Himself, by His Spirit, that proceeds from the Father and the Son, so operated upon the flesh and blood of the virgin Mary, that she conceived in her womb, and brought forth her firstborn Son. Eliminating the will of man, the Person of the Son of God, prepared His own human nature, and that, too, from the flesh and blood of the virgin Mary. And this means, seeing that the Persons in the holy Trinity can never be separated, that the triune God is the Father of our Lord Jesus Christ, also in His human nature. It also implies that Christ is flesh of our flesh, and blood of our blood. As to His Person, He came from without, from above, out of eternity, to unite Himself with us for ever; as to His human nature, He is of us, not especially created, but conceived and born. "Forasmuch then as the children are partakers of flesh and blood, he also himself likewise took part of the same; that through death he might destroy him that had the power of death, that is the devil; And deliver them who through fear of death were all their lifetime subject to bondage." Heb. 2:14, 15.

Thus understood the words with which the angel concludes his message to Mary become intelligible, and receive a new meaning: "For with God nothing shall be impossible." The impossibility is the virgin without a man. The divine possibility is realized by the wonder of God expressed in the words of the *Apostolicum: conceived by the Holy Ghost.* And in the light of this revelation, through faith, the Church calls "that holy thing" that was born of Mary the Son of God! For "every spirit that confesseth that Jesus Christ is come into the flesh is of God: And every spirit that confesseth not that Jesus Christ is come into the flesh is not of God: and this is that spirit of antichrist, whereof ye have heard that it should come; and even now already is it in the world." I John 4:2, 3.

II

The Flesh And Blood Of The Children

Concerning the human nature which the Son of God assumed, the Heidelberg Catechism teaches us that He "took upon him the very nature of man, of the flesh and blood of the Virgin Mary . . . . that he might also be the true seed of David, like unto his brethren in all things, sin excepted." There are, in these words, especially four elements that must always be emphasized in our confession concerning the human nature of Christ, and which we must briefly discuss in this connection, namely: 1 That it is a real and complete human nature. 2. That it is an individual and *central* human nature: He was born in the very center of the line of the promise, the seed of David. 3. That it is a weakened human nature: He came in the *likeness* of sinful flesh. 4. That it is a sinless human nature: He was made like unto His brethren in all things, sin excepted.

The *Confessio Belgica* emphasizes the same truths, when it declares that He "took upon him the form of a servant, and became like unto man, really assuming the true human nature, with all its infirmities, sin excepted . . . . and did not only assume the human nature as to the body, but also a true human soul, that he might be a real man. For since the soul was lost as well as the body, it was necessary that he should take both upon him, to save both. Therefore we confess (in opposition to the heresy of the Anabaptists, who deny that Christ assumed human flesh of his mother) that Christ is become a partaker of the flesh and blood of the children; that he is a fruit of the loins of David after the flesh; made of the seed of David according to the flesh; a fruit of the womb of the Virgin Mary, made of a woman; a branch of David; a shoot of the root of Jesse; sprung from the tribe of Judah; descended from the Jews

612

according to the flesh; of the seed of Abraham, since he took on him the seed of Abraham, and became like unto his brethren in all things, sin excepted, so that in truth he is our Immanuel, that is to say, God with us." Art. XVIII.

That our Lord assumed a real human nature means, first of all, that He was very really *born*, not created, and that, too, according to body and soul. Even though He was conceived without the will of man, and born of a virgin, His was not a strange, or specially created human nature, but He took upon Him our flesh and blood. He was organically connected with us. As to His human nature, He did not come from without, but was brought forth by us. He did not stand next to men, but among them, and was of them. He partook of the flesh and blood of the children. He was flesh of our flesh, blood of our blood, bone of our bone. This must be maintained, because it is the plain teaching of Scripture. According to the message of the angel to Mary, she would conceive in her womb, and bring forth a son, Lu. 1:31. That which was conceived in her developed in the womb of Mary like the seed of any other human being, and its growth required the same length of time, for while Joseph and Mary were in Bethlehem, "the days were accomplished that she should be delivered. And she brought forth her firstborn son." Lu. 2:6, 7. When Mary visited her cousin Elisabeth, before the birth of Jesus, the mother of John the Baptist, filled with the Holy Ghost, greeted her in the following words: "Blessed art thou among women, and blessed is the fruit of thy womb. And whence is this to me, that the mother of my Lord should come to me?" Lu. 1:42, 43. Moreover, Scripture teaches us that "when the fulness of time was come, God sent forth his Son, *made of a woman,* made under the law, to redeem them that were under the law, that we might receive the adoption of sons." Gal. 4:4, 5. And "forasmuch then as the children are partakers of flesh and blood, he also likewise took part of the same; that through death he might destroy him that had the power of death, that is, the devil; and deliver them who through fear of death were all their lifetime subject to bondage." Heb. 2:14, 15.

From the above passages of Holy Writ, it is also evident that the organic unity of Christ with us was necessary unto our redemption. He must bear our sin, and suffer death in our stead. If this were to be done, the punishment of sin must be borne in our nature. The same human nature that had sinned must bear the wrath of God to the end. If Jesus had not been of us, if His human nature had been especially created, He might have been similar to us, but He would, nevertheless, have stood outside of us. And even as He would have been extraneous to us, so His death would have been suffered entirely apart from us. It could not have been *our* death. In that case, God would really have left the human race in Adam in their sin and condemnation, and created something entirely new. Then we did not die with Christ, neither were we raised with Him, and our life cannot possibly be hid with Christ in God. The truth, therefore, that Christ really assumed the flesh and blood of the children, is essential to the gospel of our redemption.

But, in the second place, the truth that Christ assumed a true and real human nature also implies that this human nature is complete, that is, consists of body and soul. We must not conceive of the incarnation of the Son of God in such a way that by this wonder of grace the divine nature came to inhabit a human body, took the place of the human soul; or even that the Person of the Son of God took upon Him a human body and a human soul, but that the divine nature took the place of the human mind or spirit. The whole human nature He assumed in His incarnation. He was completely human, even as He is truly divine. That this is true is evident from all we read of the revelation of Jesus Christ in the days of His flesh. And more than once our Lord speaks of His soul expressly. Shortly before His death, He declares: "Now is my soul troubled." John 12:27. And as He entered into the garden of Gethsemane, He complained: "My soul is exceeding sorrowful, even unto death." Matt. 26:38.

It would seem that the theory of Creationism meets with a serious difficulty here. According to this theory, as you know, the soul, in the case of the birth of every individual human being, is created by God, while the body only is conceived and born by and from the parents. However, in the case of the incarnation, we confess that the whole human nature, both body and soul, was assumed by the Son of God from the virgin Mary. In His case, therefore, the soul is also born, and not created. It would appear, then, that Creationism is wrong, and that we are bound to adopt the view of Traducianism, the theory that in all cases the whole human nature is brought forth through conception and birth by the human parents. And yet, we are loath to accept that also the human spirit is propagated through generation and birth, because it would seem that by adopting this view we would destroy the very spirituality of the soul, and change it into flesh and blood.

It seems to me, therefore, that we must seek to avoid both crass Creationism and liberal Traducianism. Of course, let us admit it from the outset, when we deal with the questions concerning the human soul and body, we are facing deep problems, problems that are, ultimately, impossible of solution. The relation between soul and body is a profound mystery. Yet, it may be possible, on the basis of Scripture, to formulate some conception that will cover and explain all the facts, especially that of man's creation, and that of the incarnation of the Son of God. It would seem that the theory of Creationism is guilty of completely separating soul and body; while, on the other hand, Traducianism must lose the spiritual identity of the soul. Another distinction, therefore, would appear to be more to the point here. I mean the distinction between *person* and *nature*. Certain it is that it is this distinction which we face in the incarnation of the Son of God. He was a human being without being a human person. In His case the divine Person of the Son of God took upon Himself a human nature, but not a human person. Hence, it is certainly correct to say that in His case the Person came from God, the nature from the virgin Mary. But if this is true of the incarnation, it must also be true of the birth of every human individual: the whole nature is born, the person comes into being by an act of God.

And this would seem to be in harmony with what Scripture reveals to us concerning the creation of man in Gen. 2:7. (1). God formed *man*, not merely his body but the whole *nature* out of the dust of the ground; but He also breathed into his nostrils the breath of life. And thus, that is, by this one but twofold act of God man became a living soul. He did not form a body, in order then to breathe a soul into it, but He formed the whole man, and made him a living soul. With His own fingers God formed man out of the dust of the ground, and by His in-breathing He made him a rational, a *personal* being, in distinction from the animals who also are living souls. Now, in a similar way, in the conception and birth of a human being, the *nature*, the whole nature, all that God originally formed from the dust of the ground, comes from the parents; while by a special act of God's providence, like unto the original in-breathing of God in the creation of Adam, that nature is formed into a *personal* being. The nature comes from the parents, the person from God.

At all events, thus we must conceive of the incarnation.

From the virgin Mary, the Son of God assumed, not a human body merely, but the whole human nature, both according to body and soul.

But we said, and our confessions emphasize the fact, that He assumed a concrete and individual, though a *central* human nature. He was the "true seed of David." According to the Belgic or Netherland Confession, he was "a branch of David, a shoot of the root of Jesse, sprung from the tribe of Judah, descended from the Jews according to the flesh; of the seed of Abraham."

To us this clearly implies, in the first place, that He assumed a very concrete and individual human nature. There are those who deny this, and who insist that Christ's humanity was *general*. He did not assume a certain concrete form of the human nature, but *the* human nature in general. He was not *a* man, but Man. Just as we speak of the general concept *the*

----

(1) Cf. Section I, pp. 90, ff.

tree, in distinction from all specific trees, so we must conceive of the humanity of Christ as being *the human nature.*
Thus Dr. A. Kuyper dictated to his students:
"The human nature which Christ assumed was not concrete. With us it is. With each of us the human nature bears a definite, concrete stamp, determined by our individual ego. The human nature in the abstract sense is that which is common to us all. The general human nature is, so to speak, the wax into which each man impresses his own stamp. Christ, however, assumed the abstract and unstamped human nature, while He possessed the divine nature concretely." (2).
Again:
"The view that Christ was *a* man is Nestorian . . . . To be sure, Scripture teaches everywhere that Christ was man, and that He bore the human nature, but that He was an individual, that among the variations of the seed of Adam there was also the variation — Jesus — is absurd. In the seed of Adam were all the variations of human life, of nations, generations, and persons. And over against this, the Scriptures witness and say that Christ was the second Adam; He was out of Adam *as Adam,* that is, as one who like Adam carried within Himself endless variations, namely, those of all the elect of God. Because of this every child of God knows that he is in Christ, that he died and is raised with Christ, that he draws his life out of Christ, even as the sinner out of Adam" . . . . (3).
The same view is set forth in *De Gemeene Gratie* by the same author, II, 138, 139.
The Scriptural ground on which this conception is supposed to be based is especially threefold: 1. The statement in I Cor. 15:45 that Christ is the second Adam. Let it be noted here at once that Christ is not called the *second,* but the *last* Adam, and that He is such, not in virtue of the fact that in the state of humiliation he bore a general human nature (even if this could be asserted of Adam, which it cannot, it does not apply to Christ

---

(2) Dictaten Dogmatiek, Locus de Christo, III, 33.
(3) Op. Cit. p. 7.

in the flesh) , but because He represents all His own, and, as the quickening Spirit is able to impart Himself to all the elect. 2. The fact that Christ is called the Son of man. It is emphasized that He is never called *a* Son of man, but always *the* Son of man. And this is supposed to teach us that, while we are all sons of man, He is *the* Son of man in the sense that he assumed a general human nature. He was not a man among men, but the man in the abstract sense of the word. However, if the name Son of man is derived from Dan. 7:13, as is generally accepted, it does not refer to a supposed general and abstract human nature in distinction from the specific forms of the human nature other men have, but to the Messiah as He is destined to inherit the glory of His everlasting kingdom. And this is corroborated by such passages as the eighth Psalm in connection with Heb. 2:6-9. 3. The fact that Scripture presents the Lord as the Head of the Church, His body. This implies that, even as we partake of the nature of Adam, so we also really partake of the nature of Christ. But, according to this theory, this is possible only if Christ is not a mere individual, a man among men, but *the* Man, and that He assumed a general human nature. But this argument overlooks the fact that we are not partakers of Christ according to the flesh, but according to the Spirit, and that this union became possible, not in virtue of a supposed general human nature, which He assumed at His incarnation, but in virtue of His exaltation, and through the Spirit that was given Him. According to the flesh, we are not of Him, but He is of us.

The most serious objection to this theory of a general human nature in Christ is, no doubt, that it really implies a denial of the reality of our Lord's humanity. What is a general human nature? It is something that does not concretely exist, an abstraction that exists only in the form of a conception, but that has no real, no tangible existence. Thus I can speak of *the* tree as a concept. I can probably say that *the* tree has reality in the mind of God. But in reality *the* tree is nowhere. It exists only in various forms and types of trees, oaks, maples, poplars, etc., and these various classes again exist only in individual forms.

The same is true of the human nature of our Lord. To say that it was general is tantamount to saying that it did not concretely, historically exist, that it had no tangible reality. But this is, indeed, absurd. It is evident that our Lord, according to the flesh, had a very concrete form of the human nature. In the days of His flesh He certainly could have been photographed. He had a concrete body. He was of a certain, measurable height, weighed a certain number of pounds, had a certain color of eyes, was white, not black or yellow, and possessed certain definite features by which He was recognized in distinction from His fellowmen. It may seem absurd to mention all this, but the fact is that these concrete statements could never be predicated of a general human nature. And what is true of Jesus' body is equally applicable to His soul. Even though the gospel narratives are not at all interested in a "Life of Jesus," and although it is certainly true that one looks in vain in them for a description of His character, the conclusion is not warranted that Jesus had no character, that He had a "general" human soul. That the gospel narratives are not interested in a *Leben Jesu* is due to the fact that they mean to be the revelation of Jesus Christ, the incarnated Son of God, Who died for us and rose again, and is seated at the right hand of God. But it certainly must be maintained that, both according to soul and body, our Lord possessed a real, concrete, definite form of the human nature. He was of the seed of David, the Son of Mary, and it is not at all presumptuous to say that He looked like His mother.

Rather than assuming that Jesus possessed an abstract, general human nature, we hold that the Son of God assumed the flesh and blood of the children, that is, that He took hold of the human nature in the very center. This is in harmony with Scripture. He assumed His human nature, not from the Romans, or from the Greeks, not from the sons of Ham, or from the yellow race, but from the seed of the promise, in the line of the covenant. He is the seed of the woman, the son of Adam; but in the generations of Adam, He is the seed of Seth, not of Cain. He is of Noah, but in the generations of Noah, He is of the seed of Shem. And again, in the generations of Shem, He is of the line that culminates in Abraham; in the generations of Abraham, He is of the seed of Isaac; and in the latter's generations, He is not of Esau, but of Jacob. Gradually, in the generations of Jesus Christ the line becomes narrower, and more defined. The line runs through Israel, but in Israel it is the tribe of Judah that bears the Christ in its loins, and within the tribe of Judah the house of David is pointed out as the everlasting royal line that must culminate in the Christ. And this royal line of David culminates finally in the virgin Mary. Thus the generations of Jesus Christ are like a pyramid, with its base in the seed of the woman, and its apex in the virgin Mary. And in the fulness of time, the Son of God took hold of the very heart of the seed of the promise, and thus assumed the flesh and blood of the children. A very definite and concrete, but at the same time a central human nature Christ took upon Himself in assuming our flesh and blood.

III

Very God And Righteous Man

The early Church, after a long period of controversy about the truth concerning the incarnated Word, finally expressed the faith of the orthodox believers in the *Symbol of Chalcedon,* in the year 451, as follows:

"We, then, following the holy Fathers, all with one consent, teach men to confess one and the same Son, our Lord Jesus Christ, the same perfect in Godhead and also perfect in manhood; truly God and truly man, of a reasonable soul and body; consubstantial with the Father according to the Godhead, and consubstantial with us according to the Manhood; in all things like unto us, without sin; begotten before all ages of the Father according to the Godhead, and in these latter days, for us and for our salvation, born of the Virgin Mary, the Mother of God, according to the Manhood; one and the same Christ, Son, Lord, Only-begotten, to be acknowledged in two natures, *inconfusedly, unchangeably, indivisibly, inseparably;* the distinction of natures being by no means taken away by the union, but rather the property of each nature being preserved, and concurring in one Person and one Subsistence, not parted or divided into two persons, but one and the same Son, and only begotten, God, the Word, the Lord Jesus Christ, as the prophets from the beginning have declared concerning him, and the Lord Jesus Christ himself has taught us, and the Creed of the holy Fathers has handed down to us."

Briefly expressed, the Church here formulated the doctrine, which since that time has remained unchanged, that the two natures of Christ subsist in unity of divine Person, without mixture, without change, without division, without separation.

About each of these chief elements in the doctrine concerning Immanuel, God with us, we will make a few remarks.

First of all, then, it must be emphasized that Christ is *one Person*, not two persons. In the incarnation of the Son of God, it was not a human person that was united with the second Person of the Trinity, but a human nature, body and soul, which the Son of God assumed. This truth has sometimes been expressed by stating that in the incarnation the Person of the Son assumed an *impersonal* human nature. This is, perhaps, hardly correct. Better it would seem to express the matter thus, that the human nature of Christ became and is personal only through its assumption by the Person of the Son of God. It has no personal subsistence of its own, but it is personal because the Son of God took up His abode in it. Hence, both the personality of the human nature of the Saviour and its union with the divine nature have their ground in the Person of the Son of God.

It is difficult to conceive of and to define what is meant by *person*. It has usually been defined as an individual subsistence in a rational, moral nature. Only a rational, moral being can be a person. There may be many individual trees, but a tree is not a person. There may be an endless variety of the species *horse*, but no individual horse is a person. God is personal, for He reveals Himself as having intellect and will. And so, those creatures are persons that are endowed with a rational, volitional nature, like angels and men. This description, however, is rather an answer to the question: what is *a* person? It does not define what is that mysterious something within us that we call our person, or ego. My *person* is that which I know to be the subject of all my actions, and, besides, of whose identity I remain conscious and assured no matter what radical changes my *nature* may undergo. It is not my nature, my body or my soul, my brain, my eye, my ear, my mouth, my feet, that acts, thinks, sees, hears, speaks, runs, but my person: *I* act, *I* think, *I* see and hear and speak and run, in and through my nature. And from childhood to old age, from the cradle to the grave, my nature undergoes many and great changes; yet, my person remains the same. I know that I am still the same person that once was nursed at my mother's breasts. And even through death my person remains the same, retains its identity. It is *I* that die, and will be raised again in Christ at the last day.

Now, in Christ this person is the Son of God, the second Person of the holy Trinity. In and through the human nature of Jesus it is the Son of God that is the subject of all His actions and all His experiences. It is He that is born in Bethlehem, as to His human nature, that grows up in the home of Joseph and Mary in Nazareth, that converses with the doctors of the law in the temple when He is twelve years old, that is baptized and enters upon His public ministry when He was about thirty years of age. The Person of the Son of God, Who is in the bosom of the Father as to His divine nature, appeared in the form of a servant in the human nature, tabernacled among us, spoke to us, performed His mighty works among us. The Person of the Son of God as to and in His human nature is captured in Gethsemane, condemned by the Sanhedrin, delivered over unto death by the Roman governor. The Son of God suffers death, is raised from the dead, exalted at the right hand of God, and received a name that is above every name, — all in His human nature. Always He is the same Person, "not parted or divided into two persons, but one and the same Son, and only begotten, the Word, the Lord Jesus Christ." Were He two persons, He would not be Immanuel, the union of God with us would not be established in Him, His death would have no other significance than any human death, atonement would not have been made through Him, and He could not be the object of our adoration and worship: we could not address Him as: "my Lord and my God."

The union of the two natures in Christ, therefore, is in and through the Person. Hence, the Church confesses that this union is without mixture or fusion. The two natures in Christ are not merged, blended, or fused into one nature. Christ is not a theanthropos, a God-man. Such a view would be Pantheistic. For Pantheism identifies the essence of God with the essence of the creature. It fuses the Creator and the creature into one

624   LORD'S DAY XIV

vague All. God is the world, and the world is God. The world
spirit is the spirit of God, that comes to highest expression and
self-consciousness in man. It obliterates the line of demarcation
between God and man, the Infinite and the finite. According
to this proud philosophy, the incarnation is only the natural
development of the human race: in Christ God reached self-
consciousness. Hence, He could identify Himself with the
Father. He was divine because he was truly human. This Pantheistic view, which in the course of history frequently lifted
up its proud head in one form or another, is the destruction
of all true religion. If the divine essence is not distinct from
the essence of the creature, if the Personality of God and that
of man are merged, if my life, my thoughts and my desires, are
nothing but little ripples on the swelling tide of the universal
Spirit-ocean, — then there is neither religion nor morality. Then
God is one Universal Subject in all, and there is no fellowship
between Him and us, no responsibility, no sin and no redemption. Then he does not exist, has no being, in distinction from
us, we cannot speak to Him, believe in Him, trust in Him,
enter into His covenant fellowship. Hence, it is important that
the confession of Chalcedon be maintained with regard to the
natures of Christ: they are united in the Person of the Son
unconfusedly. The Son of God, Who is co-equal with the Father
and the Holy Ghost, God of God, Light of Light, assumed the
real and complete human nature, body and soul, but so that
the two natures remain forever distinct. God and man are most
intimately united in Him, yet so that the two are never fused
into one substance or nature.

In close connection with the preceding stands the second
limitation, or negative qualification of the union of the two
natures in Christ by the council of Chalcedon: *unchangeably.*
Neither the divine nor the human nature was essentially changed
through the incarnation. The Son of God did not *leave* the
bosom of the Father to become man: He *is,* according to the
divine nature, in the bosom of the Father, while, according to
the human nature, He lies in the manger of Bethlehem, grows
up in Nazareth, walks among us in the form of a servant, dies

on the cross, is raised and exalted. For the divine nature is immutable. Nor did the Son of God put aside the divine virtues. The Infinite was not changed into the finite, but assumed the finite; the Eternal did not empty Himself of eternity, but assumed the temporal; the Lord of all did not cease to be Lord, but assumed the form of a servant. Nor did the human nature in any sense change into the divine, or assume divine attributes. In His human nature Christ was finite, temporal, limited in power, knowledge, wisdom and understanding, dependent and changeable. In it He lived our life, thought human thoughts, had human desires, and spoke our language. Yea, He even assumed our weakened human nature from the Virgin Mary. His was not the original human nature, as Adam possessed it in the state of rectitude, but the flesh and blood of the children, subject to suffering and death. The only exception to this was His sinlessness. For He came in the likeness of sinful flesh: not in sinful flesh, but yet in its likeness. Rom.8:3. And it behooved him in all things to be made like unto His brethren, and we have not an high priest which cannot be touched with the feeling of our infirmities, but one who was in all points tempted even as we are, yet without sin. Heb. 2:17; 4:15. He is eternally very God; He became truly man in time. He *is* eternally in the form of God; in the fulness of time He also assumed the form of a servant. And thus He could speak that mysterious word to Nicodemus: "And no man hath ascended up to heaven, but he that came down from heaven, even the Son of man which *is* in heaven." John 3:13.

This already implies that the two natures, the human and the divine, subsist in Christ *indivisibly*. Yet, the early fathers considered it necessary also to express this negative qualification to bar another erroneous view from entering into the Church. For the heresy had already been taught that Christ assumed only a partial human nature, that the natures of Christ were divided into parts, and that parts of these natures were joined in the incarnation. He was *really* human in as far as He assumed the human nature, but He was not *completely* human: the divine Spirit or nature inhabited a human body and a human soul, but not a human spirit or mind. The highest in man, his spirit or mind, was replaced by the divine Spirit. It is my experience that some such conception is often met with in those that believe the incarnation of Christ. Upon questioning catechumens, I frequently discovered that they had the notion that the divine nature inhabited a human body, took the place of the human soul. It must, therefore, be constantly made clear and emphasized that the whole, infinite divine nature was joined indivisibly to the whole human nature, body and soul. Christ is very God, and completely man.

And yet, although each of the natures in Christ retains its own distinct qualities, and the two natures neither are merged or fused into each other, nor supplement each other, they are united in the divine Person of the Son of God *inseparably*. Although the human nature in Christ never partook of the divine, through the intimate union of the two natures in the Person of Christ, there was a constant inner connection between His human nature and the divine, between His human mind and the mind of God, His human will and the will of God, His human spirit and the Spirit of God, His human power and the power of the Almighty, instructing Him from within, making Him obedient unto death, sanctifying Him, and sustaining Him even in His deepest afflictions. That is why He is the perfect revelation of the Father in human nature. And that is the reason why He could endure the terrible moment of the pouring out of all the vials of God's wrath without being crushed.

Beautifully this distinction and union of the two natures in Christ is expressed in the *Confessio Belgica*, Art. XIX: "We believe that by this conception, the person of the Son is inseparably united with the human nature; so that there are not two Sons of God, nor two persons, but two natures united in one single person: yet, that each nature retains its own distinct properties. As then the divine nature hath always remained uncreated, without beginning of days or end of life, filling heaven and earth: so also hath the human nature not lost its properties, but remained a creature, having beginning of days, being a finite nature, and retaining all the properties of the real body. And though he hath by his resurrection given immortality to the same, nevertheless he hath not changed the reality of his human nature; forasmuch as our salvation and resurrection also depend on the reality of his body. But these two natures are so closely united in one person, that they were not separated even by his death. Therefore that which he, when dying, commended into the hands of his Father, was a real human spirit, departing from his body. But in the meantime the divine nature always remained united with the human, even when he lay in the grave. And the Godhead did not cease to be in him, any more than it did when he was an infant, though it did not so clearly manifest itself for a while. Wherefore we confess that he is very God and very Man: very God by his power to conquer death; and very man that he might die for us according to the infirmity of his flesh."

This union of the human nature to the divine in the Person of the Son already postulates the sinlessness of His human nature. For God can have no fellowship with sin. In a corrupt human nature the Son of God could not have dwelled. He was the holy Child Jesus. He was separate from sinners. "For such an high priest became us, who is holy, harmless, undefiled, separate from sinners, and made higher than the heavens." Heb. 7:26.

This sinlessness of Christ implies especially three elements. It means, first of all, that He was without original guilt. We are born in original guilt and condemnation: the sin of Adam is imputed to us, we being reckoned in Adam forensically. But Christ does not fall under this imputation *because He is not a human person, but the Person of the Son of God.* Although as to His nature He is out of Adam, as to His Person He was not reckoned in Adam. Guilt is imputed to the *person.* And as Christ was a divine, not a human person, the guilt of Adam's sin could not be imputed to Him. Personally He did not lie under the wrath of God and under the condemnation of the human race. He was separate from sinners. Secondly, the sinlessness of Christ implies that He was not depraved, that His nature was without corruption, that He assumed a holy human nature. Being without original guilt, He was entitled to a sinless human nature, for He was personally not subject to the sentence of death. And this sinless human nature He assumed, not from a holy virgin, who herself was immaculately conceived, but because the Son of God formed His own human nature through the conception by the Holy Spirit in the womb of the virgin Mary. "The Holy Ghost shall come upon thee, and the power of the Highest shall overshadow thee: therefore also that holy thing which shall be born of thee shall be called the Son of God." Lu. 1:35. And, lastly, this implies that Christ never had any actual sin, that His whole existence, from the manger to the cross was without spot or blemish. He was tempted in all things even as we are, yet without sin. Heb. 4:15.

And in this connection it must be maintained that there was not the slightest possibility that Christ should fall into sin. The first Adam was lapsible, the last Adam was not. And this impossibility was due, not to the holiness of His human nature alone, for Adam also was righteous and holy, yet he fell; but, objectively, to God's decree that in Him all things should be made perfect; and, subjectively, to the union of the human nature to the divine in the Person of the Son. To maintain that also for Christ there was a possibility of falling into sin, is to deny God's immutable decree that He should be made perfect as the Captain of our salvation; and is tantamount to the statement that the Person of the Son could become disobedient to the Father in human flesh. And this is absurd. Hence, it must be maintained that Christ could not sin. This does not render the reality of His temptations less real. He was tempted in all things even as we are, yet without sin. The trial or test of anything does not become less real because it is certain from the outset that it will not and cannot break. The strain put upon the obedience of Christ in His sufferings and death is no less real and heavy, because it was a priori established that He could never be crushed under the strain. Also in this respect Christ was separate from sinners. He could never fall. In Him the realization of God's everlasting covenant is assured from the beginning, because He is the Word become flesh!

Thus He is our Mediator, Who is able to bring the perfect sacrifice for our sins, and to deliver us from all the dominion of sin and death. At first sight, the words of the Catechism in question and answer 36 leave a somewhat strange impression, as if only by the holy conception and birth of Christ our sins are covered in the sight of God, and that, too, only our original sins: "What profit dost thou receive by Christ's holy conception and nativity? That he is our Mediator; and with innocence and perfect holiness, covers in the sight of God my sins, wherein I was conceived and brought forth." Ursinus, in his *Schatboek* offers no further explanation of these words. The meaning cannot be, of course, that by Christ's holy birth my original sins are blotted out. However, if His holy conception and birth are brought into connection with His perfect sacrifice on the cross, all is plain. Because He had no original sin, because He was free from the guilt of Adam's sin, and from the defilement of the human nature, He could offer Himself up to God, a Lamb without spot or blemish, and perform that perfect act of obedience that constitutes the perfect *Yes* over against the *No* of the entire human race, and thus blot out the guilt of all our sins, even of the sins in which we are conceived and born. The Son of God in the flesh is the perfect High Priest, that is able to save to the uttermost all that through Him go to God. By one sacrifice He has for ever perfected all His own!

LORD'S DAY XV

Q. 37. What dost thou understand by the words, "He suffered?"

A. That he, all the time that he lived on earth, but especially at the end of his life, sustained in body and soul, the wrath of God against the sins of all mankind: that so by his passion, as the only propitiatory sacrifice, he might redeem our body and soul from everlasting damnation, and obtain for us the favor of God, righteousness and eternal life.

Q. 38. Why did he suffer under Pontius Pilate, as judge?

A. That he, being innocent, and yet condemned by a temporal judge, might thereby free us from the severe judgment of God to which we were exposed.

Q. 39. Is there anything more in his being crucified, than if he had died some other death?

A. Yes, there is; for thereby I am assured that he took on him the curse which lay upon me; for the death of the cross was accursed of God.

I

Atoning Suffering

As to the text of this fifteenth Lord's Day, we may note the following: 1. The original of "propitiatory sacrifice" can be more correctly rendered by "atoning sacrifice," or "sacrifice of reconciliation." The German text has Suhnopfer. 2. "Mankind" can be more fully translated by "the whole human race." The original has: ganzen menschlichen Geschlechts. 3. The original translated by "favor" is : Gnade, and there is no reason why this should not be rendered by "grace." All these remarks concern the answer to the thirty-seventh question. The text of the other questions and answers is quite correct.

Modernism, emphasizing the goodness of the Man of Galilee, and glorifying Jesus as an example for us to follow, cannot but be disappointed and very much dissatisfied with the account of Jesus' life and ministry as presented by the Apostolic Confession: born, suffered, crucified, dead, and buried! From the viewpoint of an attempt to write a biography of Jesus, or even to furnish the necessary material for a description of Jesus' character, the *Apostolicum,* it must be admitted, made a rather poor selection of facts. Or what human being ever lived of whom this same review might not be written: born, suffered, died, buried? There would seem to be nothing special or distinctive in all this. And yet, it is exactly in these words that one must find the revelation of Jesus Christ as far as His earthly life and ministry are concerned. It is true, many other works may be attributed to Him, and could be mentioned here, so many, in fact, that if all were written the whole world could not contain the books. He taught, and revealed the Father; He performed many wonderful works; and He stands out in the midst of all men as the One Whom no one could ever convict of sin. But all this would have no significance for us, if He had not suffered and died. And if the revelation of Jesus Christ is to be expressed in a brief confession, the words of the *Apostolicum* must surely have the preference to any *"Leben Jesu,"* or character description of the Man of Galilee. Of course, these words of the Confession dare not be divorced from the preceding declarations concerning Jesus Christ, nor from what is stated subsequently, for it is only in their connection that their special significance is discerned. Taken by themselves, they describe only what is common to all men. All men are born, suffer, and die. And although all men are not crucified, there is nothing unique even in this. Thousands of men were crucified about the time of Jesus' life, and untold thousands more have suffered even greater agonies, were tortured, sawn asunder, torn apart limb by limb on the cruel rack, burnt alive, or left to rot slowly in dark dungeons. And that was the end of them, as far as human history is concerned. But the special significance of the words "suffered, was crucified, dead and buried," must be found in the Subject of this suffering. It was *He* that was born, that suffered, was crucified, and buried. And He is Jesus Christ, our Lord, the only begotten Son of God, who was conceived by the Holy Ghost, born of the virgin Mary. God Himself came in the flesh, and was born. God Himself suffered in the flesh! God Himself was crucified in the flesh, died in the flesh, and was buried in the flesh! Therein, and therein alone, lies the altogether unique and tremendous power and significance of the words of the Confession.

Only because it is the Subject of the only begotten Son of God in the flesh that suffered, can the explanation of this suffering offered by the Catechism in its answer to the thirty-seventh question be maintained. For only the Son of God could truly bear the wrath of God in His suffering, and taste the awful reality of that wrath in all His passion; only the Son of God in the flesh could *sustain* that wrath of God to the end, without being crushed under it, and becoming utterly lost in everlasting desolation; only the Son of God in the flesh could make of that suffering *an act,* and that, too, an act of perfect obedience, so that His passion and death became the perfect *Yes* over against the *No* of sin, the only atoning sacrifice. And so, only by the suffering of the Son of God in the flesh could our redemption from everlasting damnation be accomplished, and could there be obtained for us the grace of God, righteousness, and eternal life.

Moreover, only when we first confess that it is Jesus Christ, the only begotten Son of God, our Lord, that was born, suffered, was crucified and died, is it possible to continue this confession concerning the revelation of Jesus Christ. With mere man this is impossible. You can, indeed, write the real biography of every man, no matter how illustrious a name he may have made for himself among men, in these words: born, suffered, died. For such is the reality of human existence that in these words the most important facts concerning it are related. All is vanity. Death is in all man's life and activity. And there is no way out. You cannot continue the description. Man's existence ends in death, and that, too, in everlasting death. But the revelation of Jesus Christ is not finished with death and burial. Exactly because it is the only begotten Son of God that suffered and died, the confession of the Church continues: "on the third day he was raised again from the dead, ascended into heaven, and sitteth at the right hand of God, the Father, Almighty. From thence he shall come to judge the quick and the dead!"

That, and not the modern good Man of Galilee, is emphatically the revelation of Jesus Christ.

No wonder that Modernism, which begins by denying the true and essential divinity of Christ, is loath to speak of Christ's atoning suffering and death, and rather extols Him as the great teacher, and the perfect example, from whom we can all learn to be good, and whom we may all follow to establish the brotherhood of man, and to realize the kingdom of God on earth. When a man babbles much about the goodness of Christ, and about the lovely Jesus, and avoids to emphasize His suffering and death, you must inquire of him at once whether he believes the confession of the Church that Jesus Christ is the only begotten

Son of God, co-eternal with the Father and the Holy Ghost.
If the Cross is not the cross of the Son of God, it is foolishness!

————

Turning now to the explanation of the Catechism in its answer
to the thirty-seventh question, we cannot but notice that it
elaborates upon the words of the Confession, and ascribes to
them a wider meaning than they can literally have. The *Apostolicum*, evidently, refers only to the suffering of Christ at the
end of His earthly sojourn and ministry, when it declares:
"suffered under Pontius Pilate." The phrase "under Pontius
Pilate" must probably be understood as a temporal modifier, an
indication as to the time when Jesus suffered. At all events, the
entire expression is one, and is, according to the intent of the
Apostolic Confession, not to be split up. It refers, therefore,
definitely to the final suffering of our Lord. The Heidelberger,
however, divides the phrase of the Confession, and in its answer
to the thirty-seventh question treats the words "He suffered"
separately, thus making it possible to speak of the passion of
the Saviour as extending over "all the time he lived on earth."
Further, it is to be noted that the Catechism mentions the
following elements in explanation of the suffering of our Lord:
1. The real essence of this suffering consists in the fact that He
bore the wrath of God. 2. This wrath of God He not merely
suffered, but He *sustained* it; in German: Er hat den Zorn Gottes
wider die Sunde des ganzen menschlichen Geschlechts *getragen*.
3. That He bore and sustained this wrath of God during His
whole life, but especially at the end. 4. That He sustained the
wrath of God *against the sin of all mankind, of the whole human
race*. 5. That thus His suffering constitutes the atoning sacrifice
whereby we are redeemed from damnation, and obtain the grace
of God, righteousness, and eternal life. These various truths
now demand our attention.

First of all, then, the suffering of Christ was essentially a
sustaining of the wrath of God against sin, the sin of the
whole human race, and thereby it becomes the sacrifice of
reconciliation.

For a proper understanding of this mystery of salvation, it may be well, first of all, to recall the distinction that is frequently, and very properly, made in theology between *state* and *condition*. For this distinction is important with a view to the question as to how Christ could bear and sustain the wrath of God. In popular speech the two words are often used promiscuously, but in theology they should be carefully distinguished. By *state* is meant one's legal position as determined by the sentence of the judge or magistrate, while *condition* denotes mode of being, the sum total of the accidental properties of any being at a given time. When someone enters this country as an immigrant, his *state* is that of a foreigner, under the American law he has no rights of citizenship. When, a few years later, he receives his naturalization papers, his *state* is changed. His *condition*, however, remains practically unchanged: he still has foreign blood in his veins, and his outward appearance reveals that he is foreign born. Such modes of existence, however, as sickness and health, soberness and drunkenness, integrity and depravity, are *conditions*.

Now man is a sinner both as to his *state* and as to his *condition*. As to his state, i.e. his legal position according to the judgment of God, he is guilty; as to his condition, he is totally depraved. In this state of guilt he is worthy of death, object of the just wrath of God; as to his condition, he is incapable of doing any good, and inclined to all evil.

Applied to Christ, this means that He entered into the *state* of sinners, but not into their ethical, corrupt *condition*. In God's eternal decree, He was ordained to be the head of His sinful people, so that He represented them before the law of God, and before the bar of the Judge of heaven and earth, He assumed their guilt. And in the fulness of time He willingly entered into that *state* of guilt decreed for Him in God's eternal good pleasure. For "when the fulness of the time was come, God sent forth his Son, made of a woman, made under the law." Gal. 4:4. He, Who is in Himself the eternal Lord, became a servant, entered into the *state* of a servant, so that He was obliged to fulfill the law. He, Who was above the law, placed

Himself under the law. Moreover, seeing that He placed Himself under the law, and that, too, according to God's decree,
as the representative Head of His sinful and guilty people, He
entered the *state* of guilt, and in that state He was obliged to
bear the wrath of God to the end, to fulfill all the demands of
the justice of God against the sin of His own.

It must be remembered that in and through all this His
personal state remained that of perfect righteousness before
God. He was born without guilt, for He was the Person of the
Son of God; and while under the law, and even while under
the wrath of God, He remained perfectly righteous: He was the
obedient Servant of Jehovah. And, as to His ethical *condition*,
He was and remained holy and blameless. While He entered
into the *state* of sinners, He remained separate from sinners as
to His *condition*, except in so far as He must bear the wrath of
God, and, therefore, be subjected to suffering and death. The
Son of God, Who is Lord and above the law, came under the
law, and entered into the *state* of a servant. The holy Child
Jesus, Who was personally righteous both as to His *state* and
condition, entered into the *state* of sinners, and, therefore, into
their *condition* as far as their suffering and death are concerned.
This is the meaning of that rich and profound passage in
Philippians 2:6-8: "Who, being in the form of God, thought it
not robbery to be equal with God: but made himself of no
reputation, and took upon him the form of a servant, and was
made in the likeness of men: And being found in fashion as a
man, he humbled himself, and became obedient unto death,
even the death of the cross."

If we bear this in mind, we will be able to understand a little
of the profound mystery of redemption and reconciliation.

Christ, so the Catechism teaches us, bore the wrath of God
against the sin of the whole human race.

What does that mean?

Let us put the question this way: does it mean that God was
ever angry with Christ personally? But how could this possibly
be? In His person, our Lord is the only begotten Son of God,
Who is in the bosom of the Father eternally. Certainly, it

would be blasphemy to assert that the Father is ever angry with the Son. But was He, perhaps, angry with the Man Jesus? Was His anger directed against Christ as the Servant of Jehovah personally? Again, we say that this is equally impossible, and, besides, it is contrary to all we ever read of the Saviour as Man in relation to God. If He suffered the wrath of God all His life, this certainly cannot mean that God was angry with His holy Child Jesus during His entire lifetime, and that our Saviour was conscious of this anger of God against Him. All His life is one testimony of the fact that He lived in perfect fellowship with the Father, and was conscious of His approval and favor. What was announced from heaven at His baptism, and again at His transfiguration on the mount, covers His relationship to the Father during His whole life: "This is my beloved Son, in whom I am well pleased!" Was He not the obedient Servant? And was not God always well pleased with Him, even as Man? Yea, was there ever a moment in which He was so perfectly obedient, so deeply in harmony with the will of God, as that very moment in which He cried out: "My God, my God, why hast thou forsaken me?"

What does it mean, then, that our Saviour bore the wrath of God?

It implies, first of all, that He suffered the *expression,* the concrete *effect* of the wrath of God against sin, against the sin of others, of the human race. God's wrath is the reaction of His holiness against the workers of iniquity. God is the Holy One. For He is the only Good. He is the implication of all infinite perfections. Hence, He is consecrated to Himself. He seeks Himself, knows Himself, loves Himself, glorifies Himself. He seeks His glory also in the creature. For man this means that it is his everlasting obligation to be consecrated to God only. He must love God, seek Him, and glorify Him, with all his heart, and with all his soul, and with all his mind, and with all his strength. If he does this, God embraces him in His blessed lovingkindness and favor, and he is unspeakably happy. But if he fails to do just that, if he turns against the Holy One, rejects Him, rebels against Him, ignores Him, tramples His glory under foot, He reacts against that rebellious sinner in His anger, pursues him constantly with fear and terror, makes him inexpressibly miserable, casts him down into everlasting darknesses of desolation. This is His attitude toward the sin of all mankind. And the expression of this wrath, i.e. the pain and agony, the suffering and misery, the sorrow and anguish of soul, the desolation and darkness, the fear and terror, the death and hell, that becomes the experience of him against whom God directs His wrath, Christ experienced!

That is the explanation, but at the same time the paradox of the cross!

At the moment of His deepest and most perfect obedience, He endures the agonies of the damned!

At the moment when God is most highly pleased with Him, He experiences all the terror of being forsaken of God!

But this is exactly why hell is still a question, an outcry to God for an answer! And that is the reason, too, why, even from the darkness of hell, and in the condition of utter desolation, the obedient Servant can still cry out: "*My* God, *My* God!"

He, that knew no sin, is made sin!

And that is also the reason, why his question, pressed from His utterly forsaken and agonized soul, has an answer. In the hell of mere sinners there is no question. It *is* the answer, the final answer, the answer of everlasting wrath. But the suffering Servant of Jehovah, because He is obedient and yet forsaken, has a question: *Why me?* And it receives an answer presently, an answer to which the Servant responds even at the cross: *It is finished!*

Christ, then, bore the wrath of God in that He bore all the agonies of soul and body which are the expression of that wrath.

This wrath of God, the Heidelberg Catechism instructs us, Christ *sustained.*

And this expression deserves special attention and emphasis, because it points to the deepest reason why the suffering and death of our Saviour could be an atonement for sin.

Atonement is the perfect satisfaction of the justice of God with respect to sin. This satisfaction must be an act, an act of perfect obedience in the love of God. Sin is an act; atonement must be an act. Sin is an act of rebellion and disobedience; atonement must be an act of self-subjection and obedience. Sin is an act of enmity against God; atonement must be an act of perfect love of God. For we must remember that the fundamental demand of the law of God upon man is expressed in the one commandment: "Thou shalt love the Lord thy God." This demand is unchangeable. God never relinquishes it, not even when He subjects fallen man to His wrath, to the suffering of the curse. Man must love God even in His wrath, for God's wrath is righteous and holy, an expression and revelation of His goodness and perfection. Hence, the guilt of sin can be removed only by an act of love under the wrath of God. He that would atone for sin must willingly, motivated by the pure love of God, seek to fulfill all the justice and righteousness of God against sin. He must will to suffer all the agonies of the expression of that wrath, in death and hell, for God's sake. Only such an act is a sacrifice. And only such a willing sacrifice is satisfaction of God's justice, and, therefore, atonement.

And thus I would like to understand that word *sustained* in the thirty-seventh answer of the Catechism. Christ not merely *suffered* the wrath of God against sin, He *sustained* it: "er hat den Zorn Gottes *getragen*." He suffered, but His suffering was an act. The distinction that is often made between the active and passive obedience of Christ may be accepted provided it is rightly understood. By the former, then, must be understood that Christ without fail was obedient to the law of God in all His walk and conversation, by the latter that He was obedient also in His suffering. But it must be maintained that in all Christ's suffering He was never purely passive. He was active also in His passion and death. He *willed* to fulfill all righteousness. He was determined to satisfy the justice of God against sin. Voluntarily He assumed the obligation to suffer the wrath of God. And actively, in the love of God, He bore that wrath even unto the end. And thus His suffering was the perfect *Yes* over against the rebellious *No* of sin.

This wrath of God against sin, the Heidelberg Catechism teaches us, He sustained all the time that He lived on earth, but especially at the end of His life. It is not difficult to see that Christ's suffering extended over His entire life. This does not mean that He was subject to special diseases, or even to the common sicknesses of mankind. If we consider the life of Jesus in as far as we become acquainted with it from the gospel narratives, we can find no special suffering of pain or sorrow that distinguishes Him in any respect from other men. Although He took all our sicknesses upon Himself, not once do the gospel narratives mention that He was sick. But we must remember that He sustained the wrath of God. He, the Son of God in the flesh, the sinless One, assumed the likeness of sinful flesh. And this means that He took upon Himself the corruptible human nature, in which life is nothing but a continual death. And this death He tasted as the heavy hand of the wrath of God against sin. Moreover, in the likeness of sinful flesh, He came into a world that was sinful, and under the curse of God. The creature itself was made subject to vanity, and was subjected to the bondage of corruption. And the Person of the Son of God in the sinless human nature tasted and suffered through it all the just wrath of God. Add to this that He suffered the contradiction of sinners against Himself, that He dwelled among men that loved the darkness rather than the light, with whose enmity against God and against one another He came into daily contact, and in the corruption of whose nature He apprehended the wrath of God revealed from heaven, and we need not try to discover some special suffering, sicknesses, or calamities in the life of Jesus on earth, in order to understand, that in the corruptible and mortal flesh, and in the midst of the world filled with enmity against God, and of a creation that bore the curse of God, Christ's life was nothing but a continual death, and that in this death He experienced the wrath of God during His entire sojourn in our world.

Not only so, but we should never forget that all His life Christ lived in the shadow of the cross, and that, with increasing consciousness He moved deliberately in the direction of that cross,

He had come under the law, not only under the moral law, but under the entire Mosaic institution of ordinances and shadows. And that meant that He came under the curse, and that it was His task to remove that curse. He knew the program of His suffering, as is evident from the repeated, and rather detailed announcement of it to His disciples. He had come to lay down His life, and He was aware of it all His life. In a sense, all His life was a Gethsemane, an anticipation of the hour of the righteous judgment of God, when all the vials of God's wrath would be poured out over His head.

Nevertheless, it was especially at the end of His life that He suffered and sustained the full concentration of God's holy wrath against sin, and finished it. We need not elaborate upon this final suffering now, for we must speak of this again in connection with the succeeding questions and answers. But two elements must once more be emphasized in this connection. First of all, the truth that in all that final suffering, inflicted upon Him through the wrath and fury of evil men, His passion in the garden, before the Sanhedrin, before Pilate and Herod, and on Calvary, in all His being forsaken and denied, despised and rejected of men, beaten and buffeted and scourged and spit upon, in His condemnation and death, He tasted and suffered the wrath of God against the sin of the world. And, secondly, that He bore the wrath of God voluntarily, in the obedience of love, even unto the end. And thus His passion was the sacrifice of reconciliation, by which He obtained for us redemption from everlasting damnation, not only, but also that everlasting righteousness that makes us worthy of that higher, heavenly glory which the Scriptures denote by the term "eternal life." So infinitely precious was the death of the Son of God!

A word must be said about the statement of the Catechism that Christ sustained the wrath of God *against the sins of all mankind,* of the whole human race. This dare not be understood in the sense that He suffered and died and brought the sacrifice of atonement for every man individually, nor even that it was His intention to do so. Nor may the expression that

occurs elsewhere in our Confessions (Canons II, 3) that the
sacrifice of Christ is "of infinite worth and value, abundantly
sufficient to expiate the sins of the whole world," be understood
in the sense of general atonement. Christ suffered for His elect.
Them and them alone He represented according to the counsel
of God. For His own, for the sheep His Father had given Him,
He laid down His life. He did not suffer more than was necessary
to redeem them. Not one drop of blood that was shed by the
Saviour was shed in vain. Those for whom He suffered are surely
redeemed and saved. However, also the Scriptures employ similar
expressions as occur in our Confessions. John the Baptist points
Him out as "the Lamb of God, which taketh away the sin of
the world." And the apostle John writes: "And he is the propitiation for our sin: and not for ours only, but also for the
sins of the whole world." But these expressions, as well as
similar terms, must be understood organically, rather than
individualistically. They refer to the whole organism of the
race, to the elect from every nation, and tongue, and tribe,
and not to every individual man. After all, mankind, and not
a few individuals, is saved; but it is saved in the elect. The
world is redeemed, but it is the world of God's love, not every
individual man. And it is in that same sense that the words
of the Catechism must be understood that Christ sustained the
wrath of God *against the sins of all mankind.* For those, in
whose stead and in whose behalf, He bore the wrath of God, are
surely redeemed by His blood. Everlasting righteousness and
eternal life He obtained for them. And what He obtained for
them by His suffering, He surely bestows upon them by His
sovereign grace.

II

Under Pontius Pilate

Although in the *Apostolicum* the words "under Pontius Pilate" are probably intended as a temporal modifier, the Catechism calls special attention to this phrase, and interprets it as meaning "That he, being innocent and yet condemned by a temporal judge, might thereby free us from the severe judgment of God to which we were exposed."

The question is: how must this answer of the Catechism be understood?

That our Instructor is correct in discovering a special meaning in the trial of Jesus and His condemnation to the death of the cross by Pontius Pilate cannot be a matter of doubt.

In general, it may be said, that all the phases of that final suffering of Christ, His betrayal by Judas, His agony in Gethsemane, His capture and His trial before the Sanhedrin, His being set at nought by Herod and by the Roman soldiers, have their special meaning. They all belong to the program of Jesus' passion as it was determined upon and arranged, not by man, but by God Himself. Christ must not only suffer and die, but He must suffer exactly at the time and in the way which the Father had ordained. Hence, even in the light of this general truth, the question of the Heidelberger is quite justified and to the point: "Why did he suffer under Pontius Pilate as judge?" And that the question is not repeated with respect to the other phases of the passion of our Lord is, undoubtedly, due only to the fact that the Catechism is following the *Apostolicum* in its explanation of that suffering.

All the more reason there is for asking this question, because it was evidently through God's special direction of events that the Saviour was brought before the Roman governor at all. It is very clear from the gospel narratives that it was not the intention of the Jews to lead Jesus to His death in the way of a public and official trial. Their original intention was quite different from its final execution. For when shortly before the final Passover the chief priests, and the scribes, and the elders of the people assembled in the palace of the high priest, to conspire against Jesus, they consulted "that they might take Jesus by subtilty, and kill him. But they said, Not on the feast day, lest there be an uproar among the people." Matt. 26:4, 5. That this program was frustrated, both as to time and manner, was due to several factors over which the leaders of the Jews had no control, not the least important of which was the wholly unexpected dismissal of Judas from the upper room in the night in which Jesus was betrayed. For this dismissal forced them to take action at once. It was evident that all their secret plans were known to the Lord, and that even their employment of the traitor could not serve them to realize their purpose of taking and killing the Lord by subtilty. Thus it came about that they hired a band of soldiers that night, that the capture of Jesus, as well as His trial before the Sanhedrin that same night could not remain a secret, that it had become impossible to kill Him secretly, and that, therefore, they were virtually forced to bring the Lord to the Roman judge, and seek confirmation of the death sentence they had already pronounced. All this was, of course, also necessary because the death of the Saviour must be a public spectacle, and must assume the form of crucifixion. But He must also be condemned by the temporal judge. It was, therefore, not according to the counsels of men, but according to God's own program of Jesus' suffering, and by His special direction, that Christ appeared before Pontius Pilate to be tried and condemned by him.

But why must He be tried by the worldly judge?

And what is the particular significance of this phase of the suffering of our Lord?

The Catechism answers: "That he, being innocent, and yet condemned by the temporal Judge, might thereby free us from the severe judgment of God to which we were exposed." This answer of the Catechism may simply be understood as meaning that, while He was innocently condemned to, and suffered death, He obtained for us freedom from condemnation. In this general form the same thought is expressed by our "Form for the Administration of the Lord's Supper" in the words: "that he was innocently condemned to death, that we might be acquitted at the judgment seat of God." But is there, in the trial and condemnation of our Lord by Pontius Pilate, not a deeper, and more specific meaning?

Ursinus explains this particular answer of the Catechism as follows:

"Why must Christ suffer under a judge, and be condemned in the ordinary way?

"1. In order that we might know that He was condemned by God Himself on account of our sins, and that He, therefore, made satisfaction before the tribunal of God, in order that we might not be condemned by the severe judgment of God; even as He also sustained death for us, that we might be delivered from it. For God presides over ordinary judgments.

"2. In order that He might obtain testimony of His innocence of the very judge that condemned Him. For this reason it was necessary that Christ should not be secretly put out of the way, nor killed in an uproar; but it was the will of the Father that according to a lawful process and trial, with due examination of all the indictments against Him, He should: (1) be examined, in order that His innocence might be brought to light; (2) be condemned, in order that it might be established that He, Who had first been declared innocent, was now condemned, not because of His own, but because of our guilt, and that His unjust condemnation might take the place of our most righteous condemnation; (3) be put to death, that the prophecies might be fulfilled, and it might appear that it was by Jews and Gentiles that He was killed and nailed to the cross. This phase of Jesus' suffering, therefore, we should diligently contemplate, that we may be assured that Jesus, condemned by Pilate, is the Messiah, and that through Him we are freed from the severe judgment of God." (I, 300, 301).

If we may understand this as meaning that God, "Who presides over ordinary judgments," used the judgment of Pilate, first, to establish Christ's innocence and perfect righteousness publicly and officially; and secondly, to condemn the innocent One to the death of the cross, that He might bear the sins of His people; and that our Lord did not rebel against this, as far as man's judgment was concerned, unrighteous condemnation, but voluntarily bowed under it, in order that He might bear the wrath of God on the cross, — we can agree.

But if the Catechism here be interpreted as meaning: 1. That Pilate, as the representative of the sword-power, instituted by God, expressed his judgment of condemnation upon Jesus in the name of God; 2. That, therefore, the sentence of the Roman governor, whereby he condemned our Lord to the death of the cross, was God's own sentence, and, 3. That, therefore, through Pilate's sentence God actually caused the guilt ⁹and condemnation of our iniquities to come upon the Saviour, — we must disagree.

This appears to be the opinion of Dr. A. Kuyper as expressed in *E Voto*, I, 415, 416:

"However unrighteous may be the way in which this verdict is established, it is and remains a verdict *pronounced in the name of the Lord*. The condemned is not allowed to oppose it. And thus it is, indeed, the Lord Himself, and this must receive all the emphasis, Who *in the verdict expressed by Pilate laid our condemnation upon Immanuel*. He laid on him the iniquity of us all."

To be sure, Pilate represented the sword-power. And the magistrate is God's minister to execute judgment in His name, for the praise of them that do well, and the punishment of them that do evil. As Roman governor and judge he occupied the place of power and authority that was given him from above. Whether he realized this and acknowledged his authority as being derived from the Judge of heaven and earth, or whether he denied this, makes no difference as to the reality of his position.

Formally, therefore, it may be said that Pilate rendered his verdict in the name of the Lord. And the Lord Jesus acknowledged Pilate's authority, and humbly submitted to his verdict. He did not oppose it.

But *materially* Pilate's final sentence of condemnation could not possibly be pronounced in the name of the Most High.

For, Pilate's judgment did not concern the Mediator, but the man Jesus. And concerning that man Jesus his judgment was twofold: He is perfectly innocent, and: I sentence Him to the death of the cross.

And in this deliberate, extreme, and self-confessed perversion of judgment by the instituted worldly sword-power, must be found another, perhaps, the main reason for Jesus' trial and condemnation by the worldly judge.

The condemnation of Jesus by the world was the judgment and condemnation of the world.

Thus the Lord had spoken a few days before he stood before the Roman governor, delivered by His people, to be tried by that representative of worldly justice: "Now is the condemnation of the world, now shall the prince of this world be cast out." John 12:31. And there can be no doubt about the fact that he spoke these words with a view to his own condemnation and death. What was historically, as men view the events of this world, the trial and condemnation of Jesus by the world, was in reality, and according to the purpose of God, the trial and judgment of the world.

This is to be understood, not as a figure of speech, but in the literal sense of the word.

The world, the whole of sinful humanity as it reveals itself and develops in the present world, the world in its ethically evil sense, with its lust of the flesh, and lust of the eyes, and pride of life, was tried, weighed in the balance of God's justice, exposed as corrupt and found wanting, and condemned, when it passed judgment upon Jesus the Christ, the Son of God in the flesh. It is true, Scripture teaches us that there will come a final day of judgment, a day when the ever righteous judgment of God shall be revealed, and when all that is implied in the judgment of the cross shall be openly and clearly manifested, but that does not alter the fact that nineteen hundred years

ago the world stood in judgment before God, and was condemned in the cross and the resurrection of Jesus Christ from
the dead.

And in that hour of judgment the world was well represented.

This was necessary. For in and through those that were present
at and took an active part in the trial and condemnation of
Jesus, the whole world of all ages, from the beginning to the
end of time, is judged and condemned by God. There may,
therefore, be no room for complaint on the part of the world
that it was not well represented. Its representatives must belong
to the very best the world is able to produce. Not a tribe of
ignorant savages, or a band of criminals from the lowest strata
of society, not men whom the world itself draws into its courts
to judge and condemn them, may kill the Christ of God. Not
on the outskirts of the world, far from the pale of civilization,
may this judgment take place, and the cross of Christ be erected.
Not in a period of darkness and ignorance, when human culture
stands on a low level, is the Anointed of the Lord tried and
condemned by the world. On the contrary, in the center of the
world, in the very heart of civilization, in the fulness of time,
Christ is judged, and in that very judgment the world is condemned. That center of the world, and of history, was in
Jerusalem in the year thirty-three of our era. There, indeed,
the whole world in all its culture and civilization was present.
There were the representatives, not only of culture and philosophy and human justice, but there also of the world of religion,
as it had been enlightened by the law and the prophets. There
were the leaders of the Jews, the theologians of that day, teachers
of Moses, sitting on Moses' seat, proud of their knowledge of
and keeping of the law. And there was also the Roman court
of justice, famous for its knowledge of what is right and true
among men.

That world was tried and exposed as evil through the trial
and condemnation of the Christ of God.

By that trial it was very really called before the bar of divine
justice, examined, and exposed in its corruption, its hypocrisy,
its worthiness of damnation. It was forced to cast off its mask

of goodness and nobility, of justice and love of the truth, in order to become manifest in its inner wickedness and rottenness, its love of the darkness rather than the light, its constant suppression of the truth in unrighteousness, its enmity against the living God.

For this purpose, the world must judge the Christ, God's Son, the holy child Jesus. And in this judgment they must give an answer to the question: what think ye of the Christ? Mark you well, they must give an answer to this question not in the way of theological contemplation or as a result of philosophical thought, not in a disinterested, impersonal way, but as a revelation of their ethical worth, of the intents and imaginations of their inmost heart. The question was a searching one. It was a question of life and death. It was intended to reveal whether they loved or hated the truth, whether they were in harmony with or opposed to the will of God, whether they were children of God or children of their father the devil.

Hence, it must become very plain that Christ represents the light, and that they are perfectly aware that there is no darkness in Him at all. He had gone throughout the land doing good, and revealing the Father. He represented the light in a world of darkness. And in that final hour He stood before the world without power and without defense. Freely, without fear of human might or revenge, the world could express its judgment, reveal its inmost heart, and in judging the Christ of God principally answer the question: what will ye do with God, His truth, His righteousness, and holiness, if He is represented by a weak and helpless man? And the answer they gave with one accord was: Then we will kill Him!

To that world also belonged the power of the State, the sword-power as instituted by God for the punishment of evil-doers and the praise of them that do well.

And the sword-power, the institution of the State of all ages was well represented at the time by the Roman world-power.

And the representative of that Roman sword-power in Jerusalem was Pontius Pilate.

He, too, therefore, must be confronted with the question: what wilt thou do with the Christ of God?

No, he was not the sole representative of the world that judged Christ and was itself condemned. Judas had given his answer to the question. So had the Church-institute, represented by the Sanhedrin, Annas, Caiaphas, the leaders of the Jews. So would Herod, "that fox," face and answer the question, when, by way of an intermission in the trial by the Roman governor, the Lord was sent to him. So did the soldiers, the representatives of Roman might, give an answer to the same question, when they made Him the object and victim of their ribald and cruel mockery. And so did the Church as a congregation, when they voted in favor of a murderer, and demanded that the Christ of God be crucified.

And yet, whether in the *Apostolicum* the words "under Pontius Pilate" are intended as a mere temporal qualification or not, the Confession touches the very heart of the matter in this phrase. For Pilate ultimately was the representative of the highest worldly tribunal, without whose verdict Jesus could not have been crucified.

He suffered under Pontius Pilate!

Simple words, but tremendous in their significance, when we consider that in the judgment of Pilate the whole world is finally tried, and condemned.

One of the most remarkable and striking features of this trial, as reported to us by the gospel writers, is that the judge repeatedly and most emphatically declares that Jesus is innocent. He makes it very plain that he is perfectly convinced of Jesus' righteousness. He finds no guilt in Him. When he finally renders the verdict that is to send Jesus to the death of the cross, his sentence is not the result of a misunderstanding. Nor is he finally convinced that Jesus is guilty. On the contrary, to the very last he emphasizes that the Lord is innocent. His original judgment is never changed: "I find no guilt in him at all!"

Yet, even so the way is open for the Roman judge to answer the question: what wilt thou do then with the righteous Jesus, the light in darkness, the revelation of the Father? And an answer he must give. He represented the sword-power of the world. And he is very deeply conscious of the fact that he has power to release Jesus, and power to send Him to His death. But in this particular instance he does not like his position, is not well pleased with his power. Under ordinary circumstances, he would have revealed little or no hesitancy to send the innocent to his death. And even now it was not love of truth and righteousness that caused him to waver. But he was afraid. Caring little for truth and justice as such, he was anxious about his own position. On the one hand he was afraid of Jesus. He probably had heard of Him. His calm and majestic appearance must have impressed him. And his wife's report of her dream, and her request that he would have nothing to do with this righteous man, increased his anxiety and trouble not a little. On the other hand, he was afraid of the Jews, and above all of Caesar. By all means, he must remain Caesar's friend. Tossed to and fro by these various motives and circumstances, he repeatedly seeks a way out, and tries to release Jesus. Desperately he attempts to avoid a definite answer to the question: what wilt thou do with the perfectly righteous? He places the people before the choice between Barabbas and Jesus. He tries to rid himself of the troublesome case by sending Jesus to Herod. He has Jesus scourged, and brings Him out to the people, perhaps to evoke their pity. But all these attempts fail.

Pilate must give the answer to God's question.

And the answer he finally gives: I have no regard for the righteous and for righteousness, let the blood of the Righteous be shed!

He suffered under Pontius Pilate! That means, indeed, that He was innocent and yet condemned by the worldly judge, in order that, as He voluntarily submits to this judgment, and willingly goes the way of the cross, we might have a strong assurance that He bore, not His own, but our transgressions on the tree.

But it also was the condemnation of the world, our world, the world of men. And its blood-guiltiness and condemnation can never be removed, unless its guilty stains are washed away by the very blood that was shed on Calvary.

For them that are thus washed the judgment of the cross is removed by God's verdict in the resurrection of Jesus Christ from the dead.

For He was delivered for our transgressions, and raised for our justification.

III

The Death Of The Cross

In the Apostolic Confession the fact that Jesus died the death of the cross receives special mention. Christ "suffered under Pontius Pilate, was crucified" . . . .

And to the meaning of this death by crucifixion the Heidelberg Catechism calls our attention in question and answer thirty-nine: "Is there anything more in his being crucified, than if he had died some other death? Yes, there is; for thereby I am assured that he took on him the curse which lay upon me; for the death of the cross was accursed of God."

The Scriptural reference here is to Deut. 21:22, 23 as interpreted in Gal. 3:13. In the former passage we read: "And if any man have committed a sin worthy of death, and he be put to death, and thou hang him on a tree: His body shall not remain all night upon the tree, but thou shalt in any wise bury him that day; (for he that is hanged is accursed of God;) that the land be not defiled, which the Lord thy God giveth thee." The reference is, not to capital punishment by hanging, but to the hanging and public exposure of the bodies of those that had been put to death by the sword, or by stoning. Such a public hanging was considered an intensification of capital punishment. It was, therefore, the hanging itself, and not the death by hanging, that was an abomination, and that caused the hanged one to be accursed of God. And the entire passage in Galatians is as follows: "For as many as are of the works of the law are under the curse: for it is written, Cursed is every one that continueth not in all things which are written in the book of the law to do them. But that no man is justified by the law in the sight of God, it is evident: for the just shall live by faith. And the law is not of faith: but the man that doeth them

shall live in them. Christ hath redeemed us from the curse of
the law, being made a curse for us: for it is written, Cursed is
every one that hangeth on a tree." 3:10-13.

Now, the quotation in vs. 10: "Cursed is every one that continueth not in all things which are written in the book of the
law to do them," is from Deut. 27:26. And the context of that
passage is remarkable, in as much as it shows how really "as
many as are of the works of the law are under a curse." Moses
gave commandment to the people of Israel that when they shall
have crossed over Jordan into the land of Canaan, half of the
tribes shall take their position on mount Gerizim, and the other
half on mount Ebal. And then the Levites shall read to them
the curse and the blessing, and the people shall respond by a
solemn Amen. The reading of the curse was to be as follows:
"Cursed be the man that maketh any graven or molten image,
an abomination unto the Lord, the work of the hands of the
craftsman, and putteth it in a secret place. And all the people
shall answer and say, Amen. Cursed be he that setteth light by
his father and mother. And all the people shall say, Amen.
Cursed be he that removeth his neighbor's landmark. And all
the people shall say, Amen. Cursed be he that maketh the blind
to wander out of the way. And all the people shall say, Amen.
Cursed be he that perverteth the judgment of the stranger,
fatherless and widow. And all the people shall say, Amen.
Cursed be he that lieth with his father's wife; because he un-
covereth his father's skirt. And all the people shall say, Amen.
Cursed be he that lieth with any manner of beast. And all the
people shall say, Amen. Cursed be he that lieth with his sister,
the daughter of his father, or the daughter of his mother. And
all the people shall say, Amen. Cursed be he that lieth with
his mother in law. And all the people shall say, Amen. Cursed
be he that smiteth his neighbor secretly. And all the people
shall say, Amen. Cursed be he that taketh reward to slay an
innocent person. And all the people shall say, Amen. Cursed
be he that confirmeth not all the words of this law to do them.
And all the people shall say, Amen."

From this it is evident that all that were under the law, not only were actually under a curse, in as much as no one could keep the law of God perfectly, and the people of Israel in the course of their history had trampled the law of God under foot a thousand times; but also that they had solemnly covenanted on mount Ebal to take this curse upon them. Did all this mean, then, that the promise had been made of none effect, seeing that the law and its curse had been superimposed upon it, and that no one could fulfill the demands of the law, nor bear the curse and remove it? How is it possible that the heirs of the promise could thus be made subject to the law, and that, too, as a condition unto life? And how could the curse they assumed on mount Ebal ever have any other result than that it made the promise for ever impossible of realization?

The answer is in the thirteenth verse.

To be sure, all that are under the law are under a curse. And Israel as such, by itself, could never bear that curse and live. It could never work its way through the curse, so to speak, unto the promise, and unto the inheritance of eternal life. It would seem to have been nothing short of sheer recklessness on their part to assume responsibility for the curse at all. But in Christ they could assume that responsibility. Christ was in their loins. And that Christ was able, and would bear the curse for them, in their behalf and in their stead, was demonstrated to them daily by their sacrifices. And in the fulness of time Christ did come. He, too, came under the law. And with the people, His own, the heirs of the promise, he also came under the curse, though by a voluntary act of His own. He, so to speak, took up His position on mount Ebal, and to Him, too, the curse of the law was read. And He, too, responded by a solemn Amen. And He was able to assume that responsibility, and to fulfill it. For He was the holy Child Jesus, the Son of God in the flesh. He could bear that curse in such a way that the demands of the law were satisfied, so that it would no longer curse the children of the promise. He could work His way through the curse to the promise, through death into life, through hell into eternal glory. And this He did. Figuratively speaking, His cross was

planted on mount Ebal. And there He fulfilled, once and for
ever, the curse of the law. For Christ became a curse for us, as
it is written: Cursed is every one that hangeth on a tree.

It was principally Christ that covenanted with God on mount
Ebal to assume responsibility for the curse of the law.

And it was Christ again, this time on the real mount Ebal
of Calvary, that fulfilled that responsibility, and, becoming a
curse, removed it for ever.

Such is the meaning of the cross.

No other death than that by crucifixion might the Lamb of
God, that must take away the sin of the world, die.

For Him it would not have been proper had He died suddenly
of heart failure, or of some common disease, or of the weakness
of old age.

Nor might the enemy stone Him to death, as they sometimes
sought to do even before His hour had come; or cast Him down
the precipice, as they meant to do at Nazareth; or, with the help
of the traitor, sneak upon Him unawares, and secretly put Him
out of the way, as must have been their intention when they
covenanted with Judas for thirty pieces of silver. All these
attempts were frustrated. The counsels of the enemies were
brought to nought, and by God's special direction the events
of His "hour" were so arranged that the ultimate outcome was
the death of the cross.

For Christ had to bear God's curse against the sinner. And
the death of the cross was accursed of God. Thus it was written:
"Cursed is every one that hangeth on a tree."

This is not to be understood as if this is the only meaning
of the cross, and as if it were the only reason why our Lord
must die the death by crucifixion.

There are several other reasons.

For one thing, as has already been demonstrated, the Saviour
must be brought to His death in the way of legal procedure
and of a public trial, and that, too, not only by the Jewish
authorities, but also by the tribunal of the world, represented
by Pontius Pilate.

Furthermore, Jesus' death must be a sacrifice for sin.

This implied, first of all, the shedding of His blood. In Christ the priest and the sacrificial victim were one. He was both. He must, therefore, shed His own blood, and Himself carry it in the inner sanctuary, as did the high priest among Israel on the Day of Atonement. For "Christ being come an high priest of good things to come, by a greater and more perfect tabernacle, not made with hands, that is to say, not of this building; neither by the blood of goats and calves, but by his own blood he entered in once into the holy place, having obtained eternal redemption for us. For if the blood of bulls and of goats, and the ashes of an heifer sprinkling the unclean, sanctifieth to the purifying of the flesh: how much more shall the blood of Christ, who through the eternal Spirit offered himself without spot to God, purge your conscience from dead works to serve the living God?" Heb. 9:11-14. And again: "And almost all things are by the law purged with blood: and without shedding of blood there is no remission." If the death of Christ were to be an atoning sacrifice, His blood must be shed. And this was one of the reasons why He might not die some other death, but must suffer the death of the cross.

That the death of our Lord must be a sacrifice for sin implied, secondly, that He must lay down His life voluntarily, in willing and loving obedience to the Father. His death must be an act of the High Priest. He must offer Himself. As He said while He tabernacled among us: "I am the good shepherd: the good shepherd giveth his life for the sheep . . . . As the Father knoweth me, even so know I the Father: and I lay down my life for the sheep . . . . Therefore does my Father love me, because I lay down my life that I might take it again. No man taketh it from me, but I lay it down of myself. I have power to lay it down, and I have power to take it again. This commandment have I received of my Father." John 10:11, 15,17,18. But if He were to lay down His life, if He were to shed His own blood, the very form of His death must be such that it offered Him an opportunity to do so. To this end the death of the cross was eminently adapted.

In the case of the Old Testament sacrifices the priest and the sacrificial victim were two different beings. All that was required, therefore, was that the priest should stab the victim as quickly as possible, and sprinkle the blood upon the horns of the altar, and upon the mercy seat, to realize that idea of a sacrificial offering. Precisely because the priest and the offering were not identical this was sufficient. The victim did not have to be slowly tortured to death, in order to make its death a voluntary offering, for it was the priest, not the victim itself, that brought the sacrifice.

But with our Saviour this was different.

He was the priest, but also the offering. He had to shed His own blood. Hence, the very form of His death must be such that it gave Him the opportunity to pour out His life in a voluntary sacrifice, to carry His own blood into the heavenly sanctuary, sprinkle it upon the horns of the altar, and on the mercy seat by an act of conscious obedience. Had our Lord been stabbed to death, so that He had died instantaneously, this act of voluntary and loving obedience could not have been performed. But now it was different. He died the death of the cross. And this meant, not that the enemies killed Him instantaneously, but that they merely opened His body, broke it, that He might shed His blood.

For six long hours Christ poured out His life unto death!

This was a completely voluntary act on His part. At any moment during those six hours He might have refused to remain suspended on the accursed tree, and have taken up the challenge of the enemy to come down from the cross. But He remained on the tree, and continued to pour out His life. In every drop of blood that slowly trickled from His hands and feet there was an expression of perfect obedience, of the love of God, and the love of His own. Through the death of the cross He, the High Priest, poured out His own blood, sacrificed Himself as the Lamb of God without spot, and carried the blood of atonement into the sanctuary of God.

And, finally, through the death of the cross our Lord could *taste* death, could experience the fulness of horror there is in the reality of death as punishment for sin. This, too, was necessary in order to make of His death a sacrifice for sin. He must not merely die, as quickly as possible, but He must pass through the full experience of the agony of death. Every bitter drop of death in all its misery He must taste as He drinks His cup. And the death of the cross was eminently adapted to this purpose.

And thus the death of the cross was the means through which Christ took upon Himself and suffered the curse of God that is upon the sinner.

God's curse is the expression of His holy wrath against the workers of iniquity. It is the opposite of His blessing. Both, blessing and cursing, are Words of God. The former is the Word of His favor, His grace and loving-kindness, drawing us into His fellowship, and causing us to taste that the Lord is good. The latter is the Word of His wrath and hot anger, expelling us from His house, causing us to experience Him as a consuming fire, casting us away from Him, forsaking us in utter terror of darkness and desolation, making us unspeakably wretched.

This curse of God was upon Christ as He was made sin for us, that we might be made the righteousness of God in Him.

And somehow, He experienced this awful curse through the cross.

The question may be asked: what did the cross have to do with Christ's tasting the horror of the curse of God against the sinner? Was it merely a symbol, expressive of the curse? Or did it serve as a means through which the bitter experience of God's wrath in the curse was conveyed to the consciousness of the Sufferer on Calvary?

The answer must be that it was both.

To us the cross of Christ is a symbol, a sign, expressive of the fact that He bore the curse of God that was upon us. For the victim of crucifixion was a castaway. There was no room for him in all God's wide creation. Suspended between heaven and earth, he was the embodiment of the judgment that there was no place for him on the earth among men, and no room for him in heaven with God. Men did not want him; God did not receive him. This is the symbolism of the cross of Christ. Suspended on the accursed tree, He has no name left unto Him. He empties Himself completely. By the symbol of the cross, conceived not merely as man's, but as God's cross, we are assured that Christ bore the curse that was upon us.

But for Christ it was also a means through which He actually tasted the horror of God's curse upon the sinner. For let us not forget that the cross was a Word of God. It was not man, but God Himself that had spoken the word: "Cursed is every one that hangeth on a tree." That the hanged one was accursed, therefore, was not due to an act or interpretation of man: it was God Himself Who by His own Word placed him in the category of the accursed. The category, I say, for the word of God in Deuteronomy emphatically speaks of *every one* that hangeth on a tree. There was no exception to this rule. In that category, therefore, also belonged the cross of Christ, and that, too, by the Word of God. On Calvary, through the means of the tree, God spoke His Word of wrath to the crucified One: "Cursed is every one that hangeth on a tree; cursed art Thou, even as Thou here standest in the place of sinners!"

And Christ heard that Word of God, and trembled, and became unspeakably miserable!

The Word of God's anger was in His cross, and He felt it!

He felt the oppressing hand of God's wrath in an increasing measure, as the slow moments of His dying hours were measured by the equally slow trickle of His blood from hands and feet.

More heavily laden with the wrath and the curse of God became every succeeding moment. And to every moment of God's fierce anger the Saviour responded, so to speak, by every drop of blood, sprinkled with fervent love and perfect obedience upon the mercy seat before the face of God. Accentuated was the Word of the curse by the darkness that spread its horrible wings over the scene of that judgment of God on Calvary, and the Saviour became completely occupied with the tremendous task of tasting the horror of God's cursing wrath, and of responding to it in the obedience of love through His dripping blood. Before the darkness descended He could still direct His attention to others, even while bearing the curse. But in the three hours of darkness He is silent. His own suffering, His own work of obedience, the bringing of the perfect sacrifice, the laying down of His life in perfect obedience, the amazing experience of the fierce wrath of God against sin, and the equally amazing calling of meeting this expression of God's anger without rebellion, without complaint, without drawing back, in love of God, — these require all His attention, every ounce of strength that is in Him.

And thus He descends into the depths of woe! And thus it is somewhat understandable that, at the moment when God's cursing wrath is most oppressive at the same time that His love and obedience are most perfect, the question of amazement should be wrung from His sorely vexed soul: "My God, my God, why hast thou forsaken me?"

This is the meaning of the cross!

And thus I know, through the *logos* of the cross, that my Saviour took upon Himself, completely bore, and removed for ever, the curse that was upon me!

Christ hath redeemed us from the curse of the law, having become a curse for us!

LORD'S DAY XVI

Q. 40. Why was it necessary for Christ to humble himself even unto death?

A. Because with respect to the justice and truth of God, satisfaction for our sin could be made no otherwise, than by the death of the Son of God.

Q. 41. Why was he also buried?

A. Thereby to prove that he was really dead.

Q. 42. Since then Christ died for us, why must we also die?

A. Our death is not a satisfaction for our sins, but only an abolishing of sin, and a passage into eternal life.

Q. 43. What further benefit do we receive from the sacrifice and death of Christ on the cross?

A. That by virtue thereof, our old man is crucified, dead and buried with him; that so the corrupt inclinations of the flesh may no more reign in us; but that we may offer ourselves unto him a sacrifice of thanksgiving.

Q. 44. Why is there added, "he descended into hell?"

A. That in my greatest temptations, I may be assured, and wholly comfort myself in this, that my Lord Jesus Christ, by his inexpressible anguish, pains, terrors and hellish agonies, in which he was plunged during all his sufferings, but especially on the cross, hath delivered me from the anguish and torments of hell.

I

The Death Of The Son Of God

The text of our translation of this sixteenth Lord's Day is substantially correct. However, in the answer to the forty-third question, the words "that by virtue thereof," should be changed into "that by his power" (dass durch seine Kraft). And in the forty-fourth answer, instead of the words "wherein he was plunged during all his sufferings, but especially on the cross," we should read "which he suffered also in his soul on the cross and before" (die er auch an seiner Seele am Kreuz und zuvor erlitten).

This Lord's Day is intended as an exposition of the words of the Apostolic confession: "dead and buried, descended into hell." And while treating the subjects of the death, burial, and descension into hell of the Saviour, the Catechism inserts a question and answer concerning the necessity and reason of our physical death in the light of the fact that Christ suffered death for us; and another question and answer concerning the present, spiritual fruits for us of the death of Christ.

In the *Apostolicum* the words "dead and buried" belong together. And what is more, they belong to the series: "suffered under Pontius Pilate, was crucified, dead and buried." This should not be overlooked in our discussion of the necessity and significance of the death of Christ. For this means that the Apostolic Confession mentions the various elements of the passion of our Lord in their chronological, historical order: He suffered, was crucified, died, was buried. And again, this implies that in the Confession the word *dead*, strictly speaking, refers to the fact that Christ *died*, to the moment when He gave up the ghost and laid down His earthly life.

663

We are apt to overlook this in our dogmatical interpretation
of the death of Christ.

The Catechism considers the death of Christ from the viewpoint of its necessity as a sacrifice for sin and satisfaction of the
justice of God: "Why was it necessary for Christ to humble
himself even unto death?" And the answer is: "Because with
respect to the justice and truth of God, satisfaction for our sins
could be made no otherwise, than by the death of the Son of
God." And as we explain this answer, and try somewhat to
demonstrate this necessity and significance of the death of Christ,
we are inclined to omit the physical and temporal death of
Christ altogether, or, at least, hastily pass over it, in order to
elaborate at once upon the broader and deeper aspect of death
in general, and of the death of Christ in particular. After all,
physical death, the death of the body, thus we are liable to
reason, is not the real, the only penalty for sin. The separation
of soul and body, the state of *sjeool* or *hades* is only temporal.
The essence of death is the wrath of God, the curse, separation
of our whole being from the favor of God's presence, to be forsaken of Him. If, therefore, we are to speak of the death of
the Son of God as a satisfaction for sin, we must not call attention to the moment when Christ gave up the ghost. Then His
suffering and death were finished. It is true that He was buried,
and that His body remained until the third day in the place
of corruption. But His soul was in Paradise even then, and
the suffering of the wrath of God had all been borne to the end.
It is, therefore, to the deeper meaning of His death as the
expression of the wrath of God, to His suffering of the punishment of death before "He died," that our attention must be
called, when we explain that death as a satisfaction of the justice
of God for our sins.

And this is true.

It is perfectly correct to say that the essence of death is not
to be found in the separation of soul and body, but in that
everlasting desolation in hell that consists in the being forsaken
of God. Physical death is, as separation of soul and body, only
temporal. There is also a resurrection of the wicked, a reunion

of soul and body unto damnation. And it is, therefore, also true that, if we would speak of the death of Christ as a satisfaction for sin, as a bearing of the full punishment for our sins, we must speak of its deeper meaning. The mere *dying* and *burial* of Christ, His being in *hades,* apart from the rest of His suffering, especially on the cross, cannot be the satisfaction for our iniquities.

And yet, it should be evident that in this connection we must speak particularly of that aspect of Christ's death that consisted in the departure of His spirit from His earthly house, and that was, as far as the body was concerned, finished in the burial.

This is plainly the denotation of the word "dead" in the series: "suffered under Pontius Pilate, was crucified, dead, and buried."

This is also evident from the connection between the fortieth question and answer of the Catechism with what precedes it. That Christ sustained the wrath of God against sin, and that thus He offered the only propitiatory sacrifice whereby we are redeemed from everlasting damnation, was stated in the answer to question thirty-seven, as an explanation of the words "He suffered." That by His suffering as the innocent One, he delivered us from the severe judgment of God to which we were exposed, was explained in the answer to question thirty-eight. And that His suffering of the death of the cross signifies that He took upon Himself and bore the curse in our stead, was mentioned in question and answer thirty-nine. It is evident, therefore, that in question and answer forty, the Catechism, even as the *Apostolicum,* refers to the fact that Christ *died,* that He laid down His earthly life, and that He entered into the state of *sjeool.*

What, then, is physical death? What does it mean for sinful man to die? And what is the meaning of the grave?

From the viewpoint of experience, of what we, who are on this side of the grave, can see of death, it is the complete dissolution of our earthly house, the end of our earthly existence; and the grave is corruption, our return to the dust, whence we are taken.

It is an utter loss.

In death the organism of the body collapses and is dissolved, and with it man's entire earthly existence is completely destroyed. As far as this world is concerned, he is no more. For it is through the body that man is a living soul. Through his physical organism, with its senses of sight, hearing, touch, taste, and smell, he has contact with the outside world, the world of his experience. When his body is dissolved that entire world, as the object of his experience, dissolves with it. In death he sees and hears, he tastes and touches and smells, he eats and drinks, he thinks and speaks, he desires and pursues, he craves and delights in the things of this world no more. Everything is taken away from him. His power and talents, his house and possessions, the object of his love and friendship, his position and name, the fruit of his toil and labor and invention, — all are suddenly and completely lost. His very place knows him no more. He may have been very important, he may have occupied a position of honor and great influence; perhaps, he was considered indispensable: all his importance and influence ceases absolutely and with utter finality when he dies. His very name perishes.

No, he is not annihilated. He continues to be, though he cannot possibly conceive the mode of that existence on the other side of death and the grave. For it is very really *he* that dies, and that passes through this terrible reality of dying. But in and through death, he is left utterly naked. From the viewpoint of his present existence, death means that he is deprived of all rights and privileges.

And the grave seals it all, and signifies that there is no return, means that there is no way out as far as his own knowledge and power can conceive of and effect such an escape. In the grave the corruption and dissolution of his body are finished. It becomes a mere heap of dust without form and meaning.

Such is the meaning of death as far as we can even now interpret its mystery.

But in the light of revelation we know far more about death. For the Word of God reveals to us that death is not a normal process, but a violent intervention of the hand of God to take away our name. Death is punishment. It is the wages of sin. It is the expression of the wrath of God, the revelation of His justice against the sinner. We do not simply die as a matter of fact: God kills us. And therefore, death is God's verdict over us. In death, physical death, God declares that we are unworthy, wholly unworthy, to have a place and a name in this world, that we have forfeited the right to be, to exist, and that, on the other hand, we have made ourselves worthy of destruction: "the day thou eatest thereof, thou shalt surely die!"

Still more.

Death, so Scripture informs us, is the end; but it is also the beginning. It is the end of all existence in the world; it is the beginning of eternal desolation. Physical death is only the entrance of a dark and horrible pit, the pit of hell, of outer darkness, where there is nothing but the experience of the just wrath of a righteous and holy God. There shall be weeping and gnashing of teeth, — and nothing else!

That is why man is terribly afraid of death, and, always being in the midst of death, the fear of death holds him in bondage throughout all his present living. Nor should we characterize this fear of death as cowardice. On the contrary, for mere sinners, apart from Christ, it is mere folly and also haughty rebellion to pretend that we are able to face death without fear. How can mere man speak of courage over against an enemy he cannot successfully hope to oppose, he cannot even begin to fight? We may cover our coffins with beautiful flowers, and decorate our graves, but through it all the grim spectre of death mocks our vain attempts to deny him, and strikes terror into the heart of every man!

Christ also died.

And He, too, was buried.

But His dying unto death was from beginning to end a voluntary act of His own.

From the very beginning, He, the Son of God, until He gave up the ghost at the cross, performed the act of dying. We lie in the midst of death. All our present existence is oppressed by death. Death surrounds us on every side, and the fear of death pursues us every moment. And at His incarnation He entered into this death. He became like us in every respect, sin excepted. He assumed the flesh and blood of the children. He took upon Himself the likeness of sinful flesh. And in that likeness He was, even as we are, in the midst of death. But He came voluntarily. For He is the Son of God. He came from without, though He is born of a woman. Into the prison of our death He entered by an act of His own, in obedience to the Father.

And all His life He tasted death.

He could taste death in all its horror, because He was the Son of God in sinless human nature. He knew and experienced the reality of death, for He apprehended it as the expression of the wrath of God, as the execution of God's justice against the workers of iniquity. He felt that in death the hand of God was heavy upon Him. Nor was His attitude towards death that of courage and indifference in the worldly sense of the word. He knew the fear of death. And this suffering of death and of the fear of death was aggravated as His "hour" approached. Just hear Him complain, as the shadow of the cross begins to creep over His soul: "Now is my soul troubled; and what shall I say? Father, save me from this hour: but for this cause came I unto this hour." John 12:27. Or behold Him, on the eve of His deliverance into the hands of sinners, as He casts Himself into the dust of Gethsemane, a worm and no man, His soul exceeding sorrowful even unto death, His agony so great and deep that His sweat became as it were great drops of blood, crying from the depths of fear to the Father that the cup may pass from Him if it were possible!

Yet in all His fear and suffering He never became disobedient, nor did He ever despair. His was the true courage, the only possible courage over against death, the courage that is based on the assurance that God was with Him in all His dying, even unto the end. For, first of all, His dying was an act of perfect obedience in the love of God. Knowing death as the just judgment of God against sin, and standing in the place of His sinful people, He willingly assumed the suffering of death. In all His life He died, and in all His dying He was obedient. And being obedient in dying, He never lost the consciousness of God's favor upon Him personally, even while He experienced His wrath in dying. And in the consciousness of His perfect obedience, and of the favor of His God, he trusted that God would not leave His soul in hell, nor suffer His holy One to see corruption. And, in the second place, in this consciousness He was constantly assured of the victory. He had power to lay down His life, and He had power to take it again. Trusting in God, He saw through death and looked forward to the resurrection. Hence, suffering the fear of death, He was not afraid.

And so He died.

O, yes, it was necessary that He, too, should die the physical death. He might not simply suffer the agonies of death on the cross, in order then to be revived or glorified in the sight of the enemies. He must bear the wrath of God to the end. The sentence of God in physical death is that the sinner has absolutely forfeited every right to his existence in the world. This sentence must be executed upon Christ also. God takes away His whole earthly house. His very name perishes. His body, too, collapses, and He gives up the ghost. Also upon Him the sentence is pronounced that He is unworthy to exist on the earth. Only, as the Head of His people, He agrees with the sentence of God with all His heart. He makes of death an act. His life He lays down even as God takes it. His spirit He commends to God, His body He delivers over into the place of corruption. His name and position He freely offers up to the righteousness of God. And in delivering up His soul unto death He confesses: "Thou, Father, art just and righteous, when Thou judgest that the sinner has no right to be, should be utterly destroyed from the earth, and should sink into everlasting desolation. Take my life, my name, my all. Freely I offer it in love to Thee. For even now it is my meat to do Thy will!"

And so He was buried.

The Catechism explains that He was buried to prove that He was really dead. If this may be explained as meaning that His burial set the seal upon His death, inasmuch as the grave is the place of corruption, the finality of death, the return unto the dust, there is sense in this answer. However, if it merely means that from His burial it became evident that He had died on the cross, the answer is hardly correct. One hardly buries a person to prove that he is dead. Besides, such proof was not needed in the case of the death of Christ. If there had been any doubt that He died the moment He cried out: "Father, into thy hands do I commend my spirit," it should have been completely removed by the spear thrust that pierced His heart, and caused blood and water to gush forth from His side. But Christ must die unto the end. He, too, must enter into the place of corruption. He must deliver His body to the humiliation of the grave, to the place where the sinner returns to the dust. In perfect obedience to the Father He enters into Hades, and commits His body to the grave. For let us not forget that even His burial was an act of His own. As He entered into the womb of the virgin, and thereby into the likeness of sinful flesh; as He voluntarily suffered the reality of death all His life; as He willingly entered into death finally, and gave up the ghost; so He obediently submitted to the sentence of God: "dust thou art, and to dust thou shalt return," and entered into the grave. He could do so, because He was the Son of God, and the person of the Son was never separated from His human nature, even in the grave. And so, He accomplished all of death, and fulfilled all righteousness.

And thus satisfaction was made for our sins. For, as the Catechism explains, "with respect to the justice and truth of God, satisfaction for our sins could be made no otherwise than by the death of the Son of God."

A bold expression this is: "the death of the Son of God." There are those who consider the phrase too bold. They argue that the Son of God is very God Himself, that He has life in Himself, and that, therefore, it is blasphemy to speak of His death. It was, therefore, the man Jesus that died on the cross. And even while the man Jesus died the Son of God liveth in eternal glory.

But this objection is based on a misunderstanding of the phrase, and the expression should certainly be retained. It is quite true, of course, that the divine nature cannot suffer death. God is the Lord. He is the living God. He is life. He is the most Blessed for ever. In His divine being He cannot suffer. But this is not denied by the expression: "the death of the Son of God." We must remember that Christ is the Person of the Son of God. As such He subsists eternally in the divine nature. And in that divine nature He is in the bosom of the Father, and lives the life of infinitely perfect divine friendship with the Father and the Holy Ghost in infinite bliss. But this same Person of the Son also assumed the human nature. He is not two persons, a human and divine; but He is and remains one Person, the divine Person of the Son, subsisting in two natures, the divine and the human. And it is this Person of the Son of God that suffered the death of the cross, and that was in Hades, that committed His spirit to God, and that was buried in the sepulchre of Joseph. Only, it must be remembered that He suffered all this, not in the divine, but in the human nature. And so it is perfectly proper to speak of the death of the Son of God.

And this expression must be retained, because "satisfaction for our sins could be made no otherwise than by the death of the Son of God."

If it was a mere man that died on the cross, the cross is made vain. No mere man, even though he were righteous, could ever bear the full punishment for sin and finish it. Still less could a mere man make satisfaction for others, and that, too, for countless millions of sinners. Only the Son of God could taste the depth of death. Only He could bear the full burden of the wrath of God and sustain it to the end. Only He could make of death an act of obedience, and voluntarily lay down the life He had voluntarily assumed. Only He could finish death in dying. And only He had the right and the power to take the place of the elect, and satisfy the justice of God in respect to their sins. Only His death, the death of the Son of God Himself in human nature, could be so deep, so precious in the sight of God, that by His obedience many could be made righteous. Only when the death of the cross is the death of the Son of God can we have the assurance that our sins are blotted out for ever, and that in Christ we have the righteousness of God by faith.

II

The Death Of Believers

The question arises quite naturally: why must believers die the physical death? Christ died for us. His death is the satisfaction for our sins. Now, if physical death belongs to the punishment for sin, and the death of Christ is really satisfaction, it would appear to follow that believers were also delivered from temporal or physical death. Yet, this is not the case. The Catechism, therefore, inquires into this matter, and asks the question: "Since Christ died for us, why must we also die?"

We may notice that the Heidelberger does not directly answer the question. It does, indeed, explain that the death of believers is no satisfaction for sin, and it removes the apparent contradiction between the death of Christ as an atonement for sin and the death of those for whom He atoned. But the question, why the death of believers, even though it be no satisfaction for sin, is still necessary, is not answered. The question remains: why is it that believers must pass through the suffering of physical death? Why could they not be translated without enduring this suffering? Enoch was so translated. Elijah ascended up into heaven without seeing death. The saints that shall be living at the coming of the Lord will be changed in a moment, in the twinkling of an eye. Why could not also believers be glorified, and taken up into heaven, without having to face the horror of death and the grave?

Several answers may be suggested to this question. And these answers are really all controlled by the one fact that, before the saints can be completely glorified, all things must be ready, the entire elect Church must be born and saved, and the new heavens and earth must be created in which righteousness shall dwell.

If the elect were to escape the suffering of physical death in all its implications, they would have to be completely glorified at the moment of their regeneration. And what is more, their regeneration, and also their glorification would have to take place at birth. For the reality of physical death is not limited to the moment when we give up the ghost, and our spirit leaves the body, but involves our entire earthly existence. We are born in the midst of death, with a corruptible and mortal body. Living our earthly life, we die constantly. The power of death reveals itself in all the diseases, suffering, and sorrow of this present time. If, therefore, the elect were to escape physical death, they must be regenerated and completely renewed at their coming into this world, and at once taken into heaven. But this is absurd, for in that case the Church of the elect could not be brought forth. The generations of the elect must be born. And to them we can give birth only in our present, earthy, and corruptible bodies. And in these corruptible bodies we lie in the midst of death, and must needs pass through death and the grave into glory.

Moreover, it is no doubt the will of God that the glory of His grace shall eternally shine forth in the Church of the redeemed. And this glory must be realized in the consciousness of the elect. They must know by experience from how great a depth of sin and misery and death the marvelous grace of God redeemed and delivered them. But unto this end they must have experience of the suffering and power of death. From the depth they must cry unto God, that they may for ever extol the wonder of His grace whereby they are redeemed. And, therefore, they must not at once be glorified in body and soul, when they are regenerated, but as renewed children of God in principle suffer a while and pass through the darkness of death, that they may taste the goodness and glorious grace, the mighty power and dominion of God their Redeemer, Who calls the things that are not as if they were, and Who quickens the dead.

Moreover, it is only in the body of this death that believers are able to fulfill their calling in this world, according to God's good pleasure over them. For they must, for a time, represent the cause of the Son of God in antithesis to the world of sin. They must be to the glory of the grace of Him that called them in all their walk and conversation, fight the good fight of faith, and that, too, in the midst of a crooked and perverse nation. And in this cause they are called to suffer with Christ, and so fulfill the measure of His suffering. Hence, their regeneration and glorification cannot be simultaneous. It is only in their present body, in which they are "by nature" one with the world, and have all things in common with natural men, that they can serve this high purpose of God, and be faithful even unto death. Believers, therefore, must also die, even though Christ died for them. For it is given them of grace, in the cause of Christ, not only to believe on Him, but also to suffer with Him. Phil. 1:29.

And, finally, that economy of things to which their ultimate and complete redemption belongs is not yet come. They shall be glorified body and soul, and inherit the kingdom of God, the incorruptible, and undefilable inheritance, that fadeth not away. But this kingdom of God is heavenly, and to inherit it also the body of believers must be made to bear the image of the heavenly. The heavenly kingdom and the redemption of their body belong together. The one must wait for the other. Hence, the body of believers cannot be glorified until the consummation of all things, the moment of the resurrection, when God shall make all things new, and create new heavens and a new earth in which righteousness shall dwell, and the tabernacle of God shall be with men. Until that moment, the second advent of our Lord Jesus Christ, the body of believers must rest in the grave and await the resurrection of the dead.

But the Catechism considers the question why believers must also die only from the viewpoint of its juridical ground. Death is the punishment of sin. It is an enemy. It is the expression of the just wrath of God against sin. But Christ died! He died instead of His own. And His death, the death of the Son of God, is the complete satisfaction for sin. He overcame death. He removed the ground of our condemnation. Would it not follow, then, that, the ground of death being removed, death

itself must already be swallowed up in victory, and there can be
no more death for believers? Why then is it that believers also
die?

This question the Catechism answers in a twofold way, negatively and positively.

The sting of death is gone: death is, for believers, no satisfaction for their sins.

And the enemy of death has been changed into a servant: it
is become a passage into eternal life for them that are in Christ.

This is a most glorious confession which, if we apprehend it
by faith, makes us more than victors through Him that loved us.

The death of believers is no satisfaction for their sins. Satisfaction it could never be, of course. Only the death of the Son
of God could blot out the guilt of sin. If the just wrath of God
must fall upon us, we can only perish everlastingly. For ever
we must suffer death. But the Catechism means that the death
of believers is no longer to be considered a manifestation of
the wrath of God, an execution of justice, a punishment for sin.
It is changed into something else for them that are in Christ.
And this must be understood in its full sense. It must be applied,
not only to the final moment of dying, to our descent into the
grave, but equally to all that is implied in death, to all the
suffering of this present time. For we lie in the midst of death
in this world. Dying we die. All the suffering and agony, all
the sorrow and grief of this present time are very really the
operation of death. When, therefore, we confess by faith that
our death is not meant as a satisfaction for sin, it also implies
that all our present sufferings of soul and body are no longer to
be considered as punishment for sin and expressions of the
righteous judgment of God.

For believers, the sufferings of this present time have lost
their real sting.

They are no longer experienced as righteous retribution.
Even those sufferings that appear to be the direct result of certain concrete, personal sins, dare no longer to be considered
as punishment for sin. If a man is regenerated and called to the
light of life in later life, and if in his unconverted state he should

have lived a life of dissipation, of drunkenness and adultery, the effects of this former life of sin are not removed by his regeneration. He must suffer them. Yet, even that suffering is no longer punishment for sin, and may not be regarded as such. For Christ died for all our sins. He died all our death. His death is a complete satisfaction for all our iniquities. The debt has been paid in full. And God in His justice will not exact payment twice.

It is very important that believers apprehend this glorious truth by faith, fully and clearly.

They often fail to lay hold of this comfort. In the midst of suffering, they will often express themselves in a way that clearly reveals their failure to consider their misery and death in the light of the cross and of the perfect satisfaction of Christ for all their sins. They feel that they have "deserved" it all, and that they suffer exactly because they are worthy of death. They declare that God is righteous in visiting their sins upon their head, and that they have made themselves worthy of His wrath. They often seek a connection between their specific suffering and certain sins in their past life, and feel that the former is the expression of God's just wrath upon the latter. They must still make satisfaction for their sins!

And thus they err, because they fail by faith to lay hold on the perfect satisfaction and atonement of Christ.

Let us not misunderstand this.

The error in this attitude is not that they apprehend in their suffering the displeasure of God against sin. God is, indeed, displeased with sin, also with the sins of His children. It is, therefore, very well that we humble ourselves before the face of God in our suffering and misery, and confess that, if God should deal with us according to our transgressions, we would not be able to stand before Him, but would have to perish in eternal desolation. But the error is that in our suffering, and in our apprehension of the righteous judgment of God, we do not lay hold upon Christ by faith, and lack the joyous assurance that all our sins are blotted out, so that our death is no longer to be considered a punishment for sin. As soon as, and in the measure that we do take all our sins and sufferings to the cross, we do, indeed, confess:

> *"Lord, if Thou shouldst mark transgressions,*
> *In Thy presence who shall stand?"*

But we also triumphantly shout:

> *"But with Thee there is forgiveness,*
> *That Thy name may fear command."*

God does, indeed, chastise His children, and there is an element of chastisement in all their suffering in this present world.

But there is a great difference between punishment and chastisement. The former is the expression of God's just and condemning wrath, the latter is an operation of His paternal love. "For whom the Lord loveth he chasteneth, and scourgeth every son whom he receiveth. If ye endure chastening, God dealeth with you as with sons; for what son is there whom the father chasteneth not? But if ye are without chastisement, whereof all are partakers, then are ye bastards, and not sons." Heb. 12:6-8. If we are punished for our sins, there is no hope. For punishment means to be just retribution. And the just retribution for our sins is death, eternal death. But if we are chastised, we may rejoice in the chastisement, for it is meant for our good, and it tends unto life. Punishment for sin the suffering of this present time is for the reprobate wicked; chastisement is the same suffering for God's elect children. Punishment is that suffering as it is mixed with God's fierce and holy anger; chastisement is the same suffering mixed with saving grace. Punishment ends in destruction; chastisement is for our good, for our correction and sanctification. For thus the Scriptures teach us: "Furthermore we have had fathers of our flesh which corrected us and we gave them reverence: shall we not much rather be in subjection unto the Father of spirits, and live? For they verily for a few days chastened us after their own pleasure; but he for our profit, that we might be partakers of his holiness. Now no chastening for the present seemeth to be joyous, but grievous: nevertheless afterward it yieldeth the peaceable fruit of righteousness unto them which are exercised thereby." Heb. 12:9-11.

And all things work together for good for them that love God, that are the called according to His purpose. Rom. 8:28.

Although, therefore, also believers still lie in the midst of death, and taste death in all the sufferings of this present time, yet, for them it is no punishment, no satisfaction for sin. Christ died and rose again. He fully satisfied for all their iniquities. And the sufferings they endure must be their servant and tend unto their eternal good.

And thus it is with respect to their final, physical death and the grave.

The Catechism teaches us that the death of believers is: 1. no satisfaction for sin; 2. an abolishing of sin; 3. a passage into eternal life.

Those that are in Christ die in faith. And even though judging from outward appearances their death appears the same as that of unbelievers, even though they pass through the same struggle, and suffer the same agony in departing from this present world, their death is essentially different. For as in that hour of death they cling by faith to their crucified Lord, they know that it is not the retributive wrath of God that is upon them in all the agonies of death, but His elective love, delivering them from death into life, and beckoning them home to the house of many mansions. By faith they may truly die in peace.

For them death is, indeed, an abolishing of sin. The death of believers in Christ is not simply a separation of soul and body. It is much more. It is the final deliverance of the "inward man" from the bondage of the "outward man" and from all that pertains to it. Thus the apostle Paul teaches us in II Cor. 4:16: "For which cause we faint not; but though our outward man perish, yet the inward man is renewed day by day." When the believer dies his outward man perishes completely. To that outward man belong many things. The earthly house of this tabernacle it is called in II Cor. 5:1. His body and all his earthly life, his earthly experiences, his joys and sorrows, his earthly relationships, his name and position in this world, belong to the "out-

ward man." But to it also belongs the old nature, in which the
motions of sin are still active, in which operates the "law of
sin," that wars against the "law of his mind" and brings him
into captivity to the law of sin that is in his members. In death,
this outward man perishes. It is completely and finally destroyed.
And even though it is true that death is suffering, and that the
believer as well as the unbeliever, as long as he is in this earthly
house, does not want to be "unclothed" but "clothed upon," so
that he too dreads and hates the dissolution of his earthly house
from a merely earthly viewpoint, yet by faith he may rejoice in
the very suffering of death. For, all his life he had to fight
against the motions of sin in his members, and frequently he
seemed to suffer defeat. The sin that is within him was a cause
of profound sorrow and misery to him. And now, as he finally
lays his weary head upon death's pillow, he may rejoice in the
prospect of final deliverance from the body of this death, and
of the enjoyment of the perfect liberty of the children of God.

And so, the death of the believer is a passage into eternal life.
The inward man does not perish. It is the new principle of life,
of the life of Christ in him. And that cannot die. It is resurrection-life. Death has no dominion over it. With regard to the
believer from the viewpoint of that inward man our Lord said
to Martha: "I am the resurrection and the life: he that believeth
in me, though he were dead, yet shall he live: And whosoever
liveth and believeth in me shall never die." John 11:25, 26.
According to his inward man, the believer is firmly rooted in
Christ, the resurrection. He passes through death, but himself
cannot die.

This is not the place to speak about eternal life, and of the
passage into heavenly glory of the believer immediately after
death. For of this the Catechism speaks in Lord's Day twenty-
two, in connection with the article of the Apostolic Confession
on life everlasting.

All that need be emphasized here is that the character of
death, in case of the believer, has radically changed through the
power of the death of our Lord, the Son of God.

It is no longer satisfaction for sin, it is a means to deliver us from the power of sin.

No longer is death a terrorizing lord: he is become a servant, opening for us the gates into the glory of eternal life.

And the grave, that dreadful tyrant that swallowed us up into everlasting desolation, has become a passage into the glory of the resurrection.

We are conquerors, yea, more than conquerors, through Him that loved us. For death has no longer dominion over us. Our very enemies have become subservient to our salvation.

Nothing can separate us from the love of God which is in Christ Jesus our Lord!

III

Dead To Sin

In question and answer forty-three the Catechism calls our attention to a present, spiritual fruit of the death of the Son of God: the crucifixion, death, and burial of our old man, so that the corrupt inclinations of the flesh may no more reign in us, but we may now offer ourselves a sacrifice of thanksgiving to the living God.

Already we remarked that the better translation is: *"That by His power* (instead of: "That in virtue thereof") our old man is crucified, dead, and buried with him." The translation as it is in our Psalter might leave the impression that the Catechism favors the moral theory of the power of Christ's death. It is not in virtue of the death of Christ merely that our old man is crucified, but by the power of the very Lord that died for us and rose again.

Nevertheless, this crucifixion, death, and burial of our old man, which is accomplished by the power of His grace in us, is somehow the result, the fruit of the death of Christ, a spiritual benefit that was merited by Him in His death. Centrally, the death of Christ is the death of the old man of all the elect. When He died, they all died as to their old man; when He arose, they all arose in newness of life. And it is the application of this power and value of Christ's death to the individual elect in this world, that causes the old man to die in him, so that the inclinations of the flesh no longer reign in him, and he may offer himself a sacrifice of thanksgiving to God. We, therefore, confront two questions. First of all, we must ask in what sense the death of Christ is the death of the old man. And, secondly, how does the application of this death of Christ to the elect reveal itself in their life in this world? In what sense is their old man even now crucified, dead, and buried with Christ?

The teaching of the Catechism in this forty-third answer is directly based on Scripture. The instructor refers us to Romans 6. The apostle introduces this chapter with a question that might be raised by those that would oppose the doctrine he had presented in the preceding chapters, that of justification by faith alone, without the works of the law: "What shall we say then? Shall we continue in sin, that grace may abound?" The conclusion from the doctrine of free grace and justification by faith that is implied in this question would seem to be inferred quite logically. The death of Christ is the satisfaction for all our sins. When we are ingrafted into Him by a true faith, and accept all His benefits, we lay hold upon this satisfaction, and, so to speak, by faith have a general indulgence, the forgiveness of all sin, the sin we ever committed, still commit, or shall commit in the future. In Christ we are perfectly righteous, and that, too, without any work of righteousness which we have performed or might perform. No amount of good works can possibly increase our righteousness, or make us more perfectly righteous before God than we are by faith in Christ; no sin on our part can possibly deprive us of the perfection of the righteousness we have in Him. Now, then, what would appear to be more logical than the conclusion that we had better continue in sin, seeing that there is no condemnation for them that are in Christ anyhow? Yea, to continue in sin would yield the benefit that thereby the power of Christ's satisfaction and of the grace of God would shine forth more gloriously. Let us sin that grace may abound!

This question, however, the apostle most emphatically answers in the negative.

He does so, first of all, by an indignant "God forbid!"

The apostle is horrified at the very thought that such a conclusion should be drawn from the doctrine of justification by faith. Not only so, but in this well-known, emphatic exclamation, he also expresses what must rise spontaneously from the heart of every justified believer when the possibility is suggested to him to continue in sin, in order that grace may abound. Such a possibility is far from his mind. It is directly contrary to his very experience of the grace of justification. For he that is freely justified by grace through faith is not at all inclined to abide and continue in sin. The very opposite is true. He principally hates and abhors sin, and fights it, that he may walk according to the precepts of the living God. Hence, he is at once ready to take the exclamation of the apostle on his own lips: God forbid that I should assume so profane an attitude as to have any desire to continue in sin.

But the apostle does not consider this mere exclamation of emphatic denial sufficient. The opponent, who by his question would calumniate the truth of justification without works, must have an answer. And, therefore, the apostle continues to explain that he that is justified by faith is also dead to sin, and that, therefore, it is for ever impossible that he should abide and continue in sin. "How shall we, that are dead to sin, live any longer therein?"

But how is the believer dead to sin? This the apostle expounds in the verses that follow: "Know ye not, that so many of us as were baptized into Jesus Christ were baptized into his death? Therefore we are buried with him by baptism into death: that like as Christ was raised up from the dead by the glory of the Father, even so we also should walk in newness of life. For if we have been planted together in the likeness of his death, we shall be also in the likeness of his resurrection: Knowing this that our old man is crucified with him, that the body of sin might be destroyed, that henceforth we should not serve sin. For he that is dead is freed from sin. Now if we be dead with Christ, we believe that we shall also live with him: Knowing that Christ being raised from the dead dieth no more; death hath no more dominion over him. For in that he died, he died unto sin once: but in that he liveth, he liveth unto God. Likewise reckon ye also yourselves to be dead indeed unto sin, but alive unto God through Jesus Christ our Lord." Rom. 6:3-9.

We need not enter into a detailed exposition of this passage. Two points, however, are evident. First of all, that the old man of believers is crucified. And, secondly, that this crucifixion of the old man is the direct result of the death of Christ. Believers are ingrafted into Christ. And thus they are partakers of His death. They are crucified, dead, and buried with Him. And thus the passage does, indeed, support the teaching of the Catechism, that from the sacrifice and death of Christ on the cross we receive this further benefit that "our old man is crucified, dead, and buried with him."

Now, this must mean, first of all, that the death of Christ is the crucifixion of the old man; and, secondly, that when the power of the death of Christ is applied unto the elect, the old man also dies in them.

Let us try to understand this a little more fully.

What is "the old man" that is crucified, dead, and buried with Christ? It is man in his corrupt and sinful nature, in the human nature as we are all partakers of it in Adam. In this nature man lives unto sin. He is not free from sin, but bound in and to sin. Sin has dominion over him. Sin is the queen that is enthroned in his heart, that issues her precepts, to whom he is enslaved, willingly enslaved to be sure, but enslaved nevertheless; and whom he does obey, whose will he honors, whose direction he follows, whose wages he receives. For the human nature in Adam is wholly corrupt. The understanding is darkened, the will is perverted, the heart is obdurate, the desires and inclinations are impure, it is motivated by enmity against God throughout.

But more must be said in order to understand how the crucifixion and death of Christ are the death of the old man. We must remember that this corruption, this being enslaved to sin of the old man, is *death*. And as such it is punishment of sin. The "old man" is guilty, and guilt is liability to punishment, and the punishment of sin is death. And to this death also belongs the corruption of the human nature. The "old man" is man as he has no right to life, no right to be delivered from the bondage of sin and death. He is legally, that is, according to the very sentence of the Judge of heaven and earth, a slave of sin. He is under "the law of sin and death." In this sense, it may be said that sin is legally his lord, that it is the power that is legally enthroned in his heart, and that it cannot and may not be dethroned, until the guilt of sin is blotted out.

Such is "the old man."

If we bear this in mind, we will be able to understand that and how the death of Christ is the crucifixion, death, and burial of "the old man" for all the elect. For the death of Christ is the satisfaction for sin, the complete and final blotting out of the guilt of sin for all the elect, for the whole Church of all ages, and the establishment of a basis of eternal righteousness. Hence, the very basis of sin's dominion in the human nature of the elect was removed by the death of Christ. Legally sin has no more dominion over them. On the basis of righteousness, of the righteousness of Christ, the throne of sin in the human nature cannot stand, it must fall. When Christ died, therefore, all the elect were freed from sin, as the apostle writes: "he that is dead is freed from sin." Rom. 6:7.

This is the meaning of Scripture in Rom. 8:3: "For what the law could not do, in that it was weak through the flesh, God sending his own Son in the likeness of sinful flesh, and for sin, condemned sin in the flesh." Notice that it is *sin*, not the sinner, that is here said to be condemned. Notice, too, that this condemnation of sin in the flesh could not be accomplished by the law, on account of the weakness of the flesh. And, finally, observe that this condemnation of sin in the flesh was accomplished by God, through the sending of His Son in the likeness of sinful flesh, and that, too, for sin, that is, for its destruction. In what respect, then, was sin condemned? It was juridically deprived of its dominion in the flesh, deprived of its right to rule in human nature. This the law could not do. Seeing that it can only condemn the sinner to the slavery of sin, it rather sustains sin in its claim of dominion over the sinful nature of guilty man. But when God through His Son had blotted out the iniquity of His people, sin was condemned. It could no longer reign in human nature.

Thus, then, the "old man" of all God's own is crucified, dead, and buried for ever through the death of the Son of God.

And it is by Christ's own power that this freedom from the dominion of sin through the sacrifice of the cross is applied to the individual elect in this world.

For Christ is raised, and death has no more dominion over Him. And He is exalted at the right hand of God, clothed with all power in heaven and on earth. And having received the promise of the Spirit, He poured out that Spirit into the the Church, and through Him dwells in His own, and makes them partakers of all His benefits. He gives them the justifying faith, and by that faith they become partakers of His death and resurrection. They receive the forgiveness of sins, and the everlasting and perfect righteousness He obtained for them by His perfect obedience even unto death. And in this righteousness they possess their legal liberation from the dominion of sin over them, and they are conscious of this freedom. And being legally freed from sin's dominion, they are also actually delivered from the power of corruption, raised with Christ, and inducted into the glorious liberty of the children of God, through the power of grace and by the calling of the gospel. And thus it is "by his power" that "our old man is crucified, dead, and buried with him; that so the corrupt inclinations of the flesh may no more reign in us; but that we may offer ourselves unto him a sacrifice of thanksgiving."

In the light of all this, we can understand the intimate and inseparable connection between justification by faith and a walk in newness of life.

It is clear now why, in answer to the question, whether those that are freely justified had not better continue in sin, Paul so emphatically exclaimed: "God forbid." For exactly in being justified the believer is freed from the dominion of sin, that he may live unto God.

An indulgence granted by mere man, though he be the pope, may induce the sinner to live wantonly in sin; the mighty power of the death of Christ has the very opposite effect. By it, sin is condemned, dethroned, its power destroyed, and the believer is become dead to sin. The corrupt inclinations of the flesh no

more reign in him. He may now serve the living God, and
offer himself a living sacrifice unto Him.

But it may not be superfluous to ask the question: how does
this freedom from the dominion of sin reveal itself in the present
life of the believer in this world? What does it mean, then, to
be dead to sin, and no longer to live in it?

In answer to this question we may state, negatively, that to
be dead to sin does not mean that sin is dead in us. Bitter
disappointment must needs be the result, if we imagine that
when we are ingrafted into Christ, crucified and raised with
Him, the death of sin follows, is the sure fruit. For sin is not
dead in the believer as long as he is in this life. It does not die,
until he dies. Till then it is very much alive. The motions of
sin are in our members. In fact, in opposition to the new beginning of life in the believer, they are often more active, assert
themselves more emphatically and insistently, as the believer
grows in the knowledge and grace of the Lord Jesus. He has
but a small beginning of the new obedience, and a small beginning it remains even in the very holiest of God's children.
And the believer must understand this, that he may watch and
pray, lest he fall into temptation. Paradoxical though it may
sound, though the old man is dead and buried with Christ, yet,
throughout his whole life in this world, until the very moment
of his death, he must constantly fight to put off the old man,
and to put on the new man in Christ Jesus.

And yet, though sin is not dead, he is dead to sin. The old
man is very really dead and buried. That old man was characterized by his being legally and ethically enslaved to sin, and
the believer is a free man: death has no longer dominion over
him. The old man was known by his inner harmony with sin.
Sin was his proper sphere. He lived in sin. He loved iniquity.
He found his delight in the service of unrighteousness. He
hated the light and loved the darkness. Though he often was
filled with the sorrow of the world, and dreaded the wages of sin,
he was a stranger to the sorrow after God, and never knew repentance. After forgiveness and righteousness he did not yearn.
The kingdom of God he could not see. In the world he found

his delight, and the things that are above he did not seek, neither did he perceive them.

That old man is dead!

He that is in Christ Jesus is a new creature; old things are passed away; behold, all things are become new.

Yes, the motions of sin are still in his members, but he hates them. He still sins, but he is sorry for his sin, and the cry for forgiveness is on his lips daily. He does not live in sin, abide in sin, find his proper sphere in sin anymore. Where formerly he agreed with sin, there is now in his inmost heart a deep, a radical disagreement between sin and him. Whereas formerly he found his delight in sin, he now abhors it, eschews it, opposes it, and takes God's side in the judgment of his own iniquities. And he has an inner delight in the precepts of his God. He hears His Word, he tastes that the Lord is good, he seeks His fellowship, and he is a companion of all them that fear Him. And he seeks the things that are above, where Christ sitteth at the right hand of God. It is true that he often finds himself doing what he would not, but fact is that he does not will it. He frequently must confess that he does that which he hates; it is true, however, that he hates it. And he longs in hope for the day when he shall be delivered from the body of this death, and be like unto his Lord in perfection, that he may offer himself for ever unto God a sacrifice of thanksgiving!

Such is the manifestation in this life of the fact that the old man is crucified, dead, and buried with Christ.

And it is all the fruit of the death of the Son of God!

IV

The Descension Into Hell

The final article of the *Apostolicum* that speaks of Christ in His humiliation concerns His descension into hell. And this article our Catechism explains in the forty-fourth question and answer: "Why is there added, 'he descended into hell?' That in my greatest temptations I may be assured, and wholly comfort myself in this, that my Lord Jesus Christ, by his inexpressible anguish, pains, terrors, and hellish agonies, in which he was plunged during all his sufferings, but especially on the cross, hath delivered me from the anguish and torments of hell."

We may note here that the Catechism only indirectly and by implication explains the article as it occurs in the Confession, laying all the emphasis on the spiritual benefit believers derive from this part of the work of Christ: assurance of salvation and full comfort even in their greatest temptations. Nevertheless, the implication is that the article about the descension into hell as it occurs in the Apostles' Creed signifies that on the cross Christ suffered "inexpressible anguish, pains, terrors, and hellish agonies." This is Calvin's explanation of the article, and this interpretation was generally adopted by the Reformed Churches.

The article itself is not found in the older copies of the Apostles' Creed, though the matter itself was believed by the Church, and the expression occurs in some isolated confessions. In our Apostolic Confession it was not introduced until the beginning of the sixth century. Our readers may have noticed that in the worship of many American churches, when this creed is recited, the words "he descended into hell" are omitted. And, let it be remarked that if they are explained as referring to the agonies and hellish sufferings of Christ during His whole life, and especially on the cross, there is little reason why they should not be omitted. It must be evident that, after all that the Catechism has explained concerning the sufferings and death of Christ in this and in the preceding Lord's Day, there is little or nothing to add. In the answer to question thirty-seven, the Heidelberger already explained the suffering of Christ as meaning "that he, all the time that he lived on earth, but especially at the end of his life, sustained in body and soul, the wrath of God against the sins of all mankind." But what else is this bearing of the wrath of God than the suffering of pain and terror and hellish agonies? In answer to the question concerning the special significance of the death of the cross, the Catechism explained that through the cross God laid the curse upon Him, and that He took it upon Himself, for the death of the cross was accursed of God. But is not the curse of God the suffering of hellish terrors? If, therefore, we adopt the explanation of the Catechism, the omission of this article from the recital of the *Apostolicum* in public worship is not a serious one, the more so because, as we have said, in the older copies of this creed the article does not occur.

The article has been explained in more than one way.

One explanation gives to it the meaning that Christ was in the state of the dead. The Greek word for "hell" is *Hades,* a word that is translated and that, too, usually correctly, in our English Bible by hell, but which may signify the same as grave, or the state of the dead before the resurrection. Hence, the explanation is linguistically possible: *he descended into the state of the dead.* The context in which the article occurs, however, would seem to be opposed to the idea that this was actually the meaning of the article historically, that is, according to the faith of the early Church. For it occurs at the end of the series: *suffered, was crucified, dead, and buried.* The last of these terms already declares that Christ descended into the place of the dead, and to add another article virtually expressing the same thing, would appear to be a rather useless repetition.

The second explanation is that offered by our Heidelberg Catechism, that Christ suffered the agonies of hell in our stead. We have, of course, no objection whatever to the doctrinal contents of this explanation. And as part of our Catechism, we shall have to refer to it again. Nevertheless, in view of the position of this article in the *Apostolicum*, between the burial and the resurrection, it may be seriously doubted, whether this was the intention of the early Church.

The third possible explanation of the article concerning Christ's descension into hell, and the one which, according to Dr. Philip Schaff (Creeds of Christendom, II, 46), presents the meaning of the early Church, is that it refers to "an actual self-manifestation of Christ after the crucifixion to all the departed spirits." And Dr. Schaff continues: "As such the descent is a part of the universality of the scheme of redemption, and forms the transition from the state of humiliation to the state of exaltation."

Whether or not "this is the historical explanation, according to the belief of the ancient church," as Dr. Schaff thinks, we have no means to verify. However, the explanation is rather vague, and it is rather difficult to see how the "descent into hell" in this sense could be a part of the universality of the scheme of redemption. Besides, it opens a wide field of speculation as to the purpose and effect of this self-manifestation of Christ to all the dead in hades. Why should Christ thus manifest Himself to all the dead, and what could such a self-manifestation add to the revelation of Jesus Christ as the Saviour of His people?

We need not seriously consider the view that our Lord, after His crucifixion, descended into the place of desolation in order to suffer the tortures of the damned, neither can this have been the meaning of the early church, if the explanation of Dr. Schaff given above is correct. Whatever the early church may have understood by *hades*, it certainly cannot have been the place of eternal punishment, for it was to *all* the departed spirits that Christ is supposed to have manifested Himself. Besides, the notion that the Saviour suffered the torments of hell after His crucifixion is contrary to the plain teaching of Scripture. Evident it is that the Lord, after He gave up the ghost, cannot have suffered the torments of hell *in body and soul*, for His body rested in the grave of Joseph of Arimathea. Besides, such a view would be in conflict with the word our Lord addressed to the malefactor from the cross: "Today thou shalt be with me in paradise." And had He not announced in His next to the last cross-utterance: "It is finished"? Surely, this triumphant outcry was uttered in the consciousness that the work of redemption, the sacrifice of reconciliation, had been completed and perfected, and that no more suffering remained to be endured.

Nor can this possibly be the meaning of Ps. 16:10, as quoted by the apostle Peter on the day of Pentecost, Acts 2:27: "Because thou wilt not leave my soul in hell, neither wilt thou suffer thine Holy One to see corruption." The reference here is not the place of eternal torture, but to *hades*, the bodiless state of the dead. In that state the Lord's soul was in paradise, and His body lay in the grave. And the meaning of the passage is that God would not leave Christ's soul in that disembodied state, neither would He allow His body to be swallowed up by the corruption of the grave, but He would glorify His Holy One in the resurrection. This is evident from the following: 1. It may not be ignored that in Ps. 16 it is David that is speaking. True, he speaks as a type of Christ, and ultimately his words are applicable to Christ only. Nevertheless, what is true of the antitype principally, and in the full sense of the word, is certainly predicated of the type in the first instance. The words, therefore, must also be applied to David. The psalmist was confident, and that, too, with his eye on the Holy One that was to come, that God would not leave his soul in hell, but through death would show him the pathway of life. But it follows that David cannot be speaking of the place of eternal damnation, but that he refers to *sjeool*, the state of the dead. 2. On the day of Pentecost, the apostle Peter is not speaking of Christ's deliverance from the place of the damned, but of His glorious resurrection. This is evident from the twenty-fourth verse: "Whom God hath raised up, having loosed the pains of death: because it was not possible that he should be holden of it." In proof of this, namely, that it was not possible that Christ should be holden of death, he refers to the passage from the sixteenth psalm. The very purpose for which it is quoted, therefore, proves that the apostle Peter was not thinking of a descent of Christ into the place of the damned, but simply of *hades*, the state of the dead, and of Christ's deliverance from it. 3. And this is also the application made of this text from the sixteenth psalm by the apostle, when he says: "Men and brethren, let me freely speak unto you of the patriarch David, that he is both dead and buried, and his sepulchre is with us unto this day. Therefore being a prophet, and knowing that God had sworn with an oath to him, that of the fruit of his loins, according to the flesh, he would raise up Christ to sit on his throne: He seeing this before spake of the resurrection of Christ, that his soul was not left in hell, neither his flesh did see corruption."

In the light of Scripture, therefore, the view that Christ personally descended into the place of the damned there to suffer vicariously the pains of eternal torture, cannot stand.

Roman Catholic theologians appeal to I Peter 3:19, 20, to support their view that Christ descended into what they call *Limbo*, a portal of hell, in order to deliver thence the Old Testament saints, to whom heaven was not opened until Christ's own ascent from death into glory. Thus in "Radio Replies," the Rev. Dr. Leslie Rumble gives the following answer to the question why Christ descended into hell: "Christ did not go to hell in the modern and restricted sense of the word. At the time when the Apostles' Creed was composed, the word hell was used to designate any state of existence lower than heaven. After his death, our Lord's soul went, says St. Peter, to preach to those spirits that were in prison. That is, he joined those souls which were detained from the fulness of heaven and who were awaiting the opening of heaven to mankind by Him. This descent of Christ's soul into hell was obviously not to the hell of the eternally lost, but to what we call the Limbo or detention place of the souls of the just who lived prior to our Lord's coming into this world."

However, this bit of Roman Catholic exegesis cannot stand for a moment, even though there may be room for difference of opinion as to the true meaning of the passage in I Peter 3:19, 20.

This well-known passage reads as follows: "By which also he went and preached unto the spirits in prison; Which sometime were disobedient, when once the longsuffering of God waited in the days of Noah, while the ark was a preparing, wherein few, that is, eight souls were saved by water." Now let us note: 1. That the apostle is not speaking here at all of a personal descent of Christ into "prison," after His crucifixion and before His resurrection, but of a going to preach to the spirits that were in prison *after His resurrection and through the Spirit*. This is the simple and plain meaning of the words. The introductory words of vs. 19, "by which" refer back to the latter part of the eighteenth verse: "being put to death in the flesh, but quickened by the Spirit." And then follows: "By which also he went and preached unto the spirits in prison." The order of the phrases, therefore, demands that we conceive of this mission of Christ to the spirits in prison, as having taken place after His resurrection. Moreover, He went, not in His human nature, or in His disembodied soul, but in the Spirit by Whom also He was quickened from the dead. And through this Spirit He is able to send His Word down unto the spirits in prison without a personal descent. 2. That the apostle, by the phrase "spirits in prison," certainly cannot designate the Old Testament saints, unto whom heaven was not supposed to be opened until the coming of Christ. For they are described as those "which sometime were disobedient, when once the longsuffering of God waited in the days of Noah, when the ark was a preparing." Now, this so very clearly refers to the ungodly of Noah's day, when the righteous were persecuted all the day long, and God saved them by the waters of the deluge, that one can only be amazed at the curious bit of exegesis that makes Old Testament saints out of them. 3. That the apostle does not speak with one word, nor even suggest in any way, that these "spirits in prison" were delivered and taken to heaven by Christ. The text simply informs us that He "preached" to them. And the word used here for "preached" does not mean at all that He preached the gospel unto them, but simply that He proclaimed, announced something as a herald. And besides, Scripture knows nothing of a

Limbo, in which the Old Testament saints were kept until heaven was opened for them by Christ.

For all these reasons we must reject the Roman Catholic view of the descension of Christ into hell.

Nor does the Lutheran explanation, that, after His death and before His resurrection, Christ descended into hell to proclaim His victory to the "spirits in prison" find support in the text from Peter 3:19, 20. It is, indeed, quite in harmony with that passage to say that Christ announced His victory to those spirits that persecuted His people, and mocked at His cause in the world, but this word of victory was proclaimed by Christ, not between His death and resurrection, nor by a personal descent into hell, but after His resurrection and exaltation, and through the Spirit that is given Him.

We conclude, therefore, that, whatever may have been the significance of the clause concerning the descension of Christ into hell in the mind of the early church, Scripture knows of no such descent into the place of the damned, nor of such a self-manifestation of Christ to all the departed spirits.

And if the article in the Apostles' Creed that speaks of this descent is to be retained, the explanation of it offered by the Heidelberg Catechism must be adopted, in spite of the fact that this is not its historical meaning.

Christ endured "inexpressible anguish, pains, terrors, and hellish agonies."

He endured them in all his sufferings, but especially on the cross. And even on the cross there is a gradual increase in His suffering of these hellish agonies. This is evident from all that occurs on and about the cross. During the first half of the six-hour period of the crucifixion, the sun still shed its light upon the awful spectacle on Calvary, the enemies have the audacity to mock and jeer at the crucified One, and the Lord Himself finds it possible to take interest in the things about Him, praying for His enemies, committing His mother to care of the disciple whom He loved, and assuring the penitent malefactor of final salvation. But during the last three hours, the cross is completely taken out of men's hands. Darkness, that dreadful symbol of God's wrathful presence, descends on the scene; the enemies, amazed at the fearful omen, cease from mockery, and grow silent; and for the space of three hours the crucified One is completely wrapped up in His own suffering: not a word is heard from His lips. Then, almost at the end of these last three hours of His passion, He makes it known that He has been descending into the depths, that He has, indeed, reached the very bottom of hell, in the question of amazement: "My God, my God, why hast thou forsaken me?"

What does it mean?

The answer follows presently: "It is finished!"

The measure of suffering, and of obedience, is filled. All that was to be borne of the wrath of God against the sin of all the elect, had been endured even to the end. Nothing, emphatically nothing, remains to procure for us eternal righteousness and life.

The Son of God had tasted all there is to be tasted in the agony of death as the expression of God's just wrath.

That is the meaning of the descension into hell.

Hence, the Catechism, contemplating this descent into hell in its relation to and significance for the believer, explains that it assures the latter, even in his greatest temptations, that he is saved, delivered from the wrath of God and the torments of hell.

Many are the temptations. And let us remember that the German word that is translated by "temptations" here is *Anfechtungen*. It has a slightly different connotation from temptations. It denotes that the believer is assailed, from within and from without, to move him from his sure ground of confidence in Christ, of his assurance that his sins are forgiven, and that he has obtained eternal righteousness and life by mere grace. His own conscience accuses him, sin from within would bring him to doubt, the valley of the shadow of death appears to testify that God's wrath is still upon him, the world laughs at his confidence, the devil assails his assurance.

Can he, then, be saved?

In all these temptations, however, he clings by faith to the death of the Son of God, that finished it all, which was a suffering of hellish agonies in his stead, and in his behalf.

And from the darkness of his present death, and from the depth of his greatest temptations, contemplating that death of the Son of God, that death even unto the bottom of hell, and clinging to that Son of God, Who died and was raised, he knows that nothing remains to be done, and that he is for ever delivered from torments of hell.

The death of the Son of God is the sole ground of his confidence.

Nothing can separate him from His love!